S0-AYO-156

WARS OF THE 20th CENTURY

WARS
OF THE
20th CENTURY

Bison Books

First Published in 1985 by
Bison Books Ltd
176 Old Brompton Road
London SW5
England

ISBN 0 86124 261 0

Printed in Hong Kong

CONTENTS

World War I

World War II

The Modern World

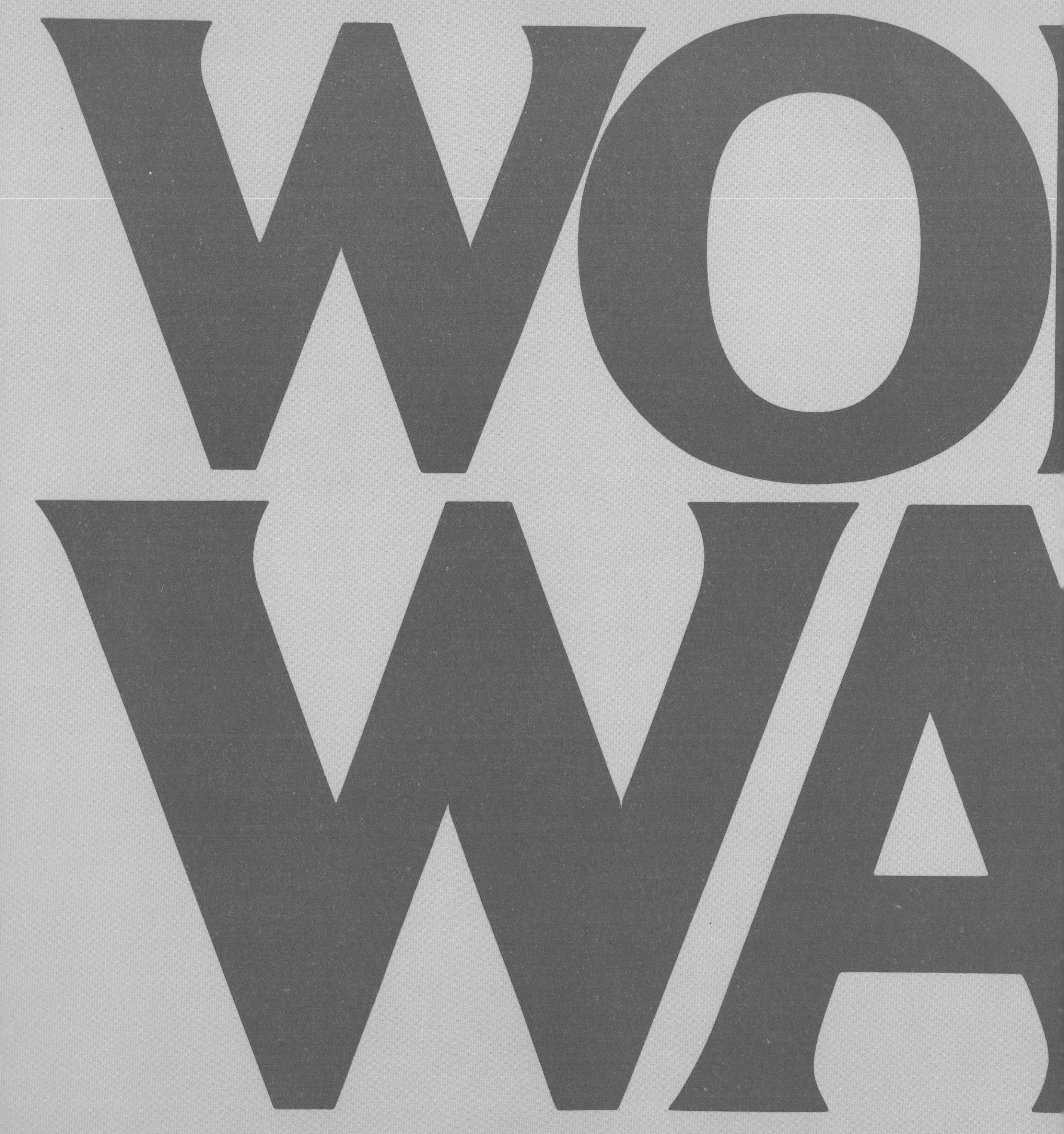

Susanne Everett
Introduction by John Keegan

RLD

Introduction by John Keegan

The First World War stole upon Europe by surprise. There had been two small Balkan conflicts in 1911–12, but neither had looked to involve the armies of the Great Powers. Before that, one had to go as far back as 1871 to find a time when international peace was sundered by fighting. The European 19th century has indeed come to appear in retrospect as an era of almost miraculous tranquility for, though we can count half a dozen sizeable conflicts between the abdication of Napoleon in 1815 and the assassination of the Archduke Ferdinand in 1914, none was protracted or very costly in life. This appearance seemed valid also to contemporaries. Peace had become a habit of mind as well as a condition of life and was expected to persist, whatever the sums spent upon armament and even though they rose year by year.

Yet we are now able to see, as Europeans of the last century were not, that there were special and local reasons restraining the Powers from waging major war against each other. Most important was the enormous expansion in the availability of resources, in Europe and beyond, which for the first time in human history not only relieved populations of the ever present fear of famine and privation, but actually offered them the prospect of better times. The hardships to which the industrial revolution condemned the new manufacturing classes have been made notorious. What is forgotten is that manufacturing provided continuous year-round work, and created a steady demand for agricultural produce, thus transforming the conditions of life both in town and countryside. Even when the exploitation of the new lands in America and Australia provoked an agricultural slump in the second half of the century, it also provided a way of escape from the consequences at home, via the open door of emigration. It is therefore perhaps the 19th rather than the 20th which deserves to be called 'the century of the common man,' since it was in those 100 years that the real transformation of his conditions and expectations occurred.

This 'peaceful progress,' which was the ideal of 19th-century liberalism, by definition precludes war. There were other factors at work to distract the peoples of Europe from hostility toward their neighbors. The most important turned on the belief that people of the same language should share a common statehood. That belief could lead to war, as between Austria and Savoy in 1848 and 1859 and Austria and Prussia in 1866. Since these conflicts were normally between states of unequal strength, none persisted enough to become general. They were emotionally important enough, however, to the parties concerned to nullify quarrels with neighbors of a different language group. Nationalism therefore served, for a time at least, to overlay the danger of quarrels between neighbors speaking different languages.

In the case of three of the powers – Britain, France and Russia – there were the attractions and rewards of imperialism to draw their military efforts away from a European focus. Britain's rise to great empire in the 19th century is a familiar story. It is less well-remembered that France acquired enormous colonial possessions in the same period, in the Far East and in North and West Africa. Russia, whose pioneers had carried the outposts of Czarist power to the shores of the Pacific in the 18th century, turned southward thereafter, and subjected the Muslim kingdoms and khanates of Central Asia to her control. Thus distracted, the states of greatest war potential had little energy left to waste in struggles within the European heartland, and indeed little motive. It was only when their imperial ambitions conflicted, as they did over the future of the enfeebled Turkish Empire in 1854, that they found cause to fight each other. Then their geographical locations, at the periphery of Europe, ensured that they fight at arm's length, without the means to do each other serious or lasting harm.

These invisible and beneficent influences had run their course by 1914. The imperial powers had completed their expansion; there were indeed few new lands to conquer by that date. The new states of Europe were also complete. Italy had thrown off the power of foreign rulers and united under the House of Savoy. Germany had ceased to be a cluster of small kingdoms, under the thrall of more important powers, and become an entity, with the King of Prussia at its head. The enormous expansion of the European economy had also lost its first wind. Cheap resources were harder to come by, easy markets more difficult to find. Economic competition took on a new edge, sharpened by the military powers of those states which felt threatened most keenly by the new commercial climate. Britain was the first to suffer. Though in dimensions of empire by far the greatest power in 1914, she had already ceased to be the most productive manufacturing country, and was losing her status as the world's leading merchant and carrier. France too felt economically disadvantaged. Her start in the industrial revolution had been slow and her industry did not compete well in foreign markets. These were increasingly dominated by the Germans, who had the inventiveness, energy and discipline to make and sell at a price and in volumes which the older industrial powers could not match.

Trade war had therefore become a condition of life in the European world of 1914. Peace might have survived that development. What fatally threatened it was the transplantation of nationalist urges from the large peoples to the small, those whose weakness and backwardness had left them within the boundaries of the empires which the large peoples had created or preserved. The Poles of Russia and Germany felt a bitter sense of deprivation. They were an isolated case which could be contained. That of the peoples of the Austro-Hungarian empire could not, for they formed a majority which could be deprived only by the artificial superordination of two of them – Austro-Germans and Hungarians – over the rest. Yet the maintenance of that superordination was essential: internally, because to give autonomy to the 'nationalities' would leave Austria and Hungary as tiny rumps; externally, because the liberation of the 'nationalities' would provoke instability elsewhere, notably inside the German Empire itself.

Germany was therefore compelled to defend Austria-Hungary against any danger of dissolution, even to the point of going to war, but she had other reasons for thinking the risk of war bearable. The disparity between her economic power, which was great, and her overseas possessions, which were small, was a constant source of national discontent, heightened by the traditional powers' determination to treat her as a newcomer to their table and to exclude her from it as much as possible. Hence her indulgence in state investments which were not really necessary to her well-being, like the enormous High Seas Fleet, built to remind Britain of the fragility of her naval supremacy. That fleet, by 1914, was almost large enough to proffer the chance of victory at sea. The German army, in efficiency if not in size, was a force which made the prospect of victory on land highly realizable. Discontent, ambition and new-found strength therefore combined to turn Germany into a warlike power by 1914, and worked on the fears of her neighbors to generate a complementary motivation. It needed only one incident, at the wrong place and time, to set these motivations into action.

The Sarajevo assassination was that incident. Its immediate outcome had been foreseen. Its long-term consequences had not. Men of power, military as well as civilian, held it as a dogma that any large European war must be short, with victory going quickly to the side which could best mobilize its resources. They were nearly right. Germany did almost win in August 1914, because she brought to the battlefronts, east and west, a better army than her neighbors could find in the time. The mistake the men of power had made was in their definition of 'mobilization.' They had grossly underestimated the resources, material, human and spiritual, of the societies at the head of which they stood. The campaigns of 1914 devastated the armies which fought them. However, such were the reserves of manpower, so deep the resources, so flexible the economies, so fervent and obedient the populations of Britain, France, Germany and even Russia, that their governments found themselves able to create new armies for the next round, to which the logic of circumstances bound them without opportunity of escape.

A war of quick victory was thus transformed, against all expectation, into a struggle of attrition, of which the lives of millions of young men were to be the raw material. 'World war' it became, because the imperial states carried the fighting to wherever their colonial possessions impinged; 'world war' because the clients and allies of the European powers – Turkey foremost among them – were bribed or compelled to join in; 'world war' because in the penultimate year, America judged it her duty and necessity to intervene. The strangeness of the war, and its best-known, most-reviled quality, was its narrow geographical confinement. Its only great sea battle, Jutland, was fought within a few miles of the British and German coasts. Its great land battles were fixed within even narrower limits. All the fighting on the Eastern Front was played out in a belt 100 miles wide north and south of the Carpathians, or on the crests of the Caucasus. Gallipoli, where the Turks defeated the British and French attempt to destroy their power at a blow, was a pocket handkerchief battlefield. The Italian Front, which opened up in 1915, clung to a few strategic peaks in the Tyrol and the Julian Alps. In the west, parts of the front fixed in 1914 did not move a yard throughout four years of offense and defense. It was in these narrow strips, defined by the range of the artilleries of the two sides, and so never more than 10 miles wide at any one time, that 'attrition' did its work. The results remain for all to see. They reside in the great war cemeteries which cluster together along the trace of the old Western Front in France and Belgium. In them lie buried nearly a million British, over a million German and nearly two million French soldiers. Nearly a million Germans lie buried elsewhere, in less solemn surroundings, and with them millions of Russians, Turks and soldiers of the Habsburg armies. A majority of the victims of the war probably have no known grave.

They demand a memorial. Their deaths require an explanation. The best memorials have come from the pens of the survivors, in whose lives their months or years at the front remained overwhelmingly the most important event. The best explanations paradoxically tend to emerge with the passage of time, as passions cool and the tragedy which the war was find its place among all the other tragedies which civilized men obstinately visit on themselves. This book is an attempt at an explanation. It looks for it particularly in the nature and quality of the fighting which, like the ascent of a mountain of small gradient, offered those who took part a succession of illusions, a replacement of one false crest of conquest with another, toward which the dwindling band of survivors constantly struggled forward in the belief that victory lay just beyond it. That illusion was one of which the soldiers of the war were themselves bitterly conscious and yet from which, being human, they could not liberate themselves. Unable to believe that next day, next week, next month would not reward their efforts with success, they soldiered on. Some of them, in the end, won a sort of victory. We all live with the defeat which they inflicted on the world of the hundred year peace.

French *poilus* are cheered on the way to the front at the beginning of the war, August 1914.

1 Europe Blunders to War

The Ancients believed that wars were made in heaven. World War I was made on earth and, in particular, in the dangerous triangle of central Europe where, in 1914, three empires met. Eastward stretched the great empire of the Czar of all the Russias; west and north lay the empire of the German Kaiser; south along the Danube ran the hereditary lands of the Archduke of Austria, inhabited not only by Germans but by Hungarians, Rumanians, Poles, Czechs, Slovaks, Slovenes, Ruthenians, Croats and Serbs. The two other empires had their minorities – Poles in Germany, Finns, Letts, Estonians and more Poles in Russia, not to mention the myriad Asiatic tribes and mountain peoples of her deep interior. Both were states unmistakably founded upon a majority. Austria was not. It was an empire of factions, some major, some minor, some enthusiastic over their standing in society, and a few outrightly dissatisfied. Foremost among the last were the Austrian Serbs, who wished above all to be united with their independent brethren inside the borders of the kingdom of Serbia.

The government of the Austro-Hungarian Empire was, however, adamantly opposed to releasing them. Not only would the cession of the territory inhabited by the Austrian Serbs diminish that of the empire in a place of great military vulnerability; not only would it add greatly to the power and pretensions of the Serbian kingdom, itself a potential ally of Russia rather than Austria; but it would fan the flames of nationalist and separatist ambitions burning inside every one of the other communities of which the empire was composed. Austria was caught in a vice. Although in the grip of a domestic organization both cumbersome and illogical she was nevertheless obliged to maintain the status quo, in the fear that any attempt to improve the situation would merely heighten problems for which the empire, however inadequately, provided a solution. Vienna and Budapest, twin capitals of the Dual Monarchy, could only hope that by refusing to move in any way to meet nationalist demands the whole gigantic artifice of empire could be held immobile against a day of reckoning that might, with luck, never come.

The worm in the apple of their hopes was the impatience of the most fervent of the Serb nationalists. Like others before and since, their thoughts had turned to terrorism for they felt it was only through violence that their dreams of a day of liberation could be realized. It was by no means an easy task. Not only were such practical idealists few and far between, they were inexperienced and, more important, lacked opportunities for a dramatic gesture to promote their cause. By 1914 the ancient emperor, Francis Joseph, barely travelled beyond his palaces, and, in any case, his immense popularity made his assassination unthinkable even to the most fanatical of nationalists. A more promising target presented itself in the form of the Emperor's nephew and heir, the Archduke Franz Ferdinand, who was out of favor with his uncle due to an ill-judged marriage and universally disliked throughout the empire. On 28 June 1914, together with his wife, he was to visit Sarajevo, capital of the formerly Turkish province of Bosnia, the disputed area, scene of many uprisings, which had been administered by Austria-Hungary since 1898 and annexed in 1908. A fraternity of adolescent Serb patriots led by a schoolboy, Gavrilo Princip, decided that the moment had come to take action, and resolved to make an attempt on the Archduke's life. Their first efforts were not promising. As the royal pair drove into the city two of the young conspirators faced with the 'enemy' could not bring themselves to shoot him, a third threw a bomb and missed. Princip, presented with a second chance thanks to the imperial chauffeur's mishandling of the Archduke's car, took it with determination. Three shots killed Franz Ferdinand and, probably unintentionally, his wife. Princip was arrested alive and taken for trial – the empire he hated so much proved to be no tyranny. The Austrian intelligence service, however, had clearly decided that its counterpart in the Kingdom of Serbia lay behind the outrage, and the Austrian government accordingly decided to punish its neighbor so severely that it would not in future foment disorder within the imperial borders.

The punishment was not to be military but moral; Serbia was to be obliged to apologize for the assassination, to give guarantees of good behavior in the future and to permit representatives of the Austrian police to enter Serbian territory in order to track down the conspirators still at large. If she accepted these terms, Serbia would, in effect surrender an important part of her sovereignty to her great neighbor. If she refused, she would give Austria the pretext for justifiable military action against her. Austria would, in fact, have been content with either outcome, but in anticipation of refusal had, before issuing her ultimatum to Serbia, taken the precaution of extracting from Germany an assurance of her support should an Austro-Serbian military confrontation threaten to develop into something wider.

That such a development was threatened was made highly probable by the prevailing pattern of European alliances. For Austria was not the only state in Europe to enjoy the protection of a stronger neighbor. So, too, did Serbia itself – that of Russia, which, in turn, was linked by treaty to France. This state of affairs, the so-called 'interlocking pattern of alliances,' had come about in the past 20 years and in the following fashion.

Germany, under the Chancellorship of the great Otto von Bismarck, had always been careful to avoid enmities on both her frontiers,

Bottom: **The aging Kaiser Franz Joseph of Austria in the Hofburg grounds. His heir apparent was Franz Ferdinand.**

Below: **The Royal couple pass through Sarajevo prior to their fatal meeting with Princip.**

Below: **Archduke Franz Ferdinand of Austria and his wife arrive in Sarajevo on 28 June 1914 followed by General Oskar Potiorek, who was military governor of Bosnia. He met the fated couple at the station and travelled with them in an open sports car.**

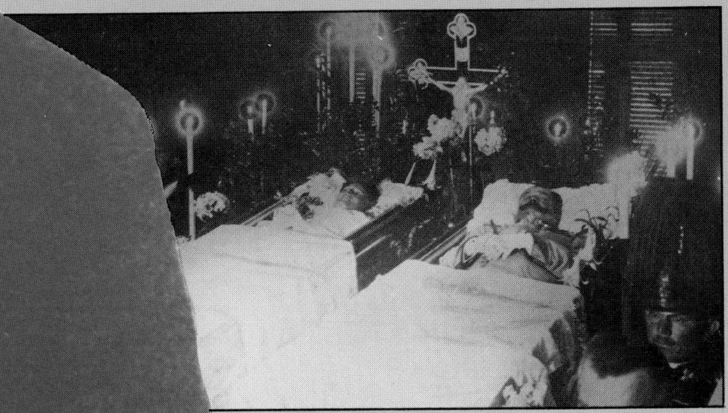

Right: Gavrilo Princip, assassin of the Archduke and his wife. His actions on 28 June 1914 led the world to war.

Far right: Czar Nicholas II and Czarina Alexandra of Russia.

Below right: The Archduke and Archduchess lie in state in Sarajevo after their assassination.

eastern and western. Enmity on her southern frontier, with Austria, might have seemed unavoidable after the War of 1866. The two German-speaking courts had too natural an affinity and their empires too many common interests for the aftermath of that quarrel not to be quickly forgotten. The rancor of France, defeated in 1870 and stripped of her frontier provinces of Alsace-Lorraine, could not be so easily dissipated. It had, therefore, seemed essential to Bismarck that Germany should always be on good terms with Russia, thus avoiding any prospect of the Czar and the French President co-ordinating plans for military action against Germany of an offensive, or even a mutually defensive, nature. Bismarck, however, had been removed from office in 1888 by the young Kaiser, who had subsequently failed to renew Bismarck's 'reinsurance' treaty with Russia. The failure had not been an oversight, but a deliberate omission, designed to increase Germany's diplomatic freedom of maneuver, from which Wilhelm II hoped to reap wide benefits on the world, rather than the nearby European scene.

The immediate effect of the Treaty's lapse had, however, been to excite Russian fears of isolation in European affairs and to turn her toward exactly that reinforcement of her strategic position which Bismarck had most dreaded: an alliance with France. Tentative negotiations between the two countries fared well and in 1894 they consolidated their understanding. It had remained intact throughout Russia's war with Japan in 1904–1905, which had, in one way or another, soured her relations with the rest of the great power community, and it had been renewed and refreshed since. Germany was thus confronted on her eastern and western frontiers with powers each of which, Berlin had reason to suspect, would react to a German attack by assisting the other.

However Germany's diplomatic predicament did not end there. More recently Great Britain had been drawn into the system of military precautions against Germany. No formal undertaking had been arranged, but since 1910 British officers had been conducting staff talks with their French opposite numbers and had agreed on a plan to integrate the deployment of a British Expeditionary Force (BEF) with the French field army if both should be called upon to resist a German invasion of France.

Politicians and diplomats in France and Britain remained remarkably ignorant of the details of these discussions, though aware that they were in progress. The isolation of soldiers from politicians was however a feature of public life at the time. It was even more marked in Germany, where control of the armed forces rested not with the Minister of War or the Reichstag but with the Kaiser. His chief military servant was the Chief of the Great General Staff, who was answerable to him directly. The war plans of the German army, which the Chief drew up, were not, therefore, necessarily known in all their details to the Chancellor, who was head of government. As things stood in Germany in 1914, the current war plan had not been drawn up by the then Chief of Staff, General Graf Helmuth Johannes von Moltke (the Younger) but by his predecessor, Graf Alfred von Schlieffen, and its details had remained almost unaltered since his retirement in 1906. Chosen by the Kaiser for his name (his great uncle was the victor of 1870) rather than for his qualities of command, which were slender, Moltke was a reluctant Chief of Staff. He had not wanted the job, and he filled his post badly, entirely failing to convey to Chancellor Theobald von Bethmann-Hollweg a proper understanding of the consequences of a German mobilization. Perhaps, as one historian has suggested, he did not understand them fully himself.

They were dramatic enough. Schlieffen had lived during his long tenure of office (1891–1906) with the nightmare of the 'war on two fronts,' which he feared the Kaiser's new foreign policy might bring about. He feared Russia – whose vast spaces and great reserves of manpower would, he thought, engulf any German army which marched eastward – more than he feared France, but only in the longer term. In the short term his fears were exactly reversed. His solution of the military predicament was, therefore, to engage Germany's main force first against France rather than against Russia and to pit the German army against the latter only after the former had been defeated. But how was this to be achieved? France, defeated by an attack across the common frontier in 1870, had since spent large sums on frontier fortification, filling the gap between southern Belgium and Switzerland with a dense belt of forts and obstacles. A passage in the middle – the so-called 'Trouée de Charmes' – had been left open, but only with the idea of funnelling any German invading force into a space so constricted that it would emerge through it helplessly exposed to decapitating thrusts by mobile French flanking forces. He was determined to avoid this deliberate trap. But what other approach was there? He could not contemplate a seaborne invasion. He dared not risk a move through Switzerland, whose mountainous terrain was the best guarantee of her diplomatic status as a permanently neutral state. He therefore had to look at Belgium.

What he saw was another inconveniently neutral country with the additional problem that her neutrality was guaranteed not only by Britain and France but, as the inheritor of the obligations of the Kingdom of Prussia, by Germany also. This diplomatic conundrum was originally sidestepped by Schlieffen when he first put his mind to it in 1891. Only a small violation of Belgian neutrality, 'no more than was necessary to outflank the French line of forts in Lorraine' would, he considered, be needed. Such a limited move, he felt, would not only be acceptable to the international community but, even more important, would not provoke Britain into rallying to the defense of her small ally. However, further deliberations drew Schlieffen to the awkward conclusion that a small violation would not be enough to answer Germany's military needs – he felt he had to place at least two armies, each of 150,000 men, on the left flank of the French, and that required the use of a plentiful road network on a wide front. Southern Belgium was hilly, wooded and badly provided with communications. Any violation would therefore have to be executed in the northern Belgian plains. On the principle that he might as well be hanged for a sheep as a lamb, Schlieffen decided to make the whole of Belgium the scene of his outflanking maneuver, and to commit the greater part of the German army to it.

By 1906, when ill health forced his retirement, the plan was complete. Such was Schlieffen's prestige that his successor did not dare to question its logic or tamper with its details and it therefore remained the blueprint for Germany's part in a European war in 1914. Its full implications, however, had even then not been grasped. It was a recipe for dealing with a combined offensive against Germany by France and Russia united, either through an instantaneous response or by what today would be called a 'pre-emptive attack.' It left Germany with no plan for fighting either country singlehanded. Should either France or Russia attack Germany without the agreement of the other, Germany would be obliged to mobilize against both. Worse, in a diplomatic situation elsewhere than in Franco-Russian-German relations, which nevertheless threatened a confrontation between Germany and either France or Russia, she was still obliged to mobilize against both. Unlike Austria, which had a 'major' and a 'minor' war plan, the first to deal with a Russian threat, the second with a lesser danger in the Balkans, Germany had only one plan: to mobilize against both her greatest enemies. Mobilization, in the circumstances of the age, would inevitably lead to war.

That had not always necessarily been the case. Nations had mobilized in the past as a means of bringing pressure to bear on a neighbor, yet without the maneuver leading to an actual clash of armies. But developments both in the size of armies and in the speed with which they might be moved to a potential war front had recently invested mobilization with great

Below: **Count von Schlieffen, who had completed his war plan in 1906. It was to be executed as it had been laid down.**

Left: President Raymond Poincaré of France (white beard) at an airdrome near Paris just prior to the war.

Right: Kaiser Wilhelm II of Germany and his army Chief of Staff von Moltke on maneuvers prior to war.

Far right: A heroic view of the Kaiser.

Below right: Kaiser Wilhelm II in full regalia.

Below: Theobald von Bethmann-Hollweg, German Chancellor in 1914, who gave Austria-Hungary a 'blank check' to invade Serbia at will.

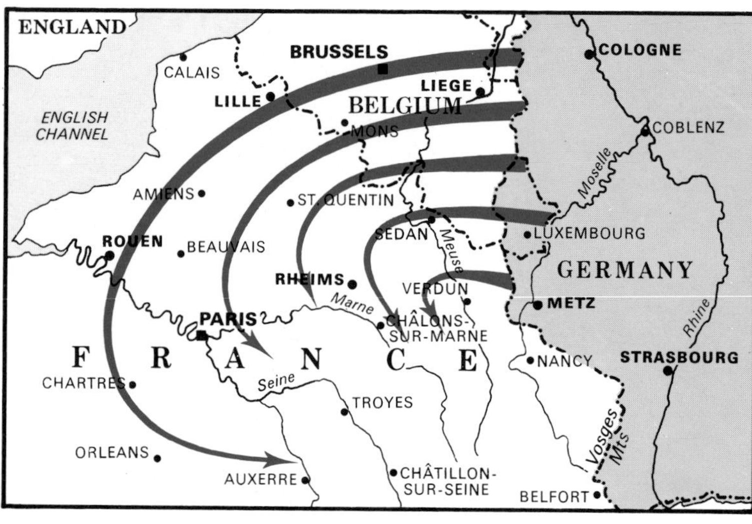

Above: The Schlieffen Plan called for a quick encirclement of Paris within six weeks of the outbreak of war, forcing a French capitulation.

Above: Provincial townspeople are called to the German colors in July 1914.

risk; where a power was threatened, as Germany was, by a war on two fronts simultaneously the danger became all the more intense.

All the powers in 1914 maintained large standing armies in peace, fed by conscription, which in turn fed very large reserves. France maintained a standing army of 500,000, Germany of 750,000, Russia of 1,200,000, and Austria of nearly 500,000. The officers and senior noncommissioned officers of these armies were long-service soldiers. The privates and corporals were conscripts serving from two to three years and then returned to civilian life, but remained on the books of the armies as reservists. With these reservists, France could increase the size of her field army to 3,500,000, Germany hers to 5,000,000. There were still more reservists to be drawn from men up to the age of 50, capable of forming second-line units – called *Territorials* in France, *Landwehr* and *Landsturm* in Germany – who, though not fit to take their place in the line of battle, were able to do tasks on the lines of communication, thus releasing younger men for the front.

These large numbers of active troops, first-line reserves and second-line Landwehr and Landsturm, allowed Germany, in the summer of 1914, to contemplate putting eight separate armies into the field. One, the Eighth, was earmarked to defend East Prussia against the Russians should they manage to mount an invasion. The other seven were to be transported from their mobilization centers to the Belgian and French frontiers, in accordance with the Schlieffen Plan.

It was expected that these armies would encounter the French about 18 days after mobilization, if war should follow. However, the principal ingredient of the Schlieffen plan was concealment. Where Germany would deploy its main force was to remain hidden – and in such a context the word 'if' could not be used. But as the Kaiser was to discover to his anguish, the sequence was that war would follow a German mobilization. He had to face up to the fearful truth that mobilization inevitably revealed the deployment plan, and that the deployment plan told all.

The Kaiser made this horrifying discovery rather late in the day. On 24 July, the day after the issue of the Austrian ultimatum to Serbia, the crisis had deepened. Certain precautionary military measures had been taken by Russia and an announcement was made on 26 July that she would pass to the 'Period Preparatory to War.' This unfortunately-phrased term, which in fact only meant that the army would prepare to mobilize rather than actually do so, laid itself wide open to misinterpretation. Straight away it was misconstrued by Austria. She had two mobilization schemes – the first (B) for a small-scale war in the Balkans, the second (R) for general war. She had implemented B on issuing her ultimatum to Serbia, anticipating a Serbian mobilization to resist it. Sergei D Sazonov, the Russian foreign minister, expected the Austrians to accept the 'Period Preparatory to War' as a purely precautionary measure, even though it involved bringing the 13 Russian corps on the Russo-Austrian border to a state of readiness. The head of the Russian mobilization office pointed out to Sazonov that he might be expecting too much: that Austria would probably feel itself forced in consequence to order full mobilization, and in that case Germany, as Austria's ally and protector, would also feel herself obliged to mobilize. Presented with this likely outcome, Sazonov, far from deciding to defer the 'Period Preparatory to War' made plans for its implementation. Not

Below: Herbert Asquith, British Prime Minister in 1914, who used the violation of Belgian neutrality by Germany as a pretext to join the war.

Below: Sergei Sazonov, the Russian Foreign Minister, warned the Czar that entry in the war might prove fatal to the monarchy.

Below: Sir Edward Grey, British Foreign Minister, who warned the world that 'the lamps were going out all over Europe.'

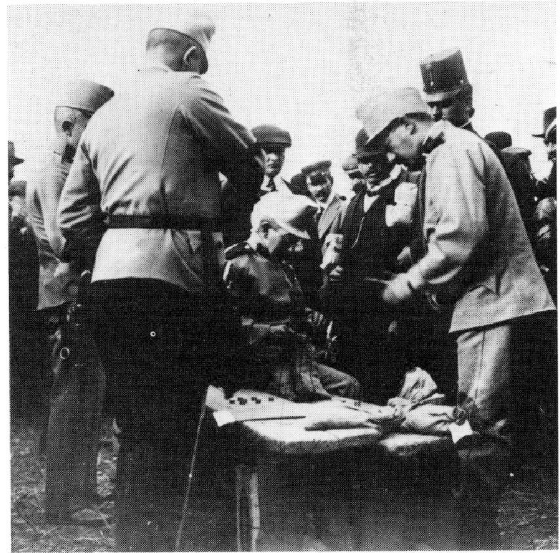

Above: Austrian soldiers receive their first pay after the mobilization in July 1914.

Above right: French crowds cheer after the declaration of war was announced.

only that, he also gave orders to prepare the full mobilization procedure, intending to lay both before the Czar for signature. Later, when he saw how the crisis was developing, he would judge which should be put into effect.

The next fatal twist to the development of the crisis was transmitted by France who, as Russia's ally, was naturally concerned by news of her preparatory measures. On 26 July the French government cancelled all military leave and the next day ordered the embarkation of the North African garrison, 100,000 strong. At the same time, the French Ambassador at St Petersburg, Maurice Paléologue began to press the Czar's government about its intentions. French anxiety about the Russian mobilization in the Caucasus differed from the Austrian in that in the event of a war with Germany French national security rested on the supposition of a major Russian offensive in East Prussia – the present Russian precautions thus represented a weakening, not strengthening of France's strategic position. During the next few days, therefore, Paléologue made it his business to move the Russians toward full mobilization. But in his hurry to maintain France's strength, he failed to see that such measures threatened to destroy, rather than preserve, peace. The flood gates of war were already being prized open.

As late as 29 July, however, Sazonov was uncertain about whether to proceed to full mobilization. On that day he received a telegram from Bethmann-Hollweg, the German Chancellor, which he took to be a patronizing and menacing ultimatum. The German ambassador, who was the intermediary, covered the note with the words that it was 'not a threat but a friendly warning,' sentiments which Sazonov chose to disregard. It implied that 'further progress of Russian mobilization measures would compel (Germany) to mobilize and then European war could scarcely be prevented.' Sazonov interpreted this to mean that Germany demanded a humiliating reversal of Russia's self-defensive precautions and accordingly advised the Czar that 'the risk could not be accepted of delaying a general mobilization.' Faced with this uninspiring alternative Nicholas II agreed to allow the whole of his army to be put on a war footing.

On the brink, however, the Czar had second thoughts. A patron of the international peace movement, his concern for peace was genuine. He decided to order not general but partial

Send Out the Army and the Navy

Send out the army and the navy,
Send out the rank and file,
Send out the brave territorials,
They'll face the danger with a smile
(I don't think)
Send out my mother,
Send out my sister and my brother,
But for God's sake don't send me!

Below: British recruits at Chatham Barracks. Some less enthusiastic volunteers sang this song.

Russian cavalry uniforms: 1 Border guard. 2 Cavalryman. 3 Cavalry officer. 4 Hussar of the Imperial Life Guard, summer uniform. 5 Ulan of the Life Guard.

Russian Cossack uniforms: 1 Don Cossack. 2 Ural Cossack. 3 Field artillery officer. 4 Kuban Cossack. 5 Field artilleryman.

Russian infantry uniforms: 1 Infantry officer. 2 Infantry officer in mufti. 3 and 4 Infantrymen. 5 Lower grade infantry officer in mufti.

Russian army uniforms: 1 General. 2 Infantry guard's officer. 3 Infantry guardsman. 4 Lower grade officer of the Life Guard. 5 Infantryman of the Life Guard.

БОЖІЕЮ МИЛОСТІЮ,

МЫ, НИКОЛАЙ ВТОРЫЙ,

ИМПЕРАТОРЪ И САМОДЕРЖЕЦЪ

ВСЕРОССІЙСКІЙ,

ЦАРЬ ПОЛЬСКІЙ, ВЕЛИКІЙ КНЯЗЬ ФИНЛЯНДСКІЙ,

И ПРОЧАЯ, И ПРОЧАЯ, И ПРОЧАЯ.

Объявляемъ всѣмъ вѣрнымъ НАШИМЪ подданнымъ:

Слѣдуя историческимъ своимъ завѣтамъ, Россія, единая по вѣрѣ и крови съ славянскими народами, никогда не взирала на ихъ судьбу безучастно. Съ полнымъ единодушіемъ и особою силою пробудились братскія чувства русскаго народа къ славянамъ въ послѣдніе дни, когда Австро-Венгрія предъ[явила] Сербіи завѣдомо непріемлемыя для державнаго государства требованія.

УКАЗЪ

ВОЕННОМУ МИНИСТРУ

Признавъ необходимымъ привести на военное положеніе армію согласно данныхъ МНОЮ вамъ указаній, повелѣваемъ вамъ нынѣ же сдѣлать по сему всѣ распоряженія.

Первымъ днемъ мобилизаціи назначить 17-е Іюля.

Николай

mobilization. The telegram reached the four military districts bordering Germany and Austria at midnight on 29 July. His soldiers, dismayed at this back-pedalling, then decided to take matters into their own hands. Realizing that international tension had become so acute that a partial mobilization would have the same effect as a general, they prevailed on the Czar to change his mind once again, and order general mobilization for 31 July. Their analysis of the mood of the other Great Powers was correct. Moltke, the Chief of the German General Staff, was acutely alarmed by Russia's partial mobilization in the four western districts and had immediately urged Franz Conrad von Hötzendorf, his Austrian opposite number, to move himself from partial to general mobilization – a departure, he pointed out, which under the terms of their treaty agreement would automatically compel Germany to mobilize also in Austria's support. He had also been working on the Kaiser, explaining that, in his professional judgment, Germany was now in a deteriorating military position in relation both to France and Russia and that she too must proceed to a preparatory phase. On 31 July, therefore, a state of 'imminent danger of war' (*drohende Kriegsgefahrzustand*) was proclaimed throughout the German empire.

Austria had actually been at war with Serbia since 28 July, though neither as yet had taken military action. On the news of the *Kriegsgefahrzustand*, however, Conrad von Hötzendorf declared general mobilization – from state (B) to state (R) – and thus created the situation which guaranteed a full Russian mobilization. The departure taken, pressure was renewed on Moltke and the German general staff. Since the plan hinged on Russia and France going to war simultaneously, thus asking Germany to attack France with seven-eighths of her armed forces, the German General Staff needed to take measures which would delay French mobilization. The German foreign office, acting on the initiative of the Crown Council, accordingly issued ultimata to both countries at the same time. Russia was to cease mobilization within 24 hours, France was to announce her neutrality within 36 hours and, for the duration of the crisis, to hand over two of her greatest frontier fortresses, Toul and Verdun, as a guarantee of goodwill.

As the Germans knew perfectly well, this demanded too much of French goodwill, whose sensitivities had never recovered from the humiliation of defeat by Germany in 1870 and the government rejected Germany's terms without discussion. Since 30 July her covering troops – the portion of her army which was kept permanently on a war footing – had been deployed along the Franco-German frontier, though 10 kilometers short of it in order to avoid further incidents. On 31 July, however, Joffre, Chief of the General Staff, warned the cabinet that:

'any delay in calling up our reservists will have as a result the withdrawal of our concentration points from 10 to 12 kilometers from each day of delay: in other words, the initial abandonment of just so much of our territory.'

A mobilization army order, the equivalent of the *Kriegsgefahrzustand*, had been issued the same day. On the next, 1 August, Joffre advised the Cabinet that it was unsafe to delay issuing the order for full mobilization any longer, and the posters *Ordre de Mobilisation Générale*, calling all reservists to report to their units, began to be posted up in the streets of Paris at 1555 that afternoon. Five minutes later, Germany ordered her own mobilization.

In the meantime, however, the Kaiser had had his personal moment of anguish. Although long informed of the Schlieffen Plan, he had not faced its full implications. Suddenly, on the evening of M-Day (general mobilization), he could not bring himself to take the responsibility of ordering a major attack on France when the weight of the crisis lay in the East. He summoned Moltke to him at short notice and demanded that the troop trains now loading for departure toward the Rhine, should be redirected and their passengers deployed against the Russians. Moltke, so appalled as to be unable even to remind the Kaiser of France's obligation to attack Germany if she should attack Russia, was reduced to a simple confession of impossibilities. The timetables, he said, perfectly accurately, had been prepared for years. The mobilization plan was designed to proceed almost literally by clockwork. Any attempt to interfere with it now would only render Germany defenseless, both on the Eastern and Western Front. Their responsibility, therefore, was to push on with the plan, and not to hinder its unrolling; with this reminder of inevitability, the Kaiser acquiesced.

The only major power not yet drawn into the crisis was Britain. She had no alliance which automatically engaged her support to one side or the other. However she was a guarantor of Belgian neutrality under the treaty of 1832. She had been made deeply antagonistic to Germany by the latter's creation of a large battle fleet, whose only visible purpose was to challenge the

Above: **A lull in the fighting in a French trench near the Hultebise farm, painted by Albert Boisfleury. This was a typical scene once the fronts had stabilized following the First Battle of the Marne.**

Below: **French postcard shows the latest models of cars and bikes to be used at the front. Mobilization problems caused a severe strain on the transportation system.**

Far left: **Czarist announcement of the declaration of war on Germany.**

Left: **Decree signed by Czar Nicholas II ordering the mobilization on 31 July 1914 (17 July, Russian date).**

Above: German troops are festooned with garlands as they march to the Belgian frontier.

Top: Austrian soldiers say goodbye to their families as they leave for the Serbian Front.

Above right: The 2nd Scots Guards leave the Tower of London for the mobilization center in the New Forest.

Below: French cavalry parade down the Rue de Rivoli on their way to the front.

Royal Navy for supremacy at sea. Also her soldiers had, since 1911, been conducting staff talks with their French opposite numbers to agree on how the British army might act in concert with the French if the British government decided to come to the aid of France in a defensive war against Germany. The outlines of that defensive war now loomed before the Cabinet in London. On the personal responsibility of Winston Churchill, First Lord of the Admiralty, the Grand Fleet had been kept together at Scapa Flow at the end of one of its trial mobilizations on 29 July. The Admiralty had also issued notice of a 'Precautionary Period.' On 1 August, requested by the French government to take incentives to protect the sea lines for troop movement across the Channel, it had ordered full mobilization, which called in the naval reservists and activated older ships of the fleet which did not normally take their place in the squadrons. The Cabinet were not yet ready, however, to order the mobilization of the army, or to give France a firm guarantee that it would come to her aid. Cabinet discussions from 1 to 3 August were sharply divided between those who felt that Britain's vital interests were threatened by the developing crisis on the continent and those who held true to the traditional principles of the Liberal Party – peace and isolation. Sir Edward Grey, the Foreign Secretary, a devoted Liberal and lover of peace, increasingly came to see no way out of the crisis for Britain but a declaration against Germany. 'The lamps are going out all over Europe,' he remarked to a colleague; in that deeply depressed mood he revealed to the House of Commons on 3 August the news both of the existing understanding between Britain and France for military co-operation, and firm news of Germany's violation of Belgian neutral territory. Later that day the Cabinet instructed the War Office to order General Mobilization and, the following morning, after all diplomatic representations had failed to take effect, Britain formally declared war on the German empire.

The Europe of the Great Powers was now at open war. Spain, as politically isolated as she was geographically, economically and culturally, would take no part, neither would Portugal. Italy, newest of the Great Powers, a club to which she only marginally belonged, was calculating her interests on the principle of *sacré ègoisme* – divine selfishness. She would later decide to join the Allies rather than the Central Powers, to which she had earlier been diplomatically committed. The Scandinavian states, Denmark, Sweden and Norway, the last an independent kingdom of only nine years' standing, were neutralist by popular mood, aspiration and diplomatic custom. Holland, whose territory Schlieffen had considered using for the passage of his armies westward toward Paris, was grateful to have been left alone. The smaller Balkan powers – Rumania, Montenegro, Bulgaria and Greece – had as yet no reason to enter the war for reasons of their own, and the interests of none of the Great Powers yet threatened to engulf them. Turkey, propelled by reaction away from Russia, her age-old enemy, toward Germany, trembled diplomatically on the brink of involvement, but had not yet toppled. Switzerland would remain an island of neutral middle ground, physically almost impregnable. Luxemburg had been engulfed without choice by Germany's military necessities. All other countries were at war: France, Russia, Serbia, Britain and, willy-nilly, Belgium, against Germany and Austria-Hungary.

In the East, Austria was finding Serbia a tougher enemy than she had complacently expected. The Serbs, a compact, proud and warlike nation, had mobilized simply and, when three Austrian armies, the Second, Fifth and Sixth (comprising the 'B Contingent' of Austria's War Plan) advanced into her western provinces across the River Drina they were roughly handled. Between 12 August and 20 August they were heavily counterattacked by the Serbs who, fighting on their own territory and with their national survival at stake, outperformed the invaders and forced them back, eventually compelling them to recross the Drina. The Second Army was, in any case, required under Plan R to move from Serbia to Galicia, to take its place in the line against Russia. Thereupon it suffered the humiliation of defeat and was instantly removed from the field of action without having had a chance to revenge its setback. In a week of fighting the Austrians suffered over 23,000 casualties, against an inferior enemy and

Above: **Viennese citizens hold up portraits of Wilhelm II and Franz Joseph as they celebrate the outbreak of war.**

Below: **Russian civilians demonstrate their patriotism at the outbreak of war in front of the Czar's Winter Palace in St Petersburg.**

Below: **Conrad von Hötzendorf, General of the Austrian armies at the start of the war.**

Above: **General Pau, French commander of the Army of Alsace in 1914.**

for no territorial gain. Indeed soon, there were no Austrian soldiers at all inside the Serbian frontier, which was to remain quiet for the next year of the war.

Elsewhere the action was dramatic and large scale. On the Eastern Front, the Germans found themselves almost instantaneously with a major crisis on their hands. All Schlieffen's calculations had rested on the assumption that Russia would mobilize much less quickly than France and would not move to the offensive until her armies were at full strength. His deliberations showed, on paper, a delay of six weeks between M-Day and the first Russian offensive, and it was in those six weeks that he planned to defeat France. Alas for the calculations – for which, of course, he could no longer be brought to book – Russia behaved in a fashion quite different from that which he had predicted. Far from waiting for the completion of mobilization, a procedure which Schlieffen had rightly calculated would be far lengthier in underdeveloped Russia than in the modernized West, the Czar's Stavka (Grand Staff) decided to attack with its covering force from the outset of hostilities. This force comprised two large armies, First and Second, deployed against the German Eighth Army in East Prussia, as well as four others, Fourth, Fifth, Third and Eighth, which were to face the Austrians in Galicia. The Austrians found the virtually roadless countryside of Galicia difficult terrain in which to develop an offensive, and were slow to move against the Russians. Equally hampered, the Russians were also slow to deploy but, as they planned no offensive action yet, were at less of a disadvantage. In the north, however, they pressed on against all difficulties – First and Second Armies determined to make the most of the opportunity that the German weakness offered them. Russian strategy, which aimed to win a victory not only to safeguard their own territory but also to materially aid the Western Allies in their struggle with the mass of the German army, was one for which France and Britain had the strongest reasons to be grateful. However for the Czar and for Russia, it would have dire consequences.

Below: **Serbian women hung by the Austrians in Macva, August 1914.**

The officers commanding First and Second Army, Pavel Rennenkampf and Alexandr Samsonov, were on bad terms, which hardly augured well for smooth co-operation between their two armies. Even worse, their staffs, separated by a hundred miles of almost roadless countryside, required to co-ordinate a complicated enveloping maneuver and obliged to communicate by radio, chose not to encode their messages. Radio was an entirely novel means of signalling and the Russians trusted to the fact that they changed their frequencies and varied their transmission times to shield their messages from the Germans – who, they hoped, might not be searching the air waves. The Germans, however, were. At first the knowledge they gleaned did not do them much good. Max von Prittwitz, the Eighth Army's commander, had unrealistic orders: to stand on the line of the Eastern frontier and hold it fast, if possible by offensive action in Russian Poland. Outnumbered, his three corps commanders – Otto von Below, August von Mackensen, Hermann von François, all to become famous as the war progressed – were defeated on 20 August in the frontier battle of Gumbinnen and forced to withdraw to the line of lakes (the Masurian Lakes) which bisects East Prussia. He also

Above: **General Otto von Bülow, Commander of the German Second Army in 1914.**

Above: **General Erich Ludendorff, Chief of Staff of the German Eighth Army.**

Above: **Field Marshal Paul von Hindenburg, Ludendorff's commander and head of the German Eighth Army at Tannenberg.**

decided his next move would be to retreat to the River Vistula, thus abandoning most of East Prussia to the Russians.

The thought of the historic heartland of the German military class falling to the despised Slavs put the German High Command into a controlled panic. Moltke was aghast. 'This was the result,' he raged, 'of leaving that fat idiot in command of the Eighth Army. . . .' Prittwitz, once described as the German version of Falstaff ('impressive in appearance, conscious to the highest degree of his self-importance, ruthless, even coarse and self-indulgent') had long been disliked by Moltke, who considered him unfit for his assignment. Now that he could legitimately be relieved Moltke did not hesitate. He nominated Erich Ludendorff, victor of the recent *coup de main* at Liège, to succeed Prittwitz's Chief of Staff. Shortly afterward he recalled Paul von Hindenburg from retirement to replace Prittwitz. On 23 August the two reached Marienburg, headquarters of Eighth Army and prepared to tackle the crisis. To their considerable relief they found that the Eighth Army's operations officer, Colonel Max Hoffmann, had already formulated a plan which offered the chance of a solution. This was to leave the 1st Cavalry Division to delay Rennenkampf's First Army on the coast, while the bulk of the infantry was transferred on a wide detour by railroad to attack Samsonov's Second Army, whose movements could be anticipated by radio interception. Hoffmann had, indeed, already set the plan in motion and, so impressive was the confidence with which he expounded it, that Hindenburg and Ludendorff at once adopted it as their own. After all, it might achieve the 'classic double envelopment' of Schlieffen's dreams.

The detraining place of François' corps was near Tannenberg, site of the great battle in 1414 in which the Slavs had won a rare victory over the crusaders of the Teutonic Order. That defeat was about to be avenged. Radio intercepts now revealed that Rennenkampf, impeded by poor roads and lagging supply columns, had actually halted short of the Masurian Lakes and

Below: **An Austrian encampment in northern Serbia near Belgrade.**

Above: **The Russian attack at Tannenberg. The Czarist armies pushed into swampy ground, preparing their encirclement.**

that Samsonov was accordingly at their mercy. His soldiers, 'exhausted and semistarved troops who had barely managed to stumble to the frontier,' fighting among the birch woods and small lakes which dot the sandy countryside of East Prussia, nevertheless gave François four very difficult days. But on 27 August von Below's corps arrived to attack Samsonov's northern flank, with Mackensen following him. Samsonov now realized that he was enveloped and decided to withdraw. Hindenburg was content to let him go, but the fire-eating von François, descendant of one of those Huguenot families which had found refuge from Louis XIV's persecution in Protestant Prussia, pressed his men forward. On 30 August two of Samsonov's five corps were surprised on the march and 60,000 prisoners taken. The total eventually reached nearly 100,000.

Samsonov, appalled at the fate of his offensive, shot himself on the field of battle. The gesture did as little to help Rennenkampf as the latter's hesitant advance had helped him in the crisis of Tannenberg. Now isolated in every sense, Rennenkampf dug his soldiers in on the line of the Masurian Lakes, hoping to ride out the storm of the German counteroffensive. His luck was in. The Eighth Army and its commanders, all tired from the emotional strain and physical exertion of the previous month, moved very slowly to the attack. The Russians resisted their efforts to envelop their right flank and, although eventually forced to withdraw across the Niemen, did so in good order. The Battle of the Masurian Lakes was a German victory, not of the stature of Tannenberg but enough to complete the liberation of East Prussia, and to establish the German army, even in the inferior numbers by which it was represented on that front, as the dominant force in the war in the East. As for Hindenburg he was, as Barbara Tuchman said, 'transformed into a titan by the victory.' For the Russians it was nothing short of a disaster. The Second Army virtually ceased to exist, its commander was dead, two corps commanders had been captured and three cashiered for incompetence. The French, however, were well satisfied that German strength on the Western Front had been weakened – the Russians had, indeed, as their Commander in Chief put it, made a sacrifice for their allies.

Above: **The German counterattack at Tannenberg, which forced the Russians to surrender hundreds of thousands of men.**

It remained to be seen whether the German armies in the west would have a Tannenberg of their own to celebrate. Walter Bloem, marching southward with the 12th Brandenburg Grenadiers, looked forward to entering Paris, *la ville lumière*, 'the city of light,' as a conqueror. He had reason to be optimistic. All had gone so well since mobilization and deployment that it was impossible to foresee anything but a conclusion to the campaign as successful as that now unfolding in the East.

The campaign had begun with a dramatic success. Long before the war, the German

Below: **Serbian victims of the reprisals by Austria after the assassination of Franz Ferdinand.**

Below: **The Russian advance guard in Poland which was preparing for the disaster at Tannenberg.**

Great General Staff had determined that the Schlieffen Plan could only succeed if the gorge of the Meuse, the great river which passes through northern Belgium, could be crossed by its existing bridges, at Liège and Namur. A plan had accordingly been drawn up to seize the former at the very outset of the war by *coup de main*, with a specially picked task force of 13 infantry regiments and a siege train of 210mm howitzers.

The man chosen to command the attack was Ludendorff, a fanatical devotee of Schlieffen on whom he modelled himself carefully, even down to his forbidding personality. A staff officer of some brilliance he was now to demonstrate that his idol's theories could be put into practice, and also to demonstrate his own considerable powers of leadership. Liège was a 'ring fortress,' a central citadel in the city surrounded at a distance by a circular chain of smaller forts. The spaces between the outer forts was supposed to be filled by 'interval troops,' infantry allotted to the fortress commander. Leman, the Belgian general had, however, only been asked to render four of these forts impregnable. Work had not progressed very far before on 6 August the Germans broke in after some stiff fighting. Ludendorff put himself at the head of the leading column and marched down into the center of the city where, with the pommel of his sword, he battered for admission on the door of the citadel. To his frustration, however, the outer fortresses refused to surrender in sympathy, and he was obliged to bring up his big howitzers and reduce them one by one. The explosions of their giant shells as they were 'walked up' to each while the range was found drove some in the fort garrisons mad. Not Leman however, who, bloody but unbowed, was extracted from the ruins of the last fort to fall, on 13 August. He was allowed by Ludendorff, in an uncharacteristic gesture to keep his sword.

Above right: **Some of the first members of the British Expeditionary Force take up positions in a Belgian wood.**

Right: **Belgian infantrymen pause for chow prior to the German onslaught.**

Below: **Swarms of German infantry cross the rolling hills at the Belgian frontier in the first days of war.**

Above: **Marshal Joffre on the cover of a French illustrated magazine.**

Above far left: **The cover of a German youth magazine depicting Crown Prince Rupprecht of Bavaria.**

Above left: **General Sir John French, leader of the BEF.**

Left: **'The Last Gunner,' the legendary defense of the British retreat at Mons, where one gunner held off the advancing Germans until the British forces were safely out of gunfire.**

Above: **The French General de Castelnau, who commanded the Second Army which guarded the Ardennes.**

The week-long resistance of Liège had threatened to set back the departure of the 'great wheel' on Paris. In the nick of time, its fall allowed the preordained schedule to be met. It had also threatened to unveil to the French the true center of the German concentration and the direction in which their armies would deploy. However Joffre, at GQG (Grand Quartier Général, French Headquarters), remained resolutely convinced that the focus of German concentration was not in the north, but in the center of France's eastern frontier at Metz. Therefore he considered that the right strategy to pursue was precisely that offensive one which the Supreme War Council had decreed before the war. Plan XVII divided French forces into five armies. Of these the First was to stand on the defensive on the right in the mountainous Vosges. The Second was to attack into Lorraine, toward Metz. The Third and Fourth were to advance into the Belgian Ardennes. All were trained tactically to prosecute the offensive with great vigor, indifferent to enemy fire, and to attack off the line of march with or without artillery support. Colonel Grandmaison, principal advocate of this tactical doctrine, preached that 'infantry which went forward boldly must conquer.'

General Charles Lanrezac, commanding the Fifth Army, subscribed to the tactical doctrine but not to official strategy. He had long believed that the Germans could not resist making use of the open avenue into northern France which Belgium offered and, positioned as he was nearest the Belgian border, prevailed on Joffre to allow him to extend his flank in that direction. It was toward that flank that the British Expeditionary Force of six divisions of infantry and one of cavalry was making its way. Lanrezac privately arranged with the BEF to bar the approach of the German armies, which he suspected to be descending on the currently unprotected northern plains. While he stealthily sidled northward, however, the experience of other armies tended to reinforce his diagnosis. Between 6 and 11 August the First Army's probing operations in the Vosges encountered strong German opposition. The Second Army, which had begun an advance into Lorraine toward Metz, was resisted by German covering forces and had to fight hard to progress. Though its commander did not know it, the Germans were deliberately drawing the Second Army on and on 20 August, overextended in difficult country under a fierce counterattack, it was thrown into full retreat after a two-day battle. On that same day, the French Third and Fourth Armies, pushing through the forests of the Ardennes, came up against major German forces – in fact the Fifth and Fourth Armies, which were wheeling southwestward in conformity with the Schlieffen plan.

The French had not expected to meet the Germans; the Germans, however were more than ready for such an encounter. As a result,

Below: **Belgian troops camouflaged their hats with straw at the start of the war.**

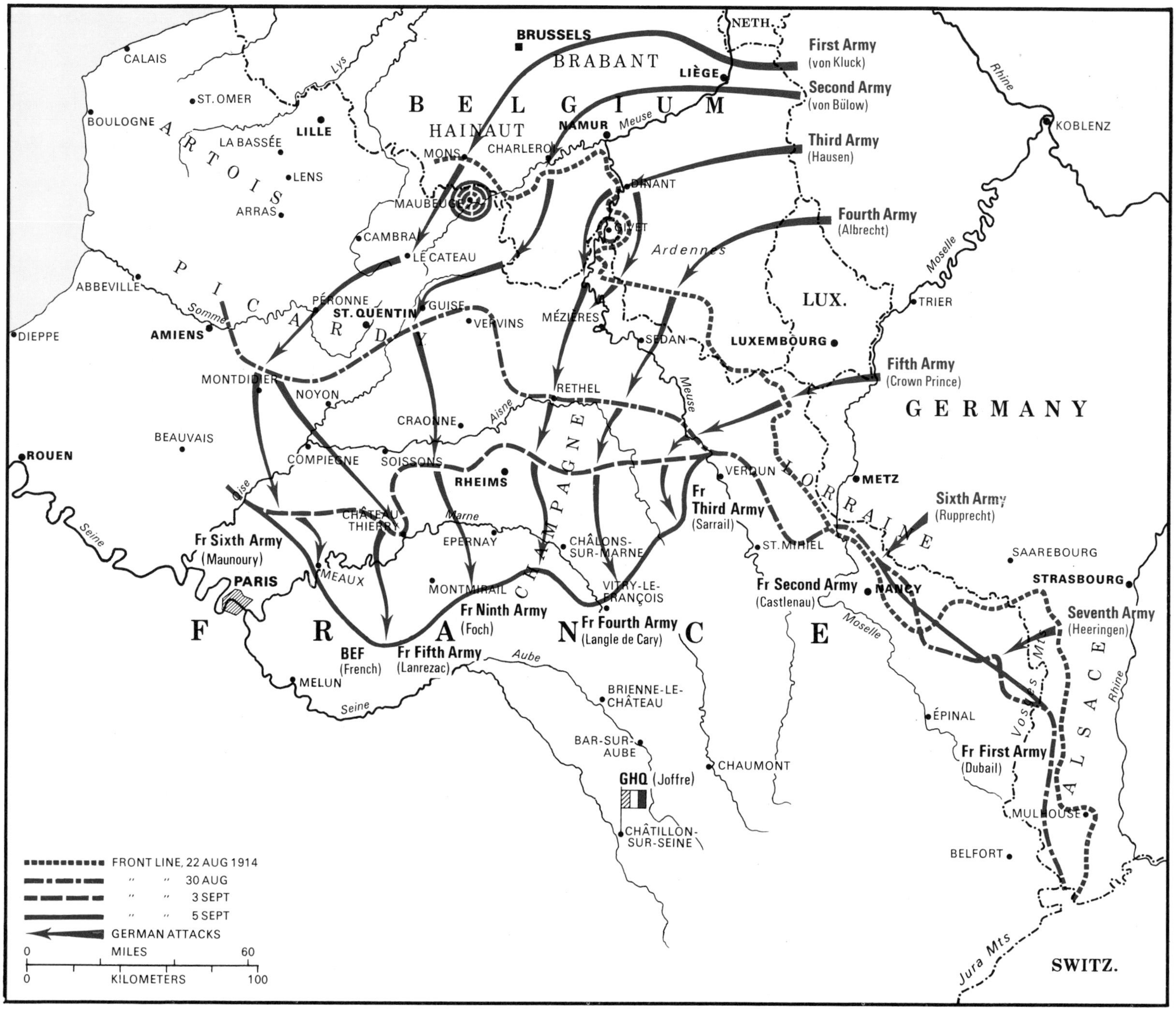

Above: The German sweep into France violated the basic tenet of the Schlieffen Plan. Instead of encircling Paris the Germans hoped to drive toward it and, almost inevitably, failed.

Left: Belgians defend the Willebroeck Canal near Antwerp.

the battle went disastrously for the French who were forced into a hasty retreat. General Sordet's Cavalry Corps, which had been reconnoitering to the north in an empty tract of countryside, also fell back frustrated, announcing that it had seen no major German forces.

In fact, it had simply been in the right place at the wrong time. As it withdrew, the major weight of the German wheeling armies, supplied by Third, Second and First, came hurrying forward. All that now stood in their way was the British Expeditionary Force and Lanrezac's Fifth Army. By constant entreaty, Lanrezac had prevailed on Joffre to allow him to move his army further and further northward, but now it and the BEF were deployed to defend the most important water line guarding the northern approaches – the Sambre-Meuse line between Dinant-Namur-Charleroi and the Mons Canal. On 23 August both were heavily attacked in their positions, the French at Charleroi, the British at Mons. In both places the Germans suffered heavily. They, like the French, em-

Above: Belgians watch as the 2nd Scots Guards advance.

Right: A Belgian armored car and infantry wait for the Germans to arrive.

Below right: Victorious Germans cross the Place Charles Rogier in Brussels, 26 August 1914.

ployed their infantry in direct frontal attacks against the Allies' hasty entrenchments, which were reinforced both by machine guns and plentiful field artillery. The British were expert marksmen and the young German conscripts paid the price. So, too, did they against the French at Charleroi. But their numbers were overwhelming and eventually the weight of their supporting artillery told.

Even so, they might have held the position but for the withdrawal of the French Fourth and Third Armies from the Ardennes. Threatened by that development on their right flank with a German envelopment, both Sir John French, commanding the BEF and Lanrezac came to the conclusion that they must abandon the Sambre-Meuse line and accordingly gave orders for a retreat to begin the following day, 24 August. A similar retreat was taking place all down the French line, as far south as Nancy, where the Germans had relaxed their pressure. The retreat was not, however, a rout. Joffre continued to retain control of his subordinate armies' movements and they stood and fought whenever and wherever they could: on 26 August the BEF fought a successful delaying action at Le Cateau; on 29 August Lanrezac held the Germans for a day at Guise – and there were other, small, successes. But the trend was inexorably southward. Joffre first hoped to hold the line along the Somme, 60 miles north, but his forces were pushed off that river without the chance to make a stand. By 1 September, after 10 days of ferocious marching, the Germans were approaching Paris. There was only one defensible obstacle which lay between them – the line of the Marne. Moltke, who was secure in the German High Command, firmly believed that it would offer no more serious impediment than any of the others his victorious armies had overcome so successfully in the course of their onslaught. True, his armies were tiring and his lines of supply were drawing thin, but that had been foreseen. There now seemed no reason why the culminating act of the Schlieffen Plan, a battle of annihilation before the walls of Paris, should not be triumphantly concluded.

The French Model 1875 artillery gun in action.

2 The Clash of Arms

The walls of Paris was not merely a literary phrase. Alone among the historic capitals of Europe, Paris retained in 1914 its girdle of fortification. London had overgrown its walls in the sixteenth century; Vienna's had been razed to the ground in the 1850s in order that revolutionaries should never again hold the city against the Emperor; Berlin's had been buried in the enormous building boom which followed its elevation to imperial status in 1871; Rome's had never been restored since their breaching by Victor Emmanuel's soldiers in 1870. Paris, besieged in 1870 by the invading Prussians, had been judged by successive French governments to be too tempting and too vulnerable a target and the walls had been allowed to remain. For Paris, strategically as much as politically and culturally, was France. All roads, all railroads, led to it. He who held the capital held the country.

Schlieffen had been aware of the central significance of Paris throughout the years of work on his plan. He accepted from the first that his decisive battle would have to be fought near it, but he could not decide what to do about the obstacle that it presented. He knew that in a crisis its garrisons would come out to fight beside the French field army, unless there was some way of confining it within the walls. His first idea, therefore, was to allot extra troops to the marching mass of his 'great wheel,' whose task would be to invest the city. Try as he might, however, he could not find a surplus of troops to undertake it. The imperial parliament was reluctant to vote funds to raise yet more men but, even if they could have been persuaded to do so, Schlieffen found that however hard he stared at a map of France there was simply no way of accommodating the extra troops in the 'wheel.' There were just not enough roads. The whole road network of Belgium and northern France was required solely to move the armies of the 'great wheel.' For the moment Paris would have to be left uninvested.

This had, however, raised another difficulty which Schlieffen had tinkered with, failed to solve, and finally bequeathed to his successors without disclosing the threat it offered to the great plan's success. It was General Alexander von Kluck, commanding the German First Army at the beginning of September, who had to grapple with the consequences. Paris was dead ahead of his line of advance. The Second Army, commanded by Bülow, was keeping static to his right. On 31 August they crossed the River Aisne and were now approaching the Marne, the last major water obstacle on the route to Paris. Kluck was following the retreat of the British Expeditionary Force but found as he

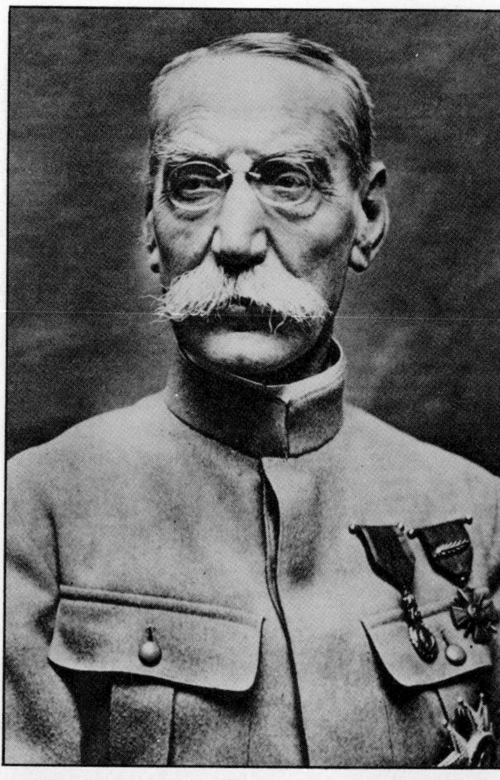

Above; **General, later Marshal Galliéni, military governor of Paris.**

Above: General Franchet d'Esperey, commander of the French Fifth Army.

Above: French *cuirassiers* in Paris on their way to the Marne.

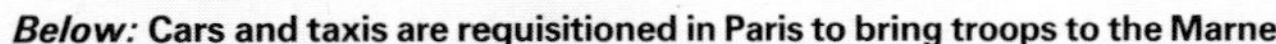

Below: Cars and taxis are requisitioned in Paris to bring troops to the Marne.

Above: **French troops advance through a village near Paris during the Battle of the Marne.**

came inward that the line of march drew him away from Bülow in a direction which threatened to take him west of Paris. At once he saw that if he persisted he would find himself cut off from the rest of the German army by the intervening obstacle of the Paris fortress – with the strong possibility of being attacked by its garrison. On 3 September pilots of the Royal Flying Corps, who the day before had observed Kluck's columns heading southwestward, now reported that they had turned southeast, and that some had turned east to regain contact with the outer flank of Bülow's army. Kluck's army would now pass Paris to the east.

This news quickly filtered to GQG, where Joffre had been busy forming a new army near Paris (to be called the Sixth, under General Joseph Maunoury). General Joseph Galliéni, the Military Governor of Paris, and once Joffre's superior in Madagascar, at once pointed out to the Commander in Chief that Kluck's change of direction offered a magnificent opportunity to launch an attack into his flank with Maunoury's new reserve. Joffre, who had been sitting all day under a tree in a village schoolyard at Châtillon, rose to the occasion. Enormous in bulk, ponderous in speech, (and apparently in thought) his massive calm had served France better in the terrible days of August than, perhaps, the qualities of a more obvious leader would have done. He now demonstrated that he was able to profit from, as well as survive, a crisis. Orders were given that on the following day the French armies should turn about and counterattack along the whole length of the front from Verdun to Paris. The Battle of the Marne was about to begin.

In retrospect the Marne was not a spectacular battle. Fought along a front 100 miles long, few of those taking part were conscious that they were actors in a dramatic turning point of European history. Few of the army commanders in action had grasped any full picture of events. There was little, if any, maneuver during the four days the battle lasted. The Germans simply went on with their frontal offensive, but now they found that the French, instead of turning their backs, showed their faces to the front and attacked. At the eastern end of the battleline the reaction achieved little effect. At the western end, however, the BEF launched a determined counteroffensive spearheaded by the newly-formed Ninth Army under the dynamic Foch ('My center is giving way, my right is falling back. Situation excellent. I attack.') It was, though, the outflanking move of Maunoury's Sixth Army from Paris which did most to unhinge the German position. Kluck and Bülow, at OHL's orders, first halted and then found front to the west, so as to meet this new threat, a change of activity which spelled doom to the Schlieffen plan.

During the ensuing battles, both against Foch and Maunoury (some of whose troops had been brought to the battlefront in taxi cabs, thus giving birth to a potent legend), the Germans actually established a supremacy. However the appearance of the BEF in the gap which had opened between Kluck's and Bülow's armies, and the paucity of information filtering to OHL over the crackling field telephone, threw Moltke into a panic. 'Where,' he kept asking, 'are the prisoners? Where are the captured guns?' He was convinced that the battle was lost, and on 8 September dispatched a junior staff officer, Colonel Richard Hentsch, from his headquarters at Spa in Belgium to the battlefront, with authority to take the decision to retreat should he judge it to be necessary. Hentsch motoring along the battlefront from headquarters to headquarters soon became persuaded that the situation near Paris was, indeed, critical and accordingly ordered a retreat to the Aisne, to begin the following day. The intention was that it should be only temporary and that, from firmer positions, the Germans should resume their offensive. But, though they could not foresee it, Hentsch's decision was to consign them to those long years of defensive warfare in the trenches, which within a few days, they would begin to dig.

They reached the Aisne on 14 September, exhausted but in good heart. The retreat had been orderly and their defense of the line on arrival was so successful that hopes were still high at the prospect of resuming the offensive. Just as the French, during the Battle of the Marne, had been able to bring reinforcements from either end of the front – Paris and Alsace – along their shortened line of communications, so now the Germans could find extra troops to thicken their line. In September the BEF, the Sixth Army (Maunoury) and the Fifth, now commanded by Franchet d'Esperey, Lanrezac having paid the penalty for having been right too soon, attacked across the Aisne to the heights on the north bank, only to find the German First and Second Armies reinforced and the gap between them now solidly filled. Nothing was achieved in the ensuing three days of fighting except for heavy casualties.

Joffre and Foch, (now promoted to be his deputy after the magnificent display of moral courage he had shown at the Marne) accordingly decided to dislodge the Germans by an attack upon their open flank. More troops had been brought from the eastern end of the front, where the old frontier fortress towns of Nancy, Toul and Verdun stood as bastions against a German advance, and with these reinforcements the French applied pressure first at Roye, then Arras, then Lens, then La Bassée. Though they did not realize it, they were fighting a hopeless battle. The railroad system was against them. For the Marne, it had worked in their favor, when the Reine–Verdun line had been used to shift troops east–west along the battlefront. Now, however, they were fighting an enemy who could use, as the French put it, another *ligne de rocade*, from Metz to Lille, running north–south at about 50 miles from the successive points of encounter. The superior speed of reinforcement which this facility conferred on German strategy (now directed by Erich von Falkenhayn, who had succeeded the disgraced Moltke on 14 September) nullified any French offensive effort. Fortunately for the Allies, their hold on the coast was secure. British reinforcements landed at Ostend in late September, and the Belgian army, which had fallen back from Antwerp to join them, held the little river Yser which runs through the wet coastal plain of Flanders to the sea at Nicupat. In between, however, lay the small city of Ypres – offering, as it seemed, a last chance to break through into the German rear area. The BEF, transferred from the Aisne to La Bassée by rail on 10 October, and having seen little action on the Marne, was still in fine fighting fettle. They at once began to push forward and, quite by accident, encountered an equal and opposite reaction.

For the Germans had, in the nick of time, managed to form those new divisions for which Schlieffen had searched in vain during the days when he was designing his master plan. Raised from students of all ages who had volunteered at the outbreak of war, they comprised six new corps (XXII–XXVII) to add to the 37 (I–XXI, Guard, I–III Bavaria, and 12 reserve corps)

Right: **The rush from Paris by Galliéni's men enabled the BEF to drive between the German First and Second Armies and force a retreat at the Marne.**

Right: **General Falkenhayn was brought in as German Chief of Staff to replace the disgraced General von Moltke.**

Far right: **German soldiers take up machine-gun positions near the Aisne, to which they withdrew after the Marne maneuver.**

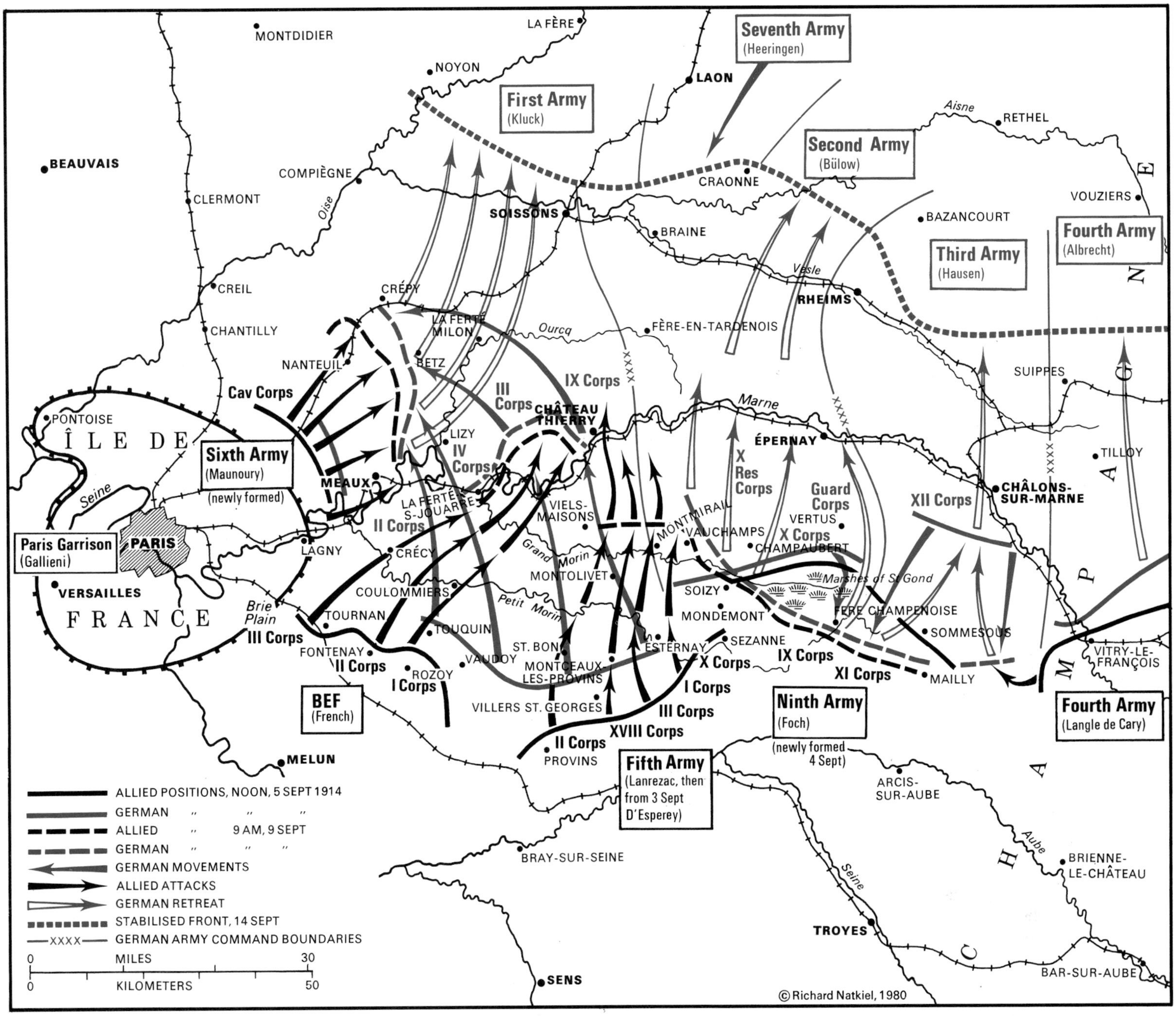

Seventh Army (Heeringen)
First Army (Kluck)
Second Army (Bülow)
Third Army (Hausen)
Fourth Army (Albrecht)
Sixth Army (Maunoury) (newly formed)
Paris Garrison (Gallieni)
BEF (French)
Fifth Army (Lanrezac, then from 3 Sept D'Esperey)
Ninth Army (Foch) (newly formed 4 Sept)
Fourth Army (Langle de Cary)

MONTDIDIER
LA FÈRE
NOYON
LAON
RETHEL
BEAUVAIS
COMPIÈGNE
CRAONNE
CLERMONT
VOUZIERS
SOISSONS
BRAINE
BAZANCOURT
CREIL
CRÉPY
RHEIMS
CHANTILLY
LA FERTÉ MILON
FÈRE-EN-TARDENOIS
NANTEUIL
BETZ
SUIPPES
PONTOISE
ÎLE DE FRANCE
CHÂTEAU THIERRY
ÉPERNAY
TILLOY
LIZY
MEAUX
CHÂLONS-SUR-MARNE
LA FERTÉ-S-JOUARRE
VIELS-MAISONS
MONTMIRAIL
VERTUS
PARIS
LAGNY
CRÉCY
VAUCHAMPS
CHAMPAUBERT
MONTOLIVET
Marshes of St Gond
VERSAILLES
COULOMMIERS
SOIZY
TOURNAN
MONDEMONT
FÈRE CHAMPENOISE
TOUQUIN
SEZANNE
SOMMESOUS
FONTENAY
ST. BON
ESTERNAY
VITRY-LE-FRANÇOIS
VAUDOY
ROZOY
MONTCEAUX-LES-PROVINS
MAILLY
VILLERS ST. GEORGES
PROVINS
MELUN
ARCIS-SUR-AUBE
BRAY-SUR-SEINE
BRIENNE-LE-CHÂTEAU
TROYES
SENS
BAR-SUR-AUBE
CHAMPAGNE
Aisne
Oise
Vesle
Ourcq
Marne
Seine
Grand Morin
Petit Morin
Aube
Brie Plain

Cav Corps
III Corps
IV Corps
IX Corps
II Corps
X Res Corps
Guard Corps
X Corps
XII Corps
III Corps
II Corps
I Corps
X Corps
IX Corps
XI Corps
I Corps
III Corps
XVIII Corps
II Corps

ALLIED POSITIONS, NOON, 5 SEPT 1914
GERMAN " " "
ALLIED " 9 AM, 9 SEPT
GERMAN " " "
GERMAN MOVEMENTS
ALLIED ATTACKS
GERMAN RETREAT
STABILISED FRONT, 14 SEPT
——XXXX—— GERMAN ARMY COMMAND BOUNDARIES
0 MILES 30
0 KILOMETERS 50

© Richard Natkiel, 1980

Entente cordiale.
"PATRIE"
15

Far left: A Tommy and a *poilu,* multiplied by millions, made the Entente Cordiale a reality.

Center left: Artillery fire in the hills near Paris, painted by François Flameng.

Left: 'Papa' Joffre, whose masterly patience saved Paris and France at the Marne.

Right: General von Kluck, whose German First Army failed to sweep around Paris as Schlieffen had planned.

Below left: The trenches near Notre Dame de Lorette after a thunderstorm, painted by Francois Flameng.

Below: Messine Ridge in early 1915.

Above: Lewis gunners of the BEF in position near the Marne. Their crash helmets and guns were brought up quickly by the rail line behind them.

Below: Men of the 1st Middlesex struck by shrapnel at the Marne, 8 September 1914.

Far left: Belgian troops land at Ostend.

Left: British reinforcements near Ostend.

Right: French troops in the trenches in Belgium in 1915. By this time their colorful uniforms had been replaced by the horizon blue uniforms which made a less obvious target.

already in existence. Inspired by the ideals of youth and patriotism, these young men came up against the British at Ypres on 20 October. It was indeed a dreadful baptism of fire. Advancing in massed columns, they were repelled with heartrending ease by the rapid shooting – 'the mad minute' of 15 aimed shots per rifle – of the trained British marksmen. Their sheer numbers, however, determined that the British could not break out through the Ypres gap and the BEF dug itself in to resist a fresh onslaught. It came on 31 October with the same result. In those two battles, and a third final assault by the Prussian Guard at Nun's wood directly outside Ypres on 11 November, the Germans lost, killed and wounded 135,000 men, including 41,000 from the volunteer corps. Little wonder that the Germans call this First Battle of Ypres the *Kindermord* (Slaughter of the Innocents).

Meanwhile, the French army had, on a limited scale, gone over to the offensive. From 14 December to Christmas Eve, it attacked in front of Arras and on 20 December it opened a siege offensive in the Champagne, east of Reims, its prewar training area and destined to be the scene of continuous trench warfare throughout the war. There were limited offensives at other points, all also destined to become familiar names in the communiques: The Argonne, a wet, wooded sector north of Verdun; Les Eparges, east of the city; St Mihiel, further south, where a German salient interrupted a vital military line; and the mountains of the Vosges, where French *chasseurs alpins* and German *Jäger* battled it out for possession of crests and peaks (like the Hartmannweilerkopf – *le vieil Armand*) of jealously loved significance.

Little effect was made on the increasingly dense structure of the French line, now continuous from Nieuwpoort on the North Sea to Switzerland. Both sides had exhausted their prewar reserves of ammunition, neither had really large reserves of artillery with which to batter an entrance into the entrenchments. All

Above: French troops pass through the ruined village of Soisy-aux-Bois near the front in early 1915.

armies had suffered appalling casualties – the BEF 80,000 on a strength of 160,000, the Germans and French each nearly a million. In the British and German armies, Christmas 1914 brought on a mood of war weariness and reconciliation. Neither side had yet any real reason to inflict hurt on the other, and at dawn on Christmas day British soldiers in the lines around Ypres were roused by the sound of carols sung across no man's land and the sight of candle-decked Christmas trees rising over the parapets. Behind them appeared the figures of German soldiers, who, in a steady stream, made their way to the halfway line, calling out Christmas greetings and offering schnapps and cigars. They were shortly joined by friendly partners from the British side and, by noon, the whole of the British front had given itself over to fraternization.

In some places the Christmas truce lasted for nearly a week, and it took the intervention of British headquarters to bring it to an end, to the regret of ordinary soldiers in both armies. No such truce, however, had broken out on the French front. Even if the Germans had wished to offer it, the French army was in no mood to respond. Besides their own losses, there were other reasons for which they could not forgive the invaders: the destruction of much that was beautiful and historic in their country, the occupation of an eighth of the national territory, including the most heavily industrialized regions, the imposition of military government on the population of the occupied areas and, above all, the obvious threat of a renewed offensive against Paris which the German presence held out.

Far from wishing to fraternize, therefore, the French army sought to repay in kind what it had suffered. But, as yet, it had not the means to do so. Asked to decide his strategy by the politicians in meetings of the war cabinet, Joffre, impenetrable and incommunicative as ever, replied *'Je les grignote'* ('I am nibbling the Germans to death'). With his reserves of men and munitions exhausted, he could do no more. But, with the approach of spring, prospects of renewing the offensive brightened. The colonial garrisons yielded an important increment of

Above: **Digging of trenches finally began after the race to the sea. Here Germans dig near the Argonne Forest.**

Above right: **No man's land between Neuve-Chapelle and Armentières.**

Above far right: **A British field hospital.**

men, augmented by the tightened screw of the conscription machine. The universities and the *grandes écoles* offered a source of replacement for the casualties among regular officers. The cadets of St Cyr, commissioned on the steps of Madame de Maintenon's academy for young ladies on 1 August 1914, swore on oath to meet the enemy in the white gloves and egret feathers of their ceremonial uniforms. All had done so, and most had paid the price. Their places would be taken by students of Science-Po and the Ecole Normale who, in peace, made a cult of their nonmilitary attitude to life. Most important of all, the factories of America, fuelled by the gold reserves which patriotic loan subscriptions had coaxed from the safe deposits of the French bourgeoisie, had begun to tool up for war production and were beginning to make good the vast expenditure of artillery ammunition which the Battle of the Frontiers, the Marne and the Aisne had imposed on the French army.

In May, therefore, Joffre was able to issue detailed orders for a great offensive, whose objects were nothing less than the recovery of the national territory. The map provided a suggestion as to how that might be achieved. On it, the German line described a horizontal S about 450 miles long, one end in the sea, the other touching Switzerland near Basle. At its southern end, high broken country made the line unsuitable for offensive operations. At the other, where the Belgians had let the North Sea into the flood plains of the Yser, an offensive

Right: **A British 18-pounder near Armentières, 7 December 1914.**

Far right above: **Wounded from the Marne arrive at Charing Cross Hospital, London. Medical facilities on the front were virtually nonexistent in 1914.**

Far right below: **British start to dig trenches near the Ghent-Antwerp road, 9 October 1914.**

CHARING CROSS HOSPITAL
CHARING + HOSPITAL
ENTRANCE
FOR
PATIENTS

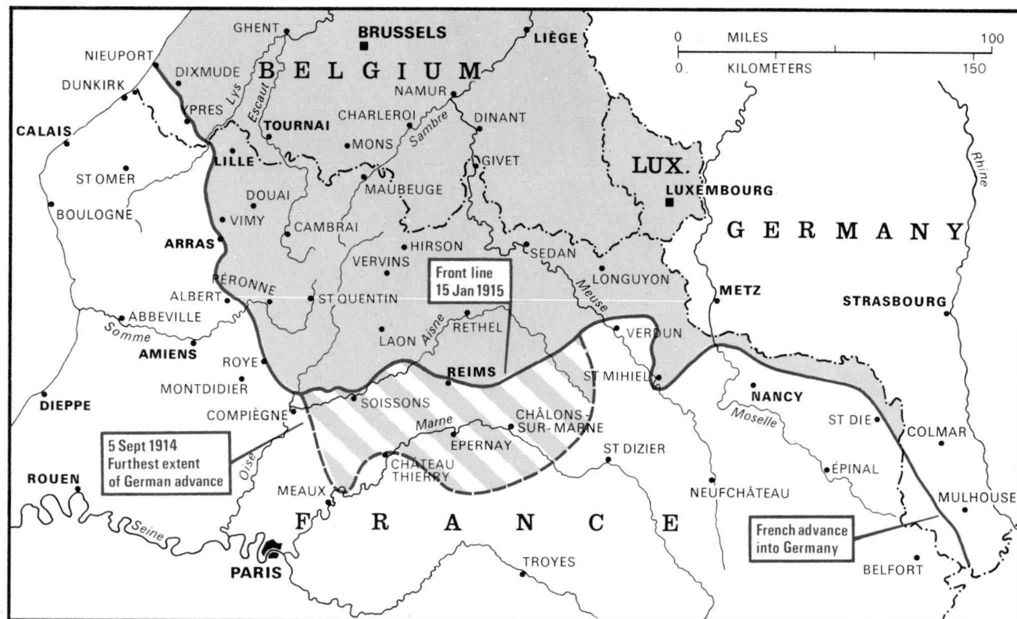

Above: **The Western Front at the end of 1914.**

would have had to be amphibious to succeed. In between, the countryside offered several routes eastward particularly favorable for an offensive, and Joffre had, as early as December 1915, mentally selected two of them as decisive. They were Arras and the Champagne, on each of which he had already made interim assaults. For May 1915 he planned a large-scale attack at Arras, designed to capture the key feature of Vimy Ridge, from which he could look down into the German positions in the plain of Douai. He had assembled a new army, the Tenth, a great stock of ammunition, and much heavy artillery. That army, despised before the war by French gunners since it could not accompany the infantry in the field on the lightning attacks with which they planned to win the war, was now seen to be the key ingredient of successful strategy. Arsenals and forts had been stripped of every heavy gun, new or old, that could be found. The collection, often more suited to a museum than for action at the front, was fitted with wheels and carriages, in order that it would be able to add its weight to the shoals of 75mm field guns which, against trenches and barbed wire, were proving of little use.

Below: **An Austrian hospital, obviously far better than most. Conditions were usually abysmal.**

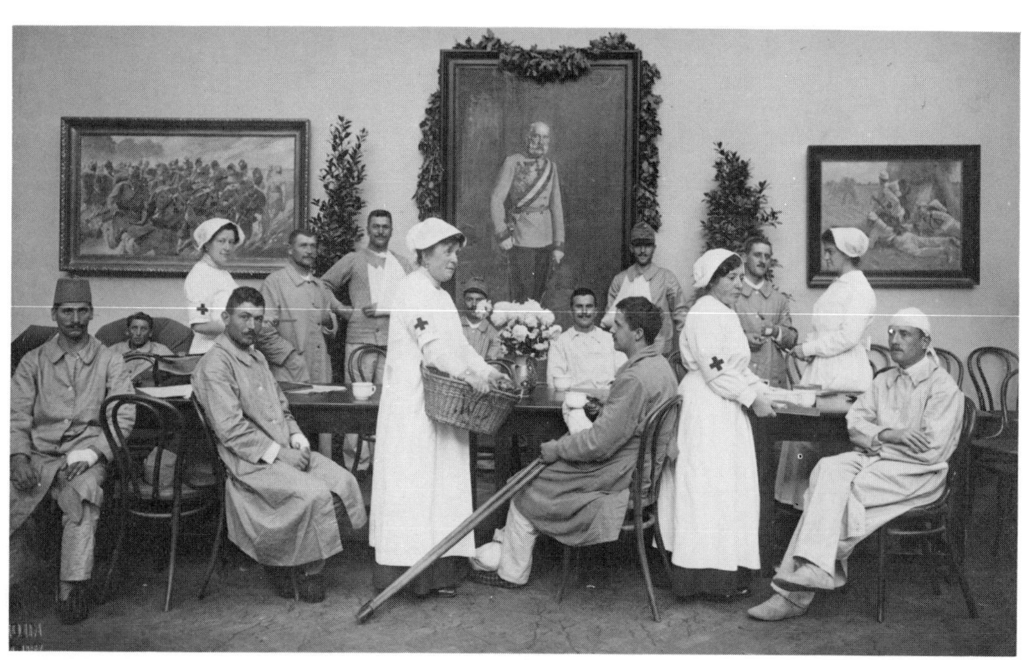

On 9 May the Tenth Army attacked. Among its formations was XXXIII Corps, commanded by General Henri Philippe Pétain, and composed largely of white regulars of the colonial army, hardy and experienced soldiers. Their target was the church which crowned the summit of the Ridge, Notre Dame de Lorette and, within two hours of attacking, they had penetrated two and a half miles into the German lines and seized the crest. Five days of preliminary bombardment, however, had so cut up the ground that Tenth Army's reserves (positioned in any case too far from the front) could not reach the first assailants before they were counterattacked. Once they were under attack, the prospect of deepening the break-in disappeared.

The divisions on either side of XXXIII Corps had done less well, reporting slow progress in what came to be called the *Labyrinthe.* All up and down the Western Front, however, the pattern was the same. The trench system was being transformed, of necessity, into a labyrinth. Official policy on both sides was for a simple layout of entrenchments. A front line, 'traversed' (dug in right-angled zigzag paths, to prevent an enemy who entered at one point firing down the length of the trench); a 'support' line, two or three hundred yards behind; perhaps a 'reserve' line, further back still; and the whole connected transversely by 'communication' trenches, also traversed, which led from the rear into the front trench. Trenches were dug at least six feet deep – the Germans (whose strategy was defensive in the West) furnishing theirs with deep dugouts excavated under the parapet which went down to a depth of, perhaps, 20 or 30 feet. On the Allied side the dugouts were shallower, due to the fact that both the British and French armies made it their official policy to declare trench positions temporary, Allied strategy being offensive. In practice these official pronouncements of dogma were often ignored. Tactically both sides were offensive at many places up and down the front. Local attacks to capture a piece of high ground, or to iron out an awkward angle, meant that small sections of trench constantly changed hands, and others were hastily dug to protect sections threatened by change of ownership. The result was the growth of a maze of trenches old and new, which to an attacker who inadvertently found himself trapped behind enemy lines presented a puzzle almost impossible to solve and made his task of finding his way out into open country an increasingly difficult one.

Never was this more clearly demonstrated than at Ypres where, sometime before Joffre's attack at Vimy Ridge, the Germans had employed a new weapon to attempt the capture of the cornerstone of the Flanders position from the British. On 22 April both they and the French, whose line abutted on the right, noticed about 1700 hours a curious blue-white mist rising from the parapet of the German trenches and drifting toward them. When it reached their wire the sentries began to cough and choke. As it passed the parapet, it sank into the trench and soon, almost everywhere, French and British soldiers were streaming to the rear, tearing at their collars and gasping for breath. The mist was xylyl bromide, a tear gas, borne by a light evening breeze, behind which the Germans advanced to capture their prize. It was not, however, the first time that gas had been used. That occasion was at Bolimow in January 1915, when the Germans had experimented against the Russians. However the Ypres attack was certainly far more spectacular and threatened devastating results. For on a four-mile front, directly in front of the city, on the evening of 22 April there were no Allied defenses at all.

Just before the Germans reached it, however, and after the gas had dispersed, Plumer, the British commander, was able to scrape together some reserves and race them out to the threatened sector. Due to the fact that it had been fought over in the autumn of 1914, they found old, abandoned trenches everywhere. They hastily improved and connected stretches with their entrenching tools and, when the German assaulting columns appeared, drove them off with rapid rifle fire.

The essential terms of the equation of trench warfare had by now been determined. Wire and trenches required the attacker to use heavy artillery to forge a way for his infantry. Heavy artillery, always in short supply, had to be brought from a distance and its arrival was difficult to disguise. Even when emplaced, its use imposed a dilemma. If employed at the last moment, simply to break gaps in the wire, it might not do enough damage to get the infantry into the enemy's positions. If employed well beforehand, to lay down a long, destructive, preliminary bombardment, or 'artillery preparation,' it would certainly attract enemy reserves to the threatened front and so determine that, whatever success the assaulting infantry had in crossing the front line, they would be counterattacked as soon as they were well inside enemy territory. Neither in a short nor in a long

Carry me back to dear old Blighty,
Put me on the train to London town.
Take me over there,
Drop me anywhere,
Liverpool, Leeds or Manchester.

Above: **Men of the 2nd Battalion, Royal Scots Fusiliers in the trenches at La Boutillerie, winter of 1914–15.**

bombardment could the artillery ensure the neutralization of the most powerful killing-agent on the defending front – the medium machine gun. In the first accurate hits on the machine-gun nests could not be guaranteed, in the second the machine guns were simply taken by their crews into the dugouts, safe from shelling, until the moment came to race up the steps when the bombardment lifted, to let the attacking infantry through.

For the next two and a half years, therefore, all trench-to-trench offensives were to lurch uneasily between hoped-for surprise and assured destruction, until new technical means were at last found to make surprise once again a feasible stratagem. In the meantime the troops at the front began to invent or resurrect a whole array of devices adapted particularly to low-level trench fighting. The Germans, impressed by Russian and Japanese experience in the war of 1904–1905, already had a number of useful devices, like flare pistols, grenades and trench mortars. There were no such things for the British and French, but they soon improvised. Grenades were made from jam tins, mortars from steel piping. There was a short-lived fashion for grenade-throwing catapults, which resembled Roman siege-engines, and a great deal of ingenuity given to the design of periscopes, wire-grappling and cutting devices and even body armor. The steel helmet, to be universal (except in the Russian army) by 1916, was still under development, and attracted the opposition of many traditionally minded officers. Neutral-colored clothing had been adopted everywhere by early 1915. The Germans and the British were already in a camouflage color. The Belgians in black and the French in blue coats and scarlet trousers made conspicuous targets, even against the background of the trenches and both quickly changed – the former to khaki, the latter to a bright 'horizon blue' which muddied itself to an indeterminate gray in the front line.

Equipped and clothed like this, the two sides visited a good deal of small-scale beastliness on each other during the long, inactive summer of 1915. Even though the Germans were on the defensive in the West, while attempting to destroy the Russians in the East, they were ready and able to mount raids, demonstrations and local offensives, and the same ingredients formed the staple diet of the Allied armies. There were French attacks at Metzeral in Alsace, in Lorraine and at Bois-le-Prêtre in the Woevre, near Verdun. On the British front around Ypres, casualties during the summer ran at about 300 a day, in an army of 300,000 infantry, and rose higher whenever there was a flare-up of activity, as at Hooge on 2 June. This château, headquarters of the BEF in the First Battle of Ypres, had a sentimental value to the British. It was recaptured on 16 June but lost again on 20 July, when the Germans attacked with flame-throwers, a new addition to the armory of trench warfare.

The summer's pause did not, however, imply any acquiescence by the Allies to the German occupation of France's 10 most productive *départements*. On 4 June Joffre sent Sir John French the draft of his plan for an autumn offensive. Like those of December, it proposed a dual attack in Artois and Champagne, intended to break the German line and converge on the headwaters of the Somme east of St Quentin. The German line in between, which formed a large salient, would thus be bitten out, its defenders encircled and forced to surrender and a large enough gap created for a victorious

Below: **A gas school at Barleux in August 1915. Gas warfare was equally devastating for both sides.**

Above: **German cavalry near Arras in 1915. Trench warfare made cavalry charges obsolete and usually fatal.**

advance to the German frontier. On this occasion, however, while the French army made the major effort on Champagne, that in Artois was to be heavily British. The Tenth Army, which had tried and failed to capture Vimy Ridge in May, would be supported on its left by further British divisions.

Joffre's proposal formed the basis of discussion at the First Inter-Allied Conference, held at Chantilly, seat of GQG, on 7 July and attended by representatives of France, Britain, Belgium, Russia, Serbia and Italy (which had entered the war on 23 May). The French dominated the proceedings, since they maintained the largest army in the West which, though smaller than the Russian, was the only one capable of offensive action against the Germans on a large scale. Joffre had opposed the landings at Gallipoli, which had led to the Mediterranean campaign currently in progress, but his failure to cancel it did not shake his power to dictate when and where the Western Offensive in 1915 should take place. The Russians were grateful for any effort which relieved the pressure on their front. The Italians were occupied with their own offensives, which amounted to the liberation of territory they believed to be theirs by divine right. The Belgians and British, both inferior in military power to the French, were prepared to accept French leadership for practical purposes.

Joffre's plan, though set back by difficulties in the assembly of men, guns and munitions (the British pleaded they would not have sufficient ordnance or artillery available for a large offensive until the spring of 1916), therefore went forward. Scheduled originally for 8 September, it had to be postponed on 31 August, because General Pétain, in the light of his experience at Vimy in the spring, demanded more time to train his artillery more thoroughly. The need to extend the road network in the prewar French training area in Champagne also required more time than had originally been anticipated.

So extended were the Allied preparations that they inevitably came to the attention of the Germans, who, using conscripted French labor as well as the older soldiers of their Landwehr and Landsturm regiments, began in August to construct secondary positions in the rear of the two threatened sections, at distances of two to four miles from the front. They also summoned from Russia an extra four divisions to act as a counterattack reserve. It was against this reinforced line that the Allies began, on 21 September, the first large and prolonged artillery preparation yet unleashed on the Western Front. In Champagne the French had 47 heavy guns to the mile, in Artois 35, the British only 19. Day after day their crews toiled round them, winging shells of 100 to 200 pounds onto the German communications trenches and battery positions deep in their rear, while the 75mm and 18-pounders of the field artillery poured shrapnel and high explosives into the wire and trenches of the front line in order to open the door for the infantry. The German artillery replied as best it could, until beaten into silence or deliberately ceasing to answer, so as to survive until the infantry attack developed.

The attack in Champagne – called by the French the Second Battle – began at 0915 on 25 September. Two armies, Second (Pétain) and Fourth (de Langle de Cary), 20 divisions against six, attacked side by side. They did not attack in what had become conventional trench fashion, silently and surreptitiously. The two Armies had convinced their soldiers that 25 September was the beginning of the end of the war. The regiments had brought their bands onto the front line to sound the men off to *Ca ira! Sambre-et-Meuse* and the *Chant du Départ*. Many had also brought their colors, those gold bedecked and fringed tricolors, painted with the battle honors of a hundred years of victories, which enshrine the heart of a French regiment. One colonel seized the color from the young officer whose duty it was to carry it, and himself bore it forward over the parapet.

He fell dead within a few feet. The bands, the shouting and cheering, as well as the cessation of the bombardment as it lifted to play on targets beyond the German front line, had given the German defenders all the warning they needed for the 'race to the parapet.' The Germans' starting point was their dugouts, that of the French the other side of no man's land. When the Germans reached it they found their view obscured by clouds of smoke and gas, into which they were forced to fire blind. The result was that along wide sectors of the front the French were suddenly on top of them before they could organize effective resistance. Along a front of 18 miles, the French quickly broke in to a depth of 1000 yards on the left and 2500 yards on the right, capturing in all 10.5 miles of the front line. Some of the strongpoints taken would become catchwords in French military history – the Butte de Tahure and La Main de Massiges, where five projecting spurs of a ridge resembled the fingers of a hand. Some of the bravery shown on that day would also become legendary – by no one more strikingly

Above: **British artillery in action near Chusseau–Flaviens.**

Below left; **German troops carry their heavy machine guns past a French farmhouse.**

Below: **French troops storm into the plain of their lost province, Alsace.**

Left: British infantry march through Vieux Berquin after the Battle of Loos, 1915.

Below: Generals Castelnau, Joffre and Pau, 1 February 1915.

than General Marchand, the central figure in the Fashoda incident, which had brought Britain and France to the brink of open hostilities in Africa in 1900. He attacked at the head of his colonial infantrymen, was shot through the body and removed from the field to face, it was thought, certain death. However within 10 days he had returned to duty for the closing stages of the offensive.

The closing stages were reached so soon for the simple reason that the Germans were able to man their support line with reserves hastily brought forward from the rear, and to cover it with the artillery fire the French had been unable to silence. The attack in Artois (Third Battle) was not sustained for even that long. There the French had brought their reserves close to the front, hopeful of early success. It did not come, and the German artillery counterbarrage fell into the crowded trenches of the front line, causing terrible casualties and prompting Joffre through his deputy, Foch, to terminate the attack next day.

On the left of this French attack, the British had also opened an offensive at 0630 on the same morning. It became known as the Battle of Loos, after the little village astride the front. This time the BEF was a different attacking force from the one that had opposed the Germans the previous year. Then it had been an army of regulars. There were still prewar regulars in the BEF, but many fewer than the year before – about three-quarters had become casualties. Their places had been taken partly by newly-enlisted men, but mainly by Territorials and new volunteer divisions. The Territorials (not to be confused with the elderly French reservists who also went by that name), were a peculiarly British breed. They were part-time volunteers, who also gave up their Saturdays in peacetime to train for war. They formed in all 14 divisions of infantry and 14 brigades of cavalry, at the outbreak too deficient in equipment and skill to be sent to the front, but now acclimated to the Western Front. The new volunteer divisions were not yet fully deployed to France. Their time would come in 1916. One, the 15th Scottish, however was ready for Loos and, together with the 47th London Territorial Division, and the 1st, 2nd, 7th and 9th of the old regular army, set off across no man's land on 25 September.

Haig, commanding the British First Army, placed especial confidence for the operation's success in the discharge of a gas cloud. He had calculated on a 20mph wind to carry it across no man's land, but unfortunately the morning dawned calm. Reluctant to cancel the discharge, he told his aide-de-camp to light a cigarette in the garden of his headquarters and, when he detected a slight eastward drift of the smoke, decided that conditions justified letting his order stand. At the front the breeze was either non-existent or carried the gas in the wrong direction. At best it drifted slantwise across no man's land. At worst it actually blew back into the British trenches. Where it touched the German line, south of Loos, the 47th Territorial Division was able to cross. Elsewhere it actually hindered the attack, hanging about in pockets, so that where the British infantry took off their masks to get a breath of fresh air, they were overcome.

Haig nevertheless judged the attack to be going so well by the early afternoon that, from his headquarters eight miles behind the line, he ordered the reserves forward. They consisted of another two of the new volunteer divisions, 21st and 24th, which had never before been into action. They did not reach the front line until dark, and prepared themselves to attack the following morning. When they did so, a soldier in the German 15th Reserve Regiment reported seeing '10 columns of infantry between Hulluch and Hill 70, each about a thousand men, all advancing as if carrying out a parade-ground drill.' Unable to believe their eyes, the defenders of the position, who had been driven from the front line by the gas the previous day, stood up on the parapets to open fire with rifles and machine guns. The effect was devastating. The army could be seen falling literally in hundreds, but they continued their march in good order and without interruption. Despite the terrible punishment inflicted on them, they went doggedly on, some even reaching the wire entanglements in front of the reserve line which had scarcely been touched by their artillery. Confronted by 'this impenetrable obstacle, the survivors turned and began to retire.' In their advance the two divisions' infantry, about 24,000 strong, lost 8000 killed and wounded. 'Sickened by the sight of the massacre,' the 16th Reserve Regiment's history reads, 'no more shots were fired . . . so great was the feeling of misery and compassion after such a victory.'

Above: The mine craters at Aubers Ridge were home for these men of the BEF.

Below: The barbed wire of a captured German trench at Loos, 28 September 1915.

Hanging on The Old Barbed Wire

If you want to find the old battalion,
I know where they are, I know where they are,
If you want to find the old battalion,
I know where they are,
They're hanging on the old barbed wire,
I've seen 'em, I've seen 'em,
Hanging on the old barbed wire,
I've seen 'em,
Hanging on the old barbed wire.

Above: **Marshal Galliéni studies a map on the Western Front, in the company of other French officers.**

Above: **The fire and smoke of the Western Front in 1915, as the war took on an increasingly ghastly tone.**

Loos was to be last offensive effort of the Allies on the Western Front in 1915. Not only had the September offensives exhausted their reserves of manpower and munitions, they had also cast an incurable blight both upon reputations and the optimistic forecasts of those who had advanced them. In the first months of the war Joffre had dismissed a third of the generals in the French army, at first posting them, as a sop, to Limoges, the command most distant from the front (the origin of *limogé*) then, when the fiction became transparent, simply sending them direct into retirement. The men whom he had promoted in their stead, notably Foch, but also Pétain, Maunoury, d'Urbal, Gourand, Franchet d'Esperey and Debeney, had proved themselves. They had shown themselves capable of taking decisions and of remaining resilient even in the face of the terrible casualty returns which every attack they organized produced. Joffre's own reputation, however, that of Papa Joffre, unpretentious, imperturbable, had begun to crack – if not with the army and the people, then with the politicians. They found his reticence infuriating and his calm a mark of complacency. On the German side, Moltke's removal had brought a soldier of energy and vision, Erich von Falkenhayn, to the head of OHL and he, too, had replaced the dinosaurs of August 1914 with younger, more efficient men. In the British army, Sir John French, Commander in Chief of the British Expeditionary Force, was about to be deposed. His extreme range of mood, emotional approach to military planning and hidden but powerful despair at the failure of the offensives and their human cost had raised a virtual conspiracy against him among his more immediate subordinates. Foremost was Douglas Haig (commanding the First Army), who, through private correspondence with King George V, transmitted 'the feeling of the army' to the highest government circles. On 16 December 1915 French paid the price of his shortcomings and his brother officers' disloyalty and was removed. Haig took his place.

In Britain the war was having its inevitable effect – the phrase 'on the home front' became current. In May 1915 Herbert Henry Asquith, whose heart had never been in the war, had abandoned the attempt to run the government with only the support of his own Liberal party. Thenceforth he became Prime Minister of a coalition, with eight Conservatives in his Cabinet. The new cabinet's most important member was the Liberal Minister of Munitions, David Lloyd George, who brought to the newly-created post a dynamism noticeably absent from other government offices – from the War Office, where Kitchener's early creativeness had petered out, and even from the Admiralty, whose First Lord, Winston Churchill, was eclipsed by the failure of his ill-conceived campaign on the Gallipoli peninsula.

France also had its man of the hour in the Ministry of Munitions, Albert Thomas. Like Lloyd George, he saw that the war needs would be met not simply by exhorting national industry to meet the production targets set it, but by direct governmental intervention to change its structure. In Britain Lloyd George's Munitions Act concentrated the power to distribute orders to the munitions factories into a single office. This power determined that inefficient factories would not receive orders while new enterprises which promised to deliver would. The result was a burgeoning of new engineering workshops in places where industrial work had never before been made available to the population, particularly in the South of England, nearest to the fighting front. At the same time the Munitions Act restricted the right to strike in factories and created a new force of itinerant workmen who had to go wherever labor was shortest.

The labor force was not exclusively male. The migration of enormous numbers of young men to the front, or to the training camps which were staging posts on the way, meant a sudden dismantling of the barriers to female employment in many traditionally male occupations. In July 1914 only 212,000 British women had been employed in engineering. By July 1915 the number had increased to 256,000. A year later, under the impact of Lloyd George's Act, it had doubled to 520,000. A veteran of the mobilization recalled her experiences 60 years later:

'I was in domestic service and hated every minute of it when war broke out, earning two pounds a month working from six in the morning to nine in the evening. So when the need came for women "war workers" my chance came to "out." I started on hand cutting shell fuses at the converted war works at the ACs Thames Ditton, Surrey. It entailed the finishing off by "hand disc." The machine cut thread on the fuses that held the powder for the big shells, so had to be very accurate so that the cap fitted perfectly. We worked 12 hours a day apart from the journey morning and night at Kingston-upon-Thames. Believe me I was very ready for bed in those days and as for wages I thought I was very well off earning five pounds a week.'

Another branch of munition work, filling shells, was commoner than the skilled task of cutting fuses. By the end of 1915 it was done almost entirely by women, the largest concentration being at the national cordite factory at Gretna, on the Scottish border. There 11,000 women worked and were accommodated in purpose-built hostels. A survey revealed that, out of each hundred, 36 had formerly been in domestic service, 20 had lived at home, 15 had been shop assistants and 12 had been laundry workers, farm hands, dressmakers, school teachers or clerks. Soon they were all 'munitionettes.' Those who worked with TNT, which discolored the skin yellow, became known as 'canaries.' They were a familiar sight in the streets of Southeast London surrounding the great armaments complex at Woolwich and Deptford.

Women had also begun to infiltrate occupations long defended as male preserves – tram driving, bus conducting, postal delivery and so on. Between 1916–18 the number of women employed in transportation rose from 18,000 to 117,000. Similar shifts were apparent in the much more traditional society of France. By October 1915 there were 75,000 women employed in the munitions industry, and they had also begun to appear in uniform on the vehicles of the public transport system. Yet, at the same time, those already disenchanted by the war – and they included many soldiers on leave from the front – were offended by the lack of feeling

Above: British girls make up soldiers' rations. Women were used extensively in European factories as the men were taken off to war.

Top left: A howitzer shop in the Coventry Ordnance Works.

Top: A German girl makes cartridges.

Left: Packing fuse heads at the Coventry Ordnance Works.

Below: A French female welder at work making cartridges.

Above: **General Ferdinand Foch surveys the fighting near Arras; his destiny was yet to be realized.**

for those undergoing the war's harshness displayed by many in the great cities.

In December 1915 the Ballet Russe gave a five-hour performance at l'Opéra, for which a fashionable Paris couturier had previously advertised jewelled gowns at prices of up to 3500 francs. An American, J G Coolidge, said of the packed audiences 'Never in ante-bedlam days have I seen anything more magnificent. The general feeling is that it was a mistake.' However such mistakes were an integral part of the France behind the lines. Restaurants, hotels, theaters and casinos flourished, not only on the pocket money of soldiers snatching a leave from the front. The war had generated a flood of cash and credit, and the earning classes, old and new, were spending unprecedented amounts on entertainment and adornment. A popular department store in the rue de Rennes reported selling a million more articles in 1915 than in 1914, mainly scent and fancy underwear. The war wounded were fêted, but the more realistic accepted that their acclaim would be short lived. 'This year,' said an officer who lost both legs, 'I am a hero. Next year I shall be a cripple.'

In Germany the mood was different. Resistance there to the employment of women in war work was strong, as befitted the most traditional society in Europe. There was little behind-the-lines enjoyment – indeed there was little to rejoice about. Cut off from the Allies' ready access to the resources of the world beyond Europe by an efficient naval blockade, Germans had already been subjected to bread rationing in January 1915. Importing 20 percent of their foodstuffs, they quickly found that other staples started to fall into short supply, or even disappear completely. Butter was scarce as was fresh meat. The quality of meals, even in an hotel as good as the Berlin Adlon, was, to an American visitor, noticeably poor by March 1915. The hardships of war in an encircled nation made themselves felt in other ways. Nonferrous ores, copper, zinc and tin, were now in particularly short supply, at a time when military demand for them was insatiable and unprecedented. As a result German families were ordered in October 1915 to supply lists to the local authorities of all articles in their possession made of these materials and households were then stripped of them by official collectors. Melted down, the product went to make driving bands for shells, wire for signal cable and electrical contacts.

Yet rumors of the imminent imposition of rationing of all foodstuffs did nothing to shake German commitment to the war or belief in swift victory. 'The people are still well in hand,' wrote the American ambassador, James Gerard, in November 1915, 'constant rumors of peace keep them in hand.' In France, too, enthusiasm, if not for the war then certainly for the gratification of victory of the hated *Boche*, remained high. *'On les aura'* was the catch phrase not only of commanding officers but also of the civilian population. Next year would bring victory, a victory which would wipe out all the humiliations of the past 50 years. In Britain, where Kitchener's New Armies were reaching the peak of their strength and training, there was unbounded public confidence in the belief that the British Empire, once it put forth its strength, would puncture swiftly and completely the pretensions of Germany to dictate the future of Europe by Christmas 1915. *'A Berlin'* had become as popular a watchword as *'Nach Paris'* had been the year before.

Above right: **French troops halt for a rest on a march to the front.**

Right: **Germans watch as a village burns in northern France.**

Above far right: **Crown Prince Rupprecht of Bavaria and Lieutenant General von Krafft von Dellmensingen in Alsace in 1914.**

Far right: **German troops in the newly-built trenches in France late in 1914.**

Below: **An encampment of Moroccan *spahis,* a colorful addition to French forces on the Western Front.**

When this Bloody War is Over

When this bloody war is over,
O, how happy I shall be!
When I get my civvy clothes on,
No more soldiering for me.
I shall sound my own reveille,
I shall make my own tattoo:
No more NCOs to curse me,
No more bleeding army stew.

Transports at Lemnos in April 1915 which took part in the fiasco at Gallipoli.

3 The Widening War

On to Berlin was not the only watchword in the Allied camp during 1915. Constantinople – Istanbul as the Turks call it – seemed an equally glittering prize. It could be reached far more quickly and cheaply than the German capital and offered a strategic reward almost as valuable. Turkey had come into the war late. It had been counted in the German camp for years before the war, if only because it had the same natural enemy, Russia. The Ottoman Empire was crippled by weaknesses so severe that even its ambitious and energetic leaders, the Young Turks (all military men) had hesitated to expose it to the strains of a great military effort. They had signed a treaty with Germany on 2 August, pledging Turkish support to the Austro-German cause. However, the unexpected entry of Britain into the war, the poor Austrian showing against the Russians and, particularly, the Serbs, and the French victory on the Marne had further weakened the Young Turks' resolve. Germany had however found a means of tightening the screw.

On 3 August 1914, while their two flag-showing ships in the Mediterranean, the battle-cruiser *Goeben* and cruiser *Breslau*, were racing for the straits of Gibraltar to rejoin the High Seas Fleet, the German admiralty signalled Admiral Wilhelm Souchon to turn about and seek haven in Constantinople. Evading a British pursuit, he did so. A comic pantomime followed, Souchon and his men formally enrolled in Turkish service, exchanging their naval caps for the fez, and the two ships prepared to join the Turkish Navy's order of battle. However, once transpatriated, their mission was to be one of calculated disobedience. Enver Pasha, the War Minister and most pro-German of the Young Turks, collaborated in a scheme whereby the *Goeben* led the few seaworthy elements of the Turkish Navy into the Black Sea. On 28 October, on a slim pretext, they opened fire on such Russian vessels as they could find and bombarded the Russian seaports of Odessa and Sebastopol. The Sultan, Mahommed V, a cypher in the hands of his ministers, thus found himself a formal ally of Kaiser Wilhelm II and Emperor Franz Josef in the war against Russia, France and Britain.

The French and even the British, despite their compelling Mediterranean interests, might have been content to treat hostilities as a formality had it not been for the supplications of Russia. The Czar had men in millions, more men than any of the combatant powers, but he lacked the guns and the munitions with which to feed them. Outside his own dominions were industrial powers which could supply the goods he needed. After October his sea lanes were blocked by the enemy, the Baltic ports by Germany, the Black Sea ports by Turkey. The answer to the question of how to get supplies through was of importance not only to Russia but to the Western Allies, who had vested large hopes in a Russian steamroller which was now almost broken down for lack of fuel. When, on 2 January 1915 the British ambassador in Petrograd forwarded a request from the Russian government for some diversion to be made to draw off troops from Turkey's invasion of the Caucasus, it prompted an immediate response. Kitchener at once thought of a landing at Gallipoli, gateway of the Dardanelles which led to Constantinople, and Churchill, First Lord of the Admiralty, was equally enthusiastic. While intentions were pondered and plans prepared, Churchill persuaded the War Cabinet to let his Mediterranean fleet attempt to 'force the Narrows' on its own and between 19 February and 18 March a bombarding force of British and French battleships bludgeoned its way up the channel toward Chanak, where the channel was only a mile wide. The naval effort went well at first and the Turkish batteries the fleet engaged were first silenced and then destroyed. Some blue jackets found that they were able to land and walk about on enemy territory unchecked. However on 18 March a succession of disasters brought the fleet's action to an end. First the old French battleship *Bouvet*, then the British *Irresistible* and *Ocean*, were shaken by explosions and quickly sank. The *Inflexible*, a brand new battlecruiser, was holed soon afterward, then the French *Gaulois* and the *Suffren* were also hit. The last three ships managed to limp away to safety. The Turks, who had inflicted all this damage with a few mines floated down on the current, had shown that the naval effort was doomed.

London and Paris, the latter reluctantly, therefore agreed to commit to a shore landing the military force which it had been gathering in the eastern Mediterranean. It consisted of a French division, which was to land at Kum Kale on the Asiatic shores and make a diversion, and two British and two Australian/New Zealand (ANZACS) divisions, which were to assault Gallipoli itself. One of the British divisions was the Royal Naval Division, which had landed at Ostend the previous October and, for reasons difficult to explain, numbered many writers and poets among its officers. Of these the best known was Rupert Brooke, whose meditation on his own death – 'some corner of a foreign field which is forever England' – had already become the most famous of the flood of war poems which World War I had stimulated and was to remain the best remembered. Writing home to a friend from the troopship, he claimed that 'all my life (I had) wanted to go on a military expedition to Constantinople.' His letter expressed the unspoken wishes of many of his companions and friends from the privileged world of Cambridge, who saw in the war the means to give point to lives which they felt were too soft and purposeless. Rupert Brooke, at the

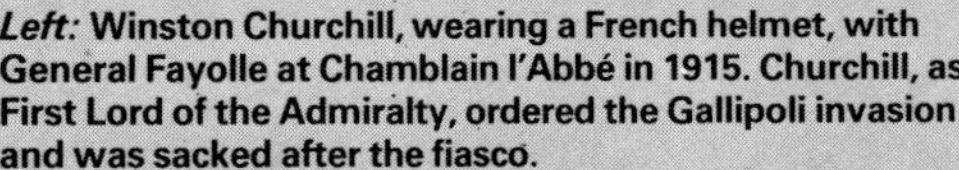

Left: Winston Churchill, wearing a French helmet, with General Fayolle at Chamblain l'Abbé in 1915. Churchill, as First Lord of the Admiralty, ordered the Gallipoli invasion and was sacked after the fiasco.

Below: The *Goeben*, which was commandeered into the Turkish Navy at the start of World War I.

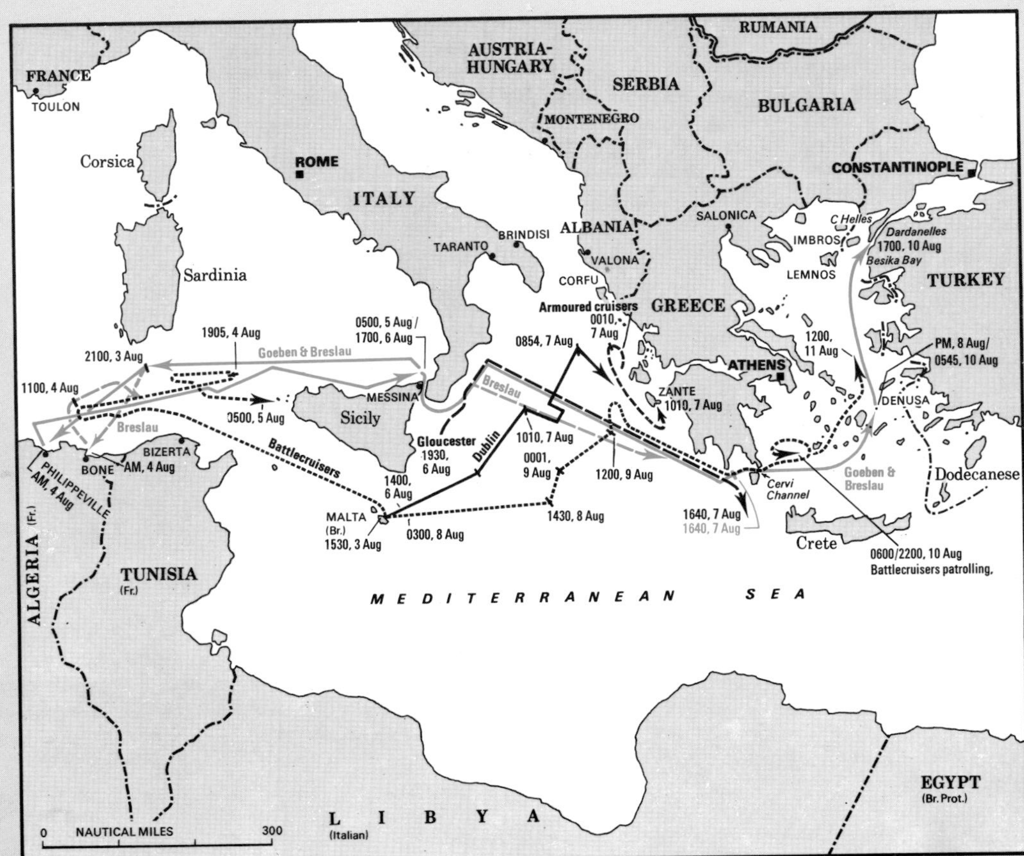

Above: The surrender of the *Goeben,* by Philip Connar. The incident took place at the end of the war.

Top left: Poster celebrating the Turkish defense of Gallipoli.

Above left: Enver Pasha, who led the Turkish defense of the Dardanelles.

Top: The pursuit of the *Goeben* and *Breslau* by the British Mediterranean Fleet.

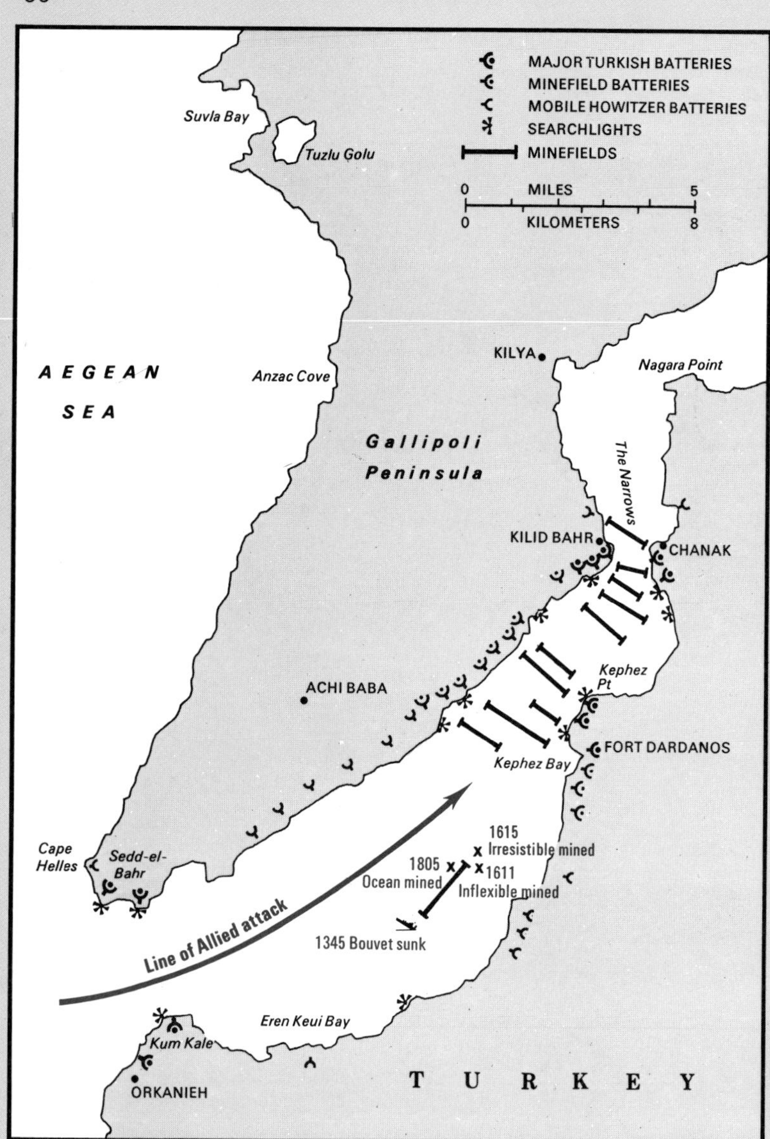
MAJOR TURKISH BATTERIES
MINEFIELD BATTERIES
MOBILE HOWITZER BATTERIES
SEARCHLIGHTS
MINEFIELDS
0 MILES 5
0 KILOMETERS 8
Suvla Bay
Tuzlu Golu
AEGEAN SEA
Anzac Cove
KILYA
Nagara Point
Gallipoli Peninsula
The Narrows
KILID BAHR
CHANAK
Kephez Pt
ACHI BABA
FORT DARDANOS
Kephez Bay
1615 Irresistible mined
1805 Ocean mined
1611 Inflexible mined
Cape Helles
Sedd-el-Bahr
1345 Bouvet sunk
Line of Allied attack
Kum Kale
Eren Keui Bay
ORKANIEH
TURKEY

last moment, was to be cheated, for an insect bite turned septicemic and he died at sea on 23 April, to be buried by torchlight on the island of Skyros among the olives and lemon trees of the Mediterranean world he had loved so passionately in life.

It was a better death than many in the Mediterranean Expeditionary Force were to suffer two days later. A month's pause in the naval bombardment had given the Turkish garrison, now under the command of the German officer Liman von Sanders, the chance it needed to fortify the beaches. When the improvised landings vessels appeared off shore, mainly naval whalers towed by steam pinnaces, but also a collier, the *River Clyde*, converted to discharge troops down ramps, a storm of rifle and machine-gun fire was unleashed on them. At those beaches, lettered S, X and Y, the troops dug trenches at the top of the cliffs they had captured. Had they advanced inland, they would have taken in the rear the Turks who, at the tip of the peninsula, were massacring their comrades at beaches V and W. Alongside the *River Clyde* the sea literally turned red with blood and the expedition commander, General Ian Hamilton, a writer with a sensitive soul, was stricken by horror. He described the sight as 'monstrous; too cold-blooded; like looking at gladiators from the dress-circle. . . . As men fixed in the grip of a nightmare, we were powerless – unable to do anything but wait. To be safe oneself, except for the offchance of a shell, was like being stretched upon the rack.'

Far left: **The Allied attack on Gallipoli.**

Above left: **HMS *New Zealand*, part of the Gallipoli flotilla.**

Left: **Turkish artillery which bombarded the Allies on the beaches.**

Above right: **A Turkish shell bursts near the *River Clyde*, a troopship at V Beach at Gallipoli.**

Below: **HMS *Majestic* sinking off the Gallipoli peninsula. U-Boats were in evidence throughout the assault, harassing Allied shipping.**

Gradually, the Turkish resistance on the two stricken beaches was beaten down and the landings consolidated. However that did not mean that the tide had turned and the operation had ensured success. Subordinate to von Sanders, whose nerve had been badly shaken, was a young Turkish divisional commander, Mustapha Kemal, later Ataturk. While von Sanders rode distractedly about the peninsula, Kemal sent for replacements and led them down tó seal off the landings made by the ANZACs, most threatening because of their proximity to Constantinople. British inaction in the south then allowed their beaches to be contained also. By 30 April the 'military expedition to Constantinople' had resolved itself into a battle for two tiny footholds on a rocky coast 100 miles from the city.

On 11 May the Turks mounted a mass attack against the beach-heads. So ferocious was the attack, with soldiers dying in their thousands, and so horrifying was the aftermath of suffering among the wounded that the two sides agreed

to a truce in order to recover the survivors and bury the dead. The conference was held in a dugout at the beach called ANZAC after its devil-may-care Australasian garrison – one of whom interrupted the conference between Generals Birdwood and Braithwaite and Mustapha Kemal, to enquire, 'Have any of you bastards got my kettle?' Aubrey Herbert, friend and comrade-in-arms of Rupert Brooke, accompanied a Turkish captain to oversee the work of mercy:

'We mounted over a plateau and down through gullies filled with thyme, where there lay about 4000 Turkish dead. . . . There were two wounded lying in that multitude of silence. The Turkish captain said, "At the spectacle even the most gentle must feel savage and the most savage must weep." The dead fill acres of ground. They fill the myrtle grown gullies. It was as if God had breathed in their faces. I talked to some Turks, one of whom pointed to the graves. "That's politics," he said. Then he pointed to the dead bodies and said, "That's diplomacy. God pity all of us poor soldiers."'

The truce did not end the battle, though the initial disaster had ended the current careers of Lord Fisher, who resigned on 15 May, and Winston Churchill, who was removed from office on 26 May. After a summer of small-scale trench fighting, no different from that on the Western Front except for the heat, flies and unfamiliar diseases, the Allies launched what was to be a final large-scale offensive on 6 August. The troops at the tip of the peninsula were briefed to attack simultaneously with the launch of a new landing at Suvla, 20 miles along it to the north. The landings were successful, but then, as on 25 April, many of the soldiers who had got ashore believed they had achieved all that was expected of them. They sat down, sunbathed, lit fires to make tea and even went swimming. Once again, Mustapha Kemal, now established as the lionheart of the defense, rode about summoning reinforcements until he could be sure that he had sealed off the new landing.

The coming of winter to Gallipoli brought bad weather and despair. On 27 November there was, according to one survivor:

'a terrific thunderstorm, followed by 24 hours of torrential rain, during which the men got soaked to the skin. Then came an icy hurricane; the rain turned into a blinding blizzard; then heavy snow, followed by two nights of bitter frost. . . . At Suvla, trenches were soon flooded, water-courses became roaring torrents and a wall-like spate of mud and water, several feet high, bore down the corpses of dead Turks and pack ponies into our lines. . . . Streams of exhausted men struggled down to the beaches, many collapsing and freezing to death where they fell. . . . At Suvla alone, during these three dreadful days, there were more than 5000 cases of frostbite. No such storm had been known in these parts for more than forty years.'

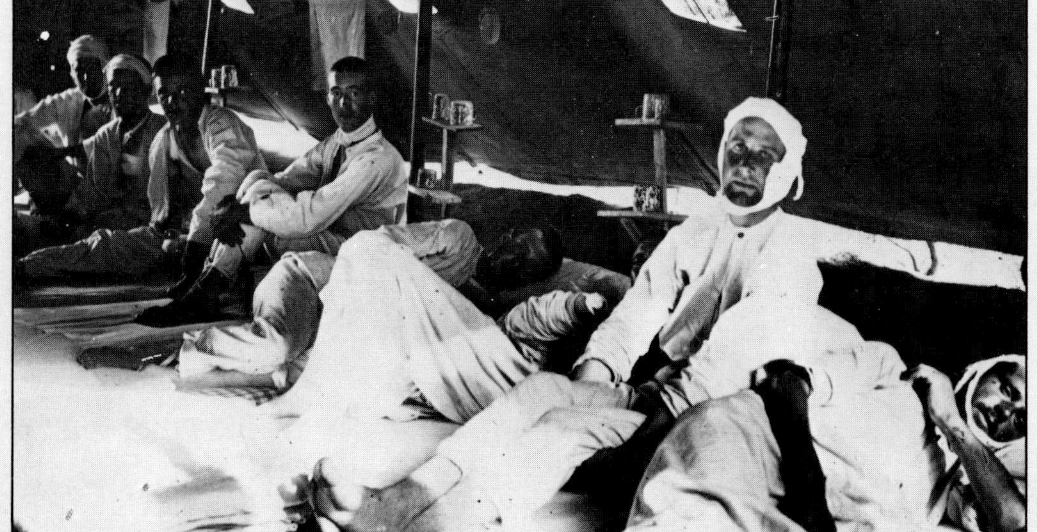

Above: **Turkish troops in their trenches near Gallipoli.**

Left: **British POWs in a Turkish hospital after they had been captured in the Gallipoli campaign.**

Kitchener himself had just left the peninsula after a tour of inspection and, before the climatic catastrophe, had decided that conditions were so bad, and prospects of breaking through to Constantinople so slim, that all the beaches but those at Cape Helles, on the tip of the peninsula, should be evacuated. By 20 December this had been accomplished. Liman von Sanders attempted an all-out assault on Helles when he found that the rest of the garrison had been evacuated. However, under naval fire and without the overbearing presence of Kemal (who had been transferred) to drive them to battle, the Turks turned and fled. While they remained disorganized, Birdwood, now commanding in place of the sensitive and artistic Hamilton, decided to get the rest of his men off Cape Helles. The last 16,000 were lifted by the navy in a single night on 8 January 1916.

Gallipoli had raised high hopes in those like Churchill, who had planned it as 'a way round,' a 'back door into the fortress of the Central Powers' and in those like Rupert Brooke and Patrick Shaw-Stewart, who had gone there in a spirit of crusade. Their emotions were perfectly captured in Brooke's poem to The Dead:

These hearts were woven of human joys and cares
Washed marvellously with sorrow, swift to mirth
The years had given them kindness. Dawn was theirs
And sunset, and the colours of the earth.
These had seen movement, and heard music; known
Slumber and waking; loved; gone proudly friended;
Felt the quick stir of wonder; sat alone;
Touched flowers and furs and cheeks. All this is
ended.

These were not the emotions of the common soldiers who had fought and died at Gallipoli. They had learned to hate the place, to feel a grudging respect for the courage and endurance of the Turkish soldier – 'Johnnie Turk' – and to feel there must be a better place to fight a war. The romanticism of the 'Lost Generation' of young officers who felt as Brooke did, and whose feelings were shared by bold spirits in the government like Churchill, had done much to motivate the British to war, just as the wounded patriotism of the French and the frustrated nationalism of the Germans deafened their ears to reason when the pace of crisis began to accelerate. Emotion, as much as self-interest, had generated the war and sustained the warlike urge of the first 18 months.

Above: **Turkish prisoners taken in the third battle of Krithia, 4 June 1915.**

Top: **A British trench captured by the Turks with the remains of corpses and a few rifles.**

Below: **A village captured by the French shows the *River Clyde,* a British transport, run aground at Sedd-el-Bahr, May 1915.**

However by the beginning of 1916 it was realized that emotion could not fuel a war machine any longer. In the West hard decisions were being made about a new sort of battle which would defeat the enemy by allotting him an uneven share of suffering. In the Mediterranean a use had to be found for the army which the Gallipoli defeat had suddenly left unemployed. It came unexpectedly through the intervention of Bulgaria in the war. The Bulgarians were regarded by their Balkan neighbors as little better than the Turks who had so long been their masters – cruel, selfish and scarcely European. There were some reasons for this. In the Second Balkan War of 1912 the Bulgarians had fought their Christian neighbors, who had previously supported them against Turkey in the First Balkan War. They had been defeated, but that had driven them further toward Turkey. Since 1914 the Allies had been busy with flattery and bribes to bring them back to their side, but the Bulgarians demanded a price higher than the nearest of the Allies, Serbia, would pay. Moreover, Germany had her own urgent reasons for wishing Bulgaria in her camp, notably the need to safeguard her rail connections with Turkey, which ran through Bulgarian territory. On 6 September 1915 she succeeded in binding Bulgaria by a treaty which committed the two countries and Austria to an offensive which would defeat Serbia. Bulgaria at once began to mobilize; news of this prompted the French and British to send troops, partly drawn from the force at Gallipoli, to Serbia's assistance. As Serbia had no outlet to the sea, the Allies were obliged to demand passage for this expeditionary force from Greece. The Greek government lacked the power to resist, and the troops were landed at the Greek port of Salonika on 5 October and at once marched against Bulgaria.

The campaign which ensued was to be one of the most pointless and frustrating of the war. The Central Powers – as the Germans, Austrians and Bulgarians were increasingly known – swiftly disposed of Serbia by a converging attack. The Serbian army, commanded by the aged but indomitable *Voivode* (War Chief), Radomir Putnik, twice avoided encirclement. However, it was forced into an agonizing winter retreat through the mountains of Serbia into Albania, where its survivors, bearing the *Voivode* in a litter on their shoulders, arrived in December. Allied ships evacuated them to Corfu, many so emaciated that they could be carried aboard ship in the arms of the nurses, as if they were sick children. The Austrians were close behind. In January 1916 they compelled the surrender of Serbia's dwarf ally, Montenegro, and then occupied Albania.

Meanwhile the Bulgarians had driven the vanguard of the French Expeditionary Force out of their territory to join the British in their staging area south of Salonika. The two armies constructed a vast entrenched camp as a precaution against a pro-German government coming to power in Greece and sat down to await events. Their inactivity provoked critics of Allied strategy even within the alliance to ribald jests about their function. 'Gardening' it was suggested, and the force became known as the 'Gardeners of Salonika,' with its French commander, Maurice Sarrail, as head gardener. Germans and Austrians were even more cutting. Prisoners of war, their propagandists said, were usually confined in barbed-wire cages. Salonika provided the first example of an army imprisoning itself. Alas, all these jibes were to retain their force almost to the end of the war.

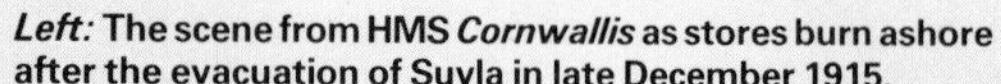

Left: **The scene from HMS *Cornwallis* as stores burn ashore after the evacuation of Suvla in late December 1915.**

Below: **British troops attempt to go over the top to extricate themselves from their beach at Gallipoli. The assault failed.**

If in this isolated backwater of the war the tide ran for the Central Powers, in others it was the Allies who enjoyed success. By the end of 1915 all but one of Germany's overseas possessions had fallen. First to go were their Far Eastern possessions. New Zealand troops had occupied Samoa on 29 August 1914, Papua and New Guinea on 17 September and the other Pacific islands – Yap, Nauru, the Peters, Caroline and Marshall Islands – had all been taken by the Royal or Imperial Japanese Navies by the end of November. There had been little or no resistance offered.

The Japanese, who had entered the war on 23 August 1914 precisely because of the pickings it offered, met a different response in September when they undertook the reduction of the most important German naval base in the region, the port of Tsingtao in Shantung Province of China. They found that the German force, which numbered 4000, had entrenched the landward approach to the port and was prepared to fight. Only 10 years before the Japanese had attacked a similar fortification at Port Arthur, Russia's naval base in the Yellow Sea. They tackled the Germans using the same

Above: French General Maurice Sarrail inspects the equipment of a Serbian unit which landed in Greece to join the Allies.

Top left: British troops land at Salonika in November 1915. The assault through Greece was meant to encircle Constantinople.

Top: The pro-Ally Greek Premier Venizelos reviews one of his regiments in Salonika.

Above: **A Montenegrin guerrilla force which fought a successful defense of mountain strongholds.**

Below: **A Sikh unit lands at Tsingtao, China's largest port, after its capture by the Japanese late in 1914.**

methods. Like an 18th-century European army, they dug trenches at a safe distance from the German perimeter, brought up heavy guns – the same heavy guns that they had used at Port Arthur – destroyed the enemy's guns and then pushed forward their earthworks. On the night of 6 November the enemy was judged to be weak enough for the delivery of a general assault. The Germans fell in the confusion, and the next morning the Rising Sun flew over Tsingtao.

A token British force, from the Hong Kong garrison, had taken part in the siege. The German possessions in Africa, with one exception, were to fall to colonial forces. Togoland, on the old slave coast, was overrun by columns of black soldiers, West African Rifles and Tirailleurs Sénégalais under white officers by 27 August 1914. German Southwest Africa, which bordered the Union of South Africa and was far larger and better-garrisoned, proved a harder nut to crack. The army, organized to occupy it, was composed exclusively of native white South Africans. Many were Afrikaners, who 10 years before had fought in the three-year war against the British Crown. Now they responded enthusiastically to the summons to march against their enemies, but they had to pause for four months to put down an internal rising led by Lieutenant Colonel Solomon G Maritz, one of the Boer generals of 1899–1902. Then, marching in four converging columns, they invaded the German colony in January 1915 from the landward and seaward approaches and between April and July encircled the enemy garrison at Otavi and forced it to surrender.

Above: The Tirailleurs Sénégalais under French command. Black African troops were used extensively.

Right: A Serbian artillery barrage against the Austrians. Serbia fought hard and well against overwhelming odds.

German resistance in the West Coast Colony of the Cameroons took longer to suppress, the dense jungle impeding the British, French and Belgian drives against the local German defense force, which was not reduced until February 1916. The most stubborn and skillful resistance of all was encountered in German East Africa (Tanganyika). The forces there were no larger, indeed rather smaller, than in Southwest Africa, and the space in which to maneuver no more extensive. However in Tanganyika the German Empire had a commander of genius. Although only a colonel, Paul von Lettow-Vorbeck had the mind of a great general and he understood from the beginning that by a strategy of evasion and delay he could tie down a far greater number of Allied troops than he had German under command, and so serve the purposes of his Kaiser. He had, in fact, only 3500 whites and 12,000 black Askaris, and his acquaintance with the territory was small, since he had only arrived in the colony in May 1914. He nevertheless succeeded in defeating the first British expedition sent against him from India in November 1914. Its landing was a disaster and, after a confused struggle made more chaotic by the intervention of swarms of vicious wild bees, which seemed to sting only the Kaiser's enemies, the expedition was forced to re-embark on 5 December 1914, only three days after landing.

The British Empire, stung by the rebuff, then gathered its forces in earnest. General Jan Christiaan Smuts, the Boer rebel who had made whole-hearted peace with his enemies, took the campaign against Lettow-Vorbeck in hand, and arrived in the colony in July 1915. Belgian and, later, Portuguese forces made up his strength and in April 1916 a strategy of convoying columns, which had proved so successful in German Southwest Africa, was set in motion. Lettow-Vorbeck eluded all of them, time after time inflicting a local defeat on his pursuers and then slipping away to double back on them in the dense bush and appear on their flank or rear. In January 1917 Smuts, now in demand in Britain as the representative of his country's contribution to the imperial war effort, left the center of operations. His successors, fellow South Africans, fared no better than he, though the force at their disposal had risen after his departure to 22 battalions of African troops, with several thousand white South Africans still present. Lettow-Vorbeck, reduced to commanding a handful of Askaris, continued to dodge and twist through the interior and was not to surrender until 12 days after the European armistice, on 23 November 1918, when he still had 1500 soldiers under his command. His name belongs to the annals of those great guerrilla soldiers who, true to the logic of their strategy, oblige a larger army to deploy a disproportionate force for an unconscionable time merely to achieve a negative object.

The most famous guerrilla leader produced by the war was T E Lawrence – Lawrence of Arabia. However his operations were a sideshow for the larger forces which tied up the main strength of the Turkish army. As an imperial power Turkey faced two major problems: many of her subjects were non-Turkish and even non-Muslim and her borders were at many points cut off from the center of power in Asia Minor. Also, as the Allies' had control of the sea, they were able to bring their power to bear in remote areas where Turkey was at a disadvantage. Even Gallipoli, because of the lack of rail communications, was difficult for Turkey to defend,

Above: South African Generals Botha and Smuts, who led the Empire's fight against the Germans in Africa.

Below: A column of East African troops under German command which fought a successful rear-guard action under Lettow-Vorbeck to retain a German presence in Tanganyika.

Below: One of Lettow-Vorbeck's German units in Tanganyika.

Below: A British 4.5cm howitzer in action in the Cameroons.

Above: Colonel T E Lawrence, the famous Lawrence of Arabia, who fought for Arab unity and independence despite British intentions to colonize the Middle East.

particularly at a moment when its offensive against the Russians in the Caucasus was going disastrously. The Caucasian border between Turkey and Russia was not served by railroads at all, scarcely surprising as the average elevation on the plateau was 6500 feet. Across it ran a series of mountain ranges with summits between 10–16,000 feet, snow covered even in summer and in winter swept by gales which drove the night temperature to 20 degrees below zero. Twice before the scene of fighting between Russia and Turkey, the Caucasus was known to be difficult campaigning country even in summer. Enver Pasha, the Turkish War Minister, nevertheless decided to attack the Russian Caucasus in winter. In December 1914 he personally led troops up onto the plateau. The Turkish Third Army totalled 190,000 men at the start of the campaign, slightly outnumbering the Russians, but the soldiers lacked winter clothing and were quickly cut off from regular supplies. They had no overcoats, blankets, fuel, tents or decent footwear. They pushed slowly into Russian territory but after a week the Russians counterattacked and defeated three of their former corps, one of which surrendered en masse. Many who escaped capture simply froze to death in the mountain snows. At least 30,000 Turks were buried and by the end of February 1915 the Third Army had been reduced to 12,000 men.

Defeated on the Russian border, the Turks in 1914 were also stretched by the need to defend the southern frontier of their empire in the Persian Gulf. As soon as she entered the war, the staff of the British Army in India conceived a plan to draw away Turkish troops from the Suez Canal region by an attack up the valleys of the Tigris and Euphrates, which it was thought, might also foment rebellion among the Arabs. An offensive strategy in the region would also directly serve to protect the outlets of the Anglo-Iranian pipe lines in the Persian Gulf which, since the abandonment of coal-firing, fuelled the boilers of the Grand Fleet. In November an Indian army expeditionary force landed at the mouth of the Shatt-al-'Arab, the confluence of the Tigris and Euphrates, and marched inland. Weak local forces opposed their advance but were pushed aside and Basra was occupied on 22 January. The Turkish units in these parts, unlike those which had fallen under the reforming influence of Liman von Sanders in Anatolia, had obsolete equipment and were commanded by officers whose ambitions were to lead the easy life of the harem, the divan and the hookah pipe. They made no effort to expel the British force – even though many of its soldiers were Muslim co-religionists, who might have been susceptible to enticement. Their inactivity actually alarmed the Government of India into reinforcing the advance guard,

Below: German machine gunners search for British planes over East Africa. Only a few aircraft were used, as most were needed in France.

Below: British unit, manned largely by Africans, attacks a German strongpoint in Tanganyika.

captured Baghdad. It was then the Central Powers' turn to fail. In September 1917 a joint Turkish-German force, code named *Yilderim* (Lightning), attempted to retake Baghdad but fell to pieces in the roadless wastes of northern Mesopotamia. However Germany and Turkey were determined to take possession of the Russian oilfields at Baku on the Caspian Sea. The Russians had earlier attempted to assist Townshend by launching an offensive from the Caucasus into eastern Turkey and northern Persia. Since Russia's army was falling apart, her two enemies agreed on a plan to take Baku by pincer movements north and south of the Black Sea. To counter them an Anglo-Indian force, named Dunsterforce after its commander General Dunsterville, model for Kipling's schoolboy hero Stalky, set off from Mesopotamia to race them to the objective. In the event, the Turks beat the British to the prize but arrived so fatigued that they were obliged to relinquish it almost as soon as it was taken. Meanwhile on 3 November 1918 the British army in Mesopotamia had captured Mosul, on the headwaters of the Tigris. On the Mediterranean coast of the Turkish Empire another army under General Sir Edmund Allenby was, in September 1918, approaching the capital of Syria, Damascus.

The British campaign in Palestine had begun in February 1915 when an expedition of 20,000 Turks, under German officers, had crossed the Sinai desert and attacked the Suez Canal. This threat to the most precious lifeline of the empire had so alarmed the British government that it thereafter kept 500,000 troops in Egypt. The majority was training for operations elsewhere, but a solid nucleus was earmarked to secure the eastern Mediterranean flank against a renewal of the Turkish menace. This did not recur until

Left: **British and Armenian artillerymen use a captured 6-inch Russian howitzer defending the Baku oil fields.**

Below right: **British artillery dig in to defend the Suez Canal. It was never seriously threatened.**

Below: **The British march into Kut, during the second attempt to take Baghdad.**

which they thought might be in danger of a secret and sudden counteroffensive. The reinforcement, on the contrary, only prompted the local commanders to push further up the rivers into Mesopotamia (modern Iraq). The Turks resisted but were outnumbered and defeated. As the advance progressed the idea seized the British of aiming for Baghdad, from which they could threaten both the Turkish positions in Palestine and Syria and the homeland of Anatolia itself.

In September General Sir Charles Townshend was put in command of a flying column which had the mission of capturing first Kut-al-Amara and then Baghdad. On 28 September he arrived at Kut with a division of infantry and a brigade of cavalry, followed by a long train of boats bringing supplies and munitions up the Tigris, and defeated the Turkish garrison. He at once pressed on, encouraged by a direction from the Viceroy of India that he might 'march on Baghdad if he is satisfied that the force he has available is sufficient for the operation.' He was satisfied, and on 11 November he set off into the desert again with his flotilla of boats following along the river and a column of 1000 mules, 240 donkeys and 600 camels bringing up the rear. On 21 November he encountered strong Turkish positions at Ctesiphon. The pilot of a scouting aircraft who noticed large Turkish reinforcements concentrating in the rear, crashed while on the flight back with the news.

Townshend, therefore, attacked under the misapprehension that his force outnumbered the enemy. He was defeated, forced into an agonizing retreat across the desert and took refuge inside Kut at the beginning of December.

Townshend had directed a siege once before, in the tiny Indian fortress of Chitral in 1895. His triumphant resistance there had made him a hero of the Empire and ensured him the promotion which led him to his Mesopotamian command. However, Kut and Chitral had nothing but Townshend in common. His opponents at Chitral had been ill-armed mountaineers, but at Kut he was penned in by a large, strong, Muslim army commanded by the senior German general, Baron Kolmar von der Goltz. The Turks, legendary diggers, soon surrounded the town with an impenetrable belt of trenches. After a siege lasting five months and the repulse of four attempts by the British outside the lines to relieve the garrison, Townshend was starved into surrender. He, in fact, showed little sign of privation but thousands of his soldiers would soon succumb to malnutrition or disease. However, there was also much disease in the Turkish camp, and von der Goltz himself was carried off by cholera at the moment of victory.

In September a new British effort, directed by the War Office instead of the inefficient Military Department in India, regained Kut. After a year of preparation, General Frederick Stanley Maude, Townshend's replacement, actually

Above: **Staffordshire troops at Baladasar after the withdrawal of the Armenians from the fight.**

Above: **General Townshend who was forced to surrender at Kut in April 1916.**

August 1916, when a probe toward the Canal was easily defeated at Rumani. That maneuver decided the British to substitute an active for a passive defense of the Canal, and in March 1917, after months spent pushing forward a railroad and water pipeline along the coast, they began an advance toward Palestine. Gaza, first city of the inhabited Holy Land, was quickly captured, but then evacuated through a misunderstanding.

A new commander, the ferocious Allenby, nicknamed 'the Bull' for his rampaging among inefficient subordinates, arrived in June 1917 with orders to avoid such misunderstandings and win victories. Lloyd George, now British Prime Minister, had given him the order, 'Jerusalem before Christmas,' wanting a seasonal gift for the British people in a year which had brought them little but sorrow and disappointment. Allenby threw himself into the necessary preparations. A cavalryman of the old school, he was delighted by the presence of large numbers of horsemen, Australian, New Zealand, British and Indian, in his Indian Expeditionary Force. He devised a sound strategy to make use of them. While the infantry and artillery pushed solidly along the coast, he arranged for the cavalry to move on wide outflanking sweeps inland. General von Falkenhayn, displaced from the Western Front by the elevation of Hindenburg and Ludendorff to the supreme command, opposed him with a force of 36,000. However Allenby had nearly 100,000 men and, in terms of quality, the disparity of strength was 'that of a tiger to a tom cat.' On 31 October he swept through Gaza. On 13 November he was under the walls of Jerusalem, and on 9 December the mayor of the city, brought the keys of the gates to the vanguard of the imperial army.

Allenby's next target was Damascus, from which he could stretch out a hand to join forces with the other British army in Mesopotamia. There was a second Turkish army in their rear, based in the far south of the Arabian peninsula, which might threaten their flanks. Fortunately since 1916 that threat had been contained by a home-grown Arab resistance campaign. It was supported and abetted by a British military mission, of which the leading light was a young temporary officer, T E Lawrence. In later life, this strange, introverted man of action was recognized as an intellectual celebrity among his generation. In 1916 he was no more than an apprentice archeologist, temporarily in Khaki. The war had provided an outlet for talents which the excavation of Syrian antiquities had left untapped. Already a fluent Arabic speaker, he had

been a natural choice to join the mission to the Arab rebels in the Hejaz, at the foot of the Turkish pilgrim railroad to Mecca. However mere liaison with the tribes had not satisfied his romantic urge. He had turned himself, in two years, into a full-bloodied guerrilla warrior, satisfying his passion for stealth and subterfuge in a campaign of surprise attacks against the railroad, ambushes of Turkish columns and storm assaults of sleepy desert forts. Under his inspiration, the *Jeish al-Arabi* – 'the army of the Arabs' – had grown into a force of 10,000 by July 1917, when they reached Aqaba, the Palestinian port at the head of the Red Sea. From there he led it along the desert border of Palestine, keeping station with Allenby's advance toward Jerusalem and Damascus.

Politically his greatest triumphs lay ahead of him, but militarily he would never achieve as much as he had in the Hejaz. He described his achievements brilliantly and ensured acclaim for decades. In early 1917 he had fulfilled a long-held ambition to blow up a troop train:

'One entire wheel of the locomotive whirled up suddenly black out of the cloud against the sky and sailed musically over our heads to fall slowly and heavily into the desert behind. . . . The now grey mist of the explosion drifted from the line towards us, and over our ridge until it was lost in the hills. . . . As I watched, our machine guns chattered over my head, and the long rows of Turks on the carriage roofs rolled over and were swept off the top like bales of cotton, which stormed along the roof and splashed clouds of yellow chips from the planking. . . . It made a shambles of the place. The survivors broke out in a panic across the desert, throwing away their rifles and equipment as they ran.'

This ambush ended, like so many Arab operations, in furious and selfish looting:

'The Arabs, gone raving mad, were rushing about at top speed, bare-headed and half-naked, screaming, shooting into the air, clawing one another nail and fist, while they burst open trucks and staggered back and forward with immense bales, which they ripped by the railside and tossed through, smashing what they did not want. . . .'

Sometimes the fighting was more purposeful. In June he had led a camel charge against a Turkish column surprised in the open desert:

'Yells and shots poured up in a sudden torrent from beyond the crest. We kicked our camels furiously to the edge, to see our fifty horsemen coming down the last slope into the main valley like a runaway, at full gallop, shooting from the saddle. As we watched, two or three went down, but the rest thundered forward at marvellous speed, and the Turkish infantry, huddled together under the cliff, ready to cut their desperate way out towards Maan in the first dusk, began to sway in and out, and finally broke before the rush, adding their flight to Ouda's charge. . . . They were too bound up in the terror against their rear to notice us as we came over the eastward slope; so we also took them by surprise and in the flank; and a charge of ridden camels going nearly thirty miles an hour was irresistible.'

Two years of campaigning in the desert culminated for Lawrence (el Urenz to the Arabs) in the approach to Damascus. Lawrence served as adviser to Faisal, son of the Sharif of Mecca, who desired to make Damascus the capital of a new Arab kingdom. He and Lawrence were acutely anxious to seize it ahead of Allenby's army, which the Arab leadership now saw as the instrument of a policy hostile to their interests. Anglo-Arab antipathy had crystalized in November 1917, when the British government had issued, through its foreign minister, a promise – the Balfour Declaration – to the Zionist movement. This declared that it would assist them in the creation of a national home for the Jewish people in Palestine. Word had also reached Faisal of an earlier understanding, the Sykes-Picot agreement between the British and French, which would retain Palestine and Syria under their control once those territories had been won from the Turks. Therefore, while Allenby's regular armies slogged through the Turkish defenses of populated Palestine during the summer of 1918, Lawrence, Faisal and the Arab army sought a way to Damascus through the desert. On 19 September 1918 Allenby won a major victory over the Turks, now commanded by the Gallipoli team of Liman von Sanders and Mustapha Kemal, at a place called Megiddo, identified with the biblical battle site of Armageddon. He broke across the mountain barrier into Syria and the Lebanon, but the Arabs were ahead of him. On 2 October, Lawrence and his confederates found themselves on the outskirts of Damascus. They believed that the Turks and British had already fought through the city:

'But, instead of ruins, the silent gardens stood blurred green with river mist, in whose setting shimmered the city, beautiful as ever like a pearl in the morning sun. . . . We drove down the straight-banked ridge through

Left: **British troops pass the Ctesiphon Arch, the site of General Townshend's defeat in November 1915.**

Left: **General Allenby, who led the successful attack on Palestine and Syria.**

Right: **King Faisal of the Hejaz (later Saudi Arabia) leads his men who helped the British conquer the Middle East.**

Far right: **Faisal at Wejh in March 1917.**

Below: **The British troops, led by General Maude, march Turkish prisoners through the streets of Baghdad after its capture, cheered by Arabs who thought this meant their liberation.**

the watered fields in which the peasants were just beginning their day's work. A galloping horseman checked at our headcloths in the car with a merry salutation, holding out a bunch of yellow grapes. "Good news, Damascus salutes you. . . ."'

At their approach to the town hall, they found it:

'packed with a swaying mob, yelling, embracing, dancing, singing. Every man, woman, child in this city of a quarter million souls seemed in the streets, waiting only for the spark of our appearance to ignite their spirits. Damascus went mad with joy. The men tossed up their tarbooshes to cheer, the women tore off their veils. Householders threw flowers, hangings, carpets, into the road before us: their wives leaned, screaming with laughter, through the lattices and splashed us with bath-dippers of scent, poor dervishes made themselves our running footmen in front and behind, howling and cutting themselves with frenzy. And over the loud cries and the shrilling of women came the measured roar of men's voices chanting "Faisal, Nasir, Shukri, Urenz."'

Alas for Faisal and Urenz. Their claim to have beaten Allenby's Australians into Damascus was rejected by the British, who were, in any case, determined and equipped to deny the Arabs any claim to right of conquest. The essential weakness of a guerrilla army was demonstrated as starkly as it could ever be by the steamroller refusal of the British to accept the Arabs as anything but picturesque auxiliaries to their conventional military power. They stuck unapologetically to their plan of dividing Palestine and Syria with the French and admitting Jews

freely to settle in Eretz Israel – 'the land of Israel' as the Zionists call the Holy Land. Lawrence, admitted as spokesman for the Arabs to the peace conference, struggled valiantly to win their case before the court of world opinion, but he was defeated there as decisively as he had been robbed of the fruits of battle on the ground.

There was a sort of justice in his defeat. Every guerrilla leader trafficks as much in propaganda as in deeds. Lawrence must be reckoned one of the great propagandists of the 20th century, a master of both instant personal effect and of lasting literary appeal. In retrospect his achievements appear increasingly transient and insubstantial. He engaged nothing but a small fraction of the Turkish army in Arabia and he inflicted little real damage upon it. Without the prop of Allenby's regulars his 'army of the Arabs' would have been blown like chaff before the wind of the Turks' impatience whenever they had chosen to fill their lungs. He can claim no common standing with Lettow-Vorbeck, whose brilliant campaign of evasion in Tanganyika complemented instead of depended upon the strength of the regular army, and will remain as a classic example of how a guerrilla commander can almost infinitely postpone defeat.

Defeat or victory in these 'outer theaters' ultimately counted for nothing in the scales of World War I. The German colonies, even the territory of the Turkish empire, were peripheral to the forum of the real struggle, which remained where it had begun, on the eastern and western borders of Germany. While Lettow-Vorbeck had been drawing his British and South African pursuers ever deeper into the forests of East Africa and Lawrence had been preparing his spectacular debut on the stage of Arabian politics, the armies of Germany, France and Britain had been gathering their strength for the great battles of 1916 which each believed would bring the conflict to an end. These were to be the battles of Verdun and the Somme.

Above left: **Red Cross units carry away the wounded in the fight for Palestine, October 1918.**

Left: **Indian Bengal Lancers in General Chauvel's march through Damascus after the conquest of Syria, October 1918.**

Above right: **A British armored car being shelled in Palestine.**

Top: **The triumphal march into Aqaba.**

Above: **The triumphal British entry into Baghdad after its capture, 11 March 1917.**

Below: **Lawrence's forces march into Palestine aboard their camels.**

The first British tank unit in action in World War I at Flers, September 1916.

4 Verdun and the Somme

The French High Command, though it had made a token contribution to the Gallipoli expedition, had set its face from the outset of trench warfare against campaigning by the Allies outside France. Its view of the war was simple: that Germany was the strong man of the Central Powers, without whom that alliance would collapse, that the best portion of its army occupied French territory, which was intolerable, and that the right strategy therefore was to attack and keep on attacking until the Germans had been sent packing. As early as 29 December 1915 Joffre had outlined to Haig a plan for a great attack on either side of the River Somme, where the British Expeditionary Force and the French army joined hands. Its objects would be different from those of his earlier offensives, which had been designed to strike at the left and right shoulders of the great bulge which the German line formed in France. The coming battle was to be a straightforward test of strength, in which he who could stand the attrition – *usure*, or 'wearing down' as the British called it – would emerge the victor. Joffre had chosen the Somme precisely because it was there that the two Allied Armies stood side by side, and could bring their strength fully to bear on the enemy. He suggested that they open the offensive on 1 July 1916 on a front 60 miles wide, and sustain it until the Germans could take no more.

French casualties by the end of 1915 already amounted to 1,900,000, of which a third had been fatal. Joffre nevertheless chose to believe that in the coming offensive he could inflict more casualties than his armies would suffer – a very doubtful belief, since the attacker almost always incurs losses faster than the defender. He buttressed his dubious calculation by his expressed confidence in the superior power of the Allies' artillery which he believed would win ground and kill Germans without proportionate risk to their infantry. Already in French staff circles the idea, later to become an article of dogma, had begun to circulate that 'artillery conquers, infantry merely occupies.'

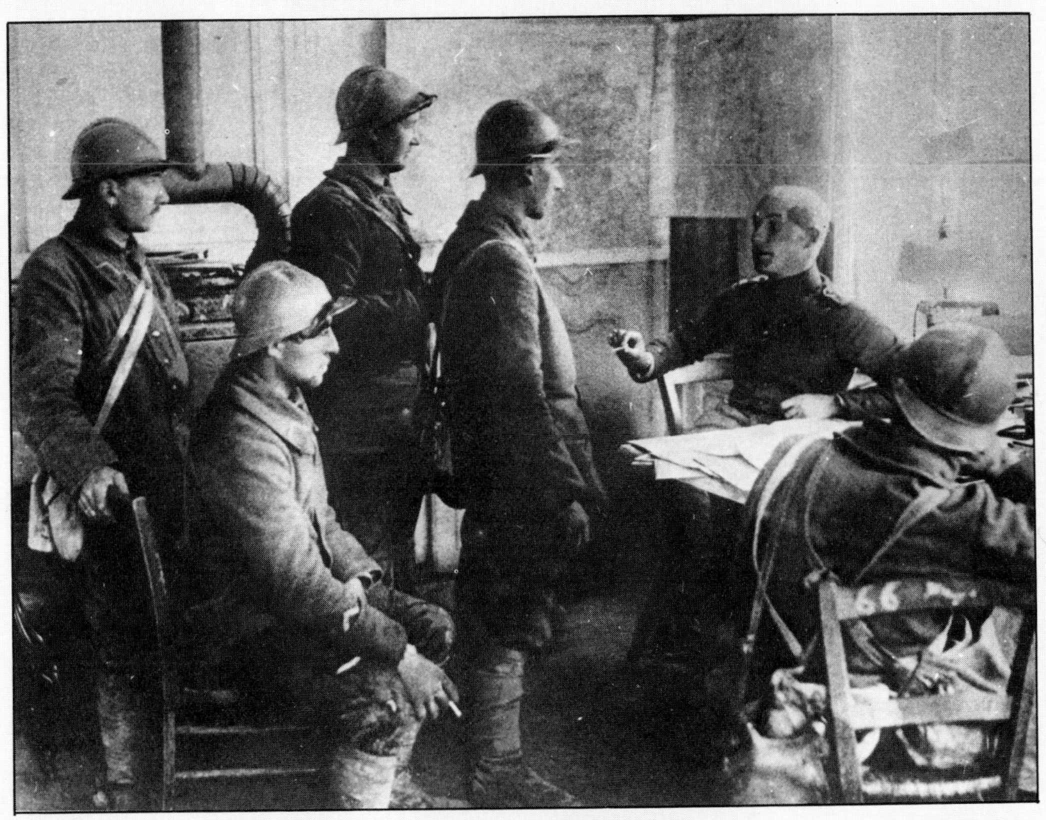

Above left: **The Archduke Friedrich of Austria and General Conrad von Hötzendorf.**

Above center: **French prisoners captured at Verdun are interrogated.**

Above right: **General Sir Douglas Haig, who planned the brutal and devastating Somme offensive.**

Below: **Some of the many thousands of French POWs seized by the Germans at Verdun.**

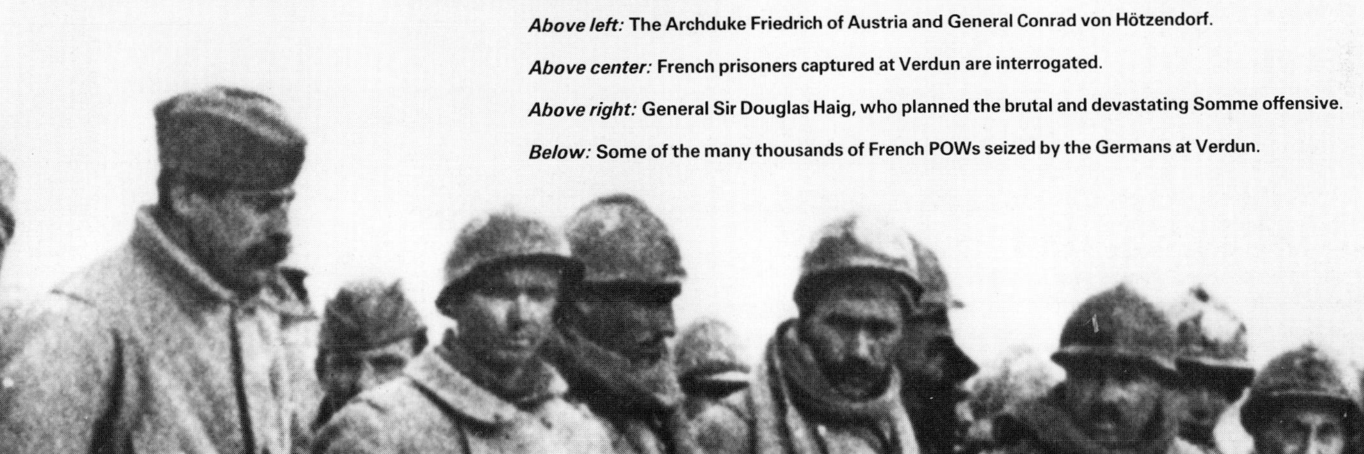

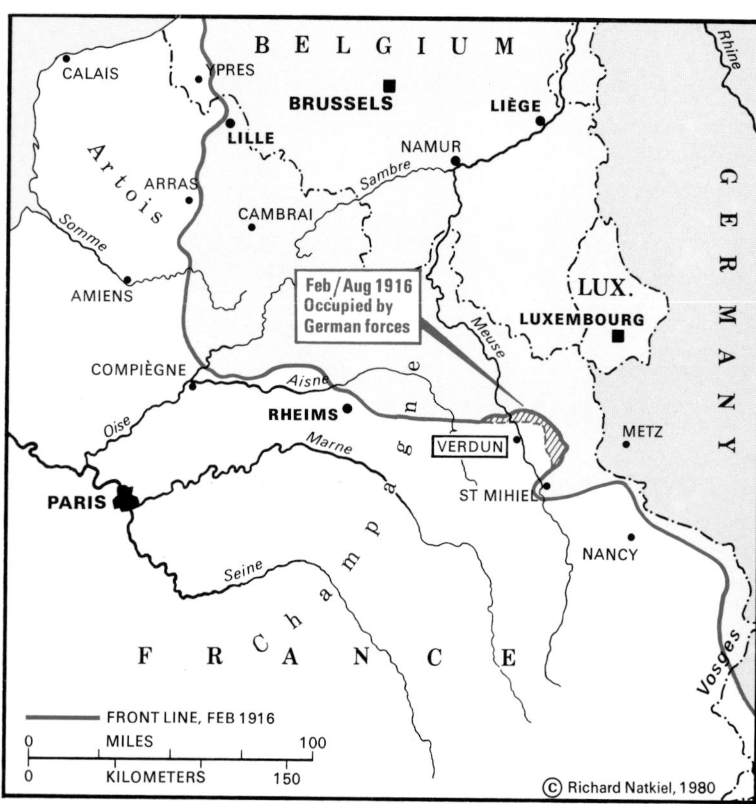

Above left: **The front line at the start of 1916.**

Above: **The remains of a French soldier after Verdun.**

Above right: **Germans dig in at Verdun.**

Above far right: **A German soldier fights on in a trench abandoned by the French at Fort Vaux, Verdun.**

Right: **A French soldier who fell at Verdun.**

During December 1915 on the other side of the lines a similar idea and a complementary strategic analysis were projecting General von Falkenhayn and his staff toward a decision for an offensive of their own. Over Christmas the German Commander in Chief prepared for the Kaiser an exhaustive survey of the military situation and the options it presented. He now identified the British as 'the arch enemy – the soul of resistance – who must be shown that they had no chance of success.' Since the blockade had begun to bite hard and limited Germany's ability to hold out indefinitely, Britain could only be disheartened by a German offensive, and the only question was where to attack. A landing on British territory was made impossible by her naval strength and the outer theaters, Egypt, Mesopotamia and India, were too remote for German power to be brought to bear. In France, on the other hand, the British were too strong to be attacked directly for though the BEF was smaller than the French army it fought better. It remained therefore to attack one of Britain's allies. Falkenhayn had discussed with Conrad von Hötzendorf, the Commander in Chief of the Austrian Army, which to choose. They agreed that a heightening of the offensive against Russia would be fruitless, for the same reasons which had dissuaded Schlieffen from attacking her in the first place; the distances were too great and the communications a nightmare. Conrad was keen to attack Italy, which had stepped into the war in May 1915 with the unconcealed intention of robbing Austria of her remaining Italian-speaking provinces when she was unfitted to defend them properly. However Falkenhayn did not follow his argument that an Italian campaign would shortly allow the Central Powers' full strength to be turned against France. He thought it would all take too long and it would be better to get at Britain through an attack on the strongest of her allies, France, which was so weakened by the agonies of 1914–15 and likely to collapse under one more heavy blow. Conrad and he therefore agreed to differ. The Austrians decided on a separate attack of their own against Italy in the Trentino. Falkenhayn turned to the map of the French front to choose a spot for an executioner's stroke at the neck of Marianne.

The spot he eventually selected was Verdun. Historically one of the great frontier fortresses of eastern France, its fortification had gradually fallen into decay since the last rebuilding in 1885 and since 1914 its strongpoints had been stripped of their heavy artillery to equip the armies in the field. The High Command had judged it safe to take that risk because Verdun seemed to have become a backwater. It stood in a remote angle of the trench line where it crossed the River Meuse south of Rheims, but there had been no heavy fighting there since September 1914. The German garrison on the east bank appeared ready to live and let live and in consequence the French held the area with troops resting from heavier fighting elsewhere. The Germans, nevertheless, enjoyed important advantages in the area. Only a single French railroad ran into the city, and it lay within the range of German artillery. The Germans enjoyed the use of no less than 11 railroads, all of which lay past the heights of the Meuse and so beyond the range of the French guns. In a 'battle of build up,' therefore, the advantage would lie heavily, if indeed not conclusively, with the Germans.

The Germans did not intend to allow the French to build up anything. Overwhelmingly strong in artillery – 221 batteries to 65, theirs included numbers of the 305mm and 420mm heavy howitzers which had devastated Liège and Namur in 1914 – their plan was to challenge the French to commit their unsupported infantry in large numbers to a battle of exhaustion. On 21 February 1916 they opened an enormous surprise bombardment, which included gas and tear-smoke shells. It fell on the positions of the two French divisions which held the eight miles

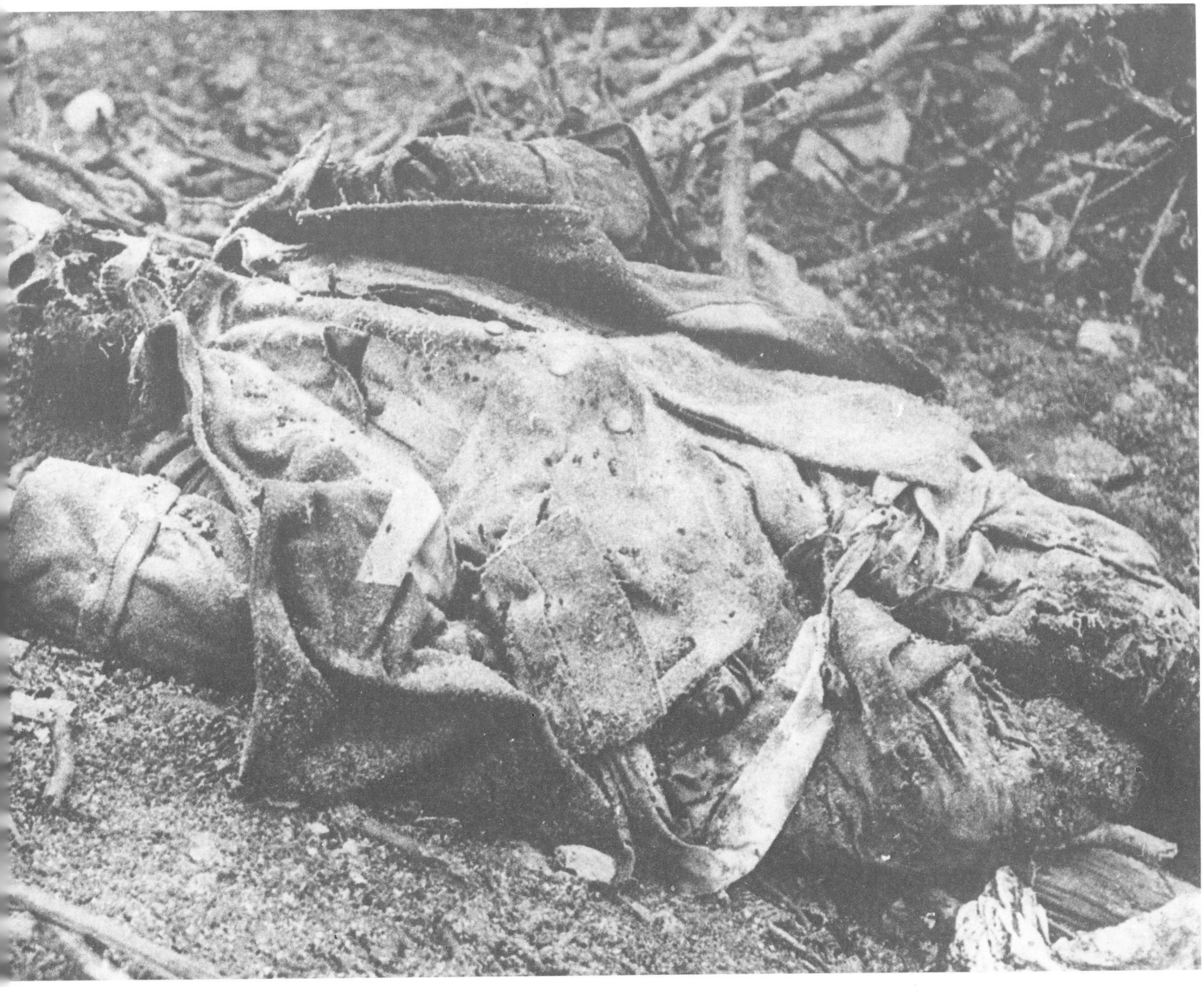

Above: French troops attack during the Battle of Verdun.

Left: No man's land at Verdun.

Above right: Germans storm across no man's land in the opening stages of the Battle of Verdun.

Far right: Grenades pock-marked the earth at Verdun.

Below: Germans crawl through the barbed wire at Verdun.

of front on the right bank of the Meuse. Nothing like it had been experienced on the Western Front before. Whole trees were uprooted and flung into the air in the woods around Verdun and along mile-long stretches of the front the trenches were completely obliterated. The bombardment was at its heaviest in the Bois des Caures, held by two Chasseur battalions commanded by Lieutenant Colonel Driant. The opening of the battle was doubly bitter for him. Not only did he see his battalions progressively wiped out under his eyes, he himself, who sat in the National Assembly for the Verdun constituency, had been warned of the danger which threatened the sector and had protested against the failure to strengthen its defenses. He was the most famous French imaginative writer about future warfare and had described in graphic detail the particular horrors which a great battle of artillery would inflict on its victims. His understanding of the power of modern armies ensured that his position was the best laid out of any on the Verdun Front, and so paradoxically the agony his Chasseurs suffered in the Bois des Caures was particularly prolonged. It was later circulated that over 100,000 shells fell into his position during the preliminary bombardment, but the concrete shelters and deep dugouts he had had constructed were so strong that most of his men were still alive when the Germans appeared. They were so heavily outnumbered, however, that although able to hold back the Germans on the first day, on the second their strongpoints fell one by one under sheer weight of numbers. Driant, who had taken absolution from the regimental Chaplain at the opening of the bombardment and behaved throughout the succeeding hours with an almost priestly calm, recognized in the afternoon of 22 February that he would have to abandon his line, which was now being assaulted by flame-thrower teams. Gathering his remaining officers about him he set off for the rear. On the way, he paused to give first aid to a wounded Chasseur, was hit and died with a prayer on his lips. His extraordinary courage and tenacity in the defense of the Bois des Caures impressed not only his own countrymen but also the enemy, one of whom arranged to have Driant's personal effects, which he had found in the command post, sent to his widow via a neutral party in Switzerland.

Thereafter Verdun was to become an increasingly anonymous battle, as the French, responding to the challenge in the style Falkenhayn had hoped they would, began to feed divisions into the stricken fortress, keeping them there until each had suffered the maximum possible level of casualties and then withdrawing it to refit.

Above: Part of the wreckage of Fort Douaumont at Verdun.

Above right: Fort Douaumont before the action.

However, in this opening stage there was to be the opportunity for one more display of individual achievement, this time on the German side. On 24 February the French second line, which had come under pressure as soon as the first had been pierced at the Bois des Caures, suddenly gave way and the Germans were able to rush to the third, formed by the outer line of 19th-century forts – Douaumont and Vaux – and the trenches which had been dug between them. At Douaumont they were only four miles from the city of Verdun itself and, if they could take it, would have only one more line of obstacles to cross in order to achieve victory.

Douaumont was a formidable position. Two fields of barbed wire 30-feet deep were backed by a line of spiked railings eight feet high on the edge of a dry ditch 24 feet deep. Inside stood a low concrete structure 200 yards long and 100 yards wide dominated by armored gun turrets and loopholed for machine guns. Inside was a labyrinth of tunnels and strong chambers with accommodation for 500 men. On the wall of the principal tunnel was inscribed the slogan, 'Rather be buried under the bricks of the fort than surrender.' On 25 August a German sergeant called Kunze appeared on the lip of this forbidding structure. He was in command of a section of pioneers whose task was to remove obstacles for the infantry regiment they were supporting, the 24th Brandenburgs. By some chance he had lost touch with them and now found himself in the shadow of their principal objective, which seemed uninhabited. Deciding to explore, Kunze found a way through the wire and the spikes, dropped into the moat and crept along the wall of the fort itself. Finding an open loophole, he got his men to form a human pyramid, climbed to the top and entered the fort. No one challenged him and he set off to find the enemy. In fact the fort was held by only 60 elderly gunners, some of whom he quickly collected and made prisoner. After he had been in the fort for about an hour he was joined by an officer with his platoon, and between them they rounded up the rest of the garrison and secured the position. For the loss of none of their men, they had cracked the French position.

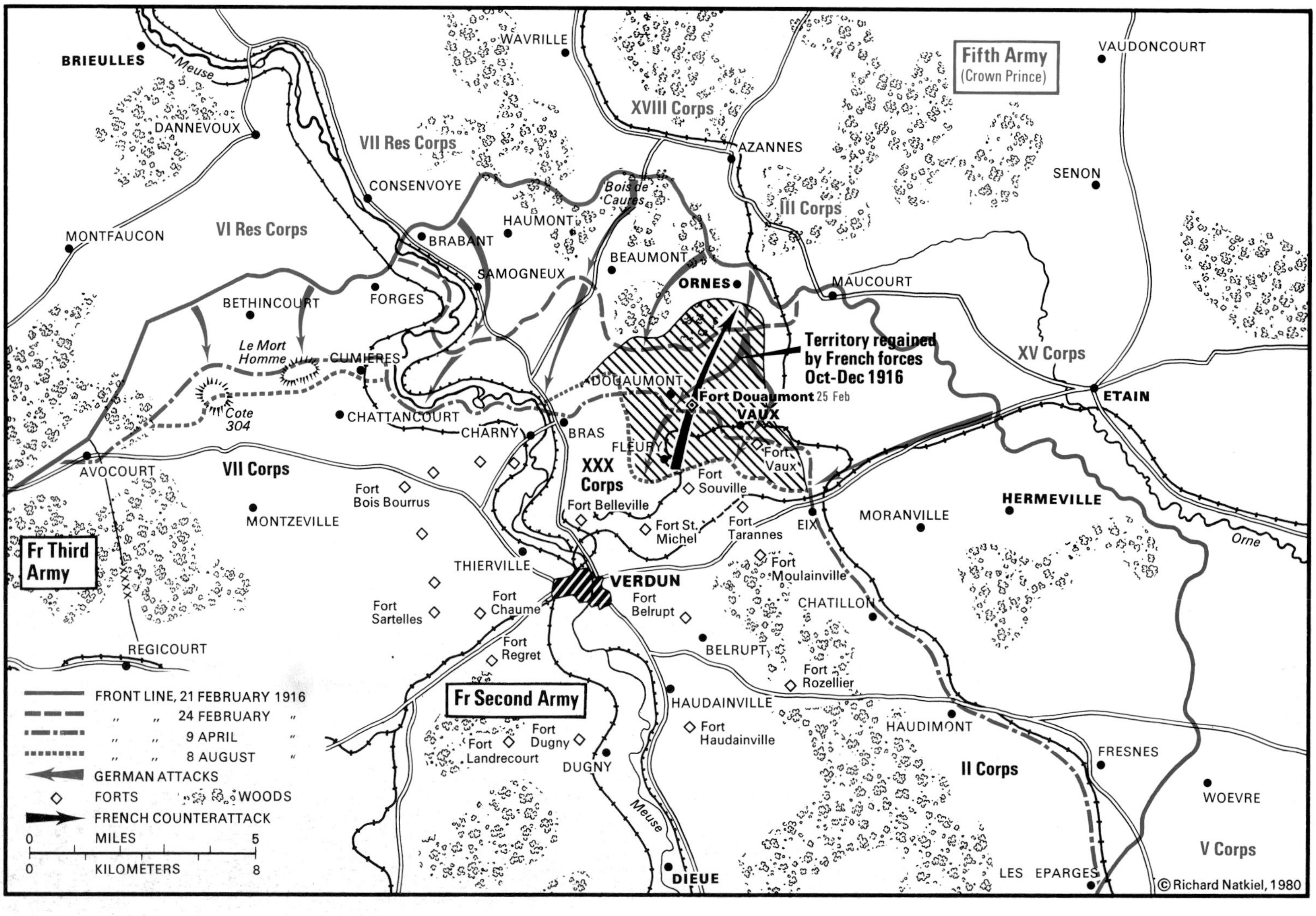

Above: Fort Douaumont afterward.

Above right: The gunfire at Mort-Homme ridge near Fort Douaumont.

Right: Germans inside the wrecked fort.

Below right: French wounded inside the main corridor of Fort Vaux.

Below left: The action at Verdun.

The Germans were slow to grasp the implications of the advantage which Kunze had won for them (and he was to be cheated of the credit, appropriated by an officer who arrived later), and were even slower to decide how to exploit it. By the time they had done so, a new and decisive factor had entered the situation. Philippe Pétain had been appointed to command on the Verdun sector. Pétain was an odd man out in the French army. Extremely individualistic, and contemptuous of fashionable ideas, he had not had a successful prewar career. He was, indeed, on the point of retiring as a 58-year old Colonel at the outbreak of war, and was kept on only as an emergency measure. However his success in commanding a brigade during the Great Retreat quickly won him a division, then a corps and later an army. By early 1916 he had emerged as the general best attuned to the problems of trench warfare and most understanding of the common soldier's problems. By 25 February it was clear that the local commander, General Herr, had lost his nerve. Joffre had chosen Pétain to replace him.

The effect on French morale in the threatened sector was instantaneous. 'Pétain is in control' were the words which ran round the trenches. 'France has her eyes on you' was the message of his first order of the day, but his intervention depended on more than his personal qualities for its effect. He focused at once on the two outstanding problems of the defense; artillery and supply. The French defenders were not only short of guns, those they had were badly coordinated. He ordered all the artillery put under a single command, appealed urgently to the High Command for more heavy-caliber pieces and made his first enquiry every morning, 'What have your batteries been doing? Leave the other details till later.' The garrison was also critically short of supplies. The only railroad into the fortress was single-line and narrow-gauge. He at once ordered the construction of a new standard gauge spur to lead into the city, but meanwhile concentrated his energies on the maintenance and improvement of the single road which provided the only other means of supply. Ten thousand military laborers were brought to widen the road to seven yards, just enough for a column of trucks to pass in each direction. Quarries were opened to provide gravel which was constantly thrown on to the surface – 750,000 tons during the course of the battle – and trucks assembled from all over France. There had been only 700 in the district when the offensive opened, enough to provide 1250 tons of supplies daily. The garrison needed 2000 tons and another 100 tons for every extra division committed. Within days Pétain's transport Chief, Major Richard, had found another 2800 trucks, which he set to work in a continuous flow from one end of the *Voie Sacrée* (Sacred Way as the road came to be called) to the other, day and night, week after week without stopping. At maximum density a truck started on to the road every five seconds, but the pace along the 50 miles was so slow that a driver might spend 50 hours at the wheel to complete the journey.

By these desperate improvisations Pétain assumed that the Germans would not take Verdun in the first impulse of their attack. 'They shall not pass' (*Ils ne passeront pas*) became the watchword of his strategy. The formation of the initial assault did not cause the Germans to think again. Falkenhayn had code named the plan *Gericht* – Execution Place – and evidence that the French were willing to prolong the battle, at what he believed would be unbearable loss to themselves, was exactly what he wanted to detect. On 6 March, therefore, he opened a new effort against the tortured fortress. Hitherto he had attacked only on the right (eastern) bank of the Meuse. He now intended to march down the left bank as well, while striking to seize the fort next to Douaumont, Fort Vaux. With that in his hands and the French left-bank positions pushed back, he believed that Verdun could be held only at a progressively intolerable loss in French lives.

The new push won an immediate and spectacular success. The French infantry on the left bank were taken by surprise and one division broke under the shock. Most of one of its regiments was taken prisoner – an ominous indication of shaken morale to Pétain, who was himself weakened by an attack of pneumonia which had struck him within days of assuming command. To add to the misery of the battlefield, already beginning to assume that appearance of contiguous and overlapping shell-craters which would leave an unforgettable impression on all who saw it, unseasonable snow had begun to fall. The French fell back in the flurries which blinded their artillery observers from one critical point to another, but on 9 March the triumphant Germans found their attack beginning to falter. It had carried them to the northern slope of le Mort-Homme (Dead Man) ridge and the hill called Côte 304 and here they encountered fresh French troops who refused to budge. During the rest of the month the battle raged on for these two beleaguered

Below: **French on Mort-Homme ridge at Verdun turn a German machine gun against their enemy.**

Above left: **Crown Prince Wilhelm, the Kaiser's son and heir to the German throne.**

Above: **The wreckage of the Fort Moulainville.**

Bottom left: **Crown Prince Wilhelm in full regalia.**

Bottom right: **British postcard satirizes German bayoneters.**

features. The Germans won ground in the Bois d'Avocourt, between the Mort-Homme and the Meuse, but the two hills held.

The cost was terrible, to both sides – each had lost over 80,000 casualties so far – but the French suffered particularly. A victim of the battle described men coming out of the line:

'Yesterday . . . I saw some regiments returning from the trenches. . . . When you see those mud statues, steps painfully dragging, those hollow faces, haunted eyes and tortured glances, those moving hulks, those bundles of agony on the march, anger possesses the calmest man. What shame! That's what you can make out of men, machines for suffering. Nothing so abominable has ever been seen before. That isn't heroism. That is degradation.'

Above: **French troops retreat from Fort Vaux along *la Voie Sacrée,* the vital supply line the French kept open to Verdun.**

There was more to come, and yet more anxiety for the French commanders. On 1 May Pétain, promoted to command the Group of Armies of the Center, had left Verdun to his brilliant subordinate General Georges Nivelle. During May he saw French casualties climb to 185,000 and despite heroic defense both the Mort-Homme and Côte 304 fell to the enemy. At the end of the month the Germans renewed the offensive for the third time in an effort code named May Cup. Its main weight was directed on the right bank in the direction of Vaux, the outermost of the forts. Since the loss of Douaumont the French had taken care to see that the forts were properly garrisoned, and Vaux was held by 300 men under the command of a Major Sylvain-Eugène Raynal. The Germans had also learned that the capture of a fort could not be left to the chance presence of a hero like Kunze. They had prepared an enormous bombardment and an assault by a special force of the 50th Division, commanded by Major General Weber Pasha, who had distinguished himself in the defense of the Turkish forts at Gallipoli.

Within minutes of the attack beginning on 1 June they were inside the fort, but their leaders had reckoned without Raynal. This rock of French stubborness and courage was determined that Vaux should not fall and, yard by yard contested every corridor and chamber of the interior with the overwhelming numbers which had invaded it. The Germans used flame throwers, gas and grenades to blast their way forward, called down the fire of the terrible 420mm howitzers and, when the fort was still holding out after three days, began mining under the concrete walls in order to blow them up. Still their losses mounted and French resistance held. Handfuls of reinforcements made their way through the murderous barrage to bring strength to Raynal's dwindling band and the French artillery from miles away put down curtains of fire on the German attackers around and on top of the concrete carapace. On 4 June, however, Raynal lost his means of communicating with the rear when he sent off

Below right: **German Crown Prince Wilhelm inspects his troops at Verdun.**

Far right: **The tunnel at Fort Vaux that became the grave of its defenders.**

Below: **Relief units pour up *la Voie Sacrée* to assist in the defense of Verdun.**

his last carrier pigeon, which delivered the message 'relief is imperative' and dropped dead in the hands of its pigeon master. (The pigeon was decorated with the *Légion d'Honneur*.) Shortly afterward he received word from his chief subordinate that the fort could no longer depend on its own resources. The cistern gauge was inaccurate and the garrison had only a quarter of a pint of water per man for a few days more. The heat inside, under a June sun, was intense and the garrison began to suffer agonies of thirst. On 6 June the men's thirst became unbearable and at 0330 hours on 7 June Raynal decided that he must surrender. He sent out a white flag party and shortly afterward he was himself ushered into the presence of the German Crown Prince, commanding on the Verdun sector. Even his enemies were prepared to recognize the extraordinary heroism he had displayed and with a gallantry which Allied propaganda would not admit 'Little Willie' was capable, he presented the weary and smoke-stained hero with a captured French sword to replace his own lost at Vaux.

His magnanimity perhaps derived from the victory he felt to be so close, for his army group was now preparing for the fourth and what was believed to be the final offensive. Large quantities of a new gas, phosgene, which the French gas masks could not filter out, had been issued to the artillery and on 22 June a disabling bombardment was fired into the French front on the right bank south of Douaumont and Vaux. The infantry assaulting behind it, which included the crack Alpenkorps division, found the French gasping for breath and already dying from gas-poisoning. They pushed quickly on to the fort of Thiaumont from the roof of which a small party of reckless attackers actually glimpsed the twin towers of Verdun Cathedral, hitherto hidden from them by the hills of the Meuse valley, gleaming in the afternoon sun. However their elan was not to win them

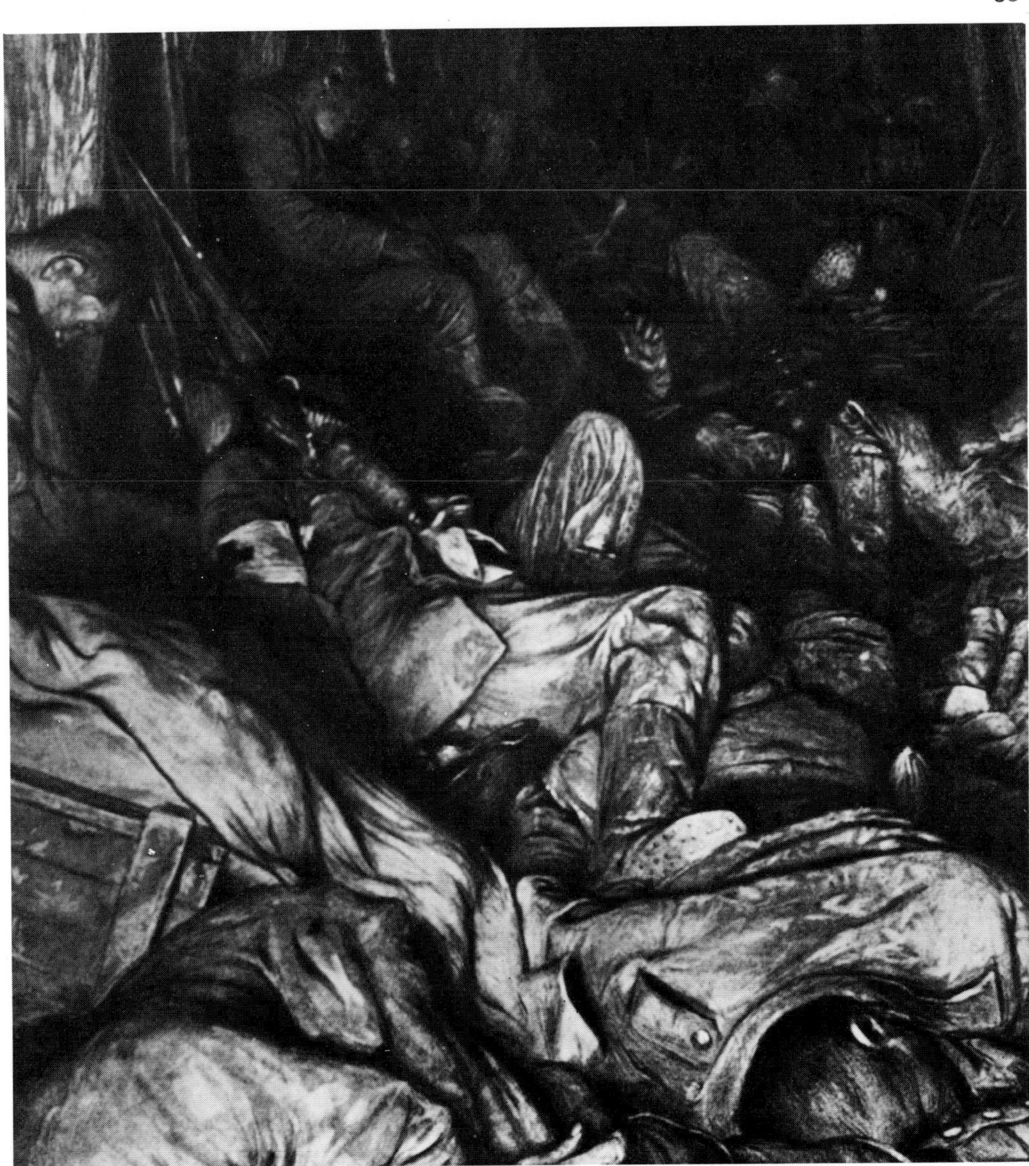

Above: **French General Charles Mangin.**

Above right: **A French trench near Verdun in the winter of 1916–17.**

Right: **British soldiers in a dugout on the Somme.**

Souville as it had won Vaux and Douaumont. General Charles Mangin, the trap-jawed colonial soldier who acted as Nivelle's subordinate commander, reacted with supreme resolution to the crisis and sent forward reinforcements which just held the line. Throughout that day and the next the pressure was unrelenting, but, out in the sunbaked wilderness of broken trenches and shell-swept ground, the Germans began to crave for water which could not reach them. Messages were sent rearward that unless they got water they would have to retire, they certainly could not go forward. At that moment the first of Mangin's counterattacks began. He was to organize eight during the next week and, though he regained little ground, the French were to lose no more important strongpoints to the Germans. At a cost of 275,000 soldiers, the French had held Verdun. Whether the indirect object of the German plan to 'bleed their army white' had succeeded, events of the following year would show.

Even had the stroke of 22 June succeeded, it would have been impossible for the Germans to continue their offensive, for they themselves became the victims of the enterprise which Joffre and Haig had been planning since the previous December. Their position on the Western Front was essentially defensive and the implications of their numerical inferiority could not be endlessly evaded by spoiling offensives of the Verdun type. The moment of truth now arrived. After two years of war, the British had assembled an army of a size sufficient for them to take over a major stretch of the Allied line and from it to launch with the French a weighty offensive.

This army was both a military phenomenon and a popular social movement, a contingent of a million volunteers who had spontaneously come forward in late 1914 and early 1915 to provide the manpower for 30 new divisions of infantry. The impulse had been provided by Lord Kitchener, hero of the Sudanese and Boer Wars, who had called in September 1914 for '100,000 volunteers' to join the regular army for three years. His appeal had been given a particular point by Lord Derby, political strongman of the industrial and commercial northwest of England, who had appealed in September for the young men of Liverpool to heed Kitchener's call, and for Liverpool to form a battalion of its own for what was already being called the New Armies. Such a battalion was formed at his first recruiting meeting and within days the city had produced three more. Kitchener promised that groups of friends joining together would be allowed to serve together, instead of being scattered throughout the army at large, and so arose the Pals and Chums battalions.

Altogether they were to make up the 9th–42nd Divisions, drawn in groups of six from Scotland, Ireland, the North Country, East Anglia, the West and the Home Counties. Inside each division the battalion titles revealed their particular local origins. The 31st Division was composed of the Leeds Pals, 1st and 2nd Bradford Pals, 1st and 2nd Barnsley Pals, the Halifax Pals, Hull Commercials (local shop assistants), Hull Tradesmen, Hull Sportsmen, Durham Pals, Halifax Pals, Accrington Pals and Sheffield City Battalion. The 34th Division had two Edinburgh Pals battalions – 15th and 16th Royal Scots – the Grimsby Chums, the Cambridge battalion and eight battalions from Newcastle-on-Tyne and its surroundings called Tyneside Scottish or Tyneside Irish. Scattered through other divisions were battalions with names like Arts and Crafts, 1st Football, Empire, Glasgow Boys' Brigade and Forest of Dean Pioneers. There had always been a strong tradition of voluntary enlistment among the British, and 28 of the divisions in the British Army of 1916 were drawn from the prewar Territorial Force, a part-time army of weekend soldiers who served in their own time without pay. It was the Territorials who had borne the brunt of the fighting during late 1915, particularly at Loos. The New Armies were different, their enthusiasm was not for soldiering as such but for service to the nation in time of crisis. They had joined to win the war and believed that they could do that where the old army and the French had failed. The coming battle was to be their chance.

The spot Joffre and Haig had jointly chosen for the offensive was the River Somme where the French line joined with the British, which had been progressively extended from Flanders as the size of the British Expeditionary Force had grown. Originally Joffre had intended that the two armies should attack in equal strength, on a front of 60 miles with the object of wearing down the Germans and eventually breaking through into open country. Falkenhayn's success in wearing down the defenders of Verdun had vitiated that intention. All that Joffre could provide for 1 July 1916, the chosen date, was eight divisions, to attack on a front of eight miles south of the river. The British, on a front of 18 miles, were to attack with 14 divisions, with three infantry divisions in reserve and five cavalry divisions positioned behind them to exploit the breakthrough when and if it came.

Below: **French *poilus* with gas masks in the mud, fire and horror of Verdun.**

Above: German troops move up to the Somme in an early example of motorized transport. Most came on foot.

Below: A 400mm rail gun prepares to fire near the Somme, June 1916.

More important than numbers of infantry was weight of bombardment, and for this the British and French had assembled more guns and ammunition than had yet been seen on the Western Front. Too many were light guns – 75mm and 18-pounders – but there was one heavy gun to each 60 yards of front on the British sector and to each 20 yards on the French, and 1,500,000 rounds of ammunition. The bombardment opened on 24 June, a week before zero-hour and every day thereafter 200,000 shells were fired into the German lines. The noise could be heard as a dull rumble as far away as the South of England where the Prime Minister, Herbert Asquith, father of two sons at the front and in his heart an opponent of the war, took refuge in endless rounds of bridge to distract himself from thought of the coming holocaust. That thought afflicted the BEF's posts, who sensed the significance of the approaching July and sought words to catch the mixture of dread and elation which word of the battle aroused. Edmund Blunden describes his Colonel's warning that his battalion is off to the Somme:

'We're going South, man'; as he spoke
The howitzer with huge ping-bang
Rocked the light hut; as thus he broke
The death-news bright the sky larks sang;
He took his riding crop and humming went
Among the apple-trees all bloom and scent.
Now far withdraws the roaring night
Which wrecked our flower after the first
Of those two voices; misty light
Shrouds Thiepval Wood and all its worst;
But still 'there's something in the air' I hear,
And still 'We're going South man', deadly near.

Much of the flower of the New Armies was to be wrecked at Thiepval Wood, which lay opposite the British front line at the point where the 32nd Division was to attack – the division which contained the 1st, 2nd and 3rd Salford Pals, the Newcastle Commercials and the Glasgow Tramways Battalions, the Glasgow Boys' Brigade Battalion and the Lonsdales raised on the Border near Carlisle from estate workers in the employment of the famous Yellow Earl.

The mood of the New Armies going south to the Somme was not one generally of foreboding but of gaiety and confidence, emotions all the more readily felt because of their inexperience. One of the New Army divisions, the 9th, which was to lie in reserve, had fought at Loos. The regular divisions committed for the offensive, the 4th, 8th and 29th, had all seen action before, but the rest of the 14 were virgin formations. Many of their soldiers had only recently arrived in France. The infantrymen had in many cases not fired their rifles at the enemy and the artillery, on which so much depended, had in many cases received its guns only at the moment of embarkation in Britain.

The morning of 1 July 1916 dawned bright and sunny, with the mist of promised heat overlying the German trenches. A pilot of the Royal Flying Corps, observing the front from the sky, saw the explosions of the shells appearing on the surface of the mist bank below like the ripples of a stone thrown into a limpid pool. A young artillery officer, Lieutenant Adrian Stephen, recorded:

'the ear-splitting bark of the 18-pounders, the cough of the howitzers, the boom of the heavy guns, sucked into a jerky roar that was flung from horizon to horizon, as thunder is tossed from mountain to mountain. It was wonderful music – the mightiest I ever heard. It seemed to throb into our very veins beating up and down and yet never quite reaching a climax, but always keeping one's nerves on the thrill. And then at last 10 minutes before zero, the guns opened their lungs. The climax had been reached. One felt inclined to laugh with the sheer exhilaration of it. After all, it was our voice, the voice of a whole empire at war.'

Above: **1st Lancashire Fusiliers tend their wounded at Beaumont Hamel on the first day of the Somme battle, 1 July 1916.**

Up and down the 18 miles of front line, the infantry had been waiting for this crescendo. When it stopped 120,000 individuals, each hunched under a load of 60 pounds of ammunition, kit and rations, climbed out of their trenches, filed through the gaps in the British barbed wire and formed up to move across no man's land. In most places it was about 300 yards wide, but at some as much as 600 yards. The Germans therefore had about two minutes from hearing the end of the bombardment to man the parapets of their trenches and open fire on the approaching British before they were upon them. Almost everywhere it was to prove time enough.

The Germans in line opposite the 14 attacking British divisions belonged to five divisions, the 2nd Guard Reserve, 52nd, 26th Reserve, 28th Reserve and 12th. For the previous eight days they had crouched in the bottom of their dugouts in the chalk, shaken by the unrelenting crash of explosions above, living on cold food and chlorined water, ears pricked for the least sign of a break in the bombardment:

'At 0730 the hurricane of shells ceased as suddenly as it had begun. Our men at once clambered up the steep shafts leading from the dugouts to daylight and ran singly or in groups to the nearest shell craters. The machine guns were pulled out of the dugouts and hurriedly placed in position, their crews dragging the ammunition boxes up the steps and out to the guns. A rough line was thus rapidly established. As soon as the men were in position, a series of extended lines of infantry were seen moving forward from the British trenches. The first line appeared to continue without end from right to left. It was quickly followed by a second line, then a third and fourth. They came on at a steady pace, as if expecting to find nothing alive in our trenches.'

The Newcastle Commercials were told, 'You will be able to go over the top with a walking stick, you will not need rifles. When you get to Thiepval you will find the Germans all dead, not even a rat will have survived.' Others were encouraged to think that they could 'slope arms, light up pipes and cigarettes and march all the way' and expect that 'the field kitchens will follow you and give you a good meal.' In fact,

Above: **Lieutenant General Sir Henry Rawlinson at his HQ on the first day of the Battle of the Somme.**

Below: **Men of the 2nd Australian Division near Armentières in 1916.**

Above: A trench at the Somme. Britain suffered some 60,000 casualties in the first hours of the battle.

two of the British divisions did have a reasonably easy time getting across, because their commanders had ordered their men out into no man's land to lie down close to the German wire while the bombardment was still going on. The rest, who emerged in the long lines noted by the German observer quoted above, were quickly brought under fire by the defenders and began to suffer horrifying loss before they could get to grips with the Germans. As the leading British line approached the rattle of machine-gun and rifle fire broke out all along the whole line of craters and a hail of lead swept into the advancing lines. Some Germans fired kneeling so as to get a better target over the broken ground, while others stood up in the excitement of the moment, regardless of their own safety, to fire into the crowd of men in front of them. Red rockets sped by into the blue sky as a signal to the artillery and immediately afterward a mass of shells from the German batteries in the rear tore through the air and burst among the advancing lines. Whole sections seemed to fall and the rear formations, moving in closer order, quickly scattered. The advance rapidly crumbled under this hail of shells and bullets. All along the line men could be seen throwing their arms into the air and collapsing, never to move again. So terrible was the loss of life in front of many of the German divisional positions that at noon white flags were shown and the German doctors allowed British stretcher bearers to come forward to evacuate such of the wounded as they could.

Douglas Haig and Henry Rawlinson could not as yet know the results of their offensive. The experienced French, south of the Somme, had taken all their objectives for comparatively little loss. On the British sector the two divisions next to the French had benefited from their advance and also got well into the German lines. Another success had been won by the 36th Ulster Division, recruited from the Protestant Ulster Volunteer Force which had opposed the Irish Home Rule Bill of 1914. Their fiery militarism – perhaps fed by the only just quelled rebellion in Dublin of Easter Week – had won them a success unmatched by any other formation under Haig's command. In every other case, the divisions had either been checked at the German front line or actually halted in no man's land, and the casualties were appalling. All the divisions engaged had lost at least a quarter of their men. The 8th, at Thiepval, had lost half – 5121 killed or wounded. By comparison the German regiment it attacked, the 180th, had lost a mere 280 casualties. Some battalions had effectively been wiped out. The 1st Newfoundland Regiment, one of those bands of colonial volunteers which had responded to the call of the country in her hour of need, had suffered 684 casualties out of 752 men who had gone over the top. In all, 60,000 British soldiers had been hit on 1 July and 20,000 had been killed. The first day of the Battle of the Somme was a tragic disaster.

When this truth eventually dawned on the British High Command, it did not deter preparation for the next stage – an advance from such ground as had been won to the German second position. As it happened, it came off, largely because it was launched at night and took the Germans genuinely by surprise. It was to be the last success won by conventional artillery/infantry methods during the battle, which still had nearly four months to run. The Germans had hurriedly begun to send in reinforcements of men and guns – so weakening their effort at Verdun, as Joffre had hoped – and their numbers rose toward parity with the attackers as each week passed, thus making the likelihood of a

Right: The 10th Worcesters bring in some German POWs at La Boisselle on 3 July 1916.

Below: Tommies with some wounded German prisoners at the Somme, 3 July 1916.

Below: British casualties at the Somme.

break out even more remote. Haig seems eventually to have recognized the true situation and to have reconciled himself to Joffre's blood-chilling idea of simply settling for *usure*, wearing-down or attrition.

The battle dragged on during August and into September, with casualties running at about 4000 a day and divisions returning to the battle for the second time, sometimes for a third after the gaps in their ranks had been hastily plastered up with new men, fresh from English training camps. Some, in the autumn of 1916, were conscripts, brought in by the new law of January. The volunteering impetus had already begun to run out. Nothing like the New Armies would ever be seen again.

In September there was a flicker of renewed hope for a breakthrough. The first tanks made a brief but spectacular appearance on the battlefield. These new engines of war were the fruit of

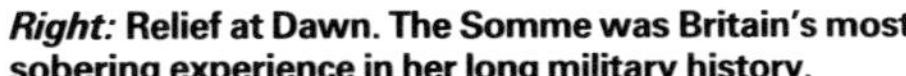

Right: **Relief at Dawn. The Somme was Britain's most sobering experience in her long military history.**

several like-thinking British minds, who had identified the principal problems of trench warfare as early as Christmas 1914. Perhaps first to do so was Colonel E D Swinton, who thought they would be overcome by an armored version of the caterpillar tractor which he had heard of but not seen. The specification for the design was actually written by Maurice Hankey, the Secretary to the Cabinet, and taken up by Winston Churchill, who instituted a Landships Committee at the Admiralty in February 1915. An experimental model ('Little Willie') had been constructed by the following September and the prototype of the Mark I Tank (a code name) was ready in December. It had been immediately put into production and the first 25 were shipped to France in August 1916 where they were taken over by the newly-formed Heavy Section, Machine Gun Corps. Haig, initially unenthusiastic, was quickly converted to the new weapon, perhaps because he was prepared to clutch at straws to save his Somme offensive.

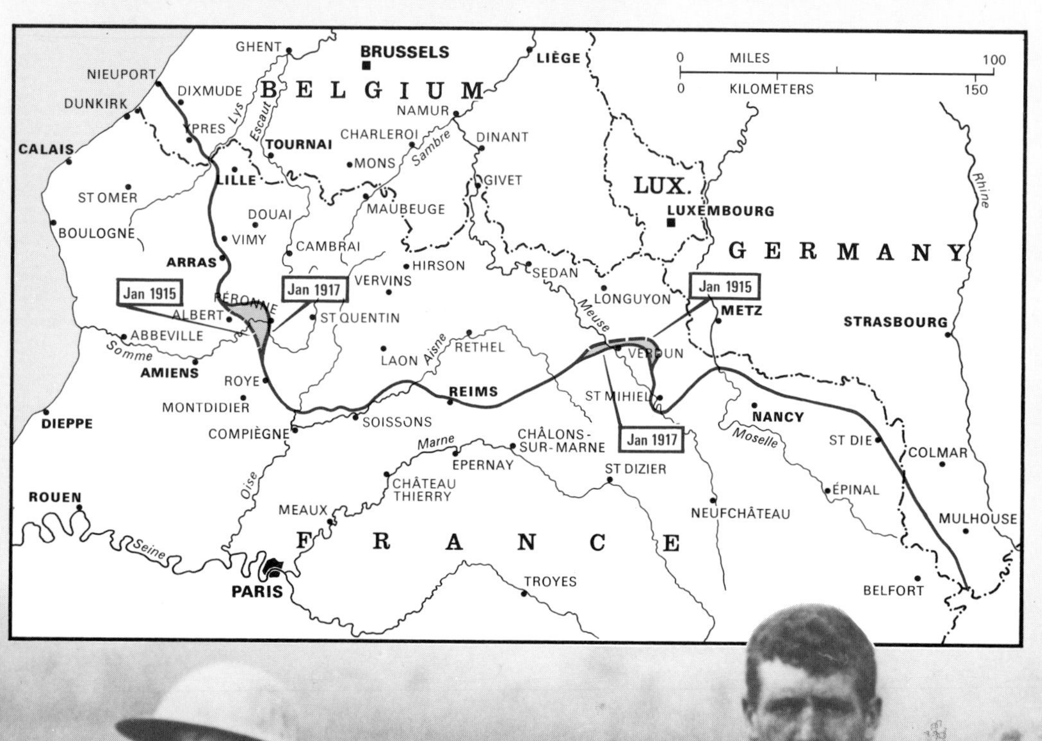

He included them in the third renewal of offensive effort, called the Battle of Flers-Courcelette, which began on 15 September. It was an attack on a 10-mile front with 12 divisions against six German; as many as had held the original front, but a fraction of the total they had subsequently concentrated there – 30 in all. As usual, the conventional assault was quickly checked by the Germans with machine guns and artillery. However at Flers, when the 36 operational tanks were deployed, the Germans gave up at the sight of these futuristic monsters and the British infantry of the 41st Division followed the leaders deep into the German lines. The Germans who were taken prisoner, Bavarians who normally displayed remarkable stolidity, were described as blue and shaking with fright. The success proved to be very brief. The tanks were too few in number and too slow – their speed was only 3mph – to create a real break in the line and the little hole they made was quickly filled by sending reinforcements to the danger spot.

Haig renewed the offensive on 25 September, again in October and twice in November, the last episode being called the Battle of the Ancre. By then winter rain had turned the churned-up surface of the battlefield into a quagmire and the infantry struggled toward their objectives caked in mud and soaked by freezing rain and wet fog. The battle petered out at last on 18 November; about 125 square miles of territory, a strip 20 miles long by six deep, had been wrested from the enemy at a cost of 420,000 British and 194,000 French casualties. German losses were optimistically calculated as equal, but were certainly many fewer.

At Verdun the summer and autumn had also cost the French dear. By 15 December, when the battle was also brought to an end by the onset of winter, they calculated their casualties at 362,000. The Germans, who had been attacking and also undoubtedly suffered as hard and, assaulted by a succession of French counter-attacks in October and December, had been forced to surrender much of the ground won at such terrible cost in the spring. Even Fort Douaumont had gone, recaptured in a push engineered by General Mangin on 24 October.

As the third winter of the war descended on the Western Front, therefore, neither side had reason to feel grateful or even optimistic about what had passed. Certainly not Falkenhayn, once the Kaiser's favored general. He too, like Moltke, had incurred the imperial displeasure. The official reason given for his removal was the entry into the war of Rumania, which had yielded to the Allies' diplomatic pressure to join

Above: Royal Australian Battery use their 9.2-inch Mark VI howitzers near the Somme.

Far left: The Western Front at the end of 1916, virtually unchanged from the previous year despite the millions who died.

Below: British and German wounded trudge toward the field hospital during the Battle for Bazentin Ridge near the Somme, 19 July 1916.

Mademoiselle from Armenteers (Armentières)

Mademoiselle from Armenteers,
Parlez-vous,
Mademoiselle from Armenteers,
Parlez-vous,
Mademoiselle from Armenteers,
She hasn't been kissed for
forty years,
Hinky-dinky parlez-vous.

them in August. Falkenhayn was sent to organize a riposte to that unwise decision, his place in the West being taken by the titans of the Eastern Front, Generals Hindenburg and Ludendorff. The real reason was a belief that his successors would succeed where he was held to have failed, in miscalculating the possibility of waging a one-sided battle of attrition at Verdun and in exposing the defenders on the Somme to the terrible losses they had suffered there.

The discomfiture of individual generals, who retained their health and whole skins, must be counted for little against the suffering which 1916 had visited on their soldiers. The German army might have emerged from the two great Western battles of the year still fit to fight. The ordeal had marked it dreadfully nonetheless. Ludendorff would later say that the summer offensives marked the end of the old German army so heavy were the inroads it made in the ranks of the regular officers and particularly the noncommissioned officers, the backbone of the military establishment. The French army, which had borne a terrible toll in each one of the three years of the war, had been brought to the verge of breaking point, as the crisis of the coming spring would show. The British Expeditionary Force, so buoyant with optimism only six

Above: **Corpse of a German soldier at Beaumont Hamel, the Somme.**

Bottom left: **Men of the 4th Worcestershires pause for a rest behind the lines at the Somme.**

Bottom right: **Weary British troops return from the trenches near Bernafay Wood, the Somme, in November 1916.**

Below: **Canadian troops go over the top at the Somme.**

months before had been turned in a single season into a grimly hardened legion of veterans, who expected nothing from the war but the chance to do an increasingly burdensome and dangerous duty. 'Where tongues were sound and hearts were light, I heard the Ancre flow,' wrote Edmund Blunden of days spent on the little tributary of the Somme before the battle. Afterward, recalling the grief he had learned there, his lines ran differently:

The struggling Ancre had no part
In these new hours of mine,
And yet its stream ran through my heart;
I heard it grieve and pine,
As if its rainy tortured blood
Had swirled into my own,
When by its shattered banks I stood
And shared its wounded moan.

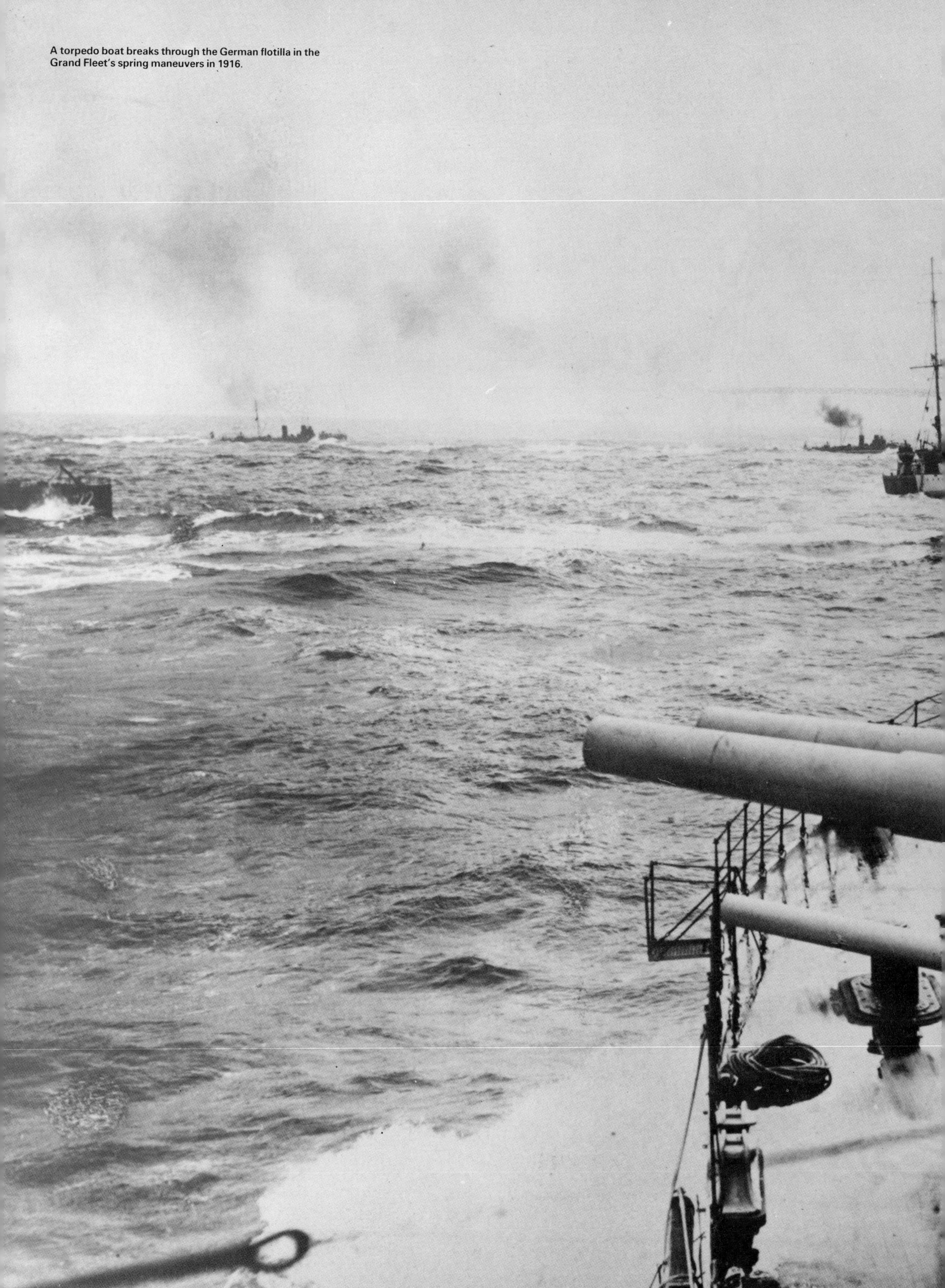

A torpedo boat breaks through the German flotilla in the Grand Fleet's spring maneuvers in 1916.

5 War on the Seas

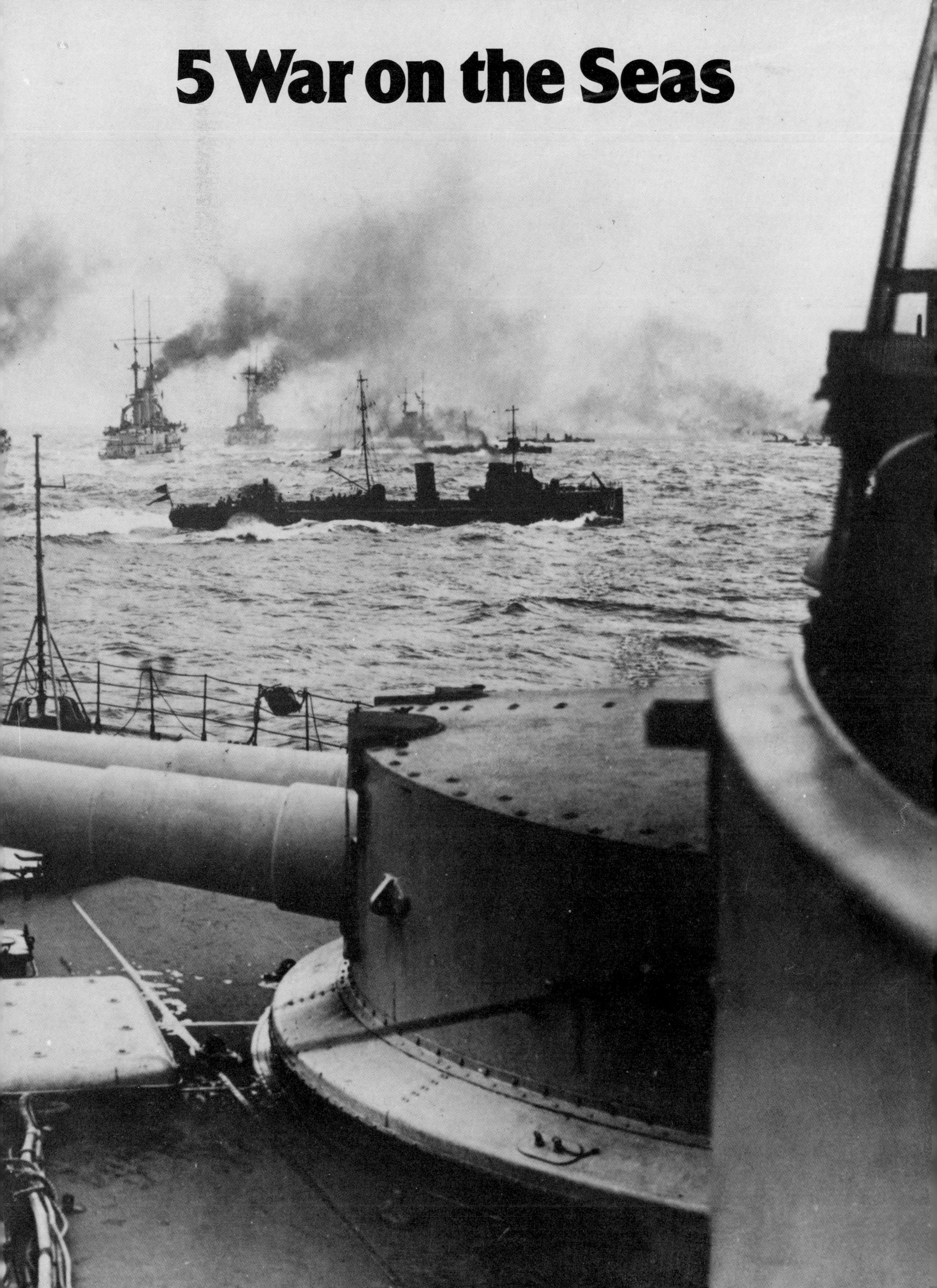

Three weeks before the guns had begun to speak for the opening of the Battle of the Somme, greater artillery had shouted across the gray wastes of the North Sea in the encounter for which the Royal and Imperial Navies had prepared for two decades. Called Jutland, after the land nearest to the Grand and High Seas Fleets' meeting place, the battle had yielded a result so dubious that as yet neither side could decide who had won and who had lost – though both claimed a victory. Even if each suspected that the result contained an element of defeat, there were no regrets. Jutland was preordained, a battle which had to be fought sometime, somewhere. Its event was as much a relief as an ordeal.

If there was a single reason for Britain's decision of August 1914 to join France against Germany, it lay in the insult and threat to her naval supremacy which Germany's building of the High Seas Fleet presented. Throughout the 19th century, indeed since the evening of 21 October 1805, when Nelson had gasped out his life in the cockpit of HMS *Victory* at Trafalgar, the Royal Navy had been unchallenged ruler of the seas. It had consistently maintained a two-power, sometimes a three-power, standard for most of the century, by which was meant that the Royal Navy was maintained at size equal to the two next biggest navies – usually the French and the Russian. However in 1900 the German government had declared its intention of transforming the Imperial Navy from a small coastal defense force into a first-class fleet. The implication of this announcement, by a power which already outproduced Britain in steel and coal and threatened to overtake her in volume of overseas trade, was that the two-power standard could not be maintained in future. An immediate effect was that Britain reconsidered her policy of 'splendid isolation'; in 1902 she signed an alliance with Japan and in 1904 an agreement with France about spheres of influence in the Mediterranean. She also looked to her naval preparedness. It was an age of technical innovation and by 1904 it was clear that a revolution in battleship design trembled on the brink of realization, a revolution which would at a stroke rob Britain of her superiority both in numbers and quality of first-line ships.

Such a revolution had occurred once before, in 1859, when the launching of the first ironclad, *La Gloire*, by France had instantly outdated the whole of the British wooden-walls navy. This new revolution was that of the 'all big-gun

Above: **The British Grand Fleet at the Coronation naval review in 1911**

Above left: **The last moments of the *Scharnhorst* and *Gneisenau,* which were sunk off the South American coast in the Battle of the Falklands in December 1914.**

Left: **The German High Seas Fleet on exercises in 1914.**

ship,' which would make obsolete all the ill-planned late Victorian models, crammed to capacity with guns of every caliber. The Royal Navy, at the behest of its emphatic First Sea Lord, Admiral 'Jackie' Fisher, boldly decided to pre-empt the Opposition and in 1906 launched the first example of the new type, from which in future it would take its name, HMS *Dreadnought.* Armed with 12 12-inch guns and engined with turbines which drove it at over 20 knots, it did indeed make the rest of the Royal Navy's battle fleet obsolete – but also that of every other navy. Britain, moreover, had cleverly geared herself to follow *Dreadnought* with a family of sister-ships and so was quickly set fair to make the leap from superiority in an old technology to superiority in a new. However Germany was not slow to respond. In 1908 the Reichstag voted the money to build 12 Dreadnoughts over the next four years, and at the same time to widen the Kiel Canal, allowing the new, bigger ships to make the transit from the training waters in the Baltic to the potential battle area in the North Sea without entering foreign territorial waters.

At the outbreak of war, which came while a sustained armaments race was in full spate, Germany had built 13 Dreadnoughts and five of the new battlecruisers, a ship with a battleship's guns and a cruiser's speed (though without, its critics emphasized, a battleship's armor protection). Britain had, however, managed to keep ahead and had eight battlecruisers and 20 Dreadnoughts in service, while far outstripping Germany in numbers of cruisers (102:41), destroyers (301:144) and even submarines (78:30). Most of the ships in the Imperial German Navy were in home waters forming the High Seas Fleet, based at Cuxhaven, Bremen, Wilhelmshaven and Emden, and ready to strike in the North Sea if the Grand Fleet should be caught at a disadvantage. The British Grand Fleet was stationed at Scapa Flow, in the Orkney Islands to the north of Scotland. The strategic logic behind the choice of base was impeccable. Southward, the exit from the North Sea lay through the Straits of Dover, which could be made impassable by mining. As the danger which the Admiralty most feared was the escape of the High Seas Fleet into the Atlantic merchant shipping lanes, the correct place to position its counterpoise was therefore at the other exit, between Scotland and Norway. In the circumstances Scapa Flow, a large archipelagic anchorage, offered the best home for the Grand Fleet.

The Grand Fleet was to spend most of the war in that land of sheep, seagulls, seals and short winter days, watching its shadow image across the North Sea. However, the Grand Fleet

Below: **German battleships in a line on exercises, with the *Bayern* astern.**

Above: German sailor cleans the gun of a warship of the High Seas Fleet.

Above right: The engine room of a German warship in 1915.

was not the whole Royal Navy. As the maritime arm of an imperial power, the Navy was deployed around all the world's oceans in four squadrons – East India, China, Australia and New Zealand – and also in smaller formations in the West Indies, in the West Coast of Africa and at the Cape of Good Hope, and a large Mediterranean Fleet, based on Malta and Gibraltar. The latter contained four of Britain's battlecruisers. Elsewhere the distant squadrons were composed of cruisers and smaller vessels, including a few remaining gunboats on which British diplomacy had been held to depend in the non-European world during the 19th century.

Germany also had a colonial fleet, based in the few Asiatic or African possessions she had acquired during the last century, as well as some detached cruisers, whose mission would be to raid British commerce when war broke out. The strongest element of the colonial fleet was the East Asian Cruiser Squadron, based at Tsingtao and consisting of the armored cruisers *Scharnhorst* and *Gneisenau*, and the light cruisers *Leipzig*, *Nürnberg*, *Dresden* and *Emden*, all under command of Admiral Maximilian Graf von Spee. As soon as Japan entered the war, on 15 August 1914, she forced the surrender of Tsingtao and Spee took his fleet (except the *Emden*) into the vast emptiness of the Pacific to evade the much larger Japanese fleet and begin his campaign against Britain's commerce.

News of their departure, and intercepted radio signals of their location, inaugurated the first and most dramatic episode of the naval war. The British Admiralty ordered Admiral Sir Christopher Cradock's South American Squadron to find and destroy them. It was a miscalculation to think that Cradock's ships could match Spee's. They could not, and when the two squadrons met off Coronel, Chile, on 1 November 1914, Spee sank two of the British cruisers without difficulty. News of this humiliation outraged the British public and the Admiralty, repairing a deficiency of which it should have been aware, at once sent two of the Grand Fleet's battlecruisers, *Invincible* and *Inflexible*, to repair it. Their destination was the South Pacific, but Admiral Doveton Sturdee commanding, called first at the Falkland Islands in the south to coal before proceeding round the Horn. On 8 December Spee appeared there, miscalculated the opposition he faced and moved in to attack. As he got closer he detected the battlecruisers' silhouettes and turned tail. All through a long southern hemisphere

Above: 'Jackie' Fisher, Lord Fisher, who created Britain's Dreadnoughts and masterminded the Grand Fleet in 1914.

Below: The Japanese destroyer *Shirakumo* in 1914. She was built in Britain.

Above: King George V aboard HMS *Queen Elizabeth*.

Left: The British battleship HMS *Barham* at Scapa Flow.

Below: The British Fleet in review, July 1914.

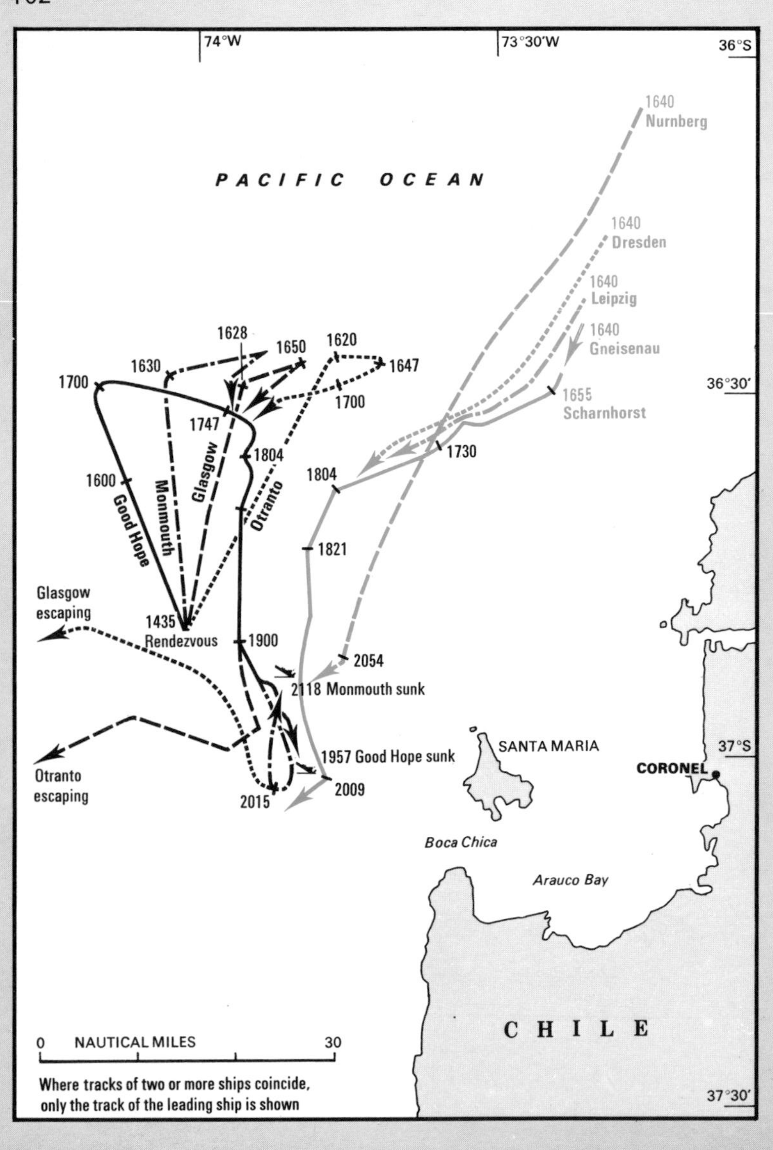
74°W
73°30'W
36°S
PACIFIC OCEAN
1640 Nurnberg
1640 Dresden
1640 Leipzig
1640 Gneisenau
1655 Scharnhorst
36°30'
1628
1650
1620
1647
1630
1700
1700
1747
1804
Glasgow
Monmouth
Good Hope
Otranto
1600
1804
1730
1821
Glasgow escaping
1435 Rendezvous
1900
2054
2118 Monmouth sunk
1957 Good Hope sunk
Otranto escaping
2015
2009
SANTA MARIA
37°S
CORONEL
Boca Chica
Arauco Bay
CHILE
0 NAUTICAL MILES 30
Where tracks of two or more ships coincide, only the track of the leading ship is shown
37°30'

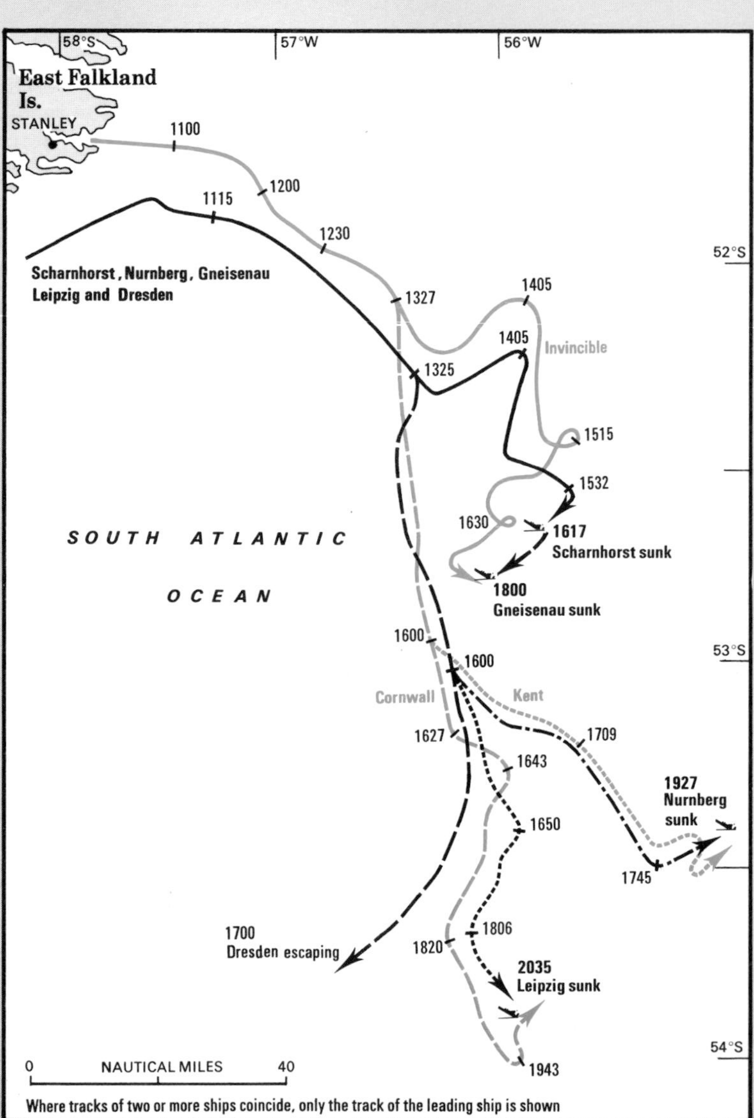
58°S
57°W
56°W
East Falkland Is.
STANLEY
1100
1200
1115
1230
52°S
Scharnhorst, Nurnberg, Gneisenau Leipzig and Dresden
1327
1405
1405
Invincible
1325
1515
1532
SOUTH ATLANTIC OCEAN
1630
1617 Scharnhorst sunk
1800 Gneisenau sunk
1600
1600
53°S
Cornwall
Kent
1709
1627
1643
1927 Nurnberg sunk
1650
1745
1700 Dresden escaping
1806
1820
2035 Leipzig sunk
54°S
0 NAUTICAL MILES 40
1943
Where tracks of two or more ships coincide, only the track of the leading ship is shown

Above: HMS *Inflexible,* which helped track down Graf Spee in the Falklands.

Below left: The Grand Fleet patrols the North Sea.

Left: The battles of Coronel and the Falkland Islands tied up part of the British Fleet in the first months of the war.

summer's day the British battlecruisers remorselessly pursued, their greater speed gradually winning back the start the Germans had had. Eventually they closed the range and between 1541 and 1723 hours four of Spee's five cruisers were sunk. Only the *Dresden*, swallowed by approaching darkness, escaped to continue the campaign of commerce destruction.

Her search for prey was to be fruitless, and she was eventually hunted down and sunk at Juan Fernandez – Robinson Crusoe's Island – in March 1915. The disaster at the Falklands still left three German cruisers and four armed merchant ships at sea. The latter, in peacetime high-speed liners, carried only light armament and inflicted little damage before being eliminated. The *Cap Trafalgar* was sunk by the British armed merchant cruiser *Carmania* in the South Atlantic in September 1914, the *Kaiser Wilhelm der Grosse* by the light cruiser *Highflyer* on 26 August off Spanish Morocco, while the *Kronprinz Wilhelm* and *Prinz Eitel Friedrich* were both interned in American ports in the spring of 1915. The true cruisers were harder to eliminate. *Königsberg*, based in the Indian Ocean, threatened British shipping using the Suez Canal for several months until a converging force of British cruisers drove her up the Rufifi River in German East Africa, where she was scuttled. *Karlsruhe*, operating off the bulge of Brazil, sank 14 British ships before being destroyed by a mysterious internal explosion on 4 November 1914. *Emden*, based in the eastern Indian Ocean, was also sunk in November, but only after she had inflicted serious loss on British shipping and property. In September she shelled and set ablaze the oil storage tanks at Madras, then sank 13 British ships, made use of port facilities at Diego Garcia, a British island so remote that the inhabitants had not yet heard of the war, and sailed out refreshed to sink seven more merchant ships, a Russian light cruiser and a French destroyer. Overconfidence then betrayed Captain von Müller, the *Emden*'s remarkable commander. He entered the harbor of Cocos-Keeling Island to destroy its important radio station. However before he did so, the operator summoned the heavier-gunned Australian cruiser *Sydney*, which in a few hours on 9 November 1914, blew the *Emden* to pieces.

Germany was to revive her commerce raiding later in the war and the cruise of her armed

Above: Admiral Graf von Spee (left) commanded the Germans in the South Atlantic.

sailing ship, the *Seeädler*, was to magnetize the interest of the German population at a dark moment. After April 1915 surface – as opposed to submarine – attack on Allied merchant shipping lost almost all its importance.

The German Navy had never invested its real hopes for success in attacks on British shipping. Those were pinned on the High Seas Fleet, smaller admittedly than the Grand Fleet, but in quality, ship for ship, perhaps its superior. The German admirals, Alfred von Tirpitz, Secretary of the Navy, von Ingenohl, commanding the High Seas Fleet, and Franz von Hipper, commanding its battlecruisers, were certainly willing to back their confidence in their ships and men by taking the fleet regularly to sea from the outbreak of the war in the hope of meeting the British on advantageous terms. The first encounter took place on 28 August, in an action which came to be known as the Heligoland Bight. The terms had been miscalculated by the Germans. The Royal Navy's Channel Squadron submarines had been calculating their patrolling pattern and their commander, Commodore Keyes, had decided that it offered an opportunity to strike unexpectedly at the cruisers which escorted the patrolling destroyers. A cruiser

Below: British battle cruisers *Indomitable* and *Inflexible* which led the fight in the Falklands.

ambush, supported by some of Admiral David Beatty's battlecruisers, was accordingly arranged and the trap sprung. Due to misunderstandings, various British Squadrons failed to co-ordinate their actions. However the German ships were well and truly surprised and driven into flight, during which a destroyer, *V-187*, and three cruisers, *Mainz*, *Ariadne* and *Köln*, were sunk by heavier weight of metal.

This setback shocked the German admirals into caution, but the news of the Falkland Islands, which revealed the absence of the battlecruisers *Inflexible* and *Invincible* from home waters, encouraged them to try again – with greater success. In October their aggressive mining policy had caused the sinking of the Dreadnought *Audacious* off the Irish coast, which slightly narrowed the odds. On 16 December, therefore, the High Seas Fleet sallied forth to bombard the British coast, a repeat of a small-scale raid against Yarmouth on 3 November. In fog, the German battlecruisers caused considerable loss of life along the Yorkshire coast and got clean away from the Grand Fleet, which had come out to intercept. Public outrage so stung the Admiralty's pride that it decided it must retaliate. It began to make reconnaissance in force into the North Sea. The provocation worked, tempting the High Seas Fleet out on 23 January. Next morning, their scouting forces met near the shallows of the Dogger Bank and shortly afterward fire was opened between the leading main units. These were the battlecruisers performing their function of covering the battleships, and soon a full-scale gun duel flickered along the line of the two squadrons. It was an exchange to which the stouter German ships stood up better than the British. The *Blücher*, not truly a battlecruiser, was hit and eventually sunk but the big German ships absorbed punishment better than the British, among which HMS *Lion*, Beatty's flagship, was so badly damaged that he was forced to transfer his flag to a destroyer. In the resulting confusion of command, the Germans made good their escape.

The loss of the *Blücher* enraged the Kaiser, and he enforced on Tirpitz and Hugo von Pohl, who succeeded the disgraced von Ingenohl, a policy of extreme prudence. They abandoned their policy of raiding toward the British coast, scarcely venturing out of the Heligoland Bight during the rest of 1915 and exercised the Fleet by taking it through the Kiel Canal to the safe waters of the Baltic, into which the Russian battleships based at Tallinn and Kronstadt did not venture. They also pressed ahead their naval construction program, though they could not outbuild the British. Between 1914 and 1916 they added five Dreadnoughts to the High Seas Fleet, making 18, and two battlecruisers, making seven. The British in the same period built ten and requisitioned three already built for, but not delivered to, other navies, making a total of 33 Dreadnoughts. They also completed another battlecruiser – a type for which only Fisher and Beatty had had enthusiasm – to give them 10.

It was a natural demand of the public in both countries to enquire what all these ships were doing, a question lent edge in Germany by the sharpening pangs of shortage imposed by the British blockade. Under this criticism, the Kaiser relaxed his ban on offensive operations and replaced Pohl with an officer more temperamentally inclined to carry action to the enemy, the energetic and aggressive Reinhard Scheer. In Britain too, where the growing affront of German submarine attack was generating

demands for retaliation, there was pressure on Sir John Jellicoe, Commander in Chief of the Grand Fleet, to engage the High Seas Fleet.

These demands were heightened by the reappearance of Scheer's bombardment force off the East Coast in April 1916. Its cruisers and destroyers had had several brushes with light ships of the coastal flotillas in February and March. Now he brought in his battlecruisers to hit the seaside towns of Lowestoft and Yarmouth – the latter for the second time. The Grand Fleet came out, but missed them. Jellicoe set about planning a trap to make certain the next time. Obviously, Scheer too was planning a trap for the Grand Fleet in the same place, between Jutland and Norway, and news of his departure on 31 May from the German estuaries, detected by British interception of his radio, ensured that these two plans would coincide.

The Grand Fleet steamed southwestward in two large groups. The main force comprised 24 Dreadnoughts and three battlecruisers, with an attendant screen of 20 cruisers and 52 destroyers. Well ahead speeded Beatty's battlecruiser force with six battlecruisers and four Dreadnoughts of the *Queen Elizabeth* Class, almost as fast as the former and as heavily armored and gunned as the most modern battleships – which indeed, was what they were. The High Seas Fleet, also with a battlecruiser force of five deployed ahead (Scouting Group

Far left: **Admiral Sir David Beatty.**

Left: **Damage suffered by SMS *Frauenlob* in the Battle of the Heligoland Bight.**

Below left: **Raiders recalled to the *Emden*, which led a merry chase across the world before she was destroyed.**

Below: **The battlecruiser action, which opened hostilities in the late afternoon of 31 May.**

Above: **HMS *Warspite*, active both at Jutland and at Matapan in World War II.**

Above right: **Admiral von Tirpitz, creator of the German High Seas Fleet.**

Right: **Admiral Lord Jellicoe, with Beatty the architect of the Jutland victory.**

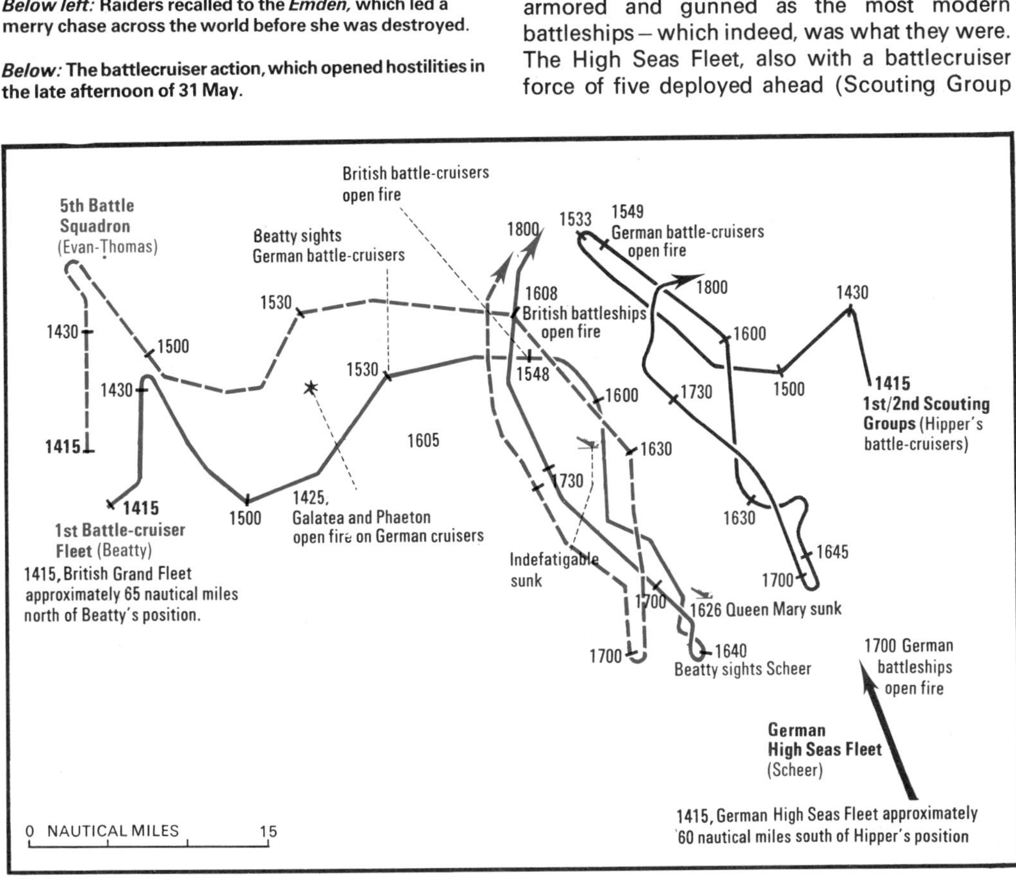

I), had 16 Dreadnoughts at sea, but had also brought along six older battleships to make weight.

As yet, neither knew for certain that the other was at sea, and their encounter was to be accidental. At about 1415 hours one of the German light cruisers with Scouting Group I spotted a Danish merchant ship and altered course to question her. A British light cruiser of the Battlecruiser Force had also seen the Dane's smoke and gone to investigate. When the cruisers sighted each other they opened fire and radioed news of the encounter. Their supporting battlecruisers turned to back them up and at 1500, to their mutual surprise, came into visual contact. Altering course to shorten the range, Beatty plunged at the Germans, while Hipper turned about to draw the British down onto the heavier guns of the battleships, still 55 miles behind. At 1548 hours the Germans opened fire, and Beatty's ships responded.

A young officer in HMS *Lion* – one of the 'big cats' as she and her sister ship *Tiger* were called – described what he saw:

'My station was in the conning tower and I remember thinking how splendid the enemy battlecruisers looked when they turned to the southward. . . . Both squadrons opened fire almost together, the Germans appearing to fire in ripples down their line starting from their leading ship. The first salvo at us was about 200 yards short, and the next straddled us – one shot short, two hits aft and one over, the two hits temporarily knocking out 'Q' and 'X' turrets.

The German shooting at this time was very good and we were repeatedly straddled but, funnily enough, we were not being hit very often. I remember watching two shells coming at us. They appeared just like big bluebottles flying straight towards you, each time going to hit you in the eye, then they would fall, and the shell would either burst or else ricochet off the water and lollop away above and beyond you, turning over and over in the air.'

German shooting was indeed very good. Their gun crews were impeccably drilled, their range-finding equipment superior to the British and their shells of better quality. When German shells hit they both penetrated and exploded, which, as the British were later to discover, theirs did not always. The difference was to tell almost immediately. HMS *Indefatigable* was hit

Top: **The Grand Fleet moves into action as the first German salvos are fired at Jutland.**

Above: **The Grand Fleet moves into line a few moments earlier.**

Below: **Battleships HMS *Royal Oak* and *Hercules* with guns trained to starboard in the afternoon of 31 May 1916, at Jutland.**

early in the exchange, failed to follow a change of course and then suddenly blew up. The main explosion started with sheets of flame, followed immediately afterward by dense, dark smoke, which obscured the ship from view:

'All sorts of stuff was blown into the air, a 50-foot steam packet boat for example, being blown up about 200 feet, apparently intact though upside down.'

Shortly afterward, another accurate German salvo hit *Queen Mary.* The same observer noticed:

'a small cloud of what looked like coal-dust come out from where she was hit, but nothing more until several moments later when a terrific yellow flame, with a heavy and very dense mass of black smoke showed ahead, and the *Queen Mary* herself was no longer visible. This second disaster was rather stunning, but the only sign from the flagship was a signal, "Battle-cruisers alter course two points to port," – that is towards the enemy.'

Beatty also said to the captain of *Lion*, standing beside him as he issued the signal, 'There seems to be something wrong with our bloody ships today.' *Lion* herself had been saved from destruction by a hair's-breadth when a fire had started in a damaged turret. It is probable that *Queen Mary* and *Indefatigable* had blown up because turret fires had tracked down the ammunition lift into the magazines, a disaster made possible by a design fault. Beatty nonetheless had relentlessly gone on, with the bravado which was to make him the most celebrated naval commander of the war, until at 1648 he spotted the enemy, the German battleships, and turned northward to lead them toward Jellicoe.

As the gap between the two fleets closed, the screens of lighter ships exchanged fire and suffered losses. However it was the clash of giants which was to count and this occurred at 1815 when Hipper's battlecruisers, now just ahead of Scheer's Dreadnoughts, got within range of Jellicoe's covering squadron of battlecruisers under Rear Admiral Sir Horace Hood and recommenced their accurate shooting. Within minutes *Invincible*, sister to *Indefatigable*, had gone her way. She broke in half and the separated pieces ground on the shallow

Top: **The British line is broken in the day action at Jutland as the Germans fire with all guns.**

Above left: **Admiral Hipper, who, with Scheer, led the German High Seas Fleet at Jutland.**

Above right: **Prince Henry of Prussia (with glasses) and Admiral von Scheer, Commander in Chief at Jutland.**

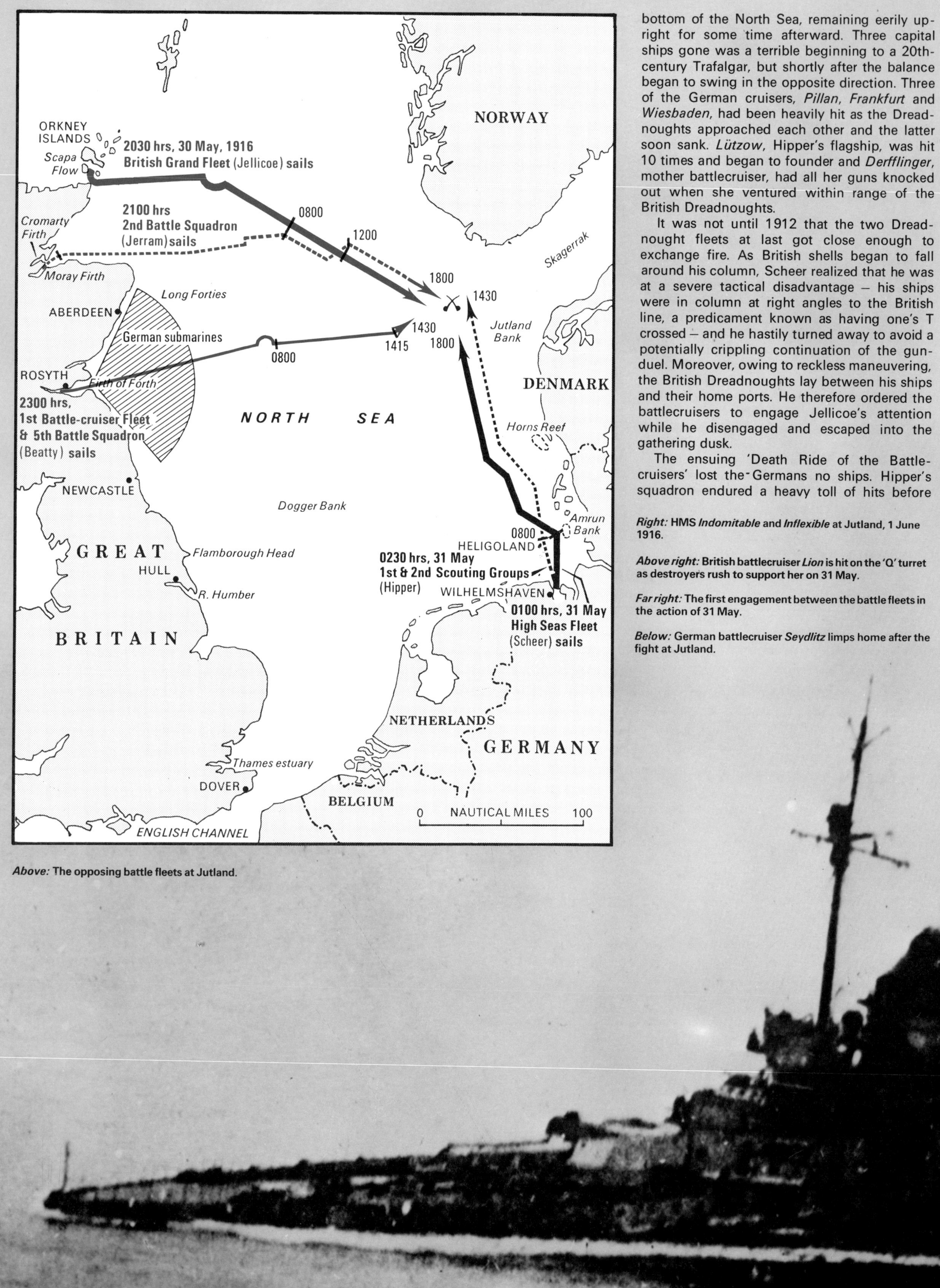

Above: The opposing battle fleets at Jutland.

bottom of the North Sea, remaining eerily upright for some time afterward. Three capital ships gone was a terrible beginning to a 20th-century Trafalgar, but shortly after the balance began to swing in the opposite direction. Three of the German cruisers, *Pillan*, *Frankfurt* and *Wiesbaden*, had been heavily hit as the Dreadnoughts approached each other and the latter soon sank. *Lützow*, Hipper's flagship, was hit 10 times and began to founder and *Derfflinger*, mother battlecruiser, had all her guns knocked out when she ventured within range of the British Dreadnoughts.

It was not until 1912 that the two Dreadnought fleets at last got close enough to exchange fire. As British shells began to fall around his column, Scheer realized that he was at a severe tactical disadvantage – his ships were in column at right angles to the British line, a predicament known as having one's T crossed – and he hastily turned away to avoid a potentially crippling continuation of the gunduel. Moreover, owing to reckless maneuvering, the British Dreadnoughts lay between his ships and their home ports. He therefore ordered the battlecruisers to engage Jellicoe's attention while he disengaged and escaped into the gathering dusk.

The ensuing 'Death Ride of the Battlecruisers' lost the Germans no ships. Hipper's squadron endured a heavy toll of hits before

Right: HMS *Indomitable* and *Inflexible* at Jutland, 1 June 1916.

Above right: British battlecruiser *Lion* is hit on the 'Q' turret as destroyers rush to support her on 31 May.

Far right: The first engagement between the battle fleets in the action of 31 May.

Below: German battlecruiser *Seydlitz* limps home after the fight at Jutland.

being able to disengage and turn to rejoin the Dreadnoughts which, by this sacrificial act, had been able to put a safe distance between them and Jellicoe. As night fell, the two fleets adopted courses which would, in the hours of darkness, bring them once more into gun range. Scheer's heavy ships did indeed encounter Jellicoe's rearguard of destroyers and in the melee British torpedoes found and sank the pre-Dreadnought *Pommern*. Jellicoe remained ignorant of the exchange, and plowed on in the hope of cutting off Scheer before he regained his base. In the darkness he missed contact and turned back to gather his scattered forces for a last search and so allowed the Germans safe home.

In the aftermath the Germans christened the battle the *Skagerraksieg*, the Victory of the Skagerrak. In terms of ships and men lost they had certainly come off better: one old battleship, one battlecruiser, four light cruisers and five destroyers sunk to three battlecruisers, three armored cruisers and eight destroyers; 3039 men killed to 6784. The British consoled themselves with the thought that their ships, built for comparative comfort in long oceanic voyages around their enormous empire, could not offer their crews the same standard of protection as the German ships which were internally subdivided in a much more safety-conscious

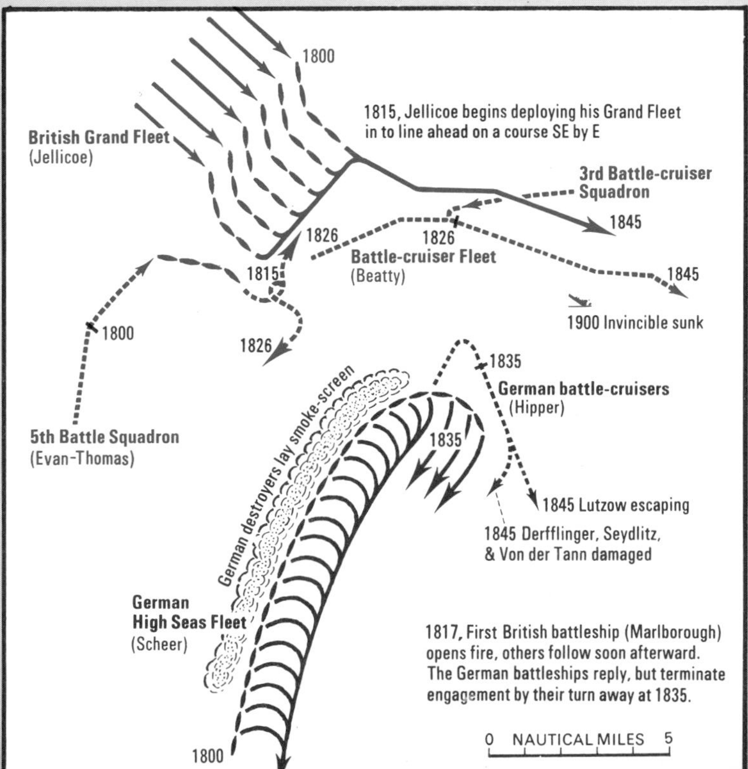

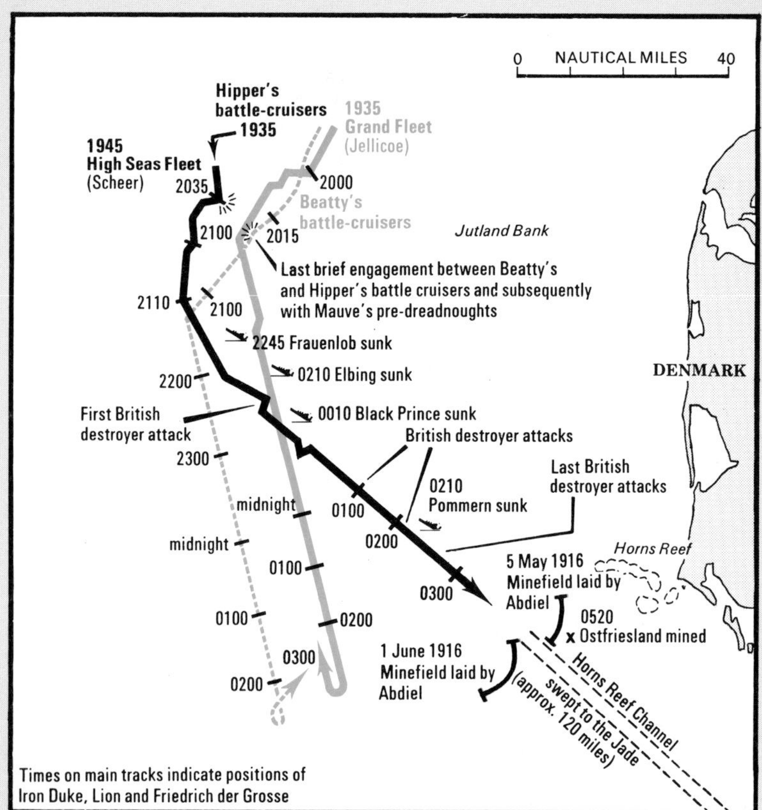

Above: The chase after the High Seas Fleet on 1 June.

Above right: British fleet crosses the German line.

Right: The second engagement of the battle fleets, which forced a German withdrawal.

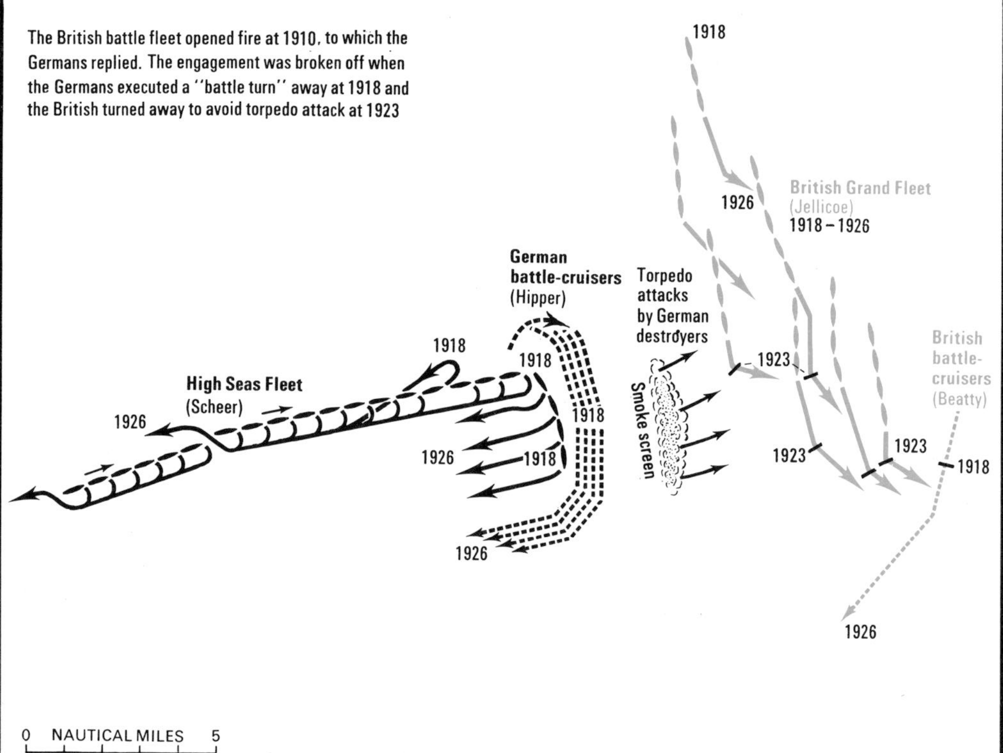

fashion. However the truth was that German guns, though generally a caliber lighter than the British, were at least as hard hitting, that German range-finding was superior and German shells more penetrating and explosive. British ships also suffered from a serious flaw in the protection of their magazines from plunging fire. But for that, three battlecruisers would not have been blown up.

What comfort the British could take from the Battle of Jutland, as they called it, lay in the knowledge that they had chased the Germans home and retreated at their own leisure – a traditional measure of victory. They could also presume that, if the Germans sought their revenge, the Grand Fleet would again demonstrate its superiority of strength, if not of quality. So Jutland, if not Trafalgar, was a success. Scheer drew the same conclusion. Bethmann-Hollweg, the German Chancellor, insisted that he should take the fleet into the North Sea again in early July and in October to demonstrate that its fighting power remained intact, but both sorties were unsuccessful and against the wishes of Scheer, who was now anxious

Below: HMS _Invincible_ goes down on 31 May. This picture was taken from HMS _Benbow_ as _Badger_ comes over to pick up the remaining survivors.

that the navy should concentrate on submarine operations of an unrestricted character.

Germany's U-Boat fleet had grown from 30 U-Boats at the outbreak of war to 111 by January 1917. In February 1915 she declared the waters around the British Isles a war zone and warned that neutral ships which strayed outside a 'safe passage' north of the Shetland Islands would be liable to attack. It was in accordance with this declaration that the great passenger liner *Lusitania* had been sunk off Ireland in May 1915, an attack which outraged the public in the United States since 128 American passengers were among those drowned. As a result, Germany abandoned the policy in August and returned to the practice of sinking ships only after the crews and passengers had been given the chance to escape – a limitation of offensive action which did not, of course, apply to naval vessels. Even within these limitations, the German submarines based in Austrian and Turkish ports in the Mediterranean were able to achieve an impressive level of success. The British were forced to route ships from Australia and the Far East around the Cape of Good Hope, so as to avoid those dangerous waters, and to deploy nearly 500 naval ships in the Mediterranean itself on antisubmarine duties.

This experience worked hard on the imagination of the German admirals. Admiral Henning von Holzendorff, of the German Naval Staff, was able to show in December 1916 that if the U-Boats could sink 500,000 tons of British shipping a month – and sinkings in November had reached half that – then within five months the British would be unable to meet their input requirements and begin to starve. As the German civilian population was going very short of necessities in the winter of 1916 there was little emotional resistance to the idea of visiting some of the same on the enemy among the German authorities. When Holzendorff went on to argue that there were no countermeasures the British could take, and that America could not intervene effectively against the Germans before such a campaign had achieved its object, opposition crumbled. Accordingly, on 9 January 1917 the Kaiser issued orders that German U-Boats should reopen an unrestricted sinking campaign on 1 February. On the day before the German government handed the United States ambassador a warning that, in waters around Great Britain, France, Italy or the Eastern Mediterranean all shipping would be 'stopped with every available weapon and without further notice.'

The effect was incredible. During the last five months of 1917, sinkings of British ships had averaged 37 per month. In February 1918 it jumped suddenly to 105 ships and in April to 127. One out of every four British ships which left port just did not return. The development transformed British attitudes to the outcome of the war overnight. Hitherto they had fought the submarines by positive methods. Antisubmarine vessels had been sent to look for U-Boats, hoping either to catch them on the surface while they were proceeding to patrol stations or to tempt them into surfacing by pretending to be unarmed freighters or fishing vessels – the so-called Q-Ships. Other ships were equipped with nets or explosive paravanes, to be towed beneath the surface in the hope of catching U-Boats under the sea.

The odd U-Boat was caught by one or other of these measures, but once the U-Boats began to attack without surfacing, and to operate far out into the western approaches to the British Isles, these antisubmarine measures rapidly became ineffective. Equally ineffective was a new policy of sailing merchant ships on widely dispersed routes, so as to diffuse the shipping lanes which the Germans patrolled. Though it spared some ships attack in the great waters, they became vulnerable as soon as they approached any of the maritime bottlenecks which led to the British Isles, where the U-Boats naturally congregated. Stationing patrol vessels in the vicinity of the bottlenecks to escort the converging merchant ships through merely guided the U-Boats to the best places to find their prey.

There was a strong school of naval thought which argued that merchant ships should be convoyed through dangerous waters, but their opponents pooh-poohed the idea. Their view was that the convoy system had worked in

Above: British anti-U-Boat propaganda, based almost wholly on fantasy rather than fact.

Below: The Grand Fleet opens fire at Jutland. Most of the paintings of the battle are somewhat fanciful and melodramatic.

Above: **Captain Turner of the *Lusitania*, which, though carrying contraband, was sunk by a U-Boat and helped the British propaganda campaign against Germany.**

sailing ship days when raiders were as visible as their victims, but now convoys would merely offer a more tempting choice of targets as the U-Boats could attack from far below the surface. Moreover, the best ships were protected by their speed, a protection which would be nullified if all ships had to travel at the speed of the slowest. Their arguments appeared convincing but, as losses continued to mount, the convoy school became more insistent. Their case was strengthened by the mounting toll of losses which, during the first five months of the new U-Boat campaign, actually exceeded the 500,000 tons a month Holzendorff had predicted would bring Britain to its knees. A strong mine barrier in the Straits of Dover had closed that exit to the shipping lanes but mining of the northern exits from the North Sea was not working. Lloyd George, now Prime Minister, had early been attracted to the convoy argument. Now he threw his weight behind it and in May 1917 this policy was adopted. The Americans, with a vast army to transport across the Atlantic, were enthusiastic supporters and transferred 34 destroyers to British ports by July. Almost at once an encouraging decline in sinkings developed. In April there had been 169. By July the figure had sunk to 99 and by November to 65.

The reason, unperceived by the anticonvoy school, lay in the characteristics of the U-Boat. Although fairly fast on the surface – with a speed of about 18 knots – it was very slow submerged, capable at best of eight knots for one hour on its electric batteries and, when it remained submerged longer, of proportionately lower speeds. If correctly positioned to intercept a convoy, it could wreak terrible havoc for the short period it was within range. If even a few miles out of position it could not move fast enough to intercept unless it betrayed its position by coming to the surface. Many U-Boat commanders, a brave and aggressive breed, would push their boats' speed to the limit in the vicinity of a convoy. However, in doing so, they revealed their presence to the listening hydrophones of the escort ships and invited heavy and immediate attack by depth charges. This newly developed undersea bomb was responsible for the increasing disappearances of U-Boats throughout 1917. At least six were being sunk each month, a depressing total which the German Admiralty carefully kept to itself.

The Royal Navy was not satisfied, however, by the haphazard results it was achieving at sea, and sought some means to strike at U-Boats where they were most concentrated: in their bases. The chief base for their operations into the North Sea and the Atlantic was at the inland port of Bruges in Belgium, from which they made their way to open waters down two canals, issuing at Ostend and Zeebrugge. Early in 1918 the Admiralty began work on plans to close these two exits and in April a carefully prepared force set out from Dover and Harwich to tackle this task. The plan was to bring five old light cruisers, filled with cement, into the narrow tidal channels, explode charges in their bottoms and so sink them immoveably in the fairway. Just before midnight on 22 April Admiral Keyes' squadron approached its targets. At Ostend, the Germans had moved the marker buoys at the mouth of the channel and the blockships grounded offshore, but at Zeebrugge they got alongside the long curving mole which protected the harbor from westerly gales and put a landing party ashore. The idea was to distract the Germans' attention, by fighting on the harbor edge, from the arrival of the blockships in the canal. German defenses of the harbor were very strong so HMS *Vindictive*, the amphibious headquarters ship, was studded with guns and crammed with marines and sailors who were to take the German strongpoints by assault.

A naval officer aboard *Vindictive*, Lieutenant Commander Young, was hit as she came alongside, went below to be dressed and came up again to hear 'sudden eruptions of din alternating with dead silence. The wet, jade-green curve of the wall was dimly visible sweeping up out of the dark, and back into it again. The last of the landing parties was going over the brows, and there was an intermittent crackling and flushing of rifle-fire up and down the mole.' Meanwhile the submarine *C-3*, loaded with explosives, slipped up the canal and, after the crew had abandoned ship, was blown up under a viaduct which crossed the harbor. Behind them three blockships entered the canal mouth and, though one was entangled in the protective nets, the other two were sunk as planned. Then, loaded with casualties, but conscious of having boldly completed their missions, *Vindictive* and her escorting destroyers backed off and made for the sea at high speed.

As an antisubmarine measure, the Zeebrugge raid was only a partial success, for the Germans

Above: A British sub is strafed by a German plane whose pilot took this picture.

Top: A British battle fleet zigzags through the water to avoid U-Boat attacks.

Below: A Japanese submarine built in Britain. They were never called into action in World War I.

quickly found a way round the blocks but as an example of derring-do it had a tonic effect on British civilian morale. The German population, though heartened by the military victories of its armies in the spring of 1918, was by contrast deeply affected by the ever-worsening effects of the blockade. In Britain at the height of the unrestricted U-Boat campaign in 1917 there had still been sugar, butter, cheese and meat to buy in the shops, even if the quantities were rationed. The Germans had been rationed for bread since January 1915 and subsequently for other staples as their supply diminished or actually disappeared. The main items of diet were now 'War Bread,' thinned out with inferior grains, swedes and, when available, potatoes. Eggs, obtainable only on doctor's orders, had almost vanished. Citrus fruits were never seen and domestic apples, pears and green vegetables were extremely scarce and costly; a cabbage for instance cost 12 marks. Meat was so scarce that the kangaroos in the *Tiergarten* had been slaughtered for the pot. Little wonder that, as they watched their children grow thin for want of milk and fats, many Germans should wonder to what point the great battles of March or April 1918 had been fought, and ask what was the purpose of the High Seas Fleet.

Above: Two Austro–Hungarian seaplanes pick up survivors from the French submarine *Foucault* which they had bombed.

Above right: Fixing a torpedo launcher on a German torpedo boat.

Above far right: A US convoy in camouflage in World War I.

There had been disorders, fomented by frustration and lack of activity, in the High Seas Fleet in July and August 1917. They were quelled by a mixture of repression and concession; two of the ringleaders were shot but leave and better food were granted to the dissidents. Popular discontent with the failure of the Imperial Navy to break the ring of the blockade led, in the summer of 1918, to the removal of the navy minister and his replacement by Scheer, who was succeeded in command by Hipper. Together, for the honor of the navy, they planned one last dash into the Channel to engage the British, but it was not to come about. When they gave the necessary orders the stokers drew forces in the stokeholds and declared their unwillingness to leave harbor. The mutiny was suppressed but then flared up again and threatened to spread into a revolt against the Imperial Government itself.

The naval war at sea was essentially, therefore, one of action threatened rather than delivered. The French, Japanese and Russian Navies had taken virtually no part. The Italians and the Austrians had scarcely put to sea – though in the closing stages, Italian swimmers had destroyed the Austrian Dreadnought *Viribus Unitis* by attaching charges to its bottom. The Turkish Navy consisted of scarcely more than the *Goeben* and *Breslau*. In January 1918 they made a last inglorious sortie into the Mediterranean which resulted in the sinking of the *Breslau*. Submarine operations apart, naval action had effectively been confined to the abortive encounters of the Grand and High Seas Fleets, always circumscribed by Churchill's warning to Jellicoe that he was the one man 'who could lose the war in an afternoon.' He had not done so, but equally he had done little positive to win it.

Right: German submarines at Kiel at the end of the war.

Below: British submarine *C-25* under aerial attack.

The last flight of Captain Ball when this air ace's SE5 was hit by a German Albatros.

6 War in the Air

It was only 11 years before 1914 that the first true airplane flight had taken place and only six years before that the pioneers, Wilbur and Orville Wright, had brought their aircraft across the Atlantic to demonstrate to some very inexpert European imitators how the trick could be managed. Yet three years after the great Rheims air meeting of 1908 the Italian army had sufficiently perfected the techniques of the new art to use airplanes against the Turks in its war in Libya. Shortly afterward other aircraft were employed in the Mexican revolution of 1911 to observe enemy troop movements and to take photographs. The Italians had even attempted aerial bombing of the Senussi tribesmen.

These developments had given the major European powers the hint. The French army purchased a Wright biplane in 1909 and established an Air Service in 1910. The Germans founded the Imperial Air Service in 1913. Britain, which had had a balloon battalion since the 1870s, created the Royal Flying Corps, with naval and military wings, in May 1912 and in June 1914 had detached the naval wing to form the Royal Naval Air Service. However the number of aircraft in all these new organizations was small. Britain had 113 military aircraft in August 1914, France 138, Russia 45, Austria 36 and Germany 384, with 30 Zeppelins. Pilots were also scarce, not surprisingly in an age when the armies found it difficult to recruit enough men who knew how to drive motor vehicles. The role of an aircraft was strictly limited to that of serving the military headquarters to which they were attached. The generals wanted their pilots to bring them information of the enemy's movements, and saw them as a useful extension of the traditional cavalry scout rather than as pioneers of a new arm in their own right. From the very beginning they were able to fulfill this role. On 22 August 1914 a British pilot operating forward of the British Expeditionary Force observed the approach of Kluck's First Army toward Mons and was able to give advance warning of the impending attack.

Shortly afterward the first recorded instance of aerial combat occurred. On 26 August three British pilots led by Lieutenant H D Harvey-Kelley observed a German aircraft beneath them. They dived on him, surrounded his aircraft and forced it slowly to the ground. Once the trench lines had been established, observation would lose its strategic importance and combat, for control of tactical observation, would become more important. The fixed trench lines made effective artillery bombardment much more practicable than in the weeks of open, mobile warfare, but required observation from the air to check its accuracy and correct the laying of the guns. Pilots began therefore to chase enemy intruders over the lines and in March 1915 a Frenchman, Roland Garros, hit on a new method of attacking. A prewar stunt pilot, and the first to fly the Mediterranean, he had been in Germany giving a flying exhibition when war broke out, and only just made his escape in time. By early 1915 he was an established French military pilot. Aware that in late 1914 two other airmen, Stribick and David, had shot down a German photographic intruder with a hand-held machine gun, he decided to make such a weapon an integral part of his machine. The obvious place to mount it was above the engine, so that he could fire it along his line of sight, but to do so would destroy the propeller when the gun fired. By experiment he found that steel plates fitted to the propeller would deflect the bullets which did not pass clear through the arc, and thus equipped he took to the air and shot down five German airplanes in two weeks in March 1915.

In April however an engine fault forced him to land behind German lines and his aircraft was captured before he could burn it. A Dutchman, Anthony Fokker, who was assisting the German Air Service with aeronautical design, was called to inspect it, and at once detected the innovation. He also recognized its principal defect, which was that prolonged use would shorten the propeller, and set himself to design a better mechanism. He quickly produced a mechanical interrupter gear which checked the gun's firing when the blades were in front of the muzzle, and so provided the first weapon specifically adapted to aerial use. At least three earlier systems had been invented, but none was as successful as his, which he at once incorporated in one of his remarkable Fokker aircraft. These, superior to any models which the Allies were yet using, were regarded as so valuable that they were not allowed to cross no man's land, but waited behind their own front to attack Allied airplanes which ventured into their air space.

The second year of the war saw the development of aircraft types specifically designed for combat in all the existing air services. France

Below: An Albatros D.V biplane in 1917.

Above: **Roland Garros after crossing the Mediterranean.**

Above left: **A German machine gunner in a Fokker E.1.**

Top: **Members of the Lafayette Escadrille before a Nieuport.**

Top left: **The wreckage of two Nieuports in France, 1916.**

Above: **This is the way bombs were dropped in 1914.**

Above: **A British airman drops a bomb with a message for the enemy.**

had entered the war with Farman pusher aircraft and Blériots, little different from the model in which the inventor had flown the English Channel in 1909. Production was soon to be dominated by two other makes, the Morane-Saulnier and the Nieuport, both fast and maneuverable, with a rotary engine attached to the propeller and rotating around the shaft. This arrangement produced strong torque and so a spectacular ability to make sharp turns in the same direction as the engine was rotating – a great advantage in the dogfighting which was increasingly common.

The Nieuport was so outstanding an aircraft that it was eagerly bought by the Royal Flying Corps when a surplus of production made them available. Meanwhile the British were producing workmanlike aircraft of their own, both from the Royal Aircraft Factory and private firms like Vickers, de Havilland and Sopwith. Most successful of the early designs was the Vickers FBJ known as the 'Gun Bus.' A two seater with a pusher propeller at the rear of the fuselage, it was equipped with a machine gun in the front cockpit which the observer could fire through a wide arc. To score a hit required fine marksmanship, but the early pilots were good shots. It took remarkable skill to achieve, as Captain L G Hawker did in July 1915, three successful attacks in one flight from an airplane fitted with a single-shot carbine fixed at an oblique angle to the fuselage.

The Germans also were busy in the race to outbuild the enemy in quality of aircraft. The Hanuschke of 1914 was soon replaced by the Fokker, at first chiefly in a monoplane form, and then the Albatros and Pfalz. The Germans' main aircraft during 1914–15 were two-seat observation models, to which the single seaters were attached entirely for protection purposes. It would be some time before the Imperial Air Service sought directly to win air superiority over the Western Front.

Moreover, the Germans had a strange social attitude toward flying. Piloting an aircraft was likened to driving a car which, before 1914, gentlemen had employed chauffeurs to do. The first pilots of the Imperial Air Service were therefore recruited from the noncommissioned ranks. Officers acted as observers, in the rear cockpit, from which they told the pilot where they wanted to be flown. The excitement of the chase quickly broke down these social taboos, as frustrated cavalrymen glimpsed the chance to experience in the sky the triumphs in single combat which the trenches denied them on the ground. Curiously, as a result, many of the German pilots who early achieved fame as fighters were ex-cavalrymen. In the French air service, which was much less snobbish, the first heroes were often ex-racing drivers or sporting heroes who translated their skills into flying expertise. They often made their reputations as corporals or sergeants before being made officers as a testimony to their prowess.

The improvement in the offensive capacity of aircraft and the emergence of highly-skilled pilots transformed the character of air warfare. During 1915 the haphazard encounters of individuals gave way to planned, purposeful air campaigns for dominance over those sectors of the front where great ground battles were in progress. This new policy produced a new sort of airman, the 'ace,' deliberately celebrated by national propaganda as his reward for victory over enemy airmen. An ace was often given command of a fighter formation whose other pilots modelled their performance on his.

The first aces were two Germans, Oswald Boelcke and Max Immelmann. The latter was famous for his extraordinary airmanship, and the development of a new diving turn which put an aircraft into an attacking position, called the 'Immelmann turn.' Boelcke was more than an individualist. Given command of one of the first German fighter squadrons in the autumn of 1915, he set about training it so that in an attack all pilots would co-operate to support the most promising opening in the enemy's formations. He had the good luck to secure one of the early production model Fokker E.1s and with it led his squadron in a series of victories over their British and French opponents which became known as the 'Fokker Scourge.'

The Germans had become so dominant by the spring of 1916 that the French reacted by imitating them and, during the battle of Verdun, formed their own elite fighter unit, which became known as the *Cigognes* (Storks). Equipped with the Nieuport II and later the very

Below: **A Nieuport Type 80 biplane.**

Above: **The funeral procession for German ace Max Immelmann, 1916.**

superior Spad VII, both armed with forward firing machine guns, the *Cigognes* – officially Escadrille 3 – quickly dominated the skies over Verdun. The *Cigogne* pilots now gained reputations to rival those of Boelcke and Immelmann, notably Dorme Deullin, Heurtaux and Guynemer. Georges Guynemer eventually achieved the distinction of 'Ace of Aces,' highest-scoring of all French fighter pilots with 54 victories. His career typified that of the extraordinary band of reckless men to which he belonged. Originally rejected for military service because of his physical frailty, he succeeded in enlisting as a mechanic, qualified as a pilot in March 1915 at the age of 21 and shot down his first enemy airplane a month after being posted to Escadrille 3 in June 1915. He himself was shot down in September, but escaped from no man's land. He was wounded in the air over Verdun in March 1916, by which time he had eight victories, and was shot down from 10,000 feet in September but survived the crash landing. Between November 1916 and January 1917 his score went from 18 victories to 30 and on 25 May 1917, he destroyed four enemy aircraft in one day, two of them within a minute of each other. The strain of his flying had now combined with his poor health to make him obviously unfit for further service. The High Command begged him to give up, so nervous were they of the repercussions of the death of someone who was by now a national hero, but he refused. On 11 September 1917, five days after achieving his 54th victory, he was shot down over Podcappelle, near Ypres. His body was never found. His death, the circumstances of which have never been explained, was indeed a national tragedy, but it was also a personal one. Guynemer had shocked his family on his last visit to them as he had become physically emaciated and nervously drawn. His father, himself a former army officer, begged him to take a rest. He countered with the argument that people would say that 'I have ceased to fight because I have won all the awards.' There was a limit, his father said, to physical strength and he had

Top: **Max Immelmann was popularly known as the 'Eagle of Lille.'**

Below: **Pilots of Escadrille No 3 *Cigognes*. Guynemer is third from the left.**

Above: **Guynemer with his mechanic on the day of his first victory.**

Above: **Heurtaux and his biplane of the Cigognes squadron.**

reached it. 'Indeed there is a limit,' was his son's answer, 'but it is only there to be excelled. If one has not given everything, one has given nothing.'

Guynemer had the charisma of the mystic. His opposite number on the German side also had charisma but it was rather that of the fire-breathing man of action. Manfred von Richthofen, a regular *Uhlan* officer, and a passionate huntsman, summed up his attitude to the air war in the words, 'I am a hunter. My brother, Lothar, is a butcher. When I have shot down an Englishman, my hunting passion is satisfied for a quarter of an hour.' Eventually Richthofen was to shoot down 80 of the enemy, most in his scarlet Fokker triplane which became his emblem and was the origin of his nickname, 'The Red Baron.' He owed his skill in combat partly to his early experiences as an observer with another pilot, Kurt Wissemann, who suffered from tuberculosis and was determined to die in the air instead of in his bed. Wissemann time and again flew his aircraft to within a few feet of the enemy he was chasing and survival of those risks seems to have convinced Richthofen that he was invulnerable. He set the highest standards of courage and discipline in his *Jasta II.* His favorite expression was that 'one must overcome the inner *schweinehund*,' and he did seem to have succeeded in suppressing within himself every trace of fear and doubt. He filled his room with trophies of the aircraft he had shot down and lit it with a chandelier constructed from the rotary engine of a British victim so that even in sleep he was reminded of aerial combat. He was eventually shot down in a fight with a comparatively inexperienced British pilot. Mick Mannock, the leading British ace, remarked on hearing that Richthofen had come down in flames, 'I hope he burned all the way down.' The Royal Flying Corps pilots who recovered his body saw that he had an honorable burial, probably a better testimonial of his standing with his enemies.

Burning was all too often the fate of pilots defeated in a dogfight. Of Richthofen's 80 victims, 54 burned in the air. The reason for this ghastly disproportion was that the fuel tank was mounted as close to the engine as possible and on most models the magnetos geared to the propeller shaft by direct drive. A hit which struck the engine almost always ruptured a fuel pipe and, even if the engine was stopped, the windmilling of the propeller would keep the magnetos sparking. Fire was the inevitable result. As the British pilots carried no parachute, they were burned to death in their airplanes or killed by the fall when they jumped free. Almost as horrible was the irrecoverable stall or spin into which some aircraft, or inexperienced pilots, would fall if their control surfaces or engine was damaged while dogfighting. Cecil Lewis has

Below: **The Richthofen Squadron after it was taken over by air ace Hermann Göring (in the center).**

Above: The Fokker D.1 triplane flown by Manfred von Richthofen. His passenger came aboard from the adjacent triplane.

Right: Manfred von Richthofen, the Red Baron.

Bottom right: An Australian honor guard attends the funeral of the Red Baron.

Below: Lothar von Richthofen (left) with his more famous brother Manfred.

described seeing a fellow RFC pilot attempt to bring down his aircraft with a damaged tail,

'Roberts was a crack pilot . . . and by shutting off his engine he almost managed to avert disaster – but not quite. He could not stop the machine spinning: but he could stop it going into a vertical diving spin. He tried every combination of elevator and bank. No good. The machine went on slowly spinning, round and round and round, all the way down from 8000 feet to the ground. It took about five minutes. He and his observer were sitting there, waiting for death, for that time.'

The worst moment for the French *Aviation Militaire* had been during the period of the Fokker dominance in the summer and autumn of 1915, when they were fighting their great offensive in Champagne. The worst for the Royal Flying Corps came in April 1917 when its pilots had to cover the front of advance during the Battle of Arras. The Germans had now formed 37 *Jagdstaffeln* (*Jasta*) of the Richthofen type, equipped and trained for offensive action, and they were flying a new model, the Albatros D.III, which outclassed the RFC's Sopwith 1½ Strutters, BE2s and RE8s. German tactics, moreover, were not to cross the front but remain over the lines, idling at a high altitude, so that when British airplanes crossed they could dive to attack them out of the sun. If hit, and not burned, they could retrieve a landing place by turning and gliding eastward. As a result, British losses during April amounted to a third of the crews, inevitably falling heaviest on the replacement pilots and observers. Some squadrons attempted to extend the novices' lives by distributing them among the experienced, putting a new gunner with an old pilot in a two-seater, or giving an experienced flight-leader a tyro as a wing man. The old hands, whose survival depended on the quick reactions they had developed, naturally resisted this seeding. They particularly objected that new pilots had the greatest difficulty in seeing the enemy, a trick learned only by those who had survived at least one close encounter.

Left: **A British squadron of SE5As in France.**

Above: **A Sopwith Pup biplane, mainstay of the Royal Flying Corps.**

Emergency measures had to be taken to restore the RFC's effectiveness. The Sopwith Triplane flown by the Royal Naval Air Service near the Belgian coast was known to be a match for the Albatros and a squadron was summoned hastily for the Arras Front. It impressed the Germans by its climb and maneuverability so much that Fokker at once set about designing a copy, in which Manfred von Richthofen would cap his reputation, but the numbers deployed were too few to turn the balance. That came later in the summer with the appearance of the SE5 and the Bristol Fighter. It was a remarkable feature of aircraft design and production in those early days that a small improvement in structure or in engine power could instantly outclass existing models and be translated into large numbers of machines very quickly. Aircraft were cheaply and speedily built – the SE5 cost only £837 – and, while they preserved their superiority of perhaps an extra 10mph or half a minute less to 10,000 feet, could make their opponents' machines virtual deathtraps. The SE5, the Bristol Fighter (Brisfit) and the Sopwith Camel, which all appeared in France in mid-1917, were to redress the balance and hold it for the British until the arrival of the Fokker D.VII in 1918 gave technical ascendancy back to the Germans.

The Bristol Fighter was a two-seater, at first distrusted by its crews because all two seaters had got a bad name from the cumbersome qualities of the 1914–15 models. Its speed, agility and fire power quickly disproved that reputation and many pilots came to regard it as

Below: **A Sopwith Camel F-1 biplane.**

Below: **A Sopwith Camel in France doing a loop.**

the best aircraft in British service of the whole war. The SE5, difficult to fly until its tricks were learned, was fast – 126mph – and powerful: 10 minutes to 10,000 feet, against the 12 minutes of the Albatros. It had an in-line engine, which robbed it of turning ability but was a very stable gun platform and carried two machine guns and a lot of ammunition. The Camel, with a rotary engine and all its heavy components mounted in the front seven feet of the fuselage, was extremely maneuverable and was to remain unchallengeable for the rest of the war. Pilots flying Camels shot down more aircraft – 1294 – than any other airplane.

Robbed of technical superiority over the Western Front during 1917, the Germans sought to compensate for it by organizational improvements. The French *Cigognes* had been the first fighter unit formed to win aerial battles (it was now receiving the Spad XIII, which also outclassed the Albatros). The Germans had fought back with the *Jasta*. Now they grouped *Jasta*s to form *Jagdgeschwader* of 50 or 60 aircraft. The most famous, formed on 26 July 1917, became known as Richthofen's Circus after its first leader. Its aircraft were painted scarlet and flew together in large sweeps to catch inferior formations of British or French intruders over their lines and destroy or disperse them. The British, whose air units were tied to the military headquarters over whose sectors they operated, could not at first respond, since corps or armies were unwilling to lend their airplanes to others. As a result, the Germans were able at times to dominate their own skies, so making impossible the work of the artillery observer and reconnaissance aircraft.

While the spectacular battles of the fighter individualists were taking place over the Western Front, another form of aerial warfare had been gathering pace far to the rear. Germany, thanks to the engineering and commercial genius of the pioneer aeronaut Count Zeppelin, had entered the war with a fleet of 30 airships – always known to the British as Zeppelins. Their own efforts at building them had proved remarkably unsuccessful and it was perhaps for that reason that they underrated the danger which the Zeppelins posed. At first, the German High Command did not venture to use them against the British Isles. In January 1915, however, some British aircraft raided Germany and the Kaiser decided that provided a pretext for an attack on civilian targets in Britain. Previously there had only been a little bombing of the Channel ports, used by the army for movement to France. On 31 May 1915 the first Zeppelin raid on London took place.

Below left: **The Sopwith F-1 Camel, with its 130hp Clerget 9-Bc engine.**

Right: **Searchlights over London in the first Zeppelin raid in 1915.**

Below: **A Sopwith Camel after a forced landing at Noyelles-sur-l'Escaut, 8 October 1918.**

It was not spectacular. Only one Zeppelin was used, but five people were killed and fires started. By September, however, groups of Zeppelins were penetrating the heart of London and in one raid £500,000 worth of damage was done. On 31 January 1916 nine Zeppelins flew to the north Midlands and killed 59 people. A month later two Zeppelins positioned themselves over Hull, on the North Sea coast, and bombed it at their leisure.

Most of these raids took place at night and so, though timed to coincide with the bright phase of the moon, defeated the efforts of home-based British fighters to find or engage the airships. On 4 June 1915 one Zeppelin, *LZ.37*, had been destroyed while returning from a raid, but it was attacked in Belgium when it had lost height to make a landing. Another had been downed on 31 March 1916, by a combination of gunfire and airplane attack, but it fell into the sea. The first true victory over the 'monsters of the purple twilight' came on 2 September 1916 when Lieutenant W Leefe-Robinson singled out one of a group of 14, *SL.11*, and brought her down near Cuffley, in Middlesex. He was awarded the Victoria Cross for the feat. Three weeks later Lieutenant Brandon repeated the performance by downing *L.33*. By this time the defenses of the capital were extensive and the airship was

Above: An early Zeppelin under construction.

Above: Zeppelin I in a trial run over the North Sea.

Below: Imagination was worse than reality, as this sketch of a Zeppelin over Antwerp shows.

Below: Wreckage of a Yarmouth house hit in a Zeppelin raid in 1915.

Above: Airships *L. 13* (largest) with *L. 12* and *L. 10* set out for a raid on the English coast.

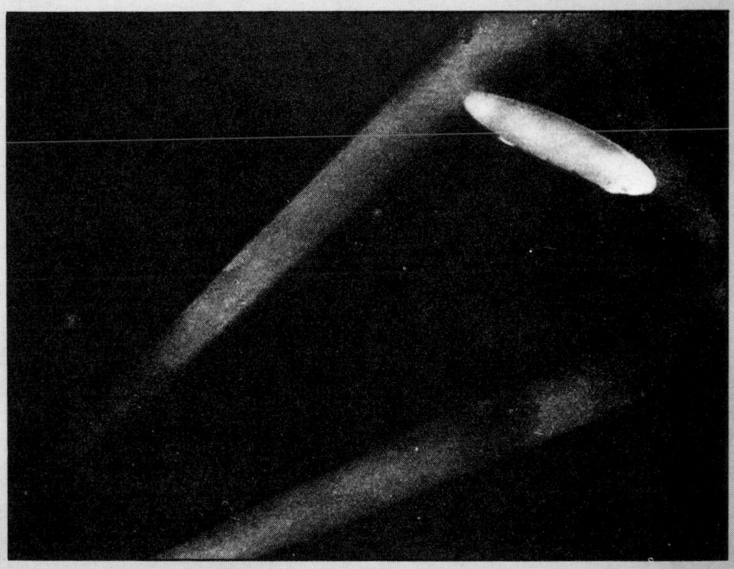

Above: A Zeppelin over London on 13 October 1915 is illuminated by searchlights.

Above: A Zeppelin in 1917, more powerful and dangerous than its predecessors.

Below: Damage caused by a Zeppelin raid on King's Lynn in 1915.

Below: King George and Queen Mary came to view the damage of an air raid on Warrington Crescent, London, in March 1918.

Above: **British dirigible over the Dover coast.**

constantly caught in the beams of searchlights. Even so, it took Brandon 20 minutes of continuous firing to bring her down. Her end came from lack of power and lift. His bullets had punctured her gas bags and damaged an engine, and she sank lower and lower until her commander decided in desperation to crash land her in Essex.

Given the size and characteristics of the Zeppelins, 5–800 feet long and filled with up to 2,000,000 cubic feet of highly combustible hydrogen, it seems extraordinary that they were not more easily brought down. They owed their invulnerability mainly to the height at which they operated and to the poor quality of ammunition used against them. Warneford, who had destroyed the first Zeppelin in 1914, had managed to catch it at a low altitude and had dropped six 20-pound bombs through its fabric. Miraculously, he had avoided the enormous burst of flame which had resulted. Such feats were difficult to repeat and it was eventually the weather, combined with the improved defenses of London, which drove the Zeppelins away. The increased density of guns and lights around London forced the Germans to fly ever larger formations of airships over the capital and on 19 October 1917 11 Zeppelins which had set out for it were caught in a violent storm. Three were destroyed by the force of the wind, a fourth by anti-aircraft fire when it dropped low for shelter. A fifth was blown out to sea, never to be found again. The other six all lost their way and came down on Allied territory or crashed. After this disaster, the Zeppelin force confined itself to attacking British submarines in the North Sea and to hit-and-run raids. In all, there were 208 Zeppelin flights, during which 5907 bombs were dropped and 522 people were killed.

Concurrently with the later airship raids, the Germans also launched numbers of raids by their large aircraft, generically known to the British as Gothas, after the most successful type. Airplane bombing began in earnest on 25 May 1917 when the 3rd Bombing Squadron, 16 aircraft strong, left Belgium and made for London. As darkness fell, the pilots lost direction and gave up their effort to reach London, but dropped bombs on Shornecliffe Camp in Essex which caused 100 casualties among Canadian troops there. On 13 June, however, bombing by day, the Squadron killed 104 people near Liverpool Street Station in the middle of London. Public outrage produced an immediate improvement of anti-aircraft defenses, so effective that by September the Gothas were also forced to make their attacks by night. For a time they succeeded in penetrating the defenses of the capital, though they caused little loss of life. The Germans pressed on with forming larger squadrons and on 19 May 1918 sent 40 heavy bombers to London. Thirteen arrived but seven were destroyed, three by fighter attack, three by gunfire and one from engine failure. Thereafter the Germans reckoned the effort too costly. In all their airships and bombers had dropped 8776 bombs and killed 1316 people.

Though the German bombing campaign failed in its attempt to shake the British people's will to sustain their war effort, it remained an impressive military effort. It might have achieved a greater effect had it been more fully coordinated. The forces engaged were divided into three, the naval airships, the military airships and the bombers, also under military control. In April 1918 the British took the pioneer step of uniting all their air units – the fighters and seaplanes of the Royal Naval Air Service and the fighters, bombers and reconnaissance aircraft of the Royal Flying Corps – into a Royal Air Force. Its first commander was General Sir Hugh Trenchard ('Boom' to all his subordinates because of his extraordinarily commanding voice).

Trenchard's career had been made by the war. At the outbreak he was an overage major who learned to fly because the new skill seemed to offer the only break in a thoroughly undistinguished career. His seniority in a corps of very young men ensured his rapid promotion as the war progressed and in 1915, rapidly promoted to Major General, he became head of the Royal Flying Corps. On its separation as an independent service this intensely ambitious man determined to find for it a truly independent role. In May 1918 he established a force of 49 heavy night bombers, 75 day bombers and 16 fighters, called the Independent Air Force. He also gave it a precise mission. Rather than simply

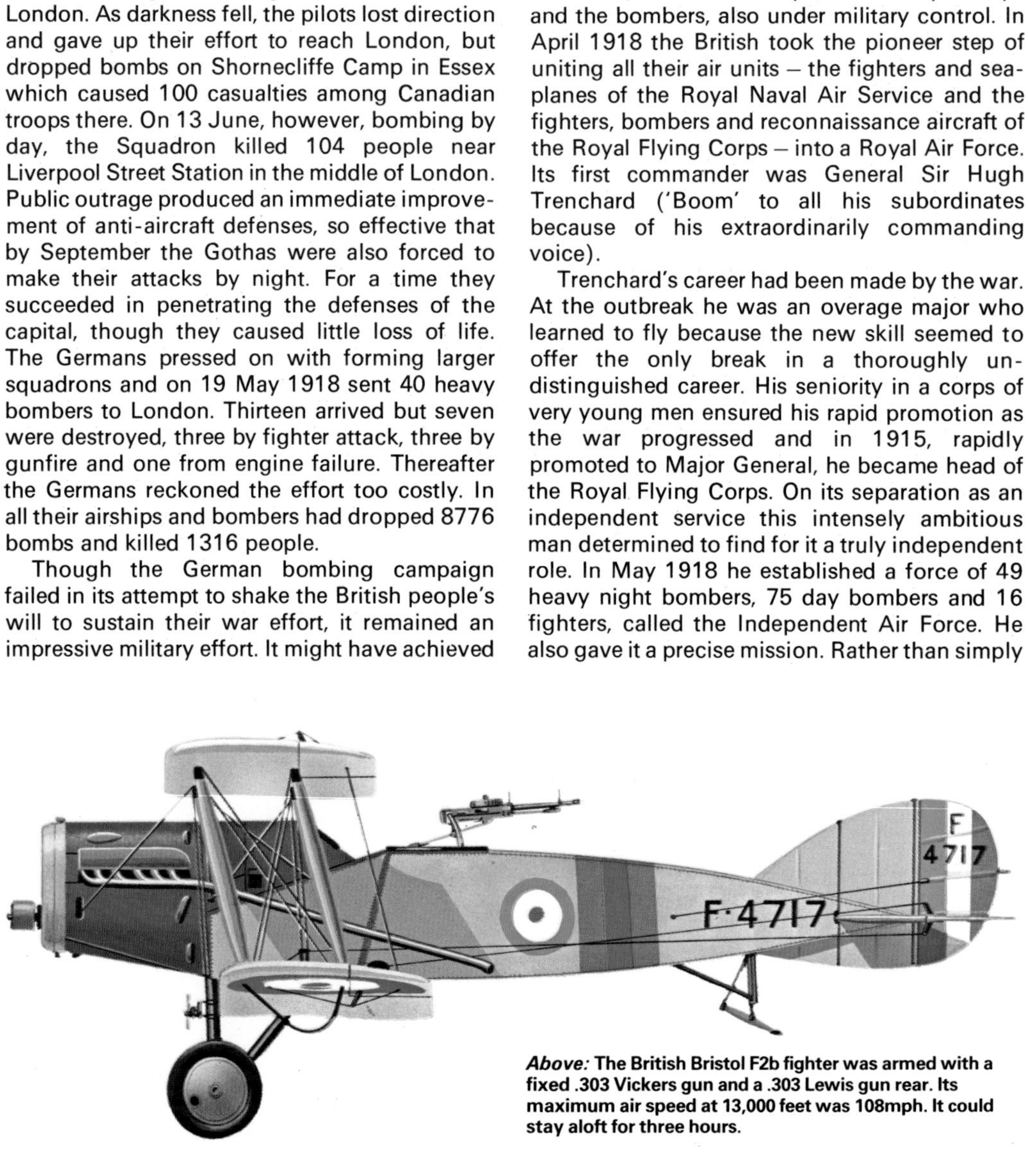

Above: **The British Bristol F2b fighter was armed with a fixed .303 Vickers gun and a .303 Lewis gun rear. Its maximum air speed at 13,000 feet was 108mph. It could stay aloft for three hours.**

Right: **Damage from a Gotha bomber over Paris on 9 March 1918. Bombing raids became more fearsome as the war progressed.**

scatter bombs haphazard into large towns, as the German Gothas and Zeppelins had done, he decided to attempt precision attacks on German industrial targets. Naturally he chose the great complex of the Ruhr as his target. In May the IAF attacked Cologne with 33 tons of bombs and between then and the end of the war dropped 540 altogether. Each raid was far heavier and more concentrated than any launched by the Germans against London. However Trenchard, as we can now see with hindsight, overestimated the effect which an offensive on that scale, mighty as it was judged at the time, could have on the economy of a powerful industrial state.

The bombers, though they caused a little public apprehension, never caught the popular imagination in the way the fighters and the pilots did. By 1918 the 'Circuses' squadrons and Escadrilles were working up to their final effort on the Western Front. To the three air forces already engaged, a fourth had now been added, the Air Service of the United States Signal Corps. Its pilots were not the first Americans to have flown against the Germans. That cachet belonged to the dashing volunteers of the Escadrille Lafayette, a squadron of the *Aviation Militaire* formed in April 1916. Despite America's neutrality, numbers of pro-Allied and adventure-hungry Americans were already serving in France, many as infantrymen masquerading as Canadians in the Canadian Imperial Force. A small group had arrived in France in 1914 to form a volunteer ambulance service, a device which kept them on the right side of America's foreign enlistment laws, but the onset of trench warfare had robbed medical rescue of its excitement. One of the ambulance volunteers, Norman Prince, was already a pilot and he conceived the idea of recruiting other American volunteers to fly for the French as an escape from their current frustration. The French authorities at first refused their application but then, recognizing the propaganda value of enlisting volunteers from America, whose neutrality Germany was trying to preserve as hard as the Allies were trying to end it, succumbed. The first seven recruits to the Escadrille Américaine were Prince himself, William Thaw, who had learned to fly at Yale, Kiffin Rockwall, a medical student from North Carolina, Victor Chapman, a Harvard man who had joined the French Foreign Legion in 1914, James McConnell and Elliott Cowdin, from the ambulance unit, and a Texas stunt flier, Bert Hall. After training the pilots were equipped with Nieuport Scouts in May 1916 and sent to Verdun, where they were given the job of attacking the German observation balloons which were directing artillery fire onto the stricken French positions.

'Balloon busting' was not the easy job an attack on a stationary target might seem to be. They were protected by batteries of anti-aircraft guns and by patrols of fighters, which circled at altitude to dive on the 'balloon busters' as they made their attacks. A Belgian, Willy Coppens, was making a speciality of this dangerous occupation and was awarded a Belgian Knighthood for destroying 37 around Ypres. The Americans quickly found how difficult the task was. Both Boelcke and Immelmann were

Right: **This biplane became a sitting duck as it straggled behind its squadron.**

Above: **No 1 Course, Central Flying School. Sir Hugh Trenchard appears on the far right, second row.**

Above: **A Gotha G.Vd heavy bomber with two 260hp Mercedes engines.**

operating Fokker Squadrons over Verdun and on 24 May William Thaw was jumped by three of these German machines and shot down. He was pulled from the wreckage with a cut pectoral artery, but survived. Next day Bert Hall was badly wounded. On 17 June Victor Chapman encountered Boelcke himself, who was shot down and wounded in the head, but in the same week five Fokkers caught Victor Chapman and shot him down. He was the first of the American squadron to die. Rockwell was killed the following day and in the same week Prince, who had been flying long hours, flew into high tension cables on his approach to the airfield in poor evening light. There were replacements – altogether 209 Americans trained as pilots with the French Air Service – but the Escadrille Lafayette was never to be the same again. It was transferred to the American Air Service in France in February 1918 and thereafter operated as a normal American fighter squadron. Its glamour and great days were behind it.

It had never included the greatest of the American aces, the extraordinary Eddie Rickenbacker. A poor boy from Columbus, Ohio, between 1910 and 1914 he became America's top racing driver, with an income of $40,000 per annum. In 1914 he broke the world speed record and after America's entry into the war became convinced that a squadron formed of America's other leading racing drivers would prove invincible. His advocacy of this idea achieved nothing and he was eventually persuaded to enlist as personal chauffeur to General John Pershing, the Commander in Chief. Some months of this duty so frustrated him that he insisted on transferring to the Air Service, learned to fly at the end of 1917 and in March 1918 joined the 94th ('Hat in the Ring') Aero Squadron. He shot down his first German plane on 29 April and within a month four more. During July and August he was away from the front with an ear infection, induced by flying at high altitude. Between the middle of September and the end of October, after his return to duty, he downed another 20 aircraft, making a total of 26 victories, a record achieved in so short a time that it made him one of the most remarkable pilots of the war. His continuing toughness and powers of survival were demonstrated in World War II when the airplane in which he was making a tour of inspection crashed and he spent 21 days on a raft before rescue.

Despite the enormous industrial might of the domestic economy almost all the American squadrons were equipped with French aircraft. Their own aircraft factories were not ready to produce home-designed models until the war was over. Thus the final effort on the Western Front remained a duel between the German and the Franco-British air fleets. In the last months of war it was the Germans who made the most important innovation in aerial tactics. This was

Below: **A Handley-Page bomber at the training depot in Halton Camp, Wendover, England.**

No. 203

AMERICAN
EXPEDITIONARY FORCES
Corps Expéditionnaire Américain

OFFICER'S IDENTITY CARD
Carte d'Identité d'Officier

Name / Nom: Harlan R. Sumner
Rank / Grade: 1st Lieut. Air Service
Duty / Fonction: Flying

Adjutant General

Signature of Holder / Signature du Titulaire: Harlan R Sumner

Above: A Gotha G.V is loaded with 110lb and 220lb bombs.

Above right: The ID card of a member of the AEF.

Right: The Handley-Page V-1500 heavy bomber had 350hp Rolls-Royce Eagle VIII engines.

the creation of *Schlachtstaffeln* (Battle Squadrons) which were equipped and trained to support ground troops in an offensive. Special aircraft, designated CL and later J types, were designed and assigned to the *Schlasta*. The J I, when it appeared, was found to be of all-metal construction and highly resistant to ground fire. The *Schlastas* had their first trial during the Battle of Cambrai, where their strafing of the British advanced positions and reporting of the progress of German infantry columns made a major contribution to the success of the counter-attack. The British had also tried 'contact patrolling,' as they called it and were to do so again, but they did not develop the specialized aircraft which the Imperial Air Service had. During Germany's first great offensives of

Above: Germans 'scramble' for their Fokker D-1 triplanes.

Left: Spad two-seater biplanes over France.

Above right: A Spad takes aim at its target.

March–July 1918, the *Schlastas* ranged far ahead of the advancing infantry and were able to indicate to the High Command in which directions it would be most profitable to exert pressure.

The Germans were also able, in the last months of the war, to win back something of the technical advantage in aerial combat which they had lost to the enemy since the appearance of the Camel, SE5, Spad XIII and Nieuport 28. The Fokker D.VII, last of the great Dutchman's designs, did not quite match the speed of the latest models of Allied fighters but it had an extraordinary ability to hang on its propeller at high altitudes while turning and climbing in a dogfight, and so get on an opponent's tail. Lieutenant J M Guder, of the Royal Flying Corps, described an encounter with a D.VII in the summer of 1918:

'There were five of us and we ran into five Fokkers at 15,000 feet. We all started climbing of course – and they outclimbed us. We climbed up to 20,500 feet and couldn't get any higher. We were practically stalled and these Fokkers went right over our heads and got between us and the lines. Gosh, it's unpleasant fighting at that altitude. The slightest movement exhausts you. Your engine has no pep and splutters; its hard to keep a decent formation, and you lose 500 feet on a turn. The Huns came in from above and it didn't take us long to fight down to 12,000 feet. We put up the best fight of our lives but these Huns were just too good for us. . . . I got to circling with one Hun, just he and I, and it didn't take me long to discover I wasn't going to circle above this one. He began to gain on me and then did something I've never heard of before. He'd been circling with me and he'd pull around and point his nose at me and open fire and just hang there on his prop and follow me round with his tracer. All I could do was keep on turning around as best I could. If I'd straightened out he'd have had me cold as he already had his sights on me. If I'd tried to hang on my prop that way, I'd have gone right into a spin. But this fellow hung right there and sprayed me with lead like he had a hose. All I could do was to watch his tracer and kick my rudder from one side to the other to throw his aim off. This war isn't what it used to be.'

Guder got away eventually, but two of his fellow pilots were shot down in this fight, and the renewed 'Fokker Menace' remained the

Left: **Officers of the 103rd Aero Squadron, formerly the Lafayette Escadrille, line up with other Allied officers to receive French decorations.**

Above: Albatros D.Va of Jasta 40 flown by Karl Degelow.

Above: Fokker DR.I triplane of Jagdgeschwader 1 flown by Baron Manfred von Richthofen.

Above: William Moorhouse was an RFC pilot of No 2 Squadron who bombed Courtrai on 26 April 1915. He was killed in this solo sortie and won a posthumous VC, the first ever Victoria Cross won in the air.

Above left: Billy Bishop, with his Nieuport.

Far left: Major McCudden of the RFC, VC.

Left: Major Mick Mannock was a leading British ace, notable for his shyness.

Below: Captain Albert Ball, RFC, VC in his SE5 two-seater. This great ace was killed in combat on 7 May 1917.

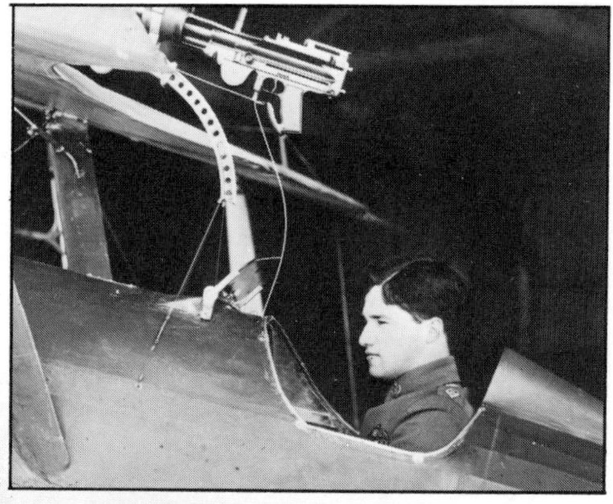

Below: Australian-born Major Roderick Dallas in his SE5A of No 40 Squadron. He was credited with at least 51 kills.

dominant factor in aerial warfare until November 1918.

Most of the German strength was concentrated during the last year of the war on the Western Front against the British. In March 1918 there were 1680 German aircraft opposite the British section and only 367 against the French, and an increasing number were Fokker D.VIIs. One of the last epics of the air war was between a formation of these aircraft and one of the heroes of the great individual dogfighting days, the Canadian W G Barker. Like many of the great pilots Barker was a slow starter and had scored only nine victories between October 1917 and January 1918. In the next nine months, however, he raised his score to no less than 49 and on 27 October was flying back to England on a home posting, when he spotted a lone observation plane far below him. Tempted by the chance of one more kill, he followed it down only to encounter no less than 15 Fokker D.VIIs flying an offensive mission. Recognizing attack to be his only hope of escape, he flew head-on into their formation and, in the first shock, shot down two before the others had coordinated their maneuvers to encircle him. He had already been wounded in one leg and was soon wounded in the other. He fainted at the controls and his Snipe (an improved Camel) spiralled groundward. The motion revived him but the Fokkers followed him down and he was wounded in the left elbow when he made a suicidal attack, which brought down another Fokker. Intermittently conscious and at ground level, he just managed to hold the machine straight enough to make a landing at 90mph which tore off the undercarriage. The wreckage came to rest close to a British position and the soldiers who dragged him clear raced him to hospital where his life was saved. When examined the remains of his aircraft, which was awash with blood, revealed 300 bullet holes. Barker was unconscious for 10 days but recovered the use of all his limbs and was on his feet to receive the Victoria Cross from King George V on 30 November 1918. His last battle raised his score to 53 and made him the seventh-ranking British ace.

Ace of aces remained Manfred von Richthofen, with 80 victories. Next came the French, Réné Paul Fonck with 75 and the British Major Mick Mannock with 73. Fifteen of the British, four of the French and 11 of the German aces had scores of over 40 aircraft shot down. The victories of the aces of the other air forces – Russian, Italian, Austrian, Belgian or American – were much lower, in the latter's case because of its late entry into the war, in the former because of the altogether lower level of activity in the skies over their fronts. The sum of these totals is the figure for casualties suffered by the opposing sides. The Germans had lost 5853 men killed, the Royal Air Force 6166.

Was the air war, in retrospect, anything more than a gladiatorial contest? The bombing of the homelands by the 'strategic' air forces clearly achieved very little and certainly inflicted damage which cost far less than the investment in the building of the airships and heavy aircraft which made the raids. It was also ineffective in depressing civilian morale. 'Zeppelins' were quickly a source of English music hall jokes. The tactical air forces achieved a good deal more. During the era of open warfare at the beginning and end of the war, roving pilots had brought nuggets of priceless information to the commanders in headquarters; whether they were used correctly was beyond their power to determine. During the long years of trench warfare, the air forces had wielded the means to make life even more uncomfortable than it already was for the suffering infantry below, by directing the fire of the enemy's artillery into their trenches, or alternatively to spare them the misery by sweeping the skies clean of prying pilots from the other side. It was in those battles for air dominance that the great aces had made their names, and the relief they had brought to humbler warriors earned the adulation that had been heaped upon them. There was another, intangible benefit they had brought. How often did infantrymen testify that, looking up from the mud of their trenches into the blue skies above, their spirits had been uplifted by the sight of airplanes duelling far above their heads; not by the victory of one side over the other, for altitude made the recognition of friend and enemy impossible, but by the reminder that the wheeling and swooping brought that there was still a realm of freedom and movement in the terrible land-locked war that the armies were fighting. Cecil Day Lewis, later Poet Laureate, a pioneer pilot managed to catch the intoxication of fear and excitement that aerial combat brought to warriors and observers in his lines from a pilot's cockpit:

Tempt me no more; for I
Have known the lightning's hour,
The poet's inward pride,
The certainty of power.

Bayonets are closing round.
I shrink; yet I must wring
A living from despair
And out of steel a song.

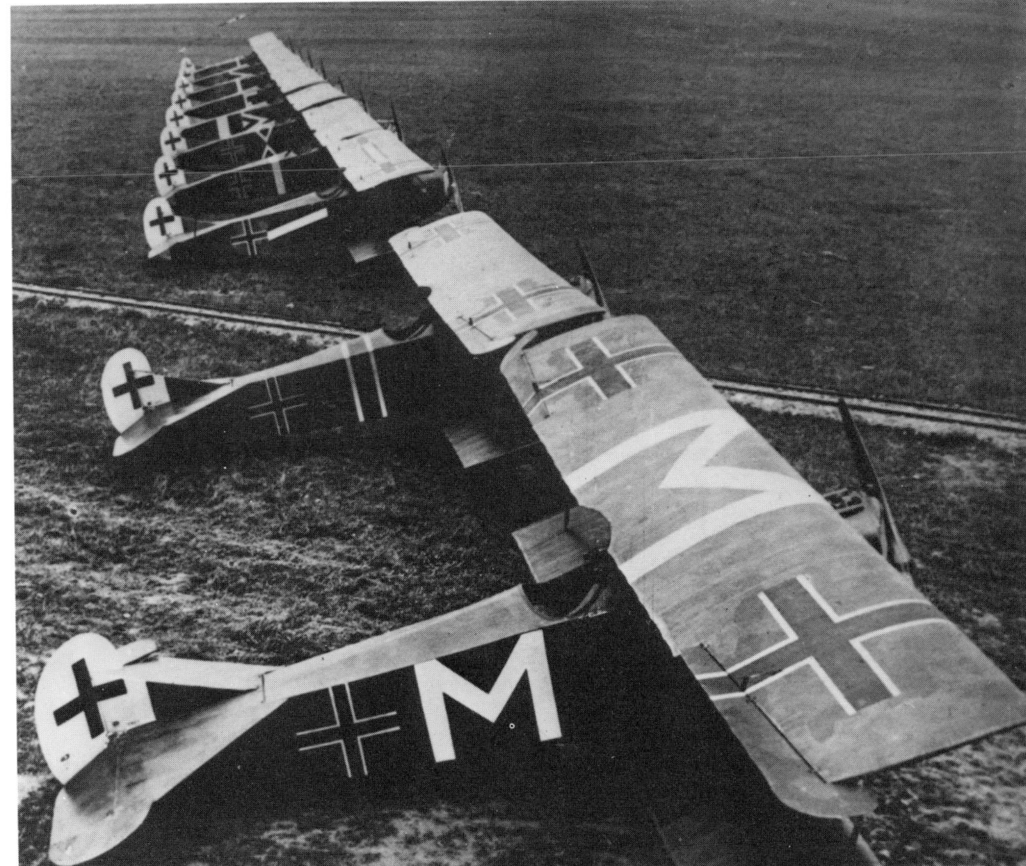

Above: A squadron of Fokker D.VII biplanes in 1918.

Below: Fokker D.VII pilots mount their aircraft in Flanders for a sortie.

Russian heavy artillerymen in position in a Polish wood.

7 The Russian Collapse

Hindenburg's great victory at Tannenberg in August 1914, life-saving though it was for Germany, by no means ended Russia's threat to East Prussia and Silesia, or to Germany's feeble ally, Austria-Hungary. Just as at the outbreak it was Russia's generous strategy of a premature offensive which had relieved the pressure on France at the critical time of the Battle of the Marne, so as autumn drew into winter on the Eastern Front French, and later British, activity in the West prevented the Kaiser and his generals from transferring thence any but a few of the divisions originally committed to the march on Paris.

The Central Powers' strategy in the East was defensive. The terrain and the ratio of men to space made defense in the East altogether more difficult than in the West. Measured along its whole length, from the border with Rumania to the Baltic at Memel, Russia's frontier with her two Teutonic enemies was 1200 miles. On 500 miles of front in the West the opposing sides deployed armies far larger than those in the East. They buttressed their lines at several points on major natural obstacles, the flats of the Yser, the heights of the Aisne, the swamps and forest of the Argonne and the mountains of the Vosges. In the East there were a few natural obstacles, like the Masurian Lakes in East Prussia and the Carpathian Mountains on Hungary's border. The Austrian positions stood well to the east of the Carpathians which thus acted as an obstacle to supply and reinforcement of their rear, while, between the northern end of their line and the southern end of the German line in East Prussia, the great salient of Russian Poland bulged forward toward the industrial and mining areas of Silesia and the great cities of Breslau and Posen. Russian Poland formed the land bridge between the plains of North Germany and the endless steppe of European Russia, itself as flat as a billiard table for mile after mile. The rivers, the Vistula, the San and the Warthe, ran barely below the level of the flats and, though wide, were easily bridged at almost any point. In the center of the salient stood Warsaw, nodal point of all military comminications in north-central Europe. Geographically, therefore, the advantages stood with the Russians, since they enjoyed the best transport network and were faced by no series of obstacles against which their enemies could buttress a stout defense.

The Russians also had a numerical advantage. They had seven armies in the field against one German and four Austrian. While the Central Powers were divided from each other by nationality, and Austria further divided by language – some scholars counted 15 spoken languages in the Dual Monarchy – the Russians were a single force united by a deep, almost mystical patriotism for Mother Russia. The infantry of the first-line were strong, brave obedient peasants, excellent marchers and busy diggers, who could entrench a strong position overnight without complaint. The cavalry was recruited from countrymen, used to horses and supplemented by light regiments of Cossacks, who made superlative scouts. The Russian artillery had always been good and its materiel was the equal of the German but, as with all classes of Russian equipment, there was not enough of it. Russian industry, though developing faster than that of any other nation's in 1914, faster even than America's, had not yet reached

Below: **General Zhilinsky (back to camera) gives out decorations to some Russian officers. Zhilinsky was an incompetent who was sacked in 1914.**

Above: Russian troops in a Galician trench. The Austrian and German offensives forced the Russians back from their frontiers. After this offensive in early 1915 the German Eighth and Tenth Armies moved forward from the Masurian Lakes and encircled 70,000 Russian troops.

the stage where it could feed a hungry army in full flush of a great campaign. Losses of materiel were therefore serious to Russia in a way which losses of men – whose reserves seemed inexhaustible – were not.

On the other hand, Russian leadership was not impressive. In business life, Russia now offered a career to talented people. In the army, as in the civil service and politics, court influence was dominant, some would have said paramount, and too many of the Russian generals owed their place to patronage. The Commander in Chief was a Grand Duke, Nicholas, uncle to the Czar, and, though a competent administrator, was chiefly distinguished by his enormous height. General Mikhail Alexeiev, the future Chief of Staff, was an adequate military technician but as the rare exception, a man of humble origins who had made his way to the top, lacked the self-confidence and court connections to dictate strategy. The Russian army was also wracked by fierce antipathies between the reformers who were the protégés of the War Minister, General Vladimir Sukhomlinov, and the traditionalists, who looked to the Grand Duke for protection and leadership. The result was that true leadership in the army was hard to find. Sukhomlinov continued the peacetime administration of the army; the Grand Duke, on the outbreak of hostilities, transformed the General Staff into an operational *Stavka* (High Command) which directed strategy. The two retained conflicting powers to appoint commanders and chiefs of staff irrespective of subordinate formations and in consequence often created situations in which the two most important men in a division, a corps or even an army, were not on speaking terms.

None of this augured well for Russian strategy and, as we have seen, its first test in the invasion of East Prussia confirmed the worst of pessimistic fears. However that was against the Germans; against the Austrians the Russians were to do better. The Austrian army, though it had an excellent Chief of Staff in Conrad von Hötzendorf, was beset by internal problems as grave as Russia's. These were complicated by the language problem and constantly threatened by the doubtful political loyalty of the Slavs, particularly the Czechs. Austria-Hungary also had its two-front dilemma, in its case posed by the need to fight the Serbs and the Russians simultaneously. Because of the deployment of 13 divisions against the Serbs it could not match the Russians' strength beyond the Carpathians where they had 1,300,000 men in the field against its 1,100,000. Moreover, weak though the Russian army was in artillery and shell stocks, the Austrian army was even weaker.

This weakness was the salvation of Russia's war effort in the early months of the war. Defeated in East Prussia, she could still achieve victories over the Austrians because Hindenburg's Eighth Army was too small and separated by the Polish salient, too far away to lend help to her ally in front of the Carpathians. Yet the Russians' victories were nevertheless achieved by miscalculation. Both they and the Austrians miscalculated each other's centers of strength and intentions. Conrad von Hötzendorf believed that the Russians did not intend to attack and on 20 August sent his left wing to march round what he had identified as an open flank of the Russian army, south of Ivangorod. On 23 August it met head on a Russian army, under General Alexei Evert, which was pressing forward to make a surprise attack. In a three-day battle at Krasnik the Russians were driven from

Above: **Grand Duke Nicholas, the Czar's uncle, was Commander in Chief of the Russian armies from August 1914 until August 1915 after which he was transferred to the Caucasus.**

Below: **Austrian Chief of Staff Conrad von Hötzendorf surveys the Galician battle front.**

Austro-Hungarian Uniforms

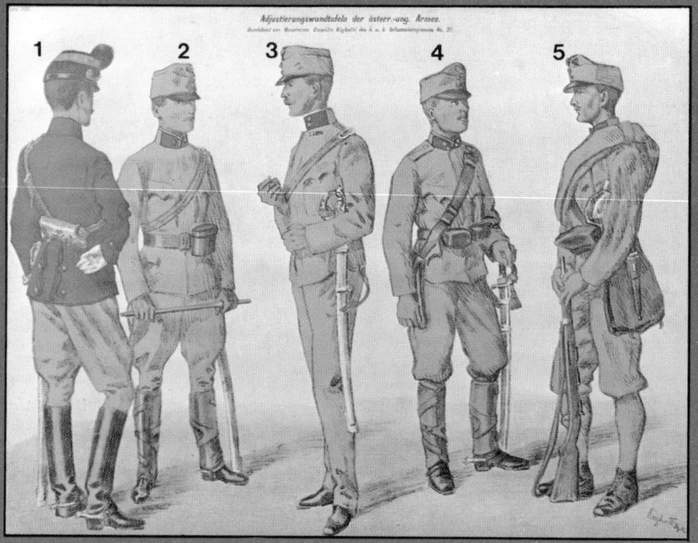

1 Field artillery officer, dress uniform. 2 Field artillery officer, field uniform. 3 Fortress artillery officer. 4 Corporal of the field artillery. 5 Cannoneer of the fortress artillery.

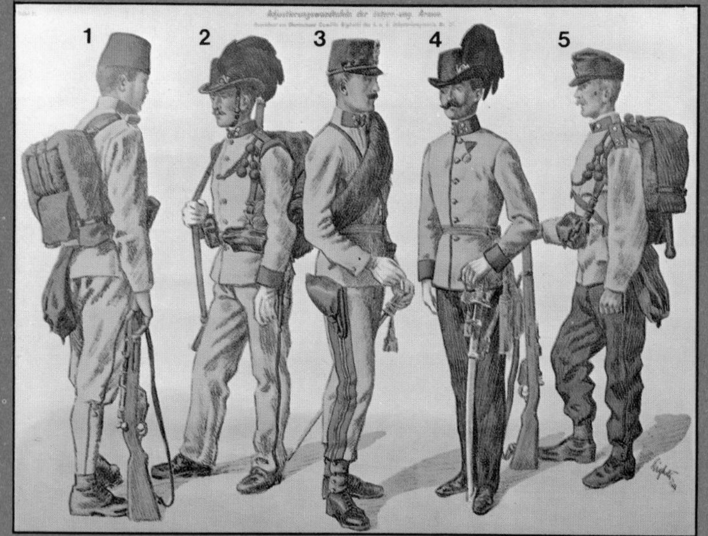

1 Bosnian-Herzegovinian infantryman. 2 Infantryman, dress uniform. 3 Infantryman, field uniform. 4 Infantry officer, dress uniform. 5 Infantryman, private, summer field uniform.

1 Captain of the infantry. 2 Lieutenant in the infantry. 3 Bugler of a Bosnian-Herzegovinian infantry regiment. 4 Foot soldier of a Hungarian regiment. 5 Infantryman, winter field uniform.

the field and Conrad von Hötzendorf believed he had won a significant victory. This belief was heightened by the fighting at Komarov, from 26 August–1 September, when General Moritz von Auffenberg, commanding the Austrian Fourth Army, almost surrounded his Russian opponent, General Plehve. Then disaster struck. The real Russian strength was further south, along the headwaters of the Dniestr River opposite the great Austrian fortress of Lemberg (Lvov) and on 26 August the advance guards drove into the Austrian lines there and quickly defeated the Austrian Third Army. Following up, the Russians quickly reached positions with three of their armies from which they could easily have enveloped almost the whole of Conrad von Hötzendorf's force in front of the Carpathians.

On 11 September, however, with disaster staring him in the face, Conrad von Hötzendorf was saved by the apparently incurable Russian fault of radioing uncoded messages. A stream of transmissions revealed to him that the Grand Duke Nicholas was planning to send troops on a wide outflanking march around his left, across the Vistula and down the valley of its tributary, the San, which would have cut him off from his escape routes into the Carpathians. He therefore ordered an immediate retreat, first to the San, 50 miles to his rear, and then to the next tributary of the Vistula, the Dunajec, 80 miles beyond that. Lemberg was abandoned, so too was the strong fortress of Przemysl, which guarded the railroad line to it at the San crossing.

Left: General Mikhail Alexeiev, Russian Chief of Staff in 1915.

Below left: Russian troops in a Galician trench.

Below: A Russian heavy gun position near Przemysl.

Above: Austrian infantrymen press forward at Lemberg (Lvov).

The Austrians now standing on the crest line of the Carpathians, which offered the last strong protection before the plains of Hungary were reached, had been forced to retreat 200 miles in two months of fighting, had lost 400,000 men, of whom 100,000 were prisoners, and had disastrously compromised the military reputation of their army.

The Germans felt that their prestige was affected by this reverse almost as much as Austria's. They were also deeply concerned by the threat which the Russians were now able to offer from the positions they had reached to vital German territory. General Nikolai Ivanov, commanding the Russian armies of the southern Front was indeed thinking of advancing into Silesia and simultaneously taking Krakow and perhaps even Budapest, capital of Hungary. Falkenhayn at OHL therefore decided that Hindenburg, now established as the strong man of the Eastern Front, must do something, quickly, to turn the tables. A new German Army, the Ninth, was formed and on 1 October began to move forward into the plains of central Poland, so outflanking the Russians who had driven the Austrians back to the Dunajec. It was now the Russians' turn to anticipate their enemy's movements. Realizing their danger,

Above: German cavalry advance during the Battle of the Masurian Lakes, February 1915.

Below: Russians prepare a counterattack at Lemberg (Lvov).

Ivanov's forces quickly disengaged and fell back, so rapidly that by 12 October the Germans had reached to within eight miles of Warsaw. The Russians did not retreat along their whole front. While Hindenburg was distracted by the thought of capturing the capital of The Grand Duchy and the Austrians by the satisfaction of retaking Przemysl, Ivanov regrouped and struck in between the Germans and Austrians to threaten Breslau. Hindenburg's nerve was gravely shaken by this offensive to which he could find no immediate answer. The Austrians again had to abandon Przemysl and had it not been for an interception of a Russian message announcing Ivanov's intention to pause, Hindenburg might have retreated inside the whole length of the German frontier. As it was in mid-November he scraped together enough troops to make a flank attack into the Russians near Lodz and so check the threat to Breslau. Having robbed the Eighth Army in East Prussia of troops for the Ninth, he could do nothing to help stem a new Russian advance which retook the Masurian Lakes region, nor to help the Austrians, who lost more ground in the Carpathians.

Help, indeed, now had to come from outside Hindenburg's resources and in December, a moment when Falkenhayn was hard pressed in the West, he found eight divisions to send eastward. They were sufficient to form a second new Army, the Tenth, with which after some preparation Hindenburg regained the ground lost in Masuria and even managed to carry the line from East Prussia into Poland. The fighting was called the 'Winter Battle in Masuria' and lasted from 7–21 February. Conditions were appalling; the attack began in a blinding snowstorm. They were even worse in the Carpathians where the Austrians, spurred on by the Germans who had contributed a small force called the *Sudarmee*, attacked on 23 January. At an elevation of 7–8000 feet, an offensive in mid-winter became what even the Austrian official historian called 'a cruel folly.'

'Mountains had to be scaled, . . . supply lines were either an ice rink or a marsh, depending on freeze or thaw; clouds hung low, and obscured the visibility of artillery targets; shells either bounced off ice or were smothered in mud; whole bivouacs would be found frozen to death in the morning. Rifles had to be held over fires before they could be used; yet even the thick mountain forests were of no great help for fuel, since there was no way of transporting logs out of those primeval forests.'

The Austrians nevertheless made some progress. After a siege of four months, Przemysl fell on 22 March, releasing eight Russian divisions which had been besieging it. This provided the commander of the Southwestern Front, Ivanov, and his chief of staff, Alexeiev, with enough extra strength to be able to recover the ground lost and threaten the Austrians with a renewed offensive across the Carpathians toward Budapest.

This great crisis required a radical solution. The Austrian army seemed threatened with dissolution. Already the Germans were talking of the alliance as being 'chained to a corpse.'

Above: Vladimir Sukhomlinov, who as Russia's Minister of War, administered the army until June 1915.

Austria had mobilized all her reserves in 1914 but had lost 2,000,000 men, many to frostbite and winter sickness by March 1915. Since she had the least efficient conscription system of all the powers, Russia included, she could not properly make good the losses. The young boys of 1915 had to be conscripted because the records of the conscription service were too badly organized to permit calling-up the older men who had been exempted from service before the war. The supply situation was worse. In the Skoda Works in Bohemia and the Steyr Works of Lower Austria, the government had the makings of a considerable war industry. The shell supply office of the War Ministry was perhaps the most inefficient department of that supremely inefficient agency, so managing to achieve even lower deliveries of munitions to the front than on the Russian side. While Germany was producing several million shells a month, Austria managed only 116,000 in December 1914 against a minimum requirement of 240,000. There were 45 different models of gun in the Austrian artillery, a situation which ensured that some models would not receive any shell at all. There was a serious shortage of the supply of other essentials. Hungary, the wheat bowl of the empire, used its political autonomy within the imperial system to supply its own needs first, with the result that workers in the great industrial centers of German Austria began to go short of the food they needed to sustain a high level of output, and even the men at the front were often hungry. The ever-present temptation to desert, in an army where the Slavs – Czechs, Serbs and Ruthenians – felt a stronger national pull toward their enemies than their rulers, began to manifest itself in actual desertion.

Left: **Germans rest in their East Prussian trench during the winter of 1914–15.**

Below left: A fanciful view of the Eastern Front.

Conrad von Hötzendorf, the Austrian Chief of Staff, quickly abandoned his pride in waging a purely national war against the Russians and by April 1915 was asking the Germans for help – while hinting at the threat of making a separate peace if it was not forthcoming. Falkenhayn had already come to the conclusion that Germany must stretch her resources that little bit further than seemed possible to save her ally and on 13 April asked the Kaiser's permission to send a force to the Carpathians for a counteroffensive. It was to consist of eight divisions, be known as the Eleventh Army and be commanded by the flamboyant cavalryman August von Mackensen, with the steely Hans von Seeckt as his Chief of Staff.

Owing to the inadequacy of railroad communications the German Eleventh Army and Austrian Fourth Army had to assemble by laborious marches along the poor roads. This meant that there was plenty of warning to the Russians that the offensive threatened. Nevertheless, the commander of the Russian Third Army which defended Mackensen's chosen front between Gorlice and Tarnow, just north of the Carpathian chain, refused to believe that he was in danger. This was disastrous, because his entrenchments were weak in the extreme; a single poor trench with a few strands of barbed wire in front of it. The German bombardment which began on 2 May 1915 tore it to pieces in four hours, and the infantry then advanced on a front of 30 miles. In the west, railroads would soon have brought reserves to seal off the danger point. In Russia the railroad had neither the capacity nor efficiency to do the job. The roads were so muddy that they prevented an easy withdrawal from the point of danger. The result was that the troops on either side of the break in were trapped in their positions and easily encircled by the attackers whose leading columns meanwhile quickly passed on through the breach. On 10 May Ivanov's Chief of Staff reported to the *Stavka*:

Above: **Field Marshal Paul von Hindenburg, victor of Tannenberg and military hero of Imperial Germany.**

Below: **French propaganda poster urges Slovaks to overthrow their Austrian masters and fight for the Allied cause.**

Below: **An Austrian army on the march in Galicia.**

'the strategic position is quite hopeless. Our line is very extended. We cannot shuttle troops around it with the required speed and the very weakness of our armies makes them less mobile; we are losing our capacity to fight.'

He suggested that Przemysl should be abandoned, together with the whole of Galicia (Austrian Poland), that Kiev should be fortified because the Germans would now invade the Ukraine and ended by declaring that Russia must 'renounce serious military activity until we have recovered.' He was at once dismissed but that did not stop a retreat to the River San by Third Army, which had lost 200 guns and 140,000 prisoners in six days.

Bad went to worse. The whole Russian Front in the west was now unhinged and a great backward movement began into White Russia in the north, the Ukraine in the south and toward the Pripyat in the center. By 13 May Przemysl had been surrendered. By 1 July Lodz, in central Poland, had been lost. On 5 August the Germans entered Warsaw. Later in the same month the great chain of Russian fortresses along the Polish rivers fell; Kovno, on the Niemen on 18 August, Novogeorgievisk, on the Vistula on 20 August, Brest-Litovsk, on the Bug on 26 August and Grodno, on the Upper Niemen on 4 September. By that date the Russians had lost at least 300,000 prisoners, some said a million. They had also begun to give up without a fight and, as prisoners, to refuse to run away even when given the chance. The army had also lost 3000 guns in the retreat, as many as it had had at the outbreak of the war.

Dissatisfaction with the High Command became so widespread and severe that the Czar, who resented any criticism of existing arrangements, could no longer ignore it and on 8 September he dismissed the Grand Duke Nicholas by announcing that he was to be appointed Viceroy of the Caucasus – where Russia's war with Turkey was having some success. The Czar alarmed even his intimates by announcing that he would in future command himself. However in practice he left strategy to Alexeiev, whom he brought in as Chief of Staff from the southwestern command. Alexeiev's main quality was a refusal to panic in a crisis, something needed all too often on Russia's Western Front. Contrarily he suffered from an inability to delegate, so that he gave himself chronic migraine by working 18 hours a day. Delegation, however, was difficult in a headquarters where the rest of the staff were, in the view of a visitor, 'either furniture or clerks,' a harsh verdict, even if true, on a group which contained seven generals and 30 colonels.

The change in command did not produce any immediate improvement at the front, even though by the end of 1915 Russia's war industry and bureaucracy had begun to remedy many of the weaknesses which had crippled her armies during the previous spring and summer. With 2,000,000 effective soldiers at the front in January 1916, Alexeiev was able to report to his French allies that they were all now equipped with rifles and the artillery, with 7000 guns, had reserves of 1000 shells per gun, reckoned sufficient for offensive activity even by Western Front standards. The fighting formations had been reorganized into three Fronts, the Northern

Above: Polish refugees and their meager belongings on the road east as the Germans pushed forward in 1915.

Above left: Kaiser Wilhelm II with General von Mackensen (on platform, right) in Campina, Rumania in September 1917.

Below: Russian POWs trudge into captivity during the German advance in Poland.

commanded by General A Kuropatkin, the Western commanded by Evert, and the Southern commanded by General Alexei Brusilov. On each the Russians now had a superiority over their German and Austrian enemies: 300,000 to 180,000, 700,000 to 360,000 and about 500,000 to rather less.

The Western Allies, particularly the French, took advantage of this increase in Russian strength to demand action which would relieve them from the pressure now being exerted by the Germans at Verdun. In March the Russians responded by mounting an attack on either side of Lake Narotch where their Northern and Western Fronts joined, but it was disastrous. Previous experience had revealed that a besetting weakness of Russian offensives was a failure to co-ordinate the effort of their infantry and artillery. The Russian gunners, who regarded themselves as an elite and their weapons as far more valuable than the lives of the infantry they were supposed to support, took no trouble to insure that their shells would disable the German defenders whom the Russians were supposed to overcome. They often fired blind off their maps at positions where they guessed the Germans ought to be, but were not, either because they had prudently evacuated their trenches or had never been there in the first place. The Germans at the end of a week's fighting, 14–21 March, removed 5000 Russian corpses from their wire. Total Russian losses were 100,000 compared with 20,000 German. It was all terribly reminiscent of the offensive at the southern end of the front against the Austrians the previous December:

> 'After artillery preparation we went about a mile forward under heavy enemy gunfire. Once we were within 500 yards, we were hit suddenly by devastating machine-gun and rifle fire that had hitherto been silent. There was the enemy in solid trenches with great parapets and dugouts sitting behind 10 or 15 coils of uncut wire, waiting for us. We lay on the frozen ground, for hours, as the snow drifted down. If we were wounded, there was no help because we were so close to the wire. But behind us there were artillery colonels and captains of the General Staff, drinking rum tea and writing their reports – "After brilliant artillery preparation, our glorious forces rushed forward to occupy the enemy trenches, but were held up by counterattack of strong reserves."'

Such strictures on uncaring commanders were altogether too true of much of the Russian army even in 1916. On the Southern Front things were changing. At the root of the changes was Brusilov, the new Front Commander. Formerly in charge of Eighth Army he had been successful in the Carpathian offensives of 1914–15 and he had important connections at court. However his success owed nothing either to patronage or reputation. Unlike almost any other Russian general of the period he had actually set himself to analyze the nature of the war he was fighting and to find answers to the difficulties which recurred whenever an initial success was gained. As he saw it, the problem in the East was that shortage of supply obviated the possibility of making an attack on a wide front, which was possible only in the more affluent West. Attacks on a narrow front always failed because the enemy could manage to move his reserves to the spot quicker than the attacker could pass his through the breach. The answer was therefore to attack on several narrow but widely separated fronts at the same time, thus confusing the enemy as to which was the main thrust, and trust to psychological factors to widen the gap. Such a strategic surprise required for success, however, radical tactical reorganization. Foreign observers had been startled to discover that on the Russian Front as much as three miles of ground separated the two sides, with still inhabited villages carrying on their business in no man's land. Supporting artillery, as a result, could not reach deep into the enemy's positions while infantry attacks were spotted and broken up long before they reached the enemy's barbed wire. Brusilov changed all that. Along his whole front the first trench was carried forward to within 75 yards of the Austrian trenches and communication trenches and deep dugouts were constructed to shelter the troops moving up to avoid waiting

for the attack. The artillery carefully registered the locations of the enemy's batteries and the concentration points of local reserves.

All promised well, therefore, for Alexeiev's offensive in midsummer. Had his intentions been followed, Evert's much stronger Western Front would have undertaken it. Evert, however, demanded more time for preparation. In the meantime Conrad von Hötzendorf launched his own offensive, the counterpart to the German's at Verdun, in the Trentino against the Italians, an enemy whom the polyglot peoples of the Dual Monarchy were united in detesting. Italy's appeals for relief had to be met, so Alexeiev gave Brusilov permission to attack independently, which he did on 4 June. There were almost no German divisions left opposite his front – only two in the so-called German *Sudarmee* – and in a few hours' bombardment the Austrians, their trenches in ruin, had been reduced to trembling helplessness. When the High Command of the two worst hit armies – Archduke Joseph Ferdinand's Fourth and Pflanzer-Baltin's Seventh – sent up their reserves, they were swept away in a rout and the whole front began to cave in, just as Brusilov had planned. The armies in between, Second and *Sudarmee*, were carried back by the retirement of the flanks and by 20 June all four had lost over 200,000 prisoners to the enemy.

Pflanzer-Baltin's worries were particularly

Above: **Artillerymen operate a Russian field gun during their defense of Poland in 1915.**

Below: **German transport crosses the Vistula in 1915. Germany conquered Russian Poland throughout that year and invaded Russia proper subsequently.**

Above: German cavalrymen enter Warsaw after its occupation in August 1915.

Top: General Brusilov became Commander in Chief of the Russian army in May 1917.

Top left: Austrian troops march into Russia watched by Russian POWs.

Left: Germans pause during their advance in Poland in 1915.

Above: German wounded prisoners are carried into captivity by Russian troops.

Below: Members of the 11th Bavarian infantry cross the Danube in 1915.

alarming because almost all his soldiers were Croats – the most *Kaisertreu* of all the Emperor's subjects – or warlike Hungarians, who were defending their own homeland in any case. Conrad von Hötzendorf appealed for help and the Germans, though scarcely in a position to help, were obliged to scrape together a relief force. It was assembled by 16 June around Kowel on the northern shoulder of the salient Brusilov had created and attacked at once though Falkenhayn did not know it. Brusilov's offensive had now run out of steam itself, after gaining up to 50 miles of territory in places so that General Alexander von Linsingen, the German commander, did not catch the Russians in disorganized movement but when they had already halted to consolidate. His counter-offensive went slowly.

What saved the situation was an intervention designed to complete the Central Powers' discomfiture, Rumania's declaration of war on 27 August. France and Russia had long been urging her to come in on their side but, surrounded as she was by Bulgarian, Austrian and Austrian-occupied territory her reluctance was understandable. Greedy for Hungarian lands inhabited by Rumanian speakers she was finally seduced by Brusilov's victory which implied an imminent Austrian collapse. Unfortunately her government and the Allies had miscalculated. Rumania's 23 divisions did not tip the balance in the East. They merely provided the Germans, who continued to display a conjuror's ability to produce reserves and move them rapidly wherever needed, with an easy target. Hindenburg and Ludendorff, who replaced Falkenhayn, disgraced by the failure of Verdun and the surprise of Brusilov's offensive, found no difficulty in assembling an army to

Left: **Russian soldiers in gas masks in 1915.**

Right: **There were no survivors in this action during the Brusilov Offensive.**

counter Rumania's invasion of Transylvania, the Rumanian-speaking province which she wanted. In fact they assembled four, the Austrian First, from the southern flank of the Russian Front, the new Ninth, under Falkenhayn in Transylvania, the Danube army under Mackensen, based in Bulgaria where most of its troops came from and a Turkish force which crossed the Black Sea to land at the mouth of the Danube. The Rumanian army which had taken some of Transylvania was thus encircled and quickly began to collapse, an outcome which surprised no Westerner, or Russian who had inspected it at close quarters. One provision of its mobilization orders was to forbid the use of cosmetics to officers under the rank of major. Between 25 September and 26 November the whole of Wallachia, Rumania's main southern province, fell into enemy hands. Bucharest, the capital, fell on 5 December and by 7 January the remnants of the Rumanian army to which the Russians had sent a relief force, had been forced back to the Sereth, a tributary of the Danube. Over half the country, and by far the most productive regions, had thus fallen under occupation and the Rumanians survived only as ancillaries to the Russians to whom they were of doubtful use.

Russia itself was now to undergo a national crisis, ultimately of far greater import to the Allied cause than Rumania's collapse. Despite Brusilov's military victory and the very remarkable adaptation to the demands of war in the domestic society and economy, Russia in early 1917 was a deeply troubled country. Although agricultural production had never before been higher, the inflation to which the government had resorted as a means of paying for the war had frightened the peasants into withholding the fruit of their labor. The factory workers of the towns had thus begun to go hungry and to their distress was added the dissatisfaction of the propertied classes on which war taxation principally fell, who also suffered because inflation eroded their fixed incomes.

On 12 March 1917 self-appointed representatives of 'workers' and 'soldiers' and some moderate and left-wing members of the Russian parliament (*Duma*) met in the Duma building in Petrograd and formed a council or Soviet. Together with the members of the Duma, it set up a Provisional Government, announcing that the Czar should be deposed. On 15 March the officers of the *Stavka*, convinced by the defection of the Petrograd regiments that the resolution was irreversible, conveyed to the Czar their belief that he must abdicate 'to save our country as well as the dynasty, and in order to have the war prosecuted to victory.'

Below: **Russian soldiers push forward during the Brusilov Offensive in the summer of 1916.**

Far left: **German soldiers lie dead during the Rumanian campaign of 1916.**

Left: **Rumanian troops on the march to Bitro in the Carpathians, 1916.**

Not a sound broke the oppressive silence. The doors and windows of the imperial train were tightly closed. 'Ah! if only this painful silence could be over,' recounted General Danilov, who acted as the *Stavka*'s spokesman:

'Suddenly with an abrupt movement the Emperor turned toward us and declared in a firm voice. "I have made up my mind. I have decided to abdicate in favor of my son Alexis," whereupon he crossed himself with an ample sign of the cross. We, too, crossed ourselves. "Thank you all," he went on, "thank you for your brave and faithful service. I trust it will be continued under the reign of my son."'

The Czar eventually abdicated in favor of his brother, Grand Duke Michael, rather than his son, but the change was of absolutely no significance because of the ineffectiveness of the Provisional Government which had demanded it. Its authority was daily challenged by the Petrograd Soviet which demanded a republic, and undermined by the unpopularity of the war, which Alexander Kerensky, the Minister of War who had become the leading man of the regime, was determined nevertheless to carry on. He appointed Brusilov Commander in Chief, with orders to repeat his success of the previous year by opening the offensive against the Austro-German front. It began on 1 July 1917, a dual blow by 31 divisions against General Felix von Bothmer's *Sudarmee* and five days later against the Austrians on the Dniestr by another 13. Although the Germans had been warned, the attack had considerable initial success. The Russian soldiers however would not resume the advance after it had been temporarily halted. When out of sight of their officers they began to drift away from the front and after the German counterattack of 19 July the drift became a flood. The Russian front line was quickly driven back to the positions occupied before the so-called Kerensky offensive, where the remaining troops subsided into listless and surly inactivity, accepting orders only from the Soviets which had been elected to represent their views to the Provisional Government:

Left: **Bulgarian trenches in 1917 as the war widened in the Balkans.**

Below: **Rumanian wounded take a bath in a field hospital.**

'The trenches are incredibly defiled,' an observer recorded, 'in the narrow communication trenches and those of the second line the air is thick and close. The parapet is crumbling away. No one troubles to repair it; no one feels inclined to do so and there are not enough men in the company. There is a large number of deserters; more than 50 have been allowed to go. Old soldiers have been demobilized, others have gone on leave with the arbitrary permission of the Soviet. Others again have been elected members of numerous committees, or gone away as delegates; a while ago, for example, the Division sent a numerous delegation to 'Comrade' Kerensky, to verify whether he had really given orders to advance. Finally, by threats and violence, the soldiers have so terrorized the regimental surgeons that the latter have been issuing medical certificates even to the "thoroughly fit."'

Despite the failure of 'his' offensive, Kerensky, who in July became head of the Provisional Government, was unwilling to make peace. The Germans, anxious to end their Eastern campaign so that they could transfer strength to the West for a decisive campaign in the coming spring, therefore decided on an offensive to break the Russian army for good. The spot chosen was Riga, on the Baltic coast, from where Major General Max Hoffman, the Chief of Staff on the Eastern Front, believed it might even be possible to reach Petrograd. He nominated the artilleryman Bruchmüller, who had organized the bombardment for the counterattack to Kerensky's offensive, to plan the blow. Its secret ingredient was the use of massed batteries of artillery which opened fire without having previously ranged their guns. Although the gunners thereby sacrificed some accuracy they preserved surprise, which was devastating. The infantry advancing after the five-hour bombardment found almost no Russians present. Nine thousand were taken prisoner; the rest had run away. This behavior spelled doom to the Provisional Government. It was now threatened from within by General Lavr Kornilov, the general who had served notice on the Czar. After Brusilov's failure in the Kerensky offensive, Kornilov had taken his place as Commander in Chief and in September marched on Petrograd with the intention of turning the Provisional Government out. The attempt failed because his troops refused to follow him but it provoked Kerensky into releasing the Bolshevik leaders from jail, as a means of breaking the rising. As a result the Petrograd garrison began to heed the words of the Petrograd Soviet in preference to those of the Provisional Government. Since May the Soviet had increasingly come under the influence of Bolshevik émigrés who had returned home on the news of the Czar's deposition. Leon Trotsky had come from America, Vladimir Illych Lenin from Switzerland at the instigation of the German government, which had provided him with the notorious 'sealed train' as a means of transport.

Above: **Alexander Kerensky, who led the Provisional government after the Czar's overthrow.**

The Germans had taken that decision because, though deeply hostile to Bolshevism they were prepared to compromise their political principles in the hope of strategic profit; the collapse of the Russian war effort from within. The result was by no means immediate, for Lenin's arrival in April was followed by months of intrigue before he was able to capture unshakeable control of the Petrograd Soviet. However when he did so, he struck decisively on 7 November (28 October Old Style). A Red Guard of workers, soldiers and sailors turned the Provisional Government out of its offices and on 8 November Lenin and his Council of People's Commissars proclaimed a Government of Workers and Peasants. Trotsky was installed as Commissar for Foreign Affairs, Josef Stalin, then a minor figure in the Bolshevik Party, as Commissar for the Nationalities.

Lenin and Trotsky proceeded, as the Germans had hoped, to open peace negotiations at once. Delegates from the two countries met at Brest-Litovsk, just behind the existing front line, and an armistice was arranged between Russia and the Central Powers to begin on 16 December. It proved difficult to move from the armistice to conclusive peace. The Russians, though threatened by imminent civil war at the hands of what were coming to be called the 'Whites' (in contradistinction to the Bolshevik 'Reds') were determined to ignore their own military helplessness and extract from the Germans an acceptance of the territorial status quo. Their terms were 'peace without annexation.' The Germans and Austrians, aware that it was not Allied policy to extract peace terms which would strip their two empires of their non-German speaking lands, signified their agreement, on the understanding that the Allies ratified the 'no annexation' clause and that the Russians excluded from it Poland and the Baltic States. Germany intended to set up an independent

Finland, Lithuania, Latvia, Estonia and a reconstituted Poland as client states of her own. Germany's hand was strengthened by the appearance at Brest-Litovsk of a self-appointed delegate from the Russian province of the Ukraine with a request that the Central Powers recognize his homeland's independence by concluding a separate peace with him.

Trotsky maneuvered with agility around the Germans' uncompromising insistence on their terms. As he had no cards to play, he was eventually compelled to withdraw from the negotiations, declaring his policy to be 'no peace no war.' However the Central Powers had meanwhile signed the so-called 'bread peace' with the Ukraine on 9 February, which gave them the right to station their troops on Ukrainian soil, and automatically transferred its produce from Russia to the hungry peoples of Germany and Austria. Defeated, Trotsky returned to Brest-Litovsk and on 3 March signed a treaty even harsher than that originally proposed, whereby Russia was obliged to cede the southern Caucasus region to Turkey. Meanwhile the Finns, under the redoubtable ex-Czarist General Carl von Mannerheim, had declared independence and a White army had put down a Red rising sympathetic to the Petrograd Soviet.

The stage was now set for the most tragic passage in Russia's 20th-century history. At least three White armies were preparing to open civil war against the Red Army – created by Trotsky – of the Workers' and Peasants' Government. With the Ukraine under German occupation, the Allies chose to regard the Bolsheviks as in the enemy's camp and so began to prepare expeditionary forces to intervene in Russia on the side of the Bolsheviks' enemies. This 'imperialist intervention' would lend substance to the Bolsheviks' claim that the Whites were antipatriotic as well as antirevolutionary and allow them to call successfully on all Russian nationalists to join them in the fight for independence. A surprising number of ex-Czarist soldiers – officers as well as men – proved ready to do so. They included Brusilov, who became Inspector General of Trotsky's cavalry, Klembovski, a Czarist Corps Commander in 1914, Karbyshev, chief engineer of the Southwestern Front in 1914, and Kirey, artillery commander of the Czar's Ninth Army.

In the prism of history the Russian Revolution now appears as by far the most important outcome of the First World War, its effects dwarfing even those of Germany's ultimate defeat and Austria's dismemberment. At the time, its importance was judged chiefly in terms of the setback it caused to the strategy of the Allies, confronting them as in 1917 with the dread prospect of a one-front war with their chief enemy the German Empire. What is forgotten in the West, and concealed in the East, is how stoutly the Russians had fought, and how near they had brought the Central Powers to disaster in both 1914 and 1916.

Top left: **The German and Austrian delegates at the Brest-Litovsk treaty signing, 3 March 1918.**

Top right: **Crowds scatter to the tattoo of sniper fire in Petrograd's Nevsky Prospekt during the first days of Russia's March Revolution in 1917.**

Above: **Germans fire at retreating Bolsheviks in early 1918.**

Retreating Italian troops during the Austrian offensive in Venetia, 1917.

8 1917: the Breaking of the Armies

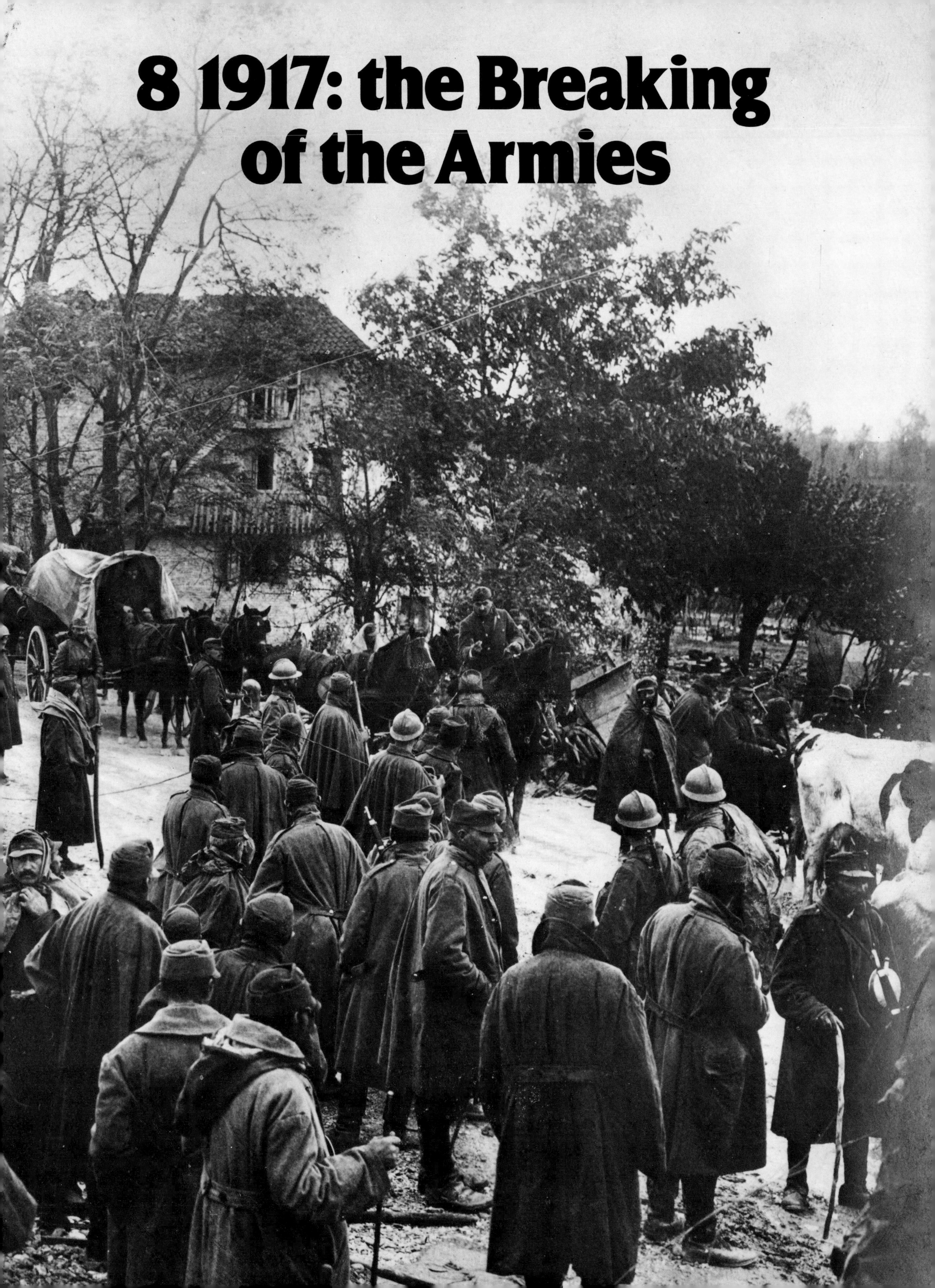

At the beginning of 1917 the Western Allies had reason to believe that the year would go well for them. Russia remained a powerful ally which was retaining most of the Austrian and a third of the German army on the Eastern Front. Italy occupied the rest of the Austrians on the Isonzo, had successfully weathered Conrad von Hötzendorf's offensive in Trentino and seemed set to wear her way gradually through the barrier of the Julian Alps into the plains of Slovenia. There was growing expectation that America would enter the war bringing to the Allies as plentiful a supply of men as she was already contributing of food and munitions. The French and British still felt that their armies were in good fighting shape. The British army was stronger than it had ever been, with nearly 60 divisions, 3,000,000 men, in the field, most of them in France. The French with 100 divisions had survived Verdun, won back much of the ground lost there and made good at least some of their losses with new young conscripts and older men 'combed out' of civilian employment and static military units. Their material power was also on the increase. While the blockade progressively starved Germany of the essential metals and minerals, as well as the food, which her war machine required, the French enjoyed a glut of world production of both raw materials and finished goods, including increasing quantities of shell from American as well as their own factories. There were new weapons to add to their armories, not just improved models of heavy guns and airplanes – during the summer and autumn of 1917 British and French pilots would establish command of the skies over the Western Front – but also the tank, tested experimentally on the Somme and now in mass production in both countries.

Above: **Poster for the French second War Loan invoking the Verdun slogan ,** ***On les aura*** **(we will have them!).**

Left: **French soldiers prepare another advance over the bodies of their fallen comrades.**

Right: **General Nivelle, whose long awaited offensive threatened to destroy the remaining morale of the French Army.**

So confident were both High Commands of their growing strength that they had planned for 1917 yet another great joint offensive. As in 1915 Joffre had called a conference at GQG at Chantilly in November 1916 to co-ordinate arrangements. Russian, Italian, Serbian, Belgian and Portuguese – whose country had declared war on Germany in March 1916 – had been present as well as British and French representatives. There was agreement to maintain pressure on all fronts, including those of the 'outer theaters' in Mesopotamia, Palestine and Macedonia. In France there was to be a renewal of the offensive on the Somme, excluding only that part of the front worst devastated by the fighting of the previous summer. Later, an offensive in Flanders would 'clear the Belgian coast,' thus unhinging the German line in the West and capturing the U-Boat bases of the North Sea. There was no thought of seeking peace on the strength of the achievements of 1916. Indeed, a peace initiative on the part of the new Emperor of Austria-Hungary, Karl I, who had succeeded the venerable Franz Josef in November 1916, met no response from the French government and a similar proposal by the Marquess of Lansdowne, a former Conservative Foreign Minister, which he circulated to the British Cabinet, was also ignored. The Pope's appeals went unheeded and, more significantly, so did those of President Woodrow Wilson of the United States who on 22 January 1917 appealed for all combatants to accept 'peace without victory.' The rejection of these appeals by the British and French is explained in part by the conditions for which they knew the Germans were still holding out; the cession of the Belgian Congo to Germany; surrender of the Briey-Longwy iron-ore area by France; establishment of German influence in Belgium or, in default, the surrender of Liège; 'improvement' of Austria's frontier with Italy, Rumania, Serbia or Montenegro – the rump of the latter was to be given to Albania; cession of some Serbian territory to Bulgaria and the further limitation of non-Turkish vessels' rights to use the Dardanelles. The seriousness of the German position was emphasized to the Allies by what they knew of the growing influence of Hindenburg and Ludendorff over the German government. As popular dissatisfaction with the hardships caused by the war grew and middle class resentment of socialist defeatism was reinforced by the war inflation's erosion of fixed incomes, the German establishment was demanding not a more conciliatory but a more extreme, triumphalist policy, since it now grasped that only through total victory could it recover all that it had lost through the war.

Joffre therefore pressed forward with his

Above: Some of the first British tanks in action near Amiens, 1917.

Below: A British tank obliterated near Cambrai.

Above: **Britain's new Prime Minister David Lloyd George visits the Western Front.**

Left: **German sharpshooter in the front line in 1917.**

plans in the confidence that he was doing the right thing for the alliance, but suddenly his own position of leadership was shaken. The military dictatorship toward which Hindenburg and Ludendorff were moving in Germany had long applied in France, at least within the war zone and the war committees of government. Foolishly, Joffre had sustained the emergency exclusion of members of parliament from the 'zone of the armies' and strictly curtailed the freedom of the press. On 13 December the Prime Minister, Aristide Briand, yielded to parliamentary protests so far as to promote Joffre to the meaningless post of 'technical military adviser' to the government, with a young general, Nivelle, as his executive representative at the front. That failed to quell dissatisfaction and he was compelled to secure Joffre's resignation on 26 December. Foch, his longtime protégé, a ferociously effective fire-eater but a man with many enemies, was simultaneously removed from command of Northern Army Group (though he was soon restored as commander of Eastern Army Group).

Nivelle's was a surprise appointment. A comparatively junior general, he had made his name under Pétain at Verdun, where he had planned the artillery tactics which had first matched and then overwhelmed the German gunnery offensive. As a tactician his star was in the ascendant. As a personality, he was favored by the politicians because his manner was open and explanatory in striking contrast to the sphinxian silence of Joffre. He enjoyed the timely advantage of speaking perfect English, the language of his mother. Moreover, once appointed he began to promise results. Joffre's caution had not allowed him to suggest that 1917 would be anything more than a year of attrition. Nivelle spoke of victory:

'Only the destruction of the principal mass of the enemy's forces,'

Left: **British Signal Service operators with gas masks at a forward position in the front line.**

Above: **Austrian troops prepare to throw hand grenades in September 1917.**

he explained to Lloyd George, who was pressing for an attack in Italy,

'can bring about the end of the war. The principal mass of the German forces is on the Western Front. . . . It comprises 130 out of 200 divisions, and includes the best troops. To beat them, it is necessary in the first place to break through the trench system. Is this operation possible? To this question the army of Verdun, in the fighting between 24 October and 15 December (1916) has given an affirmative answer.' (These were the successful local offensives which had recaptured Forts Vaux and Douaumont, so making Nivelle's reputation.) 'We will break through the German front when we wish, on condition that we do not attack it at its strongest point, and that the operation is carried out by a sudden surprise attack and is not extended beyond 24 or 48 hours.'

In private conversation, Nivelle expanded on this optimistic promise. 'I have the secret,' he exulted. After three years of war and a dozen attempts on the inviolability of the German trench system by French and British armies, he believed that he had found a formula which had hitherto escaped the questing minds of all the commanders and staff officers in the two great Allied Headquarters, as well as those of the German army which had also 'found the secret' before Verdun. In essence, his plan was to assemble an enormous mass of artillery in secrecy and open fire without warning along the whole chosen front of attack, and deep into the enemy positions behind. The intended effect was to destroy all opposing German batteries and paralyze the enemy's means of communication and reinforcement. At the same time deep masses of infantry would move forward, following a rolling barrage at a distance of only 70 meters from the curtain of exploding shells. When they had occupied the enemy trenches, a solid block of reserves would pass onward, to be followed by the cavalry which would exploit the breakthrough by debouching into open country.

Skeptics might argue that the formula looked little different from that attempted by Haig on the Somme in July 1916. Pessimists might mutter that he had selected the least promising sector of the front for his attack, since it was to be on the Chemin des Dames, the ridge where the first Allied counteroffensive of the war had miscarried in September 1914. Nivelle's optimism was unshaken – even in the face of the most remarkable event yet to occur on the Western Front; a secret German withdrawal from the center of the great salient which he planned to pinch out. Part of Nivelle's scheme was for the British to attack a week earlier at Arras, north of the Somme, so as to draw off the German reserves from the Chemin des Dames. On 16 March, however, it was noticed that the enemy's normal artillery fire was dwindling along the whole of the Somme Front and when reconnaissance was made the German lines were found to be weakly held. Bad weather and indecision inhibited any vigorous probing and 29 German divisions were thus allowed to steal back 30 miles to a new but enormously strong position, later to be called by the Allies the Hindenburg Line, which the Germans had surreptitiously constructed between Arras and the Chemin des Dames.

The British offensive, which opened on 9 April in a raging snowstorm could not therefore strike into the northern flank of the Germans' Somme salient, since it had disappeared, nor could it draw off the whole of the German reserve, since the shortening of their line had increased its size. The British chose to regard the battle of Arras as a success – which it was in terms of ground won on the battlefield – but strategically it was of no significance, and therefore a positive setback to Nivelle's plan. Moreover, he had talked. The eloquence of his

Below: **David Lloyd George is greeted by General Haig and Marshal Joffre in September 1916.**

Below: **Aristide Briand served as a War Minister and Prime Minister of France during World War I.**

exposition, which had so impressed Lloyd George, was not a talent he kept for private performances. Anxious to change the command arrangements on the Western Front so that the British Expeditionary Force should become a tool of a single unified command, he had used his charm, and his ideas, on dinner-party audiences all over London in January. Word had inevitably filtered to the Germans of a coming offensive on the French Front and aerial reconnaissance had then pinpointed the spot for them. Toward it they had moved the divisions released by their withdrawal to the Hindenburg Line, so that whereas in January there had been only 18 divisions along the Chemin des Dames, by April there were 42 with 2451 guns, to oppose 46 French divisions with 3810.

Yet, just as Nivelle's optimism remained intact, so did that of this attacking army. Corporal Georges Gandy of the 57th Infantry Regiment describes the mood in the last days of preparation:

'The air was filled with enthusiasm and a heroic mood prevailed in each of us. Officers and soldiers refused to go on leave so as not to miss the great offensive. "Boy, what an attack," the *poilus* (front-line soldiers) were saying to each other, "eighty divisions to go over the top. We've never been that many! This is it, pals! If we don't get them this time, we'll never get them."'

When the French infantry did jump off to 'get them' on 16 April, however, they found that Nivelle's promise of possessing 'a secret' meant no more than any of the other empty words of generals in the three hard years which had gone before. Observing from a distance a French officer of the new tank arm saw:

'Our men's wave, unbroken a moment ago, spread out again and then progressing in zigzag fashion. Here and there the men would crowd together without advancing, having met some obstacle which we couldn't see, most likely one of those accursed, still intact barbed-wire networks.'

Soon afterward the first wounded began to make their way back and their hasty explanations gave the observer a clue as to what was happening:

'A helmetless lieutenant, his clothes torn and a wound in his chest, walked slowly toward our group. "If only you had been with us. We found nothing but barbed wire. If it hadn't been for that, we'd have been far ahead by now, instead of being killed where we stand." "We just couldn't keep moving," shouted an alert corporal, who was using his rifle as a crutch. "Too many blasted machine guns, which we couldn't do anything against."'

In fact 16 April was a disaster comparable to the first day of the Battle of the Somme. The hospital services were overwhelmed even as far away as Paris where the trains took the wounded, and members of parliament, able for the first time to witness the effects of a battle at close quarters, were appalled. Nivelle nevertheless gave orders that the attack was to be renewed the next day, and the subsidiary offensive in Champagne ('The Third Battle of Champagne') maintained. By 20 April the Aisne valley had been regained and 20,000 prisoners taken. Nivelle, cheated of his breakthrough, was outwardly more certain than ever of victory and decided to use his reserves for a final big push on 25 April. Subordinate commanders pleaded for only a modest maintenance of pressure, but he was adamant. The government was now alarmed and insisted Nivelle wait until 5 May, meanwhile appointing Pétain Chief of Staff, a post vacant since Joffre had been made Commander in Chief at the outbreak of the war. On the appointed day, heavy artillery fire preceded the assault. A Sergeant of the 128th Regiment describes what followed:

'In the early morning of 6 May, at the appointed hour, our men were full of dash when they launched their assault. They practically reached their objective, at least in the gap where our artillery had opened a gap in the enemy's defense zone. This was very little, as no

Above: A French attack on German positions near the Aisne, 16 April 1917.

Above right: 5th Australian Infantry Brigade parades through the Grande Place of Bapaume in March 1917 in utter disregard of the ruins around them.

Below: German storm troops train near Sedan in 1917.

Top far left: Camouflaged British armored car and gun near Arras in 1917.

Center far left: The battlefield at Mont des Sapins near the Aisne in April 1917.

Bottom far left: Aerial view of Mont Cornillet, Champagne, in May 1917.

Left: Tommies carry a wounded buddy back to their lines.

Top: French advance first wave hits the Chemin des Dames as the Germans retreat in the background.

Above: Marshal Philippe Pétain, the inspiration of French *poilus* during and after Verdun.

Above: **General Sir Herbert CO Plumer, later Lord Plumer, British commander at the Third Battle of Ypres.**

less than 16 gaps had been expected but the observations made by the Colonel and the battalion commanders had not been taken into account by the higher staff. The 2nd Battalion ran into an intact barbed-wire network and into the fire of the German machine guns, which our artillery had not been able to neutralize. The regiment was relieved on 15 May and the position it had conquered was lost. Our men were deeply disappointed. They realized that their sacrifices were useless, perhaps even needless.'

The government decided to relieve Nivelle and replace him with Pétain on 15 May. His was a name the troops trusted and the French Government hoped that he, as a man known to value the lives of his soldiers, would be able to restore the shaken morale of the divisions which had taken part in what had come to be called the 'Nivelle offensive.' Its effects had spread even wider, deeper and faster than had been feared. During the month of April the French army had lost 100,000 men by official record; unofficially the figure was put at 200,000. In the five armies which had taken part in the attack, there began an outbreak of what the High Command called 'acts of collective indiscipline' which have since been generally recognized as mutinies. The 'indiscipline' took the form of infantry units refusing to go up to the front; demonstrations against the war, particularly by men returning from leave; the flying of red flags; throwing stones at transport and rear-area troops; minor sabotage of the railroad and occasional attacks on officers, usually ones already unpopular. The disorders affected 54 divisions altogether, over half the French army, and were eventually quelled by a mixture of bribes and threats. About 55 men identified as ringleaders were shot and 300 men were sent to Devil's Island. Another 20,000 were court-martialled but their sentences were commuted. At the same time, more generous leave was promised, family allowances to soldiers' wives increased and canteens and recreation facilities in the zone of the armies improved. Loyal men held the line while the work of rehabilitation went on and the artillery, which was not affected by the mutinies, continued to keep up its program of fire into the German lines. Pétain travelled ceaselessly about the front, assuring the soldiers that he had their welfare at heart, and gradually the army was weaned from its resentment and inactivity, which in retrospect is perhaps best thought of as a large-scale military strike rather than a mutiny. Curiously, no word of it reached the Germans until it was over. Though the mutineers had, in fact, always assured their officers that they would defend their trenches if forced to do so. What they refused to do was attack.

The onus of the effort on the Western Front Army during the troubled summer of 1917 therefore fell upon the British Army. Still strong despite the losses of the Somme, and in good

Above right: **Two men of the Scots Guards in the mud of Ypres (Passchendaele).**

Top far right: **An expression of public doubt during the Third Battle of Ypres.**

Below: **Mine crater at Messines Ridge, June 1917.**

Above: **German infantrymen return from battle. German morale remained high as French and British morale declined after three years of attritional war.**

spirits even though it was now depending upon conscripts instead of volunteers to fill the gaps in its ranks, the BEF was ready for another offensive as soon as Arras was over. Haig, a strategic free agent as long as Pétain was occupied with the mutinies, had his own firm ideas about where that offensive should take place. He had made his name in Flanders, at the First Battle of Ypres in 1914; when all seemed hopeless he had strapped on his sword, mounted his horse and ridden out up the Menin Road to die among his troops. The line had held and his death had not proved necessary, but the epic moment had fixed in him an obsession with Ypres. It was a purely British battlefield, at the furthest point of the line from the French sector. Any success won there would redound solely to the credit of his army. To a fierce patriot like Haig, that prospect was extremely enticing; it

Left: **German bodies in a Passchendaele trench, July 1917.**

Right: **German POWs are paraded through a Belgian town by their Canadian captors.**

Below: **A horse-drawn water cart breaks down in the mud of Ypres, August 1917.**

was made all the more so by the narrow escape he had recently had from subordination to Nivelle.

Between 4 May and 2 June, therefore, he secured the agreement both of the French High Command – who urged him to take all the pressure he could off its front – and his own government, though the latter was now becoming very suspicious of his costly schemes, to mount an attack 'to clear the Belgian coast.' As a preliminary his Second Army, commanded by Sir Herbert Plumer, undertook to widen the Ypres salient by the capture of the Messines Ridge. This attack, which opened on 7 June had, like all Plumer's operations, been meticulously planned. Two thousand guns covered the advance of nine divisions, which was preceded by the explosion of 19 enormous mines (one failed to explode and the fusing mechanism was lost; activated by a bolt of lightning in 1956, it left a crater as large as a small field). The German defenders were either blown out of existence, stunned by the bombardment, or easily taken prisoner. Limited though it was in scale, Messines was the first wholly successful British battle of the war so far.

It augured well for the coming third battle of Ypres (Passchendaele, as it came to be called).

Haig now decided to transfer planning responsibility from Plumer to his own protégé, Hubert Gough, a cavalry general of 47 who had won notoriety before the war for his part in the so-called 'Curragh Mutiny.' Haig's apologists were later to argue that Passchendaele required a boldness which the painstaking Plumer could not manage. Boldness may well have been in Haig's mind but what the particular circumstances of the Ypres Salient required was exactly that step-by-step method which Plumer had made peculiarly his own. For here the terrain favored the defender very strongly. Beyond the little walled-fortress city the open plain rose in a series of shallow swells toward the distant Passchendaele ridge from which the Germans could observe every movement in the British positions. The ground, moreover, was waterlogged, a potential marshland which a combination of rain and heavy shelling would

Far left: **Italian propaganda poster of 1917.**

Left: **Italian magazine of 1916 depicts an idealized version of their mountain troops' struggle against the Austrians.**

Right: **Anti-Communist Italian propaganda in 1918.**

Below: **Stretcher bearers bring back a wounded comrade near Boesinghe, Ypres, August 1917.**

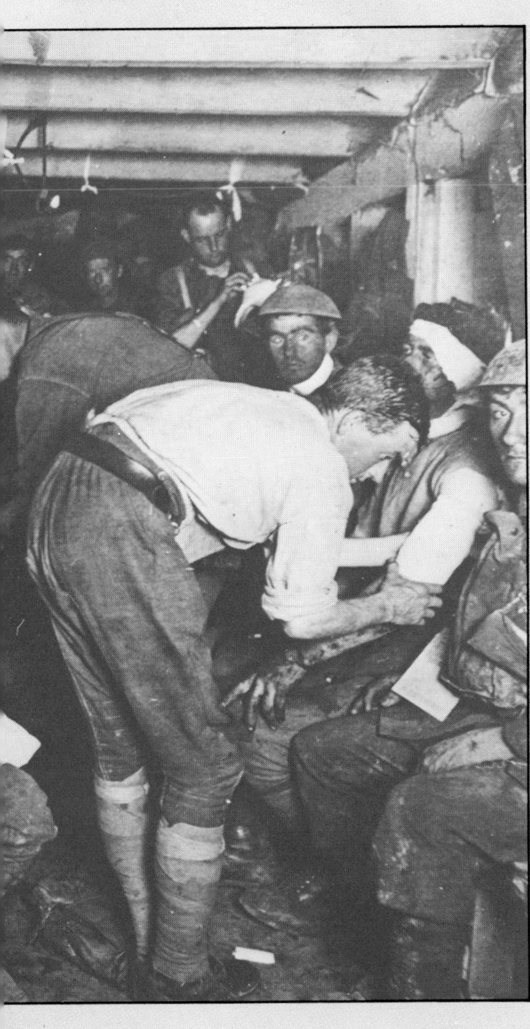

quickly turn into a quagmire. Heavy shelling was a necessity, because the Germans had fortified this part of the front in great depth, studding their trench lines with concrete pillboxes, many of which had been built inside derelict cottages and farm buildings so that their construction was concealed from British observation.

The battle began on 31 July after a week's bombardment and as it opened so too did unseasonably heavy rain. It continued until 4 August, by which time two miles of ground had been won and 32,000 casualties suffered. Gough, declaring this to be the 'first stage' of the battle, then announced a pause. The attack was renewed on 6 August and persisted for two days, but only a sliver of ground was captured. The German commander opposite professed himself unworried by the offensive, since he had ample reserves, the best of which were now held back and committed only when a British thrust had pushed in deep enough to lose the support of its own artillery.

Doubt in the wisdom of Haig's battle had now spread from the Cabinet to his own officers. Brigadier Baker-Carr, visiting General Headquarters at Montreuil from the front, expressed his disquiet with 'candor and vigorous language' over lunch, announcing that 'the battle was dead as mutton' and had been so since the second day. After lunch he was summoned to the office of General Davidson, the Director of Operations:

'On entering, I found him seated at his table, his head in his hands.

"I am very much upset by what you said at lunch. . . . A man of your knowledge and experience had no right to speak as you did."

"You asked me how things were and I told you frankly."

"But what you say is impossible."

"It isn't. Nobody has any idea of the conditions."

"But they can't be as bad as you make out."

"Have you been there yourself?"

"No."

"Has anybody in Operations been there?"

"No."

"Well then, if you don't believe me, it would be as well to send somebody up to find out."'

Baker-Carr's description had been of a battlefield reduced to a series of interconnecting ponds, water-filled shell holes, on which all roads and tracks had disappeared and men were sometimes drowned in liquid mud. Even Haig was now shaken by the lack of progress and mounting toll of lives and turned to Plumer again for a solution. That steady old soldier, asked to clear the right-hand side of the salient into which the British were attacking, demanded time so that he could make proper preparations. He was favored by a spell of sunshine and drying winds so that when his meticulous attack began on 25 September all went well for some days. A succession of short advances, each like the Messines success of June, carried the British to the crest of the ridge from which the Germans had hitherto overlooked Ypres. Haig was encouraged and ordered a similar advance on the left-hand side of the salient, to begin on 9 October. The rains of autumn, which could not be explained away as seasonal bad luck, now set in uninterruptedly and turned the last month of the battle into a soldiers' hell.

An Australian officer on 10 October found the slope below Poelcapelle:

Above far left: **Men of the 13th Durham Light Infantry on the Menin Road Ridge before their attack on 20 September 1917 near Veldhoek.**

Above left: **Wounded at an advanced dressing station near Ypres.**

Below: **British troops pull an 18-pounder out of the mud near Langemarck, 16 October 1917.**

Above: Germans cut down trees to block an Allied advance near Havrincourt, 20 November 1917.

Top: Austrian troops advance during the Trentino offensive of 1916.

Below: Canadians bring in their wounded at Passchendaele, 6 October 1917.

Above left: 'Clapham Junction,' looking toward Sanctuary Wood at Passchendaele, 23 September 1917.

Top right: A 5.9-inch naval gun is captured at Cambrai, 29 November 1917.

Above right: German prisoner is captured at Havrincourt near Cambrai, November 1917.

Above: **Leicester Regimental machine gunners in a captured second-line trench at Cambrai, 20 November 1917.**

Above: **The Kaiser and Prince Rupprecht inspect a heavy British gun captured at Cambrai.**

Above right: **Men of the 51st British Division cross a German communications trench near Cambrai in November 1917.**

Right: **British tanks pass captured German guns on the way to Bourlon Wood, Cambrai, in November 1917.**

'littered with dead, both theirs and ours. . . . I found about 50 men alive, of the Manchesters. Never have I seen men so broken or demoralized. They were huddled up behind a pillbox in the last stages of exhaustion and fear. The Germans had been sniping them off all day and had accounted for 57 – the dead and dying lay in piles. The wounded were numerous – unattended and weak, they groaned and moaned all over the place. Some had been there four days already. Finally the company came up – the men done in after a fearful struggle through the mud and shell-holes, not to speak of the barrage. The position was obscure – a dark night – no line – demoralized Tommies – and no sign of the enemy. I spent the rest of the night in a shell hole, up to my knees in mud and with the rain teeming down.'

Despite these awful scenes, Haig – and whatever his faults of stubbornness and monomania, he did go and look for himself – refused to call off the offensive until the beginning of November, justifying his persistence by the stated need to hold the best line possible for the coming months of winter. When on 10 November 'Passchendaele' was officially closed down it had cost 240,000 British casualties. At its deepest point, the advance had been pushed six miles into enemy territory on a front of 10 miles. Ypres was still in a salient, if a slightly larger one. The Belgian coast remained uncleared. The German line had not been unhinged. Haig was convinced that he had done the right thing.

He was aware that his supporters in the Cabinet had dwindled in number and that Lloyd George was anxious to be rid of him. This sense of insecurity had prompted him earlier in the autumn to take up the proposals of the new Tank Corps for a tank offensive on a part of the front as yet untouched by heavy fighting. It had been carefully prepared during the last bitter stages of Passchendaele and was ready by 20 November. The place chosen was the ground in front of Cambrai, between Ypres and the Somme, high chalk downland, dry and unpitted by shell fire. Four hundred and seventy-six tanks had been assembled and, after a brief dawn bombardment, they lumbered off into the German positions, the infantry of eight divisions following cautiously behind, with five cavalry divisions – 25,000 horsemen – waiting in the rear for the chance to ride deep into enemy territory.

The Germans whom the massed tanks found in their trenches were, almost without exception, terrorized into instant surrender by the appearance of the monsters. The Hindenburg Line was breached for little loss of life and at the end of the day the front had been advanced three miles. Yet a clear breakthrough had once again eluded the British army. The fault for that lay with the commander of the division attacking in the center of the front, the 51st Highland. Mistrusting the tanks, he had ordered his infantry to keep their distance. As a result, the tanks going forward unsupported had been destroyed by gunfire. When the infantry, who might have driven off the gun crews, came up they were shot down by machine gunners, who would have been silenced by the tanks had they still been in action.

A week after the initial success, the Germans counterattacked, reclaimed most of the ground lost and even captured an unwary British general asleep in his pajamas in his command dugout. Haig did his best to minimize the extent of the humiliation but it gave Lloyd George the excuse for which he had been looking to forbid him any more fresh troops who would, in the Prime Minister's view, only be wasted in pointless or ill-organized attacks. Further force was given to his determination by a sudden and chilling turn of events in Italy whose government had been forced by it to make urgent appeals for men and guns to the French and British.

Italy's war thus far had been an even more depressing essay in fruitless attrition than the Western Allies'. She had declared hostilities against Austria in May 1915 with the declared aim of winning from the Dual Monarchy those pieces of Italian-speaking territory which she claimed as *Italia irridenta* – unredeemed Italy. In particular she wanted the Trentino in the north, and Trieste in the east, toward which her main offensive effort was made throughout 1915 and 1916. Unfortunately, Trieste lay across the high barrier of the Julian Alps and the Italian armies had spent two years attempting to win footholds in the mountains on the far side of the Isonzo River which crossed its foothills. No less than 11 Battles of the Isonzo had been launched. Very little ground had been won if any, but enormous losses had been suffered; over 600,000 casualties. Despite that the size of the Italian army had been built up to 60 divisions, many men returning from the United States to volunteer for the patriotic war, and in the Eleventh Battle, fought between 18 August and 12 September 1917, the Italians had caused a serious breach in the Austrian line which threatened a breakthrough. General Count Luigi Cadorna, the Italian commander, at once laid plans for a new effort, word of which so alarmed Conrad von Hötzendorf and his chief Staff Officer, General Arthur Arz von Straussenburg, that they appealed to the Germans for help.

During late September and early October, Hindenburg and Ludendorff found six divisions to send to the Italian front, of which four were mountain-trained. They included the Alpenkorps, a division of Bavarian ski troops to which was attached the Württemberg Mountain Battalion. Already notable among its officers was a company commander, the young Erwin Rommel. The coming battle was to offer him the fullest opportunity to demonstrate his dash and fire in attack. Early in the morning of 24 October the German and Australian artillery opened fire on the Italian lines, using shells filled with a gas against which the Italian gas masks gave no protection. When the Fourteenth Army, the Austro-German attack force, moved into the Italian trenches it found them largely deserted. The defenders had fled before the deadly cloud. Particularly important were the footholds obtained by the attackers at Caporetto and

LA DOMENICA DEL CORRIERE

Si pubblica a Milano ogni Domenica

Supplemento illustrato del "Corriere della Sera"

MILANO

Per tutti gli articoli e illustrazioni è riservata la proprietà letteraria e artistica, secondo le leggi e i trattati internazionali.

Anno XVIII. Num. 7. 13 - 20 Febbraio 1916. Centesimi 10 il numero.

La guerra fuori delle trincee: un attacco di sorpresa, dei nostri alpini, a circa tremila metri.

Above: Italian Alpine troops depicted in a Sunday magazine.

Above: General Pietro Badoglio, who made his reputation in both world wars.

Tolmino (Karfreit and Tolmein), because there the Isonzo crossed the front, to run in a loop behind the Italian lines. Advances down its valley from either place thus acted as pincer movements around a huge chunk of the Italian garrison, and would cause their capture. Rommel was quick to see the possibilities. When his regimental commander looked like showing too much caution, Rommel simply took his leave and departed into the mountains, carrying with him his 250 Swabian mountaineers.

In the next 36 hours Rommel and his men captured 9000 Italian prisoners, including a whole regiment of 1500 which he trapped between the fire of his machine guns in a narrow valley. So outstanding were his exploits that he won the *Pour le mérite*, the order founded by Frederick the Great to honor the greatest acts of courage and leadership. The success at Caporetto, as the battle would be called, exceeded individual deeds of derring-do. The Italian reserves, marching up the roads to the fractured front, began quickly to be outflanked by enemy mountain troops who were moving behind them along the mountain ridges. Reserve positions quickly became the front line and then had to be abandoned because they had been taken by the enemy. On 25 October the situation was already so desperate that Cadorna had to order a retreat to the Tagliamento river, well inside Italian territory, and toward it the Second Army (one of the three on the Isonzo) which had taken the brunt of the Caporetto Strike, began to make its way. In truth no authority could have stopped it. Of its men, 180,000 had already been taken prisoner; the remaining 400,000 were a crowd of stragglers and fugitives. No sooner had they reached the Tagliamento than the speed of the enemy pursuit convinced Cadorna that they could not stop there. So he gave orders to fall back again to the Piave, which runs into the sea only 15 miles North of Venice. The Italian army had retreated, when it was reached on 10 November, over 60 miles in two weeks and abandoned not only all the territory it had gained in three years of war but a great swathe of the homeland to Austrian occupation.

The personal consequences of the disaster were swift. Cadorna, never a popular general as he was considered to be indifferent to casualties, was dismissed and replaced by General Armando Diaz. In Britain and France which had by mid-November dispatched 11 divisions to help shore up the Piave front, the politicians' patience with their generals, whom they felt should have taken steps to aid the Italians earlier but had selfishly ignored the danger, was growing very thin. Lloyd George would dearly liked to have sent Haig Cadorna's way. However, unable to find a satisfactory substitute, he agreed with the French Prime Minister a plan to set up a Supreme War Council, to which the generals would be subordinate, which would have the power to survey and provide for the strategic needs of all the fronts as a unity.

The French Prime Minister with whom Lloyd

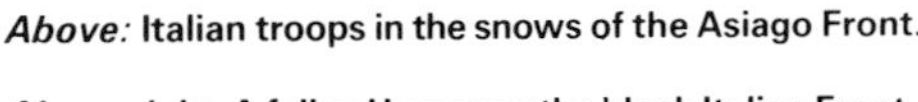

Above: Italian troops in the snows of the Asiago Front.

Above right: A fallen Hussar on the bleak Italian Front.

Right: A fanciful depiction of the skill of Italian Alpine troops.

George dealt was new: Georges Clemenceau, the 'Tiger.' Though new, he was not young, indeed at 78 he was one of the oldest members of the French parliament. His spirit was that of an impatient hothead, and his character was very much to Lloyd George's taste:

Below: Italian General Luigi Cadorna, who was quickly dismissed after the Caporetto disaster.

Below left: Victims of the Central Powers' breakthrough at Caporetto.

Far left: Italian Bersaglieri officers present a dashing appearance.

Left: An Austrian 30.5cm artillery piece in Zompicchia in November 1917.

Right: Austrian storm troopers break out of their foxholes for an assault.

Below: Italian Marines go over the top in 1917.

Right: General Cadorna was replaced by General Diaz as Chief of Staff of the Italian forces.

Above: **Clemenceau visits the front line.**

Left: **Hoisting a '75 gun up an Italian peak.**

'He had insulted every prominent politician in France and conciliated none. He had no party or group attached to him. I once said of him that he loved France but hated all Frenchmen. That is a substantially fair account of his personal attitude throughout his career.'

By the end of 1917 there was no French politician who commanded wide respect in parliament. Clemenceau's offensiveness was therefore irrelevant. His fighting temper very much was not. Raymond Poincaré, the President, had decided that the choice of leader lay between Clemenceau and Joseph Caillaux, who was a notorious defeatist and would probably organize a peace party out of like-minded deputies. Therefore, though he cordially disliked the 'Tiger' (he had suffered his insults), he decided to entrust him with the government, a decision he communicated on 15 November.

Five days later the old man stood before the chamber of deputies and delivered a battle cry of a speech which quashed all German hopes of bringing France to a negotiated peace:

'We stand here before you,' he declaimed, 'with but one thought; to pursue the war relentlessly. No more pacifist campaigns, no treachery, no semi-treachery. Only now, nothing but war. Our armies are not going to be caught between two fires. Justice shall be established. The country shall know that it is being defended.'

Left: **Italian Alpine soldiers in position atop a rocky crag near the Austrian frontier.**

His arrival transformed the atmosphere of French politics and also its personnel. Caillaux was imprisoned for treason in January 1918, and Jean Malvy, the Minister of the Interior, was sentenced to five years in exile. Bolo, a political intriguer believed to be in German pay, was guillotined for treason in April 1918 and scores of other lesser agents of defeatism or espionage were also executed or imprisoned. Most exotic if probably least significant of the victims of the purge was Mata Hari, the dancer and courtesan, who was shot in the moat of the Château of Vincennes. She made a dramatic impression by refusing to be blindfolded and blowing a kiss to her lawyer from the execution stake.

The French army, rested during the summer months, had been weaned back to the offensive in October by Pétain, who had arranged a few carefully prepared small attacks which were calculated to be successful. The appointment of Clemenceau ('Foreign policy? – I make war. Home policy? – I make war. Everywhere, always, I make war.') had a further heartening effect on its morale. The mood of the British army was less certain. Wilfred Owen, writing an epilogue to the year, remembered that:

'last year at this time . . . I lay awake in a windy tent in the middle of a vast terrible encampment. It seemed neither France nor England but a kind of paddock where the beasts are kept a few days before the shambles. I heard the revelling of the Scotch troops, who are now dead, and who knew they would be dead. I thought of the present night (31 December 1917) and whether I should indeed survive . . . but I thought neither long nor deeply, for I am a master of elision. But chiefly I thought of the very strange look on all the faces in that camp; an incomprehensible look, which a man will never see in England; nor can it be seen in any battle. It was not despair, or terror, it was more terrible than terror, for it was a blindfold look, and without expression like a dead rabbit's. It will never be painted and, no actor will ever seize it. And to describe it I think I must go back and be with them. We are sending seven officers straight out tomorrow. I have not said what I am thinking this night, but next December I will surely do so.'

Wilfred Owen would not live to see December 1918. He had already written his own epitaph, and that for the men whose faces he had watched with such clinical pity at base camp:

Above: Digging trenches atop the Dolomites.

Above right: Austrians capture an Italian town in the Alps.

Above far right: The Kaiser visits the former Doge's Palace in Passariano on the Italian Front.

Below: Wilfred Owen, the Welsh war poet.

Right: Italian POWs march into captivity near the Piave.

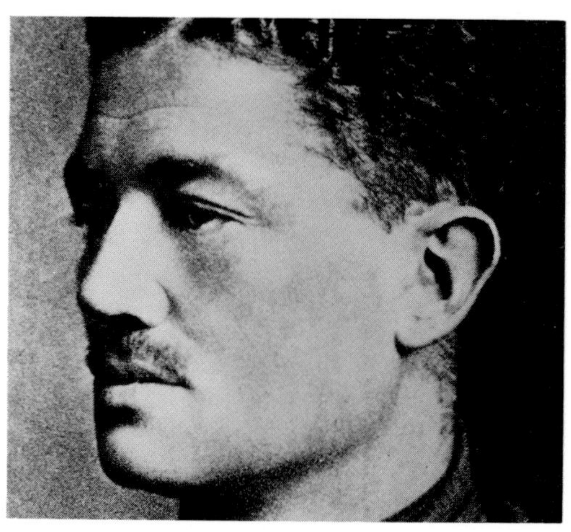

What passing bells for those who die as cattle?
– Only the monstrous anger of the guns.
Only the stuttering rifles' rapid rattle
Can patter out their hasty orisons.
No mockeries now for them; no prayers nor bells;
Nor any voice of mourning save the choirs –
The shrill, demented choirs of wailing shells;
And bugles calling for them from sad shires.
What candles may be held to speed them all?
Not in the hands of boys, but in their eyes
Shall shine the holy glimmer of goodbyes.
The pallor of girls' brows shall be their pall;
Their flowers the tenderness of patient minds.
And each slow dusk a drawing-down of blinds.

The British army had not broken in 1917, but it had been brought to the brink. Too many of its soldiers had now died like cattle for the remainder to hope for anything much more from the war but survival, national or perhaps personal. They were waiting on both for the coming of the Americans. So too was the other great intact army of the World War, the German. It had work to do before the doughboys arrived.

Some of the first American troops sent to France arrive at St Nazaire.

9 The Yanks are Coming

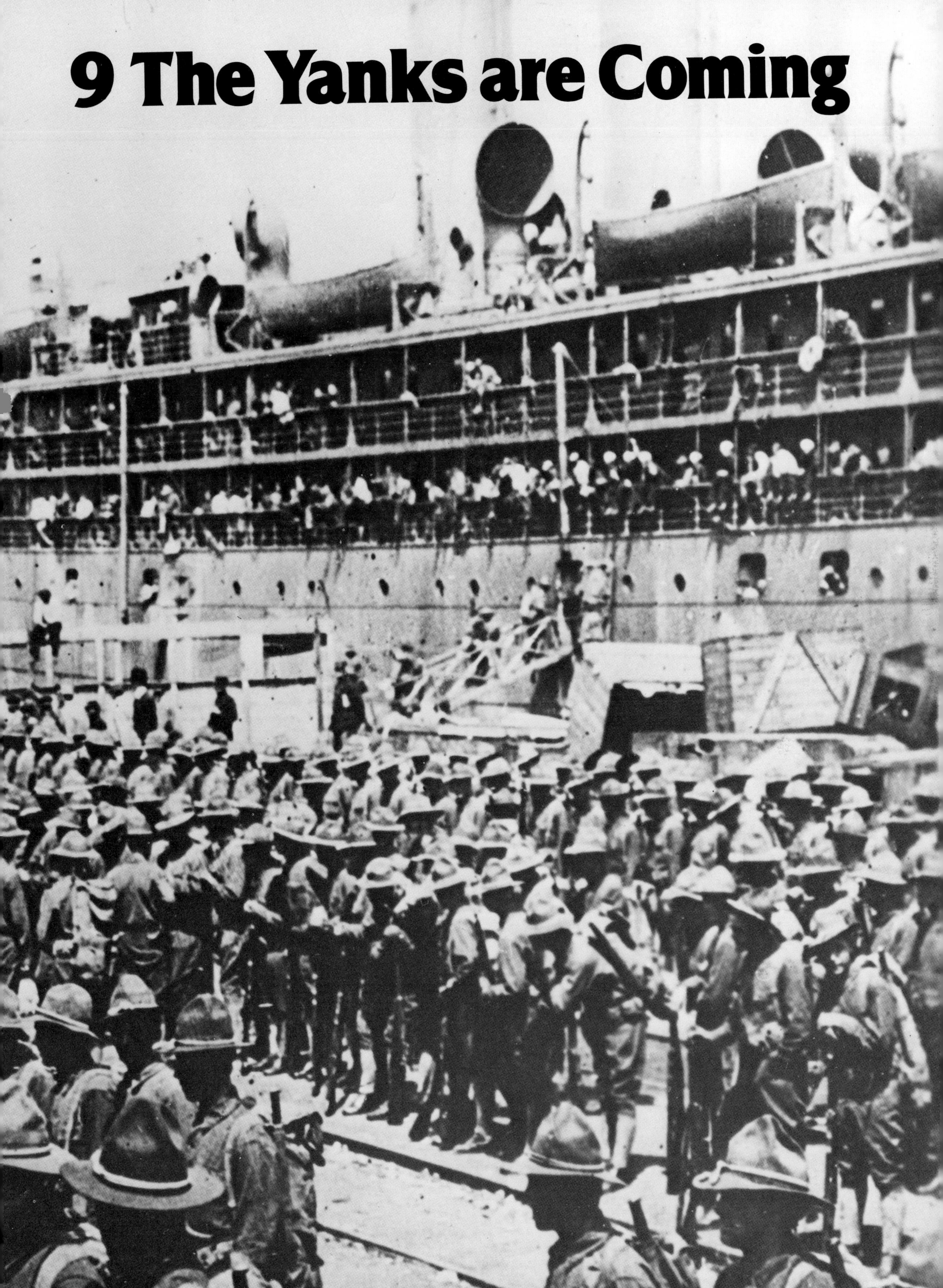

America had struggled against entering the war. It was being fought far from her shores. It threatened neither her territory nor, apparently, her vital interests. The large German minority in the United States, descendants of immigrants who had sought the good life there in the 19th century, were vociferous in opposition to American entry, against which the traditional voice of American isolationism also spoke loud. There were other minority groups, particularly the Irish, who had good reason to oppose any change of policy which would benefit Britain. Had Germany played her diplomatic cards sensitively she might well have ensured the continuance of American neutrality even if that neutrality had favored Britain or France rather than Germany. Germany chose not to do so. Since she could not benefit from the commercial connection with the United States, while the Allies could, she sought to interrupt it by attacking the mechanism of blockade which the Royal Navy had created even though such interruption had inevitably to lead to the sinking of American ships, or the loss of American lives carried in foreign ships sailing to European ports. The first great incident of the sort was the sinking of the *Lusitania* off Southern Ireland on 8 May 1915 which, though a British liner, carried many Americans among its 2000 passengers. The attack, coming only three years after the sensation of the *Titanic* sinking seemed like a deliberate re-enactment of a natural disaster, and outraged American opinion which, for a time, led to the cessation of 'unrestricted' sinkings by U-Boats in the war zone. However, the *Lusitania* was carrying munitions and Germany did not violate international law in sinking the ship. Only American sensitivity was violated.

As the blockade bit deeper, German prudence wilted. The hardships it caused led to a resurgence of left-wing opposition to the war to which the right and the government reacted to by hardening their war aims. What had been started as a war for national self-interest was increasingly seen by the directing class of the German Empire as a war for national survival in which the stakes justified the taking of higher and higher risks. Effective power passed, with the approval of the industrial, commercial and

DEFEND
YOUR COUNTRY
Tom Woodburn
ENLIST NOW in the
UNITED STATES ARMY

Right: **US call to the colors in 1917.**

Below right: **A consignment of Americans arrives in Lorraine as newsreel cameras record the event.**

Below: **A doughboy befriends some French children.**

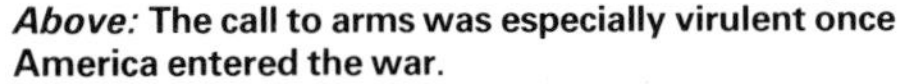

Above: **The call to arms was especially virulent once America entered the war.**

professional sections of society from civilian politicians to the High Command. Where Ludendorff enthusiastically pursued a total war policy, Holzendorff, the chief of the Naval Staff, had easily persuaded him at the beginning of 1917 that a return to unrestricted sinkings was essential and that by those means Germany would make British sue for peace before the autumn harvest 'even taking into account a break with America.' Accordingly the step was decided upon, and a note declaring it delivered to the American Secretary of State, Robert Lansing, on 31 January, only 24 hours before it was to be put into effect. President Wilson naturally regarded the discourtesy as insulting. On 3 February he announced the severing of diplomatic relations with Germany. A week later the staff of the American Embassy in Berlin left for home:

'The train which left Berlin on the night of 10 February carried the happiest group of Americans who had been in Europe since the war began,' wrote an American journalist who accompanied the party. 'When the Swiss border was reached the Stars and Stripes was hung from the car windows and Americans breathed again in a free land. They felt like prisoners escaping from a penitentiary. Most of them had been under suspicion or surveillance for months. They were delighted to escape the land, where everything is "verboten" except hatred and militarism.'

Many Americans remained steadfastly opposed to any further move toward war. The transmission to the American government by the British Secret Service of secret communications between Germany and Mexico further converted public opinion to the inevitability of intervention. The key document was the Zimmermann Telegram, made public by Wilson on 1 March. In it the German Foreign Secretary promised the Mexican government an alliance in the event of further American violations – undertaken in response to raids into the United States by the Mexican patriot, bandit Pancho Villa – plus large financial support and the mutual restoration of its former territory of Texas, New Mexico and Arizona. This cleverly unveiled threat to American sovereignty turned the tide and on 2 April 1917 Wilson visited Congress to announce the momentous 'change of policy' for which he felt his people now to be ready:

'With a profound sense of the solemn and even tragic character of the step I am taking and of the grave responsibilities which it involves,' he said, 'I advise that the Congress declare the recent course of the Imperial German Government to be in fact nothing less than war against the Government and people of the

Above: **President Wilson and his wife, who took over many of his duties when he was stricken in 1919.**

Top: **The drive to buy Liberty Bonds raised billions from American citizens.**

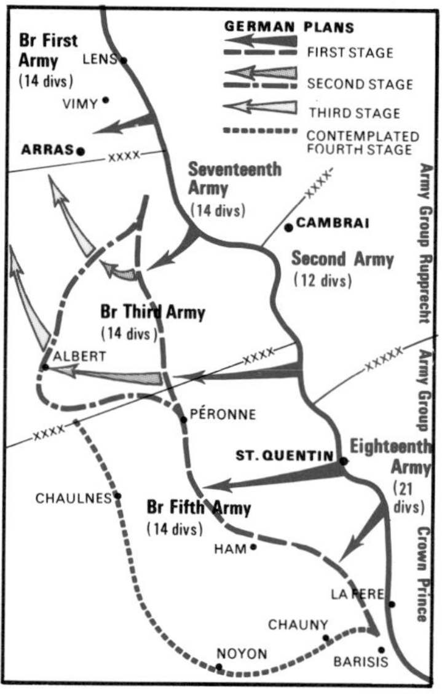

Above: **The German offensive of March–July 1918.**

Above right: **Mule teams bring up American supplies to the Argonne Front.**

United States . . . (and) to exert all its power and employ all its resources to bring the Government of the German Empire to terms and to end the war. . . . It is a fearful thing to lead this great, peaceful people into war – into the most terrible and disastrous of all wars, civilization itself seeming to be in the balance. But the right is more precious than peace and we shall fight for the things which we have always carried nearest our hearts – for democracy, for the right of those who submit to authority to have a voice in their own government, for the rights and liberties of small nations, for a universal dominion of right by such a concert of free people as shall bring peace and safety to all nations and make the world itself at last free.'

Four days later Congress formalized a state of hostilities between the United States and the Central Powers.

Enormously heartening though the news was to Britain and France, it could not at first bring anything more than moral comfort to the Alliance (which America did not technically join, remaining an Associated Power). The United States army was only 150,000 strong and without trained reserves. The United States Navy, the world's second largest, could and did at once play a major part in the antisubmarine war. By 5 June 1917 34 American destroyers were based at Queenstown, Ireland, to help with convoying Allied ships. Until the vast reserves of American manpower had been conscripted and trained, there would be no appreciable American military effort in France to make good the weakening physical and moral strength of Britain and France.

That factor was nowhere more strongly appreciated than in Germany. Indeed by the autumn of 1917, when the failure of the U-Boat campaign to starve the British to the peace table had become undisguisedly apparent, it formed the chief element in strategic planning. With the effective collapse of Russia as a military force in September 1917, the way stood open to achieve for the first time an actual superiority in numbers on the Western Front. In January 1918 there were 56 British divisions in France, but Lloyd George's policy of denying Haig reinforcements, which he suspected would be thrown away, had necessitated the reduction of the infantry battalions in each from 12 to nine (a step the French and Germans had taken a year earlier). The French were losing 40,000 men a month, whom Pétain declared himself unable to replace, and could field only 100 divisions. At that time the Germans had 124 divisions in the West and the number was increasing. By March 1918 it had reached 194, with more still to come from the Russian Front. To offset the growing preponderance, the Allies could expect as a first installment of American help only nine divisions, which were to be in place in April.

By October, however, there would be 42. American divisions were large, almost twice the size of German divisions, and were filled with enthusiastic and physically-robust patriots, longing to do their bit. 'Lafayette, we are here' may not have been the words which their commander, General John 'Black Jack' Pershing, pronounced on setting foot on French soil, but the idea was in the American doughboys' hearts. They were coming to fight on the side of liberty, which Lafayette had helped their ancestors to win, and they intended to fight with the mythical fervor of Washington's embattled farmers.

Ludendorff – for it was he, rather than the 'wooden titan' Hindenburg, who now more and more openly directed German strategy as secretly as he did domestic policy – had therefore to win the war with his new superiority of numbers quickly, before it was eroded by the arrival of Americans en masse. A calculation suggested that he had until midsummer. However to win decisive results in that time required either new weapons or new methods. Of new weapons he had none. Foolishly the German High Command had formed a low opinion of the tank when it had first appeared and had not, until too late, embarked upon the construction of a model of their own, the A7V. The few which had appeared were even slower than the first British tanks and the Germans eagerly pressed the later British models into service whenever captured. From both sources Ludendorff had only dozens of tanks at his disposal, instead of hundreds like the British and French.

He had therefore to trust in new methods – unless he was to subject his own infantry to the pointless martyrdom suffered by their enemies on the Somme and the Chemin des Dames. As it had happened, the German army did have new methods. They principally concerned the artillery, and were the work of Bruchmüller (now nicknamed *Durchbruch* Müller – Breakthrough Müller), who had organized the successful surprise attack at Riga against the Russians in September 1917. What he had overcome was the weakness which had hitherto always robbed

Top center: **American conscripts leave New York.**

Top right: **Georg Bruchmüller, the artillery expert.**

Right: **Doughboys off to the front in French railroad cars.**

YAPHANK

Right: American convoy enters British waters to the cheers of fishermen in the Western Approaches.

Below: American convoys broke the back of the German U-Boat campaign by mid-1917.

great artillery bombardments of the element of the unexpected. It arose from the need to 'register' the guns when they arrived on a new front by firing trial shots so that their future fire would be accurate. Sound-ranging and flash-spotting techniques, now very refined, were always translated by an alert enemy into signals that the opposing artillery was being reinforced and therefore that an attack might be expected. In view of this expectation, artillery chiefs had always previously thought it better to make bombardments very long, thereby hoping to make up in terms of physical destruction what was lost in moral surprise. A big bombardment also gave the enemy time to assemble his reserves close to the front of attack – but of course not in it – so that even if the attacking infantry should be able to capture the destroyed area they would be unable to break out of it.

Bruchmüller's achievement was to find ways of measuring a gun's accuracy before it arrived on a chosen front of attack, details which were then entered on a graduated list. It was subsequently necessary to fire only a few guns to establish the data from which the fire of all might be corrected to 'register' an entire artillery force, however large. Once assembled – which was done at night – the guns were to remain silent until the opening of the bombardment, which was to be very short. Bruchmüller took the view that the shock effect of a sudden, intense unheralded earthquake of shells would 'open' a front just as certainly as a long, heavy pulverization. The enemy infantry, in brutal terms, would be terrorized into inactivity. All who had experienced a bombardment testified that the first hours were the worst, when the noise and concussion temporarily robbed men

Left: **Germans take up their mortar positions during the spring breakthrough of 1918.**

Below: **Storm troops advance across open fields as the French retreated to cover Paris.**

of the power to control their nerves, while indeed their nerves were not yet accustomed to the unremitting racket. His bombardments were planned to last no more than four hours, to be unprecedently heavy – 7000 guns firing together – and to 'neutralize' rather than kill the defenders.

As it lifted, no man's land would be crossed first by specially picked squads of storm troops (*Stosstruppen* or *Sturmabteilungen* – Adolf Hitler would later appropriate both terms for his personal bodyguard, some of whose members had served in such units in 1918). Their task would be, like the Panzers of *Blitzkrieg* 20 years later, to pass through weak spots in the enemy's defenses and to keep on going, without stopping to fight pockets of resistance. 'Infiltration' was the key word of these infantry tactics, the corollary of 'neutralization.' The elite storm units had been given special light equipment for their role and were allowed to dress and behave with a freedom not accorded the ordinary infantry of the line:

'He did not march with shouldered rifle,' wrote a propagandist of the *Sturmtruppen*, 'but with unslung carbine. His knees and elbows are protected with leather patches. He no longer wears a cartridge belt, but sticks his cartridges in his pockets. Crossed over his shoulders are two sacks for hand grenades. Thus he moves from shell hole to shell hole, through searing fire, shot and attack, creeping, crawling like a robber, hugging the ground like an animal never daunted, never surprised, always shifting, cunning, always full of confidence in himself and his ability to handle any situation.'

Their officers were especially chosen for their pitiless bravery:

'The turmoil of our feelings,' one of them wrote, 'was called forth by rage, alcohol and the thirst for blood. As we advanced heavily but irresistibly toward the enemy lines; I was boiling over with a fury which

Below: **Germans move their 28cm rail gun into position during the Ludendorff offensive.**

Below: **British field guns in action during the German Somme offensive, 28 March 1918. For the first time since 1914 a war of movement had reopened on the Western Front.**

Above: **Germans storm through Bailleul in March 1918, for whom rudimentary barricades proved no barrier.**

gripped me. The overpowering desire to kill gave me wings. Rage squeezed bitter tears from my eyes. Only the spell of primeval instinct remained.' Officially the stormtroopers were hailed as 'the New Man, the storm soldier, the elite of *Mittel Europa*, a completely new race, cunning, strong and packed with purpose.'

Behind the storm troopers would march the massed columns of the ordinary infantry. They too had been trained to move in small groups, seeking cover and following the trail of the storm troopers to find the gaps in the enemy's lines and press onward deep into his rear. Overhead, the ground-attack squadrons (*Schlastas*) of the air force would patrol, to bomb and machine gun surviving enemy points of resistance.

During February the reinforcements of infantry and guns were moved forward close to the front. Ludendorff, after much thought, had decided on 21 January where the first strike was to be made. It was to be against the British, because they were still the Germans' toughest if not largest enemy and because, as one of his staff officers put it, 'the French will be in no hurry to run to the help of their Entente comrades,' a cynical but accurate judgment, as events were to show. The place he had selected was on the Somme, in a sector the British had recently taken over from the French, where the line was consequently in a poor state of repair and, most important, where a split could be made along the seam of the Anglo-French Front. Once through, the Germans were to turn northward and 'roll up' the British line. Subsequently he planned to attack in the north toward the railroad junction of Hazebrouck, from which all British supplies and reinforcements moved to Ypres. A blow there would split the British Front in two. This double stroke should, he calculated, be sufficient to end the war, if not victoriously then on terms acceptable to Germany. Beyond the putative success of this strategy he did not yet think.

The British Fifth Army on the Somme was in an even worse state than Ludendorff had supposed. Lloyd George's policy of keeping reinforcements in Britain so that Haig could not use them in a new offensive had hit it particularly hard and it was the weakest of the four British armies in France. It had only 12 divisions, disposed on a front of 42 miles. Its trenches had been reorganized in imitation of the system which the Germans had used so successfully to keep the British out of their positions the year before, but the staff had misunderstood the German theory and crowded the infantry far forward in exactly the zone which Bruchmüller's 'neutralizing' bombardment was planned to hit. It was commanded by Hubert Gough, the slapdash cavalryman whose tactics had been so disastrous at Ypres the previous autumn.

The Germans, by contrast, were able to mass 43 divisions on Gough's front, a superiority of nearly 4:1, and had a superiority of 5:2 in heavy guns. They also planned to attack General Sir Julian Byng's Third Army at the same time, though there the superiority was less. Whatever the proportion of attackers, all were supremely self-confident. Whether old Western Front hands or new arrivals from the East, they had been told, and believed, that this was the *Kaiserschlacht*, the Emperor's Battle, which would end the war. At 0440 hours on 21 March when mist lay thickly all over the valley and plain of the Somme, they heard their guns open up, and tensed themselves to push forward into the curtain of explosions and gas. They knew that the bombardment was to last for exactly four hours and that then all would depend upon their courage and dash.

On the other side of the front, a colonel of the Royal Scots Fusiliers was asleep in his dugout when:

'a tremendous roll of fire brought us to our feet; even in the depths of the shaft we could distinguish the thunder of gas projectors being fired in enormous quantities. . . . At first only projectors were being fired, and we thought it might betoken merely a big-scale raid. Then our uncertainty was dispersed by the instantaneous crash, the like of which has never been heard before by land or sea, from thousands upon thousands of guns roaring on a front of 30 miles, and we knew that the hurricane had broken on us at last. The noise transcended anything I had ever conceived. . . . . We were stunned by the concussions of literally thousands of bursting shells, and although the light was uncertain, for there hung a mist, we could see that all our front stood wrapped in a sea of smoke, and flame, and the earth heaved and twisted under our feet.'

Below: **The Monterail-Château-Thierry Road: refugees passing troops going to the front, by George Harding.**

The German general, Oskar von Hutier, commanding the spearhead Eighteenth Army, recorded the immediate results of this tremendous bombardment:

'The enemy's first position was quickly captured at all points. By the evening the infantry of the divisions of the first wave, closely followed by their escort batteries had penetrated to an average depth of six kilometers into the enemy's defensive system. The English suffered terribly heavy losses, both in men and prisoners, guns and war materiel. With ruthless energy the Eighteenth Army's attack was continued during the night of 21–22 March, and on the following day along the whole line. The impetus and enthusiasm of the troops were such that they did not need the Army Order I issued on the evening of 21 March enjoining them to keep up the pursuit. I shall never forget the scenes I witnessed in those days. For the first time after more than two years of heavy defense in the waste of trenches in the West, the hour of liberation had struck and the command had gone forth to Germany's

Right: **General Hubert Gough was one of those blamed for the German breakthrough in 1918.**

Far right: **President Woodrow Wilson.**

Below: **The German Big Bertha.**

Above: A doughboy explains how his rifle operates.

Below: British 60-pounder in action near La Boisselle in the First Battle of Bapaume in March 1918.

sons to strike for final victory in the open field. As if shaking off some horrible nightmare my infantry had risen from its trenches and crushing all resistance with unexampled vigor had broken through the enemy's defensive system.'

Von Hutier did not exaggerate. In two days' fighting, the Germans had captured the whole of the British defended zone on either side of the Somme and were poised to push out into open country. By 24 March they won through and had advanced 14 miles in four days, the greatest gain of territory since 1914, better even than the British had done at Cambrai with massed tanks. Before them the British Fifth Army was in full retreat. The Third Army to its north was being drawn into the rout:

'The journey seemed endless,' wrote a gunner officer, who was evacuating his heavy battery. 'It soon grew dark. The road was flanked by great trees which loomed up and faded away in endless succession. Dust and petrol vapour were everywhere. It filled ears and eyes, nose and mouth. Kilometre stone after kilometre stone went by. It was impossible to grasp the fact that we were in flight.'

Haig was seized by panic at the sight of the way his front was collapsing. He had earlier agreed with Pétain that each should come to the other's assistance if the promised German offensive should provoke a crisis. He had shrunk from a more formal arrangement, his fierce isolationism warning with proper military prudence even at this late stage of the war. Pétain had, in earnest of his promise, sent a single division to stand behind the crumbling British right flank on 22 March, but no more. The German gibe that the 'French would not hurry to help' was proving all too true in practice. On 24 March Haig received unequivocal evidence that such was the case. Pétain came to his headquarters at 1100 hours, revealed that he did not feel able to help the British more than he had

Above: **The Americans move forward in one of their first actions near Coutigny in late May 1918.**

Top left: **General Oskar von Hutier.**

Above left: **General Hubert Gough, Fifth Army Commander.**

Top: **6-inch howitzers in action near Boues, April 1918.**

Over There

Over there, over there,
Spread the word, send the word, over there,
That the Yanks are coming, the Yanks are coming,
The drums drum drumming everywhere.

So prepare say a Prayer,
Send the word, spread the word to beware
We'll be over, we're coming over,
And we won't come back, till it's over over there.

Right: Poilus return to an abandoned mine shaft near Riffencourt which became their trench in April 1918.

Below: A doughboy surveys the ruins of the town square of Château-Thierry.

Above: **A new German tank, the monstrous A7V in action in April 1918, one of the spearheads of the breakthrough.**

already and handed him an order, just issued to the French armies, which revealed that he accepted the probability of the Germans' dividing the Allied front, in which case his troops would fall back to cover Paris. When asked if that was his policy, Pétain merely nodded his head.

In an instant, all Haig's objections to subordinating British troops to foreign command dissolved. He at once signalled London, asking that Lord Milner, the war minister, or General Sir Henry Wilson, the Chief of the General Staff, should at once come to France and make it clear to the French government that 'unless General Foch or some other determined general were given supreme command, there would be a disaster.' On 26 March the two arrived at the little town of Doullens, a little north of the great bulge the Germans had pushed into the Western Front where Haig was waiting. From Paris, which for the last three days had been under bombardment from a range of 75 miles by a gigantic German gun, already nicknamed Big Bertha, came President Poincaré, Clemenceau and Foch. Pétain arrived from his headquarters. As he entered, Foch whispered to a neighbor that he had the look of a man who was preparing himself for defeat in the open field. His obvious defeatism spurred all present toward a decision. The necessary formula was quickly arrived at:

Below: German heavy tanks plow through open country as the way to Paris seemed clear. Germany hoped to win the war before the effect of a million fresh American troops was felt.

'General Foch is charged by the British and French governments with the co-ordination of the action of the Allied Armies on the Western Front. He will make arrangements to this effect with the two Generals in Chief, who are invited to furnish him with the necessary information.'

This was sufficient to give him power over their reserves, which could now be switched wherever danger threatened most. Clemenceau remarked to Foch as the document was distributed 'Well, you've got what you want.' Foch answered 'A fine present. You give me a lost battle and tell me to win it.' However, his real feelings were not so pessimistic. As he sat down to lunch with the party, his mind was already turning on victory. Haig did not join them. The humiliations of the last few days, culminating in subordination to a Frenchman, had robbed him of appetite both for company and food. 'Lunched from sandwich box,' his diary gloomily recorded. Humble pie was on the menu.

As Foch already detected from the situation reports, the worst of the crisis was already over. The Germans had already begun to experience the phenomenon Clausewitz had recognized a hundred years before and termed 'the diminishing power of the offensive,' brought about in this case partly by their lack of tanks and other mechanical means to sustain the speed of their advance, partly by the obstacles of the old Somme battlefield of 1916, which now lay before them, and partly by the temptations of the British supply dumps which their troops were now capturing. These supplies should have fuelled their onward progress. Rather than fill their knapsacks and press on, the German infantry, after three years of blockade, preferred to fill their stomachs:

'Today,' recorded Rudolf Binding on 28 March, 'the advance of our infantry suddenly stopped near Albert. Nobody could understand why. Our airmen had reported no enemy between Albert and Amiens. . . . I jumped into a car with orders to find out what was causing the stoppage in front. . . . As soon as I got near Albert I began to see curious sights. Strange figures which looked very little like soldiers, and certainly showed no sign of advancing, were making their way back out of the town. There were men driving cows,

Above: **A US Marine recruiting poster. The Germans called them 'devil dogs.'**

Below and below right: **The German breakthrough and the five major drives which were stopped short of Paris.**

another who carried a hen under one arm and a box of notepaper under the other, a man carrying a bottle of wine under his arm and another one open in his hand. . . . More men with writing-paper and colored notebooks. Evidently they had found it desirable to sack a stationer's shop. Men dressed up in comic disguise. Men with top hats on their heads. Men staggering. Men who could hardly walk. When I got into the town the streets were running in wine. Out of a cellar came a lieutenant, helpless and in despair. I asked him "What is going to happen?" It was essential for them to get forward immediately. He replied solemnly and emphatically "I cannot get my men out of this cellar without bloodshed."'

Moreover the static troops of the British rear areas, railroad engineers, tunnellers and transport drivers, were now being collected together as the bases they occupied were threatened and turned into temporary fighting units. One of these held a hastily improvised line of trenches outside Amiens, which Ludendorff was now making his target with great bravery and success. Ground was lost elsewhere. Foch, whose powers were widened to include 'the strategic direction of military operations' on 3 April was manipulating the reserves with great skill. After two attempts at renewal of the advance, on 28 March at Arras and on 4 April in front of Amiens, Ludendorff accepted that the *Kaiserschlacht* had run into the sand and ordered the attackers to rest. They had lost over 250,000 casualties in two weeks, but so too together had the British and French.

His men's losses did not mean that Ludendorff could not still try again elsewhere. His 'battering train' of heavy artillery was intact, and he still had a surplus of infantry. He was also still convinced that he must hurt the British rather than the French, and so moved his attack formations northward to the valley of the River Lys, just below Ypres. Hazebrouck, the railroad junction he had selected as his target, lay only 15 miles from his jumping-off point. Moreover, as luck would have it the center of the 12 miles of front he had chosen was held by a tired division of cold, homesick Portuguese, who had little idea of why their government had sent them to join England's war and little desire to stay and find out when attacked. Under the first breath of German fire on 9 April, they dispersed leaving a hole through which the *Stosstruppen* pushed hard toward the Channel. The gap was cordoned off by the British who even captured the band behind which the overoptimistic Germans were planning to make a triumphal entry into Béthune, but some of the units used in the cordon had been brought down from the Somme and were still recovering from the battering they had received there. So next day the attack made more ground. By evening it had reached to within five miles of Hazebrouck and Haig saw the fragmentation of his army staring him in the face. He issued an Order of the Day; 'With our backs to the wall and believing in the justice of our cause each one must fight on to the end.'

He appealed to Foch for reinforcements, but that hard and shrewd old warrior did not believe

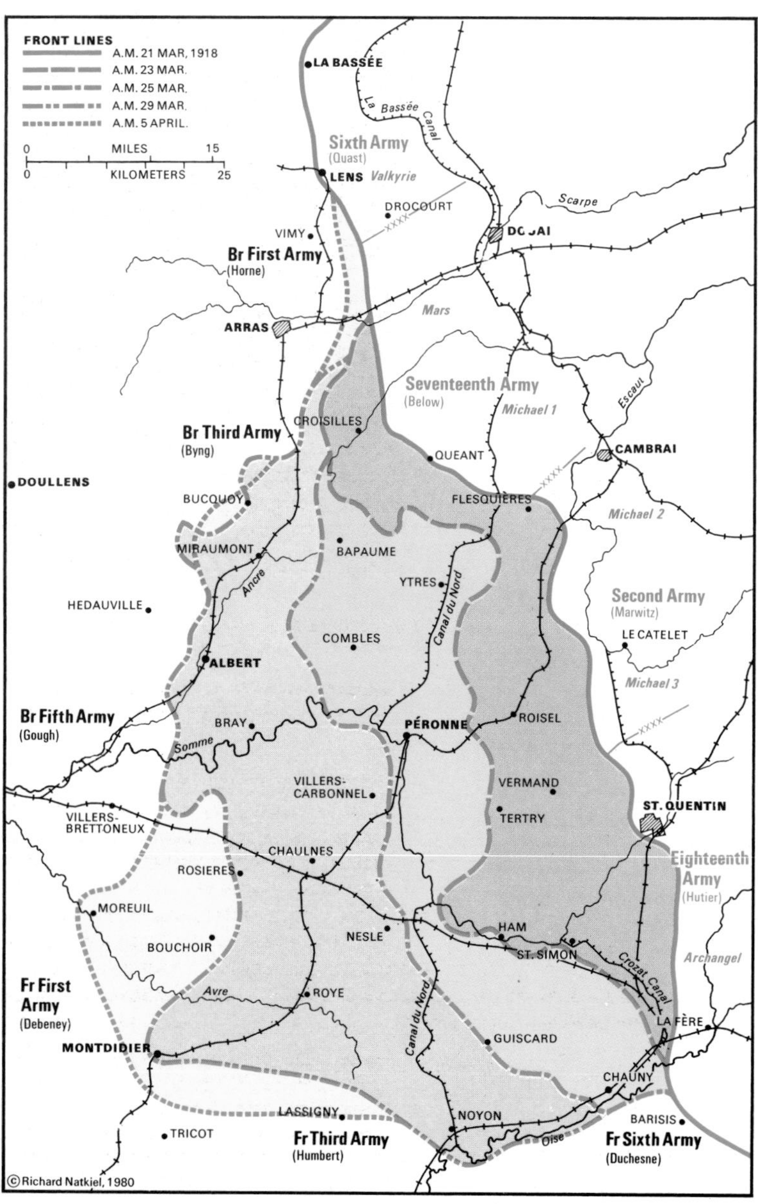

Above: **An American machine-gun emplacement near the Argonne Forest.**

Douglas MacArthur

Douglas MacArthur (1880–1964) was America's greatest war hero both in World War I and II. After his graduation from West Point he served in the Canal Zone and Texas as well as on the General Staff in Washington before he saw his first active service during the American intervention in Mexico. He was appointed Major in 1915 after his return to Washington but when America entered World War I in April 1917, General John J (Black Jack) Pershing was chosen to lead the American Expeditionary Force. MacArthur, who was impressed by Pershing's soldierly bearing and strength of character, was assigned to the Rainbow Division, so-called because it drew its members from all parts of the United States rather than from one state or territorial unit, an innovation at the time. By the end of 1917 only four of the 24 divisions Pershing promised the Allies were complete, and the Rainbow Division was one of them. At this time there were only 175,000 American men in France.

One of the first actions taken by any American unit in World War I was in the Luneville-Baccarat area in February 1918, where the Rainbow Division relieved a French unit. In his first action MacArthur led a raiding party through the barbed wire. For this action MacArthur received the American Silver Star and the French Croix de Guerre, which General de Bazelaire presented to MacArthur, and after pinning it on his tunic, kissed him on both cheeks.

In March 1918 MacArthur led a raiding party into German lines and was decorated with the Distinguished Service Cross, a battle honor second only to the Congressional Medal of Honor. MacArthur was given another DSC later in the War.

The Rainbow Division was withdrawn from action on 19 July, after having suffered over 1500 casualties and MacArthur won his second Silver Star. Thrown back into action on 25 July along the Marne, MacArthur led his 42nd Division from the front during a particularly costly action involving hand-to-hand fighting. MacArthur was given a second Croix de Guerre, a third Silver Star and was made a Commander of the French Legion of Honor.

During the St Mihiel offensive MacArthur's 42nd Division led a breakthrough of a line held by Germans since 1914 which resulted in the capture of almost 15,000 prisoners and 450 guns. Brigadier General MacArthur was awarded two more Silver Stars.

In the Meuse-Argonne campaign, which the 42nd Division entered on 11 October, Major General MacArthur led a successful attack and received his second DSC. Pushing forward to Sedan the 42nd Division was finally withdrawn on the night of 9/10 November. MacArthur was awarded his seventh Silver Star and the next day the Armistice ended the War.

There were some who were jealous of MacArthur's many awards as well as his idiosyncratic methods such as leading from the front and walking around the battlefield unarmed. When Pershing was informed of these criticisms he was said to have replied, 'Stop all this nonsense. MacArthur is the greatest leader of troops we have.' MacArthur's Commanding Officer wrote to Pershing that 'he had filled each day with a loyal and intelligent application to duty such as is . . . without parallel in our army.'

At the age of 38 MacArthur proved his merit as a soldier and as a leader of men and was praised by both his men and his superiors. MacArthur's reputation as America's greatest soldier was secure at the end of World War I.

that things were as dangerous as they looked. He also held to the view that it was better in a crisis to leave tired troops where they were rather than risk their total collapse by the promise of relief. So, while he sent some French troops in the direction of Hazebrouck, he ordered their commanders to make haste slowly. Events proved him right. Many of the German attackers were veterans of the Eastern Front where some shelling and gas usually made the enemy run. When they found the British more stubborn, their will to victory wilted and the offensive began to run out of steam. By 30 April it had petered out altogether.

The most significant incident of its closing stages was the encounter at Villers-Brettoneux on 24 April of British and German tanks. It led to the first tank-versus-tank battle. Four British tanks met three German. Of the British tanks, No 1 tank of No 1 Section, A Company, 1st Battalion, Tank Corps was commanded by 2nd Lieutenant Frank Mitchell. He was warned by a British infantryman that German tanks were about and opened a loophole to keep watch. Some 300 yards away he saw a round, squat-looking monster advancing, behind it came waves of infantry and further away to the left and right crawled two more of these armed tortoises. So the rivals had met at last! For the first time in history tank was encountering tank. Miller's gunner, whose eyes had been badly affected by a barrage of mustard gas through which he had earlier driven, fired two shots at it but missed. It replied with armor-piercing

Above: **French tanks in action. They proved less effective than their British counterparts.**

machine-gun bullets which 'filled the interior with a myriad of sparks and flying splinters.' The gunner again fired twice and missed twice. Meanwhile, the German tank was engaging Mitchell's two accompanying tanks and hit them, forcing them to withdraw. Mitchell decided therefore to halt his tank, to give his gunner a steady platform:

'The pause was justified; a well-aimed shot hit the enemy's conning-tower. Another round and yet another white puff at the front of the tank denoted a second hit! Peering with swollen eyes through his narrow slit, the gunner shouted words of triumph that were drowned by the roar of the engine. Then once more he fired with great deliberation and hit for the third time. Through a loophole I saw the tank heel over to one side, then a door opened and out ran the crew. We had knocked the monster out!'

However, not until the next war would tank duels become of strategic significance. In 1918 Ludendorff still had to win with men – and by May he was running short of reserves. His two 'knock-out' blows against the British having failed, he decided that he would next make a diversionary attack against the French in order to draw Foch's reserves southward and then return to the north for a final stroke at Haig. On 27 May, therefore, after careful preparations, the now familiar 'neutralizing' bombardment fell on the Chemin des Dames. The high ridges and broken terrain, most of which was in German hands, had facilitated the concealment of his troops – he could still find 41 divisions – and Bruchmüller's fire plan was more hellishly refined than ever before. Defending were only four French and three British divisions which had actually been sent thither as a 'rest' from the battering they had taken in Flanders. The central French division disappeared under a flood of five German divisions, which pounded over their positions and downhill to the Aisne. There they found the bridges unblown, so complete was the surprise, they crossed them and set off into open country. By the second day they had gone 15 miles and by 3 June, while French reserves were still struggling down from the north, were at Château-Thierry, only 56 miles from Paris.

There the Germans received the first ominous warning note of a timetable in trouble. Among the hastily-assembled reserves into which they eventually ran were Americans, United States regulars of the 3rd Division and Marines of the 2nd. At Belleau Wood on 6 June the Marines counterattacked. The place has become one of the Corps' most cherished battle honors and an officer who was present explains why:

'It was a beautiful deployment, lines all dressed and guiding true. Such matters were of deep concern to this outfit. The day was without a cloud promising heat later but now it was pleasant in the wheat and the woods around looked blue and cool. Pretty country, these rolling wheatlands northwest of Château-Thierry, with copses of trees and tidy little forests where French sportsmen maintained hunting lodges and game preserves. Since the first Marne there had been no fighting here. . . . The platoons, assailed now by a fury of small-arms fire, narrowed their eyes and inclined their bodies forward, like men in heavy rain and went on. Second waves reinforced the first, fourth waves the third, as prescribed. Officers yelled, "Battle-sight – fire at will" – and the leaders, making out green-gray clumsy uniforms and round pot-helmets in the gloom of the woods, took it up with Springfields, aimed shots. . . . Men crawled forward; the wheat was agitated and the Boche, directing his fire by observers in treetops, browsed the slope industriously. Men were wounded, wounded again as the lines of fire swept back and forth, and finally killed. It helped to bag the *feldwebels* in the trees; there were men in that line who could hit at 750 yards three times out of five. Sweating, hot and angry . . . the Marines worked forward. They were there and the Germans, and there was nothing else in the clanging world.'

The French reserves which had been hurried to the front here fought as well as the Americans, no doubt under the stimulus of the cry, not heard since 1914, of 'Paris in danger.' The Germans for a moment did actually get a foothold across the Marne. Clemenceau had to calm the Chamber of Deputies by dismissing some subordinate generals, just as Joffre had done in the terrible August of four years before, but the crisis quickly passed. The German offensive outran its transport and came to a halt at the end of the first week of June. A small subsidiary offensive on the River Matz, a tributary of the Oise, was launched on 9 June, with the same diversionary object of drawing reserves away from Flanders, where Ludendorff still hoped to launch a knockout against the British, but was contained within a week.

The war was now moving to a supreme crisis, foreseen by both sides. Foch, Haig and Pétain sensed that if they could but ride the storm for another month or two at most, the gathering weight of American manpower would crush the life out of the German army. Ludendorff knew that he had strength enough for only one more

Right: **British tanks on the offensive in September 1918 as German prisoners are rounded up near Bellicourt.**

Right: **What might have happened had two tanks collided head-on.**

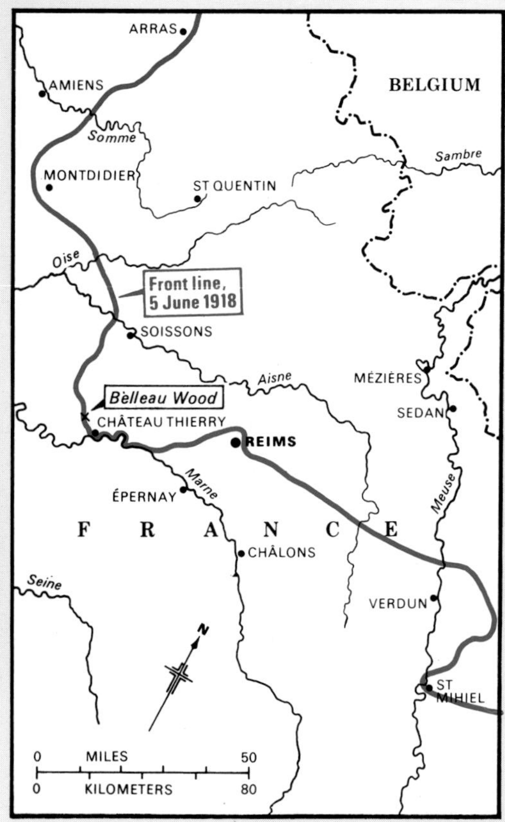

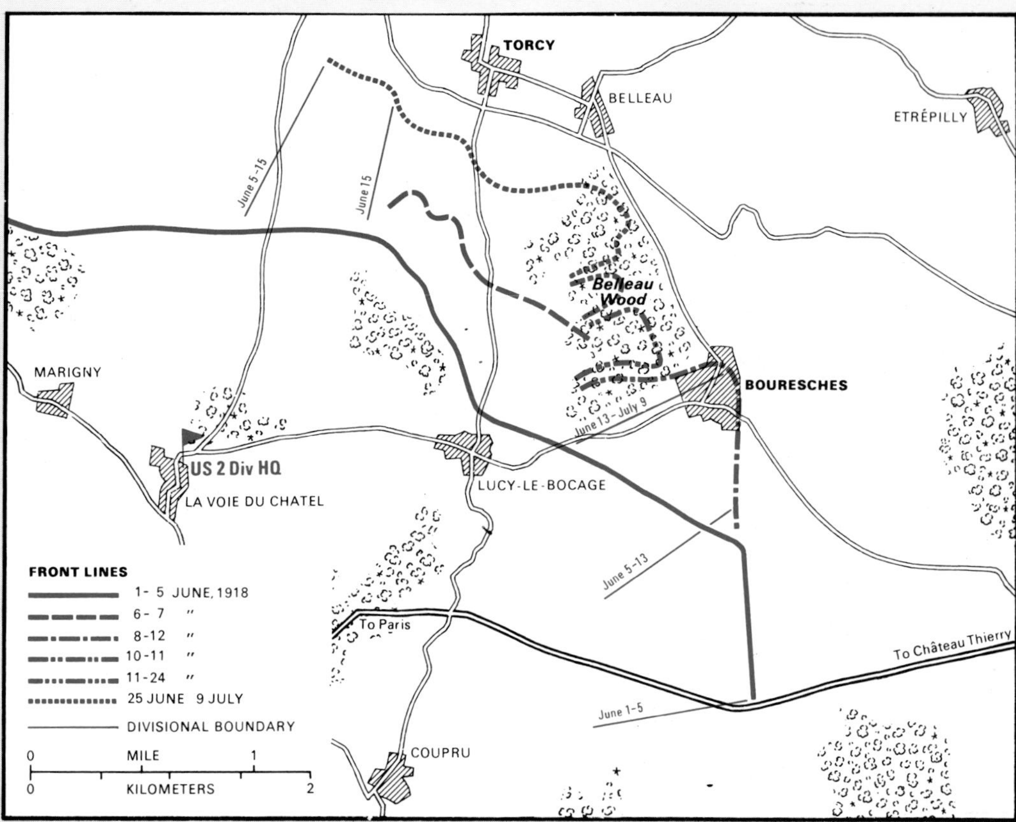

***Above:* The situation as the Americans entered the fray at Belleau Wood in June 1918, their first major action in the war.**

great throw. So stretched were his nerves that he even tinkered with the temptation of playing politics, discussing the desirability of offering the Allies the possibility of a compromise peace in order to confuse them and weaken their will to resist. However, when von Kühlmann, the foreign minister, outraged the Reichstag by airing this suggestion on 24 June Ludendorff threw him to the wolves. The Kaiser, speaking at the Headquarters at Spa on 15 June, at a dinner to celebrate the 30th year of his reign, revealed the mind of the German governing class more accurately. Renouncing any idea of surrendering the conquests made by Germany since 1914, then at their greatest extent, he went on:

'Either the Prusso-German-Teutonic world philosophy – justice, freedom, honor, moral – persists in honor, or the Anglo-Saxon – which means succumbing to the worship of the golden calf. In this struggle, one or the other philosophy must go under. We are fighting for the victory of the German philosophy.'

His characterization of what 'the German philosophy' stood for might have surprised Western liberals, who believed that their way of life enshrined justice and freedom, but the naked combativeness of his outlook would not. There spoke the voice of the militarism they feared.

It was supremely still Ludendorff's voice. After much reflection, he decided that before risking all on *Hagen*, the code name (that of the sinister dwarf of the Nibelungen) for the culminating offensive against the British in Flanders, he would give Foch and the French one more bad fright on the Marne, thus ensuring that the Allied reserves were irretrievably in the wrong place at the hour of decision. Once more the 'battering train' was wheeled forward to prepare the attack. Gas and high explosives were poured into the makeshift French positions on the morning of 15 July and, as day broke, 52 divisions moved forward in two groups, between Soissons and Reims. The more northerly was to aim for the Marne, 15 miles distant, the other to cross the Marne, which was close at hand and join up with the first in a large pincer movement.

Initially the Germans had some success. At a point held by the Italian divisions, sent to France in exchange for Allied divisions moved to the Italian front after Caporetto, they cracked the front and were held only by the hasty arrival of some British troops. Above Reims they reached and crossed the Marne. The steadfast defense of

***Top right:* German morale showed no sign of slacking as the men marched to the front in April 1918.**

***Above right:* Germans storm into Embermesnil in the Champagne country in May 1918.**

***Below:* Germans advance through barbed wire near the Aisne.**

John Joseph Pershing

John Joseph Pershing was born in Laclede, Missouri on 13 September 1860, to a family of modest means in the rural Middle West. He graduated from the United States Military Academy at West Point in 1886 as president of his class.

His first active service was in the last series of Indian wars fought in the American West, when Pershing served in the cavalry. He received a Bachelor of Laws degree in 1893 while teaching at the University of Nebraska, and later taught military tactics at West Point. His academic career was interrupted by the outbreak of the Spanish-American War in 1898, when Pershing went to Cuba and won a Silver Star. Soon afterward he was transferred to the Philippines where he joined the hard campaign the Americans waged against the Moros in Mindanao, winning the praise of the then-President Theodore Roosevelt. He was sent by Roosevelt to act as an observer in the Russo-Japanese War of 1904–05. Roosevelt rewarded him for his work in Manchuria by elevating Captain Pershing to the rank of brigadier general in 1906 over the heads of hundreds of senior officers, an act which created considerable bitterness against Pershing among his fellow officers for many years. After another tour in the Philippines Pershing was rushed back to the United States in 1916 to lead a military expedition into Mexico to pursue Pancho Villa, the Mexican revolutionary who had recently made a surprise attack on the town of Columbus, New Mexico. Arriving at El Paso, Texas, to join his troops, Pershing received the news that his wife and three small daughters had burned to death in San Francisco, his son Warren, being the only survivor. Grimly Pershing led his punitive expedition across the border on 15 March 1916, and his troops plunged deep into Mexican territory. Although the Mexican troops which attempted to repel the Americans were easily swept aside, Pershing was unable to capture Villa after 10 months of wandering through the hostile countryside of northern Mexico. But President Wilson appeared satisfied and made him a major general.

Pershing's expedition was recalled in February 1917, and three months later, after the United States had entered World War I, Pershing was sent to France with a hand-picked staff to command the American Expeditionary Force (AEF) which, at the time, did not yet exist. Pershing was given a free hand by Wilson to organize his forces, although he was cautioned by a Presidential directive to maintain his troops intact and not to allow them to be merged into a combined Allied unit. When he arrived in France Pershing discovered that the Allies wanted no untested American army; they preferred to have American manpower slowly fill their own depleted ranks. Pershing insisted on training a separate American force and on keeping them aloof from the fighting until they were prepared to wage an offensive. He was determined to prevent the Americans being dragged into the wastefulness of trench warfare, and envisioned an army of 1,000,000 men under his own command by spring 1918. Supported by the Secretary of War, Newton D Baker, Pershing achieved his ends, much to the consternation of the Supreme War Council, composed of Lloyd George, Clemenceau and Orlando. Severe pressure was put on the Americans by the Allies to relieve Pershing, but Baker protected him.

When the German threat became increasingly serious during their massive offensive in 1918, Pershing volunteered some reinforcements to Foch, and American action at Château-Thierry and Belleau Wood stopped the Germans on the Marne and opened the eyes of both the Germans and the Allies to the combat readiness of the American divisions. In mid-August 1918 the newly-formed American First Army, with the approval of Foch, was concentrating on the St Mihiel offensive. At the last minute Foch called off the attack, arguing that American reinforcements were needed elsewhere along the front. Pershing refused to break up his unit, and the struggle between Foch and Pershing was settled only through the mediation of Marshal Pétain. The AEF eliminated the St Mihiel salient and a few days later almost 600,000 men were shifted to the Meuse-Argonne area, where they advanced against fierce German opposition. In 47 days of continuous fighting the American forces had pushed forward to Sedan, chewing up German divisions as fast as they were thrown in. The armistice came three days after the AEF reached the outskirts of Sedan.

Pershing's organization of the American forces from scratch was one of the greatest feats of World War I. Starting from nothing Pershing produced an army of 2,000,000 men within 18 months. The entry of the Americans on the Western Front was decisive in the winning of the war. The iron discipline and stern military bearing which he maintained earned him the nickname of 'Black Jack,' and he won respect, if not affection, from his comrades. On 3 September 1919 Pershing was made General of the Armies, a rank unique in American military history. He was made Chief of Staff in 1921, a post which he held until his retirement in 1924. He died in 1948 at the age of 88, honored by most of the European nations as well as his own; his body rests at Arlington National Cemetery.

the American 3rd Division prevented them from enlarging their bridgehead. Other things went wrong. All the observation balloons on which his artillery depended were shot down by Allied 'balloon-busting' airmen and a force of 20 tanks which he had painstakingly assembled was knocked out by gunners firing over open sights.

Worse was to come. Pétain, who had come close to dismissal by Clemenceau during the crisis of the May offensive of the Aisne, had heeded the urgings of Foch and prepared a counterattack force. Its command was given to Mangin, his trap-jawed, fire-eating subordinate of Verdun days. Mangin was irrepressibly aggressive, a veteran of the French Colonial wars in Africa and a ferocious patriot who had never wavered, unlike Pétain, in his belief in French victory. He now had 25 divisions, positioned west of the German break-in. He also had a large force of tanks, and he was to enjoy the supreme tactical advantage of surprise. The Germans, who believed they held the initiative, were not prepared for what now struck them, a well-planned drive into their flank by rested troops under a commander determined on success and ready to dismiss any subordinate who would not carry out his orders.

On that critical morning Ludendorff was driving north to plan the offensive in Flanders, where his heavy artillery was already on its way. Isolated in his motor car, he did not hear the news of his forward infantry collapsing under the thrusts of aggressive French tank-infantry columns, moving concealed among the woods and wheat fields of countryside untouched by war for four years. By the time he arrived at Mons for his conference, the damage had been done. Four miles of territory had been lost and the bridgeheads over the Marne threatened. A steady retirement was in progress which would not end until the Germans had reached the line of the Chemin des Dames. On 6 August, Clemenceau, in recognition of success in what would be called the Second Battle of the Marne, promoted Foch to be Marshal of France.

Top left: **General Pershing arrives at Boulogne to take command of the AEF.**

Right: **US troops in action in Villers-sur-Fère, July 1918.**

Below right: **Men of the 62nd Division advance near Reims, 24 July 1918.**

Below: **General Haig greets Premier Clemenceau at Doullens.**

Doughboys of the 7th Division celebrate the Armistice, 11 November 1918.

10 Illusion of Victory

Germany's peril at the end of July 1918 could not be measured by the naked eye. Unlike Hitler's Reich in the last four months of its power before defeat, both the Empire's territory and conquests stood almost intact. The coastline of the Baltic as far as Riga, the whole of the Ukraine and much of Russia proper, the line of the Caucasus and the northern shores of the Black Sea were garrisoned by German troops. All her allies remained at her side, and their troops generally stood beyond their own frontiers and still in active contention with the forces of the Alliance. In Italy the Austrians were still on the Piave, a little above Venice. In Macedonia the Bulgarians overlooked the 'Gardeners of Salonika' in their entrenched camp on the River Varda. Rumania, Serbia and Montenegro were occupied. So too was most of Belgium and as much of France as had been captured in the first campaign of 1914. The Russian Bolsheviks, who could be counted as Germany's reluctant collaborators were preparing a campaign of extirpation against the Whites, who represented all that was left of Allied might east of Moscow. Only in the Ottoman lands had British troops pushed any distance toward the center of power. There the Anatolian heartland, recruiting ground of the peasantry who manned the ranks of the Turkish army, still stood far from Allenby's vanguards.

Yet Ludendorff, and the group around him who now manipulated imperial power in Germany, knew that the hands of the clock stood at five minutes to midnight. The U-Boat campaign, which should have starved Britain to the conference table the year before, had been defeated. The young Austrian emperor, Karl I, remained as anxious to make peace as he had shown himself to be the year before, with the difference that he heard his throne creaking beneath him; the subject nationalities – Serbs, Czechs, Slovaks, Poles – would now be satisfied only by independence, not internal autonomy. The opposition to the war within Germany had become bolder and more vociferous. In February there had been a wave of large-scale strikes, when 250,000 workers had come out in demand for larger food rations (in June the potato ration stood at one pound a week), amnesty for

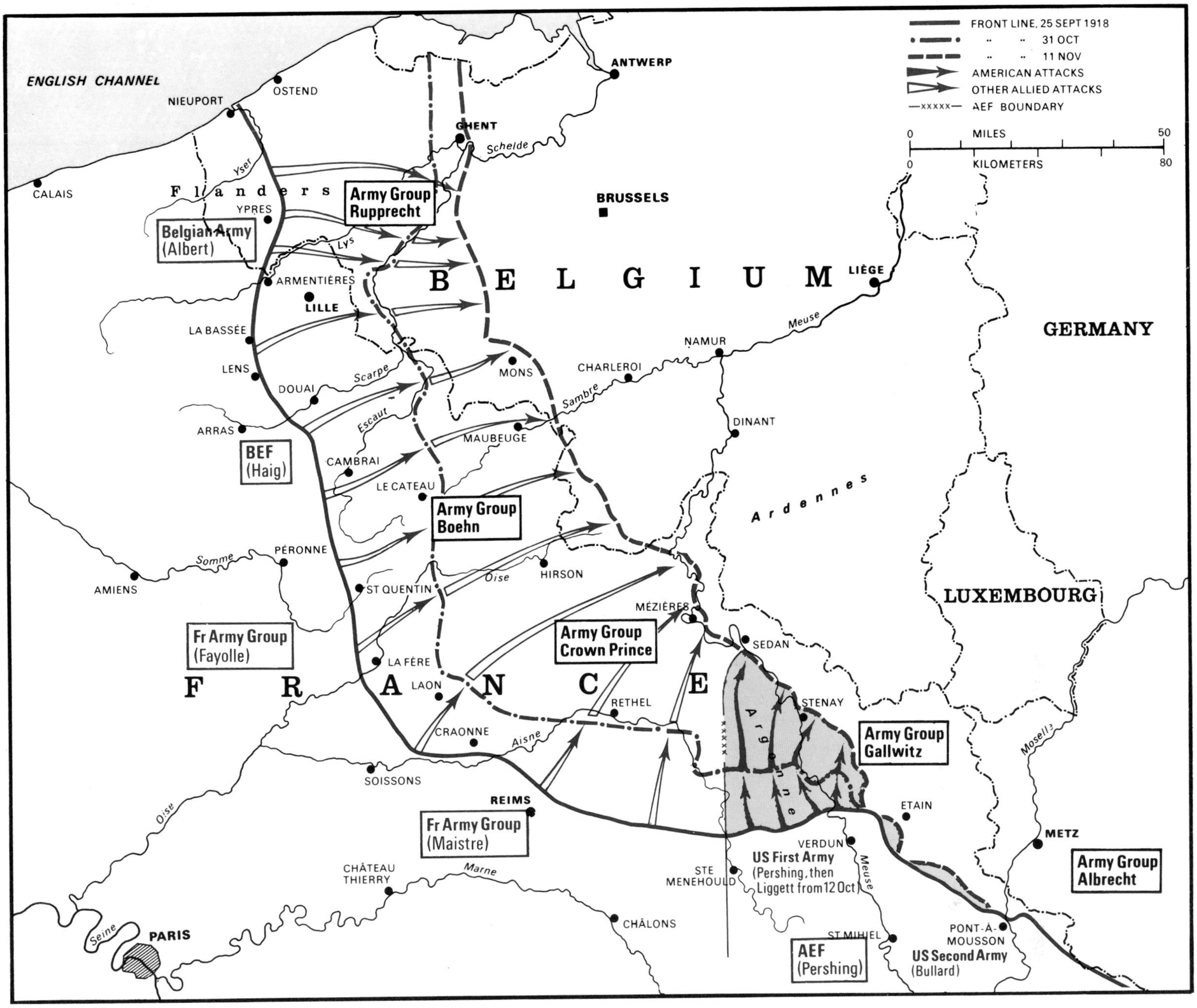

FRONT LINE, 25 SEPT 1918
.. .. 31 OCT
.. .. 11 NOV
AMERICAN ATTACKS
OTHER ALLIED ATTACKS
—xxxxx— AEF BOUNDARY
0 MILES 50
0 KILOMETERS 80
ENGLISH CHANNEL
NIEUPORT
OSTEND
ANTWERP
GHENT
Scheldt
CALAIS
Yser
Flanders
YPRES
Army Group Rupprecht
BRUSSELS
Belgian Army (Albert)
Lys
ARMENTIÈRES
LILLE
BELGIUM
LIÈGE
GERMANY
LA BASSÉE
NAMUR
Meuse
LENS
DOUAI
Scarpe
MONS
CHARLEROI
Sambre
ARRAS
Escaut
MAUBEUGE
DINANT
BEF (Haig)
CAMBRAI
LE CATEAU
Army Group Boehn
Ardennes
PÉRONNE
Somme
AMIENS
ST QUENTIN
Oise
HIRSON
LUXEMBOURG
MÉZIÈRES
Fr Army Group (Fayolle)
Army Group Crown Prince
SEDAN
LA FÈRE
FRANCE
LAON
RETHEL
STENAY
Argonne
Army Group Gallwitz
CRAONNE
Aisne
SOISSONS
REIMS
Fr Army Group (Maistre)
ETAIN
Moselle
VERDUN
METZ
US First Army (Pershing, then Liggett from 12 Oct)
CHÂTEAU THIERRY
Marne
STE MENEHOULD
Meuse
Army Group Albrecht
Seine
PARIS
CHÂLONS
ST MIHIEL
PONT-À-MOUSSON
AEF (Pershing)
US Second Army (Bullard)

Above: **The final Allied advances.**

Above left: **Irish Rifles in action in Belgium in August 1918.**

Left: **British Whippet tanks pass a column of New Zealand troops at Maillet Mailly.**

Right: **Hindenburg and Ludendorff, who in September 1918 were forced to tell the Kaiser that the war was lost.**

political offenders, restoration of civil rights, democratization of the government and peace on the basis of 'no annexations and no indemnities.' Worst of all, there was the American menace:

'People here may well look grave,' Princess Blücher wrote in mid-July from Berlin. 'The meaning of America is coming home to them at last. They comprehend now that it means an increase of the French reserves at a rate of 300,000 fresh, well-equipped men (that is, Americans) per month, while Germany can bring up no fresh reserves.'

In fact by the end of July, the Americans had 27 divisions in France, each 28,000 strong and so twice the size of a French or German division. Their very inexperience added to their formidability. British and French officers who had found American dead lying in long rows in the open wheat fields at Château-Thierry had whispered to each other that the newcomers had a great deal to learn. Precisely because they

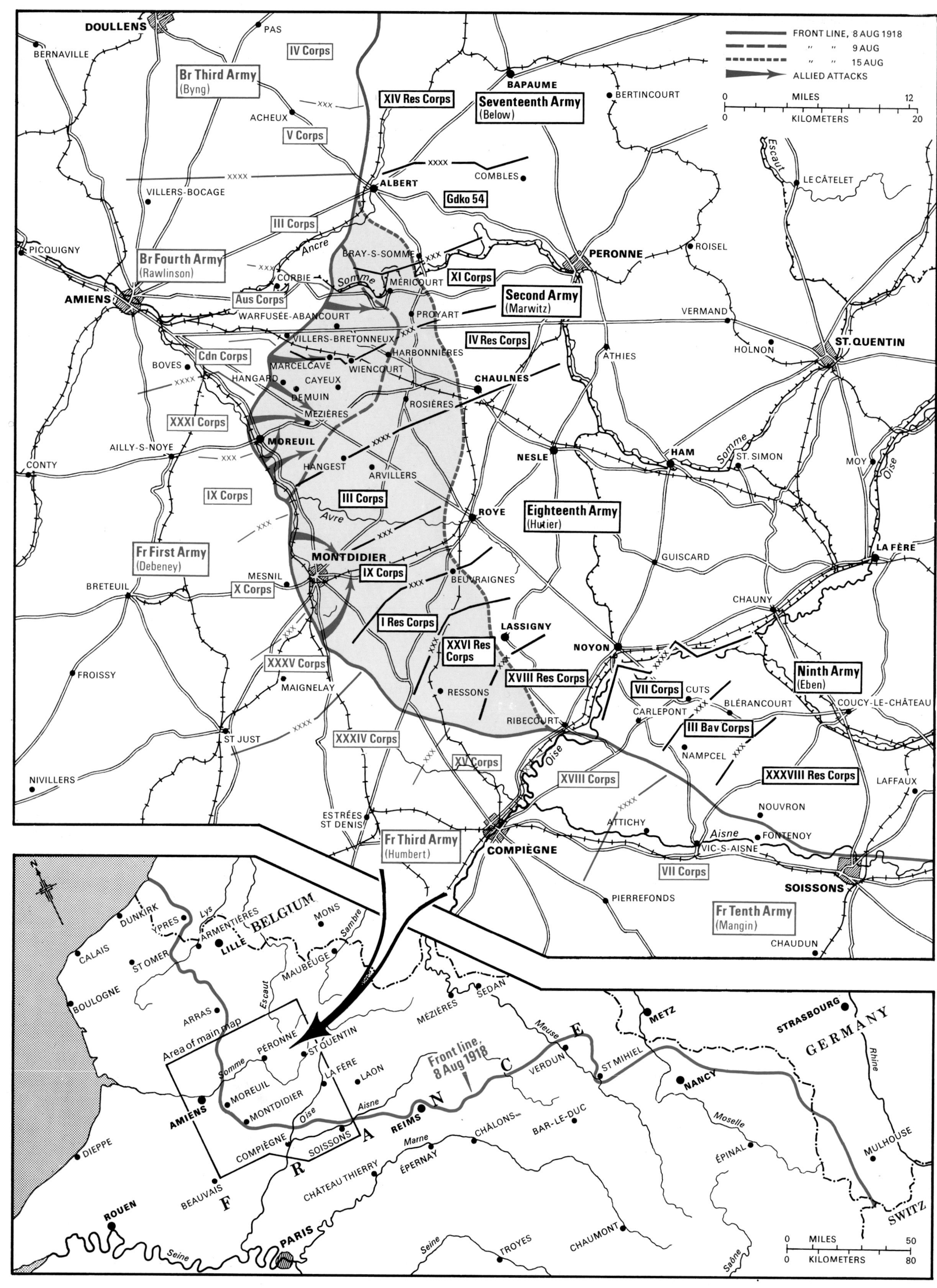
FRONT LINE, 8 AUG 1918
" " 9 AUG
" " 15 AUG
ALLIED ATTACKS
MILES 0 12
KILOMETERS 0 20
Br Third Army (Byng)
IV Corps
V Corps
III Corps
Br Fourth Army (Rawlinson)
Aus Corps
Cdn Corps
XXXI Corps
IX Corps
Fr First Army (Debeney)
X Corps
XXXV Corps
XXXIV Corps
XV Corps
XVIII Corps
Fr Third Army (Humbert)
VII Corps
Fr Tenth Army (Mangin)
XIV Res Corps
Seventeenth Army (Below)
Gdko 54
XI Corps
Second Army (Marwitz)
IV Res Corps
III Corps
IX Corps
I Res Corps
XXVI Res Corps
XVIII Res Corps
Eighteenth Army (Hutier)
VII Corps
III Bav Corps
Ninth Army (Eben)
XXXVIII Res Corps
DOULLENS
PAS
BERNAVILLE
ACHEUX
BAPAUME
BERTINCOURT
ALBERT
COMBLES
VILLERS-BOCAGE
PICQUIGNY
Ancre
BRAY-S-SOMME
CORBIE
Somme
MERICOURT
PERONNE
ROISEL
AMIENS
WARFUSÉE-ABANCOURT
PROYART
VERMAND
VILLERS-BRETONNEUX
HARBONNIÈRES
ATHIES
HOLNON
ST. QUENTIN
BOVES
MARCELCAVE
WIENCOURT
HANGARD
CAYEUX
DEMUIN
CHAULNES
MEZIÈRES
ROSIÈRES
AILLY-S-NOYE
MOREUIL
CONTY
HANGEST
ARVILLERS
NESLE
HAM
ST. SIMON
MOY
Oise
Escaut
LE CÂTELET
Avre
ROYE
MONTDIDIER
GUISCARD
LA FÈRE
MESNIL
BRETEUIL
BEUVRAIGNES
CHAUNY
LASSIGNY
NOYON
FROISSY
MAIGNELAY
RESSONS
CUTS
BLÉRANCOURT
COUCY-LE-CHÂTEAU
CARLEPONT
RIBECOURT
ST JUST
NAMPCEL
NIVILLERS
LAFFAUX
NOUVRON
ESTRÉES ST DENIS
ATTICHY
Aisne
FONTENOY
COMPIÈGNE
VIC-S-AISNE
SOISSONS
PIERREFONDS
CHAUDUN
DUNKIRK
YPRES
Lys
ARMENTIÈRES
BELGIUM
MONS
CALAIS
LILLE
Sambre
ST OMER
MAUBEUGE
BOULOGNE
ARRAS
SEDAN
MÉZIÈRES
METZ
STRASBOURG
GERMANY
Area of main map
PÉRONNE
ST QUENTIN
Front line, 8 Aug 1918
Meuse
VERDUN
ST MIHIEL
Rhine
NANCY
LA FÈRE
LAON
MOREUIL
MONTDIDIER
REIMS
Moselle
CHÂLONS
BAR-LE-DUC
COMPIÈGNE
ÉPINAL
MULHOUSE
DIEPPE
Marne
ÉPERNAY
CHÂTEAU THIERRY
BEAUVAIS
F R A N C E
ROUEN
PARIS
Seine
TROYES
CHAUMONT
Saône
SWITZ
MILES 0 50
KILOMETERS 0 80

were ready to attack with a disregard for danger no German had seen since the early days of the war, they inspired a fearful respect which the more cautious British and French did not.

Recollecting his thoughts of late July, Ludendortt later wrote:

'the attempt to make the Entente peoples ready for peace by defeating them before the arrival of the American reinforcements had failed. The impetus of the army had been insufficient to deal the enemy a decisive blow. I realized clearly that this made our general situation very serious.'

How serious was shortly to be brought home to him, not, however, by the Americans but by the British. At the beginning of August Pershing's divisions were still scattered about the Western Front, where he had lent them as reserves during the worst of the spring and summer crisis. He was now urgently reassembling them for 'an American offensive.' Meanwhile Haig had found a surplus of troops of his own and, more important, a surplus of tanks. He had also been given a clear brief as to where they were to be used. On 24 July Foch had held a meeting with the British and American commanders at which he laid down a scheme to free certain strategic railroad lines whose possession would

Left: **The Allied breakthrough on the Black Day, 8 August 1918, which ended all German hopes of victory.**

Right: **German artillery in action on the Black Day.**

Below: **Following the Battle of Amiens German POWs are escorted to the rear, 8 August 1918.**

Above: British troops storm forward on the Black Day. The horse-drawn artillery had trouble keeping pace with the British advance.

Above left: British troops fire into a German dugout to roust any German stragglers during the retreat from Delbar Wood near Roye, 29 August 1918.

Below: New Zealanders fire a captured German gun as they advance on the Black Day.

Below: Australian field artillery in action in open country on the same day.

ease the rapid transfer of force about the front. One was the Paris–Verdun line, in fact cleared by Mangin's counteroffensive of July. Another was the Verdun–Avricourt line at St Mihiel, which was eventually to be Pershing's objective; the third was the Paris–Amiens line, from which Haig was now to drive away the Germans.

His tactical plan mimicked that of the German spring offensives in every respect; short 'neutralizing' bombardment, infantry infiltration and aerial ground attack, to which was added the special ingredient of a massed tank vanguard. In all he had 554 tanks, of which 72 were the new 'Whippets,' light and fast enough to move at a cavalry pace into the German lines once the front had been broken. The bulk of his infantry were 'Colonials,' Canadians and Australians whose spirits had never been depressed as those of the home divisions had been by the trauma of March and April.

The ground favored the enterprise. It was a large plain called the Santerre, without hedges or large waterways, across which the tanks could advance at a uniform speed. The German defenses, having been dug only since April, were thin and poorly protected. Their occupants were taken completely by surprise on the morning of 8 August. Some had reported earlier hearing the sound of tank tracks, but higher authority had dismissed the reports as 'phantoms of the imagination or nervousness.' This may have been correct, for extraordinary trouble had been taken to disguise tank noise, special flights of airplanes had been employed to drown it by low-flying exercises. Whether alerted or not, the German infantry were overwhelmed by the tank armada when it emerged from the British lines:

'The barrage had lifted,' a tank commander remembered, 'and moved on, so had the smoke curtain; the blanket of fog breaks up into wraiths, and these drift away over the undulating ground. The sun comes out through the mist, and before us is waving corn and figures disappearing in the distance, brandishing rifles as they run. The hunt is up!'

As they ran, the German infantry abandoned not only their front but also their support and reserve lines, quickly exposing their artillery to direct attack. A German gunner, deserted in this way, suddenly heard his battery sergeant major shout 'a tank, straight ahead':

'A light tank was roaring toward us at great speed, plunging into craters and climbing over trenches while his machine guns kept firing at our battery. Our men feverishly set the sights and fired one, two shells in rapid succession. Before us, there was a shattering roar followed by a dark cloud the size of a house; the tank had been destroyed. But this was only the beginning. Two more tanks appeared and were knocked out, then three more, the third of which was hit only 300 yards from the gun line. Only two German guns had survived the action and the battery officers were preparing to evacuate the position when one more warning cry rang out. "Tank on the right." A large gun tank, the seventh in a matter of minutes, came speeding straight toward us and opened a murderous fire when only 200 yards distant. Sergeant Wesel's gun was disabled while being trained on this new enemy. Its commander was badly wounded, its crew either wounded or killed. Our last gun's shield and sights were seriously damaged in the attack, but the crew did not give up the fight. Crouched behind the steel shield under a hail of bullets they turned the gun-carriage. The cool-headed pointer took aim and, at the very instant the tank plunged into the sunken path ahead of us, the fatal shell crashed through its side. Nothing but dense smoke and flying pieces of iron could be seen. The tank's destruction was our last-minute salvation. Now it was high time to fall back. The British assault troops behind the tanks were surging in all directions in small groups. Machine guns began rattling, bullets whizzed all round us. We dashed away from shell hole to shell hole.'

By evening, the tanks were seven miles beyond their start lines. Of the German defenders, 15,000 had been taken prisoner, many without having fired a shot. Four hundred guns had been captured. Six out of the 10 German divisions in line had ceased to exist. 'As the sun set on the battlefield of 8 August,' the German official history recorded, 'the greatest defeat which the German army had suffered since the beginning of the war was an accomplished fact.' Ludendorff himself called it 'the Black Day of the German army.' It marked the first moral collapse of the men under his command. Some reinforcements going up to the front even experienced being bleated at like sheep by those coming down, with cries of 'sheep to the slaughter' and 'war-prolongers!' There was more to come. The French also had a large force of tanks now, light models of Renault design, and during 9–11 August they pushed abreast of the British advance on the right, recapturing Montdidier. Then the whole line north of the Marne began to move. The salient above the Somme, on the flank of the gains of 8 August was retaken by the British in the last week of August. The French armies south of the Oise pushed steadily forward to reoccupy all the ground lost to the Germans in the May retreat until they were back on their original line. The Germans recorded this time as one of 'days spent in bloody fighting against an ever onstorming enemy and nights passed without sleep in retirement to new lines.'

On 14 August the Kaiser held a conference at Spa to consider the implications of these alarming events. It was attended by all Germany's military and political leaders and they now revealed a reluctant unanimity to seek an early peace: 'We have reached the limits of our endurance.' Ludendorff did not yet believe that this entailed asking for an armistice. Although his offensives had failed, and he had squandered

Left: **Australian troops rest in an abandoned German trench near a German field gun left behind in their retreat, 10 August 1918.**

The ruins of the Cloth Hall at Ypres after the last Germans had been driven from the area which had been under siege for almost four years.

Above far left: Flame throwers in action by the Czech legionnaires of the Italian Army, 21 September 1918.

Above left: Czech legionnaires with their flame throwers on 3 August.

Above: The Austro–Hungarian *Sankt Stefan* sinks in the Adriatic, 10 June 1918.

Left: British cavalry pass the ruined basilica in Albert, Belgium in September 1918.

in them all the reserves with which to retain the initiative, he still believed that Germany was powerful enough to maintain a long defensive and so to 'gradually paralyze the enemy's will to fight.' He was thus thinking of a war which would last into 1919 at least. Paul von Hintze, the Foreign Secretary, was authorized to put out peace feelers. They were not to be direct – Spain and Holland were to be the intermediaries – and they were to be tried only at 'a suitable moment,' that is, when the military situation had stabilized. Moreover, no one present – Kaiser, the Chancellor Georg von Hertling, Hindenburg, Ludendorff and Hintze to name only the most prominent – was ready to relent from the war aims stated at the last headquarters conference which again were little different from those Germany had held throughout the war: protectorate over Belgium, annexation of the French iron fields, occupation of Liège and maintenance of the war frontier in the east.

On the same day, however, Emperor Karl I of Austria, his foreign minister, Count Burian, and his Chief of Staff, General Arz von Straussenburg, arrived at Spa with demands that the Central Powers make an immediate appeal for an end of the war to all belligerents without waiting for 'a suitable moment.' The Austrians had recently tried and failed in a last offensive on the Piave against Italy, the one enemy whom all the subjects of the empire were enthusiastic to fight, and the evidence of the declining power and unity of the Habsburg army had frightened its leaders into a desire for an immediate peace. Their visit began weeks of wrangling between the two empires over diplomatic policy. Not until 10 September did German headquarters – now the seat of all power – agree to 'arrange a conversation' with a neutral power.

By then events were moving faster than Ludendorff could control. On 12 September Pershing, who had at last succeeded in his aim of assembling an independent American army, launched his own offensive against the St Mihiel salient, which had been in German hands since September 1914. In fact, Ludendorff had decided to evacuate it four days before, but the local commander was slow to carry out his instructions and the Americans' 12 divisions caught the defenders in the act of retirement. The offensive was thus a complete success, bringing 15,000 prisoners and great kudos for little cost. In the next two weeks the British army pressed forward along the whole length of the Hindenburg line, gradually penetrating the outworks and winning positions from which to make a final breakthrough. The French army reconstituted its forces to provide a reserve for a similar breakthrough battle on its part of the line. If and when the Hindenburg line was broken the situation of the German army in the West would be insupportable.

The breakthrough was now planned for 26 September and its key action was to be a drive by the American army into the Argonne, north of Verdun, a tangled wilderness of forest and streams. The Americans attacked with the panache that had now become their trademark, but were quickly impeded by the fallen trees and patches of marsh. Only outside the forest did their progress meet the timetable. On the next day the British First and Third Armies attacked north of Arras, on 28 September the British, French and Belgians attacked in Flanders and on 29 September the British Fourth and French First Armies advanced on the Somme. In all 160 Allied divisions moved to the attack and though the Germans counted 113 in the front line, Allied intelligence reckoned only 51 as fit for combat. All were well below strength, some with only 3000 infantry instead of the 9000 required by establishment.

The attack of the Fourth Army was decisive. At the end of the day's fighting it had cracked the Hindenburg position, the infantry crossing the huge, deep trenches via brushwood bundles dropped into them by tanks which led the attack. This bad news for German headquarters was reinforced by worse from the Balkans. On 29 September the Bulgarian government, whose army had been under continuous pressure by the Allied Salonika force throughout the month, sued for an armistice. Its defection laid open the way to the Danube and so to the back door of the Austrian empire, whose leaders were now frantic to make peace on almost any terms they could get. Under this double assault from front and rear, Ludendorff's nerve cracked. Taking Hindenburg with him for support, he sought an interview with the Kaiser and announced that President Wilson must be asked to arrange an armistice, 'at once, as early as at all possible.' Hintze, the Admiral who had recently been made Foreign Minister to replace the more moderate Kuhlmann, revealed how this maneuver was to be used to gain time without surrendering concrete strategic advantages. The High Command would impose a 'revolution from above' by appointing ministers from the ranks of the liberals, thus persuading Wilson that Germany had been democratized and so become a legitimate partner in his search for peace based on the Fourteen Points he had enunciated in January as a basis for a just and lasting settlement. While appropriate negotiations proceeded, the High Command would 'concentrate all the nation's resources for a final defensive struggle.' Next day Hertling, the High Command's nominee as Chancellor, was replaced by the liberal Prince Max of Baden. Matthias Erzberger and Gustav Stresemann, liberals from the parliamentary group, were also admitted to the Cabinet.

Wilson's Fourteen Points, which by no means carried the full support of his British and French cobelligerents, were a statement of high diplomatic and political idealism. Their aim was to reorder Europe so that the rights of small nations should henceforth be respected by large ones and to reform the practice of diplomacy so that secret agreements should not suddenly overwhelm the world in war as had happened in 1914. The freedom of the seas was to be guaranteed, armament to be reduced, colonial questions to be settled with regard to the interests of the peoples concerned, free trade to be fostered and an international body to safeguard peace established. None of that disfavored Germany. Those points which did, and they required the evacuation of all Germany's conquests, the re-arrangement of the Austrian and Turkish empires by 'self-determination' of the minority peoples and the creation of an independent Poland, might, it was hoped, be deferred until Germany had sufficiently recovered her military strength to oppose their application.

Curiously, during October the German army's strength did revive. Civilian labor had been used to construct a new defensive line toward which the armies fell back in easy stages. Bad weather and shortage of transport heightened among the Allies the 'diminishing power of the offensive,' which had now set in. The soldiers also seemed to have rediscovered the will to fight as the frontiers of the homeland appeared to be threatened. Certainly all Allied generals reported a stiffening of enemy resistance as they bumped up against the 'Flanders Position' in mid-October. By then, however, peace negotiations were in full swing. Ludendorff had instructed Prince Max to request an armistice and he had done so on 4 October, though of President Wilson not Marshal Foch. In his request he announced that Germany accepted the Fourteen

Above right: **Americans advance near the Somme in September 1918.**

Below: **American troops in French tanks in the Argonne Forest.**

Above: Tommies have a sing-song in a ruined church in Exermont.

Above left: Doughboys on the march in the Argonne.

Above: American wounded watch German POWs march into captivity in October 1918 in the Argonne campaign.

Left: The ruins of Cambrai on 19 October 1918.

Right: The British enter Lille, October 1918.

Points, which France and Britain had not yet done. Delighted, Wilson replied that he was ready to negotiate an armistice provided the acceptance was genuine and that Germany evacuated all occupied territory. Before Prince Max could clinch the deal a stroke of bad luck deflated his trial balloon. On 12 October a U-Boat sank a passenger ferry in the Irish Sea, drowning 450 civilians, some of them Americans. Public outrage, and his own anger, forced Wilson to adopt a firmer line. On 16 October he told the German Chancellor that submarine warfare must stop at once, that an armistice would have to be arranged with the Allied military commanders, and that there must be firmer evidence shown of Germany's democratization. Next day the German government and High Command debated these demands. Ludendorff, encouraged by the improving situation at the front, was for rejection and fighting on. Prince Max, after hearing all views, overruled him and announced accep-

Above: Generals Rawlinson, Byng, Horne, Lawrence and Birdwood surround their C in C, Field Marshal Sir Douglas Haig in Cambrai, 31 October 1918.

Above: Marshal Ferdinand Foch, C in C of the French army.

Right: Americans pause in the remains of the Argonne Forest.

Below: Americans press forward into the St Mihiel salient in early October 1918.

tance of Wilson's terms. He assured the President that Germany had indeed become democratized and on that basis Wilson asked the Allied generals on 23 October to draft armistice terms. At the same time he invited their governments to accept the Fourteen Points.

Both invitations prompted inter-Allied bargaining. Pershing, curiously, was against granting an armistice at all, since he believed he could win full victory with his fresh and untested army. Haig wanted no more than the Germans' withdrawal from occupied territory since he felt that his own army was flagging before the Germans' renewed strength. Foch was determined to get a French army into the Rhineland, which it had long been a secret French war aim to annex, and he persuaded the British to accept the condition in return for agreeing with their admirals that the High Seas Fleet should be interned in British waters. All parties agreed that the enemy must hand over large numbers of guns, machine guns and aircraft to prevent them renewing the struggle.

The Allied politicians also differed among themselves. They eventually accepted the Fourteen Points but rejected, on British insistence, the freedom of the seas. Clemenceau persuaded Lloyd George to demand German reparation of the war's cost, which was not in the Wilsonian spirit. Wilson would no doubt have argued the point, since he was still committed to a 'peace without victors or vanquished,' but his power to do so almost instantly evaporated as a result of the current congressional elections which promised to return a Republican and therefore Hun-hating but isolationist majority. The Republicans wanted no part of the League of Nations which was Wilson's dearest ideal. His potential role as protector of a 'democratized' Germany was further undermined by the sudden and progressive collapse of the Kaiser's allies. The 'easterners' who had always believed in 'knocking away the props' now saw their policy bearing fruit; the 'westerners,' who had believed in grinding away in France, would have said that it was the result of their policy. Certainly it seems to have been the spectacle of the great pillar of the Central Powers, Germany seeking a way out of the war which prompted her weaker partners to beat her to the post. On 30 October Turkey signed a local armistice with the British in the Middle East, which allowed the Royal Navy to steam up the Dardanelles and a British garrison to occupy Constantinople.

In Austria a stranger turn of events began. The Habsburg Government, following Germany's example, asked Wilson to arrange an armistice on its fronts, which principally meant with Italy. Since enunciating the Fourteen Points Wilson had been persuaded by representatives of the Polish and Czech nationalists to promise his support for their independence as well as that of the Rumanians and Serbs within the empire. That being the case, he said it was for the representatives of those peoples to make their own terms with the Allies. Glimpsing the chance not merely to become independent but to end up on the winning side, Czechs and Poles immediately set up provisional governments of their own. The Hungarians, though a ruling not a subject people of the empire, tried the same trick, leaving only Austria proper as a combatant. Totally disoriented, the government in Vienna made no further move to disengage from the war until, on 23 October, the Italians took advantage of the empire's internal collapse to launch an offensive from the Piave. It was spectacularly successful, if chiefly because the Poles, Czechs and Slavs took the attack as an excuse to run for their new homelands as hard as they could. Shocked into sense, Vienna hastily begged an armistice, which was signed on 2 November, to come into effect 24 hours later. In the interval the Italians took 300,000 prisoners, many of whom would starve to death or die of disease in the coming winter.

In Germany, things were moving the other way. The spectacle of collapse in the East and suspicion of how harsh an armistice the Allies would impose had further hardened Ludendorff's determination to fight on. On 24 October he attempted a direct appeal to the army over the head of Prince Max, who immediately presented the Kaiser with a demand for Ludendorff's resignation against the threat of his own. The Kaiser, who knew that the Socialists in the Reichstag were calling for a republic, swiftly chose Max against Ludendorff, whose resignation he accepted in person on 26 October. He was now to experience identical trouble from his admirals. Knowing that the High Seas Fleet was to become a pawn of the armistice, they had begun to urge each other toward one last sortie into the North Sea, where by battle they might just improve the chance of settling the war on terms of equality. 'Better an honorable death than a shameful peace' was the nub of their argument.

American and French troops celebrate their victory in the streets of Paris, 11 November 1918.

Above: WACs and tanks behind the lines in June 1918.

Above left: British troops celebrate the end of their long war.

Below: Soldiers are carried aloft in the joyous frenzy of Armistice Day in Paris.

Left: Londoners celebrate their victory.

Below left: Presidents Wilson and Poincare salute the Parisian crowd upon Wilson's triumphal arrival in the capital.

It did not appeal to their crews, who had not been out of harbor for two years and among whom trade unionism and socialism were strongly established. At the rumor of this 'death ride' on 29 October, the stokers of the Third Battle Squadron extinguished boiler fires and many of the other crew men announced that they would not raise anchor. Loyal sailors and marines removed the mutineers and took them ashore. That step merely transferred the trouble from the comparative isolation of the fleet to a more fertile seedbed. On 3 November the streets of Kiel filled with sailors and their allies among the dockyard workers, demanding the release of the prisoners. There was firing outside the prison, some demonstrators were killed and next day Kiel was in the hands of a Sailors' Soviet.

The disturbances at Kiel convinced the Berlin government that it had a revolution on its hands, which could only be checked by securing an immediate armistice. It would pacify popular opinion and also bring home the army in whose absence the government was without means to quell disorder. On 7 November, therefore, the German armistice Commission radioed Foch with an appeal for an immediate meeting and that evening sent its two civilian members, Erzberger and Oberndorff, to meet the Generalissimo at Rethondes in the forest of Compiègne. There Foch read them the terms next day, but by the time they returned to Berlin, revolution had caught fire. The Socialists, both radical and moderate, were demanding the Kaiser's abdication and the declaration of a republic. Prince Max himself was now convinced that only abdication could stave off disaster. That evening on the telephone, he advised, speaking:

'as a relative; your abdication has become necessary to save Germany from civil war. The great majority of the people believe you are responsible for the present situation. The troops are not to be depended upon. This is the last possible moment.'

The Kaiser, at his HQ in Spa, still refused.

He had gone to Spa from Berlin on the day he had dismissed Ludendorff, in order to be with his troops, the ultimate protectors of the House of Hohenzollern. Now even they were weighing their devotion to the All-Highest against the survival of more substantial things, not only domestic peace but the life of the army itself. On the night of 8 November Hindenburg – his old authority restored by the departure of Ludendorff – and General Wilhelm Gröner, the latter's successor, decided that they too felt as Prince Max did. Gröner immediately took the precaution of summoning to Spa 50 senior officers from the fighting line. Each was asked in strict secrecy if the Emperor at the head of his troops could 'reconquer the Fatherland by force' and if the troops would 'fight the Bolsheviks on the home front?' Only one answered yes to both questions, the others either no or an equivocation. Armed with this evidence, the two most senior officers of his army confronted the Kaiser in his office at Spa on the morning of 9 November and intimated to him that the war was lost and he must go. A prolonged and painful argument ensued, in which Crown Prince Wilhelm joined to challenge the evidence of the army's disaffection. Ultimately the Kaiser rounded on Gröner – the sacrilege of the proceedings had reduced Hindenburg to suffering silence – and demanded 'What of the oath on the Colors.' The

Right: Lloyd George, General Sir Henry Wilson and Marshal Foch in Paris.

Below right: Austrian Kaiser Karl I visits Kaiser Wilhelm's HQ at Spa in the last days of the war.

Oath (*Fahneneide*) was the personal word of loyalty until death sworn by every one of the Kaiser's officers on commissioning. Gröner shrugged and answered with exasperation, 'Today the Oath on the Colors is just words.

This shaft of appalling truth reduced the Kaiser first to silence and then to an offer to abdicate as Emperor but not as King of Prussia. Almost immediately word was brought that Prince Max had anticipated him and proclaimed the republic in Berlin. The officers now went on to warn that they could not guarantee the Kaiser's personal safety even at Imperial Headquarters and that he must at once go into exile. Holland was the obvious place of refuge as the nearest neutral country. He took his private train there the next morning. He was never to set foot on German soil again.

In Berlin, where socialists, disaffected soldiers, the hungry and the merely feckless were busy throwing down the symbols of monarchy from public buildings, the new republican government was so occupied with the business of asserting its authority that it scarcely had time to consider negotiating the armistice. Despite the harshness of the terms – surrender of Alsace-Lorraine, occupation of the Rhineland, annulment of the treaties of Brest-Litovsk with Russia and Bucharest with Rumania, transfer of main war stocks to the Allies and internment of the High Seas Fleet – Frederich Ebert, the new socialist Chancellor, simply instructed Erzberger to return to Compiègne and sign. There at 0500 hours on 11 November, in a railroad carriage parked in a siding in the forest, he did so. The armistice came into effect six hours later.

'On the morning of 11 November, remembered a British cavalryman, 'there were rumors of an armistice, but we did not take much notice of them.' It is not surprising that the British troops did not, for the German High Command had kept its rearguards full of the best, loyal troops who continued to fight even though giving ground throughout the first weeks of November:

'At about 1045 we were in action against the Germans east of Mons, and one of our troops had just charged some German machine guns. A private soldier came galloping toward us. He was much excited, had lost his cap, and could not stop his horse. As he passed us he shouted. 'The war's over! The war's over!' We thought undoubtedly the poor fellow was suffering from shell-shock.'

In the Vosges, a French officer still in the trenches noticed that his own men:

'retained their composure and self-control in these solemn moments. The attitude of our conquered armies was quite different. At 1100 hours sharp they surged out of their trenches, shouting and flourishing a red flag, and carrying big signs with the word 'Republic' written on them. Many Germans wore republican cockades in their caps. They were all eager to engage in conversation with our soldiers but, to their intense surprise, were disdainfully ignored by them. Having been rebuffed, they began celebrating the armistice in their own trenches; they threw grenades, blew up the ammunition dumps and in the evening fired all their star shells, illuminating the sky with an incomparable fireworks display. They also began to sing merry songs and played instruments, apparently not realizing that the armistice meant their country's complete collapse, the deepest humiliation ever suffered by Germany.'

Curiously the crowds celebrated too in the great German cities, welcoming back the first soldiers from the front as if they were victors; and, like victors, the soldiers came home with flowers in their buttonholes and rifle-muzzles, just as they had done when the regiments marched away in that distant August of 1914. In the cities of the Allies, celebrations were more unrestrained:

'There was great liveliness, calls, cries, whistles and hooters sounding, noise and crowds grew as we proceeded' a traveller from the suburbs to inner London recorded. 'Chancery Lane was very lively. Going out for lunch about one o'clock, great excitement prevailed. Every vehicle going along the Strand was being boarded by people, most of whom waved flags. Boys and girls flung themselves on anywhere and boarded as best they might. One scene was more unusual than others. A stout policeman on point duty was surrounded by girls all clamouring to dance with him. The London bobby rose to the occasion – without a word he took on one after another for a turn round on the narrow pavement as they stood, while his countenance remained absolutely impassive. Custom and convention melted away as if a new world had indeed dawned. Officers and privates mixed in equal comradeship. Privates drilled officers, munitionettes commanded platoons made up of both. The spirit of militarism turned into comedy. Never in history perhaps have such great multitudes, experienced such restoration of joyousness in the twinkling of an eye.'

Was there to be 'a new world' of which this Londoner had glimpsed the dawning in the rejoicing crowds? Wilson was determined that there should be. Lloyd George had promised one ('A land fit for heroes'), while far away in Russia Lenin believed he had begun to build one. In the lands between the leaders of the new independent nations – Poland, Czechoslovakia, the Kingdom of the Serbs, Croats and Slovenes (Yugoslavia) – were disputing with the old and with each other the exact shape each of their people's new worlds should take. While peace broke out in the West, war continued or found new outlets in the East. The leaders of the Baltic minorities, Latvians, Lithuanians and Estonians, whose independence the Bolsheviks had recognized along with Finland's, were soon at war with their own Reds, through whom the Bolsheviks hoped to work a widening of the Revolution. In Hungary there shortly was to be a new Bolshevik government, under the leadership of Bela Kun. Poland had begun or was on the point of fighting three enemies, the Ukrainians for the possession of eastern Galicia, the Germans for Lower Silesia, Posen and West Prussia, the Russians for an eastern border – and eventually for the survival of their new state. Italian patriots, under the leadership of the poet-demagogue Gabriele d'Annunzio, had staked their kingdom's claim to the head of the Adriatic, while the Greeks were set on pushing the boundaries of the Kingdom of the Hellenes, deep into Anatolia. In its remote fortresses, Kemal, the defender of Gallipoli, was gathering some scraps of the broken Ottoman army to oppose them. Strangest of all the wars were those of 'intervention' against Russia. The Allies' decision to support the Whites against the Reds, while the latter seemed to be co-operating in Germany's war effort, had led to the landing of some British, French, American and even Japanese troops at the Whites' supply ports, Archangel, the Crimea and Vladivostok, while British naval flotillas operated in the eastern Baltic.

This sea of confusion was too wide and too troubled for the peacemakers to make their concern. They could not even yet begin to consider what peace they should offer Turkey or Austria (what remained of it) or Hungary. During December and January of 1918–19, it was as much as they could do to agree on a policy for peace-making with Germany. That country had more or less restored internal order by 18 January 1919, when the Peace Conference was convoked at Versailles. The Spartakist revolt in Berlin had been put down. The German army, which had dissolved itself overnight as soon as its columns had marched into their home barracks, had been replaced with a makeshift but efficient stopgap, recruited from right-wing *Freikorps* raised to buttress the authority of the republican government. Without an army capable of defending the national frontiers, the republic was at the mercy of the victors' goodwill when it came to meeting them at the Conference table, and there was to be little goodwill at Versailles.

France, who had suffered most, insisted on extortionate terms. She wanted the permanent and almost total disarmament of Germany, long-term occupation of the Rhineland, which she actually hoped to establish as a separate state under her influence, and reparations of a size calculated not merely to make good the devastation of her territory but also the expense she had incurred in defending it. The British were almost equally as demanding. They were determined to keep the High Seas Fleet (which, in a sense, they did when its crews scuttled their ships in the anchorage of Scapa Flow on 21 June 1919). Their dominions – Australia and South Africa – were also anxious to possess the adjoining German Colonies, New Guinea and Southwest Africa, so Westminster chummily offered to annex the rest in East and West Africa. A device, known as a League of Nations Mandate, was invented to regularize this imperialism, and the French made use of it to divide the Turkish Middle East with the British. They took Syria and the Lebanon, their ally Iraq (Mesopotamia) and Palestine, where thousands of European Jews had now begun to settle under the provision of the Balfour Declaration. The Americans, whose foreign policy was still determined by Wilson, demanded nothing for themselves, not even reparations, but were intent on all parties accepting their League of Nations, even Germany who was not to be admitted to it.

When Wilson was satisfied that his fellow peacemakers – Lloyd George, the Italian Vittorio Orlando and Clemenceau (who at 79 survived the wound of a would-be assassin while the Conference was in progress) – would form the League he readily agreed to their individual demands. The Germans were scarcely consulted. Democratized or not, they were regarded and treated by the Allies as enemies, and the blockade was maintained throughout the spring of 1919 to ensure that they would accept the Allied terms. In May these terms were presented. France had reduced her financial demands to the indemnification of war damage, as long as Germany admitted 'war guilt.' The Rhineland was to be occupied for 15 years and thereafter permanently 'demilitarized.' The frontier with Poland was fixed very much where the Poles asked for it, though a plebiscite was allowed in Silesia. Austria, against the wishes of its German-speaking population, was forbidden to unite with Germany. Above all, Germany was disarmed. The air force was abolished, the navy forbidden submarines or heavy ships, the army forbidden tanks or heavy artillery and reduced to a strength of 100,000 men, who must all be 12-year volunteers. There was to be no chance of building up hidden reserves with rapidly-trained conscripts. Allied inspectors, with wide powers of entry, were to police these provisions.

German opinion was outraged by the treaty. It seemed to make a mockery of the sacrifice each social group had made in ending the war; that of the monarchy by the traditional right and center, that of self-defense by the threatened peasants and landowners of the eastern frontier, that of political popularity by the socialists and liberals who had created the republic. Reparations threatened the pockets of all classes, the confession of 'war guilt' stuck in the throats of all patriots – and Versailles made every German a patriot. Even the peace-loving Ebert, now President, was driven to ask Hindenburg what chance there was of resuming the war as an act of protest. Through Gröner, his spokesman in every awkward moment, Hindenburg replied that 'the Army might hold its own against the Poles in the East. It could not resist an Allied advance in the West.' On 28 June 1919, a silent and embittered German delegation signed the treaty in the Hall of Mirrors at Versailles.

So ended the First World War. Men had already begun an attempt to reckon its cost in lives. Men still continue today. The British Empire had lost 1,000,000 dead; indeed, a tablet placed in every French cathedral records that fact: 'To the Glory of God and in memory of One Million men of the British Empire who fell in the Great War, and of whom the greater part rest in France.' About 750,000 were British and Irish, the rest Australians, Canadians, South Africans, New Zealanders, Indians and Africans. The French, with a smaller population, had suffered worse. About 1,700,000 Frenchmen had died. German casualties were usually recorded at the same figure, but may have exceeded 2,000,000. The Americans had suffered only about 125,000 casualties, quite enough considering how short their active war had been. Russia's losses were counted at over 1,000,000 before the February

Left: Italian patriot Gabriele d'Annunzio (right) seized Fiume for Italy in a daring coup after the war.

Below: Austrian President Carl Renner replies to the peace terms offered by Clemenceau and Wilson (background).

Below: Thomas Masaryk, President of the new Czech Republic.

Below: Bela Kun, who headed a Communist government in Hungary for four months in 1919.

Revolution, but were certainly many more, perhaps three times that. The peoples of Austria-Hungary suffered over 1,000,000 deaths, the Italians over 600,000. Turkish losses were never counted. In total there were probably 10,000,000 battle deaths in the First World War. Civilian casualties by privation, atrocity and disease, in particular through the great 'Spanish' flu epidemic which swept through the under-nourished populations of Europe in the winter of 1918, were higher. In all the war caused directly or indirectly the deaths of at least 20,000,000 people.

It had also transformed the map of Europe, inaugurated revolutionary regimes in new and old states which would never have come to power in the settled days of pre-1914, and shaken the industrial and financial world to its foundations. Grievances and rancors far more bitter than those which had animated the selfish and aggressive foreign policies of the powers in the last years of Imperial Europe had taken deep root and would fester on. The Bolsheviks, mis-used by the Germans, attacked by the Allies and then made a diplomatic pariah, would feed their belief in eventual ideological triumph on the discharge of these wounds. The Balkan peoples and their Turkish neighbors would each resent either what they had lost by the war or the bigger prizes of which they had been cheated. The Italians above all would see in its outcome a frustration of their 'divine selfishness,' and look to dictatorship for a chance to indulge it again. The Germans were not yet thinking of dictator-ship. Their belief in the unreality of defeat, in the 'crime' of Versailles, in their right to primacy in continental Europe was absolute and they would use any means to achieve them. Their provinces teemed with violent men who had learned the philosophy of struggle in the trenches, applied it in the Civil Wars of 1918–19 and were ready to use it again against Germany's foreign neighbors, to east or west, north or south, if struggle would make Germany great once more. One of them was an ex-corporal of the 16th Bavarian Reserve Infantry Regiment, thrice wounded on the Western Front, called Adolf Hitler.

The war had changed more than people's nationalities, political status and economic expectations. It had also changed their way of looking at the world. The Europe which died on 31 July 1914 was not a fairyland. Its peoples knew inequality, oppression, exploitation and injustice. They also knew peace and order and expected to die in their beds. The First World War had carried violent death into every family circle. To those who had fought, it had shown the skull beneath the skin, often by direct and unforgettable confrontation. The men of the trenches might seek to obliterate from their minds the horrors but few ever managed, some chose not to and none could ever feel again an absolute respect for the sanctity of human life. A terrible ugliness had been born on the Somme, at Verdun, on the vast nameless battlefields of the Carpathians and the Ukraine, along the choked stream beds of the Argonne and Ypres, which lent a dreadful and profane irony to the most beautiful and best-loved of all First World War poems by John McRae.

In Flanders fields the poppies blow
Beneath the crosses, row on row
That mark our place; and in the sky
The larks, still bravely singing, fly
Scarce heard amid the guns below.

We are the Dead. Short days ago
We lived, felt dawn, saw sunset glow,
Loved and were loved, and now we lie
In Flanders Fields.

Take up our quarrel with the foe;
To you from failing hands we throw
The torch; be yours to hold it high.
If ye break faith with us who die
We shall not sleep, though poppies grow
In Flanders Fields.

Right: Renner at St Germain during the peace talks.

Far right: The victory parade down the Avenue de la Grande Armée in Paris.

Below: Orlando, Lloyd George, Clemenceau and Wilson.

C. Duvent

A victorious Tommy on his way home.

Casualty Figures

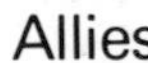

Balance of Casualties 1914-1918

Allies

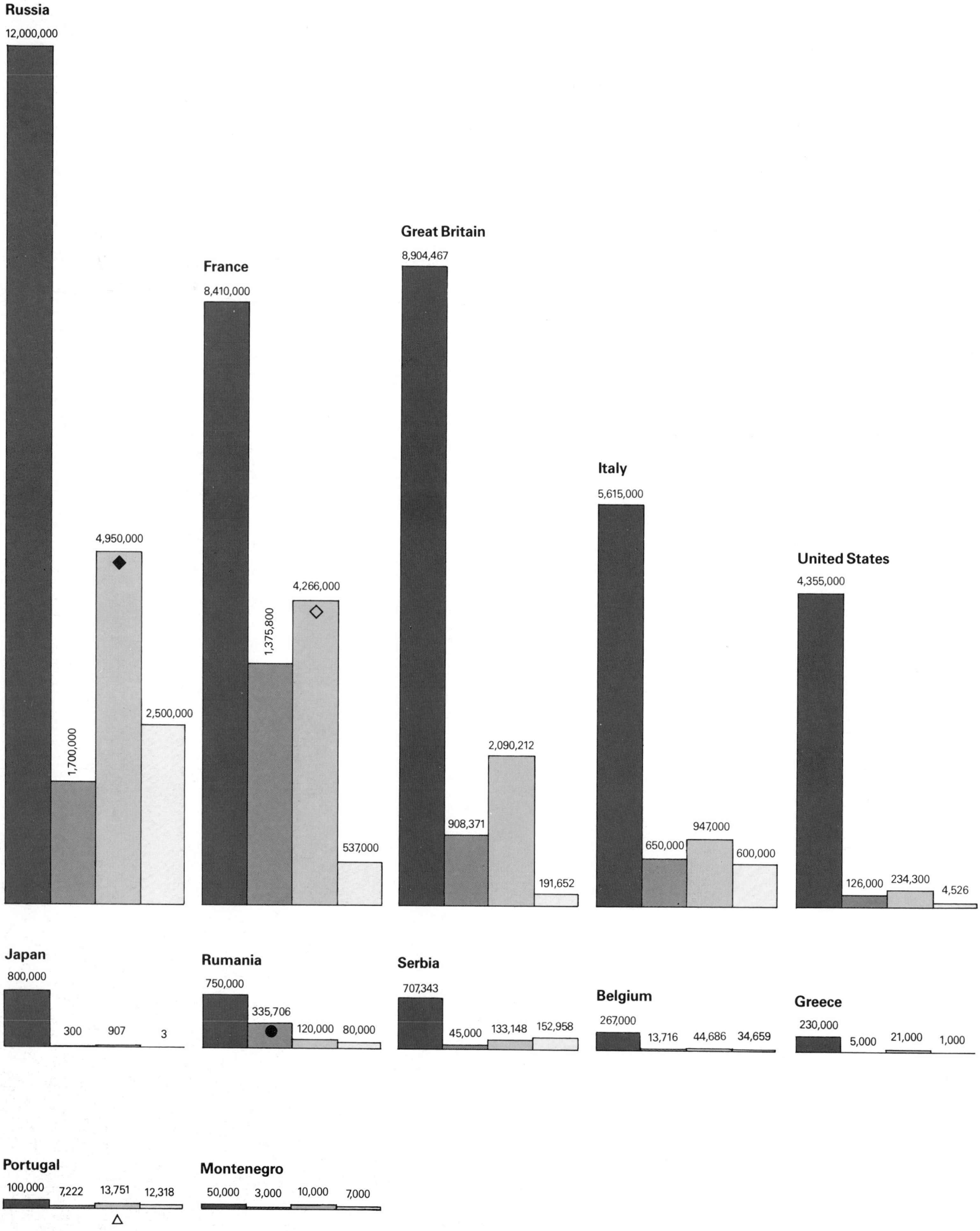

Russia
12,000,000
1,700,000
4,950,000
2,500,000
France
8,410,000
1,375,800
4,266,000
537,000
Great Britain
8,904,467
908,371
2,090,212
191,652
Italy
5,615,000
650,000
947,000
600,000
United States
4,355,000
126,000
234,300
4,526
Japan
800,000
300
907
3
Rumania
750,000
335,706
120,000
80,000
Serbia
707,343
45,000
133,148
152,958
Belgium
267,000
13,716
44,686
34,659
Greece
230,000
5,000
21,000
1,000
Portugal
100,000
7,222
13,751
12,318
Montenegro
50,000
3,000
10,000
7,000

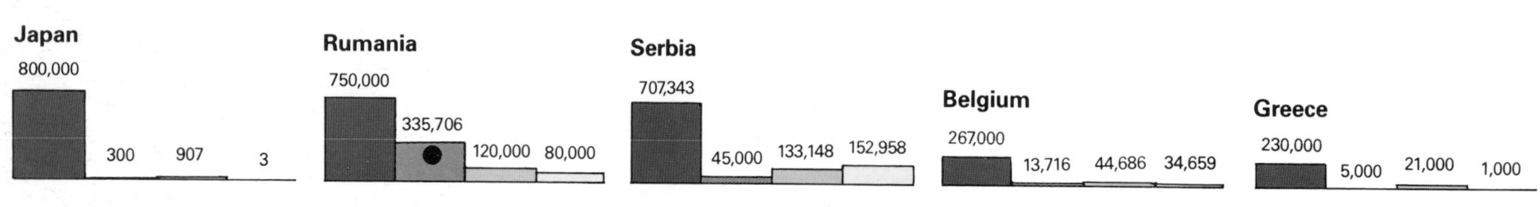

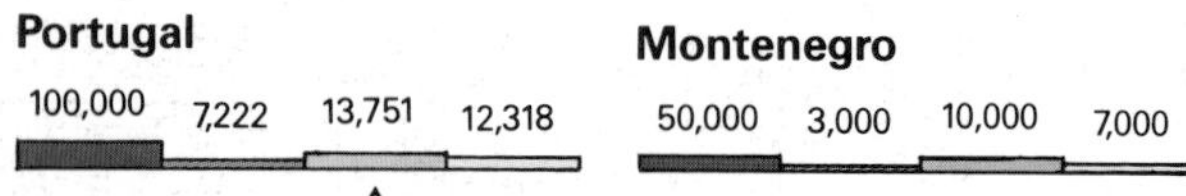

Central Powers

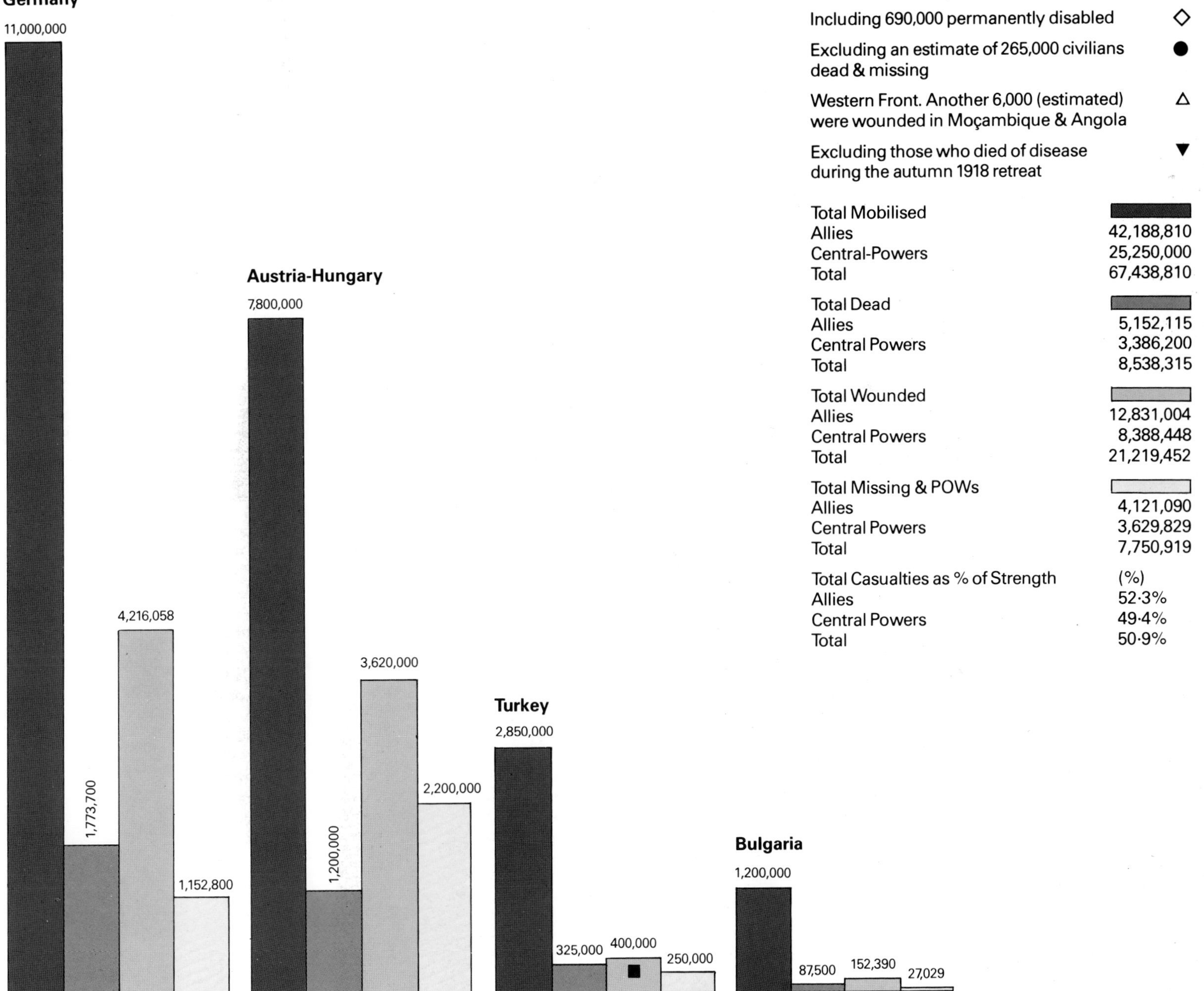

BRIGADIER PETER YOUNG

RLD
RII

List of abbreviations

ARP: Air Raid Precautions.
BBC: British Broadcasting Corporation.
BEF: British Expeditionary Force.
CINCPAC: Commander-in-Chief, Pacific.
COMSOPAC: Commander South Pacific.
COSSAC: Chief of Staff to the Supreme Allied Commander (Designate).
E-BOAT: British term for German motor-torpedo-boats.
FFI: French Forces of the Interior.
LCA: Landing Craft, Assault.
LVT: Landing Vehicle, Tracked (Amphtrac).
OKH: Oberkommando des Heeres – High Command of the Army.
OKW: Oberkommando der Wehrmacht – High Command of the Armed Forces.
RA: Royal Artillery.
RAF: Royal Air Force.
SHAEF: Supreme Headquarters, Allied Expeditionary Force.
USAAF: United States Army Air Force.

INTRODUCTION

Eighteen years have passed since the first publication of this work. In those days I was Reader in Military History at the Royal Military Academy Sandhurst, and I owe a great deal to my colleagues in the Military History Department, who helped in its preparation. We have been lucky that, despite countless alarums and excursions, we have survived another sixteen years without some new Führer plunging us into yet another World War, whose death rolls might well have exceeded the 30,000,000 claimed by Hitler's War. Yet we still await some hopeful sign that Mankind is coming round to the view that it is time to reject violence as the means of attaining political ends. The fact is that the study of past wars, their history and lessons, is one which statesmen as well as soldiers should make their own. But what do we find? On every side the same mistakes which led up to World War II are being repeated. The democratic World still has its Daladiers, its Chamberlains and its Reynauds. We look back in horror to 1939 and find France and Britain declaring war, when the one had no Air Force worthy of the name and the other could not put so many as 15 divisions in the field. How well would the Western Powers perform were a similar crisis to confront us tomorrow – or today? Let us ponder the doings of the older generation. Let us prepare to emulate their good deeds. Let us strive to avoid their mistakes.

This work is now produced in a somewhat abridged form, but it has not otherwise been altered. That is not to say that it is beyond improvement. I do not believe, for example, that I made it sufficiently clear in Chapter One that the Poles, though conquered in only 18 days, faced an impossible task, and made a staunch resistance with virtually no support from their allies, France and Britain. Moreover, numbers escaped to continue the war. The part that Polish pilots, for example, played in the Battle of Britain was of incalculable value, quite apart from the exploits of their countrymen by land and sea.

I am grateful to Mr Ignacy Dargiewicz for pointing out to me that Chapter 2 is too short and superficial and 'so evidencing the British inability to understand the position of East European countries Poland included at the first place'.

I accept his rebuke. I should have mentioned the heroic General Kleeberg, who after beating two Panzer divisions near Kock, was only compelled to surrender, on 6 October 1939, for lack of ammunition. The defenders of Hel Peninsula, who did not surrender until 2 October, also deserve mention. I should also have remarked upon the brave defence of the Westerplatte, at Gdansk (Danzig) by a single company, which held out until 7 September. It was here that World War II began.

I was, myself, a soldier by trade, and I find myself slightly surprised at the chapters dealing with the war at sea. With no wish to be immodest I find I do not wish to alter a line, nor do I think that any seafaring man has just cause to complain that I have underrated the importance of naval warfare.

With the war in the air it is another matter. I yield to no man in my admiration of the fighter pilots of 1940. If I am not absolutely sold on the great bomber offensives, both German and Allied, by which with crude and mighty blows first one side and then the other tried to end the war, it is only that having been decently brought up at Oxford by C T Atkinson and Major General Sir Ernest Swinton on 'The Principles of War' and all that, I just prefer something a little more subtle than pushing over Germany acre by acre. If for me the deed of the *Enola Gay* lacks charm you must attribute it to my old-fashioned outlook. I have often thought that I would have been happier had I been at Dunkirk in 1658, rather than in 1940. Still one must not speak lightly of one's first campaign and it cannot be denied that the so-called Blitzkrieg of 1940 was an education. I am sure I learned more in those three weeks than in the six months I later spent at the Staff College.

Looking once more through that chapter I think perhaps that the number of civilians killed

The B-17E *Yankee* is refuelled prior to another mission. The B-17s were the backbone of the Allied Strategic Bomber Force over the Third Reich.

at Rotterdam on 14 May was rather less than the figure I give, but where atrocities of this sort are under discussion, it is the brutal intent that matters rather than the actual number of unhappy victims. I trust I gave sufficient emphasis to the point that frightfulness was as much an ingredient of the Blitzkrieg as were the Stukas and the Panzer divisions, the parachutists and the Fifth Column.

Dunkirk certainly had its miraculous side, not only in the wonderful work of the Navy and its auxiliaries in bringing out men of the BEF and the 1st French Army. I do not think that I emphasized sufficiently the importance of the battle of the Ypres-Comines Canal (26-28 May) when Generals Brooke and Franklyn, greatly outnumbered, held up von Reichenau's 6th Army at the moment when by all the Rules of War it should have given Gort's Army and its Allies the *coup de grâce*. Without the officers and men of the BEF Britain would have had a very indifferent army in the years ahead.

Moving on to Operation Barbarossa, the invasion of Russia, I feel that it ought perhaps to be pointed out that the authorities do not all agree as to the number of divisions, which the Germans had on the Eastern Front on 22 June 1941. It may be that they did not have 145 but as many as 149. Be that as it may, it should also have been noted that not all were German. There were 14 Hungarian and Rumanian divisions included in the total, and it is doubtful whether we should regard these as having the same military value as German divisions. Later on Spanish and Italian troops were also used on the Russian front.

Passing on to Singapore, it may be worth adding a few statistics to the story of the end of the Battleship Age, when Admiral Tom Phillips, that old seadog who was one of those who thought that capital ships could beat off enemy aircraft with their own Ack Ack, was lost with the *Prince of Wales* and the *Repulse*. The number who lost their lives was about 840. This victory cost the Japanese precisely three aircraft and 18 men. It was indeed the end of an era.

When I wrote this chapter I was not aware of the work of the Fujiwara Organization and the way it helped Captain Mohan Singh and Rash Bihari Bose to build up the Indian National Army in Siam and Malaya. No doubt by working on the doubts and fears of half-trained Indian troops, not only in the battle, but afterwards in captivity, they paved the way for the initial Japanese successes in Burma. Fujiwara was a most able and interesting man, who survived the purge of the Japanese staff after their repulse at Imphal. By 1969 he had risen to be a general, and there were those among his countrymen who thought he was very much the cleverest they had.

An odd point, which I would have mentioned had I known it, is that apparently General Percival never had any copy of the terms of the surrender of Singapore in his possession. The surrender of Singapore, look at it as you will, was a disgrace to British arms. However, it must be said for General Percival that he insisted on the retention of 1,000 armed men to maintain order, and to protect the women and children. This was not a mere verbal afterthought, but something upon which the unfortunate General had insisted on in writing, before ever he came to the conference table. The whole question is perhaps academic. Generally speaking, when one reads of an enormous surrender, whether great or small, it is not too difficult to think of some way in which the fight could have been carried on. It is a question of one's attitude of mind.

In Singapore the Army was, I suggest, taking too much notice of the Governor and the

civilians. When the Japanese – greatly outnumbered be it noted – reached the Island it was time to use all the troops, who are vulgarly called 'tail', as 'tooth'. A counterattack – preferably by night – was worth a try.

Percival had proved his gallantry in the 1914-18 war and he was a good staff officer. But can one see Lord Gort letting things come to such an end? And he, after Dunkirk, was given no field command: only the Rock of Gibraltar and later the Island fortress of Malta. And, *en passant*, in 1943 Mason-Macfarlane, a very different sort but a real fighting man, and full of ideas was also Governor of Gibraltar. One wonders whether one of these two might not have galvanized the defenders of Singapore into deeds worthy of the British name.

I admit that I reread with distaste the story of the Bomber Offensive against Germany. But what else could we have done? What other means could that great and strong man 'Bomber' Harris have devised? With the weapons he had the answer is none. If ever a man was wronged it was Harris, who when the peerages were bestowed at the end of the war did not receive a barony.

If you like statistics let us add to Chapter 21, the point that on 7 May 1945 Bomber Command had 1,600 aircraft, mostly Lancasters, and that with the USAAF the Allies had 4,000 bombers. We had come a long way since 1939. But it does show that the Germans have a certain resilience, toughness, staunchness. . . . It is my opinion that no man who has not fought the Germans – and got the better of them – need boast of his soldiership.

Well, I have reread my own book, and I find that I still agree with my own prejudices. I hope I have been charitable to friend and foe alike. Oddly enough I think I have. War is a terrible ordeal, but speaking for myself I do not in the least regret having gone through this one. To a

The result of the B-29 raids over Japan: the main street of the city of Nagaoka, which had 66 per cent of its urban area destroyed.

man in his twenties extraordinary events such as these are immensely stimulating. Indeed they teach you something about yourself.

I have been fortunate in my time to meet many men of distinction, of learning, and of courage. But to tell the truth the ones I esteem most are the ones with whom I have served in war, and who thought as I do, that when it comes down to it, strategy, and administration and organization count for nothing if your platoons do not beat the enemy's platoons. My friends in the Commandos did not believe in a policy of 'Live and Let Live'. Quite the contrary – their idea was that the No Man's Land belonged to us, and was out of bounds to the Germans or the Japanese, or whoever it might be. The only way to deal with the Germans was to thump them, wherever they were met, and as often as possible.

We live at a time when democratic politicians are unwilling to spend money on Intelligence and on the Armed Forces. This may be parsimony rather than pacifism. In any case there could be no greater mistake. For one thing it sows doubts in the minds of one's Allies, and leads to the sort of mutual recriminations which bedevilled relations between France and Britain in 1940. When one is dealing with the successors of Josef Stalin it is well to consider the old Roman maxim: Let him, who desires peace, prepare for war. *Qui desiderat pacem, praeparet bellum*. VEGETIUS. *De Re Militaris*.

Queen Victoria confided to her Diary that she had 'learnt that history was not an account of what actually happened, but what people genuinely thought had happened.' Here you have what I think happened between 1939 and 1945.

Peter Young

TWYNING MANOR

I THE COMING OF WAR

'The angel of peace was murdered, killed consciously and deliberately in 1939.' *Dr Walter Hofer*

Hitler's War is not a bad title for the Second World War, for he was its architect. But in fact two wars waged quite separately, though more or less simultaneously, made up the struggle. These could be called the German War and the Japanese War. The German War lasted from 1 September 1939, when Hitler's armies invaded Poland, to 8 May 1945 when they surrendered. This was in effect a continuation of the 1914–18 'Kaiser's War': it was the German's second throw to achieve their national aspirations – the hegemony of Europe and perhaps eventually of the world. The Japanese War ran from 7 December 1941 (the date of their attack on Pearl Harbor) to their surrender on 15 August 1945. Their aim was simply to establish Japanese domination of the Far East.

Although the Germans and Japanese were allies, their two wars hardly impinged on each other at all, except that the Allies, especially the United States, had to decide which to fight first. In a positive sense the main responsibility for these two wars rests squarely on the Germans and the Japanese, for it was they who took the initiative. They were prepared to use war as a means of attaining the objects of their state policies.

In the First World War (1914–18) the Central Powers – Germany, Austria-Hungary, Turkey and Bulgaria – had fought France, Russia, Great Britain, Italy, the United States and their allies and had been defeated. In consequence the ancient Austrian Empire had been carved up along lines dictated by 'Self-determination'. The Imperial Russian government had been succeeded by the Communist system, the Imperial German government had given way to a Republic. But the only major power to disappear altogether was Austria-Hungary.

In 1918–19 the Germans, who had no mean opinion of their soldiership, were bewildered to find themselves on the losing side. They felt themselves cheated by the settlement, the *Diktat* of Versailles. War is a political act. Therefore the degree of violence employed must always be governed to some extent by considering the settlement that is to follow. The settlement after the First World War may have solved certain problems; it also produced a fresh crop.

Hitler had no difficulty in stirring up German

Below: **From left to right, Dr Ley, Karl Hermann Frank, Konrad Henlein, Wilhelm Frick, von Tshammer-Osten, and Adolf Hitler attend a gymnastics display in 1938. Henlein was the leader of the Sudeten German Nazi Party.**

Left: Hermann Göring, Rudolf Hess, Benito Mussolini, Hitler and Galeazzo Ciano at a meeting in 1938.

Right: Following the German occupation of the rest of Czechoslovakia, Hitler drives through Brno greeted by 'enthusiastic' crowds.

resentment against the Versailles 'slave treaty'. It had deprived the Fatherland of all her colonies, given back Alsace-Lorraine to France, internationalized the Saar, made Danzig a Free City and left the Allies in occupation of the Rhineland. Reparations too had been heavy – £6,000,000,000 – and failure to pay had led Poincaré, violently anti-German as he was, to order the occupation of the Ruhr in 1923. Even after the Lausanne Conference (1932) put an end to reparations, Hitler found no difficulty in keeping German resentment alive.

'This is not Peace. It is an Armistice for twenty years' had been Marshal Foch's comment on the Treaty of Versailles, and in a way it had been a remarkably accurate forecast. Yet the provisions of Versailles were laid aside long before 1939. Only the bitterness remained, valuable propaganda material for Hitler on his avenging progress. That Hitler was encouraged by the feeble politicians of neighbouring countries, by pacifists everywhere and by the woolly-minded dreamers of the League of Nations Union cannot be denied. But their responsibility was a negative one, whether born of good intentions or merely of ignorance and fear.

The overwhelming majority of the people living in Europe in the 1920s and 1930s, and their leaders, hated the thought of a Second World War. Yet, given the conditions prevailing after the Peace Treaties, it would have been strange indeed if the legacy of the First World War had not been a second. 'War is the continuation of state policy by other means,' General Karl von Clausewitz, the author of *Vom Kriege*, calmly assures us. However logical his

Right: **Prime Minister Neville Chamberlain makes his 'peace in our time' speech on his return from Munich, 30 September 1938.**

Below: **Vyacheslav Molotov signs the Nazi-Soviet Pact of Non-Aggression on 23 August 1939.**

aphorism may have seemed to one who had served in the Napoleonic Wars, many who had been through the First World War thought it wholly unreasonable. The idea that they had fought 'the War to end War' was widely held, at least among the English-speaking contestants. But Hitler was a disciple of Clausewitz.

Few indeed among the victors were willing to consolidate their political position at the risk of the sort of losses they expected in a further war. People everywhere were profoundly impressed by the development of modern weapons, especially bombing aircraft, though these last were as yet far less formidable than they believed. And, whatever one may have thought in 1939, the Germans themselves were not without misgivings as to the possible consequences of their leader's policies, much as they enjoyed their earlier fruits. Without Hitler to lead them the Germans would hardly have set out a second time to conquer Europe. In the words of Professor Trevor-Roper: 'The Second World War was Hitler's personal war in many senses. He intended it, he prepared for it, he chose the moment for launching it; and for three years, in the main, he planned its course.' In that sense the Second World War was certainly Hitler's War. Yet the causes of the struggle were complex and the fighting took place in many theatres widely dispersed over the face of the earth.

In 1914 war had blown up practically unheralded, but the steps that led to the explosion of 1939 were clearly marked. We need trace its origins no further back than the day when Adolf Hitler became Chancellor of Germany. It is true that in the Far East Japan was already pursuing a course of comparable violence, and that in Mussolini the new dictator seemed to have a model and a mentor, but neither Japan nor Italy would have risked a Second World War had Germany remained peaceful.

Adolf Hitler was born at Braunau in 1889, the third child of an Austrian customs official. His father, who was over fifty when the boy was born, had a stubborn though passionate nature. He wanted Hitler also to become an official and sent him to a secondary school. But the boy wanted to be an artist, and left school in 1905 without the customary Leaving Certificate. His report described his command of the German language as inadequate. From this period dated his love of Wagner's operas, which he first heard at Linz, and his intense German nationalism.

His father died in 1903 and in 1907 his mother allowed him to enter the Academy of Fine Arts in Vienna. His progress was unsatisfactory. He returned to his home where with great gentleness he nursed his mother through her last illness – cancer of the breast. Her death and the consequent break-up of the home left him badly shaken. Returning to Vienna he eked out a pitiful existence as a casual labourer and a painter, sometimes without a roof, sometimes without an overcoat. In 1910 an acquaintance described him: 'From under a greasy, black derby hat, his hair hung long over his coat collar. His thin and hungry face was covered with a black beard above which his large staring eyes were the one prominent feature.' He was 'lazy and moody . . . he disliked regular work. . . . He had none of the common vices. He neither smoked nor drank and . . was too shy and awkward to have any success with women. His passions were reading newspapers and talking politics.'

'One evening,' Hanisch relates, 'Hitler went to a cinema where Kellermann's *Tunnel* was being shown. In this piece an agitator appears who rouses the working masses by his speeches. Hitler went almost crazy. The impression it made on him was so strong that for days afterwards he spoke of nothing except the power of the spoken word.' It was from this period also that his anti-Semitism dates. 'The black-haired Jewish youth lies in wait for hours on end,' he wrote, 'satanically glaring at and spying on the unsuspecting girl whom he plans to seduce. . . .' It has been suggested that sexual envy was at the root of Hitler's hatred of the Jews. It is certainly not unreasonable to suppose that frustrated sex was the mainspring of his paranoia.

When Hitler was 25 the First World War broke out. Although an Austrian national, he was allowed to enlist as a volunteer in the 16th Bavarian Reserve Infantry Regiment, and served throughout the war as a company runner. He won the Iron Cross, Second Class (November 1914) at the first battle of Ypres, and was at the front until he was wounded during the battle of the Somme (7 October 1916). He returned to the front in March 1917, as a lance-corporal, and was at Arras, at Third Ypres, and in the Ludendorff offensive in the spring of 1918. Before he was gassed in October 1918, he had won the Iron Cross, First Class, a rare distinction for an N.C.O. Despite his good record as a soldier he was never recommended for a commission. One of his comrades thought him 'a peculiar fellow. He sat in the corner of our mess holding his head between his hands, in deep contemplation. Suddenly he would leap up, and, running about excitedly, say that in spite of our big guns victory would be denied us, for the invisible foes of the German people were a greater danger than the biggest cannon of the enemy.' Such an eccentric, however brave and patriotic, was hardly likely to commend himself to officers of the Kaiser's army.

After the war he plunged into politics, founding the Nazi party and developing his talent for demagogic, almost hypnotic, oratory. The Munich Beer Hall *putsch* of 1923 put him in Landsberg prison for 13 months and gave him time to set down his political testament in *Mein Kampf*, a work which outlined his immoral views and unscrupulous methods quite plainly. Unfortunately his turgid prose was too boring to attract the close attention of Western politicians, who remained ignorant of the menace which his rapid rise brought in its train.

Germany was hard hit by the depression: there were 9,000,000 unemployed in the winter of 1931–32; among the middle classes many were bankrupt. Hitler's clearcut solutions to the miseries attributed to Versailles had a fresh appeal. By 1932 the Nazis had 14 million votes and, as leader of the majority party in the Reichstag, Hitler was entitled constitutionally to his appointment as Chancellor (January 1933). The Reichstag fire the following month – which, incidentally, may well have been started by the Communist van der Lubbe – gave him a splendid opportunity to pose as a crusader against Bolshevism. Now followed a reign of terror not only against Jews, Liberals, Socialists and Communists but also against his own Brownshirt followers, many of whom were liquidated on the Night of the Long Knives (30 June 1934). Hitler's followers had butchered not only Captain Roehm and a number of his Nazi Brownshirts, but General von Schleicher and his wife, and General von Bredow. Yet there were still responsible French and British statesmen who supposed that we could exist in peace side by side with a dictator who could treat his own nationals in such a way. The Gestapo, censorship, arson, beatings and the concentration camp were the instruments of the new régime. Indoctrination – most efficiently run throughout the Nazi era by Dr Goebbels – fought the battle for mens' minds. Mass rallies captured the minds of the German people, who were caught young and enlisted in the Hitler *Jugend*. School text-books were rewritten. But the best propaganda of all was full employment. Little the Germans cared that the Nazis were taking up the slack by the expansion of the armaments industry.

Hitler, like Bismarck before him, had certain long-term national aims. How these were achieved was relatively unimportant to him. The course of his strategy was settled; his tactics were entirely opportunistic. His general objective being clear in his mind, he had the advantage over opponents who did not know where he meant to go. Those who believe that he intended nothing more than a revision of the Treaty of Versailles are very much mistaken, he fought for nothing less than the hegemony of Europe. It was his intention to establish a land empire double the size of the existing Reich, a world power comparable with the United States.

That is not to say that world domination was necessarily his aim. Though the French and British Empires might be dismembered in his triumphant progress, this would be incidental to his Grand Design. It was said of Napoleon I that like the witches of old his power ceased at running water. In a sense this was true of Hitler also for he himself distrusted the water. 'Cyprus would be lovely,' he once said, 'but we can reach the Crimea by road.' He was talking of nothing more grave than the holidays the German people were to have when his war was over, but still it was to the East that his strategic thinking led him. It was the black-soil region of South Russia and East Europe that was marked down as the *Lebensraum* of the German people. The 1914 frontiers figured prominently in his speeches, but not in his thinking, for the frontiers of his Reich would lie far beyond. And what he could not get by peaceful means, he planned to take by war.

Hitler expounded his long-term plans on 5 November 1937. His audience consisted of the service chiefs, Generals Blomberg and von Fritsch, Admiral Raeder, Göring, and the foreign minister, von Neurath. Hitler stated his main assumptions: that Germany must have more territory and that it was necessary to take it by force. The question was When? He himself had come to the conclusion that 1938 or 1939 would be the time to strike. By the period 1943–45 Germany would be much stronger, but her foes would have completed their rearmament and would be even stronger. He would concentrate on building aircraft and tanks, the weapons for quick victory. The shortcomings of his more conventional arms were to be clouded by the barrage of propaganda that surrounded his warlike preparations.

Hitler was going to be 50 in 1939. He felt that he could not wait much longer. Thus by his usual mixture of instinct and calculation the Dictator faced the risks inherent in his designs. And in 1933 when Hitler had at last come to power the risks were by no means evident, for it was in 1932 and 1933 that the wave of pacifism had been at its peak. It was in 1933 that the Oxford Union passed its motion 'That this House would not fight for its King and Country.' This pronouncement by the young men who were to provide, at least in part, the leaders of the next generation of Britons gave comfort to our enemies everywhere, especially Mussolini. The young gentlemen had little inkling that their maiden political joustings would be taken seriously. The assumption that the intelligentsia of any generation really speak for the inarticulate mass of Britons is in any case to be regarded with suspicion. As Churchill said 'It was easy to laugh off such an episode in England, but in Germany, in Russia, in Italy, in Japan, the idea of a decadent,

Above: **Foreign Minister von Ribbentrop announces that Bulgaria has joined the Axis powers in March 1941.**

Below: **Prime Minister Winston Churchill reviews the US 6th Marine Regiment in Iceland, 16 August 1941.**

degenerate Britain took deep root and swayed many calculations. Little did the foolish boys who passed the resolution dream that they were destined quite soon to conquer or fall gloriously in the ensuing war, and prove themselves the finest generation ever bred in Britain. Less excuse can be found for their elders, who had no chance of self-redemption in action.' The British, like any other people, need leadership. They need someone they can trust to tell them what they are thinking! When rearmament first began, it had no real popular support. But the Spanish Civil War changed all that. At long last men realized that some things can be resisted only by force. Franco's form of Fascism was one of these. Nothing that Hitler had done thus far had had anything like the psychological impact of this Spanish sideshow. Yet Hitler was already far on his sinister journey.

In 1935 Germany accelerated the pace of conscription and in 1936, against the advice of his own generals, the Dictator got away with his first great international coup when he broke the Locarno agreement, which guaranteed existing frontiers and renounced the use of force. He then proceeded to reoccupy the Rhineland, which the Allies of 1918 had meant to demilitarize for ever. Hitler did not expect that this reoccupation of his own back garden would mean war. And he was right.

There followed the *Anschluss* with the Dictator's own homeland (1938), which stirred up comparatively little resentment, at least in Britain. Again Hitler did not expect war, and again he was right. Meanwhile Mussolini, not to be outdone, was overrunning Abyssinia. The dismemberment of Czechoslovakia followed in 1938–39, with Mussolini, now the pupil rather than the master, trying to keep up by invading Albania. Meanwhile, unhindered by the distracted powers, Japan pursued her conquering course in China. The long torment of the Spanish Civil War, with Fascist and Communist support making one side as unattractive as the other, dragged out its weary course from 1936 to 1939 – the bloody curtain-raiser to a bloodier tragedy.

Through all this, British and French politicians, with the notable exception of Winston Churchill, retained their trust in the continuance of peace with a doggedness worthy of a more hopeful cause. Thus they served to reflect rather than to lead the opinion of their nations; and this, in a nutshell, was that a government should 'seek peace and ensure it'. In Britain this idea had actually led to disarmament, but none of the other European Powers had been so idealistic – or so simple – as to follow her lead.

After 1918 successive British governments had assumed that there would be no major war for ten years, an assumption that did not die in 1928. Not until 1934 was it decided that a measure of rearmament was desirable, but by 1936, the time of the Rhineland crisis, no great progress had been made. By that time neither Italy nor Germany was attempting to conceal that they were building up huge armies, while it was calculated that Japan was spending 46 per cent of her national income on armaments. No British government thought for a moment of preparing public opinion to accept similar sacrifices. Economic rather than strategic considerations dictated the nature of the rearmament programme, which was devised purely for *defensive* war. By April 1938 the government had reached the conclusion that in a war with Germany the British should confine their contribution to naval and air forces. A large expeditionary force should not be despatched to the Continent; the role of the Army would be home defence and the defence of British territories overseas. The rearmament programme provided for increases of coastal and air defences, but for a minute field force of five divisions. No provision was made for its reinforcement, and the Territorial Army was only to be supplied with training equipment.

It was obvious that, should a second World War come, France and Great Britain would be allies, but it was not until six months before the declaration of war that Staff talks began. The French made it clear that their first objective would be the defence of French territory. They intended to remain on the defensive, maintaining an economic blockade until they had built up sufficient forces for an offensive against Germany.

The Anglo-French staff assumed that they would probably be opposed by Italy as well as Germany, and that the enemy, while greatly inferior to us at sea and in long-term economic strength, would be superior on land and in the air. It would be years before allied military strength could be built up. Thus in the days of air forces, tanks and mechanization, the best the planners could hope for was to compel the Germans to indulge once more in the static trench warfare of 1914–18. Such a war would obviously demand a great number of divisions. The French were not unnaturally dismayed to learn that the British proposed to contribute at the outset no more than two regular divisions.

It was not until the end of March 1939 that the British government abandoned its belief that, in a war against Germany, it could avoid sending an army to the Continent. On 29 March the Cabinet decreed the doubling of the Territorial force, following this on 27 April by the introduction of conscription. That summer army reservists were called up for training and the Fleet and the Royal Air Force were partially mobilized. All this was some comfort to the French.

Above: **In September 1940 Japan joined the Axis by signing the Tripartite Pact. The Pact had only a symbolic value since Germany and Italy could not afford to send aid to Japan. In the picture von Ribbentrop (centre) confers with General Oshima (left) and Dino Alfieri (right).**

Right: **The President of Czechoslovakia, Edouard Benes, resigned after the Munich Agreement. He left Czechoslovakia and after Hitler invaded his country, he formed a government in exile. His Foreign Minister in exile, Jan Masaryk, stands behind him.**

Meanwhile Germany had taken Bohemia and Moravia under her protection (15 March), and seized Memel, the chief port of Lithuania. Hitler had denounced not only his non-aggression pact with Poland but his Naval Agreement with Great Britain, besides signing the so-called 'Pact of Steel' with Mussolini. There was little in all this to surprise the most innocent observer, but the news of Germany's agreement with Russia (the Moscow Pact of 23 August) was totally unexpected. Chamberlain's government riposted with the Anglo-Polish Defence Alliance (25 August) a bluff which Hitler called with stunning speed.

The Führer did not take this guarantee seriously, for he was convinced that his war with Poland could be localized. The British declaration of war, however, took him by surprise. Dr Paul Schmidt, his interpretor, recorded his reaction. 'Hitler was petrified and utterly disconcerted. After a while he turned to Ribbentrop and asked "What now?" '

Whatever the truth of this report, Count Ciano's diary records the following exchange, which took place at Salzburg on 11 August 1939.

Ciano: 'Well, Ribbentrop, what do you want? The Corridor or Danzig?'
Ribbentrop: 'Not any more. We want war.'

And so at 11 a.m. on the morning of 3 September Great Britain and Germany went to war for the second time.

2 POLAND, 1939

'Fall ich in Donaustrand? Sterb ich in Polen?'
Hugo Zimmermann, 1914

Hitler's forces conquered Poland in eighteen days. Europe had seen no such thunderbolt of war since Napoleon struck down Prussia at Jena. From a professional viewpoint the German soldiers had excelled even their ancestors of 1866 and 1870. The famous Schlieffen Plan had failed to win the First World War in 1914 and to earn its title of the new Cannae. Now General von Brauchitsch really brought off a double envelopment worthy of the name. It was a strategy which the Polish dispositions greatly favoured. Marshal Rydz-Smigly, not unnaturally, wanted to protect Poland's industrial areas, and to do this he deployed the greater part of his forces along the 1,700 mile frontier. This meant that he was strong nowhere.

It was not Polish morale that failed. The Poles simply were not strong enough. General Ironside had been impressed when, just before the outbreak of war, he had witnessed 'a divisional attack-exercise under a live barrage, not without casualties' – not the sort of manoeuvre practised in the British Army of 1939. But patriotism and *élan* were simply not enough: the Germans poised to strike from East Prussia and Pomerania, from Silesia and Slovakia, outnumbered the Poles in everything but horsed cavalry. The German fleet commanded the Baltic as effectively as the *Luftwaffe* was to command the skies. East Prussia, despite the Polish Corridor, was not really cut off from the Reich. Against nine armoured divisions the Poles could pit a dozen cavalry brigades and a handful of light tanks. Even in artillery and infantry the Germans outnumbered the Poles by at least three to two. And in any case the defending army was not given time to complete its mobilization. In addition the Germans, whether in the air or on the ground, were incomparably better equipped.

Even had Polish morale been higher than German, which was not the case, sheer force of numbers would have redressed the balance. But it was not physical considerations alone that made the German victory a foregone conclusion. Their whole approach to warfare was fresh. The Poles were fighting by the rules of 1918: the Germans had invented a new set.

Left: SS troops move into Danzig. Between the wars Danzig, which had been part of Germany, was a free port at the end of the Polish corridor which gave Poland access to sea routes.

Below: German troops remove a Polish frontier post on the first day of the Blitzkrieg in Poland.

Bottom: Hitler visits the front line in Poland. Among those who accompanied him were, from left to right: Bodenschatz, Wolff, Bormann, Keitel (standing between Hitler and the binoculars), Rommel and von Reichenau (holding the other binoculars).

Above: Hitler watches German troops crossing the San on 21 September 1939

Above right: Hitler and his generals discuss the situation prior to the final onslaught on Warsaw.

Below: The Polish population tried to hold up the German advance by destroying supplies. The Germans entering this village found only a cow left behind.

This new concept was the *Blitzkrieg*, which could be summed up as Surprise, Speed and *Schrecklichkeit* (Frightfulness). Surprise was achieved partly by means of the Fifth Column – there were two million Germans living in Poland – and partly by the simple device of striking without a declaration of war. The novel tactical combination of armour with the support of dive-bombers rather than conventional artillery was another surprise. So was the way in which the Germans were prepared to drive their armour deep through the crust of the Polish defences, bypassing pockets of resistance, and disregarding the fact that their flanks were unprotected.

Schrecklichkeit was a matter of deliberate policy. The bombing of towns and villages got the population on the move. On the roads they obstructed the movements of such reserves as the Poles possessed. Machine-gunning the columns of refugees added to the confusion – a confusion deepened by the activities of the Fifth Column.

At dawn on 1 September the Germans launched their invasion. Two days later the Polish Air Force had ceased to exist, much of it destroyed on the ground. A week later the Germans were in the outskirts of Warsaw, and the defending army was already split up into groups. The Poles had fought bitterly and not altogether without tactical successes. Polish infantry made night attacks on the head-quarters and parks of armoured divisions, compelling the Germans to provide their tanks and armoured cars with powerful searchlights so as to blind their assailants and light up the field of fire. Yet such successes were rare.

As early as 5 September Guderian's corps had had a surprise visit from Hitler, who had driven along the line of the previous advance. At the sight of a smashed Polish artillery regiment Hitler said: 'Our dive-bombers did that?'

'No, our panzers,' Guderian replied.

Hitler was astonished to be told that the Battle of the Polish Corridor had cost Guderian's four divisions no more than 150 killed and 700 wounded. Again the Dictator was amazed. In the First World War his regiment had had over 2,000 casualties on its first day in action. Guderian explained that even against a tough and courageous enemy tanks were a life-saving weapon. And resistance was not tough everywhere. Lieutenant Baron von Bogenhardt describes the advance of the 6th Motorized Regiment from Slovakia:

'There was virtually no resistance. . . . There was a certain amount of sporadic fighting when we got to the river barriers, but the *Luftwaffe* had already cleared the way for us. Their Stuka dive-bombers were deadly accurate, and as there was no opposition they had it all their own way. The roads and fields were swarming with unhappy peasants who had fled in panic from their villages when the bombing began, and we passed hundreds of Polish troops walking dejectedly towards Slovakia . . . there were so many prisoners that nobody bothered to guard them or even tell them where to go.'

General Tadeusz Kutrzeba, whose forces at Poznan had been bypassed, drew in troops from Torun and Lodz and boldly counter attacked towards Warsaw with twelve divisions. The Germans reacted violently and by the 19th the battle of the Bzura was over. Still it was a gallant effort. Meanwhile the battle of the Vistula was being fought out. Lvov fell on the 22nd, and on the 17th the German pincers closed near Brest-Litovsk. The Russians had crossed the eastern frontier on the 17th, taking Vilnyus next day. The Polish government was compelled to flee to Rumania. Warsaw held out until the 27th and the fortress of Modlin until the 28th. In this way a nation of 33 million people with an army that might, fully mobilized, have numbered 1,700,000 men, was crushed almost before the war had begun. The cost to the Germans was 10,572 killed, 5,029 missing and 30,322 wounded.

On the Western Front the German and Allied armies sat and looked at each other. The Poles had hoped, not unreasonably, that their Allies would show some signs of life, but it was not to be. Having spent a great deal of money on the Maginot Line the French were not attracted by the idea of leaving it behind them.

The victors lost no time in arranging the fifth partition of Poland. On 28 September the Foreign Ministers, Ribbentrop and Molotov, met to revise the Moscow Pact. The Russians annexed 77,000 square miles of Poland, with most of her oil and 13,000,000 inhabitants. The other 73,000 square miles, with 20,000,000 people and most of the manufacturing areas, came under the 'protection' of the Reich. By the end of the year the conquerors had executed 18,000 Poles for 'offences' of one sort and another. But the Poles had not fired their last shots in the war. Disaster did not break their spirit any more than it had done in the days of Dombrowski. At the capitulation of Warsaw a Polish general made a remark to von Manstein which may be translated: 'The wheel always turns full circle.'

Left: **The garrison of one of the fortified outposts in the suburbs of Warsaw surrenders after the Germans entered the city.**

Below: **German troops enter Warsaw. The city was subjected to intensive air and artillery bombardment and after 56 hours of resistance the Polish troops surrendered.**

Polish POWs await deportation. In some ways those captured by the Germans received better treatment than those taken by the Soviets.

3 SIDESHOW IN FINLAND

'The Russians have learnt much in this hard war in which the Finns fought with heroism.'

Marshal Timoshenko

Germany and Russia had rewarded themselves more or less equally for their very unequal share in the Polish campaign, but the Russian military machine remained untested. It was soon to show its form: a watching world found it singularly unimpressive, especially when compared to that of the Germans in Poland.

On 30 November, Russia, bent on securing territory which she considered vital for her own strategical security, invaded Finland. It seemed obvious that a nation of 180,000,000 would make short work of one of 3,200,000. But in fact Finland held out for three and a half months. A comparison of the initial strength of the two armies does nothing to explain this:

	Russia	*Finland*
Divisions	100	3
Officers and men	*c.*1,000,000	33,000
Tanks	3,200	?
Aircraft	2,500	96 (mostly obsolescent)

The Russians were very far from showing any mastery of the new German technique of the *Blitzkrieg*. They hoped to gain their ends by bombing, in order to break the morale of their victims. They also counted on a rising of the Finnish workers. The Finns, like the French, had their Line, called after their able Commander-in-Chief, Field Marshal Mannerheim. This covered the Karelian Isthmus between Lake Ladoga and the Gulf of Finland. The defensive works were far less elaborate and expensive than those of the Maginot Line, but they served their turn. It was not particularly intelligent of the Russians to attack in November. An elementary knowledge of their own history should have shown them that it was in the cold of November 1812 that Napoleon's Grand Army had dissolved.

The Red Army ploughed forward through a terrain of wooded ravines cloaked in deep snow, its tanks and transport compelled to stick to the miserable forest roads. Finnish ski patrols, the 'White Death' (Bielaja Smert), in their white winter garb, harassed the flanks, shot up convoys, cutting off not merely stragglers but entire formations, which had to be supplied by air. Russian casualties were heavy. Still they had almost complete command of the air. According to Douhet's (see Chapter 21) theories the Finns should not have lasted a fortnight. When the end came it was not the bombing tactics of Douhet or the *Blitzkrieg* tactics of Brauchitsch that brought it about, but the techniques of 1916.

In February, Marshal Timoshenko concentrated 27 divisions against the Mannerheim Line, and the biggest barrage since Verdun preceded the assault. Mannerheim records that in the fighting that followed, the Soviet armour, which hitherto had been a disappointment to the Russians, supported their infantry effectively.

Left: **The Finnish Army proved to be better prepared for the 'Winter War' than the Soviet Army.**

Above: **The Soviet Seventh and Thirteenth Armies attacked Finland through the Karelian Isthmus. The fortified Mannerheim Line, seen here, held up the Soviet advance for two and a half months.**

Right: **Soviet tanks did not function well in the cold and this one had to be abandoned by the 44th Division of the Ninth Army outside Suomussalmi. The Ninth Army attacking from Soviet Karelia penetrated as far as Suomussalmi but was subjected to intense counter-attacks.**

'Their twenty-eight and forty-five-ton tanks, armed with two guns and four or five machine guns, contributed decisively to their penetration of our lines.' The Finns held out with the greatest resolution but were gradually overrun. By the middle of the month the Russians had broken through and surrender was inevitable. Finland was compelled to cede the Karelian Isthmus, as well as the town of Viborg (Viipuri) and a military base on Hangö (Hanko) Peninsula.

Mannerheim's estimate of the losses is of interest. According to him the Russian losses were about 200,000 killed. Thousands of the wounded died of cold while waiting for medical attention. The Finns lost 24,923 killed, missing and died of wounds, and 43,557 wounded. The Finns never at any period had more than 287 planes (162 fighters); they lost only 61. The Russians lost at least 684 planes and perhaps as many as 975, besides about 1,600 tanks.

Allies and Germans alike sympathized with Finland. Both were delighted to see the poor showing of the Russian army, and so the real lessons of the campaign were lost. It seemed that the Russians were no more efficient in 1939 than they had been in 1917. But Mannerheim was well aware of their good points, which included a 'phenomenal ability to dig themselves in'. The Russian infantryman was brave, tough and frugal, but lacking in initiative. The artillery, an élite arm in the old Tsarist army, had suffered from the loss of its old officer corps. Still they had an astonishing mass of modern guns of great rapidity of fire and range and apparently inexhaustible supplies of ammunition.

The Finns, like the Germans in Poland, had underlined the value of mobility, which could offset lack of numbers. The influence of climate and terrain on tank warfare was demonstrated. Douhet's ideas on bombing were shown to be suspect. Mannerheim tells us that about 150,000 explosive and incendiary bombs (7,500 tons) killed 700 civilians and wounded 1,400. Considerable destruction was done. 'Total air war was in our country met by a calm and intelligent population whom danger merely steeled and united more strongly.' Stalin, whose purges had done so much to impair the efficiency of the Soviet Army, now set Timoshenko to work to overhaul it.

4 THE WAR AT SEA, 1939-40

'The Royal Navy of England hath ever been its greatest defence and ornament; it is its ancient and natural strength – the floating bulwark of our island.'
Sir William Blackstone: Commentaries 1765–1769

On 3 September Mr Chamberlain appointed Mr Winston Churchill First Lord of the Admiralty as well as a member of the War Cabinet. 'On this the Board were kind enough to signal to the Fleet, "Winston is back".' Half-hearted measures were to characterize the first six months of Allied operations on land and in the air. But there was no phoney war at sea. As if to emphasize this, the SS *Athenia* was sunk without warning by *U-30* off the coast of Donegal on the very day that war was declared. There was heavy loss of life. Oddly enough this atrocity was in direct contravention of Hitler's own orders. It has been suggested that the submarine's captain, Lemp, mistook the liner for an armed merchant cruiser. It is more probable that he believed such attacks to be permitted by his government.

Unilateral abrogation of international treaties was habitual with Hitler. Nevertheless it is worth recording that in 1936 his representatives had signed the London Protocol, and had joined the other powers in denouncing submarine warfare against merchant shipping. When on 12 December 1939 the British submarine *Salmon* intercepted the *Bremen* off the Norwegian coast she forbore to sink the 52,000-ton German liner. 'Magnificent, but not war,' one might say, and as late as 1941 unrestricted attacks on German merchantmen were only permitted in certain declared areas. Later in the war British and United States' warships became less inhibited.

In the early campaigns of the war the Germans enjoyed a marked superiority both in the air and on land. At sea they were outclassed from the first, for British maritime power, though insufficient to meet every possible call, was still a very formidable instrument. The French navy, too, was both powerful and efficient. When war broke out in 1939 the Allies had, generally speaking, the means to control the seas and oceans of the world for their own purposes and to deny them both to the German enemy and to his potential allies. Even so its personnel rather than its material resources was the Royal Navy's strong suit in those days.

Below: **Admiral Erich Raeder was Commander-in-Chief of the German Naval Forces until he was replaced by Admiral Dönitz in January 1943.**

The Royal Navy was manned by long-service volunteers. Most officers began their careers at 13 and the majority of the men started their shore training at 16. At 18 the men signed a 12-year engagement. They could re-engage for a further 10 years and so qualify for a pension. Men in their second term of service provided most of the Petty Officers and Leading Rates. These men, masters of their special crafts, deeply imbued with the traditions of the service and with knowledge of the sea, were the backbone of the Navy. The numerical strength of the Royal Navy was not very great. It amounted to nearly 10,000 officers and some 109,000 men and 12,400 Royal Marines. The reserves called up on mobilization were about 73,000 officers and men. Some were pensioners; others belonged to the Royal Fleet Reserve, which consisted of men who had not re-engaged after their initial 12 years' service, as well as men from the Merchant Navy. The Royal Naval Volunteer Reserve, 6,000 strong, consisted of enthusiastic amateurs who had trained in their spare time. Including reservists the Royal Navy totalled some 200,000. As the war went on the Navy expanded to four times this size and at its peak in mid-1944 it totalled 863,500, including 73,500 of the Womens' Royal Naval Service (Wrens).

The parsimony of successive governments had seen to it that these splendid men should hazard themselves to a great extent in obsolescent warships. This is especially true of Britain's 15 capital ships, 13 of which had been built before 1918. When war broke out in 1939 four new battleships (the *King George V* Class) were building, but they would not be ready for another 18 months. The position as regards cruisers, destroyers and submarines was not nearly so black. Britain and the Dominions had 25 large and 38 small cruisers, with 19 more on the stocks. All but 21 had been completed between the wars. Of the 168 destroyers, about two-thirds were relatively modern. There were 69 submarines, mostly of recent construction.

But by 1939 command of the sea was a question of air as well as purely maritime strength. Unfortunately senior officers, as well as politicians, were peculiarly reluctant to observe that flying as well as floating bulwarks were essential. The traditions of Nelson's day could still be a strength, when the techniques of Jellicoe's were already outdated. War found us with a mere six aircraft carriers. Of these 'one was a very small ship, four were conversions from battleship or battle-cruiser hulls, and only one (the *Ark Royal*) was new and had been specifically designed as a carrier. Six new fleet carriers of 23,000 tons, capable of operating 35–55 aircraft, had been laid down since 1937; but, . . . none could be ready to join the fleet for many months'. This was an extremely unsatisfactory position at the outset of a war in which carrier-borne aircraft were to play a leading part.

Above: **The *Altmark,* carrying 299 British prioners, was driven into Josen Fjord by the *Cossack.* Captain Vian secured the release of the prisoners by entering Norwegian territorial waters.**

Aviation was another weak point in the Royal

Navy's panoply. Here again the conservatism of the Admiralty hierarchy was to blame. In 1918 2,500 naval aircraft had been transferred without demur to the newly formed Royal Air Force. For twenty years the Admiralty had been responsible for the development of carriers while the Air Ministry had been responsible for the design of their aircraft! Under this Gilbertian arrangement it was hardly likely that the latter would spend its meagre funds on producing torpedo-bombers. It is not unfair to say that in 1939 the Royal Navy was in possession of some of the finest museum pieces in the world – the Swordfish, Skua, Roc and Sea Gladiator.

Coastal Command, the Cinderella of the Royal Air Force, had only achieved independent status in 1936. In 1937 it was agreed that 291 aircraft should be allotted to it for convoy escort and reconnaissance duties over the North Sea. Another 48 were to be stationed at convoy assembly points abroad. By 1939 less than two-thirds of this modest total were available, and they were slow and obsolescent Ansons. 'Unfortunately Coastal Command crews had received no training at all in anti-submarine warfare; and the belief that to destroy a U-Boat from the air was a comparatively easy matter was all too widely held. This and the fact that our anti-submarine bombs were completely useless prevented any results being accomplished for a very long time.' Fortunately the ineffectiveness of these bombs soon became obvious from the results of attacks by friendly aircraft on British submarines!

The bases of the British fleets left much to be desired. Until April 1938 it was thought that Rosyth would be the main base of the Home Fleet in any new war with Germany. Thereafter there had been a failure to push ahead with the defences of Scapa Flow, which had been demilitarized after World War I and was still far from secure. The Mediterranean Fleet was in similar difficulties. Malta, long its main base, was too vulnerable to possible Italian air attack, and in 1939 it was based, thanks to the Anglo-Egyptian treaty of 1936, on Alexandria. The Mediterranean Fleet, 'at the time the finest naval force in the world' was 'greatly handicapped by the inadequacies of the base organization which had been extemporized somewhat hurriedly in Egypt'.

In 1938 the Chamberlain government, never remarkable for its strategic foresight, had excelled itself by surrendering – voluntarily and unconditionally – rights to naval bases in Eire. Berehaven and Lough Swilly had proved invaluable in World War I. Belfast and Londonderry in Ulster were not adequately equipped as bases.

The German Navy, though outnumbered by the Home Fleet, consisted entirely of modern vessels (the Germans being generously deprived of all their older units in 1918). Moreover all their capital ships, whose displacements were supposedly limited by treaty, greatly exceeded their published tonnage. Their U-Boat strength was only 56 – slightly less, surprisingly enough, than British submarine strength – and the Admiralty actually regarded the German surface vessels as a threat to merchant shipping. While entertaining no illusions as to German regard for treaties, they did not expect that she would again indulge in unrestricted submarine warfare, because of its effect on neutral opinion, especially that of the United States. Even so, effective plans for organized convoys were laid before war broke out. German merchant shipping was 'almost immediately, swept off the face of the oceans'. A vigorous blockade of Germany was enforced and neutral ships were intercepted and searched for contraband cargoes. This interference, though long recognized as the legitimate right of a belligerent, was resented by some neutrals. On 7 November the United States declared the waters round France and Britain a war zone and prohibited American shipping from entering. This move, of course, was greatly to the disadvantage of the Allies, but was mitigated by the repeal of the Neutrality Act. This meant that the Allies could buy war material in America, so long as they could pay for it and were prepared to import it in their own ships. The so-called 'Cash and Carry' order was the first of a number of measures by which President Roosevelt began to give very real support to the Allies.

As in 1914, the Royal Navy succeeded in convoying the British Expeditionary Force to France without the loss of a single man. By June 1940, 500,000 men and 89,000 vehicles had made the crossing in one direction or the other. By the end of 1939 the First Canadian Division had safely crossed the Atlantic. The *Queen Mary* and, later, the *Queen Elizabeth* were bringing Australians and New Zealanders to Egypt. The greatest secrecy necessarily surrounded these and similar movements. Their success was yet another proof, were any needed, of the value of sea power. By October a barrage of 3,600 mines had been laid in the Straits of Dover and only one U-Boat succeeded in passing through the straits safely, while three were lost. Thereafter the Germans sent out their Atlantic patrols round the north of Scotland. In September and October several U-Boats sent to lie in wait off Scapa Flow were sunk by destroyers before they had done any damage. Fortunately they had at this time an inefficient magnetic torpedo pistol. It was probably due to this that *Ark Royal* escaped *U-39* on 14 September.

Meanwhile from his War Room the First Lord was prodding his subordinates into a counter-offensive. 'There can be few purely mental experiences more charged with cold excitement than to follow, almost minute to minute, the phases of a great naval action from the silent rooms of the Admiralty.' It was an excitement that proved irresistible and led to interventions that were not invariably fortunate. One such probably led to the loss on 17 September of the fleet carrier *Courageous* (48 aircraft), while employed, with a small screening force, on submarine hunting. This disaster receives the strongest comment from the Official Historian, Captain Roskill, '. . . this was by no means the last occasion on which the old fallacy regarding the alleged superiority of seeking for enemies in the ocean spaces instead of convoying shipping with the greatest possible strength, and so forcing the enemy to reveal his presence within range of immediate counter-attack, reared its hoary head in British circles. Half a century previously Mahan had condemned it; and after World War I both Admiral Beatty and Admiral Sims, USN, went on record with similar opinions based on their recent experiences; yet in 1939 the whole massive weight of historical evidence was again ignored.'

Having the initiative, the Germans were able to send out every U-Boat fit for sea before hostilities began. By March 1940 they had sunk 222 ships of 764,766 tons – about 100,000 tons per month. The Germans had lost 18 – about one-third – of their U-Boats. Only 11 new boats had been commissioned, for the *Führer* had not as yet given high priority to their construction. That he meant Britain ill, none need doubt, but desire oft outruns performance. Not the least of Hitler's blunders was his failure to comprehend that to destroy a maritime power you require a fleet.

In the first few months of the war Hitler had considerable success with one of his 'secret weapons' – the magnetic mine. These were sown by aircraft, and by the end of October 1939 they had already sunk 50,000 tons of Allied shipping. In November only a single channel into the Thames was open and 27 ships (120,958 tons) were lost. Then on 23 November one was dropped on land. It was dissected by Lieutenant-Commander J. G. D. Ouvry. His courage enabled the Admiralty to devise an effective counter-measure, known as degaussing. A belt of energized electrical cable was installed with the object of neutralizing the ship's magnetic field by a counter-current so that the magnetic needle in the German mine would not detonate its explosive charge.

On 8 October a German flotilla, including the battle-cruiser *Gneisenau* and the light cruiser *Köln*, made a brief foray into the North Sea. Admiral Sir Charles Forbes swiftly positioned his force to cover the passages to the Atlantic, and the Germans beat a hasty retreat to Kiel. At the end of this operation the battleship *Royal Oak* anchored in Scapa Flow, and there on the night of 14 October, *U-47* sent her to the bottom, with the loss of 833 lives. One is compelled to admire the boldness of Lieutenant Prien's exploit. This disaster had the effect of hastening our efforts to complete the defences of Scapa.

On 23 November another German foray led to the sinking of an old converted liner of the Northern Patrol, the *Rawalpindi* (Captain E. C. Kennedy), by the battle-cruisers *Scharnhorst* and *Gneisenau*. In the best traditions of the service the liner fought to the last. The Germans were jubilant, but it was not much of a victory although they escaped they had failed to dislocate Allied Atlantic shipping. Their superior intelligence at this time was due to German cryptographers having broken the British naval cipher.

The *Graf Spee* had already sunk nine British ships (50,089 tons) when three British cruisers under Commodore H. Harwood, who had always believed that she would eventually be attracted by the traffic off the River Plate, concentrated 150 miles east of the estuary. The *Graf Spee* appeared 24 hours later (13 December). The German pocket battleship outgunned the three British ships, but Harwood had long since thought out his tactics, and engaged from two different directions so as to compel Captain Langsdorff to divide his main armament. A running fight followed in which *Graf Spee* crippled the *Exeter* so severely that he had a good opportunity to finish her off. The concentrated fire of the 6-inch guns of the *Ajax* (Captain C. H. L. Woodhouse) and the *Achilles* (Captain W. E. Parry) was sufficient to distract him. Langsdorff, whose ship had suffered considerable damage, now steered for the coast, harried by the two light cruisers. At 7.25 an 11-inch shell put both *Ajax's* after turrets out of action and Langsdorff had his second chance to clinch the deal. Harwood turned east, making smoke, but finding that the German was still in flight, resumed the pursuit towards Montevideo.

Langsdorff was impressed, 'You English are hard' he said afterwards. 'You do not know when you are beaten. The *Exeter* was beaten, but would not know it.' Surely, he thought, the cruisers would not have pressed home their attack if heavier ships were not coming up to their support? He made for Montevideo.

Feeling in Uruguay was strongly pro-Allied and Langsdorff did not get permission to stay in port beyond the legal limit of 72 hours. The British let it be known that *Ark Royal* and *Renown* were at Rio de Janeiro. They were in fact thousands of miles away. Harwood had only been reinforced by the cruiser *Cumberland*. Langsdorff considered that he needed at least two weeks to make his ship seaworthy for he had received some 70 hits, but on 18 December, watched by great crowds of spectators, he put to sea. The British cleared for action only to be informed by their single spotting aircraft that the *Graf Spee* had been blown up and scuttled by her own crew. Langsdorff, perhaps unduly pessimistic, had become convinced that to continue the fight would be to run the risk of his ship falling into British hands. On 20 December he committed suicide.

The moral effect of the Battle of the River Plate was out of all proportion to its size. To the British people, so far starved of victories, there was something about the sureness with which Commodore Harwood's weak squadron hounded its mighty adversary to her watery grave that recalled the great days of British naval history. It seemed an earnest of better times. Neutrals too, began to wonder whether the British were really as effete as they had been led to believe.

The humane Captain Langsdorff had transferred the crews of his victims to his supply ship, the tanker *Altmark*. In February Admiral Forbes received warning that she was moving down the Norwegian coast. She was escorted by two Norwegian destroyers whose senior Norwegian officer alleged that the *Altmark* had been searched at Bergen, was unarmed and was making lawful use of territorial waters. Mr Churchill now intervened and with his strong backing Captain P. L. Vian laid the destroyer *Cossack* alongside the tanker and boarded her as in the days of old. The ship was found to be armed, but, after a feeble resistance, 299 prisoners were rescued. It would be idle to deny that this action was an infringement of Norwegian neutrality, but this evidence of resolution was no bad thing in the eyes of neutrals as well as the British public. The howl that went up from Goebbels' propaganda machine was gratifying!

In December 1939 the submarine *Salmon* made a patrol in which she sank *U-36* and torpedoed the light cruisers *Leipzig* and *Nürnberg* which were covering a mine-laying foray to the east coast. Little success came the way of the Allies in the first six months of the war, but such victories as they did enjoy were won by the Royal Navy.

Above: **The *Exeter* under way following the sinking of the *Graf Spee*.**

Right; **Captain Langsdorff of the *Graf Spee* with some of his crew in Montevideo.**

Below: **The *Admiral Graf Spee* blows up off Montevideo.**

5 NORWAY, 1940

A 'campaign for which the book does not cater'.
General Carton de Wiart

The Norwegian campaign is one of the most illuminating in the whole war, showing at every stage how chance and *friction de guerre* influence the decisions of commanders and throw their plans out of gear.

Hitler was not fond of the sea, nor have the Germans any tradition of amphibious warfare. Nevertheless in Norway, albeit at the cost of the greater part of their surface fleet, they brought off a combined operation on the grand scale. As usual there was no declaration of war. Surprise was achieved by a mixture of treachery and timing. The Fifth Column organized by Major Vidkun Quisling played its part. Trojan Horse tactics were used: German soldiers concealed in innocent-looking coal-ships were in position before the fighting began. Far more important was the teutonic precision of the staff work which achieved simultaneous landings at all the main Norwegian ports. It was only by the narrowest of margins that they failed to end the campaign at a stroke.

Curiously enough it was the Allies who moved first. On 8 April they laid minefields in order to deny the use of Norwegian territorial waters to vessels carrying contraband of war to Germany. British relations with Norway had already been strained by the *Altmark* incident. Now Norwegian suspicions that they were being dragged into the war were deepened. With a population of 3,000,000 and an army of 13,000 they were not anxious to cross swords with the Third Reich. On 9 April the Germans, despite a non-aggression treaty for which Hitler himself had asked, invaded Denmark. In Copenhagen the Palace Guard opened fire on the invaders, but King Christian X, unwilling to witness the massacre of his army of 14,550, ordered a cease-fire.

Meanwhile the German plan to seize the main Norwegian ports was unfolding itself. The Admiralty had got wind of a German foray as early as the 7th, though a report from a neutral minister in Copenhagen of a German expedition to Narvik and Jutland was unfortunately deemed 'a further move in the war of nerves'. Sir Charles Forbes sailed from Scapa Flow at 8.15 p.m. on the 7th. The Home Fleet seems to have had three capital ships, six cruisers and 21 destroyers at sea – no aircraft carriers be it noted. 'On the last occasion when the Germans were known to be advancing through the North Sea in strength, in the same month twenty-two years earlier, we had been able to deploy thirty-five capital ships, twenty-six cruisers, and eighty-five destroyers.' Small wonder that the only surface contact on the 8th came about by accident. The destroyer *Glowworm*, after a running fight with two German destroyers, rammed the heavy cruiser *Hipper* and tore a hole forty metres wide in her side, an exploit for which Lieutenant-Commander G. Broadmead Roope was posthumously awarded the Victoria Cross.

About midday on 8 April the Polish submarine *Orzel* sank the German transport *Rio de Janeiro* off Lillesand. Survivors told the Norwegians that they had been on their way to 'protect' Bergen. At 4 a.m. on the 9th *Renown* had an hour's duel with *Scharnhorst* and *Gneisenau* in snow squalls and very heavy weather about 50 miles west of the Norwegian coast and damaged the latter. The same evening the submarine *Truant* torpedoed the light cruiser *Karlsruhe* off Kristiansand. But nowhere had the British succeeded in bringing a German force to a general action. So, by the night of 9 April the Germans had seized Oslo, Bergen, Trondheim and Narvik. The main Norwegian

Below: **The German attack on Norway took the Allies completely by surprise. A Norwegian port was devastated by an early morning attack.**

Above: **Artur Axmann (left), Colonel General von Falkenhorst (centre), Commander-in-Chief of German troops in Norway, and Vidkun Quisling, leader of the Norwegian Nazi Party.**

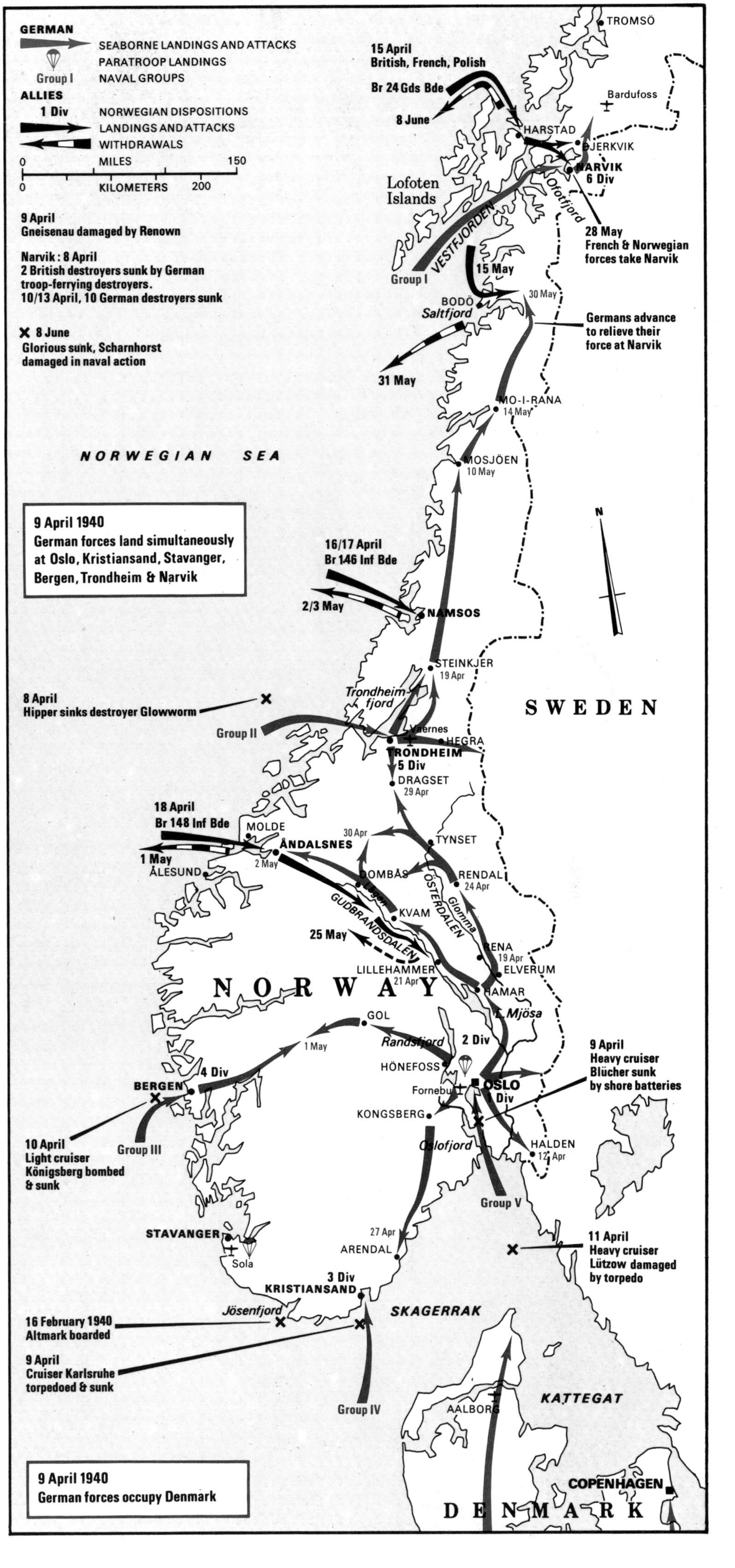

towns and mobilization centres were all in their hands. But the German plan was not one hundred per cent successful.

At Oslo the Norwegians got considerable warning of the German attack, for at 11.06 p.m. on the 8th the Norwegian patrol boat *Pol III*, a 214-ton whaler, rammed a German torpedo boat and managed to raise the alarm before she was sunk. Later the minelayer *Olav Tryggvason* gallantly attempted to defend the naval base at Horten. But it was the fortress at Oscarsborg, built at the time of the Crimean War, which did the most damage. 'Here the Norwegian batteries, armed with three 28-cm. guns (Krupp model of 1892), some 15-cm. guns, and torpedo tubes, and manned with particular enthusiasm, scored a success of some significance to the naval war at large as well as to the time-schedule for the occupation of Norway. Germany's latest cruiser, the *Blücher*, was set on fire, torpedoed, and sunk with the loss of about 1,000 men, including most of General Engelbrecht's staff for the occupation of Oslo.' The pocket battleship *Lützow* was damaged, and the expedition was compelled to land on the east bank of the fjord and continue the advance on foot.

The capital, with its 250,000 inhabitants, fell to six companies of airborne troops who landed, despite anti-aircraft fire, at Fornebu. But the Norwegian Government had just time enough to escape to Hamar, 70 miles inland, and to order mobilization. Quisling, who soon gained control of the broadcasting station, caused some confusion by ordering its cancellation. Kristiansand was taken with little resistance. Stavanger fell to 120 paratroops. At Bergen, the second largest town, fighting lasted only an hour, though the forts did serious damage to the cruiser *Königsberg*. The Germans took Trondheim, opposed only by the forts, which caused a destroyer to be beached. At Narvik the Germans were opposed only by two 4,000 ton ironclads, *Norge* and *Eidsvold*, 1900 vintage. General Dietl permitted the action of the German flotilla leader who torpedoed the *Eidsvold* at 100 yards range, on a signal from his ship's boat which was returning from a parley. *Norge* got off 17 rounds before suffering

Left: **A recruiting poster for the Waffen SS.**

Right: **Unloading supplies in a Norwegian harbour.**

Right below: **Wehrmacht troops watch a supply ship arrive in a Norwegian fjord.**

a similar fate. The garrison, only 450 strong, was being reinforced, but the commander, Colonel Sundlo, declined to fight.

With all the main ports in enemy hands it would have been difficult for the Allies to fight back, even if they had had a corps already in existence and earmarked for such a purpose. No such reserve existed. It was only with the greatest difficulty that a few brigades could be scraped together to oppose a well-found force of seven German divisions. At sea the British struck back with vigour and in two actions at Narvik, on 10 and 13 April, wiped out ten German destroyers for the loss of two.

Landings were made at Namsos and Andalsnes in Central Norway with the object of recapturing Trondheim, and at Bodø, Mo i Rana and Mosjøen to deny those places to the enemy. Lacking air support and consisting to a great extent of partially-trained Territorials these forces were quite inadequate. Andalsnes and Namsos were evacuated on 2 and 3 May respectively. Only at Narvik did the Allies meet with any substantial success. A force consisting of British, French and Polish troops took the town on 28 May, the first clear Allied land victory of the war. But by this time events in France and Flanders had compelled the Allies to abandon the struggle in Norway. The successful evacuation of Narvik was marred by the loss of the carrier *Glorious* on 8 June.

By this campaign Hitler had acquired naval and air bases flanking the British Isles, and had loosened Britain's grip on the northern approaches to the Atlantic. It was now much easier for the Germans to attack Allied commerce either with warships or submarines. From an economic point of view Norway was of value to Hitler, although her merchant navy, the fourth largest in the world, did not fall into his hands. The iron-ore route to Sweden via Narvik was working again by January 1941. Heavy water was another Norwegian product which might have proved vitally important. Outside Scandinavia the moral effects of this campaign were quickly overshadowed by the German triumphs in France and the Low Countries. The casualties on land were not very heavy. The Allies lost 1,869 British, 1,335 Norwegians and about 530 French and Polish. The Germans admitted a loss of 5,296. The Germans lost 242 planes, of which about 80 were transport aircraft. While British losses were fewer, no loss of Allied planes at that time could be afforded.

The Royal Navy, despite its chronic lack of air support, had done well. Its losses, especially the *Glorious*, had been severe, but the German Navy had been very hard hit. By the end of June her cruisers had been reduced to three and her destroyers to four. Her losses in merchant shipping had also been heavy, and they were never made up. The Germans had no surface ships for operations in the Channel or for *Operation Sealion,* the invasion of Britain. The British were left with an increased margin of superiority which enabled them to reconstitute the Mediterranean fleet.

The Germans were to occupy Norway for five years, and at first it was of great value to them as a base. The campaign, so far from breaking the spirit of the Norwegian people, nerved them to resist. Had they not, led by their wise and steadfast General, Ruge, held out for two whole months against the army that struck down Poland in 18 days? Thanks to their spirit and to British raids, such as those on the Lofoten Islands (4 March 1941) and Vaagso (27 December 1941), Hitler became convinced that the Allies would attempt to reconquer Norway. He built up the garrison until at the end of the war it numbered 300,000 men. By that time they could hardly have been less use to him had they been in Allied prison camps. In the long-term Hitler's Norwegian campaign turned out to be the strategic blunder that Winston Churchill declared it was in the House on 11 April 1940. In the short term, the British people, not without reason, showed themselves very ill-satisfied with the conduct of the campaign. This feeling led to the fall of Chamberlain, and the assumption of power, in the nick of time, by Churchill.

The British troops were well led in Norway by commanders who included Generals Auchinleck, Paget and Carton de Wiart. The troops, to be frank, were of mixed quality. General Auchinleck, who had recently returned from long years with the Indian Army, considered their morale 'had often been lower than that of other troops working under comparable conditions'. While emphasizing the effects of inferiority of equipment and, above all, of the absence of adequate air support he concluded, with justice, 'that our existing methods of training lacked realism and did not do enough to inculcate habits of self-reliance'. General Carton de Wiart found that his soldiers in their fur coats and winter clothing 'were scarcely able to move and looked like paralyzed bears'.

It is only fair to say that some units, for example the 1st Scots Guards and the 1st Irish Guards, lived up to their ancient traditions. To a great extent it was to be the task of General Paget, as G.O.C. Home Forces, to remedy the defective training of the British army.

The campaign in Norway emphasized the need for special landing craft and special training in Combined Operations. It was as well that this lesson was re-learnt early in a war, where seaborne landings were to be a feature of operations in every theatre.

The scene in a Norwegian port during the German invasion.

6 SITZKRIEG

'Nothing doing yet.'
'Looks like another bloody hundred years' war.'
(Heard in a Blackpool pub)

For six months after the fall of Poland the armies on the Western Front remained practically motionless. The French, who during the Polish campaign had advanced a few miles into Germany, retreated into the Maginot Line as soon as the main German army moved back from Poland.

The Maginot Line was the real key to Allied land strategy during these months. It had been begun in 1929 and called after the War Minister, André Maginot. France had lost 1,500,000 killed in the First World War, many of them victims of the *offensive à l'outrance* school of military thought. Except for a few months of 1914 and of 1918, the war on the Western Front had been a business of trench systems and the slow methods of siege warfare. But the trench systems had been improvised. Techniques forgotten since the days of Vauban and Marlborough had had to be re-learnt. It seemed logical to have a perfect defensive system carefully devised beforehand. Fortifications would redress the balance of manpower if France, with her population of 42,000,000, should find herself facing the German nation of 78,526,000. The fortresses of the Maginot Line contained every feature that the generals of Verdun could have wished for. Underground barracks, ammunition dumps, cookhouses, hospitals, telephone exchanges and power stations: miniature railways, ammunition hoists, drainage systems – everything had been thought of. Elaborate charts showed fire plans covering every square foot of terrain in front of the line.

All this had cost about £160,000,000,000. Yet, incredible as it may seem, the Line covered only that part of the French frontier from Switzerland to Montmédy. It is true that there were pill-boxes along the rest of the frontier to the sea, but these were not to be compared with the Maginot Line proper. It was as if Schlieffen had never been. Against an enemy

Below: **German soldiers wave to their adversaries over the Rhine during the *Sitzkrieg***

Above: German troops stockpile munitions in preparation for an offensive.

Left: General Gamelin (left) was the Commander-in-Chief of the Allied Forces and General Gort (right) was the Commander-in-Chief of the BEF.

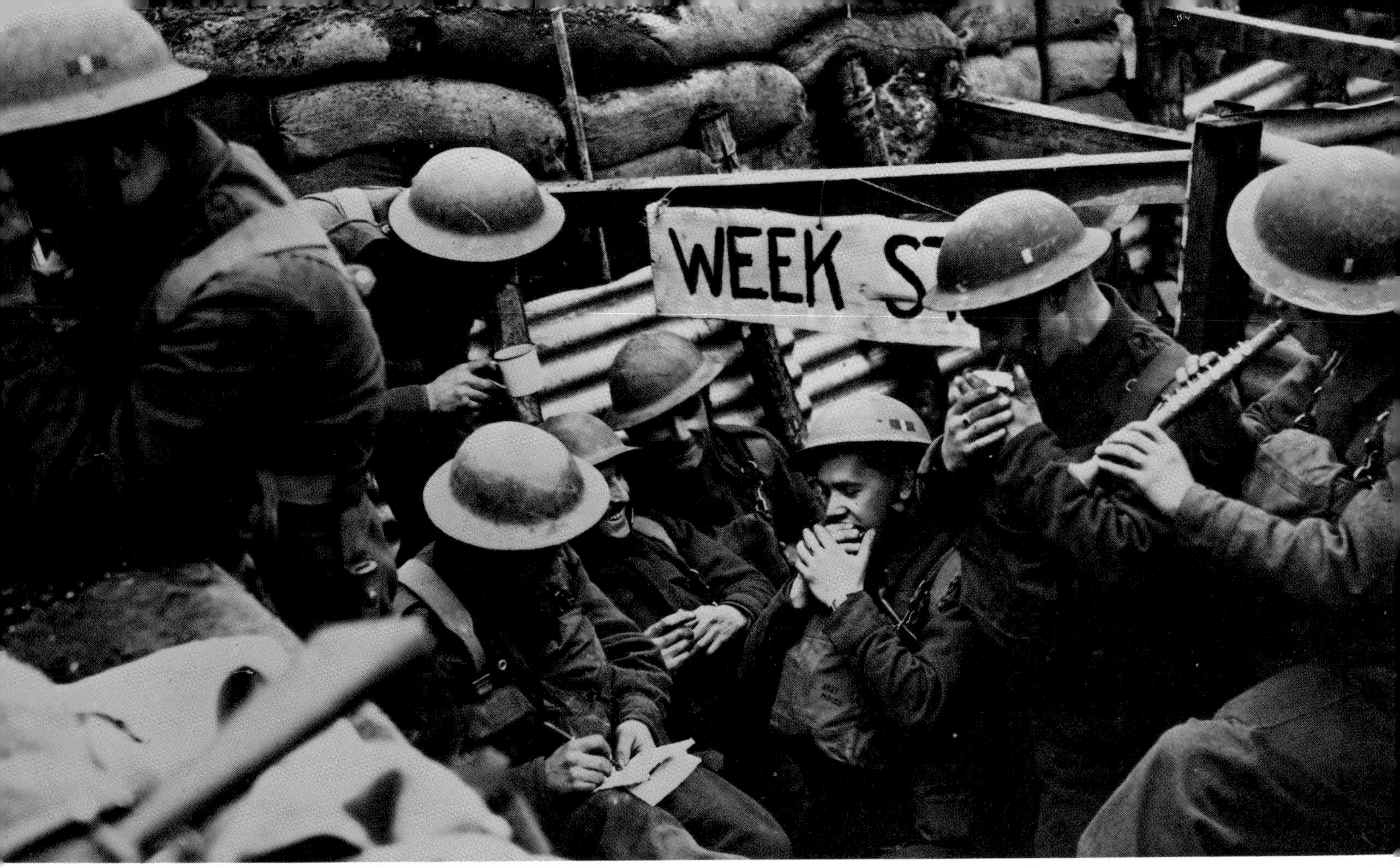

WEEK

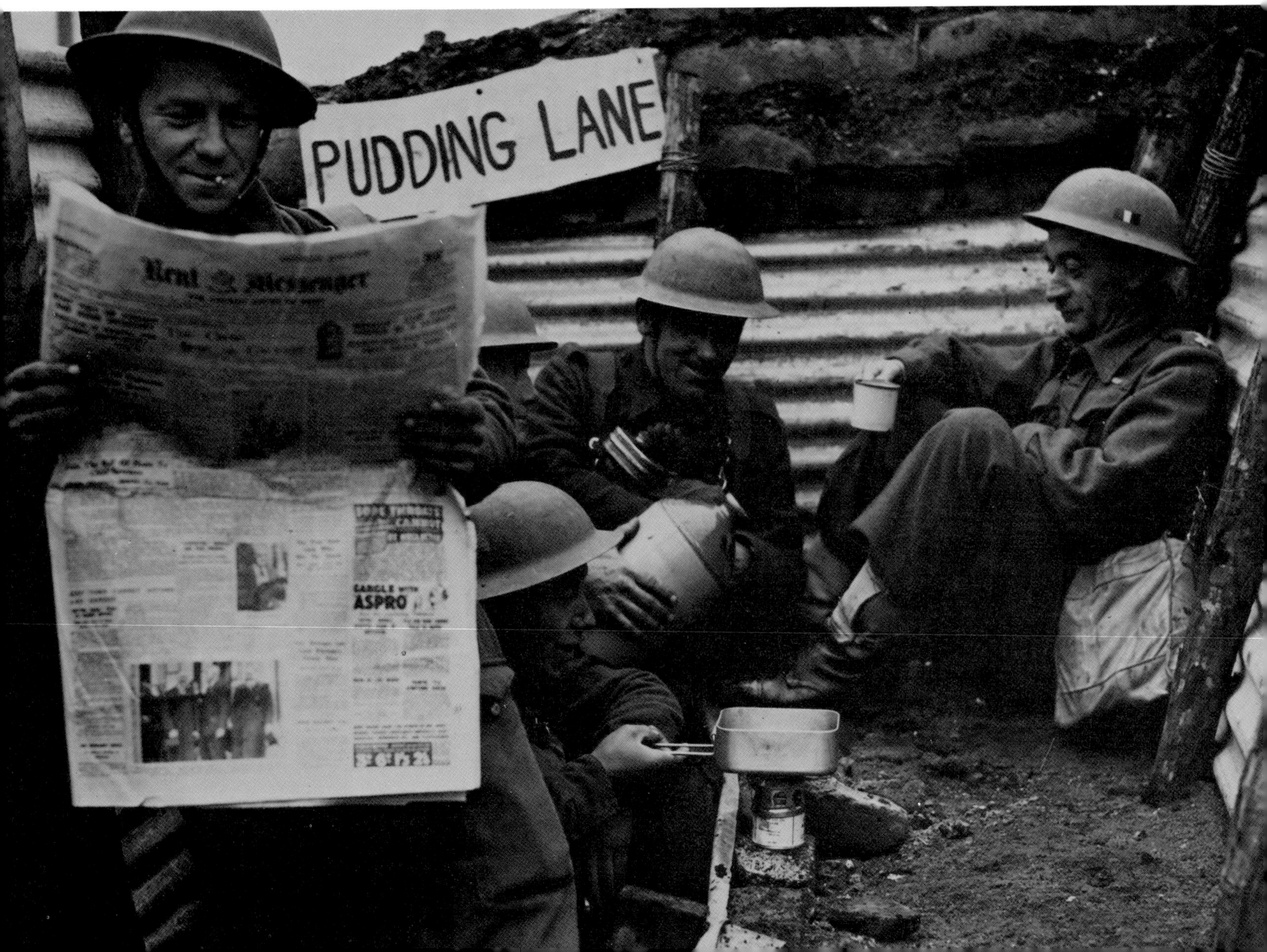

PUDDING LANE
GARGLE WITH
ASPRO

who had violated Belgian neutrality in 1914, the French had put their serious defences only on that part of their frontier which actually marched with Germany. The Line required a garrison of some 300,000 men, but since the French could put 2,776,000 in the field this was not necessarily a disadvantage. So long as their dispositions elsewhere were sound, all might yet be well. This is not to say, however, that the money would not have been better spent on tanks and planes, especially the latter.

Despite their new *Blitzkrieg* tactics, the Germans too made use of fortifications – the Siegfried Line. This was by no means as elaborate as the Maginot defences: some indeed have described it as a gigantic bluff, and it had certainly been built in a hurry. A labour corps of half-a-million workers, toiling under the supervision of Dr Fritz Todt, had built three lines of fortifications and anti-tank defences. This effort had served its turn by enabling Hitler to hold the Western Front with 23 of his 75 divisions while he concentrated against Poland. General von Mellenthin, who first saw this West Wall after the bluff had worked, was unimpressed. 'The West Wall had been built in such a hurry that many of the positions were sited on forward slopes. The anti-tank obstacles were of trivial significance, and the more I looked at the defences the less I could understand the completely passive attitude of the French.' It was indeed an attitude hard for a general in Hitler's army to comprehend, for Hitler was nothing if not a leader, and it was precisely in this quality of leadership that the Allied statesmen and politicians were lacking. They found themselves saddled with a war which they did not want, and did not know how to go about winning. The French were the senior partners on the Western Front, but it is too easy to lay all the blame on the weak governments of Daladier and Reynaud. The British contribution was unimpressive. A nation of 45 million could find only ten infantry divisions to put into the field beside her French allies. The 33 million Poles had produced thirty. And Chamberlain did not know where he was going any more than his allies did. Montgomery has recorded how the Prime Minister visited his division on 16 December, 1939: 'He took me aside after lunch and said in a low tone so that no one could hear, "I don't think the Germans have any intention of attacking us. Do you?".'

Despite their triumph in Poland, the German High Command approached the problems of the Western Front without either enthusiasm or originality. But Hitler spurred them on. Their first inspiration was to revive the Schlieffen Plan of 1914. General von Manstein, with the technical advice of the tank expert, Guderian, and the approval of his superior, Colonel-General von Rundstedt, produced a far deadlier plan. This 'involved a strong tank thrust through southern Belgium and Luxembourg towards Sedan, a breakthrough of the Prolongation of the Maginot Line in that area and a consequent splitting in two of the whole French front'. This memorandum was ill-received. The High Command wanted to use only one or two of the nine panzer divisions for this attack, and in consequence of the row that followed, Manstein, the Germans' 'finest operational brain', found himself commanding an infantry corps. But as luck would have it, the Schlieffen Plan was hopelessly compromised when a *Luftwaffe* officer-courier who, contrary to standing orders, was flying by night with papers referring to it, came down in Belgium.

Hitler heard Manstein's views when the latter reported to him on taking command of his corps. The upshot was that the Manstein Plan was tried out in War games in February 1940. Halder, the Chief of the Army General Staff, was present on both occasions. Guderian records that neither he nor even Rundstedt 'had any clear idea about the potentialities of tanks'. The idea of driving a wedge deep and wide into the French front so that they need not worry about their flanks did not appeal to them. It was not only French and British generals who conceived this new war in terms of 1916. It takes a strong-minded commander to reject or improve upon the methods of his early campaigns. Those who can build on their experience are the true masters of war.

Left below: **The Royal West Kent Regiment were prepared, like other Allied forces, to fight the Germans from their trenches. The lessons from the Polish Campaign had not been learnt.**

Left: **Members of the Royal West Kent Regiment entertain each other during the long months of inactivity before the Battle of France.**

Below: **The Germans tried to demoralise their French opponents with propaganda.**

7 BLITZKRIEG, 1940

'Le printemps rappelle aux armes.'

'Les parfums du printemps le sable les ignore!
Voici mourir le mai dans les dunes du Nord.'

Louis Aragon

When Hitler invaded Norway there was no lack of military experts to proclaim this to be his spring offensive. Yet a casual acquaintance with the remarkably accurate Intelligence Summaries then distributed in the British Expeditionary Force (BEF) showed that the German force sent to Scandinavia had subtracted nothing from their Order of Battle on the Western Front.

On 10 May the *Sitzkrieg* came to an abrupt end, with the German invasion of the Low Countries and France. This was almost a complete surprise to the victims, though why this was so is not clear, since from about 7 May onwards German aircraft had been flying over the Lille area at night, unmistakable from the interrupted buzzing of their engines. Surprise or no surprise the Germans were going to be hard to beat. Little that had happened so far in the war, still less during the months that led up to it, had fostered the morale of the Allies. The German soldier was rapidly becoming a superman in the eyes of his opponents *'Ils ne passeront pas'*, said the French soldiery with ever diminishing conviction, while a surprising number would confess without shame to having *'frousse'*, which could be translated as 'cold feet'. 'The rather inactive behaviour of the French during the winter of 1939–40 seemed to indicate a limited enthusiasm for the war . . .' wrote General Guderian, in one of the great understatements of all time.

'Le matériel est bon' the French would say enviously as the vehicles of the BEF rolled by. Their own, for the most part, would not have been out of place on the battlefields of 1870. The problems of morale and *matériel* should not, however, be overstressed. The BEF which had endured a particularly cold, dull and cheerless winter in Northern France, doing the maximum of digging and the minimum of training and shooting, cheered up with the promise of spring. Its most obvious weakness was its very small proportion of tanks. That a major power should field an army of but ten divisions was unimpressive; to provide it with no more than one armoured brigade was pitiful. This was not a balanced force. The French did not lack tanks; they seem to have had about 3,000 to the Germans' 2,700. The imbalance of their forces was due to the almost incredible state of their aviation.

But when all is said and done it was leadership, in which must be included military thinking, that lost and won the campaign of 1940. In England Mr Churchill took the reins on the very day the fighting began, and for the rest of the war onwards, at the highest level, the British were unusually well led. But the BEF also was, on the whole, well commanded. Lord Gort was a man with the courage to take decisions which many a cleverer soldier would have shirked. The other generals included Brooke (II Corps), Alexander (I Div.), Montgomery (III Div.), Johnson (IV Div.), Barker (10 Bde.), Dempsey (13 Bde.) and many other stout-hearted and war-wise soldiers.

Of the French war cabinet none can deny

Below left: The Commander-in-Chief of the BEF, Lord Gort, with his two Corps Commandants General Sir John Dill and Lieutenant General Alan Brooke.

Bottom left: Despondent French troops surrender in Lille, May 1940.

Below: The Junkers Ju 87 Stuka terrorized soldiers and civilians when it appeared in the skies over the Low Countries and northern France.

Above: General Maurice Gustave Gamelin.

Below: Dunkirk harbour under attack.

Below right: German paratroops on the outskirts of Rotterdam, 10 May 1940.

Below far right: The Germans enter The Hague.

that Reynaud and Mandel had some fight in them, or that the much-maligned Admiral Darlan was a man of courage. As to the rest, the less said the better. The real weak point in the Allied set-up was little General Gamelin, who as a Staff Officer in 1914 had followed the massive figure of Marshal Joffre through the anxious days of the Marne. If ever a man had had a chance to learn his trade it was Gamelin. But what do we find? In 1940 he assigned all but a fraction of his tanks to the infantry divisions spread out along the whole length of his front. Not only was there little armour in reserve, there was no reserve at all – no *masse de manoeuvre.* Without a reserve, especially when the enemy has the initiative and can strike where he wills, a commander cannot hope to influence the battle. In general the Allied commanders, as Guderian puts it, 'were pre-occupied with the concepts of positional warfare'.

Their experiences in the First World War had taught the French the value of fire, but not the value of movement. Their doctrine, based on the idea of methodical positional warfare, was well known to the Germans. And it was clear from their dispositions that they not only expected the Germans to try the old Schlieffen Plan once more, but scarcely considered any other possible.

On the German side the generalship was highly professional, but perhaps less impressive than it appeared at the time. Except for Hitler himself, and for Manstein, Guderian and Rommel, it cannot be said that the generals had any real understanding of modern mobile warfare, or that they had learned the lessons of Poland. Like the French, even able men like Rundstedt were inclined to think in terms of the previous war. At the higher echelons they too were to have their moments of *frousse*. The *Luftwaffe*, which had been built up by Hermann Göring, was as impressive over France as over Poland, though as time went by its head was to prove one of the Allies' chief assets, largely because he took on too many different jobs, and so did none well.

At the tactical level some of the BEF were to learn the elementary lessons that if you shot at a German he took cover like anyone else, and if you hit him he bled.

The campaign falls neatly into two parts, which one can call the battle of the Low Countries and the battle of France.

The line-up for the battle of the Low Countries was:

	Allies	*Germans*
Divisions	**146**	**126**
Armoured divisions	**3+**	**10**
Armoured vehicles	***c.*3,000**	***c.*2,700**

'Tomorrow at dawn. Hold tight!' Dutch agents warned their masters on the evening of 9 April. At 4 a.m. the Germans struck. Parachutists, some in Allied uniforms, descended on airfields and bridges. Dive-bombers, with their unnerving scream, plummeted out of the morning sky. The dozen squadrons which made up the Dutch air force were soon shattered. At 6 a.m. the German minister at The Hague blandly delivered the customary Nazi ultimatum. The German action had been forced on them by irrefutable evidence that Britain and France, with the knowledge of the governments of Holland, Belgium, and Luxembourg, were about to invade the Netherlands. Instant submission or annihilation were the alternatives.

Now that it was too late, Holland and Belgium appealed to France and Britain for help. But at least they fought on. The Dutch relied in vain on flooding and demolitions. The

Germans penetrated 'Fortress Holland' in a matter of days. On 14 May the centre of the open city of Rotterdam was blitzed to rubble by *Stukas*, and 40,000 civilians were killed. This the Inspector-General of the Bundeswehr explained in 1964 was 'a tragic misunderstanding owing to the failure of the Dutch and the Germans to appreciate that they were not using the same time, so that readiness to declare it an open city had not been received before the deadline expired'. The attack against the city, which was defended and occupied by troops, was, however, fully justified militarily, General Trettner said. He was good enough to add that German aggression against the Netherlands and Poland was morally unjustified. Such a delicately adjusted sense of values can only excite our admiration. Many a German city was to 'Remember Rotterdam' before the war was done. On 14 May 1940 the Dutch army surrendered. Its casualties numbering 100,000, 25 per cent of its strength, attest the courage of its resistance. Queen Wilhelmina and her government escaped to England in a British destroyer, and under their guidance the Dutch colonies remained in the war.

Meanwhile the Germans were pouring into France and Belgium, and the Allies, in pursuance of Plan D, were pivoting forward to cover Brussels, a move which to their astonishment was accomplished without interference from the *Luftwaffe*. Despite this bonus, disaster dogged the Allies from the outset. To command the bridges of the Meuse and Albert Canal the Belgians had built the seemingly impregnable fortress of Eben Emael, which lasted a mere 36 hours. Thoroughly trained on a full-scale model, a combat team of parachutists and assault engineers descended on the position. In vain the commander called down on himself the fire of neighbouring forts. At 12.30 a.m. on 11 May the garrison, still 1,100 strong, surrendered. It had suffered only 100 casualties. The attackers' losses, such is the value of briefing and training, were even lighter.

This setback was bad, but not fatal. The Belgians fell back to the line Antwerp-Louvain and joined hands with the BEF who by the 15th had a division at Louvain, and another

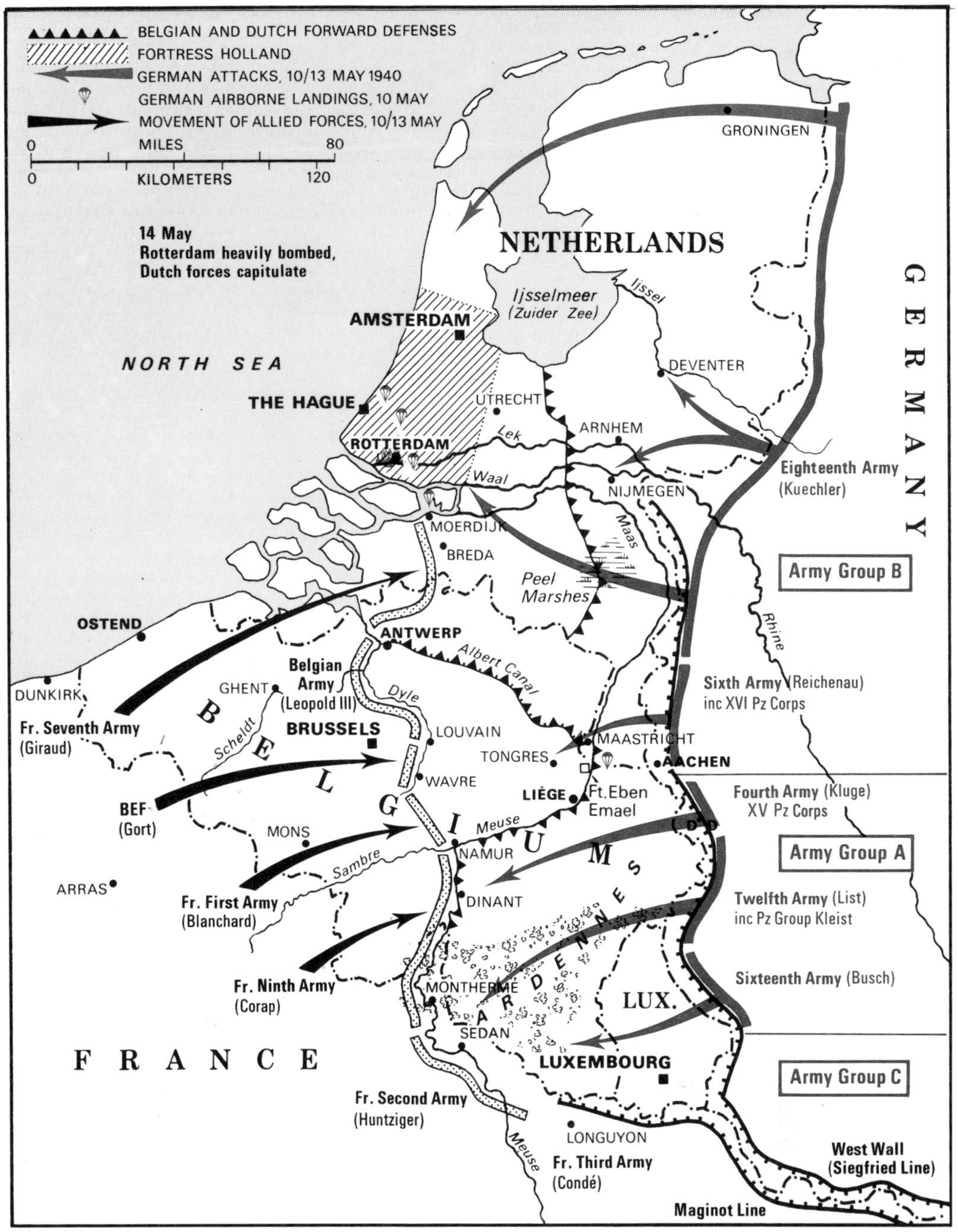

Above: **Calais fell on 26 May after heavy fighting.**

Above right: **General Winkelman surrenders on behalf of the Dutch army.**

covering Brussels – the only time in the campaign that they were to be deployed in such depth.

But already Gamelin's strategy had received a mortal blow. On the 13th Lieutenant-General von Kleist, advancing through the Ardennes, which were well-known in military circles to be impassable, had crossed the Meuse. A breach 50 miles wide was appearing in the French line between Namur and Sedan, the very hinge of the Allied position. The 14 May was for the Allies one of the black days of the war. Von Kleist now wished to halt and consolidate the Meuse bridgehead, but this did not suit his subordinate, Guderian. 'I neither would nor could agree to these orders, which involved the sacrifice of the element of surprise we had gained and of the whole initial success that we had achieved.' Heated exchanges followed during the night 15/16 May and von Kleist reluctantly approved a further advance for the next 24 hours. Captured orders told the Germans that the French High Command was seriously concerned as to the defensive capability of their infantry.

Events were moving too fast for the Allies. With this breach in the Meuse front it was now imperative that the forces in Belgium, where General Billotte was supposed to be co-ordinating operations, should withdraw. But the French command set-up was not functioning smoothly and it was only at Gort's insistence that the decision was taken. On the morning of the 16th orders were given to withdraw to the Escaut (Schelde). Brussels and Antwerp had to be abandoned. Gort had little enough up his sleeve, but there were three Territorial divisions, without artillery and with little in the way of signals and administrative units, which had been sent out to work in the rear areas. These were hastily provided with guns from reserve stores and sent to hold the Canal du Nord between Peronne and Douai: a timely piece of improvisation.

The evening of the 16th found Guderian's corps 55 miles beyond Sedan. It was a complete breakthrough. So far from being pleased, early on the 17th von Kleist berated Guderian violently for disobeying orders. It was OKH itself that had ordered the halt. However, with the connivance of Army Group (von Rundstedt) 'reconnaissance in force' was now permitted, though Corps HQ was under no circumstances to move. The wily Guderian got over this difficulty by having a telephone laid from corps to his advanced HQ. This had the added advantage that his orders could not be monitored by the wireless units of the OKH and OKW.

Opposition from the French was a lesser obstacle and by the evening of 17 May the Germans had a bridgehead across the Oise near Moy. On the 18th they reached St Quentin and next day they were pouring across the Somme battlefields of 1916. In this desperate situation the French made a belated effort to take a grip on affairs. On 18 May the Premier, Reynaud, assumed the office of Minister of National Defence. The aged hero of Verdun, Marshal Pétain, became Vice-President of the Council, and Monsieur Mandel went to the Ministry of the Interior – an excellent appointment. Gamelin was dismissed and General Weygand, who had flown home from Syria, was appointed Chief of the General Staff of National Defence and Commander-in-Chief. But the time when such resolute measures might have had effect had already passed. Weygand, like his predecessor, knew nothing of armoured warfare, besides being too old. He had been a brilliant staff officer, but this appointment at the height of the battle was probably a mistake. The French and Belgian divisions were already so shaken by the pounding they had received that their power to resist was ebbing away. The BEF was giving a good account of itself, but the British government was justifiably concerned lest it should be cut off.

Amiens fell on the 20th. 'Along the whole front the enemy is in retreat in a manner that at times approaches rout,' wrote Guderian in his Corps Order for the next day. It was a sober estimate. And every major move the Allies made was dogged by an army of refugees. In Albert the 2nd Panzer Division had captured a British battery, 'drawn up on the Barrack square and equipped only with training ammunition, since nobody had reckoned on our appearance

Top: **The damaged remains of RAF Blenheim bombers, which never got off the ground.**

Above: **Signallers work through the night to maintain communications with troops at Rouen.**

Below: **The French Army melted away before the new methods of warfare employed by Germany's Panzer divisions.**

Above: **The Panzer divisions halted outside Dunkirk to give the Luftwaffe the opportunity of finishing off the BEF. In fact it gave the British a chance to evacuate the bulk of their troops.**

that day.' Although somewhat short of fuel Guderian goaded his men into renewed activity and by 7 p.m. had them in Abbeville. Nobody could believe the German armour had got so far. Indeed the *Luftwaffe* actually bombed Guderian's HQ. The 2nd Panzer Division reached the Atlantic coast that night (20 May). The Germans wasted the 21st because Panzer Group von Kleist had received no instructions. On this day the Allies made a hurriedly mounted thrust near Arras in which two battalions and 74 tanks, with some supporting troops, attacked part of the German 7th Armoured and SS *Totenkopf* Divisions. French tanks of General Prioux's Cavalry Corps co-operated. A confused day's fighting followed. The operation was conducted with sufficient vigour to convince the Germans that there were five British divisions round Arras, and it delayed the advance of the leading German divisions. British casualties were heavy, but they took 400 prisoners and destroyed a number of tanks and vehicles. Rommel himself was persuaded that his men were engaged in a 'very heavy battle against hundreds of enemy tanks and following infantry'. The staff of Panzer Group von Kleist became remarkably nervous.

Even so the Germans began their advance on the Channel ports next day and by that evening, despite much activity on the part of the RAF, had fought their way into Boulogne, which held out until the 25th, most of the garrison (20th Guards Brigade) being evacuated by sea. Guderian tells us that the German tanks could not 'penetrate the old town walls. By the use of a ladder from the kitchen of a nearby house, and with the powerful assistance of an 88-mm flak gun, a breach was at last made in the wall near the cathedral. . . .'

At this juncture (23 May) Colonel-General von Rundstedt gave orders to the Fourth Army for a halt. Hitler, who appeared on the 24th, agreed with this arrangement, but – despite the assertions of German generals since the war – it was not his idea in the first place. When on 25 May OKH authorized the passage of the Canal front by the armour, Rundstedt still did not send it over. The Dunkirk area is not favourable for tanks and his decision may well have been correct, though Brauchitsch and Guderian did not agree with it. There was still much for the tanks to do in the South.

Calais fell to the 10th Panzer Division on the 26th. 'We took 20,000 prisoners, including 3-4,000 British, the remainder being French, Belgian and Dutch, of whom the majority had not wanted to go on fighting and whom the English had therefore locked up in cellars' (Guderian). The resistance of Brigadier Nicholson's 30th Brigade was in the best traditions of the Rifle Regiments of which it consisted. They did not fight in vain, for they contained a German force of several divisions.

Meanwhile it had been decided to withdraw the BEF to England. Lord Gort had the courage to take this decision, so foreign to his nature, in good time. The Royal Navy was not taken by surprise by the events of this campaign. The Naval Staff had laid its plans soon after the outbreak of war and in the opening fortnight of the campaign a variety of unusual but not unexpected tasks were carried out. The rescue of the Dutch Royal family; the removal of the gold reserves and diamonds from Amsterdam; the withdrawal of merchantmen, barges and tugs from Antwerp; the movements by des-

Above right: **Warehouses on the banks of the Seine in Rouen are consumed by fire during the German advance on Paris.**

Left: **Two pictures of the French delegation to the surrender ceremony. Hitler increased the humiliation by using the wagon at Compiègne which had been used for the German surrender in 1918.**

troyer of the garrisons to Boulogne and back and to Calais. In all these operations losses of warships had not been light.

A far more difficult task had now to be faced. At 6.57 p.m. on 26 May the Admiralty sent out the order: 'begin Operation "Dynamo" ' – the evacuation of the BEF. A sober view of the prospects was taken. It was thought that the operation might possibly last two days before the *Luftwaffe* and the German artillery made conditions impossible for Admiral Ramsay's force. It was hoped that 35,000 soldiers might be saved. Had this been the total it is difficult indeed to see how the British army could have been rebuilt to avenge the blow. But the operation was to last nine days, and 338,226 men were to be rescued.

The peoples Hitler had crushed watched the operation, hardly daring to hope that the BEF

Above: The victory parade down the Champs Elysées was well-documented by German propagandists and was stage-managed to produce the maximum effect.

Above: After entering Paris on 14 June these soldiers gave way to their tiredness. The speed of the German advance stunned all those involved.

would survive to play its part in their liberation. To any reasonably minded continental soldier it must have seemed that the world was about to witness the most humiliating defeat in the long history of the British Army: the surrender of a quarter of a million men. Such a defeat, followed, as already seemed inevitable, by the fall of France, must surely kill all Allied hopes stone dead. That the 'nine days' wonder' of Dunkirk seemed well-nigh miraculous is the measure of the relief it brought to the free peoples of the world – to those of the United States as well as to the peoples already in the fight.

Only a power with salt water in its veins could have brought off *Dynamo*. For it was an operation whose success depended not only on the Royal Navy and the Merchant Navy, but upon the voluntary efforts of the owners of every type of small craft. Although a swell on 31 May made boat-work impossible off the beaches, the weather was 'almost miraculously favourable' during practically the whole operation. The cost was not light. Six destroyers were lost and nineteen seriously damaged. Nine personnel ships were sunk, and eight seriously hit. Numbers of the launches and smaller craft never returned. But Dunkirk was not all loss. If the campaign on land had gone to the devil it was not the British line that broke.

But it was sea-power that baffled Hitler at Dunkirk.

Göring had expressed his confidence that the *Luftwaffe* could smash the forces holding Dunkirk, and the shipping and the beaches were heavily bombed. But the RAF, operating from home bases, intervened with great effect and between 27 May and 30 May shot down 179 German aircraft for the loss of 29. Dunkirk gave the French to the South some respite. General Weygand now attempted to organize a system of defence in depth on the Somme and the Aisne. But by this time the remains of the French army, outgunned and bewildered, was in no condition to offer prolonged resistance. Here and there individual formations distinguished themselves, notably the staff and students of Saumur, and de Gaulle's armoured division, but the majority had lost all confidence, not only in their leaders but in themselves. Nor were their allies in any condition to aid them. The 51st Highland Division serving under French orders was trapped at St Valery-en-Caux, and, after a dogged resistance, was compelled to surrender on 12 June. The 52nd Division and the 1st Canadian Division, which were sent out under Lieutenant-General Sir Alan Brooke, via Cherbourg, had to be evacuated.

The Germans were across the Seine by 10 June, and on that day Mussolini declared war. On the 12th the French government declared Paris an open city and departed to Tours. Three days later it moved on to Bordeaux. Winston Churchill now made an offer of complete union between Britain and France, but this remarkable gesture came too late to affect the issue. Reynaud resigned and his successor, Marshal Pétain, lost no time in asking for an armistice. The German terms were accepted on 22 June, at Rethondes in the Forest of Compiègne. The scene was the railway carriage in which Marshal Foch had dictated the Allies' terms in 1918.

All France North and West of a line from the Swiss Frontier at Geneva, via Bourges to St Jean Pied de Port (about 35 miles S.E. Bayonne), was to be occupied. France was to pay the cost of the occupation. Her forces were to be disarmed and demobilized. Her shipping

Left: Rouen burns and another obstacle in the path of the German war machine is dealt with. Once the Germans reached the Seine on 10 June French resistance died.

Right: The parade down the Champs Elysées.

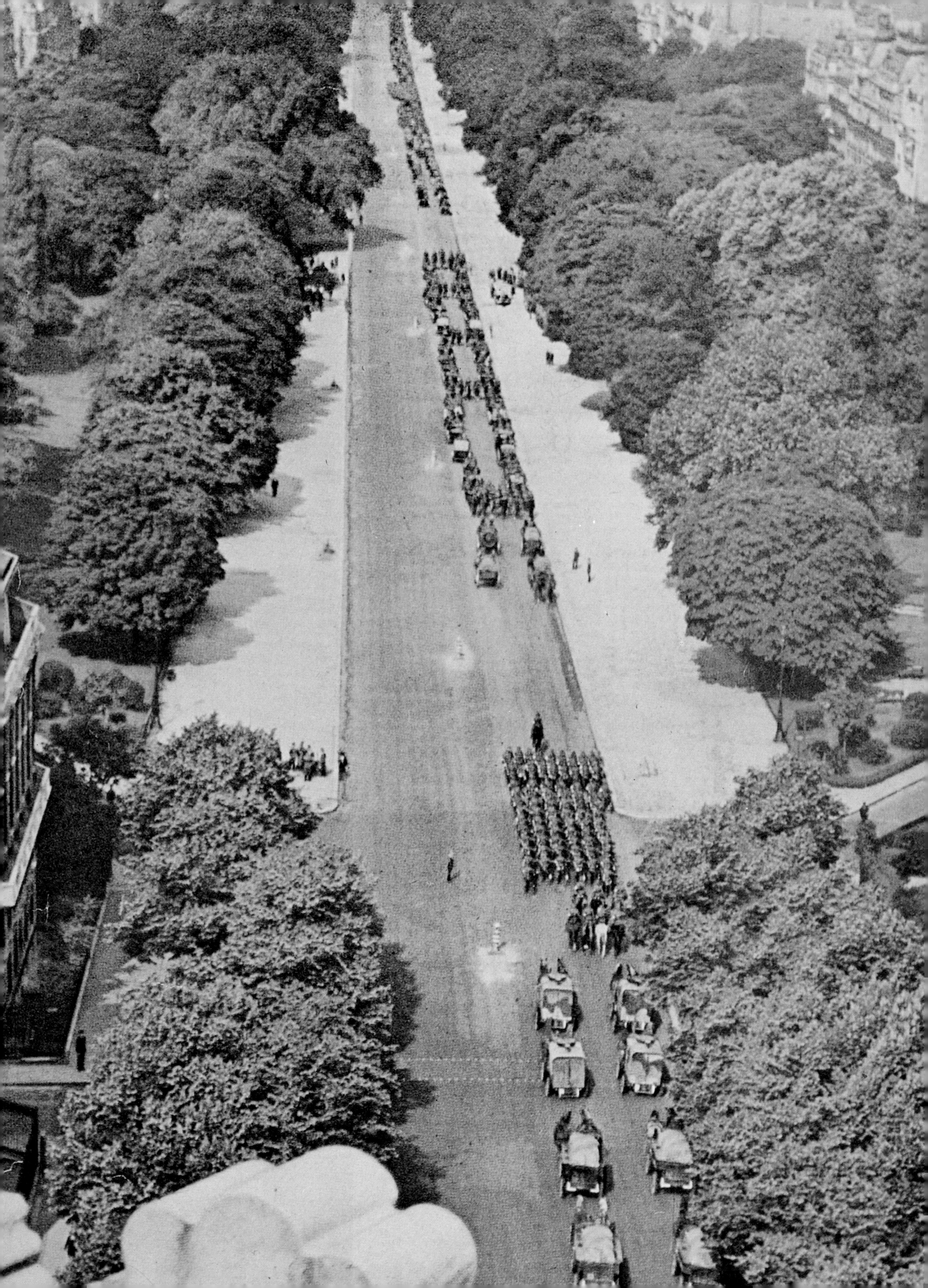

Left: **German troops march past the Etoile at the head of the Champs Elysées.**

Right: **The first station to be occupied was the Gare de l'Est. The notice on the station door announces instructions for those soldiers on leave to return to the front.**

was to stay in harbour, to be recalled, or to make for neutral ports. German prisoners of war were to be released, but French prisoners were to remain in German hands until the conclusion of peace.

The French government now set up its capital at Vichy in the unoccupied zone. General de Gaulle, who had distinguished himself in command of an armoured division, arrived in London, denounced the surrender, and set up a Provisional National Committee to work for the recovery of his country's independence and the maintenance of her alliances. This was a brave and welcome initiative. Britain now prepared to fight on alone.

On 4 June Winston Churchill spoke for his countrymen. 'Even though large tracts of Europe and many old and famous states have fallen or may fall into the grip of the Gestapo and all the odious apparatus of Nazi rule, we shall not flag or fail. We shall go on to the end. We shall fight in France, we shall fight in the seas and oceans, we shall fight with growing confidence and growing strength in the air; we shall defend our island, whatever the cost may be. We shall fight on the beaches, we shall fight on the landing-grounds, we shall fight in the fields and in the streets, we shall fight in the hills; we shall never surrender; and even if, which I do not for a moment believe, this island or a large part of it were subjugated and starving, then our Empire beyond the seas, armed and guarded by the British Fleet, would carry on the struggle, until in God's good time, the new world, with all its power and might, steps forth to the rescue and the liberation of the old.'

Right: **Some of the last members of the BEF to be evacuated from France.**

Below right: **On the whole German troops in France were restrained and did not antagonise the local people by orgiastically celebrating their victory.**

Below: **Abandoned motor transports were used to block the road to Cherbourg.**

8 THE BATTLE OF BRITAIN

'Hitler knows that he will have to break us in this island or lose the war. If we can stand up to him, all Europe may be free and the life of the world may move forward into broad, sunlit uplands. But if we fail, then the whole world, including the United States, including all that we have known and cared for, will sink into the abyss of a new dark age, made more sinister, and perhaps more protracted, by the lights of perverted science. Let us therefore brace ourselves to our duties, and so bear ourselves that, if the British Empire and its Commonwealth last for a thousand years, men will still say: "This was their finest hour".'

Above: **A recruiting poster for the Luftwaffe, Germany's elite air arm.**

With these words, declaimed in the House of Commons on 18 June 1940, Winston Churchill steeled his countrymen for the great ordeal which now began: the Battle of Britain.

This chapter tells the story of Hitler's attempt to invade England – Operation *Sealion*. He planned to clear the way for a seaborne invasion by breaking the back of the RAF, especially Fighter Command. When their casualties mounted the Germans lost sight of their target and indulged in the attack on London and other cities known as the 'Blitz'. The Germans set aside an army of some 20 divisions for the operation. It may be questioned whether the flotilla which they assembled was adequate to transport them. The German Navy, as we have seen, had been roughly handled during the Norwegian campaign, and was in no condition to escort the force even by the shortest sea passage – which we now know was the one they had selected. Clearly their safe arrival depended on the *Luftwaffe* rather than the small German Navy. If Göring's men could destroy the Royal Air Force and drive the Royal Navy out of the English Channel, the invaders had a good chance of landing without unacceptable casualties.

Once ashore they would have had to deal with some 25 divisions, all more or less up to strength, but woefully short of modern weapons, transport and tanks. Though morale was very high, this army was neither as experienced nor as well-trained as the Germans. It was, moreover, spread out from Kent to Cromarty, with no means of knowing where to expect the landing. For a long time the East coast seemed the likeliest place. It was, of course, possible that there would be several landings at once. The possibility of airborne landings had to be taken into account, but there was no likelihood that parachutists would cause the dismay and confusion they had spread in the Low Countries. The Local Defence Volunteers (soon to be rechristened the Home Guard) had sprung to life one May evening and, though armed at first with shotguns and even pikes, they were invaluable for guarding vulnerable points. Their ranks were full of determined veterans of 1914–18 who would, no doubt, have given a good account of themselves. Britain and her Empire now stood virtually alone. Furthermore it was impossible for her to deploy the whole of her meagre resources in defence of the British Isles, for it was necessary to maintain her position abroad, and especially in the Mediterranean.

But if we lacked allies we still had a good friend in President Roosevelt. There was at this time no want of Americans to proclaim that 'Britain was finished'. But the President 'scraped the bottom of the barrel in American arsenals' and provided:

500,000 rifles
80,000 machine guns
130,000,000 rounds of ammunition
900 75-mm. guns
100,000,000 shells.

And we still had some 200 tanks of our own.

The British Army exerted itself to prepare against invasion. Officers of proved ability, Generals Sir John Dill and Sir Alan Brooke, held the key positions of Chief of the Imperial General Staff and Commander-in-Chief Home Forces. It would be a long time before the army could take the offensive, but, as an earnest of better things to come, the Commandos were formed with the object of carrying out raids anywhere from Narvik to Bayonne.

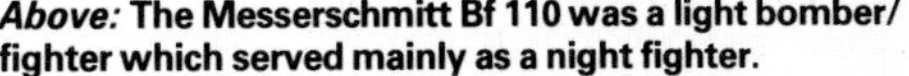

Above: The Messerschmitt Bf 110 was a light bomber/ fighter which served mainly as a night fighter.

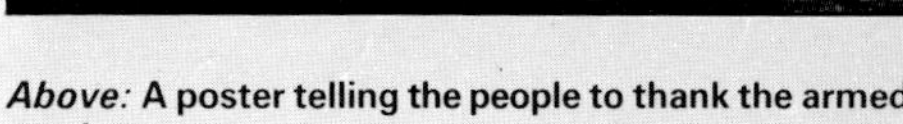

Above: A poster telling the people to thank the armed services.

Below: The Heinkel He 111s were twin-engined bombers which were very vulnerable to fighters and consequently were mainly used as night bombers.

Above: **Holborn Circus being bombed during a later raid on London in 1941.**

Above: **The famous Supermarine Spitfires of No 610 Squadron poised for action.**

None need doubt that in the mood of 1940 the British would have met German invasion with stubborn fury. Still it was just as well that the British army was not invited to take on the Wehrmacht in the fields of Kent. Keitel and other senior officers of the German Armed Forces Supreme Headquarters were convinced, after the French armistice, that England was prepared to sue for peace. So little did they understand the temper of the British people.

German air power was now at its height:

11 fighter groups	– **1,300**	**Messerschmitt 109s**
2 fighter-bomber groups	– **180**	**Messerschmitt 110s**
10 bomber groups	– **1,350**	**(Heinkel 111s Junkers 88s Dornier 17s)**
	2,830	

With skilled and experienced crews who had tasted victory, the *Luftwaffe* entered the Battle of Britain confident of success. Two air fleets took part: Second, under Field Marshal Kesselring (HQ: Brussels); and Third, under Field Marshal Sperrle (HQ: Paris). On 2 July the German High Command issued orders designed to pave the way for the invasion of Britain. Two aims were laid down:

'(1) The interdiction of the Channel to merchant shipping, to be carried out in conjunction with German naval forces, by means of attacks on convoys, the destruction of harbour facilities, and the sowing of mines in harbour areas and the approaches thereto.

(2) The destruction of the Royal Air Force.'

To frustrate this plan Fighter Command had (8 August) some 600 or 700 fighters, organized in 55 operational squadrons, including six of night-fighters (Blenheims), which took no part in daylight operations. The great majority of the planes were Hurricanes, about one-fifth were Spitfires, and there were two squadrons of Defiants. Thanks to the efforts of Lord Beaverbrook, Minister of Aircraft Production, our strength in aircraft was growing all the time, and by 30 September we had 59 Squadrons (eight being night-fighters). Pilots were, of course, more difficult to replace than aircraft, but many naval pilots volunteered, and a large number were brought in from other commands.

The Battle of Britain began when on 10 July German bombers attacked merchant convoys in the Channel. A week later (16 July) Hitler issued his instructions for Operation *Sealion*. Preparations were to be completed by the middle of August. Among them was the appointment by Heydrich of S.S. Colonel

Below left: **One of the co-ordinating centres for Air Defence during the Battle of Britain.**

Below: **Dornier 17s fly over the Thames near Woolwich Arsenal on 7 September 1940**

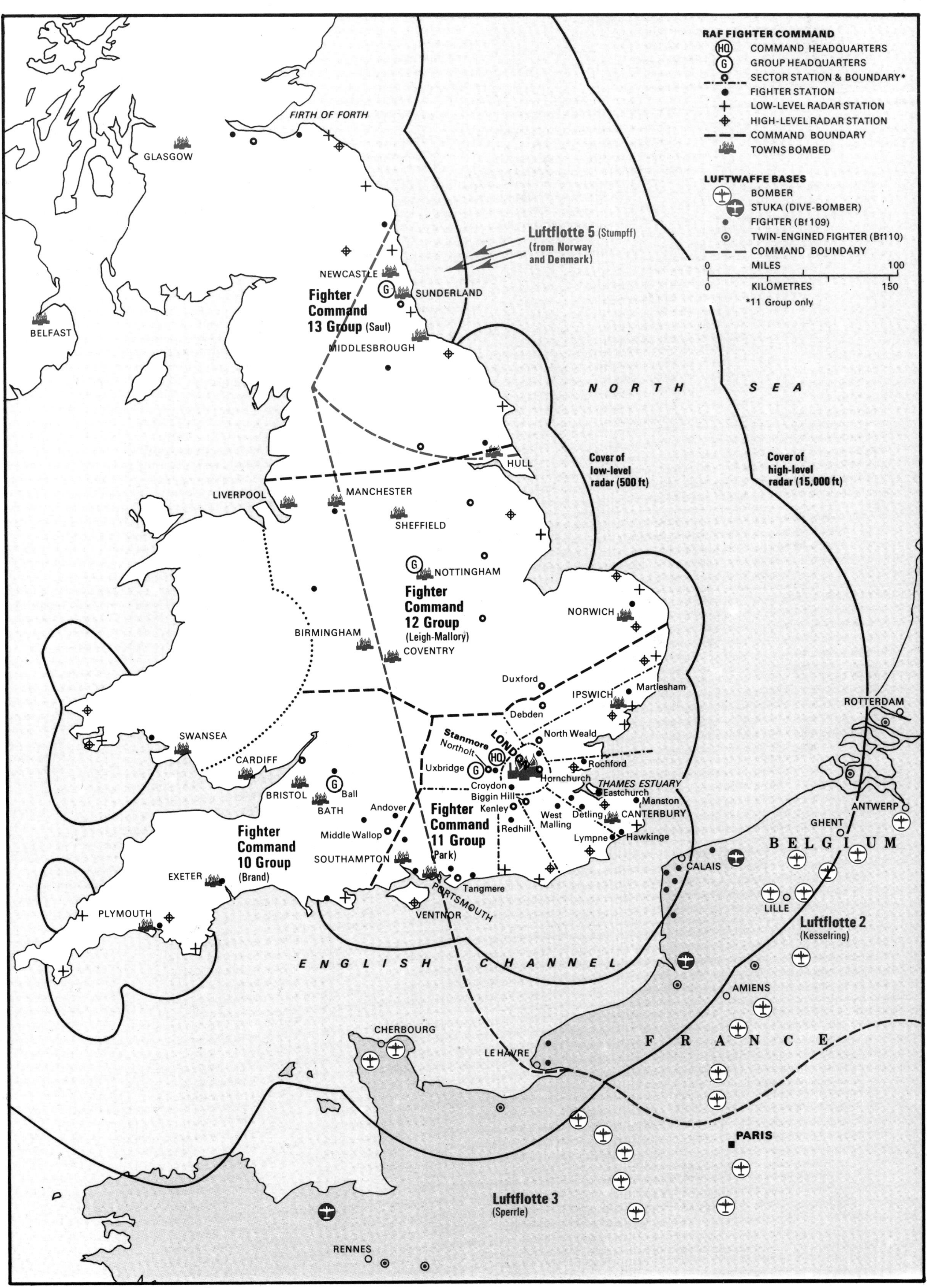
RAF FIGHTER COMMAND
COMMAND HEADQUARTERS
GROUP HEADQUARTERS
SECTOR STATION & BOUNDARY*
FIGHTER STATION
LOW-LEVEL RADAR STATION
HIGH-LEVEL RADAR STATION
COMMAND BOUNDARY
TOWNS BOMBED
LUFTWAFFE BASES
BOMBER
STUKA (DIVE-BOMBER)
FIGHTER (Bf109)
TWIN-ENGINED FIGHTER (Bf110)
COMMAND BOUNDARY
MILES
KILOMETRES
*11 Group only
FIRTH OF FORTH
GLASGOW
BELFAST
NEWCASTLE
SUNDERLAND
MIDDLESBROUGH
Fighter Command 13 Group (Saul)
Luftflotte 5 (Stumpff) (from Norway and Denmark)
NORTH SEA
HULL
Cover of low-level radar (500 ft)
Cover of high-level radar (15,000 ft)
LIVERPOOL
MANCHESTER
SHEFFIELD
NOTTINGHAM
Fighter Command 12 Group (Leigh-Mallory)
NORWICH
BIRMINGHAM
COVENTRY
Duxford
Martlesham
IPSWICH
Debden
North Weald
Stanmore
Northolt
LONDON
Uxbridge
Rochford
Hornchurch
THAMES ESTUARY
Eastchurch
Manston
Croydon
Biggin Hill
Kenley
Redhill
West Malling
Detling
CANTERBURY
Lympne
Hawkinge
SWANSEA
CARDIFF
BRISTOL
BATH
Ball
Andover
Middle Wallop
SOUTHAMPTON
Tangmere
PORTSMOUTH
VENTNOR
Fighter Command 10 Group (Brand)
Fighter Command 11 Group (Park)
EXETER
PLYMOUTH
ENGLISH CHANNEL
ROTTERDAM
ANTWERP
GHENT
BELGIUM
CALAIS
LILLE
Luftflotte 2 (Kesselring)
AMIENS
CHERBOURG
LE HAVRE
FRANCE
PARIS
Luftflotte 3 (Sperrle)
RENNES

Top: **Londoners tried to carry on as best as possible despite the Blitz.**

Above: **Pilots of a Spitfire Squadron taking a well-earned break before taking off again.**

Professor Six as Representative of the Security Police (Gestapo) in Great Britain. Intense German attacks on merchant convoys in the Channel took place between 8–12 August. Thereafter the enemy turned his attention to fighter airfields in the South and South-East. But though they did much damage, things were not going quite to plan. In the first ten days of their August campaign the *Luftwaffe* lost several times the RAF loss of 153 planes. The British losses were single-seater fighters. The enemy lost many bombers, with crews of five, and many two-seater fighters. In the severe fighting of 15 August the Germans lost 76 aircraft. The Spitfire was consistently better than the Messerschmitt 109, while the two-seater Messerschmitt 110 was faster than the Spitfire but less manoeuvrable. The slower Hurricane was proving its worth against the German bombers. It would be absurd to underrate the skill and valour of the *Luftwaffe* pilots, who included such aces as Galland and Moelders. The fact remains that the British fighter pilots, knowing how much depended on their courage and tenacity, showed even more initiative and *élan* than their opponents. Not once but many times a pilot was shot down, escaped by parachute, and went into action again the same day. There was an advantage in 'playing at home', for many RAF pilots who came down – even those who fell into the sea – were rescued. The organizational control of Fighter Command under Air Vice-Marshal Sir Hugh Dowding and No. 11 Fighter Group under Air Vice-Marshal Park left little to be desired. The development of radar had given them an advantage in that they were able to discern which German attacks were feints and which were genuine, and to deploy their resources accordingly.

The Germans now increased the proportion of fighters to bombers, and, after a brief lull, made eleven major attacks between 1 and 5 September. This time the targets were inland fighter airfields and aircraft factories. Casualties

Above: **Hermann Göring, Commander-in-Chief of the Luftwaffe.**

Left: **An Anti-Aircraft unit at Barry, near Cardiff works round the clock.**

were beginning to make the Germans lose sight of their true objective, the destruction of the RAF. Once they began to shift their targets they were beaten, though it may not have seemed so at the time. On 7 September came the first mass attack on London. 'This', quoth Göring, 'is the historic hour when our air force for the first time delivered its stroke right into the enemy's heart.' The attack came between 5 and 6 p.m. About 320 bombers, escorted by more than 600 fighters, came in up the Thames and bombed Woolwich Arsenal, Beckton Gas Works, Dockland, West Ham power station, the City, West-

Below: **A Bristol Beaufighter Mk 1 takes off.**

minster and Kensington. Tremendous fires were started, and the population of Silvertown had to be evacuated by water. At 8.10 p.m. another 250 bombers came in. The attack continued until 4.30 a.m. The civilian casualties were 430 killed and about 1,600 seriously injured. The London Fire Brigade fought all day to master the fires. At 7.30 p.m. on the 8th 200 more bombers appeared and, guided by the flames, carried on the Blitz. That night 412 people were killed and 747 badly hurt.

For 23 days the *Luftwaffe* kept up the pressure. American observers were impressed by the way the Londoners took it. 'It is pretty incredible . . .' reported Helen Kirkpatrick of the Chicago *Daily News* (9 September) '. . . to find people relatively unshaken after the terrific experience. There is some terror, but nothing on the scale that the Germans may have hoped for and certainly not on a scale to make Britons contemplate for a moment anything but fighting on. Fright becomes so mingled with a deep almost uncontrollable anger that it is hard to know when one stops and the other begins.' Serious though the casualties were, they proved by no means as severe as the disciples

Right: **Luftwaffe crews await their next orders.**

Below: **By diverting its attack to London the Luftwaffe lost the Battle of Britain giving Fighter Command a chance to regroup.**

Right: **Albrecht Kesselring and Göring. Kesselring was in command of Luftflotte II which was stationed in northeast France and the Low Countries.**

of Douhet must have expected. The biggest daylight attacks took place on 15 September, and fierce fighting between London and the Straits of Dover cost the Germans 56 planes. This was the climax of the struggle. The mounting toll of casualties was beginning to take the sting out of the *Luftwaffe*. The bombers stopped coming over in the daytime about 5 October. Raids, by heavily escorted fighter-bombers (Me 110s), flying at about 30,000 feet and carrying two bombs apiece, were not very formidable. By the end of the month the Battle of Britain was at an end.

On 12 October Hitler had cancelled Operation *Sealion*, because the *Luftwaffe* had failed to establish conditions in which the Germans dared hazard a Channel crossing. The attempt had cost the *Luftwaffe* 1,733 aircraft. It was a great British victory; one of the decisive battles of the war. It was not easily won. The loss of planes and pilots left Fighter Command exhausted, a fact which it contrived to conceal from friend and foe alike. Anti-aircraft artillery, searchlights, balloon barrages, observer corps and machine guns all played their part in the defence.

The sound of Ack-Ack fire was music in the ears of Londoners. The idea that he is hitting back – however illusory – has a tremendous effect on the Briton in battle! On 10 September General Pile, O.C. Anti-Aircraft Command, ordered that every gun was to fire every possible round. 'Fire was not to be withheld on any account. Guns were to go to the approximate bearing and elevation and fire. Searchlights were not to expose. RAF fighters were not going to operate over London, and every unseen target must be engaged without waiting to identify the aircraft as hostile.'

Right: **A later picture of Kesselring who was Commander-in-Chief of German forces in Italy and conducted a brilliant defensive campaign in 1944.**

Below: **Hugo Sperrle, Commander of Luftflotte III.**

17·RB

The centre of Coventry was destroyed following one of the most intensive raids on an English city outside London.

'The result was as astonishing to me as it appears to have been to the citizens of London – and, apparently, to the enemy as well. For, although few of the bursts can have been anywhere near the target, the heights of aircraft steadily increased as the night went on, and many of them turned away before entering the inner artillery zone . . . It was in no sense a barrage, though I think by that name it will always be known.' The brave and steady work of the ARP, firemen and the Observer Corps deserves a better tribute than this brief account can give. Still it was to all intents and purposes a straight fight between the Royal Air Force and the *Luftwaffe*, a battle of a sort that the world had never before seen. It was a struggle in which the rival navies and armies played but little part.

Though the battle was really over, the night bombing continued. London, Southampton, Plymouth, Bristol, Liverpool, Coventry, Birmingham, and Exeter were among the cities that suffered. Many civilians were killed, yet the attack on the cities merely emphasized that the Germans had failed to achieve their real aim – the destruction of the RAF. The RAF struck back against the Ruhr, against synthetic oil plants in Western Germany and against Berlin. Göring's boast that no British plane would ever appear over the Reich was proved false. Nor did the Italians escape scot free. In the autumn the RAF flew over the Alps to bomb Milan and Turin. Fantastic claims were made as to the results of this bombing and counter-bombing, 'the clumsiest, most brutal, and most wasteful of all forms of warfare'.

It cannot be said that the bombing carried out in this phase brought the end of the war one day nearer. The relatively small amount of damage done to war industry was rapidly repaired by both sides. Civilian morale was nowhere sufficiently affected to cause concern to the Government. The Churchill Government, by the Emergency Powers Act, had given itself a control over the lives and property of the British people, which was none the less formidable for being more subtle than the iron grip of a Nazi or Fascist dictator.

The year 1940, which had seen Hitler's greatest triumph, drew to a close. People everywhere perceived, however dimly, that his forces had received a defeat even more marked than the check to Napoleon's ambitions at Trafalgar. It was no longer heresy to question the myth of German invincibility. It is true that Senator Burton K. Wheeler opined at Christmas that the USA was 'doing Great Britain a great disservice in urging her to go and fight until she is exhausted. . . .' There was no sane officer, he said, who thought that England could land troops on German soil. 'And even if our own warmongers get us into the war . . . I doubt that the joint efforts of Great Britain and the United States could succeed in that project.'

But the President spoke to the American People on 29 December in a totally different sense.

'. . . The British people and their allies today are conducting an active war against this unholy alliance. Our own future security is greatly dependent on the outcome of that fight.

. . . We must be the great arsenal of democracy . . . We must apply ourselves to our task with the same resolution, the same sense of urgency, the same spirit of patriotism and sacrifice as we would show were we at war.'

Above: **A Messerschmitt fighter tails a Spitfire. The Spitfire was the most famous British fighter in World War II and made a decisive contribution to winning the Battle of Britain.**

Right: **Even after the Blitz was over raids continued on London. In this picture roof spotters watch fires from Northcliffe House.**

President Roosevelt was way ahead of public opinion in America. In Britain Mr Churchill put into words what every inarticulate Briton was thinking. And for Fighter Command he had one of the happiest tributes that ever came from that silver tongue: 'Never in the field of human conflict was so much owed by so many to so few.'

Below: **A Messerschmitt Bf 109. This fighter was as fast as a Spitfire but did not have the same manoeuvrability or range. It was also uncomfortable for the pilot.**

9 CAMPAIGN IN THE BALKANS

'Are we again going to have "Salonika supporters" as in the last war? Why will politicians never learn the simple principle of concentration of force at the vital point and the avoidance of dispersal of effort.'

General Sir Alan Brooke

Between 28 October 1940 and 1 June 1941 the Axis Powers took the Balkans in an iron grip. Rumania and Bulgaria were peacefully occupied, Yugoslavia and Greece resisted and were supported by Great Britain. Between them they put into the field some 50 divisions, about 28 Yugoslav, 20 Greek and 3 British. On paper this looks a formidable force, but it was not properly co-ordinated, and was particularly weak in aircraft and tanks, the weapons of the *Blitzkrieg*. For the most part these considerable forces were armed with obsolete weapons, and depended for transport on horses and even oxen. Still they fought with tenacity and not entirely without success. Only at sea did the Allies have the advantage and here too losses were severe whenever ships were exposed within range of shore-based aircraft.

In November 1940 Mussolini needed a victory and a cheap one. Greece seemed the most suitable victim. Not unreasonably he considered that a nation of 45,000,000 ought to be able to crush one of 6,936,000. In August 1940 Mussolini had demanded that Greece renounce the guarantee of her independence made in 1939 by Great Britain. When King George II and his premier, General Metaxas, refused, Mussolini denounced Greece for her 'un-neutral' attitude. The Italian army in Albania, 150,000 strong, began to concentrate on the frontier. The Greeks could oppose them with some 75,000. On 28 October an ultimatum was presented in Athens. It listed the 'wrongs' Italy had suffered at Greek hands, and demanded the occupation of strategic positions in Greece for the duration. In true Nazi-Fascist style the Italians then proceeded to invade Greece without awaiting a reply.

Great Britain immediately promised her support to the Greeks and established RAF squadrons in Crete, but with 200,000 Italians pouring down the valleys of Northern Greece the prospects of resistance seemed bleak. Moreover, the Metaxas Line faced not Albania but Bulgaria. It was not particularly prudent of Mussolini to choose the rainy month of November for this march through the mountains. But the Italian fiasco that followed was due not so much to weather and terrain as to the classic military fault of underrating the enemy. The Greeks were sustained by patriotism and indignation.

The Italian plan was to push up the valley of the Vijosë and, by taking Metsova, cut off the Greeks in Thessaly and Macedonia from those in the Epirus. At first they made rapid progress up the Vijosë, though another column advanc-

ing towards the Kalamas river soon got stuck. The RAF had flown in a consignment of obsolescent Boys anti-tank rifles which knocked out nine Italian tanks. On the Albanian front the Greeks, who had mobilized with creditable speed, astonished the Italians by taking the offensive and thrusting towards the supply base of Korcë. At the same time they reinforced the Pindus front and fell upon the flanks of the column on the Vijosë. Between 8 and 10 November the 3rd Alpini Division, composed of some of the best Italian troops, was caught in the Pindus gorges and lost 5,000 men. The Greeks took Korcë on 22 November with a great quantity of equipment which they sorely needed. By the end of December a quarter of Albania was in Greek hands. The RAF bombed Valona, the principal port, as well as raiding Brindisi.

Taranto, Korcë and Benghazi all came as a

Right: **A Greek general discusses surrender terms with German officers in Athens in April 1941.**

Below right: **Benito Mussolini, Il Duce of Italy. Hitler would never have intervened in the Balkans had he not been forced to by Mussolini.**

Below: **German tanks reinforce units in front of the Dikitiri Palace in Thessaloniki.**

rude shock to the Italian people, so long accustomed to Fascist vauntings. But 'the croaking bullfrog of the Pontine Marshes' was not done yet. 'We'll break the backs of the Greeks', Mussolini declared 'and we don't need any help!' But Hitler thought things had gone quite far enough, and on 13 December issued Directive No. 20 for 'Undertaking Marita. . . . In the light of the threatening situation in Albania it is doubly important to frustrate English efforts to establish, behind the protection of a Balkan front, an air base which would threaten Italy in the first place and, incidentally, the Rumanian oilfields.' He intended to build up a force of some 24 divisions in Southern Rumania and then, when the weather was favourable, probably in March, to move across Bulgaria and occupy the northern coast of the Aegean, and if necessary the whole mainland of Greece. 'English bases in the Greek Islands' were to be seized by airborne troops. On the completion of the operation the troops were to be withdrawn for 'new employment', because the denial to the British of any foothold on the continent of Europe was merely to clear the way for Hitler's ultimate aim 'the winning of living-space in the East' (Directive No. 21 for 'Case Barbarossa').

On 11 January 1941 Hitler issued his orders for supporting the Italians. 'The situation in the Mediterranean area, where England is em-

Left: **German mountain infantry march through Lambia in April 1941**

Below: **Athens under the German occupation. Resistance against the Germans continued throughout the war directed by the Communist ELAS and the royalist Free Democratic Greek Army.**

ploying superior forces against our allies, requires that Germany should assist for reasons of strategy, politics, and psychology.' The X Air Corps was already operating from Sicily against British naval forces in the Mediterranean. Now a corps was to be moved into Albania. Meanwhile the Twelfth German Army under Field-Marshal List was assembling in Bulgaria for the attack on Greece. Operations *Sonnenblume* (Sunflower) and *Alpenveilchen* (Alpine violet) were to save Tripoli and Albania respectively. But Mussolini wanted the credit of the victory in Albania for himself, and at a conference on 19 and 20 January persuaded Hitler to modify his instructions. German troops, the germ of the *Afrika Korps*, were to cross to Tripoli in mid-February, but the Albania offensive was to be left to the Italians.

Early in March Germany began to tighten her net round Greece. First she compelled Bulgaria to agree to the Tripartite Pact and to the passage of her troops. Similar pressure made Yugoslavia join the Pact on 24 March. But 'the Jugs', despite their unfavourable strategic position, with hostile forces all along their frontier except in the south where it joined Greece, did not receive this pact in any docile spirit. A military *coup d'état* led by General Simović overthrew the government of the Regent, the young King's uncle, Prince Paul (26 March). This move, which had general support in the country and was welcomed with enthusiasm in Britain, compelled the Germans to change their plans. Instead of invading Greece via Bulgaria they now determined to strike down both Yugoslavia and Greece at a blow. There was a certain amount of delay while this campaign was mounted.

Meanwhile a British force was landing in Greece. These troops were badly needed in North Africa, and it was undoubtedly a grave strategic error to send them to Greece; a violation of the principle of concentration. It may be argued that the support of Greece, an ally, was a matter of honour, but this argument would have more force had the Greeks themselves not been extremely reluctant to receive this reinforcement. De Guingand has described the way in which Mr Anthony Eden persuaded them to agree, and the shameless exaggeration of our available strength upon which he insisted.

The capture of Tripoli and the successful termination of the campaign in North Africa seems now a prize far more worth while than anything that could have been hoped for in Greece. But in fact Wavell was very far from thinking in terms of taking Tripoli, and although it is often assumed that the expedition to Greece was prompted by Mr Churchill, it is evident that the Prime Minister left the ultimate decision to his General, and that the latter expected great things from his campaign in the Balkans.

On 6 April the Germans invaded Yugoslavia with 33 divisions, six of which were armoured. The Yugoslavs could oppose them with 28 divisions, three being cavalry. They were all strung out along the frontiers, only one being in strategic reserve. Though good fighting men, the Yugoslavs were no match for the Germans in training or armament. In the air the *Luftwaffe* had everything its own way. While Belgrade and other towns were ruthlessly bombed, six strong German columns were carving through the Yugoslav defences and breaking the army

Right: **Pzkw Mark IIs cross the mountainous terrain of Greece. The British Army intervened in Greece because Britain could not allow Greece to fall unaided. However the loss of Greece was another blow to British prestige.**

into fragments. The campaign lasted a mere 10 days. On 17 April Yugoslavia surrendered.

The main body of the Greek army, 14 divisions, was facing the Italians in Albania. The British army and three Greek divisions were deployed on a line between the Aegean Sea and the Yugoslav frontier, with part of the 1st Armoured Brigade, watching the Monastir Gap. Three and a half Greek divisions manned the Metaxas Line covering Macedonia and watching the Rupel pass. It was a long and mountainous front thinly held by a largely immobile army.

Field Marshal List determined to cut the Allies in two by piercing their centre and isolating the army in Albania. At the same time he intended to force his way through the Rupel Pass and by breaking the Metaxas Line to cut off the Greeks in Eastern Macedonia. Another column, moving down Strumica and Vardar, would attack Thessaloniki from the north. For political reasons General Papagos had decided to hold the Metaxas Line, but from a military

Left: **The Duke of Aosta, Commander of the Italian Armies in Eritrea and Ethiopia, following his surrender at Amba Alagi on 16 May 1941. This was yet another humiliation suffered by Mussolini.**

Right: **Hitler's army progresses through the Balkans.**

Below: **A second wave of parachutists land on Crete.**

point of view this had nothing to recommend it.

The Germans crossed the Greek frontier at the same time as they invaded Yugoslavia. The dispositions of the Greeks holding the Metaxas Line and the British forces were unhinged from the outset by the rapid collapse of the Yugoslavs. The Greeks had prudently withdrawn from Thrace, but the enemy swiftly broke through the Rupel Pass and the Monastir Gap, which was not sufficiently strongly defended, and took Thessaloniki from the west as planned (8 April). The Greeks east of the Vardar were now compelled to surrender.

The onslaught was accompanied by heavy air bombing. In the harbour of Piraeus a ship full of T.N.T. blew up, and another with a cargo of Hurricanes was sunk. The airfields at Larissa were overwhelmed.

General Sir Henry Maitland Wilson's army, 56,657 strong, consisted of the 1st Armoured Brigade, the 2nd New Zealand Division, and the 6th Australian Division. He now withdrew with great skill from the Vardar front and under appallingly difficult circumstances got back to a position round Mount Olympus and along the river Aliakmon.

By 13 April General Wilson had completed his difficult withdrawal, but by that time the Greeks, worn down by continual bombardment, were collapsing, and the single British armoured brigade had practically shot its bolt. The Olympus line was too long for the troops Wilson had available, and he was compelled to withdraw to the Thermopylai line, though this uncovered the passes over the Pindus mountains and exposed the flank of the main Greek army retreating into the Epirus.

By 20 April the British were ensconced in Thermopylai, with the 6th Australian Division emulating Leonidas and his Spartans in the famous pass 'where the main bitumen road zigzagged up nearly three thousand feet of mountain wall.' Unfortunately by this time the RAF had been driven from its airfields in Greece, and the Germans were thrusting for Corinth. The Greek army, which had put up a truly heroic struggle, was forced to surrender on 21 April.

It seemed highly improbable that any substantial part of the British expeditionary force could escape. The situation was even worse than Dunkirk, for there was no fighter cover. On 26 April by a bold stroke the Germans seized the bridge over the Corinth Canal with airborne troops, and cut off the Peloponnese from the rest of Greece.

Temperamentally General Wilson was just the man for a crisis of this sort. With magnificent skill and *sang froid* he succeeded, despite the total lack of air cover, in evacuating the great majority of his troops. The work of the Royal Navy was beyond praise.

The Greeks too bore themselves nobly in this tragic hour. Major Seton-Watson wrote: '. . . when we drove through Athens the Greeks lined the streets in thousands, many of them in tears, yet cheering and throwing flowers and shouting, "You will be back; we'll be waiting for you." Few retreating armies can have had such a send-off.'

The Germans entered Athens on 27 April. The Swastika flew from the Acropolis. Between 24 April and 2 May 43,000 British troops were evacuated, mostly to Crete, but all the *matériel* of the expeditionary force and 11,000 men were left behind. Most of the Greek destroyers and all their submarines escaped. The King of Greece removed his seat of government to Crete. The King of Yugoslavia and his chief Ministers also succeeded in evading the Germans.

CRETE

Crete is an island about 160 miles long and varies in width from about 7½ to 35 miles. Its garrison of three infantry battalions was reinforced by 27,000 of the troops from Greece, including the 2nd New Zealand Division and part of the 6th Australian Division. A detachment of Royal Marines was landed to hold Suda Bay. There were in addition two weak and ill-equipped Greek divisions. This force had no more than 35 planes and nine tanks to support it.

On 4 May Major-General Freyberg, V.C., the famous commander of the New Zealand Division, took command in Crete. With so resolute a leader there were high hopes that the island could be held. Already on the 28th Mr Churchill had signalled to Wavell, 'It seems clear from our information that a heavy airborne attack by German troops and bombers will soon be made on Crete. Let me know what forces you have in the island and what your plans are. It ought to be a fine opportunity for

Above: **Allied transports in Suda Bay under attack from German aircraft based on Crete.**

Above left: **The inhabitants of Heraklion try to resume their lives. Because of the atrocities committed on Crete the Germans are resented and mistrusted to this day.**

Left: **German prisoners under the care of British soldiers in June 1941. Some 17,000 German soldiers were killed or wounded on Crete.**

killing the parachute troops.' This was not an unreasonable view. But unfortunately the garrison was, in its commander's words (1 May), 'totally inadequate to meet attack envisaged'. It was the old tale of the balanced force – or rather the unbalanced force. 'Unless fighter aircraft are greatly increased', went on Freyberg, 'and naval forces made available to deal with sea-borne attack, I cannot hope to hold out with land forces alone, which as a result of the campaign in Greece, are now devoid of any artillery, have insufficient tools for digging, very little transport, and inadequate war reserves of equipment and ammunition.' He urged that if the necessary support from the other services was not available the question of holding Crete should be reconsidered. There were good reasons for holding on to Crete, quite apart from the importance of blunting the edge of the German airborne corps. The triangle of naval bases, Suda Bay, Alexandria, Benghazi, might give Admiral Cunningham a grip on the Eastern Mediterranean such as he had not previously enjoyed.

Meanwhile in a room in the Hotel Grande Bretagne in Athens General Student was briefing his commanders. 'It was his own, personal plan. He had devised it, had struggled against heavy opposition for its acceptance, and had worked out all the details . . . the plan had become a part of him, a part of his life. He believed in it and lived for it and in it.' Freyberg worked hard at his defences and by 16 May could report to Wavell that morale was high. He had 45 field guns well sited, with adequate ammunition dumped, and two infantry tanks on each aerodrome. 'I do not wish to be over-confident, but I feel that at least we will give excellent account of ourselves. With help of Royal Navy I trust Crete will be held.' The Germans bombed the three airfields very severely and on 19 May the few RAF fighters that remained were withdrawn. On the 20th Student struck.

The first task of the *Luftwaffe* was to silence the anti-aircraft artillery, and in this the Germans were very successful. Next came the parachutists, supported by waves of troop-carrying gliders, landing between Canea and Maleme. Many of these first 3,500 were slain, but 3,000 more men were landed at Retimo and Heraklion, and gradually the Germans succeeded in establishing a foothold. Their capture of Maleme airfield on 21 May was the turning-point of the struggle. Aircraft began to pour in at the rate of 20 an hour. But a German attempt to follow up with a flotilla of Greek caiques met with calamity. A squadron consisting of three British cruisers and four destroyers got among them and sank almost every one either by gunfire or by ramming, including the Italian destroyer which was escorting them. A second convoy was attacked on the same day (22 May) but this time German aircraft from the Dodecanese sank the British cruisers *Gloucester* and *Fiji*, and three destroyers. Even so the Germans made no further attempt at seaborne invasion.

Although the garrison was reinforced from Egypt (350 miles away) it was clear by the 28th that the battle was lost, and once again the Royal Navy was faced with the task of evacuating a British army. They succeeded in bringing away 14,967, though some 13,000 British and 5,000 Greek troops were left behind. Crete cost the Germans 12–17,000 men and 170 troop-carrying aircraft. Never again were they to risk the Seventh Air Division troops in so hazardous an operation. General Student visited Baron von der Heydte's battalion immediately after the fall of Canea. 'He had visibly altered. He seemed much graver, more reserved, and older. The cost of victory had evidently proved too much for him. Some of the battalions had lost all their officers, and in several companies there were only a few men left alive.' If Freyberg's men were beaten they had at least blunted one of Hitler's most effective weapons, and the Royal Navy had demonstrated once more that, however desperate the situation, it was never prepared to abandon a British expeditionary force. Three cruisers, six destroyers and 29 smaller craft were lost. A battleship, four cruisers and seven destroyers were damaged. Naval casualties amounted to 2,000 men.

And so in the span of a few short weeks the Germans had crushed both Yugoslavia and Greece. Once again it was a question of air power, mobility and superior weapons rather than greater numbers. The Allies had fought with courage and determination, but the *Blitzkrieg* technique, so effective in 1939 and 1940, had not yet lost its magic. Allied armies, which would have been at home on the battlefields of 1914–18, were simply outclassed by the modern German *Wehrmacht*.

Above: **General Kurt Student inspects paratroops. Student planned and directed the parachute operations on Crete. However the high casualty rates made Hitler forbid further large-scale parachute operations.**

Above right: **Another wave of parachutists land on Crete.**

Right: **General Sir Archibald Wavell.**

Centre: **A later portrait of Student.**

Far right: **German tanks roll into Athens.**

D

10 ENTER ROMMEL

'Detachments of a German expeditionary force under an obscure general, Rommel, have landed in North Africa.'

From a British Intelligence Summary of March 1941

At the same time that General Wavell was sending 56,000 men and 8,000 vehicles to Greece, Hitler was reinforcing his ally in Tripolitania with a Light Armoured Division under General Erwin Rommel. The brilliant strategical situation brought into being by General O'Connor's campaign was being sacrificed on the altar of Allied Solidarity. With the benefit of hindsight the Greek campaign appears a very forlorn hope indeed. To many, particularly at the lower staff levels, it seemed so at the time. The advantages of finishing off a beaten enemy in one theatre before switching to another should have carried more weight with General Wavell.

At the end of March the British had a thin covering force under General Philip Neame, V.C., in a position near El Agheila, 150 miles south of Benghazi. It consisted of the 2nd Armoured Division, which had one of its brigades in Greece; the 9th Australian Division, with a brigade in Tobruk; and an Indian Motor Brigade Group at Mechili. The Armoured Division was below establishment in tanks, and many of those it had were in bad condition. Some of the units were not fully trained in the special techniques of desert warfare.

On 31 March Rommel struck. Besides his German division, he had two Italian divisions, one armoured and one motorized. He gave orders to his air force to destroy British petrol-carrying transport. Neame fell back according to plan and on 2 April was near Agedabia. On the 3rd it was reported that a strong German armoured column was approaching Msus, the main British petrol dump. The detachment guarding the place lost no time in setting fire to the petrol, so depriving Neame's armour of its mobility. Benghazi was abandoned and Neame fell back to Tobruk, which was occupied by the Australians. The Armoured Division, harassed by air attacks on its wireless and petrol-carrying vehicles, did not reach Mechili until the 6th. The 3rd Armoured Brigade got into Derna, only to be captured there. The remainder of the 2nd Armoured Division was attacked at Mechili on the 7th, and was ordered to fall back to El Adem, south of Tobruk. At dawn next morning the 1st Royal Horse Artillery and some Italian troops broke out, but the rest of the division was taken. To complicate matters still more on the night 6–7 April, Generals Neame and O'Connor were captured near Derna by an enterprising German patrol. General Gambier-Parry had already been taken.

The question now was whether to hold the port of Tobruk with the thousands of tons of supplies which had been accumulated there. Wavell decided to do so, and sent in the 7th Australian Division and a few tanks by sea. They arrived on 7 April and four days later the place was besieged. The G.O.C., General Morshead, made his intentions perfectly clear: 'There'll be no Dunkirk here. If we should have to get out, we shall fight our way out. There is to be no surrender and no retreat.' Winston Churchill too was strongly in favour of holding Tobruk: '. . . a sally port; that is what we want. . . . The further he advances the more you threaten, the more he has to fear. That is the

Above: Unloading supplies for the German Afrika Korps in Tripoli.

Above left: General Wavell, Commander-in-Chief of forces in the Middle East and North Africa, discusses the situation with General Richard O'Connor, Commander of the Western Desert Force.

Below: Pzkw Mark IVs were the means which allowed the Axis troops to regain the initiative in North Africa.

answer, a sally port.' During the siege the garrison was to average some 23,000 men, about 15,000 being Australian, few enough for a perimeter of 25 miles. From April to November their spirited defence tied up one German and four Italian divisions.

By destroying the 2nd Armoured Division, Rommel had deprived the British of their offensive power. By defending Tobruk Wavell deprived Rommel of a forward base for his further advance into Egypt. The Germans reached the Sollum escarpment, but their attack had now lost its momentum. Thus in 12 days Rommel had robbed Wavell of much of the territory won in O'Connor's campaign and had inflicted severe losses on the British.

The disaster which overtook Neame's army can be directly attributed to the absence in Greece of the RAF squadrons required to give it something like air parity, and of the vehicles necessary to ensure the mobility of its supplies – especially of petrol. Without sufficient transport the British resorted to dumping, a World War I technique. That this was inappropriate to conditions in the Western Desert is forcibly demonstrated by the calamity at Msus. To a lesser extent the absence of 1st Armoured Brigade accounts for the defeat. Had Maitland Wilson's army been in Cyrenaica instead of Greece, Rommel would hardly have progressed beyond El Agheila.

Greece, Cyrenaica, East Africa: Wavell had plenty on his plate when on 3 April there came a revolt in Iraq. The new Prime Minister, Rashid Ali el-Gailani, immediately affirmed that he intended to fulfil Iraq's treaty obligations, which permitted the presence of British troops in his country in time of war or the threat of war. This good resolution was short-lived, for on 2 May the Iraqis laid siege to the British cantonment and RAF base at Habbaniya. The situation was alarming, because in addition to the threat to the oilfields and pipelines upon which Britain so much depended, there was the risk that the Germans would establish themselves in the Middle East. Wavell's problem was to find the troops for a relief force. But Britain still had

Top: **General Erwin Rommel.**

Above: **The harbour at Tobruk under attack.**

one staunch ally in those parts, Transjordan, which even in the blackest days of 1940 had remained pro-British. The Arab Legion under Glubb Pasha, was a small but mobile force, wise in the ways of the desert. It provided 250 of the men under Major-General J. G. W. Clark, who relieved Habbaniya and took Baghdad (31 May). Meanwhile, with the connivance of General Dentz, the French High Commissioner, the Germans and Italians had established air bases at Damascus, Rayak and Palmyra in Syria. They had bombed Habbaniya. On 8 June, with the agreement of General de Gaulle, a force under General Wilson invaded Syria and Lebanon. It had been hoped that resistance would be no more than formal, but the French fought stubbornly. As the campaign developed, the force from Iraq came in from the east and took Palmyra, where the Arab Legion once more distinguished itself (3 July). An armistice, giving the Allies the right to occupy Syria and Lebanon, was signed at Acre on 14 July.

This difficult campaign was followed in August by the Anglo-Russian occupation of

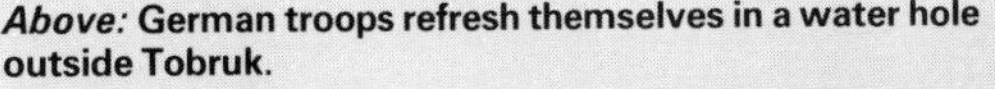

Above: **German troops refresh themselves in a water hole outside Tobruk.**

Right above: **A German tank advances through the streets of a Libyan town.**

Below: **The siege of Tobruk started on 11 April 1941 and was to continue for nearly eight months.**

Above: The first units of the Afrika Korps land in North Africa in February 1941. Generals Rommel and Gariboldi inspect the troops.

Left: The German and the British had to have supply depots situated at strategic points in the Western Desert. Advancing troops often overran the enemy's supplies.

Right: Supplies for the Afrika Korps are unloaded in April 1941.

Below: The Messerschmitt Bf 109.

Persia, which put an end to the danger of German penetration, and was executed practically without bloodshed. In order to supply Russia with vital war material the occupation of Persia was absolutely necessary. Despite his losses in Greece, Crete and Cyrenaica, Wavell had successfully cleared up the situation in Iraq, Syria and Persia. Only in the Western Desert did his generalship still meet with ill-success. An abortive attack on Sollum (15 May) was followed by a more serious offensive intended to relieve Tobruk (15 June). Some progress was made at first but Rommel counter-attacked and drove back the 7th Armoured Division at Sidi Omar. Wavell withdrew on the night of 17 June. This was the ill-fated Operation *Battleaxe*. The Panzer IV with the new 50 mm gun was too much for the British armour. Skilful use of the 88-mm anti-aircraft gun in the anti-tank role contributed to Rommel's success.

Mr Churchill was not pleased at this setback, though he himself had prodded Wavell into attacking before his army had recovered from its recent losses, and was therefore partly to blame. The Prime Minister now decided that it was time for a change in the Middle East. He was probably right. As a successor to Wavell he chose an excellent general – but the wrong one. General Sir Claude Auchinleck, Commander-in-Chief in India, was taken from a command for which his career had best prepared him, and brought to the Middle East. Wavell, whose whole career had been in the British Army, was sent to Delhi. By mid-1941 it needed no seer to prophesy that the Far East would soon be a theatre of war. The removal of Auchinleck was, therefore, particularly unfortunate. If Wavell had to go, Auchinleck was not the only possible successor. Sir Harold Alexander, one of Churchill's favourite generals, would have been a very suitable choice. (And, if you like historical 'ifs', Alexander *might* have asked for Lieutenant-General Montgomery to command his main striking force.)

The newly-formed Eighth Army was now given to Lieutenant-General Sir Alan Cunningham, who had made his name in Abyssinia. At this point Rommel's army was larger than Cunningham's, but about two-thirds of it was Italian, and, therefore, on the whole, the two armies were not altogether ill-matched when on 18 November the British boldly and confidently embarked upon yet another offensive. But though Rommel was short of Germans, in the weapons of the *Blitzkrieg* – tanks and aircraft – he had the advantage in quality.

Above: **The Commander of the 15th Panzer Division, General Neumann-Silkow (right) was killed in battle on 18 November 1941.**

	Rommel	*Cunningham*
Tanks	412	455
Anti-tank Guns	194	72

General Fuller has stressed Rommel's 'ballistical' advantage. 'Rommel's tank and anti-tank guns were of 50-mm (4½-pdr) and 75-mm calibre, whereas Cunningham's were 2-pounders, and the effective armour-piercing range of this gun was from eight hundred to one thousand yards less than that of the 50-mm gun. Besides, the armour of the British "I" tank (Matilda) was not proof against the 50-mm shell, let alone the 75 mm.'

Rommel

German
2 Panzer Divisions (15 and 21)
1 Light Division (90)
1 Infantry Division
Italian
1 Armoured Division (Ariete)
6 Infantry Divisions

Lieutenant-General Sir Alan Cunningham

XIII Corps Lieutenant-General
A. R. Godwin-Austin.
4th Indian Division
New Zealand Division
1st Army Tank Brigade
XXX Corps Lieutenant-General
Sir Willoughby Norrie
7th Armoured Division
4th Armoured Brigade
1st South African Division
201st Guards Brigade Group
Tobruk Garrison Lieutenant-General
Sir R. Scobie
70th Division
32nd Army Tank Brigade
A Polish Regiment
Army Reserve
2nd South African Division
29th Indian Infantry Brigade Group
RAF Component Air Vice Marshal
A. Coningham

	Squadrons
Light Bombers	9
Fighters	12
Medium Bombers	6

Above: **Allied prisoners of war await transportation to camps.**

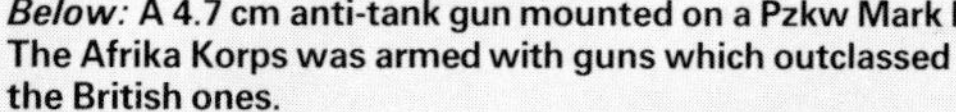

Below: **A 4.7 cm anti-tank gun mounted on a Pzkw Mark I. The Afrika Korps was armed with guns which outclassed the British ones.**

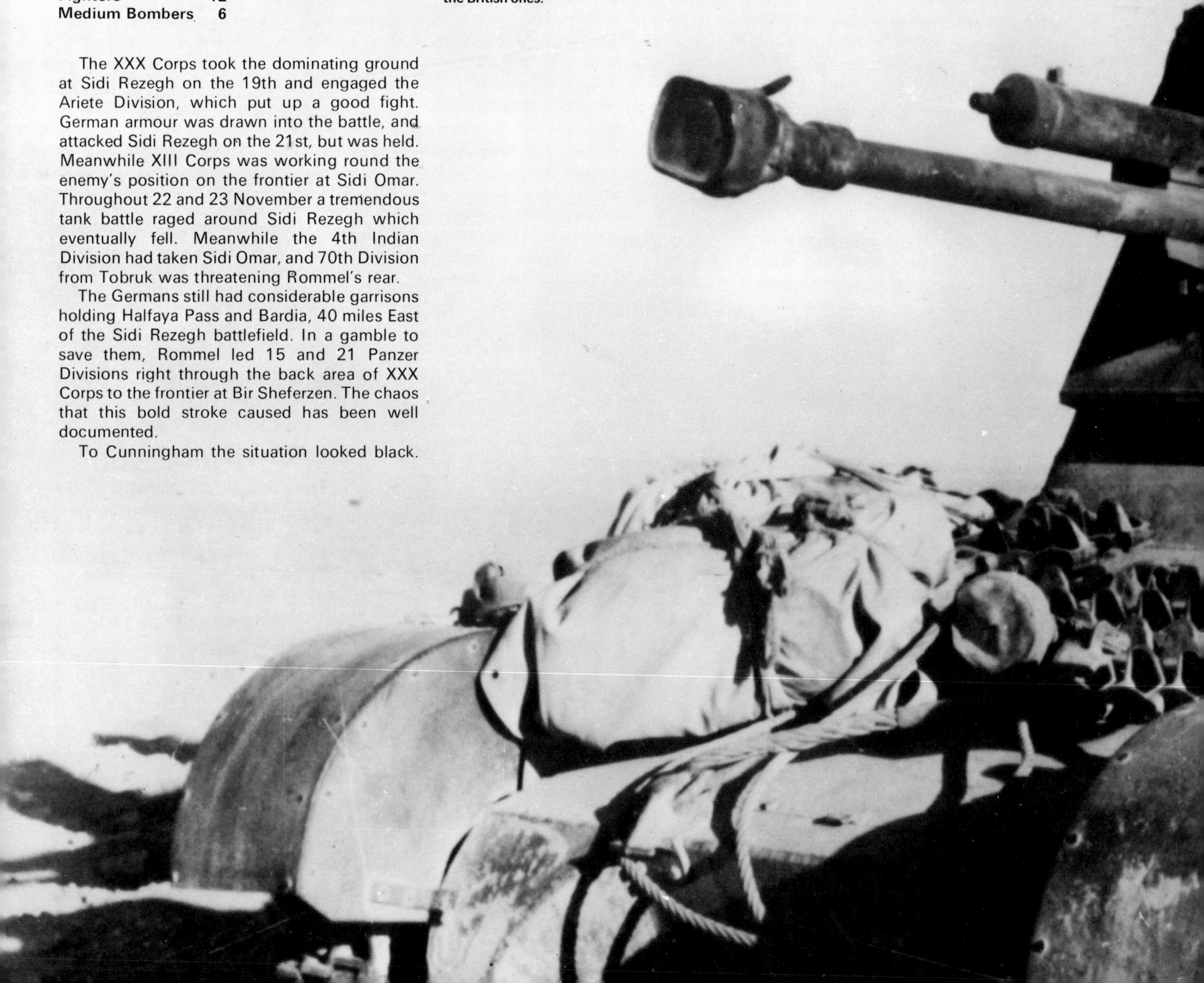

The XXX Corps took the dominating ground at Sidi Rezegh on the 19th and engaged the Ariete Division, which put up a good fight. German armour was drawn into the battle, and attacked Sidi Rezegh on the 21st, but was held. Meanwhile XIII Corps was working round the enemy's position on the frontier at Sidi Omar. Throughout 22 and 23 November a tremendous tank battle raged around Sidi Rezegh which eventually fell. Meanwhile the 4th Indian Division had taken Sidi Omar, and 70th Division from Tobruk was threatening Rommel's rear.

The Germans still had considerable garrisons holding Halfaya Pass and Bardia, 40 miles East of the Sidi Rezegh battlefield. In a gamble to save them, Rommel led 15 and 21 Panzer Divisions right through the back area of XXX Corps to the frontier at Bir Sheferzen. The chaos that this bold stroke caused has been well documented.

To Cunningham the situation looked black.

Above: **Stuka dive bombers prepared to attack English tanks outside Ghobi.**

Above left: **Tanks roll forward in the limitless desert.**

The HQ of XIII Corps was split up and out of touch; the HQ of XXX Corps had taken refuge in Tobruk. The New Zealanders had made a brief contact with the garrison at El Duda, but the Germans had reacted violently and the place was now invested once more. Its 25-pounder ammunition had fallen dangerously low. Most of the British tanks seemed to have been lost, and Cunningham thought the best course was to retreat into Libya and re-group. In war if you can make the enemy think he's beaten, you win. But Rommel had not won, for at this juncture the man to say 'Stand here' flew up to the desert from Cairo. Auchinleck absolutely forbade withdrawal. Cunningham was replaced by Major-General N. M. Ritchie.

Meanwhile, for all the confusion, the two British corps had stood firm and the RAF had battered Rommel's transport, and he, realizing that his opponents were determined to fight it out, withdrew to his supply bases between Bardia and Tobruk. The XXX Corps attacked the two German divisions as they went back, but they broke through to the West nearly cutting off the New Zealand Division as they went. The British had not yet shot their bolt, and they attacked again on 26 November, and again on 2 December. Rommel now withdrew, leaving the battlefield and 400 tanks to the victors. The British had lost 18,000 men, but they had caused 24,500 casualties and taken 36,500 prisoners. They had cleared Cyrenaica, and relieved Tobruk. It was a notable achievement against a well-led and well-equipped enemy.

The Japanese offensive in the Far East now robbed Auchinleck of expected reinforcements and Rommel, in greater strength than ever, advanced once more from El Agheila in January, driving the Eighth Army back to the line Gazala-Bir Hachim. The campaign ended with the fall of Rommel's frontier garrisons at Bardia and Halfaya Pass.

Below: **Major General Schmidt, Commander of the Bardia group, tours the front lines to assess the situation and prepare his orders.**

There followed a lull of some four months. Meanwhile the people and garrison of Malta were winning the island her George Cross. After the fall of France Britain had little enough to spare for the defence of this base. In the autumn of 1940 the garrison consisted of five infantry battalions supported by ten ancient aircraft. The best of these were three sea-Gladiators, known as *Faith, Hope* and *Charity*, which held their own very well against the Italians for some time. With great difficulty Hurricanes were flown in, and serious attacks both by submarines and aircraft were made on Italian convoys to North Africa. In August 1941 Rommel lost 35 per cent of his supplies and reinforcements and 63 per cent in October. The Germans eventually felt compelled to send a strong force of the *Luftwaffe* to Sicily, and in October 25 U-Boats, one of which sank the *Ark Royal* in the following month, were diverted to the Mediterranean from the Atlantic.

The sufferings of the inhabitants from hunger were very serious, for the island had long depended on seaborne supplies. Continual pounding from the air was their lot for 18 months. Many were compelled to live in the huge caves beneath Valletta. The Governor, General Sir William Dobbie, was a deeply religious old soldier cast in the mould that produced Cromwell's Ironsides. He regarded the struggle as a crusade. He was succeeded by Field-Marshal Lord Gort, V.C., another inspiring leader. It is typical that in those days they both lived on the lowest ration scale so as to share the privations of the people in their care. They were ably supported by Air Vice-Marshal Lloyd, who inspired the RAF to prodigies of valour and energy.

Early in 1942 Hitler stepped up the air offensive, and by the beginning of April only six British aircraft remained. Forty-seven Spitfires were flown in, but 30 of these were destroyed on the ground before they could be refuelled. By the beginning of May the end seemed near. Food, fuel and ammunition were all nearly exhausted. But at the end of the month 62 more Spitfires were flown in, and this time the ground staff got them into the air just before the bombers came over. Tremendous efforts were made to support convoys through from Alexandria and Gibraltar. In June two freighters out of six got through from Gibraltar, and in August five out of 11. The last in was the American tanker *Ohio*, full of fuel and practically disabled. By the autumn of 1942 the worst was over, and the island had survived an ordeal unequalled even by the famous siege of 1565 when Jean Parisot de la Vallette and the Knights of Malta had held out for four months against the Turks.

Above: **General Crüwell, later to be named the Commander of the Afrika Korps, congratulates Oberst Michel who had escaped from the British after three days in captivity.**

Right: **British prisoners of war wait before being sent to camps.**

II BARBAROSSA

'When Barbarossa opens, the world will hold its breath.'

Adolf Hitler

'Comrades, Red Army and Red Navy men, officers and political workers, men and women partisans! The whole world is looking upon you as the power capable of destroying the German robber hordes! The enslaved peoples of Europe are looking upon you as their liberators. . . . Be worthy of this great mission! The war you are waging is a war of liberation, a just war. May you be inspired in this war by the heroic figures of our great ancestors, Alexander Nevsky, Dimitri Donskoi, Minin and Pozharsky, Alexander Suvorov, Michael Kutuzov! May you be blessed by great Lenin's victorious banner! Death to the German invaders! Long live our glorious country, its freedom and independence! Under the banner of Lenin – onward to victory!'

Stalin, 7 November 1941

On 22 June 1941, Germany attacked her ally, Russia. The news that Hitler, like Charles XII and Napoleon I before him, had invaded Russia, certainly made the world hold its breath, but it came as a tonic to his other enemies. Now surely he was undone. Churchill lost no time in declaring Britain's full support for Russia. The people of Britain, at least since Churchill had assumed control, had never expected to be beaten. The war might go on for years but eventual victory now seemed certain. Yet Hitler's armies came within an ace of putting Russia out of the war. And unwise though it seemed to his enemies, the invasion of Russia was inherent in all Hitler's long-range plans to give Germany *Lebensraum*. The invasion may have been a blunder, but it was not one made on the spur of the moment. It was part of a deep-laid long-term scheme.

On 14 June Hitler assembled his generals in Berlin, and explained his intentions and the change of his line of operations. According to Guderian he said that he could not defeat England. Therefore in order to bring the war to a close he must win a complete victory on the Continent. Germany's position on the mainland would only be unassailable when Russia had been defeated. The audience dispersed in silence and some at least with heavy hearts. Many no doubt shared the Panzer leader's opinion. 'So long as the war in the West was still undecided, any new undertaking must result in a war on two fronts; and Adolf Hitler's Germany was even less capable of fighting such a war than had been the Germany of 1914.'

The German Army was nevertheless extremely formidable.

	Divisions
West	38
Norway	12
Denmark	1
Balkans	7
Libya	2
Eastern Front	145
	205

The garrison of Norway, then and throughout the war, was unnecessarily large, and, moreover, in 1941 there was no threat of invasion to warrant the retention of 38 divisions in the West. It would have been possible for Hitler to have employed at least 155 German divisions on the Russian front at the outset. He evidently underrated his enemy, and both OKW and OKH were confident of victory.

The Chief of the Army General Staff, Halder, calculated that the Russian campaign would require no more than 8–10 weeks. It was to be carried out by three roughly equal army groups, which would attack simultaneously, but with diverging objectives. Apparently it was not until 30 August 1941 that OKH awoke to the need for winter clothing. The *Luftwaffe* and the *Waffen-SS*, it seems, were more far-sighted, and had laid in ample stocks.

Above: Marshal Semyon Budenny, Commander-in-Chief Southern and Southwestern Army Groups.

Right: The German Army was prepared for an operation which would last a few months and expected the USSR to capitulate before the winter.

Below left: Vitebsk in flames: the Soviets practised their scorched earth policy with great efficiency.

Below: Cavalrymen were more mobile than tanks in the winter.

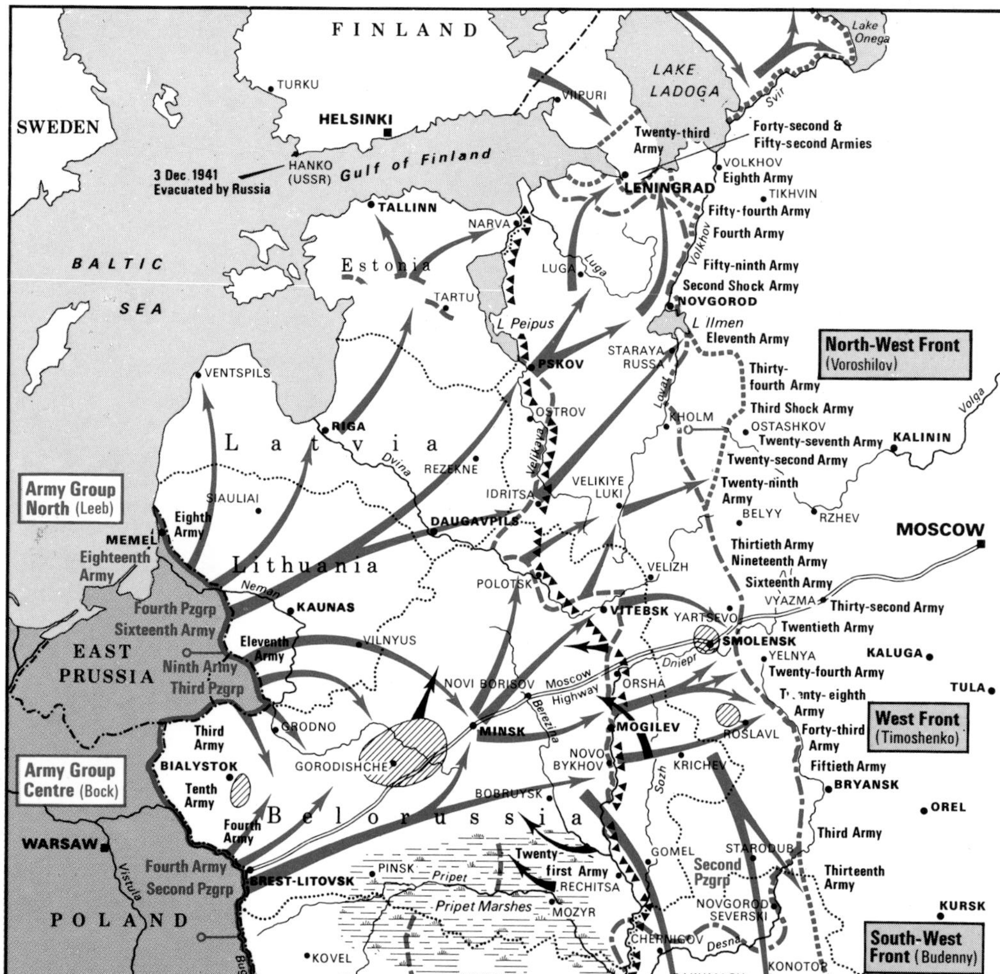

It was on 22 June 1812 that Napoleon had crossed the Niemen. It is odd that a man so superstitious as Hitler should have chosen the 129th anniversary as the day to begin his own Russian campaign. But it was also the first anniversary of the signature of the French Armistice in the Forest of Compiègne.

Stalin, whose forces had last shown their paces in Finland, was far from courting a trial of strength with Nazi Germany. He had taken care to honour the agreement of January 1941 by which Russia was to deliver food and raw materials to Germany, and this despite many German violations of Soviet air space, among other provocations. It is estimated that Russia, including her reserves, had an army of 12,000,000 men, organized in 160 infantry and 30 cavalry divisions. There were, in addition, 35 motorized and armoured brigades. But while Hitler still depended on the *Blitzkrieg* technique, which had served him so well in the early years of the war, the Russians relied on their traditional assets: numbers, space, scorched earth,

Below left: **The Wehrmacht advances on the muddy Russian roads.**

Below: **During 1941 the Soviet Army had not mastered tank tactics and used their tanks to back infantry operations.**

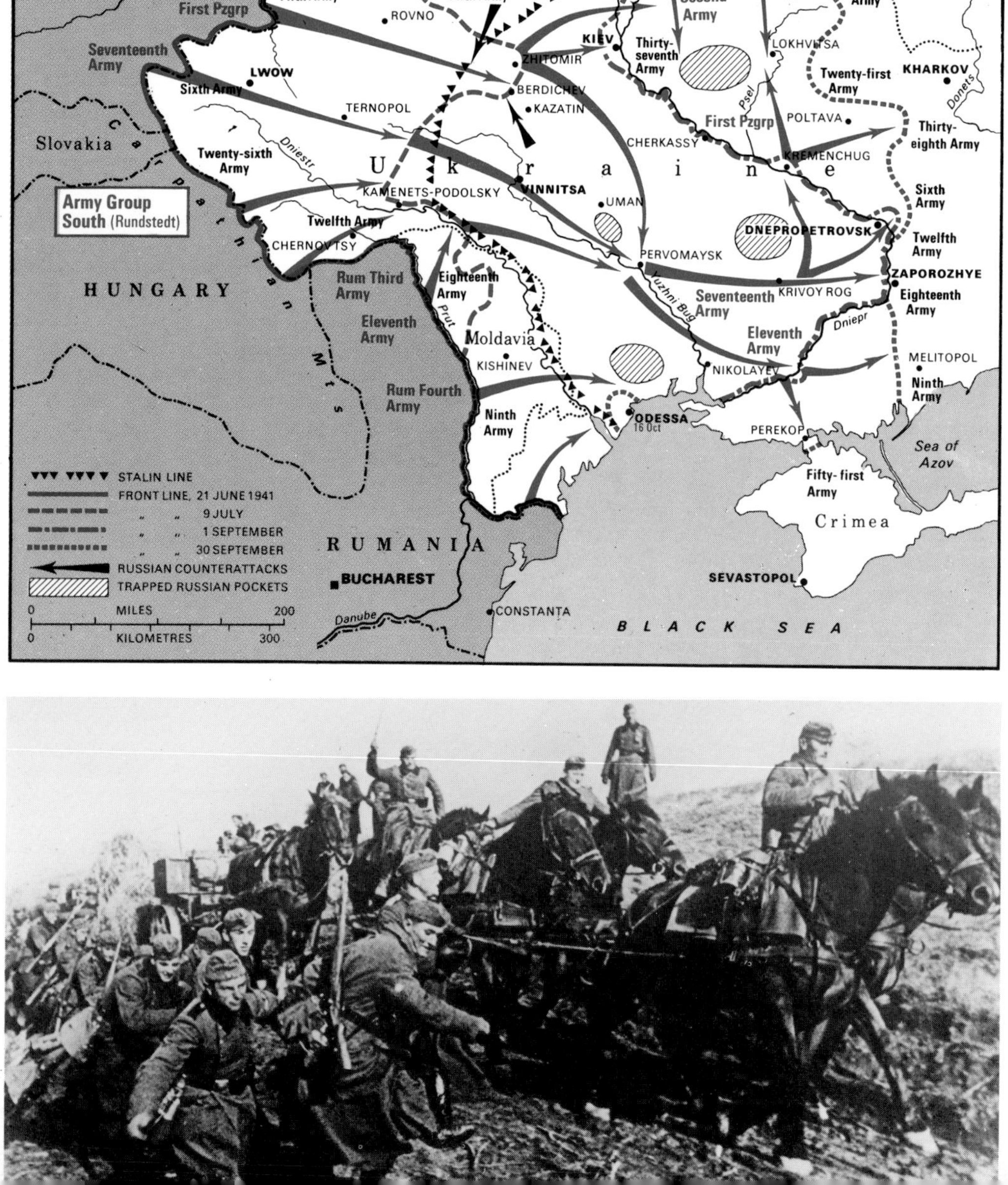

January and February. Their huge army seriously short of motor transport, was as yet quite unattuned to the pace of modern warfare Nazi pattern. And in the air, though they may have had as many as 7,500 planes, they were no match for the *Luftwaffe*, which was not only experienced but well armed.

There was a variety of reasons for the Russians' unpreparedness. The purges of 1937 had shaken the Red Army to its very soul. It did not compare with the German Army either in experience or in training. Armament too left much to be desired. Although there were perhaps 20,000 tanks, many were obsolescent. The KV and T-34 tanks only began to be produced in really significant numbers by early 1941. The Red Air Force suffered from the lack of a proper network of airfields, and from a shortage of trained pilots. Strategically the Russians, like the Poles and the Yugoslavs before them, made the mistake of concentrating too near their frontier.

But if the Russians were ill-prepared, not

Right: **Petlyakov Pe-2s on the assembly line. Almost half the Soviet Air Force was destroyed on the ground during the first week of Barbarossa. The Pe-2 dive-bomber performed most successfully in the defence of Moscow and later on at Stalingrad.**

everything was perfect with the Germans. The vehicles of the new divisions were French and unsuitable for warfare in eastern Europe. Although the old Panzers I and II had been almost completely replaced by Panzers III and IV, the number of tanks in the panzer division had been cut down. At this time the Germans were producing 1,000 tanks a year. On the Eastern front they had 3,200 tanks but even their heaviest, the Panzer IV, was not as good or as heavy as the Russian T-34, which first appeared at the front in July 1941. Incredible though it may seem, the Army Ordnance Office had failed to re-equip the Panzer III with the mark of 50-mm cannon which Hitler personally had ordered them to provide.

The *Blitzkrieg* began with successes comparable, at least in terms of prisoners and booty, with those of 1940. In the first weeks of the campaign the Soviet air force suffered fearful losses, many of them on the ground. Göring actually claimed that 3,000 planes were destroyed in the first week. By the beginning of July the Germans estimated that their fast-moving columns, piercing into the Russians, breaking them up into fragments and encircling them, had taken 150,000 prisoners, 1,200 tanks and 600 guns. By 10 July the Germans were attacking Smolensk, where at last the *Blitzkrieg* met with a decided check. So far the Nazis had covered 400 miles in 18 days. Moscow itself lay only 200 miles ahead.

But in fact it was at this very time that the

Left: **The advance to Leningrad proceeds and the Germans build a temporary bridge over the Velikaya River.**

Below: **The Soviet BT-7s were very vulnerable to German shells. They were rapidly replaced by T-34s which started to come into service in 1941.**

Russian resistance was becoming more effective. The appearance on the battlefield of the famous *Katyusha* mortars, first used near Smolensk on 15 July, had something to do with it. Moreover, the Russians were now using a few modern planes, and the *Luftwaffe* was no longer having everything its own way. The dogged rearguard action at Smolensk gave the Russian High Command a breathing space. Drastic measures were taken against Generals who failed. Dismissal or imprisonment were not enough. Army General G. D. Pavlov, who had lost his grip on the Western Front, was court-martialled along with his Chief of Staff and commander of signals. They were sentenced to death.

And successful though their tactics were, all was not well within the German High Command, nor was there the universal doctrine that one might have expected after two years of successful *Blitzkrieg*. Guderian records that on 27 July he anticipated orders to push on towards Moscow or at least Bryansk, but learned to his surprise that Hitler had ordered that his 2nd Panzer Group was to go for Gomel in support of Second Army. This meant a swing to the South-West – in fact towards Germany. 'We were informed that Hitler was convinced that large-scale envelopments were not justified: the theory on which they were based was a false one put out by the General Staff Corps, and he believed that events in France had proved his point. He presented an alternative plan by which small enemy forces were to be encircled and destroyed piecemeal and the enemy thus bled to death. All the officers who took part in this conference were of the opinion that this was incorrect: that these manoeuvres on our part simply gave the Russians time to set up new formations and to use their inexhaustible man-power for the creation of fresh defensive lines in the rear area; even more important, we were sure that this strategy would not result in the urgently necessary, rapid conclusion of the campaign.'

Right: **The Russian Polikavpov I-16 Type 24 Fighter was totally outclassed by its Luftwaffe opponents in 1941.**

Below right: **These Soviet tanks serving on the Rumanian border got stuck in marshy land when they tried to escape from a German pincer movement.**

Below: **Stalin and the Japanese Foreign Minister Matsuoka at the Soviet–Japanese Neutrality Pact in April 1941.**

On 4 August 1941 Hitler held a conference at Novy Borissov, the HQ of Army Group Centre. He designated the industrial area about Leningrad as his primary objective. He had not yet decided whether Moscow or the Ukraine would come next. He seemed to incline towards the latter target for a number of reasons: first, Army Group South seemed to be laying the groundwork for a victory in that area: secondly, he believed that the raw materials and agricultural produce of the Ukraine were necessary to Germany for the further prosecution of the war: and finally he thought it essential that the Crimea, 'that Soviet aircraft-carrier operating against the Rumanian oilfields', be neutralized. He hoped to be in possession of Moscow and Kharkov by the time winter began.

On 21 August Hitler issued orders for the Battle of Kiev. He asserted that: 'Of primary importance before the outbreak of winter is not the capture of Moscow but rather the occupation of the Crimea, of the industrial and coal-mining area of the Donets basin, the cutting of the Russian supply routes from the Caucasian oilfields, and, in the north, the investment of Leningrad and the establishment of contact with the Finns. . . . The capture of the Crimean peninsula is of extreme importance for safeguarding our oil supplies from Rumania.' Such thinking tended to lead to a dangerous dispersion of effort.

The greatest German successes came in the Kiev area. The city itself fell on 18 September. The veteran Marshal Budenny was relieved of his command, and probably owed his life to his popularity in the army. His successor, Timoshenko, could not stop the rot, and on 26 September the encircled forces surrendered, leaving 665,000 prisoners in German hands. This was a tremendous victory, yet by the beginning of October things were not looking so bright for the Germans. The roads, which were appalling, were pocked with bomb craters. The Russians were making much better tactical use of their tanks. The short-barrelled 75-mm gun of the Panzer IV could only knock out a T-34 if it attacked it from the rear. 'The Russians attacked us frontally with infantry, while they sent their tanks in, in mass formation, against our flanks. They were learning. The bitterness of the fighting was gradually telling on both our officers and our men. General Freiherr von Geyr brought up once again the urgent need for winter clothing of all sorts. In particular there was a shortage of boots, shirts and socks' (Guderian).

Notwithstanding the success of their initial thrusts, it was early October before the Germans began their final advance on Moscow. 'Today begins the last great decisive battle of the year!' Hitler proclaimed on 2 October, and certainly at this stage it was still possible for Germany to win the war. Despite an unwise dispersal of the German armour, this offensive began well for the Nazis. In three weeks von Bock was within 30 miles of Moscow, and the capital was in danger of encirclement. In the south von Rundstedt had overrun the Crimea, where resistance continued only in Sevastopol. In this crisis the Soviet government and the *corps diplomatique* removed themselves to Kuibyshev, some 500 miles to the east. There was something of a panic in the capital. But Stalin – resolute, enigmatic, cruel, but nothing if not a leader – stayed on in the Kremlin. In speeches which he made on 6 and 7 November, on the occasion of the 24th anniversary of the Revolution, he galvanized his countrymen. His Holy Russia speech ranks with some of Churchill's of 1940. It is worth noting that his references to the recent Moscow Conference, when Harriman and Beaverbrook had agreed to supply the USSR with planes, tanks and raw materials as well as a US loan of one billion dollars, were greeted with storms of applause. 'All this shows', said Stalin 'is that the coalition between the three countries is a very real thing which will go on growing in the common cause of liberation.'

And as Russian reserves massed behind Moscow in preparation for a counter-attack, the 'Napoleon weather' came. In 1941 as in 1812 the weather broke early in November. The weather which had demoralized the *Grande Armée*, brought the Germans to a halt. Of course, the weather affected both sides, but the Russians were accustomed to their winter and had prepared for it with proper foresight. Mud dominated the next few weeks, and then came the snow. Anti-freeze for the water coolers of the German tanks was not to be had any more than warm clothing. By 13 November the cold was making the telescopic sights of the tanks useless. One of Guderian's brigades was down to some 50 tanks.

But if his armies were exhausted, Hitler was not. The fate of Napoleon was insufficient to make him agree to send his frost-bitten legions into winter quarters. On 15 November the Germans launched yet another great offensive towards Moscow. Despite the weather, by 2 December they had fought their way into the suburbs, but the thermometer was below zero and by 6 December the German attack on Moscow had broken down. A prompt withdrawal to a properly prepared defensive position was the only sensible move. Far away in East Prussia the Supreme Command had other ideas.

Up to the end of November the Germans had lost about 750,000 men on the Russian Front, that is 23 per cent of their average total strength of 3,500,000 men. Of these 200,000, including 8,000 officers, were dead. In Berlin Dr Goebbels, with characteristic efficiency, organized the collection of furs and warm clothing for the troops – an appeal to which the civilian population responded with a patriotism worthy of a better cause.

On 6 December Marshal Zhukov launched a great counter-attack against his semi-paralyzed foe. Still Hitler forbade any major withdrawal. He insisted that Rzhev, Vyazma, Yukhnov, Kaluga, Bryansk and Orel must be held, and of these only Kaluga was retaken. The German commanders, many of whom advised withdrawal, were threatened with the direst penalties should they disobey. There followed a wholesale shake up in the German High Command. Generals Höpner (4 Panzer Group) and Guderian were sacked, the former being deprived of his rank and forbidden to wear uniform. General von Bock, who had been held up before Moscow, fell ill as did von Leeb, who had failed to take Leningrad. He was replaced by Küchler, a more ardent Nazi. The Russian recapture of Rostov led to the dismissal of von Rundstedt. Most important of all von Brauchitsch, the Commander-in-Chief, was relieved in his command by Hitler himself. In the long term the *Führer* was doing the Allies a great service, but in the short term he rode the storm. The Russians retook Kaluga and Kalinin, but the Dictator compelled his wretched, freezing soldiers to hold fast and gradually the front solidified leaving the Germans well-placed to begin a new offensive in the spring. In the north Leningrad had been invested since October. In the south they had overrun the best corn-lands of the Ukraine. Though their losses had been terrible, those of the Russians had

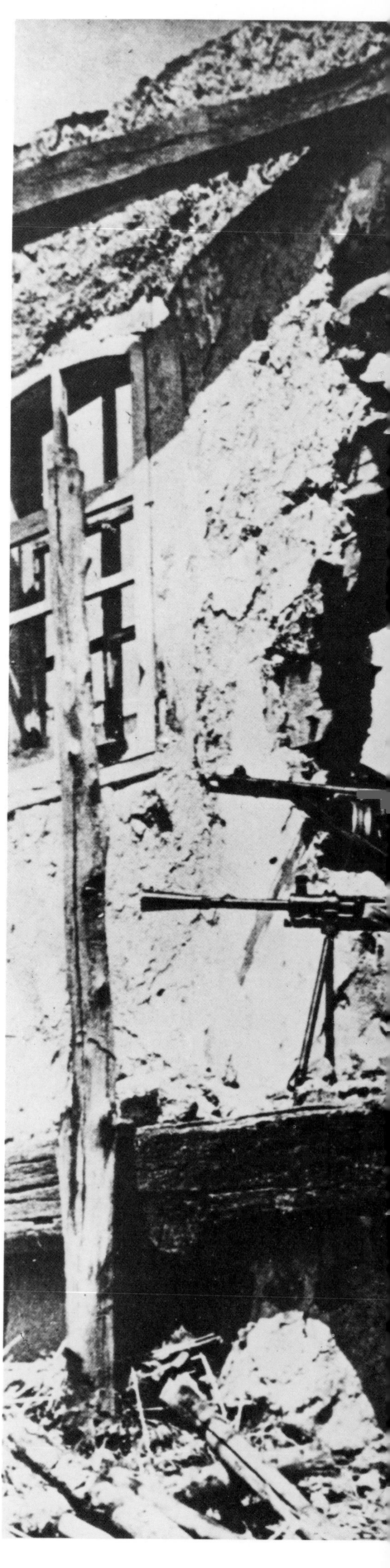

Above: Hitler consults his generals. From left to right: Keitel, von Brauchitsch and Hitler.

Right: Soviet sub-machine-gunners in action in the autumn of 1941.

Below: Soviet troops preparing to take action on Leningrad's perimeter. The siege of Leningrad began in August 1941 and was to last until January 1944.

been much worse. Moreover the German armies were reinforced by Hungarian, Italian, Rumanian and Finnish contingents, until the Russians, for all their enormous manpower, were actually outnumbered.

The Russian counter-offensive achieved a great deal, but very much less than the Soviet High Command had hoped. Rostov was recaptured at the end of November; in the Crimea Sevastopol was still holding out. It was on the Moscow front that the counter-attack achieved its most spectacular success and liberated the most territory. Leningrad remained beleaguered, but the recapture of Tikhvin had alleviated its supply position. If the Russians failed to achieve more, it was because they had no advantage in numbers or *matériel* and were still very short of transport, arms and ammunition. One is astonished not that they did not achieve more but that, after the awful blows they had suffered, they had the resilience to go over to the offensive so soon.

Shortly before the invasion of Russia the OKW had sent out an order regarding the treatment of civilians and prisoners. It laid down that German soldiers committing excesses against them were not automatically to be tried by military law. Disciplinary action was only to be taken at the discretion of unit commanders, and for the preservation of discipline. A number of generals forbade the publication of this order, but even so it led to countless atrocities and reprisals, and in due course was to play its part in the trial of German war criminals. This policy, so far from terrorizing the Russians, convinced even the most lukewarm that the Germans were as unspeakable as Stalin told them. When in the second half of December the Soviet Army retook Volokolamsk they found a gallows in the main square. Eight 'partisans', one a woman, were hanging from it. Terrorism only steeled the hearts of the Russians against the invader.

12 THE WAR AT SEA, 1940-42

'The English never yield, and though driven back and thrown into confusion, they always return to the fight, thirsting for vengeance as long as they have a breath of life.'
Giovanni Mocenigo, Venetian Ambassador to France, to the Doge, 8 April 1588

The Britain of 1940 was a moated fortress. Its inadequately armed defenders included a great many *bouches inutiles*, who could not just be banished as Montluc had banished the citizens of Siena long ago. The fortress was far from being self-supporting. Not only arms but food had to be brought in from outside. Since the besiegers' best weapon, as in 1917, was the submarine, it is not too much to say that everything depended on the success of the Royal Navy and the Merchant Navy in combatting its menace. Terrible were the losses sustained in this struggle, yet few in Britain imagined that it could end in defeat, for here again the inspired leadership of Winston Churchill met its response. Confidence in a Navy which for hundreds of years had rendered invasion impossible was unbounded.

The loss of the French fleet was a grave setback, but fortunately the Home Fleet was superior to the German surface fleet and in June 1940 it was possible to assemble Force H (Vice-Admiral Sir James Somerville) at Gibraltar. This powerful squadron included the fleet carrier *Ark Royal*, a battle-cruiser and two battleships. Its first task was its most difficult and unpleasant. It was to ensure that the French fleet at Oran did not go over to the Axis. The story of the tragedy that followed is a complex one. It is true that Somerville was told from London that if he did not 'settle matters quickly' he 'would have reinforcements to deal with' – not altogether an unreasonable view. But Admiral Gensoul signalled to his government that he had been presented with an ultimatum 'to sink his ships within six hours', which was woefully inexact. He had in fact been offered more honourable alternatives, of which he mentioned only that which his former allies least desired.

At 6 p.m. on 3 July Somerville's squadron opened fire. A number of ships were seriously damaged and 1,297 Frenchmen died. The battleship *Bretagne* blew up. The battle cruiser

Right: **The Channel Dash as seen from the German side.**

Strasbourg and five destroyers, though attacked by *Ark Royal*'s obsolescent torpedo-bombers, got safely to Toulon. Admiral Gensoul must certainly bear a share of the blame, but given time, a peaceful settlement could probably have been made. Cunningham's success in negotiating a peaceful solution with Admiral Godfroy's squadron at Alexandria strengthens this view.

At Dakar attempts to put the new battleship *Richelieu* out of action were unsuccessful. French ships in the West Indies were immobilized by lack of oil and by diplomatic pressure. The French naval commanders in Algerian ports and at Toulon honoured their undertaking not to allow their ships to fall into enemy hands. All in all Oran can hardly be justified and its effect on Anglo-French relations was deplorable. Even so it was evidence to America, and indeed to Britain, that the Churchill government was

Above: **After the Fall of France Brest became a very useful U-Boat base. The crew of *U-203* seen here at the height of the Battle of the Atlantic, July 1942.**

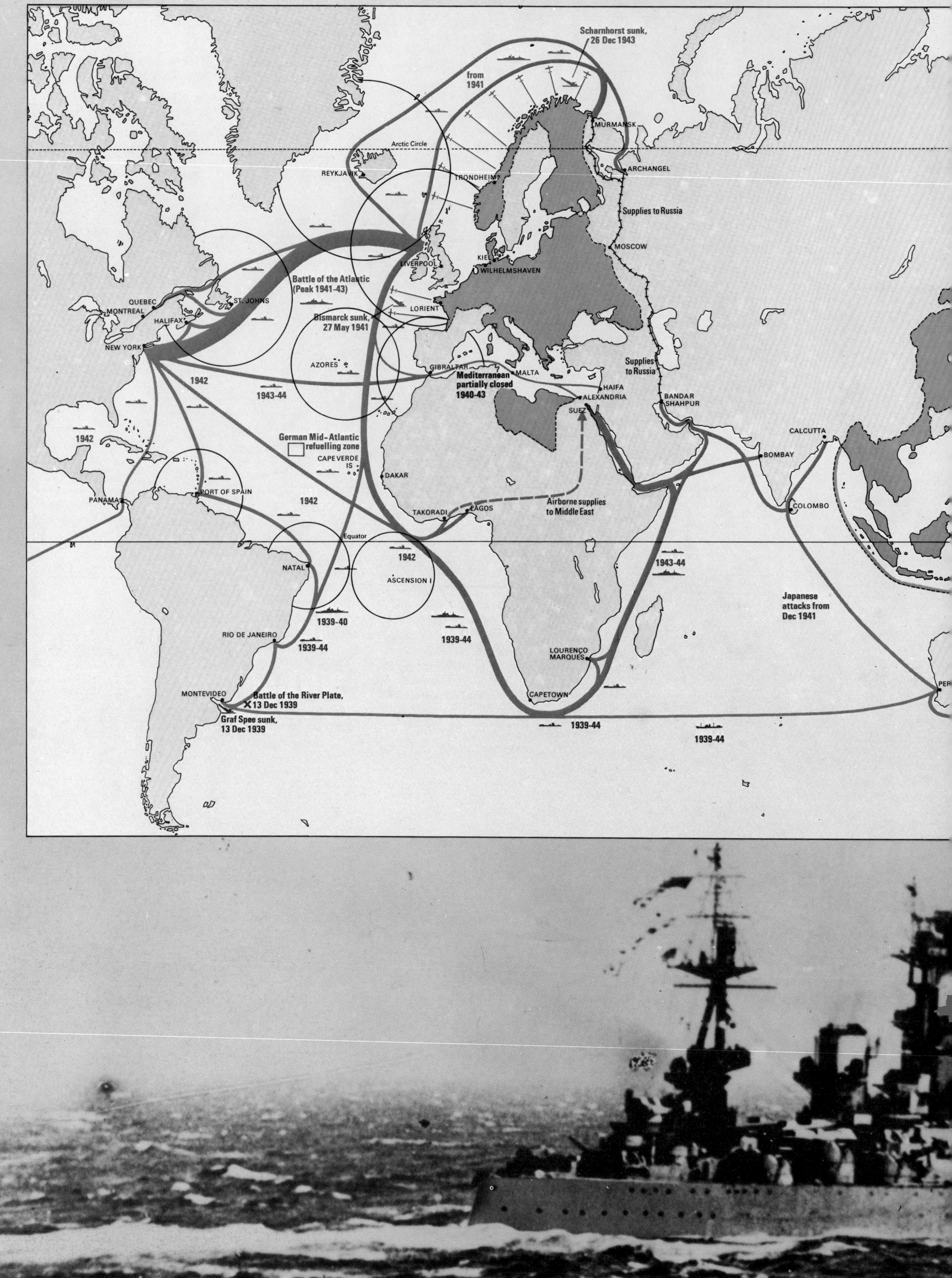

Scharnhorst sunk, 26 Dec 1943
from 1941
MURMANSK
Arctic Circle
ARCHANGEL
REYKJAVIK
TRONDHEIM
Supplies to Russia
MOSCOW
LIVERPOOL
KIEL
WILHELMSHAVEN
Battle of the Atlantic (Peak 1941-43)
QUEBEC
MONTREAL
ST. JOHNS
HALIFAX
LORIENT
Bismarck sunk, 27 May 1941
NEW YORK
AZORES
GIBRALTAR
MALTA
Mediterranean partially closed 1940-43
HAIFA
ALEXANDRIA
Supplies to Russia
BANDAR SHAHPUR
1942
1943-44
SUEZ
1942
German Mid-Atlantic refuelling zone
CAPE VERDE IS
CALCUTTA
BOMBAY
DAKAR
PORT OF SPAIN
PANAMA
1942
TAKORADI
LAGOS
Airborne supplies to Middle East
COLOMBO
Equator
1942
NATAL
ASCENSION I
1943-44
Japanese attacks from Dec 1941
1939-40
RIO DE JANEIRO
1939-44
1939-44
LOURENÇO MARQUES
MONTEVIDEO
Battle of the River Plate, 13 Dec 1939
CAPETOWN
Graf Spee sunk, 13 Dec 1939
1939-44
1939-44

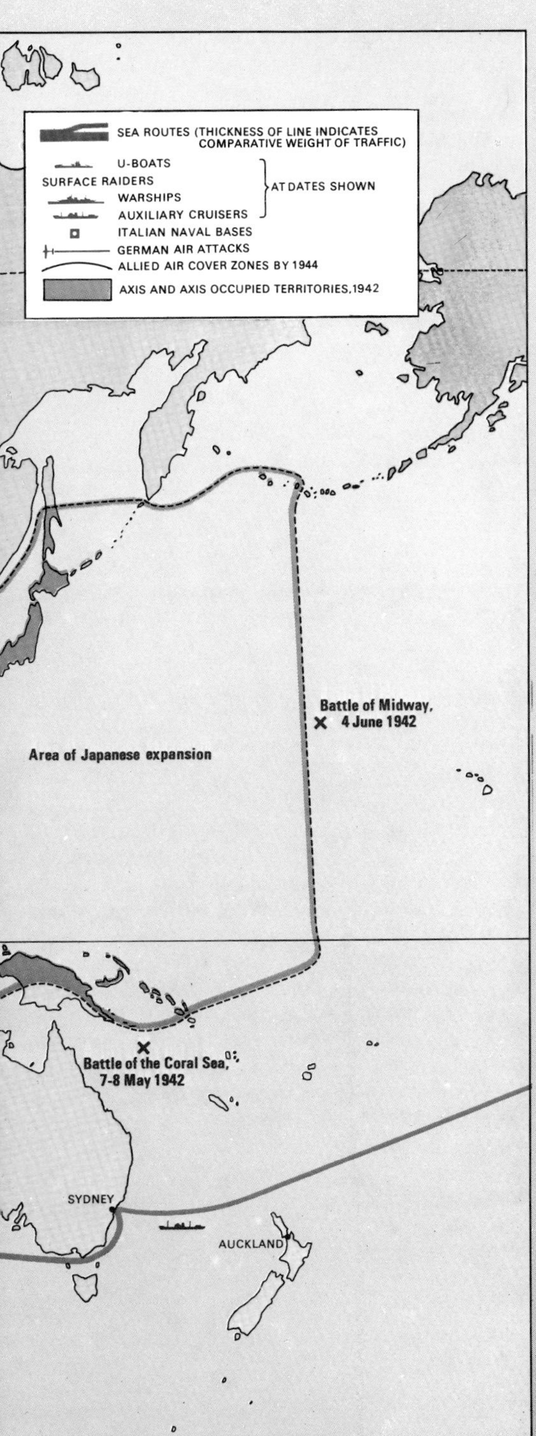

Above: **The *Scharnhorst,* along with the *Gneisenau* and *Prinz Eugen,* took part in the Channel Dash from Brest.**

imbued with a resolution quite foreign to its fumbling predecessors.

While this was going on Hitler was preparing to invade England. Since Operation *Sealion* was never launched it is easy to underrate its menace. An essential factor for its success was the defeat of the Royal Air Force, and it was the opinion of Admiral Forbes (C.-in-C. Home Fleet) that 'the correct strategy was to keep our main strength based at Scapa, whence Ireland as well as the southern coast of England could be covered; to conduct offensive sweeps in the North Sea to impress upon the enemy the extent of our control of those waters, and to continue to employ all the light forces we could spare on Atlantic escort duties. Although such a strategy had behind it the authority of centuries of experience, it was rejected both by the naval authorities in their southern commands and by the British government.' It seems now that Forbes was right. The rejection of his plan condemned the Fleet to a passive role and increased our losses in the Western Approaches, while bombardment of the German invasion flotillas, whether from the sea or the air, inflicted no crippling damage upon them.

For all their resolution it may be supposed that the British people were relieved that the Germans never ventured to launch their 13 assault divisions. Yet there are those who regret that they did not, feeling that Britain would have won a decisive victory comparable with Barfleur or Quiberon Bay. Historical 'ifs', though fascinating are not very profitable. But in this case speculation is illuminated by the fate of the German surface fleet off Norway under conditions far less favourable to the Royal Navy than those prevailing in the English Channel, where land-based air cover was within easy reach. Captain Roskill points out with justice that 'of all the factors which contributed to the failure of Hitler's grandiose invasion plans, none was greater than the lack of adequate instruments of sea power and of a proper understanding of their use on the German side.'

It is easy to forget that throughout the summer, when all eyes were fixed on the Battle of Britain, the long drawn-out and deadly Battle of the Atlantic was also going on. As yet the

Below: **The battleship *Nelson* served in the Mediterranean. She supported the Salerno landings and the Italian surrender was signed on her decks.**

Above: **A recruiting poster for the German Navy, whose cruisers and battleships were not as effective as the U-Boats.**

British, instead of using the maximum number of vessels in the escort role, wasted much effort in hunting for submarines either in the open ocean or where it was thought that they might lurk, as it were, in ambush. The German tactics of the 'wolf-pack', hunting on the surface at night like torpedo-boats, met with considerable success. Most of the escorts had not yet got radar and were in any case too slow to catch a surfaced U-Boat. Asdic (underwater detecting equipment otherwise known as Sonar) was only designed to detect the *submerged* submarine. Grand-Admiral Dönitz had forecast these tactics in a book published in 1939, but even so the Admiralty was taken by surprise. On 17 August Hitler declared a total blockade of Britain and, with his usual disregard for international law, announced that neutral as well as British shipping would be sunk on sight. In these circumstances the agreement (2 September) by which America agreed to transfer 50 ancient destroyers to Britain in return for the lease of bases in the western hemisphere was a godsend.

Astonishingly enough the factor which did most to turn the tide of success against the Germans was their own lack of foresight. Despite their tremendous success in World War I, Hitler had given U-Boat construction a very low priority. Incredible though it may seem, by the end of 1940 the Germans had lost 31 U-Boats and had 22 left! These factors, taken with the improvement both of British tactics and their production of escort vessels, eased the situation. In addition to submarines the Germans employed a number of converted merchantmen as armed raiders, a perfectly legitimate form of warfare. They operated mostly in the South Atlantic. During 1940 they accounted for 54 ships (370,000 tons) and caused much confusion and delay, being a match for any warship less powerful than a cruiser. It was not until 5 May 1941 that the *Cornwall* caught one of them, the *Pinguin*, and sent her to the bottom of the Indian Ocean.

The remaining German major warships were a further menace. On 5 November the pocket-battleship *Scheer* attacked the Convoy HX 84 (37 ships), which was escorted by a single Armed Merchant Cruiser, *Jervis Bay*. Captain E. S. F. Fegan sacrificed his ship to cover the dispersal of the convoy, and his courageous action was rewarded, since only five merchantmen were lost. *Hipper* also made a sortie into the Atlantic via the Denmark Strait, attacked a troop convoy west of Finisterre, and, having done very little damage, got safely into Brest (27 December). Her presence there was a constant threat.

Bombers from bases in France and Norway caused the British serious losses, second only to those suffered from U-Boats. They operated not only off the west coast of Ireland but in coastal waters.

Admiral Lütjens left Kiel with *Scharnhorst* and *Gneisenau* on 23 January 1941 and during a two-month cruise sank or took 22 ships (115,600 tons) before escaping into Brest. There Admiral Tovey blockaded him much as Cornwallis had blockaded Ganteaume in 1805. Both battle-cruisers were to be severely damaged in air raids, and as things turned out their commerce-raiding was over. In a five-months' cruise (October–1 April) the pocket battleship *Scheer* accounted for 16 merchantmen (99,000 tons) besides the *Jervis Bay*. This was a somewhat modest haul, but her foray into the Indian Ocean caused a good deal of dislocation on the convoy routes. The heavy cruiser *Hipper* made a brief sortie from Brest in February and sank seven of a convoy of 19 unescorted merchantmen homeward-bound from Sierra Leone. The convoy system and the sinking of their supply vessels gradually put an end to the successes of surface raiders and after the middle of 1941 they did very little harm.

With the spring the U-Boat war flared up once more. In March they sank 41 ships but lost five submarines and several 'aces', including Prien, who had torpedoed the *Royal Oak*. But they were still sinking merchantmen far more quickly than these could be replaced. In April and May, with 40 U-Boats operational, sinkings remained very heavy, but the Royal Navy scored some notable successes. On 9 May *U-110* was captured intact, a tremendous advantage for British intelligence.

Admiral Lütjens now reappeared on the scene with the formidable new battleship *Bismarck* and the heavy cruiser *Prinz Eugen*. He sailed from Gdynia on 18 May 1941. The Germans had hoped that *Scharnhorst* and *Gneisenau* would be able to sally forth from Brest at the same time, but the RAF had already cancelled that part of the German plan. After leaving Bergen on 21 May Lütjens was not sighted until his squadron was seen by the heavy cruiser *Suffolk* at the northern entrance to the Denmark Strait, steering SW. Vice-Admiral L. E. Holland, with the battle-cruiser *Hood*, the battleship *Prince of Wales*, and four destroyers, was about 220 miles away, SW of Iceland. *Hood* and *Prince of Wales* were the fastest of Tovey's heavy ships, but the former was over 20 years old and had not been properly modernized, while the latter had not had time to work up to full fighting efficiency. During the night contact with the enemy was lost; Admiral Holland detached his four destroyers, presumably for reconnaissance, and they lost

Right: **The *Tirpitz* in a Norwegian fjord. She served mainly off the Norwegian coast where her prime function was to challenge the Allied convoys to Soviet Russia.**

contact with him. At 0247 *Suffolk* again sighted Lütjens still on the same course. Admiral Holland now began to close at full speed, but, doubtless in order to obtain surprise, he would not let the *Prince of Wales* send off her reconnaissance plane, or allow his ships to use their radar. By maintaining wireless silence he deprived himself of the support of the two heavy cruisers and perhaps of his four destroyers.

At 0535 *Hood* sighted the enemy. Holland gave the Germans a distinct tactical advantage by taking his ships into action in close order. Had he allowed his captains freedom to manoeuvre they might have been able to bring more guns to bear. As it was they were outgunned. At 0552 all four ships opened fire, *Hood* engaging the *Prinz Eugen* which was leading and which she mistook for the *Bismarck*. The British missed with their opening salvos, but *Bismarck* hit *Hood* hard with her second or third, and at 0600 she blew up. No doubt one of her inadequately armoured magazines had been hit. Of her crew of 1,419 only three survived. The *Prince of Wales* was hit by four 15-inch and three 8-inch shells and turned away making smoke. She had, however, hit *Bismarck* twice and damaged some of her fuel tanks. Lütjens was compelled to abandon his foray and make for France.

Admiral Holland's disaster may be attributed to his sticking to the letter of the Admiralty's 'Fighting Instructions' (1939). It has been suggested that he had in mind this passage:

> 'Prior to deployment the Admiral will control the movements of the Battle Fleet as a whole. He will dispose the guides of divisions on a line of bearing at right angles to the bearing of the enemy battle fleet. . . .'

These tactics may have been appropriate to a great fleet action like Jutland – though Nelson had been far less rigid at Trafalgar. Military history does not lack illustrations of the danger of sticking too closely to 'the book'. *En passant* one wonders what would have happened if Harwood had fought the Battle of the River Plate on these lines.

Meanwhile the Admiralty was trying to draw a net about the quarry. Admiral Somerville was summoned from Gibraltar (24 May), the battleships *Ramillies* and *Rodney* were released from convoy duty. Even so the net was full of holes, and nobody could tell where Lütjens was going. Tovey, determined to try and slow him up, sent the aircraft-carrier *Victorious* ahead with an escort of four light cruisers. About midnight a Swordfish scored a torpedo hit on the *Bismarck*, but as it hit her main armour it did her little harm. That evening the two German warships had parted company. Meanwhile Admiral Dönitz had given orders to his U-Boats to suspend operations against merchantmen and had moved seven to positions south of Greenland in the hope of torpedoing important units of the Home Fleet.

Early on the morning of the 25th Lütjens altered course to make for western France, and in so doing shook off the shadowing British

Above right: **The heavy cruiser *Admiral Hipper*. With the *Lützow* she took part in the Battle of Barents Sea in December 1942.**

Right: **Gunther Prien was Commander of *U-47* and became a German national hero. His submarine was sunk with all hands on 7 March 1941 but the news of his death was kept secret for some time.**

cruisers. Tovey, who at about 4 a.m. was some 110 miles ahead of Lütjens, was misled by signalling and plotting errors into believing that *Bismarck* was now steering NE, and at 1047 turned in the same direction. Fortunately the Admiralty acted on the assumption that Lütjens was making for Brest and disposed Somerville's Force H, the *Rodney* and other forces to cut him off. Tovey came to the same conclusion independently, but he was now 150 miles behind his quarry. During the night 25–26 May the net tightened but nobody could tell whether there was anything in it. Everything now depended on Coastal Command's dawn patrols. It chanced that Air Chief Marshal Bowhill, its Commander-in-Chief, had served at sea as a young officer. Lütjens, he said, would not steer direct for Brest but would make for Cape Finisterre. At his insistence one patrol was sent well to the south of *Bismarck*'s direct course for Brest. At 1030 on the 26th a Catalina sighted her 690 miles west of the port, and only 30 hours steaming from safety.

In foul weather 14 Swordfish flew off from *Ark Royal*. They made a spirited attack on *Sheffield*, which was shadowing the *Bismarck*, but the cruiser was sufficiently skilful to avoid her colleagues' torpedoes. A second attack in the failing light of evening scored two hits on the *Bismarck*. One struck the armour belt, but the other damaged her propellers and jammed the rudder. Her speed fell. Captain Vian's destroyers attacked during the night and may have scored two more torpedo hits. At about 0845 on 27 May Admiral Tovey came up with *King George V* and *Rodney* and in less than two hours silenced *Bismarck*'s guns and battered her into a blazing hulk. Finally, hit by yet more torpedoes, she sank at 1036 with her colours flying. Nearly all her crew of 2,000 perished with her. Lütjens had fought a good fight, but the sinking of the *Bismarck* was a tremendous relief to the British, at a time when the war was going none too well. Morale rose accordingly.

While these exciting events were taking place, the U-Boat campaign continued on its course. Heavy losses went on, but a new phase was beginning. Escorts were becoming stronger and in consequence the U-Boats had to attack in force. Towards the end of June ten of them attacked convoy HX 133 south of Greenland. By throwing in the escorts of two outward-bound convoys the Admiralty was able to concentrate 13 warships to reinforce the threatened one. In a battle which went on for five days and nights five merchantmen were lost, but the Germans lost two submarines. Thus was born the strategy of the 'support groups', which were to play a decisive part in the Battle of the Atlantic.

On 22 June the Germans invaded Russia, an event which had an immediate effect on the Atlantic campaign, for in July and August sinkings were much reduced. To the casual observer this may seem strange. But the explanation is straightforward. Bombers which had been doing considerable damage had been moved to the eastern front. The German Navy was busy supporting operations on the Baltic coast.

A curious episode took place on 27 August when the *U-570* was captured intact by Squadron Leader J. H. Thompson in a Hudson. The submarine inadvertently surfaced immediately below the aircraft which attacked with such speed and skill that the Germans surrendered. This was no mean prize! (*U-570* continued her career as HMS *Graph*.)

After the summer lull it was sad to find the sinkings getting worse again in September. The U-Boat strength was now nearly 150. Dönitz intended to send some of his larger submarines to prey upon the distant trade routes, but the sinking by cruisers of their supply ships *Kota Pinang* (13 October) and *Python* (1 December) put paid to this. On 22 November the cruiser *Devonshire* ended the career of another predator, the disguised *Atlantis*, which had sunk 22 ships (146,000 tons) during a cruise of some 20 months. About the same time a strange fight took place off Western Australia. The light cruiser HMAS *Sydney* came upon the raider *Kormoran* disguised as a Dutch ship. Suspicious, but not suspicious enough, *Sydney* closed to 2,000 yards. She was steaming parallel to the *Kormoran* when the latter suddenly discharged her torpedoes and opened up with everything she had got. *Sydney* returned the fire but she was hard hit, and 'finally disappeared over the southern horizon a mass of flames'. She was seen no more, and it must be assumed that she blew up with all her crew. *Kormoran* too was seriously damaged and her crew had to scuttle her. Most of them reached Australia.

If the Russian campaign had brought temporary relief in the Atlantic battle it also brought the Home Fleet a serious new problem, escorting convoys of supplies to Murmansk and Archangel, often in appalling weather conditions and exposed to heavy attacks by U-Boats, bombers and surface ships during most of the 2,000-mile voyage. On 9 August Churchill and Roosevelt met in Placentia Bay, Newfoundland, and drew up the Atlantic Charter. Already in July American forces had arrived in Iceland to reinforce and later to replace the British. Now Roosevelt arranged for American warships and aircraft to 'patrol' the Western Atlantic and inform the British if they should sight any U-Boats.

Congress and the American people still hoped to keep out of the war. The President was taking a more realistic view. The Germans were furious. On 4 September a U-Boat attacked the US destroyer *Greer* off Iceland. Roosevelt retaliated by ordering US destroyers to attack any submarine on sight. On 17 October the US destroyer *Kearny* was torpedoed with 11 casualties, an incident which not unnaturally caused a tremendous outcry in the United States.

It is not easy however to see how the German commanders were to distinguish American destroyers from those which had been transferred to the Royal Navy under Lend-Lease. German writers have made a great song and dance about the help the United States gave Britain in the days before she entered the war. It is easy to forget that in 1940 the raider *Komet* reached the Pacific via the Arctic route with the help of Russian ice-breakers, and that Japan permitted the *Orion* to refit in the Marianas so that she was able to go on operating until 1941. Spain allowed U-Boats to refuel in the Canaries. It is true that these things were a drop in the bucket compared to the help Britain received

Above: **Force H including the *Valiant* on the left and the *Warspite* on the right. Force H served in the Mediterranean to fill the gap left by the French Navy.**

Left: **The battleship *Bismarck* fires a salvo at the *Hood*. The *Hood* was the largest pre-war warship and its loss as a result of this encounter with the *Bismarck* in May 1941 was a severe blow to British morale.**

from the United States. It is too much to expect a belligerent not to accept the help of a neutral if he can get it.

The co-operation of the Americans, the departure of U-Boats to the Mediterranean, and the increasing efficiency of Coastal Command, all combined to reduce sinkings during the last three months of 1941.

In November the United States, though then still neutral, sent two battleships and two cruisers to Iceland to help watch the northern exits to the Atlantic. Losses in the Mediterranean and the menace of approaching war with Japan made this move doubly welcome.

In December a new type of warship came into the service. This was the escort carrier. The *Audacity*, which helped to fight convoy HG 76 through from Gibraltar, proved her worth in closing the 'air gap' before she was sunk. Just as the Allies seemed to be getting the upper hand in the Atlantic, the Japanese struck in the Far East. In the ensuing disasters shipping losses were heavy. Nor did the fact that America was now in the war ease the situation in the Atlantic. Quite the contrary. The Americans were compelled after Pearl Harbor to send many of their best ships to the Pacific. Dönitz's submarines had a field day from January to April 1942 off the eastern seaboard of the United States against unescorted merchantmen sailing singly as if in time of peace. Many of the ships lost were tankers which the Allies could ill afford to lose. The Americans were slow to profit by the hard-won experience of their Allies and adopt the convoy system. They had shown themselves generous friends. It is gratifying to be able to record that the British were able in some measure to respond in kind. 'At the height of the onslaught against shipping in the western hemisphere we lent two dozen anti-submarine trawlers to the Americans, we released two of our mid-ocean Atlantic groups to strengthen the escorts on the American eastern seaboard, we offered to turn over ten corvettes to the United States Navy, and we transferred an experienced squadron of Coastal Command aircraft to the west side of the Atlantic,' (Roskill).

In the first six months of 1942 U-Boats sank 585 merchantmen – over three million tons of shipping. The best way to help the Royal Navy surmount this crisis would have been to strengthen Coastal Command at the expense of the bombing offensive against Germany, which – as we now know – had had very disappointing results thus far. However, the strategic views of 'Bomber Harris' carried a good deal of weight at this period, and when the matter was referred to the Prime Minister a compromise was made. Coastal Command was to be strengthened gradually, but there was to be no diminution in the bombing of Germany. Another year was to pass, and countless ships were to be sunk, before Coastal Command had the long-range aircraft needed to play a really decisive part. Although the Navy remained starved of air cover, it must not be assumed that the compromise made was unjustified.

But the tide of Axis successes was reaching its highwater mark, and by the autumn of 1942 the Allied navies had at last gained the upper hand at sea, though in 1942 the loss of Allied ships was the heaviest of the whole war: 1,664 ships (7,790,697 tons), of which 1,160 were sunk by U-Boats. But the bald summary of losses is as cold as the winter Atlantic, and recalls nothing of the hardships of countless seamen who made that long, slow voyage time and again, waiting for the inevitable torpedo, the shuddering shock running through their stricken ship, the violent explosion, the screams of scalded shipmates trapped in the engine-room: flung about like dolls, staggering in the dark, trying to launch boats suspended at a crazy angle, as their ship foundered beneath them, taking its dreadful noises with her into the deep. And then long hours in the midnight sea hoping some corvette might see the little red lights bobbing in the water.

Not that the U-Boats had it all their own way. Of 1,162 commissioned during the war 785 were sunk, mainly by surface ships (246) and shore based aircraft (245). To be attacked by a group of efficient destroyers was an experience to bring the sweat to the brow of the most stolid Teuton – the sudden desperate crash dive, instruments shattering as depth-charges exploded near, water trickling through as the bulkhead supports buckled at 100 fathoms. In the gloom of the emergency lighting many a crew waited in its steel coffin for an end as terrible as any it had meted out.

Below: **The *Bismarck* was the sistership of the *Tirpitz*. She was completed at the end of 1940 and saw limited action before being sunk in May 1941.**

13 FROM PEARL HARBOR TO SINGAPORE

'We, by the grace of heaven, Emperor of Japan, seated on the Throne of a line unbroken for ages eternal, enjoin upon ye, Our loyal and brave subjects:
We hereby declare war on the United States of America and the British Empire. The men and officers of Our Army and Navy shall do their utmost in prosecuting the war, Our public servants of various departments shall perform faithfully and diligently their appointed tasks, and all other subjects of Ours shall pursue their respective duties; the entire nation with a united will shall mobilize their total strength so that nothing will miscarry in the attainment of our war aims.'

Imperial Rescript: the 8th day of the 12th month of the 16th year of Shava

The Japanese did not await this pronouncement before beginning their war in a somewhat less formal way. Like their Nazi and Fascist allies they struck the first blow without warning.

At dawn on 7 December 1941 350 Japanese planes flew off from their carriers and attacked the US Pacific Fleet in Pearl Harbor, on the Hawaiian island of Oahu. They also attacked the Army Air Force planes on Hickham and Wheeler airfields. For the loss of 29 planes and five midget submarines they had sunk three battleships, capsized another and damaged four more. In addition 3 light cruisers and 3 destroyers, among other vessels were seriously damaged. The Americans lost 188 planes and suffered 3,389 casualties. All this was achieved within half an hour, most of it within 10 or 15 minutes. The Japanese concentrated on the aircraft first, and then on the 'sitting ducks' in Battleship Row.

'The bursting bombs, the rattle of the enemy machine-guns, and the red ball insignia on the wings were the first intimation of war that anyone had at Wheeler. In a few moments the parked aircraft, many with their fuel tanks filled, were blazing; great clouds of oily smoke were rolling up on the still air to obscure everything and hamper the frantic efforts to pull the planes apart and get them armed.'

The Americans managed to get about a dozen aircraft into the air, but out of 126 modern or fairly modern fighters on the field only 43 survived the attack. At Hickham Field it was the same story. Within five minutes of the beginning of the attack the place was a shambles.

The Pacific Fleet lying at anchor off Fort Island received equally short shrift.

'Every one of the five outboard battleships took one or more torpedo hits in the first five minutes, and the two inboard ships, *Maryland* and *Tennessee*, were hit by bombs.'

Only one thing marred for the Japanese their tactical success at Pearl Harbor; they neither damaged nor sank a single carrier, for the simple reason that they were out on an exercise. And it was the carrier, not the battleship, that was to be the vital warship of the Pacific War, for deprived of their battleships the Americans made a virtue of necessity and fought a new kind of war.

From the point of view of grand strategy Pearl Harbor was a disastrous blunder. The Americans could take hard knocks, but they did not care to be the victims of low cunning. They had not wanted war. However anxious Roosevelt may have been to aid the victims of Nazi and Fascist aggression, they did not wish to become involved. The aftermath of isolation was still strong. But now at a blow the Japanese put the nation right behind their President, and that farseeing statesman lost no time in denouncing 7 December as 'a date which will live in infamy', and in declaring that the war was all one, whether against the Japanese or against Hitler and Mussolini. Congress voted for war against Japan without a single speech or one dissentient voice.

Far away in Berlin the German Foreign Minister, von Ribbentrop, was jubilant. Mussolini too was happy. Count Ciano, more intelligent than either, saw that America would now enter the European conflict, which would be so long that she would be able to bring all her potential forces to bear. On 11 December Germany and Italy declared war on the United States, which returned the compliment.

Latin America was thoroughly aroused by these events, and within the next few days Costa Rica, the Dominican Republic, Haiti, Honduras, Nicaragua, El Salvador, Cuba, Guatemala and Panama all declared war on the Axis.

It is no more than realistic to recognize that 7 December 1941 was one of the most significant days in British history: the day that put the United States squarely in the war as an ally. The war had now been going on for more than two years, years during which Britain had won few enough victories to set off against a multitude of German triumphs. It is true that the British had

Top: **Mitsubishi Zero fighters warm up prior to take-off as part of the air strike on Pearl Harbor.**

Above: **The climax of the attack as smoke rises mainly from Battleship Row and also from the Navy Yards. By 10.00 a.m. the attack was over and the Japanese aircraft had sunk 18 warships, destroyed 188 aircraft and killed or wounded 3389 sailors.**

Below: **This Japanese Val dive-bomber was shot down during the Pearl Harbor attack and later salvaged by US naval forces.**

Above: Three sailors stationed in Chicago read a newspaper extra edition announcing the news of the Pearl Harbor attack.

Left: Battleship Row and Ford Island under attack.

Below: The damage suffered by the USS *Downes, Cassin* and *Pennsylvania.* The Japanese aircraft did not catch the American aircraft carriers, which were out on exercise.

Above: **The cover of a Japanese magazine showing a helmet, rifle and US flag left behind in the Philippines following the US surrender.**

Above: **General Masaharu Homma, Commander of the Japanese forces invading the Philippines, comes ashore at Santiago in Lingayen Bay on 24 December 1941.**

always been confident of ultimate victory; this conviction was certainly an asset but it was not altogether logical. And it is true that Hitler had dealt himself a deadly blow on the day he invaded Russia. But now by their attack on Pearl Harbor the Japanese ranged the most powerful of all possible allies on the British side. Whatever disasters lay in store – and there were plenty – the most pessimistic of Britons could no longer suppose that the Allies could lose.

But the way ahead was still a long one, and the United States, like Britain, was to pay a sorry price for years of pacifism and isolationism.

It is in no sense to excuse the conduct of the Japanese that one attempts to explain the causes that led them to make war. In the days before 1853, when Admiral Perry forcibly awoke Japan from her long sleep of isolation, that country was self supporting. In the process of Westernization she rapidly became industrialized and as swiftly became aware of her basic lack of economic resources. It may be remarked that a similar realization was coming to the Germans at much the same time.

Japan had set out on her empire-building course during the last quarter of the nineteenth century, when she acquired the Kurile, Bonin, Ryukyu and Volcano islands. Her war with China (1894–95) gave her Formosa, the Pescadores and, temporarily, Port Arthur, which Russia, Germany and France soon compelled her to relinquish. She recovered it as a result of the Russo-Japanese war, when she also won control of Korea, which she annexed in 1910, and the southern half of the island of Sakhalin. She joined the Allies in the Great War and in 1919 was granted a mandate over the Marianas, Caroline and Marshall Islands, with the exception of Guam.

Japan was hard hit by the slump of 1929, and it was partly to distract her peoples' attention from home affairs that in 1931 she invaded Manchuria, which, as Manchukuo, she added to her empire. Perhaps she thought of this as a short cut to prosperity. However that may be, it provoked the antagonism of China.

Japan, like Hitler's Germany, sought *Lebensraum* – 'The Greater East Asia Co-Prosperity Sphere'. On 7 July 1937 she invaded China. The war was long and bloody but indecisive. China was financed by the United States and also received supplies through the ports of Indo-China and via the Burma Road from Lashio to Chungking. On 21 July 1941 Vichy France, unable to protect Indo-China, agreed to its temporary occupation by Japan. Roosevelt reacted swiftly by freezing Japanese assets in the USA, some £33,000,000. Great Britain followed suit, and put an end to her commercial treaties with Japan. The Netherlands, though practically powerless to defend her Far Eastern empire, acted with America and Britain.

General Fuller sees this as 'a declaration of economic war', and 'the actual opening of the struggle', but it is more realistic to date this from the invasion of China in 1937, if not from the wanton aggression against Manchuria in 1931.

Japan now considered that she was faced with either war or economic ruin. When in October 1941 Prince Konoye's cabinet, which had favoured agreement with the United States, resigned, the new government of General Tojo determined to cut the Gordian Knot. Unfortunately for her Japan did not appreciate that by taking the initiative she was uniting America against her. But it is not easy to see how she could have provoked Roosevelt, far less Churchill, into attacking *her*.

Below: **Japanese troops celebrate at the Fall of Bataan.**

In the short term Japan enjoyed certain advantages, for although she was taking on the world's two greatest maritime and industrial powers, and although their homelands were virtually beyond her reach, many of their possessions were extremely vulnerable.

The strength of the Japanese Navy lay in its carrier fleet. Vice-Admiral Nagumo had under his command ten fast modern carriers, each carrying about 75 aircraft. Japan's early successes were in large measure due to her superiority at sea and in the air.

It had been calculated that she had 2,625 aircraft, integrated with her navy and army, and earmarked for operations:

Malaya	700
Philippines	475
China	150
Manchuria (in reserve)	450
Japan	325
Marshall Islands	50
Pearl Harbor raid	400
Fleet (seaplanes)	75
	2,625

Against this the Allies had in the Far East only 1,290 planes, many of them obsolete, widely scattered and lacking unified control.

US Navy and Army Air Forces	
Philippines	182
Wake	12
Midway	12
Hawaii	387
Royal Netherlands East Indies Af	
East Indies	200
RAF	
Malaya	332
Royal Australian Af	
Australia, Solomons and Malaya	165
	1,290

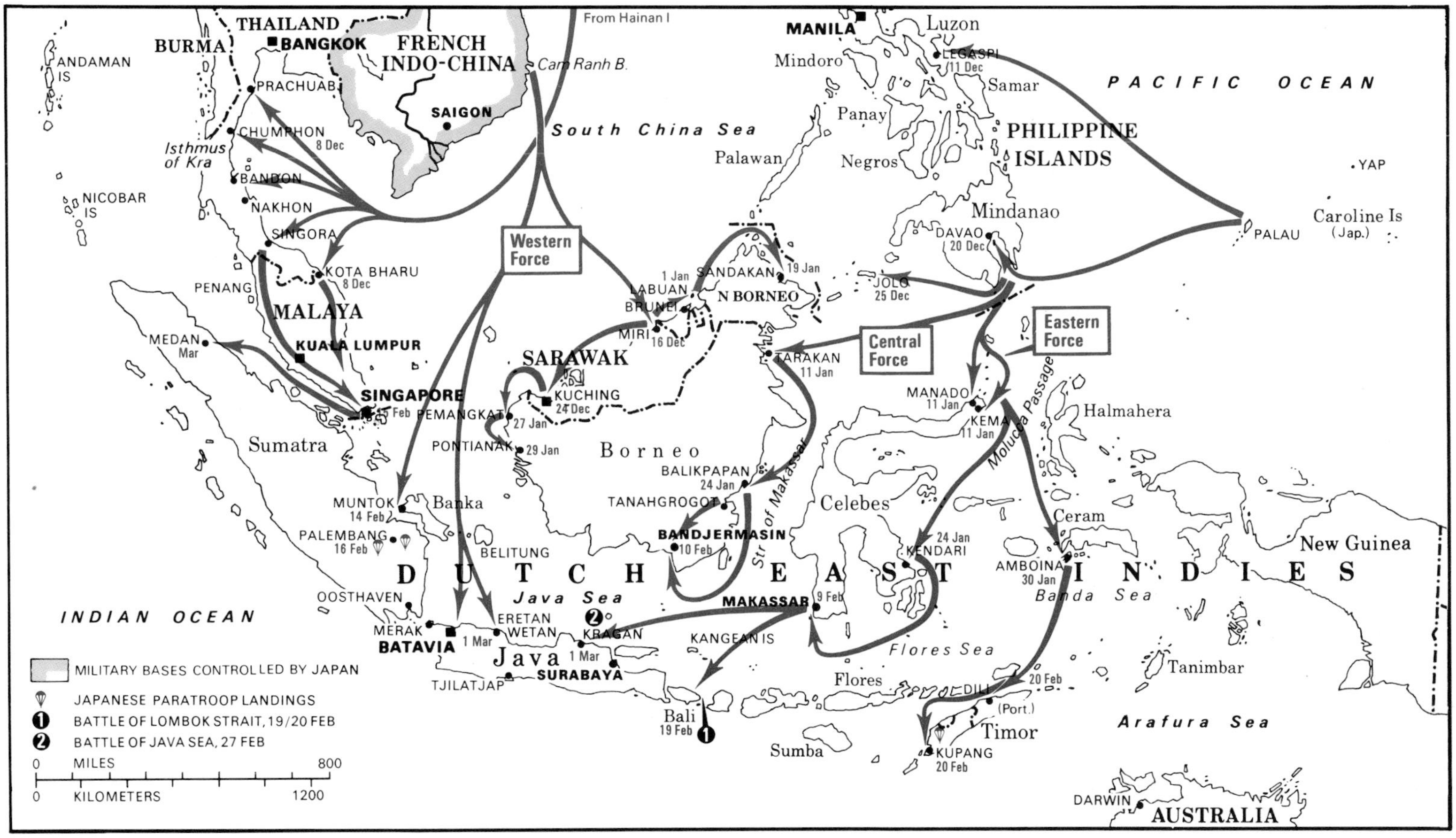

MILITARY BASES CONTROLLED BY JAPAN

JAPANESE PARATROOP LANDINGS

1 BATTLE OF LOMBOK STRAIT, 19/20 FEB

2 BATTLE OF JAVA SEA, 27 FEB

0 MILES 800

0 KILOMETERS 1200

The Japanese were swift to exploit their success at Pearl Harbor. In the Central Pacific they overwhelmed the small US garrison of Guam (10 December) and on 23 December, after one bloody repulse (11 December) and a long and heavy bombardment, invaded Wake Island, where some 500 United States Marines under Major James Devereux put up a magnificent resistance.

Next the Japanese struck at the Philippines, where General Douglas MacArthur was in command. MacArthur, who had been Chief of the US Army Staff, had no illusions as to the likelihood of war with Japan, and had done all that lay in his power to prepare his command. He had at his disposal about 200 aircraft, including 35 Flying Fortresses, 19,000 American troops and 11,000 Philippine Scouts. The newly-raised Philippine Army, which was as yet of little military value, numbered about 160,000.

The 7,083 islands of the Philippine Archipelago had been annexed by the United States after Admiral Dewey's victory over the Spanish Fleet in Manila Bay during the Spanish-American War (1898). The biggest islands are Luzon and Mindanao. The Americans had promised to give independence to this considerable part of their empire by 1946.

The preliminary air bombardment destroyed many of the American planes. On 10 December the Japanese began to land on the north coast of Luzon, following up with yet another landing on the east coast.

On 27 December General MacArthur reported to Washington:

'Enemy penetration in the Philippines resulted from out of weakness in the sea and in the air. Surface elements of the Asiatic Fleet were withdrawn and the effect of submarines has been negligible. Lack of airfields for modern planes prevented defensive dispersion and lack of pursuit planes permitted unhindered day bombardment. The enemy has had utter freedom of naval and air movements.'

On the same day Manila was declared an open city. This did not save it from a destructive air bombardment which lasted two days. On 2 January the Japanese occupied the city and the naval base of Cavite.

Below left: **RAF Brewster Buffalo aircraft at Sembawang Airfield in Singapore, November 1941.**

Below: **The Japanese advance through a Malayan rubber plantation.**

Above: **The British never expected the Japanese to advance as rapidly as they did. The Japanese used bicycles to negotiate difficult terrain in Malaya.**

In January MacArthur now withdrew some 40,000 men into the Bataan Peninsula where he had always intended to make his last stand. Bataan, which is about 25 miles long by 20 miles wide, juts out from Luzon. The Americans attempted to supply MacArthur by blockade-runners, but none got through. In February he was ordered to Australia, and much against his will went to take over the South-West Pacific Area. The Japanese broke through the Bataan position on 31 March and on 9 April 35,000 Americans laid down their arms. The prisoners were treated with bestial cruelty in the notorious death march that followed. Lieutenant-General Jonathan Wainwright held out in the old Spanish island fortress of Corregidor until 6 May, denying the enemy the use of Manila Bay, one of the best natural harbours in the East.

By their conquest of the Philippines the Japanese had destroyed an army of at least 90,000 men.

Meanwhile on 8 December the Japanese had landed in Malaya where it must be said the British resistance lacked the epic quality of the American defence of the Philippines. There were several reasons for this. Nobody need be surprised if the British lacked a leader of the calibre of MacArthur. In the early years of the war Britain had needed her best generals in Europe and the Middle East. The same applies to her troops, for few regular battalions could be spared for Malaya. The Americans, on the other hand, attached more importance to the Japanese menace than to the war in Europe, and had deployed good troops there.

The morale of the civilian population was an important factor. The population of 5,250,000 was Malayan, Chinese and Indian. Of the 700,000 inhabitants of Singapore itself 75 per cent were Chinese. The Malayans resented the presence of the Chinese and blamed the British for allowing them to establish themselves in their country. The people of the Philippines knew that they were due to become independent in 1946. Malayan independence lay far in the future. But in fact, in the early days of the campaign, especially at Penang, the native population, contrary to popular belief, stood up fairly well to merciless air bombardment, although it caused complete confusion. To be honest the morale of the white population was not altogether satisfactory. The root of the trouble was that they thought that, wherever else World War II went, it would keep away from Singapore. Men whose main concern in life was the production, in an enervating climate, of tin and rubber were not anxious to assume other responsibilities. Nevertheless one observer, writing on 13 December, recorded: 'Raffles Hotel still has dancing every night, but there are not as many dancers.

A good deal of the apathy about war has gone. In any event it is true that the certainty that war would not come to Singapore has disappeared.'

The training of the troops was vitiated by the pre-war attitude of all too many commanders, who considered that thick jungle and mangrove swamp would be 'Out of Bounds'. With the single exception of the 2nd Battalion of the Argyll and Sutherland Highlanders, none of the garrison were trained in jungle warfare. The Japanese are not accustomed by nature to work in jungle: but they had trained for it.

Even more important was the fact that the defenders were not steeled by their training against the horrors of air attack. The fate of the French in 1940 should have given the High Command notice of this problem. Later in the war German morale stood up to the complete loss of air cover. At the minor tactical level, the Japanese, travelling light, were very mobile, while the British, burdened with all the paraphernalia of European warfare, including steel helmets and gas-masks, were loaded like donkeys.

When tension in the Far East began to grow, Mr Churchill and his advisers, with admirable prescience, sent out the new battleship *Prince of Wales* and the battle-cruiser *Repulse* to strengthen our forces there. Unhappily there was no aircraft carrier available to support them. At the very outset of the campaign these two fine ships, venturing on a sortie in which for various reasons they did not have the support of shore-based aircraft, were sunk by Japanese planes from the neighbourhood of Saigon. Their daring commander, Vice-Admiral Tom Phillips, went down with his ship. It is easy to say that unwise risks were taken. The fact is that nothing in their experience against the Germans prepared the officers of the Royal Navy for the truly astonishing skill of the Japanese pilots. But by 1942 it should have been clear that capital ships should only venture within range of enemy air power with a proper air screen. A calculated risk led to unprecedented catastrophe. Far away in Britain it seemed one of the most unnerving events of a war which had not lacked black moments.

In Malaya the effect on morale was deadly. Ian Morrison writes:

'I still remember the chill sense of calamity which was caused by the loss of these two ships. It was worse than calamity. It was calamity that had the premonition of further calamity. . . . Blown clean away at one fell swoop was one of the main pillars on which our sense of security rested. Nor was our despondency in any way mitigated by Mr Duff Cooper's Churchillian heroics and well-intentioned attempt to reconcile people in Singapore to the news.'

The well-trained Japanese pushed down Malaya, seconding their thrusts with a series of amphibious landings to outflank each successive position. Their air superiority more than made up for their lack of numbers on the ground. As time went on even a 250-lb bomb could cause panic in towns with a dismayed Asiatic population and no proper Air Raid Precautions.

There was a short stand at Kuala Lumpur, but the place fell on 10 January. The 18th (British) Division, diverted from the Middle East while on the high seas, arrived when Singapore was already doomed. The fortifications and batteries on which £60,000,000 had been spent were sited, not for all-round defence, but to resist sea-borne attack. The naval and RAF bases were on the north of the Island. British and American naval losses made supply practically impossible.

On 8 February, after bombardment, the Japanese crossed the straits and established a bridgehead, from which a British counter-attack failed to dislodge them. Pushing on, the enemy seized the reservoirs in the centre of the island, and on 15 February Lieutenant-General A. E. Percival surrendered the survivors of his 85,000 British, Australian and Indian troops, by far the largest British army ever to lay down its arms.

In Britain's long military annals there is no more dismal chapter than the fall of Singapore. It is a sort of anthology of all that is worst in British military history. It is a tale of complacency, unpreparedness, and weakness, relieved only by isolated tactical successes and the firmness of a handful of units and individuals. Defeat is something not unknown in the history of any martial race. But seldom indeed has an army capitulated to one which it actually outnumbered. Lieutenant-General Yamashita and his men had, from the tactical point of view, literally run rings round the defenders. Once more in this war the better balanced force had won. Yamashita may have had fewer soldiers, but he had air and sea power.

But when all is said and done, it is probably no exaggeration to say that the one thing that could have saved Malaya was an adequate fighter force. Had the defence disposed of, say, 300 fighters, it may be doubted whether the Japanese landings would have succeeded in the first place.

The Japanese now turned their attention to Java. The Netherlands East Indies were garrisoned by 120,000 European and Indonesian troops, but without naval and air support they were to be an easy prey.

The Allies had hastily scraped together a heterogeneous squadron, the Combined Striking Force, of five cruisers and nine destroyers, under a Dutch Rear-Admiral, K. W. F. N. Doorman. The squadron had had no opportunity to train together and had no properly co-ordinated communications system, or secure base. All had been working for a long period under severe strain and Doorman considered that they had reached the limit of their endurance.

On the afternoon of 27 February Doorman attacked a Japanese force of four modernized cruisers and 14 destroyers north of Surabaya. The fighting was indecisive, though the *Exeter* was hit and the *Kortenaer* blown up. About 9 p.m. the *Jupiter* was mined and in a second encounter about 10.30 p.m. the flagship *De Ruyter* and *Java* were both torpedoed. The gallant Doorman went down with his ship.

Early next morning *Houston* and *Perth*, rounding a headland, suddenly came upon a line of anchored Japanese transports. They attacked at point-blank range sinking two and damaging others before Admiral Kurita came on the scene with three cruisers and nine destroyers and, after a hard fight, sank them both.

The damaged *Exeter* put to sea on the evening of the 28th, escorted by the *Encounter* and *Pope*. Sighted by aircraft, they were intercepted the next day by four heavy cruisers and three destroyers. The *Exeter*, of River Plate fame, fought well for an hour and a half before she was torpedoed. Both the destroyers were sunk as well.

Of the Allied ships engaged in the Battle of the Java Sea, only four American destroyers survived. They reached Freemantle, Western Australia, on 4 March. Despite their heavy losses in men and ships the Allies had only delayed the invasion of Java for 24 hours.

On the night of 28 February the Japanese effected three landings on the north coast of Java. The Dutch, who had generously sent their aircraft to help in the defence of Malaya, held out as best they could with the aid of small British and American forces. Once again mere numbers counted for little against the balanced force. On 9 March, 98,000 men surrendered at Bandung. The Japanese proceeded to mop up the other islands at their leisure, but in Sumatra and elsewhere, as in the Philippines, small bands of stout-hearted men hung on in the hills and forests.

The Japanese had now built up a brilliant strategic situation. Malaya, Java, Sumatra, Bali, Sumba and Timor formed their outpost line. It appears to have been their intention to consolidate their position in Burma, Siam, Malaya, China and the East Indies. Although it was open to them to thrust outwards against Australia or India, and although to the Allies both these offensives seemed imminent, it does not now appear that the Japanese originally had any such intentions.

The first six months of their war had gone so well for the Japanese that they were seriously misled as to its future course. The victories of their Nazi allies and their contempt for democracy alike led them to undervalue their enemies. Russia seemed unlikely to survive; Britain, on the defensive against Germany, could do Japan no harm; America, crippled by Pearl Harbor and politically decadent, would eventually come to terms.

But grave though the situation was, the Americans were already striking back. Admiral Chester W. Nimitz, who had succeeded Admiral Kimmel on 31 December 1941, had lost no time in restoring the morale of his command.

'He had the prudence to wait through a lean period; to do nothing rash for the sake of doing something. He had the capacity to organize both a fleet and a vast theater, the tact to deal with sister services and Allied commands, the leadership to weld his own subordinates into a great fighting team, the courage to take necessary risks, and the wisdom to select, from a variety of intelligence and opinions, the correct strategy to defeat Japan.'

Above: **The Japanese troops entered Kuala Lumpur on 11 January 1942 and found that the bulk of the British forces had withdrawn south of the Muar River.**

Nimitz saw that for the time being hit-and-run raids, similar to those that the British were making on the coasts of Europe, were the only form of offensive action he could take. In the Pacific the aircraft carrier took the place of the commando. On 1 February 1942 Admiral Halsey's group, built up round the carrier *Enterprise*, attacked Kwajalein in the Marshall Islands, and besides killing the Japanese commander sank a transport and damaged nine other vessels.

Admiral Wilson Brown's *Lexington* group raided Rabaul and brought on an air battle in which the Americans won the upper hand (20 February). On 10 March this force, with the *Yorktown* added, raided Lae and Salamaua on the North coast of Papua.

But the raid which really puzzled the Japanese came on 18 April, when Lieutenant-Colonel James H. Doolittle and 16 B-25 Mitchells flew 668 miles from the carrier *Hornet*, bombed Tokyo, and flew on to land in China. The actual damage inflicted was not very great, but the effect on American morale was tonic. Moreover the Japanese now allotted hundreds of planes to the defence of Tokyo, for they could not guess where the planes had flown from. President Roosevelt's announcement that the aircraft had come from Shangri-La was unhelpful.

Below right: **The official surrender of Singapore and Malaya.**

Below: **The Japanese march triumphantly into Singapore after the British surrender on 15 February.**

14 RETREAT IN BURMA

'We took a hell of a beating.'
Lieutenant-General Joseph W. ('Vinegar Joe') Stilwell

On 16 January the Japanese invaded Burma, and by mid-May they had taken Rangoon (9 March), cut the Burma Road (29 April) and driven the Allies across the Chindwin to the borders of India. The wonder is not that the Japanese won, but that the Allies were not utterly destroyed.

The defenders laboured under practically every possible disadvantage. The Japanese had command of both sea and air. When the invasion began there were only five RAF squadrons in Burma and they were equipped with the obsolete Buffalo fighter. The morale of the troops suffered gravely in consequence of the lack of air cover, and the commanders were hampered by lack of air reconnaissance. The shortage of artillery and transport, and their inexperience in jungle warfare, contributed to this sad state of affairs. The almost total lack of reinforcements was most discouraging.

The invasion of Burma offered the Japanese three possibilities. Firstly the capture of Rangoon, the capital; secondly the cutting of the Burma Road by which the Allies were sending

Above: Japanese troops enter the city of Moulmein, at the mouth of the Salween, on 30 January 1942.

Above right: The Japanese take the oilfields at Yenangyaung.

Below: The British had hoped that the rivers of Burma would hold up the Japanese advance, but the Japanese had carried with them the materials necessary to make temporary bridges.

Above: **An improvised bridge allows Japanese tanks to advance up the Burmese coast.**

Above left: **The Japanese used bicycles to speed up their advance over the uneven terrain in Burma.**

Left: **Japanese artillery units pound Burmese oilfields. The loss of these oilfields and of land access to China was a great blow.**

Above right: **Soldiers of the Japanese Fifteenth Army cross the Chindwin.**

supplies to China; and thirdly the opportunity, if all went well, to push on and invade India. Shortly before the invasion began, General Sir Archibald Wavell, Commander-in-Chief, India, had sent his Chief of Staff, Lt.-General T. J. Hutton to take command. The task he set him was to defend Burma, and particularly Rangoon, and to make plans for offensive operations against Siam. Hutton considered that Rangoon was the key to Burma, since it was his only adequate channel of supply, for as General Fuller has pointed out, the British had been in Burma for over 100 years but 'so little attention had they paid to its strategic defence that but three mule tracks – frequently impassable during the monsoon – traversed the Indo-Burmese frontier.'

Even so, Hutton realized how vulnerable Rangoon was, and with commendable foresight set up a number of supply depots in Upper Burma so that if the worst came to the worst his army could retreat into Assam. He decided that he could only defend Burma by blocking the routes from Siam, but for this purpose his forces were totally inadequate, since he had at his disposal only two divisions, 17th Indian and 1st Burma. The former was deployed initially on a front of 400 miles! Wavell had arranged with Generalissimo Chiang Kai-shek for the assistance of the Fifth and Sixth Chinese Armies, under General Lo-Cho-Ying, and the American General Stilwell. These Chinese armies (equivalent to a European corps) consisted of veteran troops, but their organization was totally different.

The Japanese crossed the frontier on 15 January and compelled the British to withdraw. The defenders fought delaying actions on the Salween and the Bilin, before making a serious stand on the Sittang (17–19 February)

where the 17th Indian Division was attacked in front and on the flank by two Japanese Divisions, and lost heavily, many men being cut off on the wrong side of the river when the bridge was prematurely blown. The Japanese had quickly captured airfields from which they could give fighter cover to their bombers attacking Rangoon. General Wavell, partly because of his successes against the Italians in North Africa, had a strong belief in offensive action. He also underrated the Japanese, whom he considered to be second-rate troops. The Viceroy of India, the Marquis of Linlithgow, now stuck his oar in. Though in New Delhi he was necessarily remote from the fighting in Burma, he had come to the conclusion that uninspired leadership at the top accounted for the poor performance of the troops, and informed the Prime Minister of his view. In consequence Churchill sent General Sir Harold Alexander to take over the command.

On 1 March Wavell held a conference with the Governor of Burma, Sir Reginald Dorman-Smith, and General Hutton, and decided that every effort must be made to hold the capital. The Chinese were advancing on Toungoo, 7th Armoured Brigade and other reinforcements were on their way by sea. Alexander arrived in Rangoon on 5 March and immediately decided to evacuate the city. It was none too soon, and the British troops only got clear because the Japanese removed a vital road-block – an unaccountable tactical error. The Governor's optimistic prophecy that the Burmese would rise up in their wrath and fight the invaders had proved nonsense. The Burmese were a peace-loving people. Most European civilians regarded the war as an unwarrantable interference with the comfortable routine of their lives. Conditions in Rangoon, which had been heavily bombed, became chaotic, partly as the result of the decision of an officer of the Indian Civil Service to release the occupants of jails and institutions, thereby leaving the city a prey to 5,000 convicts and an assortment of lunatics and lepers.

It was now decided to form the British troops in Burma into a corps, and the command of this formation was given to Lieutenant-General W. Slim who arrived at Prome on 13 March. Every kind of problem confronted him. Intelli-

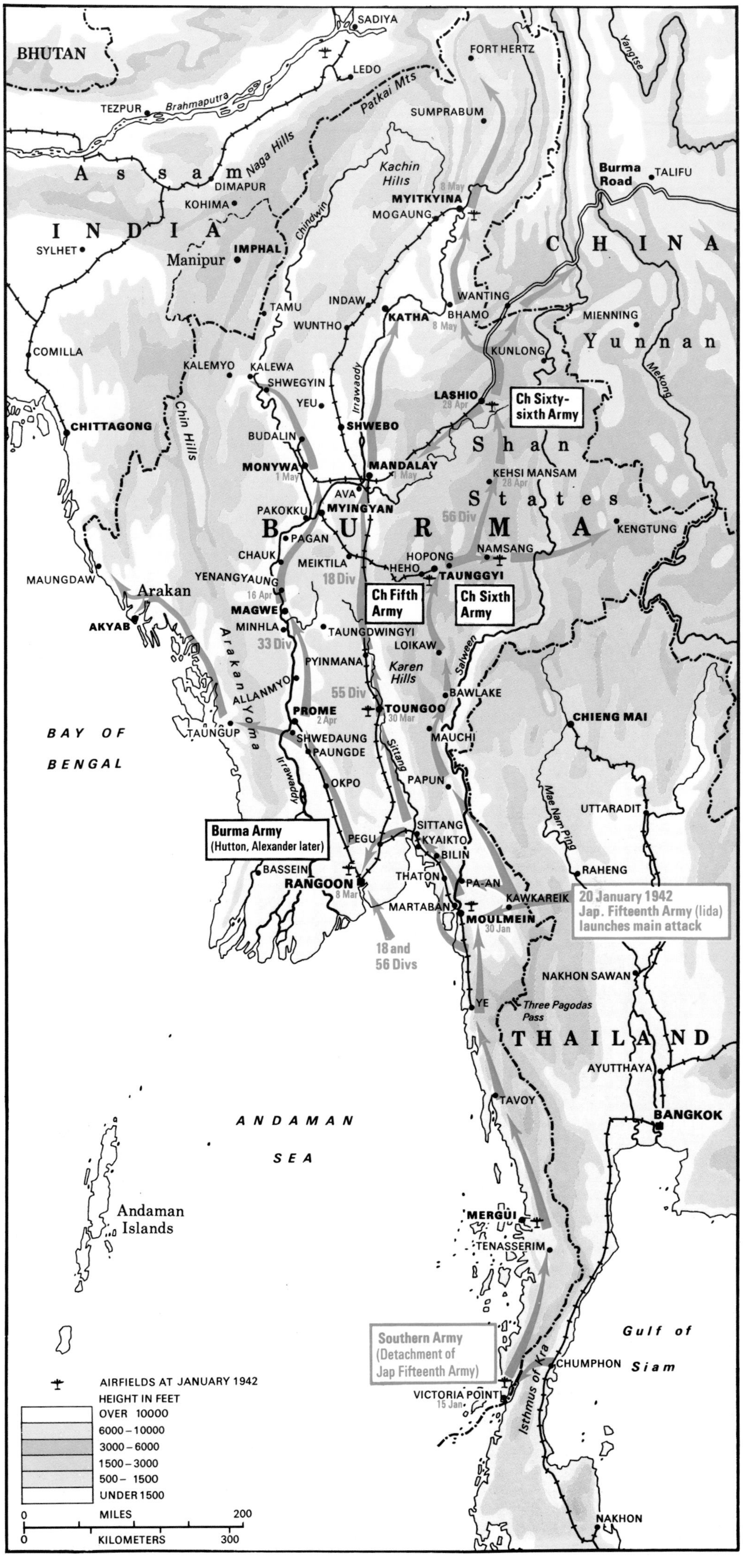

Ch Sixty-sixth Army
Ch Fifth Army
Ch Sixth Army
Burma Army (Hutton, Alexander later)
20 January 1942 Jap. Fifteenth Army (Iida) launches main attack
Southern Army (Detachment of Jap Fifteenth Army)

AIRFIELDS AT JANUARY 1942
HEIGHT IN FEET
OVER 10000
6000–10000
3000–6000
1500–3000
500–1500
UNDER 1500
MILES 0 200
KILOMETERS 0 300

gence was extremely bad; the population was unhelpful; his troops were neither trained nor equipped for jungle warfare; his units were below strength and sickness was on the increase. His two divisions were 80 miles apart. Worst of all, morale, not only in the Burmese units, was shaken. This is how Slim saw the situation when he took over:

> 'The troops had fought well, but they had had no success. Constant retreats, the bogy of the road-block, the loss of Singapore and Rangoon, and the stories of Japanese supermen in the jungle, combined with the obvious shortages of every kind, could not fail to depress morale. At this stage, the effects of the Sittang disaster on the fighting troops were evident but not irremediable, but morale in the administrative areas in our rear did not impress me as good. There were a lot of badly shaken people about.'

Above: **Japanese soldier guards a railway line to ensure communications.**

Right: **Advancing Japanese troops prepare to cross the Chindwin.**

The new commander set about putting matters right.

Despite its losses 17th Division was not prepared to let the Japanese have things all their own way. On 17 March Major Calvert with a party of commando men and Royal Marines made a bold river raid on the Irrawaddy port of Henzada and cut up a force of dissident Burmese under Japanese officers. At about the same time the 1st Gloucesters surprised and routed a Japanese battalion billeted at Letpadan, 80 miles south of Prome, driving it into the jungle and inflicting heavy casualties. These flashes of spirit gave promise of better days to come.

Thus far, against heavy odds, the Allied Air Force in Burma had done well, having destroyed 291 Japanese planes for a loss of 97. But now the Japanese, using about 250 planes, made concentrated attacks on the airfields of Magwe (21 March) and Akyab (23 and 27 March), as a result of which the RAF was driven out of the country. The cities of Burma – Mandalay, Pegu, Prome, Meiktila, Lashio-crumbled in ruins as the Japanese pattern-bombed them at their leisure. On 24 March the Japanese attacked the Chinese Fifth Army at Toungoo on the Sittang. The 200th Division defended itself well, but Stilwell could not induce the reserves to counter-attack. At Stilwell's request Alexander agreed (28 March) to attack on the Irrawaddy front in order to relieve pressure on the Chinese. This led to confused fighting around Shwedaung in which a striking force from 17th Division was cut off for a time, losing many vehicles.

The Chinese 200th Division managed to extricate itself from Toungoo on 30 March. The loss of the place uncovered the British left and made it practically impossible to hold Prome, which was evacuated (1 April). By the end of April the Japanese had completed the conquest of central Burma. On the 29th they overran Lashio, the terminus of the Burma road. Thus they had cut the only land route to China, which was now completely blockaded.

On the 30th the British withdrew across the Irrawaddy and at midnight blew up the Ava bridge. Still hard-pressed, the Burma Corps crossed the Chindwin at Kalewa, losing its tanks and much of its transport. There is no space here to recount the story of the rearguard action (10 May), which Field Marshal Slim has told so well. It must, however, be recorded that even in those days of adversity some of the troops, among them 1/7 Gurkhas and 7th Armoured Brigade, still had some fight left in them. The survivors of the corps were back across the river, but very little of its equipment remained. What was left of the Fifth Chinese Army was retreating to the north. By 20 May all Burma was in the hands of the Japanese.

Right: **Burmese women give water to their new masters.**

Below: **Prime Minister Tojo (centre) with the heads of the Japanese puppet regimes in South-East Asia. Far left is U Ba Maw, the Prime Minister of Burma during the Japanese occupation.**

15 THE DESERT, 1942

'Well, Freddie, you chaps seem to have been making a bit of a mess of things. Now what's the form? . . . I was only told I was coming out here in London forty-eight hours ago, but I have been doing a lot of thinking since. Yesterday I spent at GHQ, Cairo, and worked out with Harding how I want this Army organized. You'll never win a campaign as it is at the moment.'

General B. L. Montgomery to Brigadier F. de Guingand, 13 August 1942

In the desert the year 1942 opened with a lull of four months, while both sides prepared for another bout. Rommel's aim was to recapture Tobruk and drive the British back into Egypt. The British intended to win back Cyrenaica so as to re-establish the airfields without which they could not cover convoys from Egypt to Malta. Auchinleck was under pressure from London to attack in mid-May, but did not think much of the prospects, for he had lost two Australian divisions, the British 70th Division and 7th Armoured Brigade which, with squadrons of the Desert Air Force, had been sent to the Far East. From that quarter came nothing but tidings of woe – Corregidor, Singapore and Burma had fallen; India and Ceylon were threatened.

Auchinleck thought it might be better to send reinforcements to India and to remain on the defensive in Libya. This infuriated the Prime Minister, who was on the point of recalling Auchinleck and replacing him with Alexander. General Brooke, the CIGS, succeeded in dissuading him, but, in view of subsequent events, may well have made a mistake in doing so. Brooke in his diary gives an amusing glimpse of the Higher Direction of World War Two. He tells us that on 7 May he was on his way to a meeting of the Chiefs of Staff, when he was summoned to see the Prime Minister.

'That morning's meeting with Winston was typical of many others. He was a wonderful sight in bed, with large cigar in his mouth, hair somewhat ruffled, bed littered with papers and messages and alongside of the bed one of those large cuspidors to drop his cigar ends in. On this morning he was in one of his dangerous moods; the Auk had roused him properly with his proposed postponement of his attack. The situation required handling delicately; in his upset state he might well take some wild decision which it would then be very hard to wean him from.'

Be that as it may, the War Cabinet ordered Auchinleck to open an offensive in May or at the latest in early June. Auchinleck declined to visit London to discuss the situation, but, although relations between him and Churchill were strained thereafter, he retained his command. At this time the Eighth Army was holding the Gazala Line in front of its forward base at

Top: Ju 87 Stukas dive down over the desert.

Above: A patrol leaves the desert headquarters of the Long Range Desert Group in May 1942.

Above left: Field Marshal Erwin Rommel and his staff inspect an abandoned British tank in the Desert in April 1942.

Below: An Italian Caproni Ca315 blazes after having been destroyed by retreating troops.

Tobruk, which had now been connected with Alexandria by railway. The defensive positions were covered by extensive minefields and included several large strongpoints or 'boxes', sited for all-round defence, but too far apart to be mutually supporting. Rommel, who had watched these defences growing with some misgivings, determined to get his blow in first, before General Ritchie (Eighth Army) was strong enough to engage him frontally, while making a simultaneous 'left hook' at his lines of communications via Benghazi to Tripoli.

The British were relieved rather than otherwise when Rommel took the initiative. They would now be able to receive him on 'ground of their own choosing', instead of launching an offensive whose prospects they had always thought doubtful. Rommel advanced on 26 May and by nightfall it looked as if he was making a strong push towards the 1st Free French Brigade at Bir Hacheim. In the early hours of the 27th the mobile force of the Afrika Korps refuelled south of Bir Hacheim, planning to thrust NE towards Tobruk, Acroma and El Adem. General Carver describes this as 'a bold plan and half successful, catching Norrie's XXX Armoured Corps unbalanced, its three armoured brigades separated by considerable distances, and 7th Armoured Division, east of Bir Hacheim, still out of its battle positions.'

The British recovered quickly, however, and for a time things looked black for Rommel, who was east of the minefields, cut off from his base and short of ammunition. Captain Cyril Falls has an illuminating passage on what followed:

'A fierce armoured battle developed in this region. The enemy had meanwhile cut gaps through the minefields of the main position, overwhelmed a section of the troops holding it, and thus provided himself with a shorter supply line that round Bir Hacheim. The Army Commander (Ritchie) conceived that he was trying to retreat through this corridor, but Lieutenant-General Norrie, the first British commander to grip the tactics of armoured warfare in this country, came to the true conclusion, that he was building up strength in his "bridgehead" east of the main position and would try to smash a way out if he could first wear down the opposition sufficiently. This was, indeed, typical German tactics, already fully described in a book, *Blitzkrieg*, published in England by a Czech student of war, Captain Miksche, and therefore should have been recognized for what it was.'

On the night 1/2 June Rommel moved up to attack Bir Hacheim:

'After our summons to surrender had been rejected, the attack opened at about midday. The Trieste from the north-east and 90th Light from the south-east advanced against the fortifications, field positions and minefields of the French defenders. With our preliminary barrage there began a battle of extraordinary severity, which was to last for ten whole days.'

The *Luftwaffe* flew 1,300 sorties against Bir Hacheim. A series of tank battles followed with heavy losses on both sides. A determined British attack (4/5 June) on the 'Cauldron', as Rommel's bridgehead was named, failed, partly for lack of sufficient infantry to press it home, but still more because of the very effective German anti-tank guns. After inflicting heavy casualties on the Germans seething about in the Cauldron the British were driven back in considerable disorder by an armoured counterstroke. The battered French brigade was withdrawn from Bir Hacheim after a truly heroic resistance (10/11 June).

Once he had disposed of the 150th Infantry Brigade at Dahar el Aslaq and the Free French, Rommel set about the task of destroying the Eighth Army's tank strength. By 12 June the British had only 70 tanks left, while Rommel had still about 100 German and perhaps 60 Italian tanks. The Battle of Gazala was lost. Unable to support the Guards, who had beaten off every attack on Knightsbridge, Ritchie was compelled to withdraw them (14 June).

The fate of Tobruk now hung in the balance. As Carver puts it:

'The desire of all concerned to have their cake and eat it too undoubtedly led to misunderstandings over Tobruk. Auchinleck was determined that Tobruk should not become invested again, but also that it should not be surrendered to the enemy.'

While Ritchie was reorganizing his army on the Egyptian frontier Rommel struck. At dawn on 20 June Rommel stood with General von Mellenthin on the escarpment NE of El Adem,

where Battle Headquarters had been set up, and watched the Stukas attack Tobruk.

The German armour poured in through a gap torn in the front of the Indian brigade, and, beating off a counter-attack, began to wreak havoc in the back area which was full of 'soft-skinned' vehicles. That evening General Klopper (2nd South African Infantry Division), who had not the necessary communications to organize a break-out, surrendered the fortress with some 25,000 men and enormous quantities of stores. Part of the Coldstream Guards under Major Sainthill refused to capitulate and broke out in their transport that night.

The moral effect of the capture of Tobruk was very great. In Germany morale reached a peak that it had not touched since the fall of France. Rommel, the man of the hour, was immediately promoted Field Marshal, while his followers celebrated 'with captured tinned fruit, Irish potatoes, cigarettes and canned beer'. In Britain the shock was the more bitter for being unexpected. Nobody realized that the fortress had

Left: **The scene at Tobruk after the surrender of its garrison to the Germans.**

Below left: **The port at Tobruk on the day the city fell, 21 June 1942.**

Below: **German transports enter Tobruk.**

Bottom: **By 8 July 1942 the German offensive was spent and Rommel's troops were tired and exhausted.**

Above: **Traffic regulations in the desert had to be quite detailed and specific in order to avoid jams and undue confusion.**

been allowed to fall into disrepair since its splendid defence the previous year.

Rommel, swift to follow up his victory, crossed the frontier on 23 June with 44 tanks, and during the next few days dispersed Gott's XIII Corps near Mersa Matruh. The Eighth Army, tired, scattered and confused, was in desperate plight: Auchinleck decided to take command in person and on the 25th flew up from Cairo and relieved Ritchie. But even he could not rally the survivors until they had swept right back to the El Alamein position, where at last on 1 July Rommel was brought to a halt. It was not a moment too soon. In Cairo much of the 'bumf' of the British Embassy, the Headquarters of Middle East and British Troops Egypt, was committed to the flames on 1 July, the celebrated Ash Wednesday – a good 'flap' is not without its benefits. It was rumoured that the Navy had left Alexandria in haste. But, as so often in war, things were not quite so bad.

The so-called Alamein Line – miles of empty sand, indistinguishable from the rest of the desert, but with its flanks on the sea and on the virtually impassable Qattara Depression – was thinly enough held at first, but Rommel's men were as weak and as exhausted as Eighth Army. All through July there was fighting, but neither side could summon the strength for a knockout blow. At the end of the month Auchinleck sent a telegram to London in which he said: 'It is unlikely that an opportunity will arise for resumption of offensive operations before mid-September.' This was not music in the ears of his masters in London, who had long since come to the conclusion that it was time for a change in the direction of the desert war. In every battle since mid-1941 we had outnumbered the enemy both on the ground and in the air, and now the bewildered Eighth Army on which equipment had been lavished when it could least be spared was back on its start line.

Early in August the Prime Minister and the CIGS descended on Cairo to feel the situation for themselves. Churchill wanted Gott to command the Eighth Army, but Brooke felt that Montgomery was the man and that Gott, though the best of the old hands, was tired. Moreover he had risen from battalion to corps command since 1939 and possibly required more experience before commanding an army. On 6 August Churchill decided to give Alexander command of the Middle East and Gott the Eighth Army, but the very next day the latter was killed when two German fighters attacked a transport aircraft. It was under these circumstances that Montgomery was selected for the command of the Army with which his name will always be linked. Alexander reached Cairo on 9 August and was given a brief directive by the Prime Minister, in which his prime duty was defined:

'to take or destroy at the earliest opportunity the German-Italian army commanded by Field Marshal Rommel, together with all its supplies and establishments in Egypt and Libya'.

Montgomery flew out from England with all speed and after conferring with Alexander went up to the desert on 13 August to look round. He did not like what he saw, and decided to assume command without more ado, though this was contrary to Auchinleck's orders. He made a good beginning by cancelling all plans for any withdrawal; by deciding to form a Reserve Armoured Corps; and by giving his Chief of Staff, de Guingand, complete authority over the headquarters and all branches of the staff. Like Allenby in the days before Third Gaza his presence was 'a strong reviving wind'. Even as hardbaked an officer as Brigadier Kippenberger, the New Zealander, felt stimulated.

On the other side of the hill all was not well. In mid-July an ADC had written to tell Frau Rommel that the Field Marshal, who had not spared himself during his 19 months in Africa, was suffering from 'digestive disturbances'. In Rome as early as 6 July grave anxiety was felt. Ciano wrote:

'There is in the air a vague concern on account of the lull before El Alamein. It is feared that after the impact of the initial attack is spent Rommel cannot advance further, and whoever stops in the desert is truly lost. It is enough to think that every drop of water must come from Mersa Matruh, almost two hundred kilometres of road under bombardment of enemy aviation. It is reported to me that in military circles there is violent indignation against the Germans because of their behaviour in Libya.'

Montgomery had been in the saddle for but 17 days when Rommel struck once more. But by that time the desert fox was too late. In a famous and characteristic passage in his memoirs Montgomery drily sums up the situation, 'I understood Rommel was expected to attack *us* shortly. If he came soon it would be tricky, if he came in a week, all right, but give us two weeks and Rommel could do what he liked; he would be seen off and then it would be our turn.' Montgomery had made good use of his 17 days. Montgomery had pondered deeply over the previous battles with Rommel and with his keen tactical insight he had seen 'that what Rommel liked was to get our armour to attack him; he then disposed of his own armour behind

Above: **From February to June 1942 the German and Allied armies faced each other over the Bir Hacheim–Gazala Line.**

Left: **A PzKpfw III speeds on to the front. By this point in the Desert War Rommel's forces were not getting adequate supplies and fuel for tanks. The British now had a superiority of four to one in tanks.**

Below: **The first toops to surrender at Tobruk.**

a screen of anti-tank guns, knocked out our tanks, and finally had the field to himself.' Montgomery was determined not to let this happen:

'I would not allow our tanks to rush out at him; we would stand firm in the Alamein position, hold the Ruweisat and Alam Halfa Ridges securely, and let him beat up against them. We would fight a static battle and my forces would not move; his tanks would come up against our tanks dug-in in hull-down positions at the western edge of the Alam Halfa Ridge.'

And this is exactly what he did.

On the night of 30 August the German and Italian columns began to move forward in a 'right hook' designed to out-manoeuvre Montgomery by getting round behind his main defensive position. It just did not work, and in consequence Alam el Halfa is one of the most straightforward battles of the whole war. There was no surprise on the first night, because the RAF had spotted the enemy in their forming-up areas 24 hours earlier. Deep minefields and heavy bombing delayed the Germans, who did not seem to be coming on with their old verve. Rommel thrust at the Alam el Halfa ridge, probably not realizing that XIII Corps (Lieutenant-General Horrocks) was strongly ensconced there, and that Montgomery regarded it as the key to his position. The battle lasted a week, but Rommel could have pulled out several days earlier for all the good he was doing. He attributed his repulse to the weight of British artillery fire, the intricacy and depth of their minefields and his own shortage of supplies, especially petrol. Most of his losses he put down to air attack.

Major-General Freyberg (2nd New Zealand Division):

'attributed the enemy's failure, in a situation in which they could not find room for manoeuvre, to their inability to carry out a proper infantry attack in co-operation with artillery. He accused them of having become tank followers.'

If the Germans were getting cautious, the British were becoming cunning. Montgomery fought with his tanks dug-in, and refused to be tempted. In consequence the old Rommel magic did not work. The shortage of petrol which deprived the German of freedom of manoeuvre, was largely due to the havoc wrought to their lines of communication by the RAF.

Above: **Rommel retained the initiative in the fight with the British in North Africa until June 1942. Even after June he managed to exact a heavy price for the victory at El Alamein and then fought a brilliant defensive action in Tunisia.**

Below: **Tanks of the Afrika Korps.**

Above: **The Nazi flag was used as a marker for aircraft.**

Left: **English prisoners of war await transportation away from the front lines.**

Below: **British infantry move forward to reoccupy Tobruk.**

16 THE CORAL SEA AND MIDWAY

'Heard the heavens fill with shouting,
And there rained a ghastly dew
From the nations' airy navies
Grappling in the central blue.'

Tennyson, Locksley Hall, 1842

Above: **Admiral Isoroku Yamamoto, Commander-in-Chief of the Japanese Fleet. His plan at Midway was to lure the US Pacific Fleet into a trap and destroy the American carriers.**

By now Imperial General Headquarters was suffering from the form of megalomania which, after the war, a Japanese admiral named 'Victory Disease'. New conquests beckoned. They would capture Tulagi in the Solomons and Port Moresby in Papua. This would give them air control of the Coral Sea. Then their main fleet would seek out and destroy the remains of the United States Pacific Fleet in one operation, with Midway and the Western Aleutians as their rewards. The capture of New Caledonia, Fiji and Samoa would follow and would cut off Australia from American support. Japanese strategy was certainly correct in seeking to try conclusions with the Pacific Fleet before American war production could make it too powerful.

By mid-April CINCPAC Intelligence was already aware of the Japanese threat to the Coral Sea and Admiral Nimitz sent Task Force 17 (Rear-Admiral Fletcher) to take a hand. *Friction de guerre* – 'grit in the works' might serve as a rough translation – is a concept well-known to military commentators since the days of Clausewitz. If you have a warped sense of humour, or like illustrations of how the right thing often happens for the wrong reason, a study of the Battle of the Coral Sea may be recommended.

On 2 May 1942 a Japanese invasion force was detected approaching Tulagi. The small Australian garrison withdrew to the New Hebrides. The Japanese landed unopposed next day and began to convert the island into a seaplane base. Fletcher made for Tulagi in the carrier *Yorktown*. Early next morning he sent his planes in to attack Tulagi harbour, but they did only minor damage. The *Yorktown* withdrew and rejoined the *Lexington* and the rest of the force on 5 May. She had escaped unscathed because the Japanese carriers, *Shokaku* and *Zuikaku* were delayed for two days delivering *nine* fighters to Rabaul, and so on the 4th were too far away to counter-attack! This mission was a false economy if ever there was one.

On the 6th Fletcher, leaving the destroyer *Sims* and the fleet oiler *Neosho* behind at his refuelling point, made for the Louisiade Archipelago. Early on the 7th Japanese aircraft sighted these two vessels and reported them as a carrier and a cruiser. Vice-Admiral Takagi, not unnaturally, ordered an all-out bombing attack and sank them both. The American carriers were still unscathed. Meanwhile an aircraft from *Yorktown* had reported two carriers and four heavy cruisers 175 miles NW and Fletcher had sent every plane he could to attack what he assumed to be the main enemy force. When they had gone it was discovered that the report should have read 'two heavy cruisers and two destroyers'. But as luck would have it the American fliers sighted the light carrier *Shoho* and sank her in ten minutes, as well as a light cruiser. They lost five planes. Vice-Admiral Inouye (Commander in Chief Fourth Fleet), who was directing operations from Rabaul, was so discouraged by this loss that he ordered the Port Moresby invasion group to alter course and move around at a safe distance north of the Louisiades.

Fletcher had sent Rear-Admiral Crace, RN, with two Australian cruisers, the USS *Chicago* and some destroyers, to seek out the invasion group. He was attacked by 31 Japanese bombers from Rabaul and three American B-17s from Townsville (Queensland), but managed with great skill to dodge the lot. The Japanese pilots claimed to have sunk two battleships and a heavy cruiser. That evening Japanese aircraft tried once more to find the American carriers. Nine were shot down by fighters. After dark six did eventually find the *Yorktown* but taking her for a Japanese carrier they were lost while trying to land on her!

Left: The *Lexington* aflame during the Battle of of Coral Sea.

Below left: A PBY5a Catalina patrols the air space over Aleutians.

Below centre: A Japanese Kate torpedo-bomber flies over a US destroyer.

Bottom: The *Lexington* burns following the Battle of Coral Sea.

During the night eleven others met a similar fate on their own carriers.

The 8 May saw the climax of the fighting, when the carrier groups finally located each other. They were well-matched.

	Americans	*Japanese*
Planes	122	121
Carriers	2	2
Heavy cruisers	5	4
Destroyers	7	6

The weather favoured the Japanese. The *Yorktown* sent out 41 planes which missed *Zuikaku* in a rain squall and concentrated on *Shokaku*. They only hit her twice, but one bomb bent the flight deck so badly that she could no longer get her planes off. Half *Lexington's* group failed to find the Japanese under their cloud. The other half scored one more hit on *Shokaku*.

Meanwhile 70 Japanese planes had put in a determined attack on the American carriers, which were clearly visible in brilliant sunshine. They scored only one hit on the *Yorktown*, though it killed 66 men. The *Lexington* was hard hit – two torpedoes and two bombs. Internal explosions compelled the crew to abandon ship, and she was finally torpedoed by American destroyers. At noon on 8 May Takagi believed that both American carriers were sinking, and decided to send the damaged *Shokaku* back to Truk. Admiral Inouye now recalled the Port Moresby Invasion Fleet to Rabaul. He was unwilling to risk it South of Papua without air cover. 'Thus the battle was really won by the Americans owing to their biggest mistake, the sighting and bombing of *Shoho*; her loss led Inouye to throw in the sponge.' The Americans lost 66 planes, the Japanese considerably more. In point of tonnage sunk the Japanese were the winners, but it took them more than a month to replace *Zuikaku's* plane losses, and two months to repair the *Shokaku*, and so neither was available for the attack on Midway.

But one cannot judge the results of a battle purely by the casualties. The strategic result of the Coral Sea was that the Japanese gave up their attempt on Port Moresby, the key to New Guinea, which could itself have proved the gateway to Australia. Moreover, though the battle was by no means a decisive one, from this time forwards the Americans were no longer on the defensive. Coming immediately after the fall of Corregidor (6 May) the victory was a splendid fillip to American morale. The battle was remarkable as the first in which no surface warships engaged. The Americans had got the better in the first battle of a new era of naval warfare.

Right: **Fire-control parties cope with the damage following the first Japanese attack on the *Yorktown*.**

Below: **Torpedo-bombers warm up on the *Yorktown*.**

If the Coral Sea was a fantastic chapter of accidents and blunders the battle of Midway was one of the most brilliant ever fought, and a decisive turning point in the Pacific War. Once again the predominant factor was air power. On 5 May Imperial Headquarters ordered the occupation of the Western Aleutians and Midway Island. Midway would be valuable as a base for air raids on Pearl Harbor, and all the islands would form part of the 'ribbon defence' that was to secure the Japanese conquests. But the main object was to bring the US Pacific Fleet to battle and to annihilate it before new construction could make up for its losses at Pearl Harbor.

The operation was the biggest ever mounted by the Japanese Navy. Admiral Yamamoto's armada consisted of 162 warships and auxiliaries without counting patrol craft. The main components were:

Advanced Force:
16 submarines
Nagumo's Pearl Harbor Striking Force:
4 big carriers
Midway Occupation Force:
12 transports
5,000 men
2 battleships
6 heavy cruisers
Many destroyers
Yamamoto's Main Body:
3 modern battleships
4 older battleships
1 light carrier
Northern Area Force:
2 light carriers
2 heavy cruisers
4 big transports

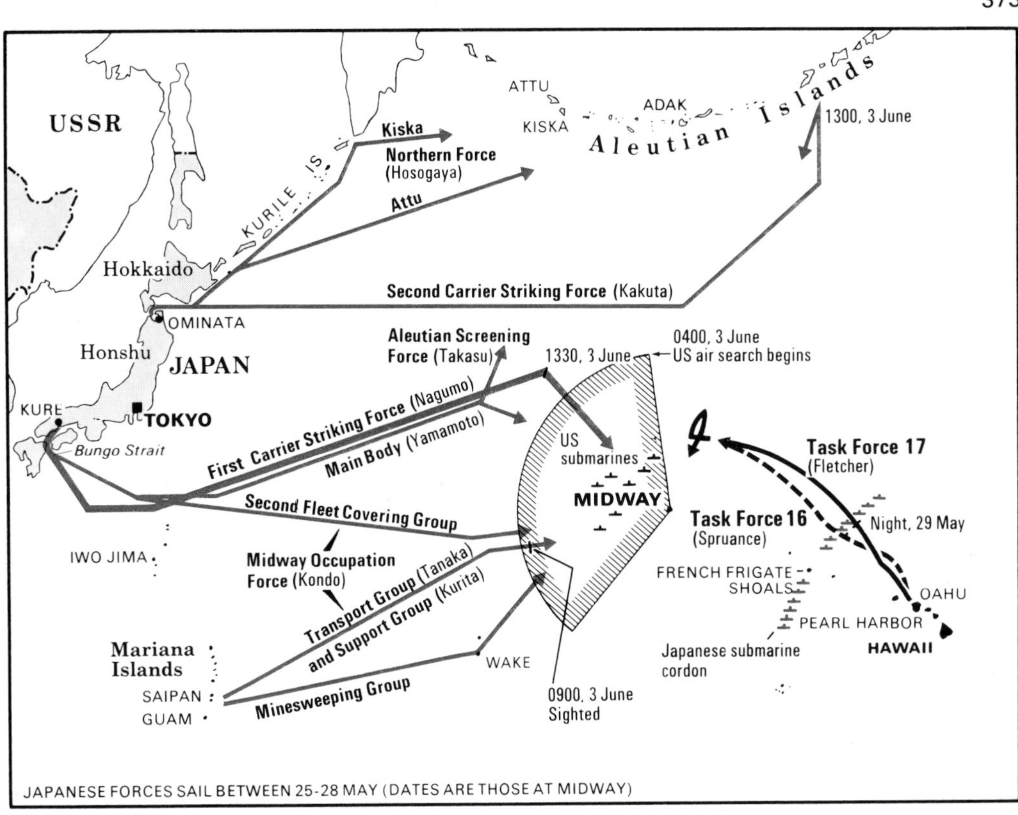

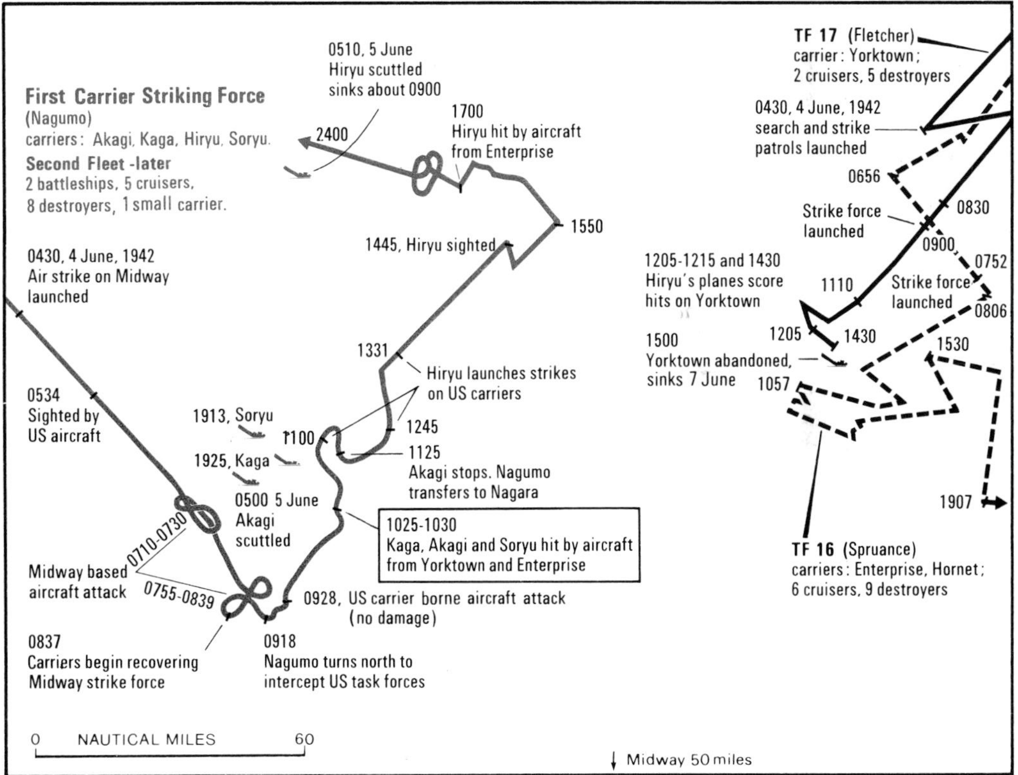

Right: **The *Yorktown* was quickly patched up at Pearl Harbor to take part at Midway.**

The object of the last force was to bomb Dutch Harbor and to occupy Adak, Attu and Kiska.

To meet this formidable armada Nimitz had only 76 ships, including the North Pacific Force. These included three carriers, *Enterprise*, *Hornet* and, incredibly enough, *Yorktown*. Nimitz had one great asset. The Americans had broken the Japanese naval cipher and he knew when and where they planned to attack. He could take his measures with a certainty which is denied to most commanders.

The battle began on the Aleutian flank. On 3 June the Japanese bombed Dutch Harbor and on 7 June they occupied Attu and Kiska. The operations are chiefly of interest as an object lesson to 'clever' commanders. CINCPAC Intelligence had given warning of the Japanese intentions as early as 28 May, but Rear-Admiral 'Fuzzy' Theobald, as usual, thought he knew better – that the enemy was going to seize Dutch Harbor. Consequently he deployed the main body of his force about 400 miles south of Kodiak, instead of trying to break up the Western Aleutians invasion force. The Japanese slipped past between him and the land and were able to bomb Dutch Harbor twice. They could indeed have captured it for all Theobald could have done about it.

Meanwhile Nagumo's carriers, protected by heavy cloud were approaching Midway unseen. On 3 June a Catalina sighted the Occupation Force, but the island-based aircraft only managed to hit one oiler in the early hours of the 4th. Before sunrise that day Nagumo sent off 108 planes to attack Midway, keeping back 93, armed with bombs and torpedoes, in case any American ships should appear. Radar picked up the Japanese when they were 93 miles away, but the Americans had not enough fighters to stop them. The bombing began at 0630 and lasted 20 minutes. Though much damage was done the runways were not put out of action. About one-third of the Japanese planes were shot down or hard hit by planes or anti-aircraft fire. The Americans lost 15 fighters. Meanwhile the Midway-based bombers had taken off to counter-attack the Japanese carriers. Fletcher had heard soon after 0600 that a Catalina from Midway had seen two Japanese carriers moving SE, and had promptly ordered Rear-Admiral Spruance with *Enterprise* and *Hornet* 'to proceed southwesterly and attack enemy carriers when definitely located'. He would follow with *Yorktown* as soon as his search planes were recovered.

Nagumo had not expected to encounter American carriers and had, therefore, sent out only a few reconnaissance planes. By 0700 these had spotted nothing. At this juncture the Admiral heard from the commander of his striking force that Midway required further attention. The point was proved almost at once when the bombers from the island started coming over. Nagumo ordered that his 93 reserve aircraft should be rearmed with incendiary and fragmentation bombs. A quarter of an hour later one of the reconnaissance planes reported 10 American ships to the NE, where no American ship should have been. The unfortunate Nagumo pondered his problem for another 15 minutes, and then decided to rearm his reserve with torpedoes. Before the planes could be got ready his striking force began to return from Midway.

Spruance launched an all-out strike (116 planes) when, at 0700, he was about 175 miles from the Japanese estimated position. At 0905 Nagumo altered course 90 degrees and began steaming ENE to seek out the American Task Force. In consequence the dive-bombers and fighters from *Hornet* missed him. But her 15 torpedo-bombers saw him and went in without fighter cover. Only one survived the Zekes and the anti-aircraft fire. They were followed by the torpedo-bomber squadrons of *Enterprise* and *Yorktown*. All but eight of their Devastators were shot down. Not a single hit had been scored when, about 1024, the third attack ended. In the words of the official historian of the United States Navy 'for about one hundred seconds the Japanese were certain they had won the Battle of Midway, and the war'.

Then at 1026 the 37 Dauntless dive-bombers from *Enterprise* came on the scene. One squadron went for the *Kaga*, the other for Nagumo's flagship *Akagi*. They struck before the Zekes, which had been dealing with the Devastators, had time to climb, and while the planes were still changing their armament. Two bombs hit the *Akagi* and Nagumo was compelled, most reluctantly, to transfer from his blazing flagship to the cruiser *Nagara*. Four bombs made an inferno of the *Kaga*.

Yorktown's 17 dive-bombers fell upon *Soryu* as she was about to launch planes, scoring three hits. She was sunk, after she had been abandoned, by the US submarine *Nautilus*. Nagumo still had one carrier, the *Hiryu*, and he now sent 40 planes to attack *Yorktown*. American fighters and anti-aircraft fire accounted for most of them, but at least seven got through. About 1445 *Yorktown* received three bombs and two torpedoes. Admiral Fletcher was compelled to shift his flag to the cruiser *Astoria*, but not before he had ordered a search mission to find the fourth Japanese carrier. At 1540 Spruance sent off 24 dive-bombers from the *Enterprise*. At 1700 they plummeted down on *Hiryu* and sank her with four hits.

Mitsuo Fuchida gives a vivid picture of the fate of the Japanese carriers.

'When the attack broke, deck parties were busily preparing the carrier's planes for take-off, and their first awareness of the onslaught came when great flashes of fire were seen sprouting from *Kaga*, some distance off to port, followed by explosions and tremendous columns of black smoke. Eyes instinctively looked skyward just in time to see a spear of thirteen American planes plummeting down on *Soryu*. It was 1025.

Three hits were scored in as many minutes. The first blasted the flight deck in front of the forward elevator, and the next two straddled the amidship elevator, completely wrecking the deck and spreading fire to petrol tanks and munition store rooms. By 1030 the ship was transformed into a hell of smoke and flames, and induced explosions followed shortly.

In the next ten minutes the main engines stopped, the steering system went out, and fire mains were destroyed. Crewmen, forced by the flames to leave their posts, had just arrived on deck when a mighty explosion blasted many of them into the water. Within twenty minutes of the first bomb-hit the ship was such a mass of fire that Captain Ryusaku Yanagimoto ordered "abandon ship!" '

The captain himself remained on the bridge. 'No ship commander in the Japanese Navy was more beloved by his men.' They were determined to save him, and sent Chief Petty Officer Abe, a Navy wrestling champion to rescue him. He found Yanagimoto 'standing there motionless, sword in hand, gazing resolutely towards the ship's bow'. The Petty Officer's entreaties were met with silence. 'Abe guessed the Captain's thoughts and started towards him with the intention of carrying him bodily to the waiting boat. But the sheer strength of will and determination of his grim-faced commander stopped him short. He turned tearfully away, and as he left the bridge he heard Captain Yanagimoto calmly singing *Kimigayo*, the national anthem.'

At first Yamamoto intended to renew the battle, but the news that he had lost all four of

his fast carriers, with their 250 planes and 2,200 men, compelled him to withdraw. Whether to save face or to cover his withdrawal he ordered a bombardment of Midway. The cruisers *Mogame* and *Mikuma* managed to collide with each other while trying to avoid an American submarine. As they made off they were attacked by aircraft from the *Hornet* and the *Mikuma* was sunk. The price the Americans paid for their victory was the *Yorktown* and 147 aircraft.

It is significant that once more a great naval battle had been fought without any action between surface ships. The day of the battleship was done. The battle left the Japanese with five carriers, including only one large one, fit for action. Six more were on the stocks or under repair. The US still had three large carriers with the Pacific Fleet, with 13 more building as well as 15 escort carriers. The Japanese were quite incapable of keeping up with the American rate of construction. It is not too much to say that from the time of Midway onwards the Japanese Navy could only take on the US Navy at night or when supported by land-based aircraft. It was a splendid achievement that within six months Admiral Nimitz could truly say 'Pearl Harbor has been partially avenged'.

Above: **Survivors from the *Yorktown* assemble on the deck of one of her escort cruisers.**

Above left: **Vice-Admiral Raymond Spruance took over direction of the battle at Midway when Fletcher's flagship *Yorktown* was put out of action.**

Below: **The last moments of the *Yorktown* at the Battle of Midway.**

17 EL ALAMEIN TO TRIPOLI

'When I assumed command of the Eighth Army I said that the mandate was to destroy Rommel and his Army, and that it would be done as soon as we were ready. We are ready *now*!'

Lieutenant-General Montgomery, 23 October, 1942

With characteristic thoroughness Montgomery had seen to it that this was no idle boast. He had refused to be prodded into action before he was ready. He had weighed up not only his enemy but his own army, for he knew well that its defects in training limited the scope of his tactical plans. The morale of the Eighth Army which had carried it triumphantly through the Crusader battles against considerable odds, had slumped after Gazala. Churchill had found it 'brave but baffled'. Montgomery's confident attitude and his firm control of the Battle of Alam el Halfa had done much to put things right.

The Axis army, so long accustomed to swift armoured thrusts and a practically continuous offensive, found itself in a novel situation. It no longer enjoyed anything like air parity. Starved of petrol at the limit of an extended and vulnerable line of communications, it was so immobile that it was condemned to act on the defensive. And Rommel himself was in hospital in Germany. The balance of forces was now about two to one in Montgomery's favour. The Axis army, temporarily under the command of the 56-year-old General Stumme, was 108,000 strong, and included 53,000 Germans. It had about 600 tanks, but 300 of them were of the type known as 'the self-propelled coffin' – the Italian M.13. Only the 38 German Mark IVs, with their 75 mm guns, were really a match for the Shermans. The enemy had 345 aircraft (216 being Italian) against some 900 British planes. There were only 24 of the powerful 88 mm guns available.

The Axis defensive position, which was very heavily mined, was five miles deep and about 40 miles long. They had about 2,000 men to a mile of front, which was not much by desert standards. The shortage of fuel meant that the armour would have to fight where it was – 21st Panzer and Ariete in the south; 15th Panzer, 90th Light and Littorio in the north; Trieste was in reserve south of 90th Light.

Montgomery had 220,000 men and 1,351 tanks. Of the 1,196 in the forward area, 1,021 were fit for action on the evening of the 23rd. Montgomery's tank force included:

285 Shermans, 246 Grants, 421 Crusaders, 167 Stuarts, 223 Valentines, 6 Matildas and 3 Churchills.

The British had 1,400 anti-tank guns (550 two-pounders and 850 six-pounders). They also had 884 pieces of artillery, including 52 medium and 832 field guns.

For once a British Army was going into battle with a clear-cut numerical advantage and, of all things, a well-balanced force! And for once the commander, like a modern Wellington, was a man of iron will, a master tactician, bold yet prudent, a far-sighted administrator. In short he was the rarest of animals in the British military hierarchy, a thoroughgoing professional. Montgomery was severely critical of the state of training in his army. 'Most commanders', he writes, 'had come to the fore by skill in fighting and because no better were available: many were above their ceiling, and few were good trainers. . . . The Eighth Army had suffered some eighty thousand casualties since it was formed, and little time had been spent in training the replacements.'

On 6 October, only a fortnight before the battle was due to start, he altered his plan.

'My initial plan had been based on destroying Rommel's armour; the remainder of his army (the unarmoured portion) could then be dealt with at leisure. This was in accordance with the accepted military thinking of the day. I decided to reverse the process and thus alter the whole conception of how the battle was going to be fought. My modified plan now was to hold off, or contain, the enemy armour while we carried out a methodical destruction of the infantry divisions holding the defensive system. These unarmoured divisions would be destroyed by means of a crumbling process, the enemy being attacked from the flank and rear and cut off from their supplies. These operations would be carefully organized from a series of firm bases and would be within the capabilities of my troops.'

Large-scale rehearsals were carried out, and careful briefing was a notable feature of the preparations. Major-General de Guingand, Montgomery's Chief of Staff, has described the

Below: **General Sir Bernard Law Montgomery and officers assess the situation at El Alamein.**

Right: **A General Grant tank of the 22nd Armoured Brigade moves up to the front line south of El Alamein.**

addresses which the Army commander gave to all officers 'right down to lieutenant-colonel'.

'Clear and full of confidence. I warrant there were no doubters after he had finished. He touched on the enemy situation, stressed his weaknesses, but was certain a long "dog-fight" or "killing match" would take place for several days – "it might be ten". He then gave details of our great strength, our tanks, our guns and the enormous supplies of ammunition available. He drummed in the need never to lose the initiative, and how everyone – *everyone* – must be imbued with the burning desire to "kill Germans". "Even the padres – one per weekday and two on Sundays!" '

If doubts remained, they were in the minds of some of the more senior officers. The three divisional commanders of 30 Corps, Freyberg, Morshead and Pienaar, had little confidence in any early breakout by the armour. In the open desert it was impossible to conceal the signs of a coming offensive. For this reason the British laid on a deception plan calculated to make the enemy expect the attack on the desert flank, which had tended to be the tactical pattern in early battles. 'All the "armour" in the staging areas, the "guns", the "dumps", and the "pipeline", in the south were stick and string, tin and canvas.' Not since Megiddo had a British offensive been so thoroughly prepared.

The opening attack won considerable success, for during the night XXX Corps fought its way on to Miteirya Ridge, and on the southern sector XIII Corps made some progress. The two deep belts of minefields and stubborn, if uneven, resistance caused a good deal of delay. There was no quick enemy reaction, for General Stumme had little idea what was happening. He drove, unescorted, to 90th Light to try and find out, was fired on – probably by the Australians – and died of heart failure while his driver was trying to get away. His body was not found for 24 hours. And so at a critical moment of the battle the *Panzer Armee* was leaderless. It defended itself with obstinacy, but there was no counterstroke.

The crisis of the battle came swiftly. Although Montgomery could not as yet be certain exactly how much progress had been made, it seemed that things had gone well; the problem was to get the armour forward through the narrow lanes in the minefields. During the night of 24/25 October Gatehouse's 10th Armoured Division tried to push forward. There was considerable

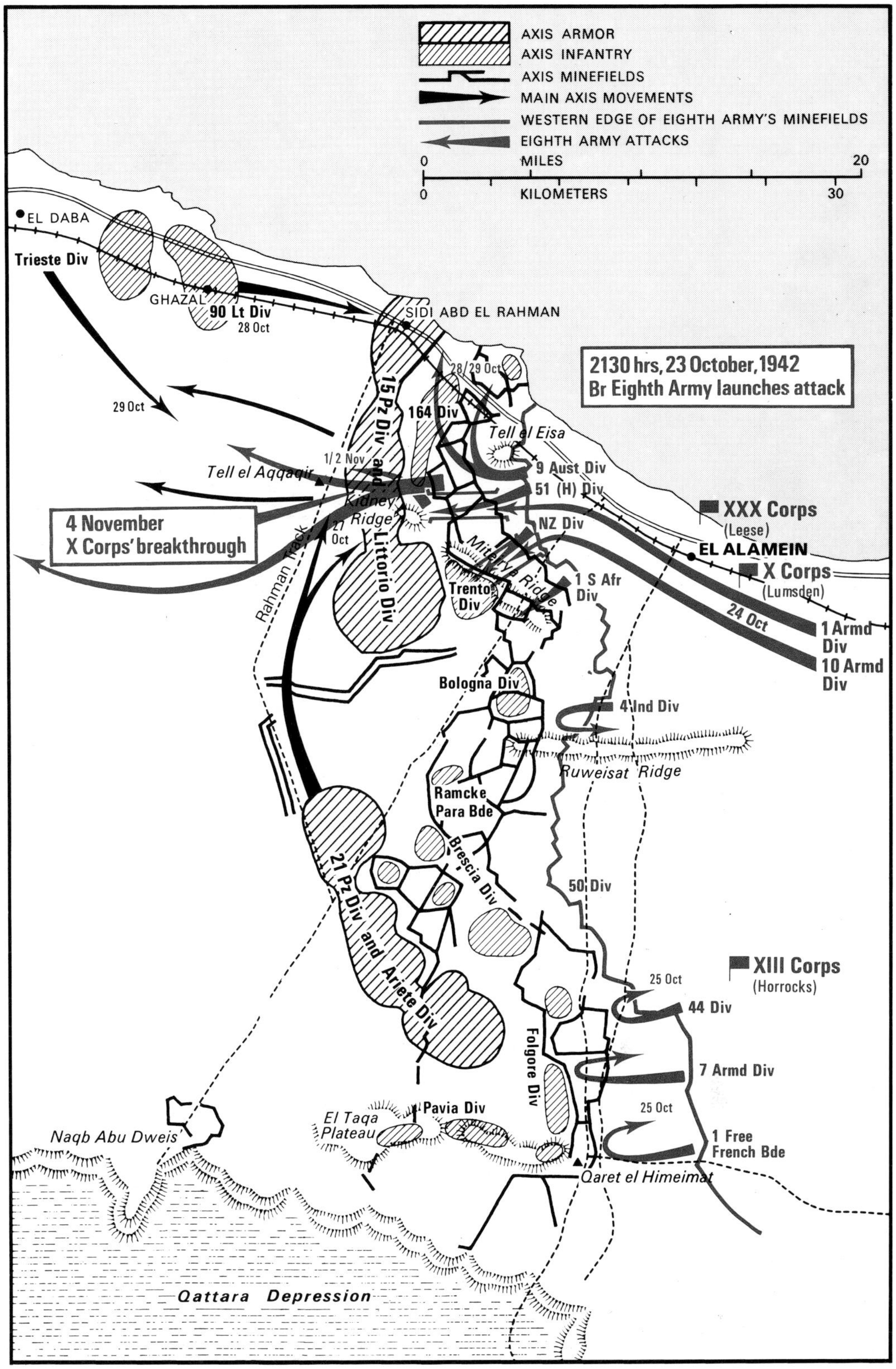

Below Left: **German troops move forward to the El Alamein line. The Afrika Korps prepared for the battle knowing that they were at a disadvantage.**

Below: **Axis troops advance on El Alamein. By this point the Germans were short of ammunition and shells.**

confusion among the gapping parties, and vehicles became double-banked nose to tail. About 10 o'clock a German bomber set fire to about 25 vehicles carrying petrol and ammunition, and started a blaze which went on all night. Gatehouse wanted to call off the attack and Lumsden (X Corps) rather agreed with him. This was the moment when the battle could be lost and won. Fortunately de Guingand, realizing this, summoned Lumsden and Leese to be at Army Headquarters at 3.30 a.m., and woke up Montgomery – an act of cool courage, for his Spartan master did not like having his slumbers disturbed. Montgomery made it abundantly clear that his original plan was to be carried out, and told Gatehouse this on the telephone. After the conference he detained Lumsden and warned him 'that, if he and his divisional commanders were not determined to break out, others would be found who were'. Montgomery himself rightly regarded this as the real crisis of the battle. Before 8 o'clock that morning one of Gatehouse's brigades was reported to be 2,000 yards west of the minefield area. The New Zealand Division had also fought its way clear. Counter-attacks by 15th Panzer Division were repulsed with loss. In the south 7th Armoured Division had got through the first minefield on the night 23/24 October, but had then been halted. Montgomery wanted to use this formation later in the battle and called off the attack before the casualties should become too serious.

By the morning of the 26th Montgomery's first onslaught had lost its momentum, casualties were mounting, about 200 British tanks had been knocked out, but XXX Corps had taken most of its objectives. The Eighth Army had taken 2,000 prisoners, 600 being German. It was estimated that the enemy had lost about 30,000 men and some 250 tanks besides a number of guns, but it now seems that intelligence was being over-optimistic. Montgomery spent the day pondering and planning.

Meanwhile Rommel had reappeared the previous evening (25 October) and had taken over from General Ritter von Thoma, who had replaced Stumme. The situation he found was not encouraging. The 15th Panzer had only 31 tanks left, petrol was short, constant bombardment from the air as well as the artillery had caused heavy casualties; morale was affected. Rommel determined to throw in his reserves, drive the British out of his main position and retake the feature known to him as Hill 28, and to the British as Kidney Ridge. His attack went in on the evening of the 27th, but was baffled by the combination of bombing, heavy armour and anti-tank guns. The 2nd Rifle Brigade, whose commanding officer, Lieutenant-Colonel Vic Turner, won the Victoria Cross, knocked out at least 37 enemy tanks.

Montgomery had thought out a new plan. Lumsden was to push on west and north-west of Kidney Ridge, while Leese was regrouping for his next major attack. The 7th Armoured

Top: **A Bf110 prepares for take-off from an airfield in North Africa.**

Above: **An armourer deactivates the fuses on a bomb in an Egyptian airfield.**

Above: A Bristol Beaufighter gets a thorough overhaul before going on another mission.

Below: A New Zealand unit which has been on a raid behind enemy lines, lead their prisoners into captivity.

Above: Enemy shells fall far short of their target.

Left: **A member of a German tank crew rushes out to surrender to the British on 27 October 1942.**

Below: Australians surge forward masked by dense smoke at the height of the battle.

Division was brought up from the south and the New Zealanders were taken out of the line. On 29 October the Australian Division launched a diversionary attack in order to make Rommel commit his remaining reserves. Advancing from the northern flank of the Kidney Ridge salient they made for the coast, threatening to cut off 164 Infantry Division. Rommel, who had already expressed his doubts as to the outcome in a letter written to his wife the previous day, reacted as Montgomery had hoped. He struck back at the Australians with his reserves, including 31st Panzer and 90th Light Division. The Australians held firm and by so doing paved the way for Operation *Supercharge*, the *coup de grâce*. Rommel was already contemplating a withdrawal to Fuka, for he had only 90 tanks left, while the British still had some 800.

Supercharge began on the night 1/2 November and was held up by the German anti-tank screen. But this was a Pyrrhic victory for the enemy, whose tanks were further reduced. The German retreat had already begun when on 3 November orders came from Hitler expressly forbidding any retirement. Thus Montgomery was granted another 24 hours in which to maul his enemies before the *Führer* changed his mind and permitted Rommel to withdraw. The British finally broke through on 4 November, but the pursuit got off to a slow start and when heavy rain began to fall on 6 November 'the bottom fell out of the desert'. Rommel, with a metalled road behind him, was able to save something from the wreck.

Nonetheless taking into account their enormous armoured superiority at the end of the battle the British might well have destroyed the Afrika Korps. The long battle had exhausted the victors and for this reason a complete triumph eluded them.

Rommel's losses cannot be accurately assessed. Of his 108,000 men, some 30,000 (including about 10,000 Germans, among whom was General von Thoma, commander of the Afrika Korps) were taken prisoner. The immobile Italians suffered particularly heavily in this respect. The Germans gave their other losses as:

	Killed	*Wounded*	*Total*
Germans	1,100	3,900	5,000
Italians	1,200	1,600	2,800
	2,300	5,500	7,800

General Carver, however, thinks it probable that they really lost 20,000 killed and wounded. In addition Rommel lost 1,000 guns and 450 of his 600 tanks. During the retreat the Italians abandoned another 75 tanks for lack of fuel. By 15 November Rommel had no more than 80 tanks left. Montgomery's casualties numbered 13,500 (8 per cent of his force). Although 500 tanks had been put out of action, only 150 were damaged beyond repair; 100 guns had been destroyed.

The tonic effect that the resounding victory of El Alamein had in Britain can hardly be believed by those who were not there to follow its course during those ten days – waiting impatiently for each succeeding BBC bulletin. At first the news was good, but then the Eighth Army seemed to get stuck. Was it to be the old desert story of hope deferred? When the breakthrough came, with the magnificent gain and the beginning of the long pursuit to Tripoli, a feeling of immense relief and indeed pride was everywhere prevalent. And the news that Britain had found a great general was not the least of it. Well might Churchill say:

> 'The Battle of El Alamein was the turning point in British military fortunes during the World War. Up to Alamein we survived. After Alamein we conquered.'

or as he put it – with pardonable inaccuracy – 'Before Alamein we never had a victory. After Alamein we never had a defeat.'

Left: **Rommel briefs his staff prior to the offensive in the summer of 1942.**

Below: **A wounded German officer is guarded by a British soldier following the infantry advance. They are waiting for an ambulance to pick him up.**

18 NORTH AFRICA

'This must not be considered as the end; it may possibly be the beginning of the end, but it certainly is the end of the beginning.'

Winston S. Churchill, at the Lord Mayor's Luncheon Banquet at the Mansion House, 10 November 1942

Above: **Lieutenant-General Dwight Eisenhower seen at his desk just a few days before issuing the orders for the invasion of North Africa. Eisenhower's appointment to command the *Torch* forces had caused much consternation since he had only held staff appointments.**

On the night of 8 November 1942 a great Allied amphibious expedition consisting to a great extent of American troops descended upon the coasts of French North Africa, with the object of seizing the widely separated ports of Casablanca, Oran and Algiers. It was hoped that the effect of this operation would be to trap Rommel between the Eighth Army and the forces advancing from the West, in a giant nutcracker. Once occupied, North Africa would serve as a base for future operations against Europe. A success here was bound to confirm Franco in his policy of neutrality, and would forestall any designs the Axis might have in the same area.

Command of this expedition was given to an unknown American officer, Lieutenant-General Dwight D. Eisenhower. A man of great charm and impartiality, he had the gift of being able to get Allies to work harmoniously together with the minimum of friction and mistrust. One has only to compare his team with the Axis partnership to appreciate his gifts in that field. But he was far more than a high-powered liaison officer. Though he had never previously commanded in the field he was well versed in the history of his profession, in staff work and in administration. Though no great tactician he has been somewhat underrated as a commander, for he was to prove on occasion that he had the power to take decisions, and to make the right ones. British history shows the value of a loyal and trusted ally; General Eisenhower was one to rank with Prince Eugène and Marshal Blücher. The naval commander was Admiral Sir Andrew Cunningham, who, because of his successes at Matapan and elsewhere, enjoyed the confidence of the Americans as well as the British. He had some 500 warships and more than 350 transports and cargo ships under his orders.

Operation *Torch* was not launched without grave misgivings. As late as September 1942 such prominent British generals as Sir John Dill (who had just been succeeded as Chief of the Imperial General Staff by Sir Alan Brooke), and Sir Bernard Paget, the Commander-in-Chief Home Forces, were still worried about the security of the United Kingdom. They feared that without the *Torch* forces it might be impossible to repel a possible German invasion in the spring. But the Prime Minister saw that the time for invasion was passed, and backed the preparations with all his tremendous energy. By the end of the month it was clear that the Americans too were backing the operation and the planners began to believe that it had a good chance of success.

The Allies, hoping that there would be no resistance from the French, tried to ensure their co-operation by diplomatic means and by sending an American, Major-General Mark Clark, by submarine to contact General Mast and others in Algiers. This cloak and dagger affair did not achieve its aim, and the landings provoked a certain amount of resistance – two destroyers were sunk at Algiers – though it proved uneven in quality and ferocity. Still there were 14 French divisions in the theatre and unfortunately the pro-Allied Commander-

Above left: **Following the overrunning of Tunisia the US Army established a base at Bizerta.**

Above: **General George Patton and Vice-Admiral Kent Hewitt prepare to go ashore on 9 November 1942.**

in-Chief, General Juin, was arrested. However, it chanced that Admiral Jean Darlan, Marshal Pétain's heir-apparent, was visiting his sick son in Algiers. Eisenhower, who neither wished to kill Frenchmen nor to lose his own men to no purpose, convinced Darlan that he should order a cease fire, and this the Admiral did on 10 November. In vain Pétain repudiated his action. Eisenhower was criticized on ideological grounds for using the anti-British Darlan in this way, and for appointing the ex-Vichy minister as French political chief in all North Africa. In war one cannot always be nice in the choice of one's instruments. This one was not to be available for long because at Christmas Darlan was assassinated by a young French patriot, and the gallant General Henri Giraud, a man who had escaped from German prisons in both World Wars, reigned in his stead.

Once established in their three main objectives, Algiers, Oran and Casablanca – the last had proved the most stubborn – the Allies cast their eyes upon Tunis. Eisenhower, decided upon an immediate advance, and troops of the British First Army swiftly occupied Bone (12 November). But already on 15 November there were clashes with German patrols, and the advance was finally checked on the 25th at Medjez el Bab, some 30 miles south-west of Tunis. The Germans had reacted swiftly, and on 9 November their first troops had landed at El Aouana airport, Tunis. Soon reinforcements were coming in at a rate of more than 1,000 a day. On 9 November Ciano had a conversation with Hitler in Munich. Laval was arriving that night. Hitler was going to insist on the total occupation of France, a landing in Corsica, and a bridgehead in Tunisia. 'Hitler is neither nervous nor restless, but he does not underrate the American initiative and he wants to meet it with all resources at his disposal. Göring does not hesitate to declare that the occupation of North Africa represents the first point scored by the Allies since the beginning of the war.'

The Germans lost no time in overrunning 'Vichy France', the southern half of the country, which had not been occupied in 1940. When on 27 November the Germans entered Toulon, Admiral de Laborde ordered that the French fleet be scuttled. The splendid battle-cruisers *Dunkerque* and *Strasbourg* were among the ships that went down.

Below: **Personnel and equipment are unloaded on beach in North Africa.**

At Hitler's Headquarters, the *Wolfsschanze*, far away in East Prussia, the staff were preoccupied with the worsening situation at Stalingrad. (See the following chapter.) Nevertheless there was a good deal of anxiety about North Africa. In mid-November General Alfred Jodl, Head of the Armed Forces Operational Staff, wrote in an appreciation:

'North Africa is the glacis of Europe and must therefore be held under all circumstances. If it is lost we must expect an Anglo-Saxon attack against south-eastern Europe via the Dodecanese, Crete and the Peloponnese; we must therefore pacify and secure the Balkans.'

General Messe had told Ciano as early as 14 November 1942 that the loss of Tripolitania was inevitable and that the attempt to establish a bridgehead in Tunisia could have no lasting success. But Mussolini, despite stomach pains probably brought on by worry, had recovered something of his old spirit by the 22nd. The effect of this swift arrival of German troops, taken with the heavy rains of early winter, and problems of supply, was to bring about a stalemate. The British First Army (Lieutenant-General K. A. N. Anderson) hung on to Medjez el Bab, but lost Jebel el Ahmera (Longstop Hill) to the north. It may be, as General Brooke thought at the time, that Eisenhower was far too preoccupied with political matters and was not paying enough attention to the Germans. However that may be, there was deadlock from Christmas until mid-February.

On the other side of the hill everything was not going as smoothly as the Allies, burdened with their own cares, may have thought. For one thing the Axis had a cumbersome command set-up: '. . . authority ran from Hitler and Mussolini, through the two high-level Defence Staffs, to Kesselring (Commander-in-Chief South) and thence to the German Army Commanders, of whom there were now two, side by side' (Rommel and von Arnim). Then at the end of November there was friction in the Axis camp when Rommel secretly left Libya to see the *Führer*. The Italians said that if one of their generals had behaved in this way he would have been court-martialled and Göring was sent to soothe them. The root of the trouble was that Rommel did not think it possible to hold Tripolitania and wanted to withdraw into Tunisia. The Italian general, Bastico, and some of the Italian General Staff, disagreed with his views. The officers of Göring's suite promised to send three armoured divisions to Tunisia and talked big about reaching Morocco in three months. The Italians – rightly as it turned out – were not impressed.

Moreover, by this time Rommel had lost the confidence of both Hitler and Mussolini. On 7 December the German Operations Staff War Diary has the acid comment that: 'just now the *Führer* considers it a positive advantage that for the moment Rommel's Army has insufficient fuel to enable it to withdraw further'. While on 5 January 1943 Mussolini spoke harshly not only of his own Chief of Staff, the shifty and dishonest toady Marshal Cavallero, but of 'that madman Rommel, who thinks of nothing but retreating in Tunisia'. In mid-January General Messe was made commander of the broken Italian forces retreating into Tunisia. So far from being pleased he was convinced that Cavallero had appointed him in the hope that he would lose his reputation in a desperate gamble and end up in a prison camp. In fact Cavallero was the first to go. On 30 January he was succeeded as Chief of Staff by General Ambrosio, an honest and respected patriot, but no thunderbolt. The Germans were not pleased at the dismissal of the obsequious Cavallero.

But despite the growing friction within the Axis, and what Ciano calls (19 January) 'the prudent but inexorable advance of Montgomery', Mussolini still had his attacks of ill-founded optimism, as on 21 January when he declared: 'Our Libyan forces are entering Tunisia and we still have many trump cards to play.' To the more realistic among his followers, however, the loss of Tripoli, which Montgomery entered in triumph two days later, was a bitter blow. If Mussolini had run out of trumps, Rommel still had a card up his sleeve. At this time his army was facing Montgomery in the old French frontier position known as the Mareth Line. His communications with von Arnim in Tunisia were threatened by two American divisions (1st and 34th) in the Sbeitla-Gabes area. Rommel had the advantage of interior lines and, while part of his army guarded the Mareth position, he rushed a strong force north and fell upon the Americans (14 February), broke through the Kasserine Pass (20 February) and sent columns towards Thala and Tebéssa, thus threatening the communications of the British First Army. He was eventually checked after fierce fighting and fell back on the 23rd.

The Kasserine battle had been a rude jolt to the Allies. General Alexander, who had just be-

Right: **A Panzer Mark IV thunders through Tunisia.**

Below: **Men of the 2nd Battalion, 16th Infantry march through the Kasserine Pass.**

come Eisenhower's deputy, made a three-day tour of the American and French fronts and was 'frankly shocked by the situation'. He found the Americans required experience and the French required arms. To the Prime Minister he signalled: 'Hate to disappoint you, but find victory in North Africa is not just around the corner.'

It was now Rommel's turn to be disappointed. Having struck his fierce blow at the Americans he turned on the Eighth Army only to get a bloody nose at Medenine, a few miles east of the Mareth Line (6–7 March). Even after this repulse Hitler remained optimistic. 'Tunis was a strategic position of the first order' and all available resources must be used to hold it.

Rommel managed to hold on to his strong position on the Mareth Line until nearly the end of March. Then Montgomery attacked. He made a frontal attack with XX Corps and pinned the Germans down, and then did a left hook with 2nd New Zealand Division and the 8th Armoured Brigade. General Leclerc's French force, which had come all the way from Lake Chad, stormed 'Plum Pass' and fell on the Germans' rear. X Corps was kept in reserve. The attack was very

Right: **Lieutenant-General Kenneth Anderson and Major-General Omar Bradley in the northern sector of the Tunisian Front.**

Below: **GIs load a 105mm howitzer as part of the defence of the Kasserine Pass.**

Above: **Lieutenant General 'Hap' Arnold visits an American air base in North Africa in January 1943.**

Left: **Medium guns in action during a night barrage in Southern Tunisia in March 1943.**

well supported by the Desert Air Force (Air Vice-Marshal H. Broadhurst), who did a 'Blitz' with bombs and cannon of the sort the Germans had so often employed. It was a fine piece of 'Army Co-operation' by bombers accustomed to giving their support by attacking airfields, headquarters and supply dumps.

The attack on 'Plum Pass' was to be heralded by a 'crump' from 40 light bombers, operating on a very narrow frontage. Sixteen Kittybomber squadrons were available and these, with Spitfires as top cover, were to range, two at a time, over the battlefield, shooting up everything in sight with bomb and cannon. A specially trained squadron of 'tank busters' was to seek out the German armour.

The 50th Division made the frontal attack on the Wadi Zigzaou at 1030 on 20 March. It had the support of a tremendous artillery barrage and gained a foothold, only to be thrown out on the 22nd by the 15th Panzer and 90th Light Divisions. Montgomery now reinforced his left hook with X Corps Headquarters and the 1st Armoured Division. The 7th Armoured Division reinforced XXX Corps and 50th Division was withdrawn to prepare for a fresh onslaught on the German centre. The New Zealanders made their way through the Foum Tatahouine Pass, but were held up at 'Plum Pass'. The 1st Armoured Division came on the scene, and following a heavy bombardment from the Desert Air Force and the artillery, broke through on the evening of the 26th. After a lull the advance was continued in the moonlight, until it was held up near El Hamma by anti-tank guns.

By this time Rommel was off and 'the desert fox' succeeded in getting his battered army away with the loss of only 2,500 prisoners. But if the bag was small, Mareth was one of Montgomery's most brilliant operations. It was Rommel's last battle in Africa. A few days later he was ordered home to Germany. The Italian, Messe, who now assumed command, fell back to Enfidaville.

The tempo of the campaign was rising. The Eighth Army captured Enfidaville on 20 April and the First Army at last took Longstop Hill. Alexander now regrouped his forces for the final assault of the Axis 'fortress'. The battle opened on 6 May with heavy bombing which in the words of General Arnold 'blasted a channel from Medjez el Bab to Tunis'. Meanwhile over 1,000 guns were pounding the defenders. At 3.30 a.m. sappers stole forward to clear mines and cut wire, to make way for the infantry, who overran the enemy outposts in the dark and by dawn had reached his main position. By 11 a.m. they were through, and casualties had not been heavy. It was now the turn of the armour, and by the night of the 7th two divisions (6th and 7th) had occupied Tunis. The same day the Americans took Bizerta.

The Axis forces, still more or less intact, but in great confusion, were beating a hasty retreat into the Cape Bon Peninsula. This is well described by General Fuller as 'an exceedingly strong position and the natural citadel of the Tunisian fortress. Like a double wall, across its base ran two lines of hills, with two main gates, one in the north and the other in the south at Hamman Lif and Hammamet respectively.'

Alexander knew that if he did not strike at once the enemy would get set in this citadel. He sent in the 6th Armoured Division at nightfall on the 8th. Its moonlight advance from Hamman Lif to Hammamet in 10 hours is one of the strangest and most impressive feats of arms in the whole history of the Second World War. Without stopping to take prisoners they thrust on right through the heart of the enemy position, striking confusion into all who saw them. British tanks seemed to be everywhere. The German communications system had collapsed. There were plenty of generals and plenty of soldiers; the orders just weren't coming through. Every man was left to take counsel of his own fears. There was a wholesale surrender. On the 12th 250,415 German and Italian troops laid down their arms. The Battle of Tunis, one of the swiftest and most decisive of the whole war, was over. The Tunisian campaign had cost the Allies some 70,000 casualties of whom 20,000 were Americans. From now on Eisenhower would be leading soldiers with some claim to consider themselves veterans. 'The troops that come out of this campaign,' he said, 'are going to be battle-wise and tactically efficient.'

Above: **An American P.38 Lightning blazes after having been shot down.**

Right: **Soldiers sleep after an exhausting night of fighting on the Mareth Line.**

Below: **Dejected prisoners of war taken during the battle.**

19 STALINGRAD

'Ich bleibe an der Wolga.' *Adolf Hitler*

'For us, there is no land beyond the Volga!'
Slogan of the Russian 62nd Army

By the end of 1941 the Russians, it is estimated, had already suffered about 4,500,000 casualties. It is idle to pretend that their long retreat was part of a subtle master-plan, though this myth was an article of faith to all good Bolsheviks while Stalin lived. Even so their heavy sacrifices had won the Russians time to organize new armies and by December 1941 the Germans had identified 280 rifle and cavalry divisions and 44 tank or mechanized brigades. The great Russian winter offensive, designed to encircle the German Army Group Centre, had lost its momentum by mid-February. Fresh German divisions arrived to fill the gap torn by the Russians between Army Groups Centre and North, and the Germans, clad in the furs and winter clothing produced by Goebbels' appeal, made a gradual recovery. Then came the spring rains, and, both sides being stuck in the mud, there was a temporary halt.

On the ground the great Russian offensive had been indecisive, but in peoples' minds it had a tremendous importance. The veteran Russian generals, January and February, had lost none of their old skill; the new ones Zhukov and Koniev had also proved their worth. The myth of Teuton invincibility was exploded. Everywhere the men who were to face the German armies in the years ahead took heart. But despite all this Hitler himself had strengthened his personal position. His will-power, he could boast, had saved the day, when his staff-trained generals had wanted to take refuge in retreat. The *Führer* was now his own Commander-in-Chief. General Halder, chief of the OKH, was no more than his personal chief of staff. By remote control this semi-educated former corporal conducted the operations involving millions of men, from his Headquarters, the *Wolfsschanze*, at Rastenburg, in East Prussia. On 5 April 1942 he issued Directive No. 41 in

Above: **General Paulus confers with Lieutenant General Pfeffer shortly after the launching of the German summer offensive.**

Below: **Stalingrad in flames as Paulus' Sixth Army reached the outer suburbs.**

which he outlined his plans for his summer offensive. His aim was 'to wipe out the entire defence potential remaining to the Soviets, and to cut them off, as far as possible, from their most important centres of industry'. All available German and allied forces were to take part in this task, but the security of occupied territories in western and northern Europe, *especially along the coast*, was to be ensured in all circumstances. The plan was for Army Group Centre to stand fast while the armies in the north were to capture Leningrad and link up with the Finns, while those in the south were to break through into the Caucasus. Hitler considered that these aims could only be achieved one at a time and therefore meant to begin in the southern sector by 'destroying the enemy before the Don'.

The Russians too were thinking in terms of the offensive and, as preliminary operations, meant to launch local attacks at Leningrad, Demyansk, Orel, Kharkov, in the Donetz bend, and in the Crimea. On 12 May Marshal Timoshenko (South-West Front) began with a thrust near Kharkov, only to find that he had run into the main German striking force. With the concurrence of his political commissar, Nikita S. Krushchev, he asked Stalin to let him call off the offensive. This permission was refused, and when on 17 May the Germans struck back his force in the Izyum bridgehead south of Kharkov was seriously compromised. On 19 May Stalin gave Timoshenko his belated permission to extricate his men, but the trap had sprung. In the fighting that followed 240,000 Russians were taken. And that was the end of Stalin's summer offensive.

Above: **Deep in Soviet territory, German troops undergo special training to equip them for the fighting in the harsh conditions on the Eastern Front.**

For the Germans this was a great start to the campaigning season, but there was now a delay of two months while they overran the Crimea. Sevastopol, which had held out for eight months, fell to the Eleventh Army on 1 July. It was not until 28 June that the main German summer offensive was begun by Army Group B. By 6 July the Second and Fourth Panzer Armies had taken Voronezh. Meanwhile on 30 June the Sixth Army had pushed eastward from Kharkov to act as the southern jaw of a giant pincer movement. The bag produced by this encirclement fell short of 100,000 prisoners, and Hitler, so far from being grateful for a respectable victory, sacked von Bock and on 13 July gave command of Army Group B to Field Marshal von Weichs. On the same day Hitler ordered Army Group A, with Fourth Panzer Army attached, to turn south, cross the lower Don and drive the Russians into a pocket round Rostov. The town fell on 23 July, but once again the *Führer* got less prisoners than he had bargained for. It was at this juncture that,

Above:* General Vasily Chuikov, commander of the Sixty-second Army during the Battle for control of Stalingrad. He recounted his experience of the battle in *The Beginning of the Road.

most unwisely, he removed about half of the Eleventh Army for his Leningrad offensive. As in 1941 he was flouting the principle of concentration of force.

The early summer of 1942 had seen some revival of the old German successes – the rapid overrunning of the Crimea; the capture of Tobruk (21 June); the air offensive which seemed to be starving Malta into submission. Certainly Hitler had reason to be pleased with these successes, but they deluded him into believing that his strategic situation was rather better than was actually the case. However Hitler did foresee that the battle for Stalingrad would be fierce.

The German successes continued in August, but already the troops were showing signs of tiredness and their tactics were becoming stereotyped. Marshal Chuikov (64th Army), who had his Second World War 'baptism of fire' on the Don Front in July, has some comments on their performance.

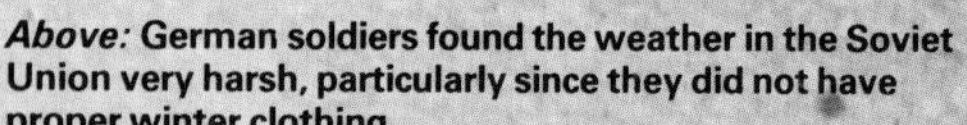

***Above:* German soldiers found the weather in the Soviet Union very harsh, particularly since they did not have proper winter clothing.**

***Below:* A Panzer Mark IV moves across the Ukrainian snow during the winter of 1942–43.**

'Observing how the Germans carried out their artillery preparation against the 229th Infantry Division's sector, I saw the weak points in their tactics. In strength and organization this artillery preparation was weak. Artillery and mortar attacks were not co-ordinated or in depth, but only against the main line of defence. I saw no broad manoeuvre with artillery cover in the dynamic of battle.'

He goes on to say:

'I was expecting close combined operations between the enemy's artillery and ground forces, a precise organization of the artillery barrage, a lightning-fast manoeuvre of shell and wheel. But this was not the case. I encountered the far from new method of slow wearing down, trench by trench. . . . The German tanks did not go into action without infantry and air support. On the battlefield there was no evidence of the "prowess" of German tank crews, their courage and speed in action, about which foreign newspapers had written. The reverse was true, in fact – they operated sluggishly, extremely cautiously and indecisively. The German infantry was strong in automatic fire, but I saw no rapid movement or resolute attack on the battlefield. When advancing, the German infantry did not spare their bullets, but frequently fired into thin air.'

On the other hand the thoroughly efficient co-operation of the *Luftwaffe* showed the familiarity of the pilots with the tactics of both sides.

'In modern warfare victory is impossible without combined action by all types of forces and without good administration. The Germans had this kind of polished, co-ordinated action. In battle the different arms of their forces never hurried, did not push ahead alone, but fought with the whole mass of men and technical backing. A few minutes before a general attack, their aircraft would fly in, bomb and strafe the object under attack, pinning the defending troops to the ground, and then infantry and tanks with supporting artillery and mortar fire would cut into our military formations almost with impunity.'

Meanwhile on the Leningrad front the Russians had made an unsuccessful attempt to break the German siege, but had at least forestalled the German attempt to capture the city.

In the south Army Group A (Field-Marshal von Kleist) had taken Maikop, but too late to prevent the complete destruction of the oilfield. German Jäger planted the Swastika on Mount Elbrus, but the Russians still held out in the passes of the Caucasus. By 21 August the *Führer* was already 'very agitated' by the lack of progress on that front. The Sixth and Fourth Panzer Armies closed in on Stalingrad, but being compelled to detach troops to guard their flanks, were gradually brought to a halt by 6 September. At last the Russians seemed to be getting the measure of the invaders. Their losses in men and territory, though grievous, had been far less serious in 1942 than in the previous year. In terms of attrition the German position was by no means brilliant. Hitler's armies on the Eastern Front numbered some 3,138,000, excluding the Finns, while Stalin had 4,255,000 men in the field. Behind the German front the partisans were active.

As the situation worsened, Hitler resorted to his old remedy of sacking generals. List was the first to go (9 September), and for two and a half months the Dictator actually commanded Army Group A in person: an extraordinary arrangement. The fact that his HQ, Vinnitsa in the Ukraine, was 700 miles in the rear of his front might have daunted a more professional soldier, but in Hitler's fantasy world such considerations went for little. On 24 September, after a series of fearful scenes, Halder was relieved as chief of OKH by General Zeitzler. Warlimont, whose position as Deputy Chief of the OKH staff gives his evidence considerable weight, assesses the *Führer*'s state of mind at this period. He tells us of a briefing conference:

Above: **German infantryman advances towards a burning farm. The German advance in the summer of 1942 was spectacular.**

'Hitler fixed me with a malevolent stare and suddenly I thought: the man's confidence has gone; he has realized that his deadly game is moving to its appointed end, that Soviet Russia is not going to be overthrown at the second attempt and that now the war on two fronts, which he has unleashed by his wanton arbitrary actions, will grind the Reich to powder. My thoughts ran on: that is why he can no longer bear to have around him the generals who have too often been witnesses of his faults, his errors, his illusions and his day dreams; that is why he wishes to get away from them, why he wishes to see people around him who he feels have unlimited and unshakable confidence in him.'

For a time the new chief of staff, Zeitzler, enjoyed great popularity with Göring and the rest of Hitler's courtiers. He certainly began well, with an address to the officers of OKH in which he said:

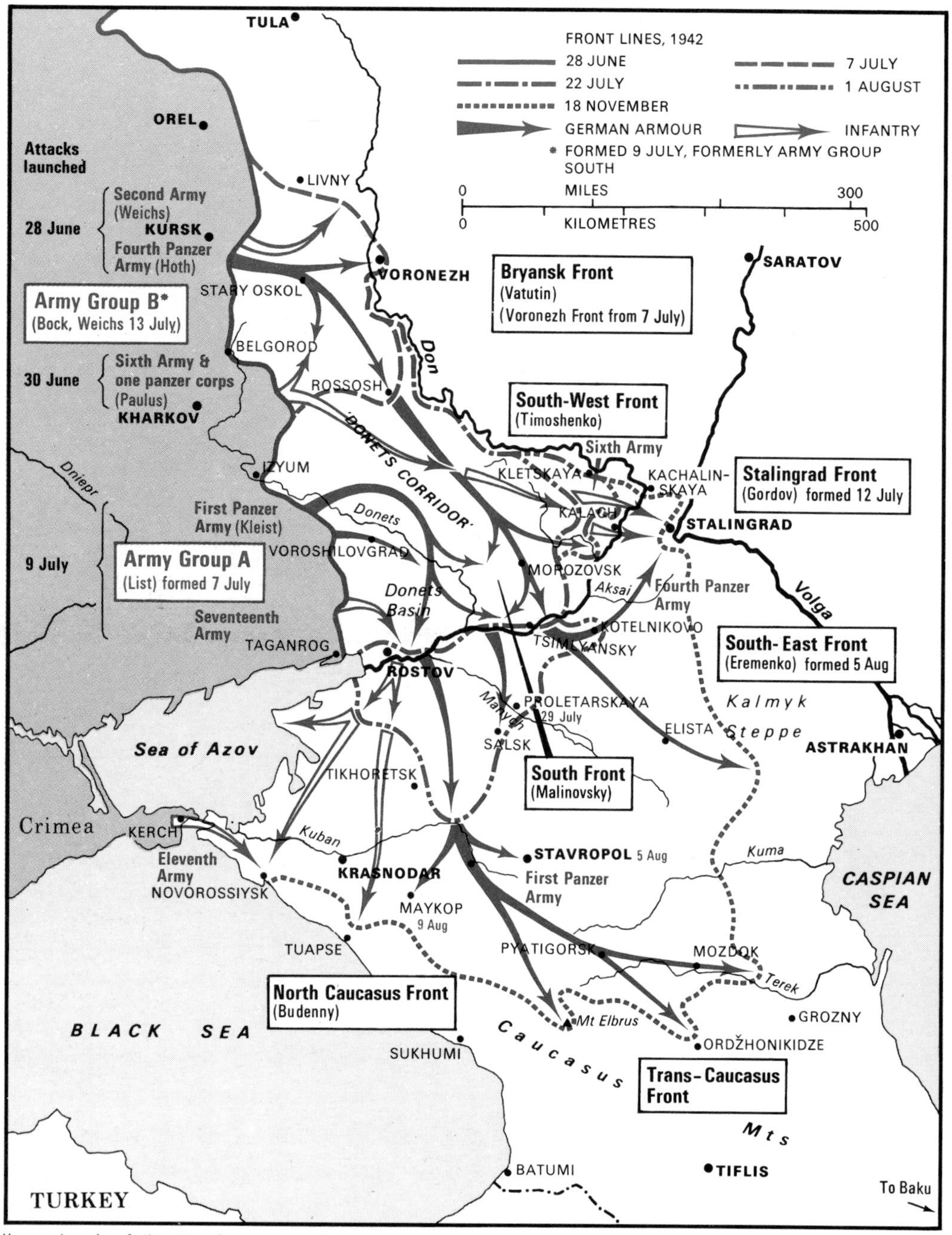

FRONT LINES, 1942
28 JUNE
7 JULY
22 JULY
1 AUGUST
18 NOVEMBER
GERMAN ARMOUR
INFANTRY
* FORMED 9 JULY, FORMERLY ARMY GROUP SOUTH
MILES 0 300
KILOMETRES 0 500

TULA
OREL
LIVNY
Attacks launched
28 June
Second Army (Weichs)
KURSK
Fourth Panzer Army (Hoth)
VORONEZH
Bryansk Front (Vatutin) (Voronezh Front from 7 July)
SARATOV
Army Group B* (Bock, Weichs 13 July)
STARY OSKOL
BELGOROD
Don
30 June
Sixth Army & one panzer corps (Paulus)
KHARKOV
ROSSOSH
South-West Front (Timoshenko)
'DONETS CORRIDOR'
Sixth Army
IZYUM
Dniepr
KLETSKAYA
KACHALINSKAYA
Stalingrad Front (Gordov) formed 12 July
First Panzer Army (Kleist)
Donets
KALACH
STALINGRAD
9 July
Army Group A (List) formed 7 July
VOROSHILOVGRAD
MOROZOVSK
Fourth Panzer Army
Aksai
Volga
Donets Basin
Seventeenth Army
TAGANROG
KOTELNIKOVO
TSIMLYANSKY
South-East Front (Eremenko) formed 5 Aug
ROSTOV
Manych
PROLETARSKAYA 29 July
Kalmyk Steppe
ELISTA
ASTRAKHAN
Sea of Azov
SALSK
South Front (Malinovsky)
TIKHORETSK
Crimea
KERCH
Kuban
STAVROPOL 5 Aug
Kuma
Eleventh Army
NOVOROSSIYSK
KRASNODAR
First Panzer Army
CASPIAN SEA
MAYKOP 9 Aug
TUAPSE
PYATIGORSK
MOZDOK
Terek
North Caucasus Front (Budenny)
GROZNY
BLACK SEA
Mt Elbrus
ORDŽHONIKIDZE
SUKHUMI
Caucasus Mts
Trans-Caucasus Front
BATUMI
TIFLIS
To Baku
TURKEY

'I require the following from every Staff Officer: he must believe in the *Führer* and in his method of command. He must on every occasion radiate this confidence to his subordinates and those around him. I have no use for anybody on the General Staff who cannot meet these requirements.'

This was to be the atmosphere at HQ during the siege of Stalingrad, in that winter when the tide of war had at last reached the turn.

November was a black month for Hitler. The news of El Alamein, followed by that of *Torch*, made it clear that sooner or later the Axis forces in North Africa were going to be crushed. This news came when Hitler was on his way to address the 'old comrades' of the Nazi party in the Munich Beer Cellar. By way of offsetting the bad tidings he could think of nothing better than to assure the veterans that he was now master of Stalingrad, where the doubtful battle had been raging since early September. On 19 November the Russian Fifth Tank Army broke through the Rumanian Third Army North of that city. By the 22nd the Sixth German Army and about half of General Hoth's Fourth Panzer Army were encircled; 280,000 men were in mortal peril.

This was indeed a reversal of fortune, for in the September days there had been desperate fighting at Stalingrad, and the Russians had barely clung to the west bank of the Volga. Marshal Chuikov, who bore much of the responsibility, had decided, as a result of his experiences against 'the Whites' in the Civil War and his study of enemy tactics,

'that the best method of fighting Germans would be close battle, applied night and day in different forms. We should get as close to the enemy as possible, so that his air force could not bomb our forward units or trenches. Every German soldier must be made to feel that he was living under the muzzle of a Russian gun, always ready to treat him to a fatal dose of lead.'

They reduced No-man's-land to the throw of a grenade. Strong-points were fortified in the centre of the city and garrisoned by 50 or 100 men. Buildings changed hands not once but many times. From 17–20 September, for example, there was a fierce struggle for an enormous building on the southern outskirts of the town, the grain elevator. Colonel Dubyanski (O.C. Guards Infantry Division) reported by telephone to Chuikov:

'The situation has changed. Before, we occupied the upper part of the elevator and the Germans the lower part. Now we have driven them out of the lower part, but German troops have penetrated upstairs and fighting is now going on in the upper part.'

Stubborn fighting marked the resistance of improvised fortresses without number. Archetype of these was the defence of 'Pavlov's House', a key strong-point in the central district held by a handful of men belonging to Rodimtsev's 13th Guards Infantry Division. Sergeant Jacob Pavlov and two of his men, Alexandrov and Afanasiev, were Russians. The rest of his garrison were Subgayda and Gluschenko from the Ukraine; Mosiyashvili and Stepanashvili, both Georgians; Turganov, an Uzbek; Murzayev, a Kazakh; Sukba, an Abkhazian; Turdiev, a Tajik; and Ramazanov, the Tartar. It was a roll call of the nationalities of the USSR! Chuikov tells us that the Germans 'unleashed a torrent of bombs and shells on to the house', which was held for more than fifty days, without sleep and rest, and remained impregnable to the end. For his dogged defence Pavlov became a Hero of the Soviet Union.

All through October the struggle went on. Those were the darkest days. But somehow the Russians hung on. Reserves were fed in across the Volga as they reached the front and eventually Paulus' seemingly inexhaustible reserves could do no more. On 29 October the battle began to die down and the next day, apart from exchanges of firing, there was no action. On the 31st the 62nd Army counterattacked from its narrow strip of land along the banks of the Volga. Advances were measured in yards, but the attack was a great success and reclaimed part of the Krasny Oktyabr factory.

Early in November the temperature dropped sharply and ice began to appear on the river. On 11 November Paulus launched a new attack, but this too was held in two days of stubborn fighting. The *Luftwaffe*, which in October had been flying as many as 3,000 sorties a day, could no longer manage more than 1,000. And thus it came about that when on 19 November the Russians counter-attacked on three fronts at once a trap closed behind the Germans which cost them 22 divisions.

Hitler entrusted to Field Marshal von Manstein the task of rescuing the Sixth Army, but he refused Paulus permission to try to break out. The supply difficulty became acute. Petrol,

Below: **General Chuikov (centre) directed the street fighting in the city of Stalingrad.**

Above: **The German Sixth Army was forced to surrender on 31 January 1943.**

Above right: **The Germans tried to bomb Soviet resistance to smithereens but the Russian troops found it easier to fight protected by the rubble.**

Right: **House-to-house fighting in Stalingrad continued for more than four months.**

shells, and firewood were hard to come by. After Christmas the bread ration was cut by half to 50 grammes a day. Many of the men existed on watery soup fortified with the bones of horses they dug up. Colonel Dingler tells us that 'As a Christmas treat the Army allowed the slaughtering of 4,000 of the available horses.' This was no help to the armoured and motorized Divisions.

The cold was bitter in December and the ground was too hard to dig. Aeroplane tyres stuck to the runways. If a position was abandoned the soldiers found themselves without

dugouts or trenches when they got back to their new line. Without petrol the armour could not manoeuvre to repulse the Russian attacks. The apertures of tanks became blocked with ice. Men froze to death in their vehicles. But all hope was not yet gone. On 9 December it was announced that the Fourth Panzer Army, which had been reinforced, would start its relieving attack next day, and by 16 December distant gunfire could be heard. Plans were made to break out as soon as Colonel-General Hoth's spearhead should be within 20 miles.

The plans for the relief were carefully examined by Field Marshal von Manstein. It was decided that Hoth, himself 'an officer with an excellent reputation', should make his thrust from the direction of Kotelnikovo some 60 miles SW of Stalingrad. At Nizhne Chirskaya on the Chir the Germans were only 25 miles away, but an attack from this direction would involve a crossing of the Don, which von Manstein rightly rejected as too hazardous an operation. From the first Hoth met with furious opposition from strong Russian forces of armour and infantry under General Vatutin. It took the Germans a week to fight their way forward 30 miles, but at the end of it they succeeded in capturing two crossings over the river Aksai by a *coup de main*. They were still 45 miles short of the beleaguered army.

At this moment Marshal Zhukov launched a massive offensive on the middle Don, tore a sixty mile gap in the front of the Italian Eighth Army, and thrust southwards towards Rostov, threatening the communications of Field Marshal von Kleist's Army Group in the Caucasus. Von Manstein had nothing up his sleeve. To check the Russian flood he was compelled to take 6th Panzer Division from Hoth's Army. On paper the latter still had two Panzer divisions, though their tank strength was now down to

Left: **The German Army found it could not rely on its allies when the going got tough. Here Bulgarian troops take part in the summer advance.**

Below left: **General Rokossovsky led the Don Front outside Stalingrad. His armies achieved the decisive breakthrough against the Axis forces.**

Above: **German troops stream forward through the endless steppes.**

Right: **The Red October factory which was the scene of some of the bitterest fighting on the banks of the Volga.**

35. Desperate fighting during the next week brought no real progress, partly perhaps because Paulus himself remained inactive. Had he also attacked, the Russians might not have been able to concentrate against LVII Panzer Corps, Hoth's spearhead. Again lack of petrol may have been the key to the tactical situation.

On Christmas Eve the Russians counterattacked the Aksai bridgehead in great force, and, keeping up the pressure night and day, had retaken both bridges by the 26th. The decimated Germans withdrew southwards.

No power on earth could now save the Sixth Army, least of all the *Luftwaffe*, which Göring had promised would keep Paulus supplied. On 15 January the Hungarian Second Army dis-

Below right: **Soviet partisans played an important role in sabotaging German communications. The German Army had left large tracts of land unsecured because of its rapid advance.**

Below: **Axis troops advance during the offensive against Stalingrad.**

integrated, and far away in the north on that same day the German siege of Leningrad was broken. On the 22nd General Zeitzler, urged on by von Manstein, plucked up his courage to ask Hitler whether the Sixth Army should now be authorized to capitulate, only to be told that the army should fight to the last man. But Sixth Army had reached the end of its tether. On 31 January Paulus, who had been promoted Field Marshal only the previous day, surrendered. Hitler had lost 20 German divisions, of which three were armoured and another three motorized, besides two Rumanian divisions – whom their allies had struck off the ration strength a fortnight before the end! The Germans lost 60,000 vehicles, 1,500 tanks and 6,000 guns. Of the 280,000 men encircled 42,000 wounded, sick and specialists were evacuated by air; 91,000 surrendered. Of these it is thought, only 6,000 lived to see their homes once more.

It has often been suggested that Hitler should have given Paulus permission to break out. But had this been attempted it is difficult to imagine it being successful. We know that petrol for the six mobile divisions was lacking. The remaining 16, with the possible exception of the Rumanian cavalry division, were comparatively slow-moving and had eaten most of their horses by the end of December. If Hitler and his entourage had withdrawn Sixth Army at the end of October, when it was clearly stuck, a large part of it might have made a reasonably orderly retreat. By the time von Manstein tried to break through, there was really very little hope of pulling Paulus back, even had Hitler consented to such an attempt. Mussolini, more

Left: **Retreating German forces left behind 80 tanks and many motor transports which were to be of use to the Red Army.**

Below: **The ruins of Stalingrad.**

clear-sighted about other people's troubles than his own, commented that Stalingrad 'makes clear to the minds of the masses the great attachment of the Russian people to the régime – a thing proved by the exceptional resistance and the spirit of sacrifice'.

No disaster suffered by the Allies in a war where disasters had not been lacking could be compared with the blow Hitler received at Stalingrad. And he was soon (13 May) to receive another at least as costly in Tunisia. Truly the tide had turned in those November days of 1942 when Montgomery emerged victorious from the field of El Alamein; when Eisenhower's host set foot on the shores of North Africa; and when, after an epic defence, the Russians encircled their besiegers on the banks of the Volga.

Above: Red Army sappers cut a way through barbed wire.

Above left: Workers defend their factory.

Top: The red flag is raised in triumph over Stalingrad.

20 GUADALCANAL

'. . . an island that neither side really wanted, but which neither could afford to abandon to the enemy.'

Samuel Eliot Morison

As early as February 1942 it occurred to Admiral Ernest J. King that it would be unwise to permit the Japanese to consolidate their gains in the Pacific. King was prepared to concede that the Allied strategic aim of defeating Germany first was correct. But at the same time he was convinced of the need for a 'defensive-offensive' strategy in the Pacific.

After the defeat at Midway, General Tojo began to build up a new Eighth Fleet in the South Pacific. A new offensive against Port Moresby was in the wind. King was aware of this design, and on 2 July, despite the objections of General Marshall, he obtained the Joint Chiefs of Staff directive for Operation *Watchtower*: the seizure, by a force based on New Zealand, of Tulagi and Guadalcanal in the Solomon Islands. It was only three days later that American reconnaissance planes reported that the Japanese were building an airfield on Guadalcanal. Without more ado King ordered that *Watchtower* should begin within the month.

This was the Americans' first combined operation since the Spanish-American War of 1898, and it was laid on in great haste. The forces available were not numerous, and to many officers it was known by the code-name *Shoestring*. The 1st Marine Division, which was to do the assault landing, was under-trained despite some rehearsals in the Fiji Islands, and lacked administrative backing. Nevertheless the actual landings on Guadalcanal and Florida Island, though carried out in daylight, were a complete surprise and met but little opposition. The airstrip, where the Japanese just melted into the jungle, was captured by 1600 hours, and was renamed Henderson Field. There were not more than 500 Japanese soldiers and 1,500 pioneers in the island.

Now began a six months' campaign by land and sea. Ashore it was fought out in a dank and malarious jungle. Throughout August and September some 17,000 Marines, under Lieutenant-General Alexander A. Vandegrift, were only strong enough to hold a narrow strip seven miles long and four miles wide and to protect the vital airstrip. Both sides strove hard to reinforce their armies, and this set the pattern of the fighting afloat, with the Americans trying to intercept the 'Tokyo Express' bringing reinforcements down from Bougainville, and the Japanese striving to avenge Midway. Seven major sea-fights mark the course of the campaign.

News of the American landings reached Vice-Admiral Mikawa (Eighth Fleet) at Rabaul early on 7 August. He decided at once to reinforce the Japanese garrisons, and several hundred troops were embarked in the *Meiyo Maru*. About midnight on 8 August she was sunk off Cape St George by the submarine *S-38*. Meanwhile Mikawa had concentrated seven cruisers and a destroyer. This force got among the Allied fleet on the night 8/9 August and in the battle of Savo Island, sank four heavy cruisers and a destroyer for the loss of 35 men killed and 57 wounded.

Ashore the US Marines were holding their own. Fortunately the Japanese thought that only 3,000 had been landed. With typical arrogance they considered that the 815 men under Colonel Ichiki, whom they landed on the night 18/19 August, should be sufficient to deal with such a force. Within two days this Japanese unit had been annihilated by the 1st Marines for a loss of 34 men killed, in the battle of Alligator Creek. The Japanese jungle-fighter had met his match at last.

The third week of August saw the inconclusive battle of the Eastern Solomons. Yamamoto, with a strong force, including three carriers, was covering the passage of transports reinforcing western Guadalcanal with another 1,500 men. The Americans sank the light carrier *Ryujo* and several other vessels, but failed to hit the *Shokaku* or the *Zuikaku*. The *Enterprise* was badly damaged and the *Saratoga*, which was torpedoed on 31 August, took three months to repair. It was not much of a victory, even though it taught the Americans a good deal about aircraft tactics and carrier construction.

In mid-September a powerful thrust by General Kawaguchi was repulsed by the Marines in the Battle of Edson's Ridge, the central feature of the American perimeter. The battle cost the Japanese 2,000 of the 9,000 men they then had on Guadalcanal. American casualties numbered only about 200, but the second Japanese assault had very nearly won the crest of the ridge. It had been touch and go. At sea a curious battle had developed. The Americans ruled the waves by day and the 'Tokyo Express' – light cruisers and destroyers full of troops – by night. Both sides were still trying hard to build up their land forces and were paying a heavy price in warships. On 15 September the Americans lost the big carrier *Wasp*, torpedoed while covering six transports which succeeded in landing the 7th Marine Regiment on the 18th.

The next crisis at sea was the indecisive Battle of Cape Esperance (11–12 October), in which the Americans, under a brilliant young Rear-Admiral, Norman Scott, got rather the better of Admiral Goto. While the sea-fight was being fought out, both sides succeeded in putting still more men ashore. By mid-October the Marine aviators at Henderson Field were desperately short of fuel. Moreover, the Americans were constantly being subjected to heavy bombardment from the sea. Well might Nimitz say (15 October): 'It now appears that we are unable to control the sea in the Guadalcanal area. Thus our supply of the positions will only be done at great expense to us. The situation is not hopeless, but it is certainly critical.'

At this juncture Nimitz replaced the conscientious but uninspiring Admiral Ghormley with Vice-Admiral 'Bill' Halsey. 'The announcement that he was now COMSOPAC was received on board ships of that force with cheers and rejoicings.' Admiral King reinforced Halsey with the new battleship *Indiana* and a task group from the Atlantic, besides 24 submarines. It was none too soon, for the Japanese, who were planning to take Henderson Field, had fixed 22 October as the day when it should be theirs once more.

At this time the depredations of German U-Boats in the Atlantic and the claims of Operation *Torch*, were engrossing the attention of the Joint Chiefs of Staff, but on 24 October President Roosevelt himself came to the support of King and MacArthur, ruling that Guadalcanal must be reinforced, and that speedily.

The Japanese land offensive, which had opened on 20 October, had been firmly met. The Marines, reinforced by Army units, beat off every attack on the airfield and gave Admiral Kinkaid time to intervene. In the battle which takes its name from the malarious island of Santa Cruz, the Japanese had the *Shokaku* put out of action for nine months and lost about 100 planes, but sank the new carrier *Hornet* and damaged the *Enterprise* at a time when the

Right: **United States transports off Tulagi, a small island near Guadalcanal, on 10 August 1942.**

Far right: **Admiral Chester Nimitz, Commander-in-Chief of the Pacific Fleet, confers with Vice-Admiral Robert Ghormley, who was in commnd of naval forces at Guadalcanal.**

Below: **Landings in the Solomons, 7 August 1942.**

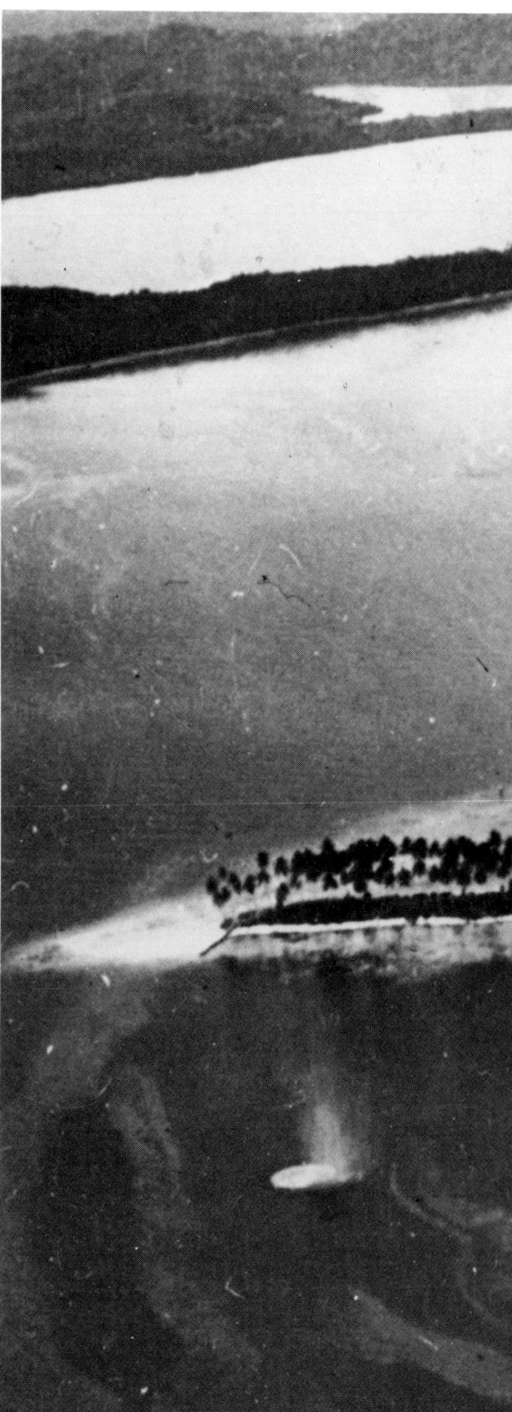

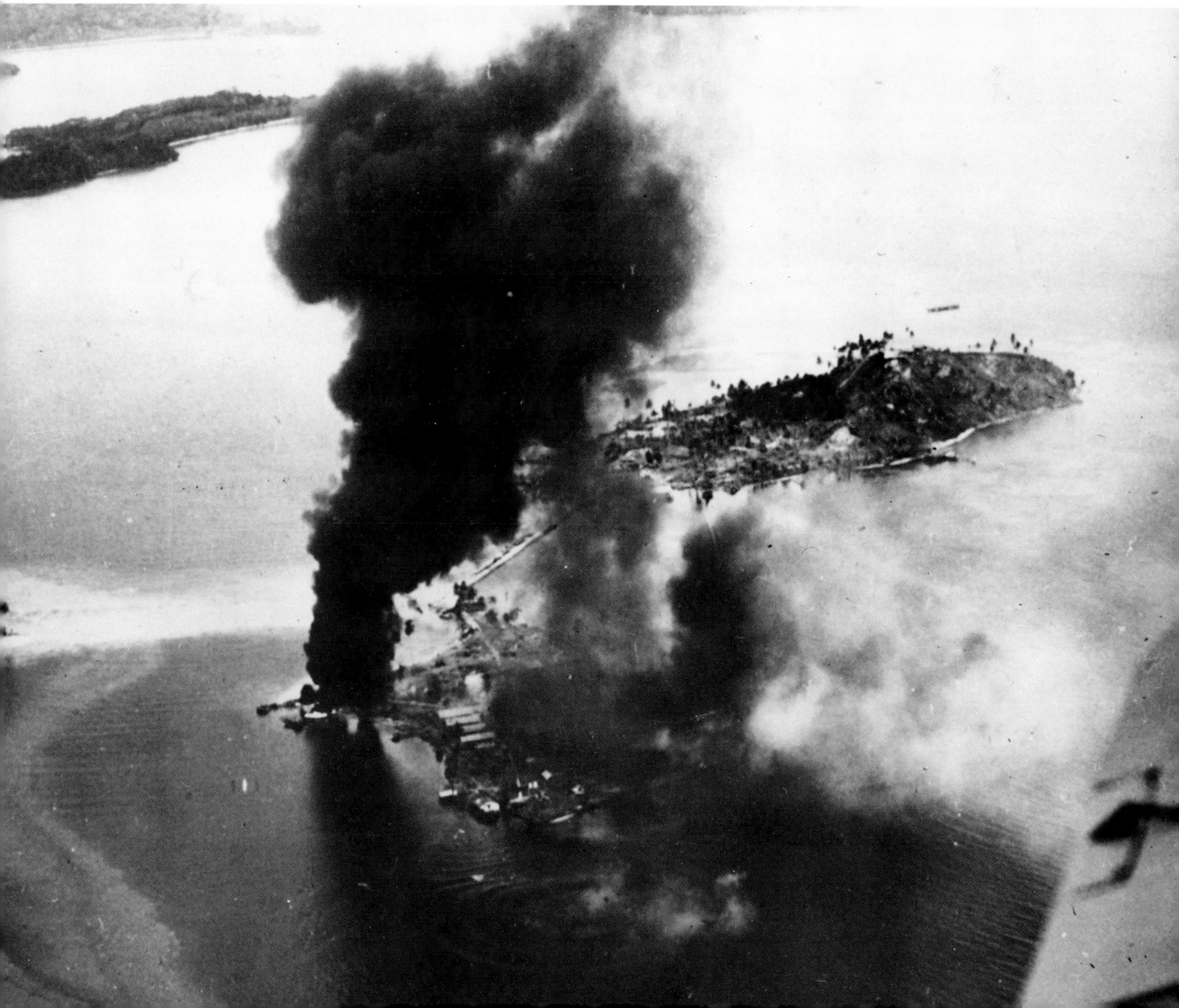

other American carrier in the Pacific, *Saratoga*, was under repair. Even so the Americans had gained time to make ready for the next crisis.

The opening round of the sea battle of Guadalcanal was fought on the night 12/13 November. It was a desperate and confused affair in which the Japanese lost a battleship (*Hiei*) and two destroyers, and the Americans two light cruisers, and four destroyers. Two Rear-Admirals, Daniel J. Callaghan, the commander of the US force and Norman Scott, were killed. In round two, Vice-Admiral Tanaka reinforced the Japanese garrison by means of a super 'Tokyo Express' – 11 destroyers and 11 transports. American airmen from *Enterprise* and from Henderson Field sank six of the transports, but Tanaka pushed on with admirable *sang froid* and actually landed the men from four of his transports by literally running the ships ashore! His destroyers picked up some 5,000 survivors from the others. Meanwhile American aircraft had sunk the heavy cruiser *Kinugasa*. Round three was yet another night battle, in which Rear-Admiral Willis Augustus ('Ching') Lee defeated Kondo and sank the battleship *Kirishima*. Things were at last beginning to go rather better for the Americans, and indeed the Japanese Navy would now have given up Guadalcanal if Tojo would have let them.

Admiral Halsey calls this 'a decisive American victory by any standard'. His comments are significant. Halsey now created a new striking force, mainly heavy cruisers and destroyers. Before this force, under Rear-Admiral Carlton H. Wright, had time to train together, it had to take on the tenacious Tanaka and another 'Tokyo Express' in the battle of Tassafaronga. It was yet another night fight, and this time the Japanese though badly outnumbered, came off best. At 2316 hours the destroyer *Fletcher*, which had the latest kind of radar

'. . . picked up Tanaka's force, broad on the port bow, steaming slowly along the Guadalcanal shore toward the jumping-off place. The squadron commander in *Fletcher* asked permission for his four van destroyers to fire torpedoes. Wright hesitated for four minutes before granting it, and so lost the battle. For, by the time the torpedoes were launched, about 2321, the Japanese column had passed the Americans on a contrary course and the range was too great for American torpedoes to overtake them.' (Morison)

The Japanese lost one destroyer. The Americans had the heavy cruiser *Northampton* sunk, while the *Minneapolis, New Orleans* and *Pensacola* were all so badly damaged that they were out of action for the next nine months. Morison, with his customary candour, describes this as 'a sharp defeat, inflicted on an alerted and superior cruiser force by a surprised and inferior destroyer force whose decks were cluttered with freight'. But at least the Japanese had been prevented from landing their reinforcements, and for this, the ungrateful Japanese higher command removed Tanaka shortly afterwards.

In December both sides continued to reinforce their garrisons. General Imamura, who had 60,000 men in Rabaul, was able to spare two divisions. But by the end of the month the Japanese on Guadalcanal were practically starving. On 19 January General Patch, who had succeeded General Vandegrift (9 December), began a two-division thrust towards Cape Esperance, driving the remnants of the Japanese before him and mopping up the island at the rate of about a mile a day. The Japanese were still dangerous. On 22 January 1943, for example, the Inagaki unit made a suicidal attack:

'On the eve of the sortie, at midnight, all the assembled men sing the *Kimigayo*, the sad and solemn hymn to the Emperor, then give three *banzais* for his eternal prosperity. The company bows in the direction of the Imperial Palace. While the American loudspeakers, which are set up above the lines, continue to repeat in Japanese the invitation to capitulate, the two hundred men, including the sick and the wounded who have still survived, rush towards death in a supreme attack. . . .'

On 4 January Tojo at last decided to evacuate the island. On 23 January reconnaissance planes reported large numbers of warships and transports at Rabaul and Buin. Halsey deduced that this portended a further attempt at reinforcement. In the hope of luring Yamamoto out, he himself sent up four transports with a strong escort. The bait was not taken, but the covering group under Rear-Admiral Robert C. Giffen was severely attacked from the air and lost the heavy cruiser *Chicago* in the so-called Battle of Rennell Island.

By 6 February the Japanese had completed the evacuation of 11,000 men. Not until the 9th did the Americans realize that they had gone, proof of the skill with which the Japanese carried out their withdrawal. Admiral Tanaka attributed the Japanese defeat to lack of an overall operation plan, committing forces piecemeal, terrible communications, unendurable relations with the Army, belittling the enemy, and inferiority in the air. 'We stumbled along from one error to another, while the enemy grew wise.'

In this long, desperate and precarious struggle Japanese losses on land, perhaps 20,000, were far greater than those of the Americans, which were not severe. At sea both sides lost precisely 24 warships. Strategically the battle turned the tide of war in the South Pacific. The myth that in the jungle the Japanese soldier was invincible had been dispelled by the US Marine Corps.

Above: **The USS *Minneapolis* was torpedoed on 30 November 1942 at the Battle of Tassafaronga.**

Right: **American transports, carrying valuable supplies come under Japanese attack on 12 November.**

Below: **The carrier *Hornet* came under heavy attack from Japanese dive-bombers during the Battle of Santa Cruz and sank later on 26 October.**

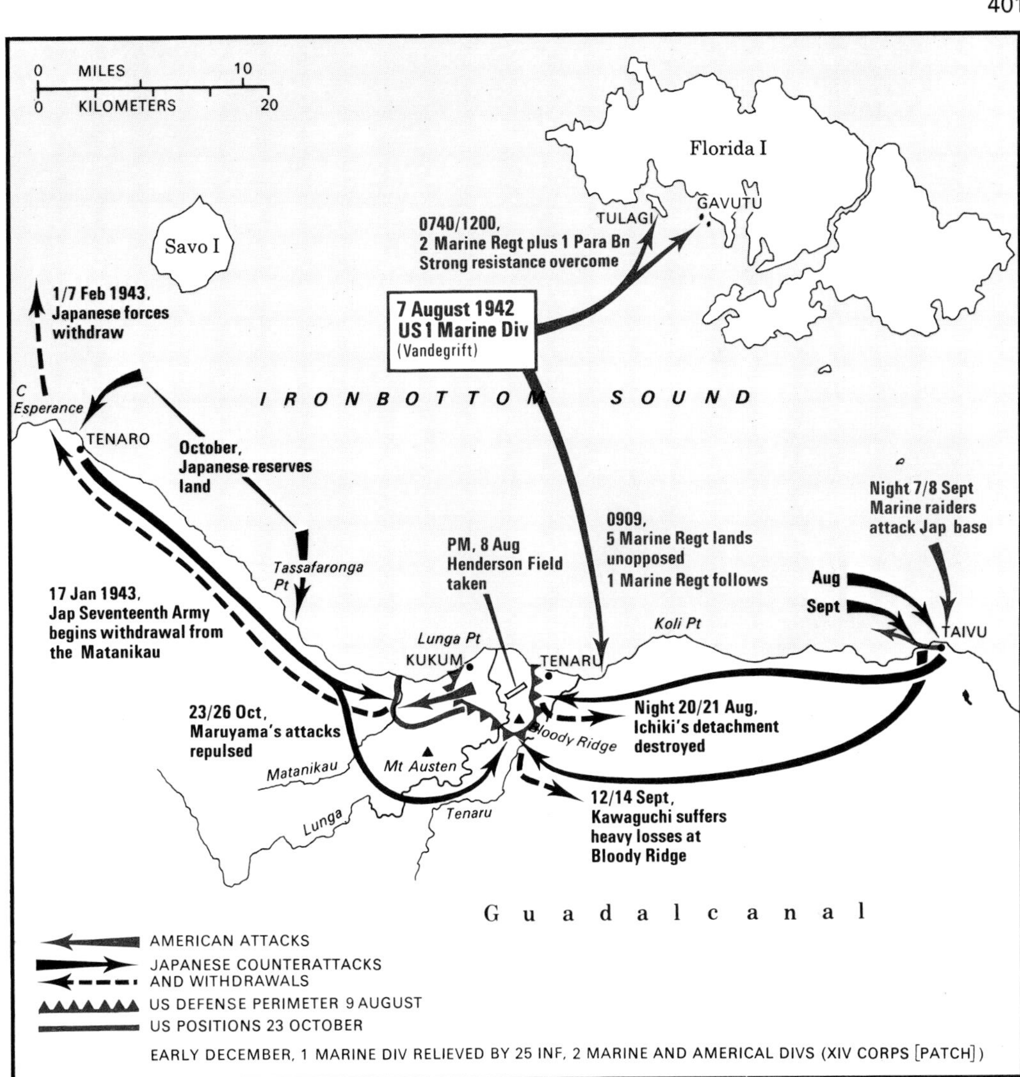

0 MILES 10
0 KILOMETERS 20
Florida I
TULAGI
GAVUTU
Savo I
0740/1200,
2 Marine Regt plus 1 Para Bn
Strong resistance overcome
7 August 1942
US 1 Marine Div
(Vandegrift)
1/7 Feb 1943,
Japanese forces
withdraw
C
Esperance
IRONBOTTOM SOUND
TENARO
October,
Japanese reserves
land
Tassafaronga
Pt
0909,
5 Marine Regt lands
unopposed
1 Marine Regt follows
PM, 8 Aug
Henderson Field
taken
Night 7/8 Sept
Marine raiders
attack Jap base
Aug
Sept
TAIVU
Koli Pt
17 Jan 1943,
Jap Seventeenth Army
begins withdrawal from
the Matanikau
Lunga Pt
KUKUM
TENARU
Night 20/21 Aug,
Ichiki's detachment
destroyed
23/26 Oct,
Maruyama's attacks
repulsed
Bloody Ridge
Matanikau
Mt Austen
Lunga
Tenaru
12/14 Sept,
Kawaguchi suffers
heavy losses at
Bloody Ridge
Guadalcanal
AMERICAN ATTACKS
JAPANESE COUNTERATTACKS
AND WITHDRAWALS
US DEFENSE PERIMETER 9 AUGUST
US POSITIONS 23 OCTOBER
EARLY DECEMBER, 1 MARINE DIV RELIEVED BY 25 INF, 2 MARINE AND AMERICAL DIVS (XIV CORPS [PATCH])

21 THE BOMBER OFFENSIVE AGAINST GERMANY

'If a single bomb drops on Berlin you can call me Meyer!'
Hermann Göring

There were some to whom the experience of the First World War revealed 'the shape of things to come'. One of these was General Smuts, who wrote in 1917 that the air arm

'can be used as an independent means of war operations. Nobody who witnessed the attack on London on 11 July could have any doubt on this point . . . As far as at present can be foreseen there is absolutely no limit to the scale of its future independent war use. And the day may not be far off when aerial operations with their devastation of enemy lands and destruction of industrial and populous centres on a vast scale may become the principal operations of war, to which the other forms of military and naval operations may become secondary and subordinate.'

The theories of the Italian Brigadier General Giulio Douhet, author of *The Command of the Air* (1921), had a very considerable influence – especially among airmen. While preoccupied with strategic bombing, he had no great opinion of aircraft as tactical weapons. He saw that command of the air must be won, but thought that this would be the result of offensive bombing rather than aerial combat. He considered that once the air force won command, superiority on the ground and at sea must follow automatically. A power that had once lost command of the air could not regain it, because the bombing of her aircraft industry would prevent any revival. Douhet considered that the rôle of armies and navies, at least initially, must be defensive, and that this should guide a nation in the deployment of its resources: 'resist on the ground in order to mass for the offensive in the air'. He saw too that an air force which has the initiative can seek out the enemy in his bases, where he is most vulnerable, and destroy his planes and installations on the ground. It followed that the side that got its blow in first had an enormous advantage. 'Whatever its aims, the side which decides to go to war will unleash all its aerial forces in mass against the enemy nation the instant the decision is taken, without waiting to declare war formally . . .'

Douhet underrated the fighter as a defence against the bomber, and grossly underestimated the tonnage of bombs required to knock out a target. 'He considered 500 tons of bombs (mostly gas) quite sufficient to destroy a large city and its inhabitants.' He gave little guidance on the vital subject of target selection, though he did point out that it is 'the most difficult and delicate task in aerial warfare.'

The beginning of the war found the RAF's Bomber Command with very little to back it in the way of reserves or training organization. It was fortunate indeed that there was no bombing campaign in the autumn of 1939 to use up the few trained crews available. In any case the 'Rules of Warfare' as agreed by the Washington Conference on the Limitation of Armaments (1922) laid down that:

'Aerial bombardment for the purpose of terrorizing the civilian population, of destroying or damaging private property not of a military character, or of injuring non-combatants, is prohibited.'

Despite this prohibition, and its own inadequate resources, Bomber Command gradually began to make itself felt from 1940 onwards. The RAF inflicted considerable damage on the invasion barges when a German invasion seemed imminent. Later good work was done against French factories working for the enemy, but the main attack on Germany did not begin until 1943. As it mounted the *Luftwaffe* was compelled to use an ever-increasing part of its strength for the defence of the Fatherland, with a decisive effect on the campaigns in Sicily and Italy and, later, Normandy as well as the Eastern Front.

After the fall of France Britain had three alternatives. One was to surrender – unthinkable; a second was to accept a stalemate which was tantamount to admitting defeat; the third was to attack Germany by a bombing offensive, for any army that Britain alone could raise was unlikely to be able to invade the continent in the teeth of the German Army. The War Cabinet, advised by the Chiefs of Staff, advised the build-up of a force of 4,000 heavy bombers – a number that was never in fact reached.

Below: **The crew of the B-17 *Memphis Belle* return from their 25th operational mission over Germany.**

Above: **A P-51H Mustang fighter. This fighter escorted bomber missions over Germany and was far superior to other operational fighters of the day.**

Left: **Wheel and tyre maintenance on a B-17 Flying Fortress. B-17s were operational in the European theatre and spearheaded the bombing offensive.**

Below left: **Boeing B-17s of the Eighth Air Force in a practice formation over the English country side. B-17s flew in 'box' formation for added protection.**

In 1940 Bomber Command was still small, and its aircraft were obsolescent. It was not in its power to strike with any precision, as General Fuller has suggested should have been done, at the sources of German industrial power, oil and coal. However immoral it may be to measure the success of a bombing offensive by the acreage devastated, the Bomber Command of those days was not a sufficiently sophisticated weapons system to have any alternative. If Mr Churchill was compelled to use a bludgeon, it was for lack of a rapier.

With only a very small bomber force it was good tactics to make concentrated attacks on one target at a time. It was not until December 1940 that Bomber Command first put this idea into action in an attack on Mannheim, which did considerable damage. Thus encouraged, they later made further concentrated attacks on Bremen, Wilhelmshaven, Kiel and other suitable targets.

With the arrival of the two German battle-cruisers, *Scharnhorst* and *Gneisenau,* at Brest in March 1941, much of the British bomber force which might otherwise have been bombing Germany was tied up in attacking them. It was a relief to the RAF when, in February 1942, they made their escape up the Channel. Soon after that Sir Arthur Harris took over Bomber Command.

Harris found that he had at his command 69 heavy, about 259 medium and 50 light bombers, a total of no more than 378 serviceable aircraft with crews. The war had been going on for about two and a half years but Bomber Command had not really begun to expand. It was obvious that the Americans would not be able to develop their full strength for another year.

On the night 28/29 March 234 aircraft dropped 144 tons of incendiaries and 160 tons of high explosives on Lübeck, an industrial town of secondary importance, and destroyed about half of it by fire, for a loss of 13 aircraft. At this time Bomber Command was receiving only about 200 new aircraft a month, so that even such relatively light casualties were serious. This was followed by successful attacks on Rostock, with its Heinkel factory. Again

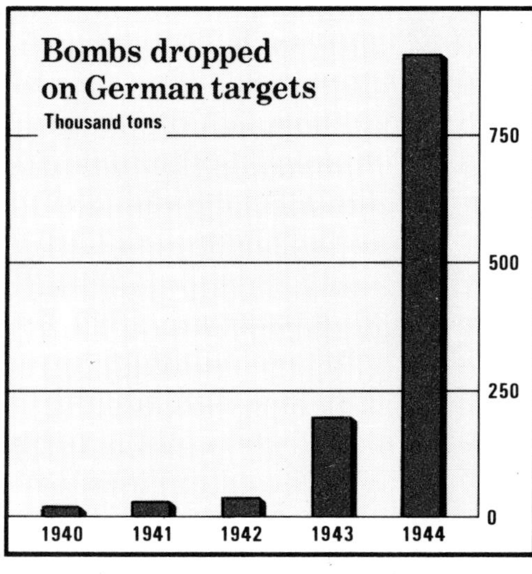

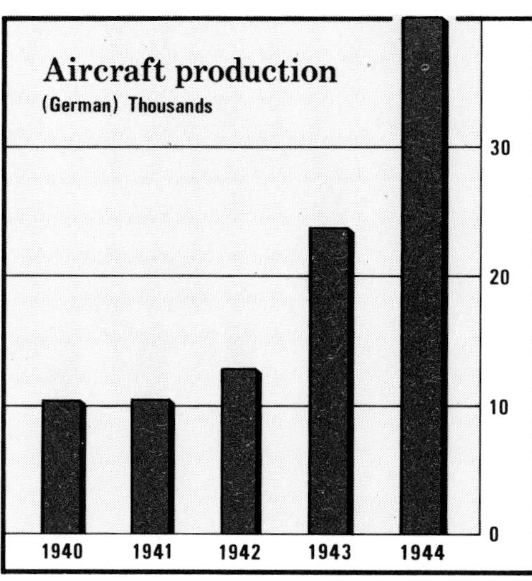

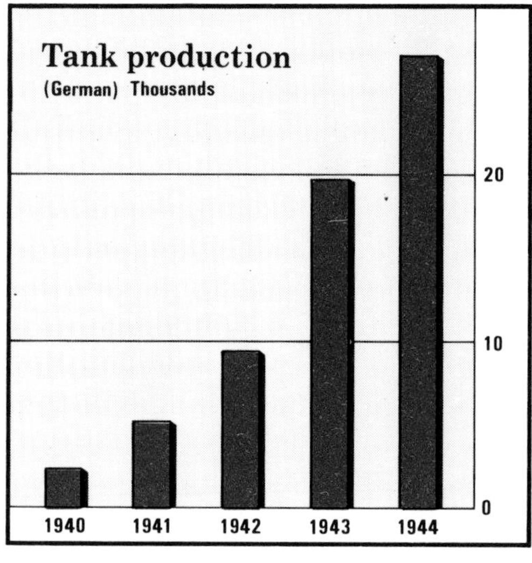

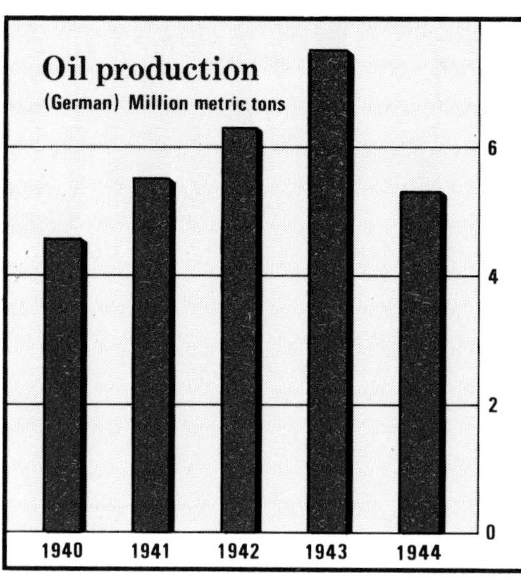

casualties were light (12 aircraft lost from 521 sorties) and the morale of Bomber Command rose as they began to get results. Already Germany had suffered about as much bomb damage as England.

The first of the 'thousand bomber raids' took place at the end of May, when 1,101 assorted aircraft including 1,074 bombers took part in an attack on Cologne. The defences were saturated and 600 acres were devasted for the loss of 39 aircraft. The Prime Minister, who above all wanted to get on with the war, was convinced that we had now 'an immensely powerful weapon'. This was the beginning of the real Bomber Offensive, and compelled the Germans to redeploy much of the *Luftwaffe*, which had been trained for army co-operation, to defend their industry. It has been estimated that when in 1941 the Germans invaded Russia, 50 per cent of their aircraft were available to help the army. By the end of 1943 this had fallen to 20 per cent.

In August a Pathfinder Force came into being, which led to more concentrated bombing. The introduction of efficient marker bombs gave a clearer aiming-point to the follow-up bombers.

By December 1942 the British had an average front-line strength of 78 medium and 261 heavy bombers. The introduction of four-engined aircraft, absolutely necessary though it was, had tended to slow down the process of expansion. The Lancaster, the best bomber the British had, was then the only aircraft in the

Below left: **A B-17 of the 381st Bomber Group flies away after dropping bombs on Kassel.**

Below and below right: **Eighth AF units took part in the raids on Schweinfurt. These are aerial views of the first raid which took place on 17 August 1943.**

Right: **Personnel of an RAF bombing squadron check their equipment following a successful raid on Heligoland.**

world which could take the 22,000 lb. 'Grand Slam' bombs, which had been designed by Professor Barnes Wallis along with the 'Tallboy' bomb. It is interesting to note that 37 per cent of the pilots were from dominion and colonial Air Forces, Canada contributing a particularly high percentage. Polish, French and Czech pilots also played an important part.

In January 1943 attacks were made on Berlin by 388 Lancasters. The weather was unfavourable with haze and snow, and the damage was scattered. To attack the German capital involved 4 hours' flying over very heavily defended country, and Bomber Command was still not really strong enough for the job.

In January and February, at the insistence of the Admiralty, the U-Boat bases at Lorient and St Nazaire were severely attacked. The towns were devastated, but in vain, for the U-Boat pens with their reinforced roofs proved too strong for any bomb then available.

The Casablanca Conference of January 1943 laid down the basic strategy for the Combined Bomber Offensive. The primary objectives were to be:

> 'The progressive destruction and dislocation of the German military, industrial, and economic system, and the undermining of the morale of the German people to a point where their capacity for armed resistance is fatally weakened.'

The Battle of the Ruhr began on the night 5/6 March 1943, with an accurate and successful attack by 442 aircraft on Essen, which hitherto had proved more or less invulnerable. Five more attacks were made during the following months and by the end of July Krupps'

Above: **Sir Barnes Wallis designed the bouncing bombs which were used by the Dambusters to destroy the Möhne and Eder dams.**

Above: **Wing Commander Guy Gibson led special squadron No. 617 which destroyed the Möhne and Eder dams. He was awarded a VC for bravery.**

factories had been severely damaged. Duisburg, Bochum, Gelsenkirchen, Oberhausen, Mülheim, Wuppertal, Remscheid, München-Gladbach, Krefeld, Münster, Aachen, Düsseldorf and Cologne were all heavily bombed.

Wing Commander Guy Gibson with 19 Lancasters attacked two vital dams, supplying water to the Ruhr, on the night 16/17 May. A special mine designed by Barnes Wallis of Vickers Armstrong was used, and Gibson's No. 617 Squadron of No. 5 Group was raised and trained for this particular rôle. The lightly defended Möhne Dam was breached and 130,000,000 gallons of water were lost. The attack on the Eder Dam was also successful and 202,000,000 tons of water were released to flood parts of Kassel. Eight planes were lost. On the night of 20/21 June the RAF carried out a successful raid on the former Zeppelin works at Friedrichshafen on Lake Constance. This was a radar factory. The defences were light, as the place was not thought to be in danger on a short June night. The bombers flew on to North Africa to refuel and rearm, and bombed the Italian naval base at Spezia on the way home.

Below: **Albert Speer was responsible for German industry's war production and the protection of factories.**

The devastation of Hamburg began on the night 24/25 July, when some 700 aircraft attacked and started terrible fires. Harris quotes a German official document which describes the results when, two days later, the British added fuel to the flames with results 'beyond all human imagination'.

'The alternative dropping of block busters (4,000 lb. high capacity bombs), high explosives, and incendiaries, made fire-fighting impossible, small fires united into conflagrations in the shortest time and these in turn led to the fire storms. . . . Through the union of a number of fires, the air gets so hot that on account of its decreasing specific weight, it reaches a terrific momentum, which in its turn causes other surrounding air to be sucked towards the centre. By that suction, combined with the enormous difference in temperature (600–1000 degrees centigrade) tempests are caused which go beyond their meteorological counterparts (20–30 centigrades). In a built-up area the suction could not follow its shortest course, but the overheated air stormed through the street with immense force, taking along not only sparks but burning timber and roof beams, so spreading the fire farther and farther, developing in a short time into a fire typhoon such as was never before witnessed, against which every human resistance was quite useless.'

When on the night 29/30 July Bomber Command attacked again, the water supply, gas and electricity failed. From the economic point of view the city was knocked out: nearly a million of the inhabitants fled. The dead numbered 40,000 and the injured nearly as many. Hamburg's four great shipbuilding yards, which had turned out many U-Boats, had been severely damaged and 6,200 acres of the built-up area had been obliterated by 7,196 tons of bombs. Bomber Command, which had thoroughly confused the defences by the use of 'Window', had lost 57 planes, or 2.4 per cent of those employed.

Colonel Adolf Galland tells us that:

'A wave of terror radiated from the suffering city and spread throughout Germany. Appalling details of the great fires were recounted, and their glow could be seen for days from a distance of a hundred and twenty miles. A stream of haggard, terrified refugees flowed into the neighbouring provinces. In every large town people said, 'What happened to Hamburg yesterday can happen to us tomorrow.' Berlin was evacuated with signs of panic. In spite of the strictest reticence in the official communiqués, the Terror of Hamburg spread rapidly to the remotest villages of the Reich.

Psychologically the war at that moment had perhaps reached its most critical point. Stalingrad had been worse, but Hamburg was not hundreds of miles away on the Volga, but on the Elbe, right in the heart of Germany.

After Hamburg in the wide circle of the political and military command could be heard the words: "The war is lost." '

Speer, the German minister for war production, thought that six more attacks might bring Germany to her knees. The attack on Hamburg was followed when the nights grew longer with another three bombings of Berlin, which was visited by 1,647 aircraft in 10 days. There was a considerable exodus of the inhabitants.

Meanwhile the Germans had been working at Peenemunde on a secret weapon. Their research establishment and factory were working on a rocket weighing 80 tons and with a warhead containing 10 tons of explosives. In an effective attack by 600 planes on the night of 17/18 August heavy damage was done and many of the scientists and staff were killed.

The American Eighth Air Force came to Europe believing in precision bombing in daylight by 'Flying Fortresses', with or without fighter escort. German fighters exacted a terrible toll, and in October 1943 the disastrous raid on Schweinfurt, coming after other heavy casualties, compelled them to call a halt. On 14 October 291 Flying Fortresses set off to attack the greatest centre of German ball-bearing production. Beyond Aachen they were outside the range of fighter cover. The Fortresses did severe damage, but 60 were shot down by German cannon and rocket-firing fighters. Of the 231 bombers that returned 130 had been damaged. The Americans retained their faith in daylight bombing, but realized the need for a long-range fighter. The P-51 Mustang, which the Americans had rejected in 1940 because of its unimpressive performance, was given a Rolls-Royce engine, and, incredible though it may seem, was in service by December. It surpassed the German fighters in speed, range and manoeuvrability, and swiftly reversed an apparently disastrous situation. Before the end of the war 14,000 Mustangs were produced.

During the winter 1943–44, despite awful weather, Bomber Command made the 16 attacks on the German capital which are called the Battle of Berlin. Cloud hindered photographic reconnaissance and it was difficult to tell how much damage was being done. Berlin was not devastated as Hamburg had been, but about 5,000 acres of the city were obliterated, for a loss of 300 aircraft. By the end the German night fighters had got the better of the bombers.

On 9 February 1944 the Bishop of Chichester, speaking in the House of Lords, condemned the area bombing of Berlin, where it was reported that 74,000 people had been killed and 3,000,000 rendered homeless. 'The policy', he declared, 'is obliteration, openly acknowledged.' His remarks were in excellent taste, though it is just as well that he was not in the War Cabinet.

In January first priority had been given to bombing the German aircraft industry. The growing strength of the *Luftwaffe* 'threatened both the bomber offensive itself and the projected invasion of Europe'. The Eighth Air Force was to attack airframe and other aircraft factories, while Bomber Command attacked industrial towns where aircraft component factories were located. Most of these were further afield than the Ruhr. In the period February to April 1944 the Allies spent most of their bomber effort against the aircraft industry. This was a good idea in theory, but it did not work very well in practice, because the Germans proceeded to disperse their plants. It may be that the Germans were deprived of as much as 20 per cent of their production by this offensive, but it was indecisive.

By April 1944 the Allies had a formidable striking force. On average 1,119 heavy bombers were available. But from April to September 1944 *Overlord* had priority and the strategic bombing offensive, which had lasted a year, had to be abandoned for the time being. This gave German industry a lull of six months in which to repair the ravages of the past year. The contribution of the air to the invasion of Normandy is discussed elsewhere: suffice it here to say that it was decisive.

On 8 June it was decided to make German oil production, which had previously been considered to be out of range, a top-priority target. Between the end of June 1944 and March 1945 the Allies made 555 attacks on 135 targets, which included every known synthetic-fuel plant and major refinery. The effect on German oil production is obvious from this simple chart:

	Average in tons
May, 1944	**662,000**
June	**422,000**
December	**260,000**
March, 1945	**80,000**

The production of aviation gasoline went down from 170,000 tons per month in mid 1944 to 52,000 in the following March. The effect on the operations of the *Luftwaffe* may be imagined.

Above: **Vacuum and pressure tanks at the I. G. Farben factories at Ludwigshafen were destroyed by constant attacks from USAAf and RAF bombers.**

Training became practically impossible. Large numbers of aircraft were grounded simply for lack of fuel. Fewer and fewer fighters were available to meet the bombers that were doing all this damage.

The Army also suffered and 'in the last stages of the war huge numbers of German tanks were unable to reach the fighting areas, or were abandoned on battlefields, for lack of fuel. Before the end, wood or coal-burning gas generators, such as had been only moderately successful on buses and trucks, had been put on some fifty tanks.'

Above: **Germany under attack: the poster advises people to go immediately for cover during an air raid. The morale of the German people did not collapse under the bombing.**

Dresden because of its beauty, was still considered safe. Perhaps 200,000 refugees had swollen the number of the inhabitants which, pre-war, had been 630,000; and it was by far the biggest German city still intact. In February 1945 it was the main centre of communications for the German armies on the southern sector of the Eastern Front. It was in addition a centre of industry. On the night of 13/14 it was attacked by 800 bombers with results that recalled those

Below: **The devastated walled city of Nuremberg seen here at the end of the war.**

at Hamburg in July 1943. The casualties have been variously estimated at 25,000 and 400,000. The effect of Operation *Thunderclap* on morale throughout the Reich was grave in the extreme.

The losses of Bomber Command throughout the war were very heavy. It has been estimated that 7,122 aircraft were lost, and that 55,573 aircrew and 1,570 ground staff lost their lives. Some 22,000 were injured and another 11,000 were taken prisoner. USAAF losses were 23,000 planes and 120,000 battle casualties in over 2,300,000 sorties.

It has been said that German war production increased, despite the bombing, between mid-1942 and mid-1944. This is to ignore the fact that Allied bombing took a long time to get into its stride. In 1942 an average of only 6,000 tons a month was being dropped on Germany. By 1944 this had gone up to 131,000 tons. And there had been a corresponding improvement in operational techniques, notably the use of radio detection devices. Again, the German war economy did not really get going until mid-1942. Until that time few women were employed, and industry was operating largely on a single-shift basis, so that it is fair comment to say that 'judged by the standard of British industrial mobilization the German economy never attained anything like its full war potential.'

The strategic bombing offensive brought the German war economy to the verge of complete collapse. It is true that this result was only achieved at the very end of the war. On the other hand the offensive was virtually halted for six months in order to support *Overlord.* There is no doubt that strategic bombing could have brought German industry to a halt much sooner, had the war leaders had more faith in its potential, and had the selection of targets been more intelligent. That this would have shortened the war and saved Allied lives cannot be doubted.

The bombing of cities, although it could affect production temporarily, is generally held now to have been indecisive, but at the time when it was begun it was the most effective technique available.

The V2, the submarine, the tank, and a multitude of other weapons, influenced the course of the Second World War, but none had a more dominating influence than the heavy bomber.

Bottom: Josef Goebbels inspects work carried out in Berlin to repair bomb-damaged buildings.

Below: The Schweinfurt ball-bearing plant.

Key Bombing Targets

Industrial

1 Le Mans (aircraft)
2 Paris
3 Rouen
4 Siracourt (V-bombs)
5 Lottinghem
6 Mimovecques (V-bombs)
7 Watten
8 Wizernes (V-bombs)
9 Lille
10 Brussels (aircraft)
11 Rotterdam
12 Amsterdam (aircraft)
13 Le Havre
14 Boulogne
15 Dunkirk
16 Metz
17 Emden (U-Boats)
18 Wilhelmshaven (U-Boats)
19 Vegesack (U-Boats)
20 Bremen (aircraft)
21 Hamburg
22 Flensburg (U-Boats)
23 Kiel (U-Boats)
24 Lübeck
25 Hanover
26 Brunswick
27 Magdeburg

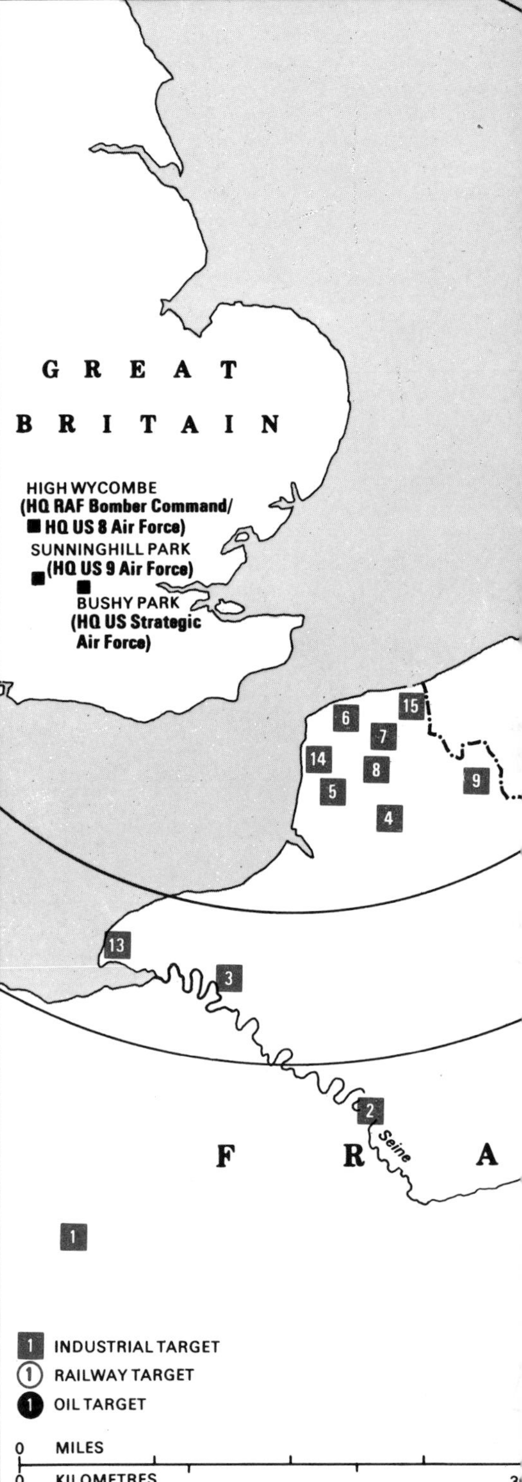

28 Oschersleben (aircraft)
29 Dessau (aircraft)
30 Essen
31 Dortmund
32 Duisburg
33 Düsseldorf
34 Cologne
35 Bonn
36 Möhne Dam
37 Wuppertal
38 Eder Dam
39 Sorpe Dam
40 Kassel (aircraft)
41 Leipzig
42 Dresden
43 Liegnitz
44 Berlin
45 Rostock
46 Peenemünde (V-bombs)
47 Stettin
48 Erfurt
49 Gotha (aircraft)
50 Schweinfurt (ball-bearings)
51 Fürth
52 Nuremberg
53 Regensburg (aircraft)
54 Augsburg (aircraft)
55 Munich
56 Ulm
57 Stuttgart
58 Ludwigshafen
59 Saarbrücken
60 Bochum
61 Karlsruhe
62 Friedrichshafen
63 Chemnitz
64 Prague
65 Wiener Neustadt (aircraft)

Railways
1 Frankfurt
2 Hanau
3 Aschaffenburg
4 Koblenz
5 Oberlahnstein
6 Giessen
7 Siegen
8 Schwerte
9 Soest
10 Hamm
11 Löhne
12 Osnabrück
13 Rheine
14 Bielefeld
15 Altenbecken Neuenbecken
16 Seelze
17 Lehrte
18 Hameln
19 Paderborn
20 Bebra
21 Stendal
22 Halle
23 Gera
24 Breslau
25 Minden
26 Mulhouse
27 Freiburg
28 Offenburg
29 Rastatt
30 Karlsruhe
31 Heilbronn
32 Treuchtlingen
33 Pasing
34 Munich
35 Rosenheim
36 Salzburg
37 Strasshof
38 Würzburg
39 Mannerheim
40 Darmstadt
41 Mainz
42 Bingen
43 Vienna
44 Munster

Oil
1 Wesseling
2 Reisholz
3 Dülmen
4 Gelsenkirchen
5 Salzbergen
6 Nienburg
7 Farge
8 Heide
9 Hitzacker
10 Dollbergen
11 Derben
12 Pölitz
13 Salzgitter
14 Lützkendorf
15 Leuna
16 Ruhland
17 Böhlen
18 Rositz
19 Mölbis
20 Zeitz
21 Brüx
22 Neuburg
23 Freiham
24 Linz
25 Moosbierbaum
26 Korneuburg
27 Floridsdorf
28 Schwechat
29 Lobau
30 Ploesti

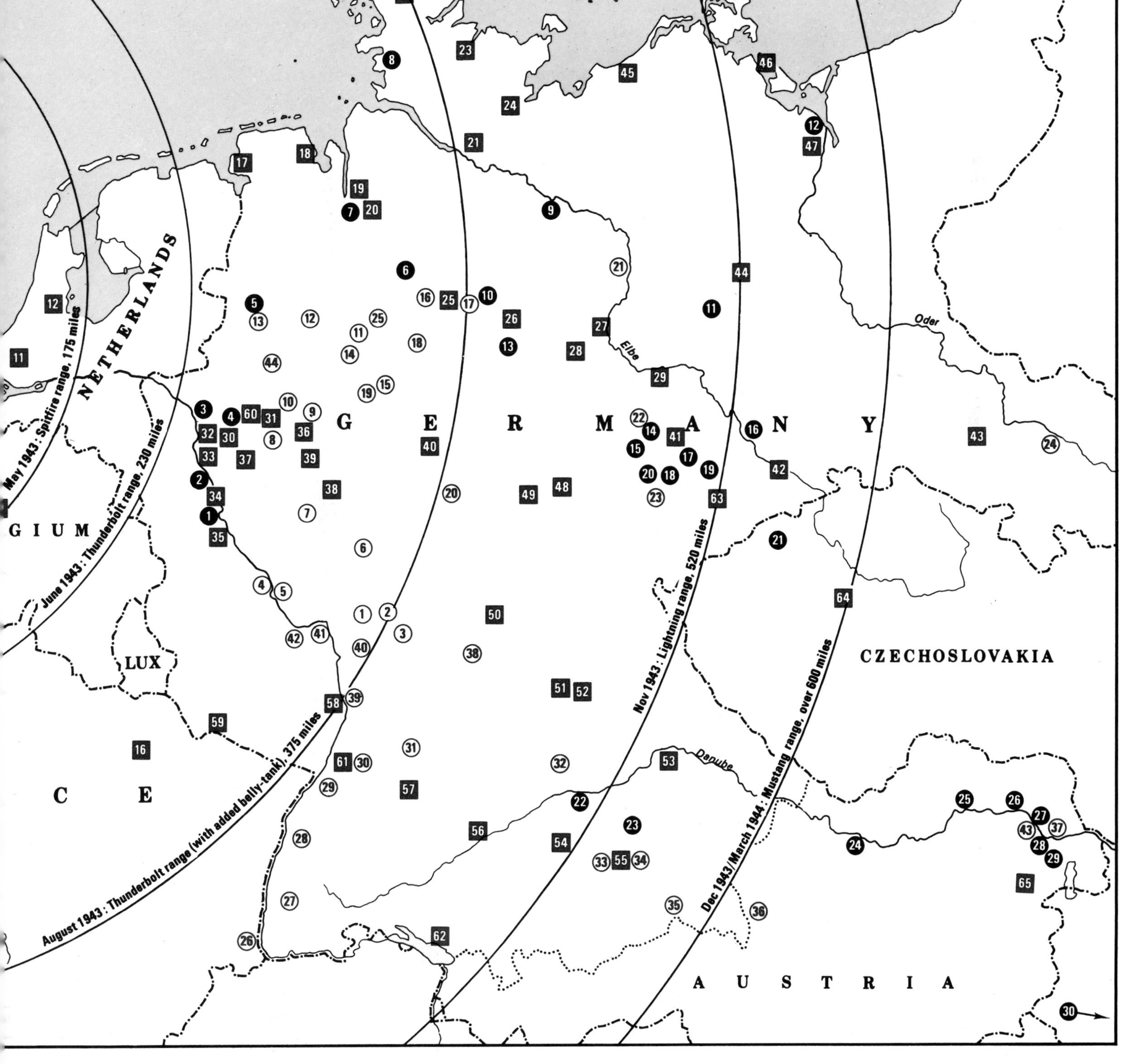

22 RUSSIA, 1943

Guderian: 'How many people do you think even know where Kursk is? . . . Why do we want to attack in the East at all this year?'
Hitler: 'You're quite right. Whenever I think of this attack my stomach turns over.'

The Allied victories of November 1942 brought a fundamental difference to the conduct of the war. Up to now Hitler had held the initiative; henceforth it was the Allies who would rough hew the shape of events.

The Stalingrad surrender had been a wounding blow to the Germans, Dictator and people alike. Hitler could not comprehend why Paulus had not blown his brains out rather than fall alive into the hands of the Russians. It was the first time a German Field Marshal had ever surrendered. The nation lamented its loss in three day's mourning.

There was to be no spring offensive in 1943. Rather it was to be a question of warding off renewed Russian attacks. By this time the Italians were demoralized. The Hungarians and Rumanians were little use except for hunting down partisans in the back areas. The Bulgarians now appeared to be the most reliable of Germany's European Allies.

The story of the Eastern Front in 1943 is the story of the great Russian victories at Kursk, Orel and Kharkov, which sent the Germans reeling back along the whole front from Moscow to the Black Sea. On the Northern front things remained quiet.

It will be recalled that on 6 February Hitler had given Manstein permission to withdraw Army Group Don to the line of the rivers Mius and Donets. The Russians followed up and took Kharkov (14–16 February). Through the gap of 100 miles between the flanks of Army Groups B and Don the Soviet armoured group under Colonel-General Popov wheeled south to cut Manstein's communications, severing the railway from Dnepropetrovsk to Stalino (13 February) and reached the junction at Sinelnikovo (19 February).

In this situation Manstein displayed his talents to great advantage. On 18 February he turned on the Russians and in eight days' bitter fighting crushed the Popov Group between First Panzer Army and the re-created Fourth Panzer Army. The Germans reached Kharkov once more on 11 March. The end of this counter-offensive left their Army of the South holding the line of the Donets as far as Belgorod, while to their north the Russians held a great salient west of Kursk. There followed the lull which the Russian spring, with the thaw and the mud, imposed on the combatants.

To the Germans, as Alan Clark shrewdly observed:

> 'The War meant the war in the East. The bombing, the U-Boat campaigns, the glamour of the Afrika Korps, these were incidentals when over two million fathers, husbands, brothers were engaged day and night in a struggle with the *Untermensch*!'

But some of these incidentals were beginning to hurt too. It was in January that U.S. Flying Fortresses first bombed the Reich in daylight. The Afrika Korps breathed its last in May. July saw the Sicily landings and the destruction of Hamburg. The tide that had turned in November 1942 was to flow with ever increasing power towards Germany throughout 1943; never again would Hitler's regiments see the Volga or the Caucasus. Yet the German position was far from hopeless. The retreat from the Don and the Caucasus and the withdrawal of Army Group Centre (February and March) had shortened the line and had allowed Hitler to build up a considerable reserve.

General Guderian had been recalled to active service and appointed Inspector-General of Armoured Troops with direct access to the

Above: **Troops of the North Caucasus Front march past the body of a German infantryman, somewhere near Mozdok in January 1943.**

Above right: **Soviet troops go onto the offensive outside Leningrad in January 1943.**

Right: **A German flamethrower in action.**

Führer (28 February 1943). With the support of Albert Speer, the Munitions Minister, he set to work to reform the German armoured formations. In April the factories at Schweinfurt, Kassel and Friedrichshafen were turning out the Panzer IV at the rate of 1,955 a month, and the new Tigers and Panthers were beginning to come into production. The anti-aircraft defences of these towns were strengthened to protect them from the bomber offensive.

As spring turned to summer Hitler's generals

Below: **The painful retreat outside Marino.**

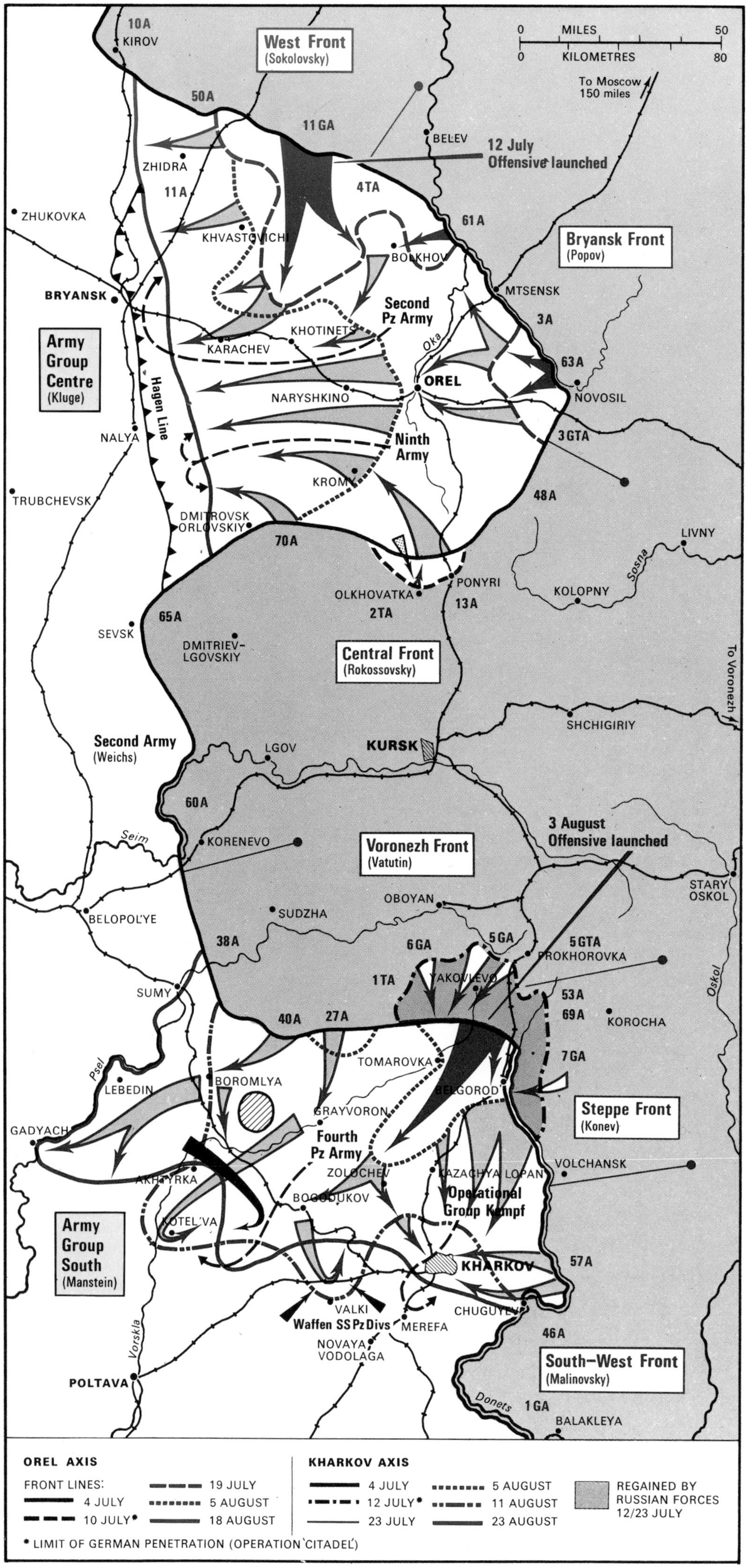

West Front
(Sokolovsky)
Bryansk Front
(Popov)
Army Group Centre
(Kluge)
Central Front
(Rokossovsky)
Voronezh Front
(Vatutin)
Steppe Front
(Konev)
South-West Front
(Malinovsky)
Army Group South
(Manstein)
Second Army
(Weichs)
Second Pz Army
Ninth Army
Fourth Pz Army
Operational Group Kempf
Waffen SS Pz Divs
Hagen Line
12 July Offensive launched
3 August Offensive launched
To Moscow 150 miles
To Voronezh
0 MILES 50
0 KILOMETRES 80
10A 50A 11GA 11A 4TA 61A 3A 63A 3GTA 48A 70A 2TA 13A 65A 60A 38A 6GA 5GA 5GTA 1TA 53A 69A 7GA 40A 27A 57A 46A 1GA
KIROV, ZHIDRA, ZHUKOVKA, KHVASTOVICHI, BOLKHOV, BELEV, MTSENSK, BRYANSK, KARACHEV, KHOTINETS, OREL, NOVOSIL, NARYSHKINO, NALYA, KROMY, TRUBCHEVSK, DMITROVSK ORLOVSKIY, LIVNY, PONYRI, OLKHOVATKA, KOLOPNY, SEVSK, DMITRIEV-LGOVSKIY, LGOV, KURSK, SHCHIGIRIY, KORENEVO, STARY OSKOL, OBOYAN, SUDZHA, BELOPOL'YE, PROKHOROVKA, YAKOVLEVO, SUMY, KOROCHA, TOMAROVKA, BOROMLYA, LEBEDIN, BELGOROD, GRAYVORON, GADYACH, ZOLOCHEV, KAZACHYA LOPAN, VOLCHANSK, AKHTYRKA, BOGODUKOV, KOTEL'VA, KHARKOV, VALKI, CHUGUYEV, MEREFA, NOVAYA VODOLAGA, POLTAVA, BALAKLEYA
Oka, Sosna, Seim, Psel, Oskol, Vorskla, Donets

OREL AXIS
FRONT LINES: 4 JULY; 10 JULY*; 19 JULY; 5 AUGUST; 18 AUGUST
KHARKOV AXIS
4 JULY; 12 JULY*; 23 JULY; 5 AUGUST; 11 AUGUST; 23 AUGUST
REGAINED BY RUSSIAN FORCES 12/23 JULY
* LIMIT OF GERMAN PENETRATION (OPERATION 'CITADEL')

Above: **General Nikolai Vatutin as Commander of the Voronezh Front at Kursk led the counter-attack against Kharkov. His army then swept into the Ukraine and took Kiev in January 1944. Vatutin was killed by anti-Soviet partisans in March 1944.**

put forward their plans for the 1943 campaign. Zeitzler and von Kluge were for a double envelopment of the huge Russian salient west of Kursk. Model opposed this on the grounds that the Russians had prepared a strong defence in great depth. Guderian was anxious to build up strength against the day of the Anglo-American invasion. At Berlin on 31 May a revealing scene took place:

'After the conference I seized Hitler's hand and asked him if I might be allowed to speak to him. He said I might and I urged him earnestly to give up the plan for an attack on the Eastern Front; . . . the great commitment would certainly not bring us equivalent gains; our defensive preparations in the West were sure to suffer considerably. I ended with the question: "Why do you want to attack in the East at all this year?" Here Keitel joined in, with the words: "We must attack for political reasons." I replied: "How many people do you think even know where Kursk is? It's a matter of profound indifference to the world whether we hold Kursk or not. I repeat my question: Why do we want to attack in the East at all this year?" Hitler's reply was: "You're quite right. Whenever I think of this attack my stomach turns over." Well it might.'

The attack took place nonetheless. Hitler decided that he needed one more big victory in Russia that would 'shine like a beacon around the world'. Operation *Citadel*, began somewhat late in the campaigning season, on 5 July, and followed Zeitzler's plan for a double envelopment, the Ninth Army (Model) striking down from the north and the Fourth Panzer Army (Hoth) thrusting upwards against the base of the Russian salient.

The attack came as no surprise to the Russians. Marshal Zhukov, whose command included more than five infantry armies (or 'Combined-Arms Armies') and a Tank Army, had made his preparations with great thoroughness. His artillery was particularly formidable and amounted to 20,000 pieces, including 920 *Katyushas* and 6,000 x 76 mm. anti-tank guns.

The training of the men and the construction of defences in depth left little to be desired. Clark quotes a Russian captain's description of the way in which his brigade took advantage of the long respite the Germans allowed them. They

'anticipated five possible places where they (the Germans) may strike and at each of them we know

Above: **Young people help clear Lenin Street in Kursk and make sure there are no booby traps.**

Right: **A gun crew in action during the artillery battle for the Kursk salient.**

alongside whom we shall be fighting, our replacements and command posts. The brigade is situated in the rear, but our trenches and shelters are ready up in front, and the routes by which we are to get there are marked out. The ground, of which we have made a topographical survey, has been provided with guide marks. The depths of fords, the maximum loads of bridges are known to us. Liaison with division has been doubled, codes and signals are arranged. Often alerted by day or night, our men are familiarized with their task in any eventuality. . . .'

Never before had the Russians had so much time in which to lay their plans and to get set before the storm. The days of improvisation were behind them.

The German Order of Battle was impressive and included 17 Panzer divisions, nine of which were with Hoth: these included such renowned formations as the *Gross Deutschland, S.S. Leibstandarte, S.S. Das Reich,* and *S.S. Totenkopf* divisions.

On 5 July this mighty force rode forth to do battle according to the well-tried *Blitzkrieg* formula of 1939–40; a formula by now as familiar to Muscovite as to Teuton. The German armour advanced in the wedge formation, known as the *Panzerkeil.* The *Tigers* at the sharp end were too well-armoured frontally for the standard Russian L.30 anti-tank gun (76·2 mm.) to do them much harm, and many got deep into the Russian position, only to find

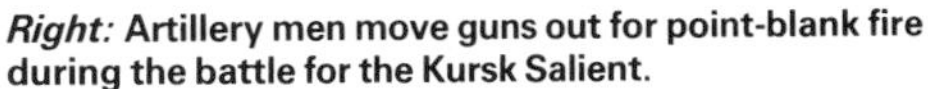

Right: **Artillery men move guns out for point-blank fire during the battle for the Kursk Salient.**

Left: **German tanks move up to the Kursk bulge in what was the last great German offensive on the Eastern Front. The battle began on 5 July but by 12 July the Soviet forces were able to launch their counter-offensive.**

themselves unsupported. For behind them the Panzer IVs had been hard hit, by mines as well as guns, and the infantry had experienced the greatest difficulty in following-up to protect the armour from the tank-killing squads ranging the battlefield by night.

The Achilles heel of some of the new German monster tanks – the 90 Porsche Tigers which were with Model – was now exposed. They had no machine-guns, and without infantry or light tanks to support them were soon in trouble. Guderian criticizes them bitterly.

'Once they had broken into the enemy's infantry zone they literally had to go quail shooting with cannons. They did not manage to neutralize, let alone destroy, the enemy rifles and machine-guns, so that the infantry was unable to follow up behind them. By the time they reached the Russian artillery they were on their own. Despite showing extreme bravery and suffering unheard-of casualties, the infantry of Weidling's division did not manage to exploit the tank's success. Model's attack bogged down after some 6 miles. In the south our successes were somewhat greater but not enough to seal off the salient or to force the Russians to withdraw.'

Rain on 5 July held up Hoth's advance, when he was about to cross a stream. The German tanks found themselves stuck in a swamp of mud under the direct fire of the enemy tanks and guns. Heavy casualties were suffered before they got going again on the 8th. In desperate fighting Hoth's men had by 11 July hacked a salient 15 miles wide and nine deep in Vatutin's line. But there had been no breakthrough and Zhukov still had his reserve, the Fifth Armoured Army, intact.

On 12 July Hoth concentrated what armour he could, some 600 tanks, and sent it in to pierce the last Russian belt of defences. They ran head-on into the fresh Fifth Tank Army – Clark aptly names it 'The Death Ride of the Fourth Panzer Army'. It was a rude shock to troops who had expected nothing worse than anti-tank guns supported by a few independent tank brigades. For eight hours the battle raged in clouds of dust and smoke. Evening found the Russians masters of the battlefield and all its booty. Next day Hitler announced to his generals that Operation *Citadel* was cancelled. The greatest tank battle in history was over, and the weapon which Guderian had striven so hard to reforge was shattered. 'It is,' wrote General Fuller, 'in no way an exaggeration to say that the defeat at Kursk was as disastrous to the Germans as had been their defeat at Stalingrad.'

Though foiled, the Germans hoped that they had done enough damage to the Russians to be able to count on a breathing-space. They were deceived. In consequence of this miscalculation they began to withdraw their surviving Panzer divisions from the Kursk front.

The Russians now advanced on a broad front towards the Dnieper and took Kharkov on 23 August. In the south von Kleist began to pull back into the Crimea.

In the centre too the Germans were going back, methodically perhaps, but nevertheless retreating. On 22 September the Russians retook Poltava, and on the 25th Smolensk. By the end of September the Germans were back

Left: **A Shturmovik which was brought down by the Luftwaffe. The Ilyushin Il-2 was a low-level armoured attack aircraft. It had a reputation for being indestructible and some 36,000 saw action during the war.**

Right: **Storming a barricade during the summer offensive on the Eastern Front.**

Far right: **General Erich von Manstein masterminded the recapture of Kharkov, February 1943.**

on their 'Winter Line' – the Dniepr – but the Russians kept up the pressure and early in October crossed the river north of Kiev, also taking Zaporozhe (14 October) and Melitopol (23 October). The passage of the Dniepr was an astonishing feat.

'They had done it *s'khodu*, that is, 'on the march'. No sooner had they reached the Dniepr than thousands rowed or paddled across in small craft, on improvised rafts, on a few barrels strung together, or even by clinging on to planks or garden benches. The Germans, who had boasted of their impregnable *Ostwall* on the right bank of the Dniepr, were taken completely by surprise.'

At this period the German army was dwindling away: it is estimated, for example, that in the three months after the end of *Citadel* Manstein's Army Group suffered 133,000 casualties and received only 33,000 replacements.

The Russians on the other hand were well up to strength and were receiving a great deal of material from the Americans:

'from sheet steel to shoe leather; clothing, blankets, tents, radio sets; enormous quantities of tinned food, iron rations (even fruit juice!) and first-aid packs. Most important of all, perhaps, were the trucks – particularly the White half-track – which began to put the Red Army infantry on wheels for the first time in its history.'

On 3 November Hitler issued Directive No. 51 in which he took a long and gloomy look at his future prospects.

'The hard and costly struggle against Bolshevism during the last two and a half years, which has involved the bulk of our military strength in the East, has demanded extreme exertions. The greatness of the danger and the general situation demanded it. But the

Right: **During the months prior to the Kursk battle the Germans built up their reserves of tanks and men south of Orel and north of Kharkov.**

Below: **Soviet minesweepers make sure that the Kharkov–Belgorod highway is safe to travel on as Vatutin's Voronezh Front and Konev's Steppe Front move forward.**

situation has since changed. The danger in the East remains, but a greater danger now appears in the West; an Anglo-Saxon landing! In the East, the vast extent of the territory makes it possible for us to lose ground, even on a large scale, without a fatal blow being dealt to the nervous system of Germany.

'It is very different in the West! Should the enemy succeed in breaching our defences on a wide front here, the immediate consequences would be unpredictable. Everything indicates that the enemy will launch an offensive against the Western front of Europe, at the latest in the spring, perhaps even earlier.'

He had decided to reinforce the defences of the West – 'particularly those places from which the long-range bombardment of England will begin.' (A reference to the V1 and V2 campaign, see Chapter 21.) Weapons, manpower and materials were to be spent in an intensive effort to put the western defences from Denmark to France in good order. No units or formations were to be withdrawn from the West or from Denmark without his approval.

Early in November the First Ukrainian Front broke out from a bridgehead west of the Dniepr and liberated Kiev, the capital of the Ukraine (6 November), driving back the Fourth Panzer Army and gravely jeopardizing the left flank of Army Group South.

By this time some 5,700,000 Russians faced about 3,000,000 Germans on the Eastern Front, and the Soviets had great superiority in guns and tanks. Hitler's best strategy would probably have been to withdraw Army Group South to the line of the Bug, but he had not abandoned hope of recapturing Kiev and going over to the offensive in the Crimea.

Manstein managed to induce his master to provide him with a few fresh divisions, but it was beyond his power to repeat his exploits of the previous spring, though in a month's bitter fighting he won a temporary delay. About Christmas the Russians resumed the offensive and recovered the ground they had lost.

That winter brought no lull, for the Russians had sufficient reserves to keep up a continuous offensive.

On 15 January the Leningrad Front came to life and after a tremendous artillery barrage the Russians drove westwards in a two-pronged offensive. The German battle line, though strongly prepared with pillboxes and minefields, disintegrated after five days' fighting and by 19 January Leningrad was no longer beleaguered. Hitler's left flank was giving. The Finns could no longer be counted upon. On 13 February Hitler ordered Army Group North to fall back to the Panther Line on the borders of Estonia – the sector of the 'East Wall' running along the Narva River to Lake Peipus and Lake PskovKoye. Here they managed to hold the Russians (1 March). Thus after a 30 months' seige the Leningrad blockade was finally broken, to the indescribable relief of the 600,000 inhabitants who still endured there. This was the first of the Russian triumphs of 1944 – the Year of the Ten Victories.

The second followed in February and March when Koniev, with the men of the 2nd Ukrainian Front, supported by Vatutin and his 1st Ukrainian Front, encircled the remnants of eight German divisions in the 'little Stalingrad' of the Korsun Salient on the Dnieper. Von Manstein broke through, but he could not keep open the escape corridor for long, and a frantic rout ensued as desperate men raced westwards. Perhaps 50,000 were killed or taken.

Meanwhile, in the centre, Vatutin took Rovno (5 February) and swung his tanks southwards to split Army Group South asunder in what the Russians called their 'Mud Offensive'. The crisis passed, for after eight months the almost continuous offensive lost its momentum. But the Russians were not held up until they had forced the Bug, the Dniester and the Prut, and reached the northern frontier of Rumania. Ironically enough it was now, when a lull was about to develop, that Hitler dismissed von Manstein, who had weathered so many storms and had shown himself full of resource in the worst days. The *Führer* graciously decorated him and von Kleist, who fell at the same time, and said: 'All that counts now is to cling stubbornly to what we hold. . . .' Hitler recognized in von Manstein a master of manoeuvre, but he felt that what was wanted now was someone who 'would dash round the divisions and get the very utmost out of the troops'. And the lot fell on that plain, blunt man, Field Marshal Walther Model.

Above: The *Hilfswillige* brigades were composed of men from European Occupied countries who bought their 'freedom' by fighting in Hitler's Army.

Above right: An enemy column on the Voronezh Front has been knocked out by Soviet aircraft.

Left: General Ivan Konev confers with a member of his Military Council, Bokov.

Below: **The first Elefant assault guns to be knocked out during the greatest tank battle of the war, Kursk.**

23 SICILY AND ITALY (TO ROME)

The paramount task before us is, . . . using the bases on the African shore, to strike at the underbelly of the Axis in effective strength and in the shortest time.'

Winston S. Churchill. January 1943

The successful conclusion of the campaign in North Africa left the Allies with powerful forces available for some great offensive stroke. The time was not yet ripe for the invasion of France, but an attack on Sicily and Italy offered an attractive alternative. The loss of his African Empire had shaken Mussolini's Fascist régime, and had demoralized the Italian army. If one of the Axis partners, albeit the junior, could be driven out of the war, the morale of free people everywhere was bound to soar. Moreover, the capture of Sicily would secure the vital Mediterranean sea route to the Far East, which, even with the North African coast in Allied hands, was still vulnerable to Axis naval forces operating from Italian ports.

It was at the Casablanca Conference in mid-January that Roosevelt and Churchill agreed upon this strategy, besides fixing the date of the cross-Channel invasion of France for May 1944. It was intended to exploit the capture of Sicily in such a way as to tie down the maximum number of German divisions, but the object of the campaign was diversionary. It was, of course, never expected or intended that it would give the *coup de grâce* to Hitler's *Reich.*

It was at this Casablanca Conference that the Allied war leaders proclaimed their demand for the Unconditional Surrender of the Axis powers. This declaration has been roundly criticized by commentators from both sides, but although Goebbels made great play with it in his propaganda, it is doubtful whether it really prolonged the war. It is easy to say that it stiffened the resistance of the Germans, but this is to ignore the fact that the German people were, with the exception of a pitifully small band of anti-Nazi officers and idealists, solidly behind Hitler. While he was still in the saddle the penalties for any weakening were painfully obvious to his followers, and the pronouncements of Allied war leaders made very little difference.

On the other hand the Italians might have surrendered sooner had it not been for this declaration. The idea behind Unconditional Surrender was not so black-hearted as some have pretended. It is worth recalling what the Allied statesmen had in mind as expressed by Winston Churchill (30 June 1943):

'We, the United Nations, demand from the Nazi, Fascist and Japanese tyrannies unconditional surrender. By this we mean that their willpower to resist must be completely broken, and that they must yield themselves absolutely to our justice and mercy. It also

means that we must take all those far-sighted measures which are necessary to prevent the world from being again convulsed, wrecked and blackened by their calculated plots and ferocious aggressions. It does not mean, and it never can mean, that we are to stain our victorious arms by inhumanity or by mere lust of vengeance, or that we do not plan a world in which all branches of the human family may look forward to what the American Declaration of Independence finely calls "life, liberty, and the pursuit of happiness".'

A great triangular rock of 10,000 square miles: that is the island of Sicily. On the north-east coast is the mighty volcano, Etna, between Messina and the broad plain of Catania with its invaluable airfields. There are no navigable rivers, but Palermo, the capital, Catania, Syracuse, Messina and Augusta are all useful ports.

To defend the island, with its 600 miles of coastline, General Guzzoni had 12 divisions, two German and ten Italian. Five of the latter were infantry and five were immobile coastal divisions. The garrison, though 350,000 strong, included only about 75,000 Germans. Even the German divisions were not fully mobile. The beach defences, pillboxes and barbed-wire, were not particularly formidable, and the defenders had few modern tanks. The rugged, rolling country, however, did lend itself to defence.

Above: **Self-propelled 105 mm Priests move up to the front in Sicily.**

Above right: **Wounded men, who had taken part in the Sicilian campaign, leave Syracuse by Hospital ship.**

Below: **Shortly after dawn on 10 July 1943 British troops land in southern Sicily.**

For this expedition General Eisenhower was the supreme commander. Directly under him were three British commanders for sea, land and air: Admiral Sir Andrew Cunningham, General Alexander and Air Marshal Tedder.

The Allied land forces consisted of the US Seventh Army (General Patton) of two and a half divisions, and the British Eighth Army (General Montgomery) of four and a half divisions.

The naval side of the operation was extremely complicated, for convoys, totalling some 2,700 ships and craft, were to approach from practically every port between Gibraltar and Port Said.

The original Allied plan was to make two widely separate landings in the north-west and the south-east of the island. Montgomery rightly objected that this violated the principle of concentration of force, and the final plan called for two closely co-ordinated landings, the British 8th Army going in on the south-east and the US 7th Army on the south coast. Meanwhile the deception plan led the Germans to believe that the Allies were planning a descent on the mainland of Greece. This was not difficult to sell to Hitler, who had declared in December 1942 that an attack on Crete and on German and Italian bases in the Aegean Sea and the Balkan peninsula might be made 'in the foreseeable future'. Even after the invasion of Sicily he thought the Allies measures in the Eastern Mediterranean indicated that they would shortly 'begin landing operations against our strong line in the Aegean, Peloponnese – Crete – Rhodes, and against the west coast of Greece with offshore Ionian Islands.' At the same time Field Marshal von Richthofen, C.-in-C. of *Luftflotte* 2, like Marshal Badoglio, felt that it would be operationally correct for the Allies to attack Sardinia rather than Sicily, and had moved the main concentration of German air defences to that island.

As a preliminary to the Sicily landings, the Allies took Pantelleria and Lampedusa, which surrendered after a severe aerial bombardment (18 May–11 June). The rock of Pantelleria, 60 miles South of Sicily, was found to have a garrison of 11,000 Italians! They might just as well have been in a prisoner-of-war camp for all the good they were doing there. Although the Allies had dropped 6,570 tons of bombs on Pantelleria the garrison suffered very few casualties, and only two out of 54 batteries were completely knocked out. These results do not seem to have led the Allied High Command to question the efficacy of saturation bombing.

A week before the landings, the Allied air forces began (3 July) to make massive air attacks on the Sicilian airfields. The work was well done: on 9 July troops in the convoy steaming towards Sicily from Port Said could already see the summit of Etna looming over the horizon, and were gratified when not a single Axis plane put in an appearance to disturb their cruise.

The Mediterranean can make itself unpleasant if it chooses and, when it was already too late to postpone the landings, an unseasonable north wind brought foul weather and a short, heavy swell to throw the soldiers' stomachs into their mouths. Such discomforts bring their compensations: no Italian soldier expected a visit that night. But through the night the airborne troops were already winging their way towards their targets, notably the Ponte Grande, whose capture was vital to ensure the British advance on Syracuse.

This, the first Allied airborne operation of any size, was not spectacularly successful. The troops, British and American, were flown from Kairouan in Tunisia in some 400 transport aircraft and 137 gliders. Conditions were difficult because of the high wind, and many of the pilots had not had sufficient training. Many of the parachutists landed far from their objectives and a large number of gliders came down in the sea. But these were élite troops and the survivors carried out much useful work.

The seaborne landings, though opposed, were everywhere successful and rapid progress was made. On the morning of D-Day troops could be seen marching up the beach in column of threes, a spectacle one had hardly expected on the first day of the reconquest of Europe.

And far away in East Prussia Hitler informed his generals that *Citadel* – their Kursk offensive – must be called off immediately. Troops must be transferred from the Russian front to deal with the invasion of Sicily.

Syracuse (10 July) and Augusta (13 July) were soon in British hands, and XIII Corps was advancing steadily towards Catania. By 13 July the leading troops were held up by an enemy rearguard at Lentini, and, to speed up the advance, landings were made that night to secure the bridges north of that town. No. 3 Commando landed from the sea at Agnone, and prevented the destruction of the Ponte dei Malati while at the same time the 1st Parachute Brigade and 151 Brigade captured the Primasole Bridge over the Simeto, and gave the British an entrance to the Plain of Catania. These results were only achieved with considerable loss, owing to the presence in the area of part of the Hermann Göring division.

Firmly established on the slopes of Mount Etna, the Germans were now able to hold up the British advance, and the plain with the Gerbini airfields was to be disputed for nearly three weeks.

Above: **A landing craft with Allied troops on its way to the shores of Sicily. The landings took place in very bad weather conditions.**

Below: **A 155 mm gun of Battery D, 36th Field Artillery goes into action against German Nebelwerfers near Cassino on 20 January 1944.**

Below: **German paratroops move up to the front lines near Anzio and Nettuno in January 1944. The first Allied landings there took place 22 January 1944.**

Meanwhile the Americans were making even more rapid progress, after beating off an armoured counter-attack by the Germans near Gela on the 11th.

On 22 July the Americans under Patton entered Palermo. The late General George S. Patton, Jr. (alias *Gorgeous Georgie*), was one of the more flamboyant characters of World War II. He was perhaps the most successful leader of armoured formations on the Allied side, combining the dash of an old-time cavalryman with the expertise of the modern Panzer leader. He was careful of his turn-out, invariably wearing a highly polished helmet and a pair of pearl-handled revolvers. He had a genius for 'putting his foot in it', and distinguished himself in Sicily when, during a visit to a hospital, he slapped a soldier whom he thought to be malingering. No doubt Patton was suffering from nervous strain. Needless to say Eisenhower was acutely embarrassed, but he managed to save his temperamental subordinate from being sacrificed on the altar of democracy. The erring general was compelled to apologize not only to his victim and the hospital personnel but ordered to appear before the officers and representative groups of enlisted men of each division under his command 'to assure them that he had given way to impulse and respected their positions as fighting soldiers of a democratic nation'. We are not told if that was good for discipline. A penitent Patton now grovelled before his chief. 'I am at a loss to find words with which to express my chagrin and grief at having given you, a man to whom I owe everything and for whom I would gladly lay down my life, cause to be displeased with me.'

It was General Bradley's opinion that the private whose face Patton slapped did more to win the war in Europe than any other private in the army! In Normandy Patton said: 'For God's sake, Brad, you've got to get me into this fight before the war is over, I'm in the doghouse now and I'm apt to die there unless I pull something spectacular to get me out.' His race across France (see Chapter 26) was to be a real *Blitzkrieg*.

By the end of July the American advance was slowing down as it approached Mount Etna. But there was to be no long deadlock. The British 78th Division, an experienced formation, was brought over from Tunisia and used to capture the key to the German defences, Adrano (6 August). When the Americans took Randazzo also (13 August) the Etna position was no longer tenable.

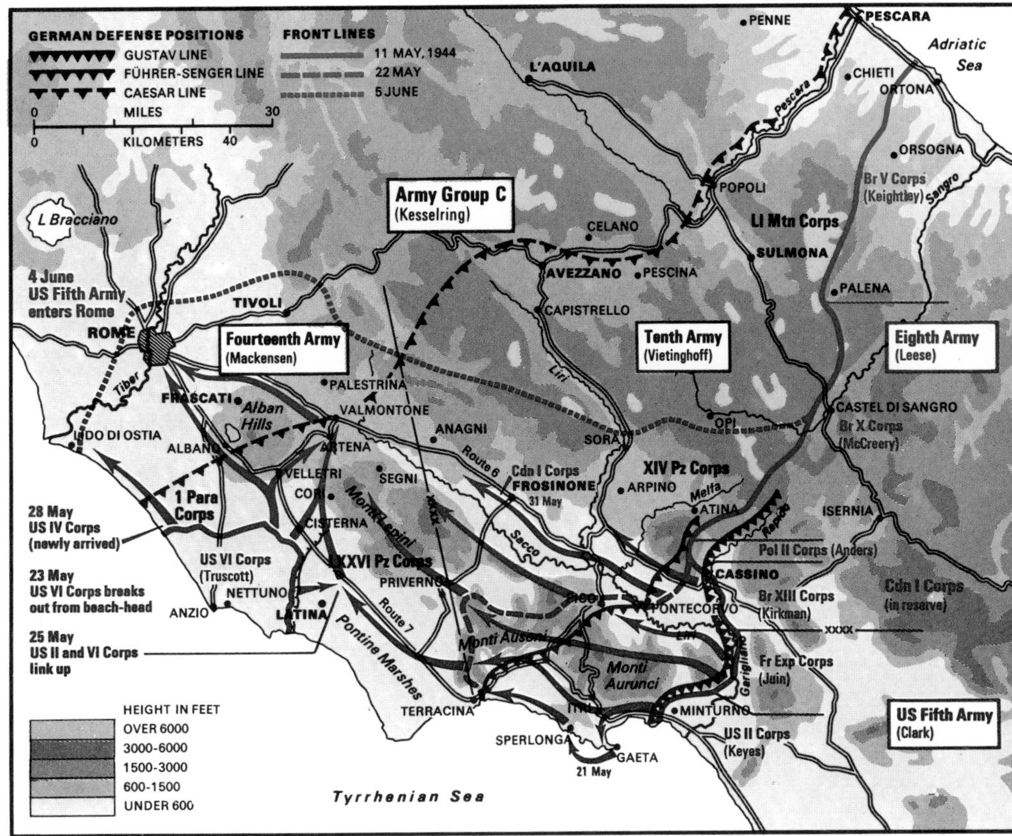

Guzzoni and his German adviser, von Senger und Etterlin, had seen from the first that their best plan was to fight a delaying action and then evacuate the main body of their fighting troops to the mainland, with as much equipment as possible. In this they differed somewhat from the ever-optimistic Kesselring (C.-in-C. South) who, 'doubtless still thinking of Dieppe,' had originally hoped for a successful counter-attack. The Axis commanders were fairly successful in getting their troops away across the narrow Straits of Messina. They are said to have concentrated 500 anti-aircraft guns astride the Straits, and by day they covered the passage by smoke. The Allied air forces sank a number of craft, but mines and coast defence batteries discouraged any attempt by naval forces to disrupt the ferry-service. When on 16 August the Americans won the race for Messina the Germans had evacuated some 60,000 men. Only 7,000 remained behind as prisoners of war.

The campaign had lasted 39 days. General Marshall estimated that it had cost the Germans 37,000 men and the Italians 130,000 – mostly prisoners. The Allied casualties in killed, wounded and missing were 31,158.

The Sicilian campaign was a mortal blow to the Axis. On 25 July Mussolini fell as the result of a palace revolution, and King Victor Emmanuel III confided the government to Marshal Badoglio. Although the Badoglio government continued to go through the motions of co-operating with the Germans, it was evident to everyone that Italy was on the verge of surrender. Mussolini was imprisoned in an inaccessible hotel in the Gran Sasso, and Badoglio opened secret negotiations with the Allies, employing the captured British general, Carton de Wiart, as an intermediary. American, British and Italian representatives met in Lisbon and an armistice was signed at Syracuse on 3 September, the very day on which the Allies, after the briefest possible lull in their operations, landed at Reggio in Calabria.

Below: **A six-pounder anti-tank gun passes through Pontecagnano, south of Salerno some time after the first landings there in September 1943.**

Above: **The monastery at Monte Cassino, which the Allies reduced to rubble. The Germans, however, found the ruins afforded excellent defensive positions.**

The Germans had been expecting the defection of their Allies for weeks, if not months, and acted promptly. Rome was seized, and it was only with difficulty that the King and Badoglio managed to evade them. Much of the Italian fleet, including four battleships and six cruisers, sailed to Malta, and surrendered early in September.

The British landing at Reggio (3 September) was not contested. It was followed by the seizure of Taranto (9 September) which, again, was not defended by the Germans.

On 9 September General Mark Clark's Fifth US Army landed in the Gulf of Salerno, South of Naples. The range of fighter cover made it practically impossible to risk a disembarkation any further north. For a time it was hoped to land an American airborne division at Rome at the same time, but the Italian grip on the airfield proved too feeble, and this bold operation was not carried out. The Allies have been severely criticized for failing to take advantage of the Italian surrender, but it must be realized that this came as no surprise to the enemy and that at least 15 German divisions were in the country. Five of these were quickly concentrated against the Salerno beach-head and at one time (11 September) it looked as if the invaders would be compelled to re-embark. The *Luftwaffe* made itself felt once more, scoring hits on the British battleship *Warspite* and the American cruisers *Philadelphia* and *Savannah* with glider bombs. But the Allies had massive air support and by 15 September the worst was over. On the 16th the advance guard of the Eighth Army, which had covered some 200 miles in 13 days, made contact with the Fifth Army about 40 miles SE of Salerno, a remarkable feat and one which strained British administrative resources to the limit.

The Eighth Army now shifted the axis of its advance to the east coast, and using Brindisi and Taranto as bases, pushed up the coast to Bari, which was taken on 22 September. Foggia, with its complex of airfields, fell (27 September) and it was not until he reached the river Biferno that Montgomery encountered serious opposition. A Commando landing seized Termoli and the town was held by 78 Division against the counter-attack of the 16th Panzer Division. The campaign now became a battle for the river lines. General Fuller, a hostile critic, describes the methodical way in which Montgomery overcame these successive obstacles:

> 'These tactics consisted in: (1) the building-up of such a superiority in every arm that defeat would become virtually impossible; (2) the amassing of enormous quantities of munitions and supplies; (3) a preliminary air and artillery bombardment of obliteration; (4) followed by a methodical infantry advance, normally begun under cover of darkness; and (5) followed by tanks, used as self-propelled artillery, to provide the infantry with fire support.'

The Germans were compelled to fall back to the Trigno and then the Sangro, where they fought relentlessly, but eventually broke. On the west coast the pattern was similar. Naples had fallen on 1 October and Kesselring had then withdrawn to the Volturno, which the Americans forced. Kesselring now fell back to the Garigliano, an obstacle whose importance is attested by its history.

At this juncture (24 December) the demands of Operation *Overlord* produced considerable changes in the Allied forces in the Mediterranean area. Generals Eisenhower, Montgomery and Bradley, and Air Chief Marshal Tedder, all went to England to take up new appointments. General Sir Henry Maitland-Wilson succeeded Eisenhower as Theatre Commander, and Lieutenant-General Sir Oliver Leese took over the Eighth Army.

Several veteran British and American formations were withdrawn to lend their experience to the cross-Channel invasion. General Alexander (15th Army Group) was left with the Eighth Army, which consisted of seven divisions, all from the British Commonwealth, and the Fifth Army (General Mark Clark) which contained five American, five British, and two French divisions, with a Polish division in reserve.

To oppose these forces Kesselring had 18 divisions. Of these five were holding down northern Italy, three were in reserve, and only 10 were actually in the line.

The Battle of the Garigliano began on the

night 17/18 January and the Allies made very little progress. On the 22nd, when it was already petering out, Major-General Lucas, with 50,000 British and American troops (VI Corps), was landed at Anzio. Instead of pushing inland to cut the communications of the Germans on the Garigliano, Lucas dug-in to consolidate his beach-head. Since he made no serious attempt to advance, the Germans did not find it unduly difficult to contain him. That so unenterprising an officer should have been chosen to command an operation calling for dash and drive is scarcely credible. The lessons of Suvla Bay were forgotten. Churchill called the VI Corps an 'army of chauffeurs' and caustically compared it to 'a stranded whale'.

But in war, as in human affairs generally, the right thing often happens for the wrong reasons. The ill-success at Anzio was to make it easier for the planners to get greater strength for *Overlord*, for it brought home to the politicians the sort of situation that might arise in Normandy.

Along the Garigliano the Germans stood fast, their hold on their great fortress of Cassino unshaken. On 29 January the Allies launched another attack on the little town, but by 4 February it had ended in failure, a failure blamed on the ancient Abbey of St Benedict, which seemed to survey the whole battlefield like a vast observation post.

It was decided that until the Abbey had been obliterated the tactical problem could not be solved. The Allies dropped leaflets on the Abbey on 14 February, warning the monks and any civilians there to depart. On the 15th 254 bombers dropped 576 tons of bombs and turned the Abbey into a heap of rubble. It was not as yet appreciated that the Germans were adept at constructing bunkers and strongpoints in buildings. When the roof fell in and the walls collapsed the bunkers were actually strengthened. This is what happened at Cassino.

After another day's bombing the Allies attacked on the 18th, following a five hour bombardment. But mere weight of metal is a crude key to a tactical problem and it did not solve this one. The infantry were soon held up. Conditions began to bear a resemblance to the Somme and Passchendaele. General Alexander, who had had vast tactical experience on the Western Front in the First World War, very sensibly called off the attack.

Many of the details of the mounting of this brief offensive have been strongly criticized, and certainly mistakes were made. The most serious, as the defending commander, von Senger und Etterlin, has pointed out, was that:

> 'The plan was so similar to the first one (in January) . . . that it could not hold any surprise. There was nothing new in it. I knew the terrain round Albaneta Farm, Hill 593 and Hill 444 from the day that I proceeded on foot to visit a battalion of 90 Pz. Gren. Div., when the trail of blood from the wounded that had been brought back marked for me the way up the track. These were all defensive positions in excellent condition, and they were being improved every day. According to German ideas, anyone wishing to continue the attack in the same direction from the terrain won in the earlier assault would have had to assemble a much more powerful mass as an attacking force. To achieve this, the attacker could have ruthlessly denuded his secondary fronts, a measure that I too was constantly compelled to adopt for my defensive operations.'

On 15 March another attempt was made in excellent weather. The preliminary bombing (1,400 tons) was not remarkable for its accuracy. Eighth Army commander lost his caravan headquarters three miles from Cassino, and the French Corps Headquarters at Venafro, 12 miles away, was heavily attacked.

Above: **The Allied bombardment of the buildings on Monte Cassino. General Eisenhower had to obtain permission from Pius XII to destroy the Abbey.**

There followed a two-hour bombardment by 900 guns; then the tanks and infantry went in, only to find the Germans still strongly ensconced in their rubble-covered strongpoints. The tanks could not get through to support the infantry because of water-filled bomb-craters that resembled ponds. Experience in Sicily, not to mention the First World War, should have shown that this would be the case. After eight days this offensive, like its predecessors, was halted.

When on 11 May yet another offensive was launched, Cassino was outflanked. Despite heavy losses the Polish Corps fought its way through to the north of the town, turning it from the rear. Cassino fell on the 17th and the next day the Poles took Monastery Hill.

Simultaneously the Allies broke out of the Anzio beach-head. But unfortunately General Mark Clark failed to cut the lines of communications of the Germans on the Cassino Front (Highways 6 and 7). Obsessed with the idea of getting to Rome ahead of his Allies, he permitted the main body of the enemy to escape with a loss of no more than 27,000 prisoners.

Rome fell on 4 June. President Roosevelt commented: 'The first Axis capital is in our hands. One up and two to go!'

Below: **The landings at Salerno, 9 September 1943.**

24 THE PACIFIC, 1943-44

'. . . This was the type of strategy we hated most. The Americans attacked and seized, with minimum losses, a relatively weak area, constructed air fields and then proceeded to cut the supply lines. . . . Our strongpoints were gradually starved out. The Japanese Army preferred direct assault after the German fashion, but the Americans flowed into our weaker points and submerged us, just as water seeks the weakest entry to sink a ship.' *General Matsuichi Ino*

Three campaigns, mutually supporting and more or less simultaneous, are outlined in this chapter. All were intended to bring the Allies within range of Japan. Amphibious operations would leapfrog across the Pacific, bypassing countless Japanese-held islands and leaving their garrisons to wither on the vine.

The first five months of 1943 did not take the Allies very far along the road to Tokyo. With the Germans still in Tunisia, and Operation *Husky* (the invasion of Sicily) in the offing, there was little shipping to spare. In particular the shortage of carriers was still acute. Even so two significant events took place in these months.

The loss of Gona and Buna led the Japanese to reinforce Lae and Salamaua in New Guinea. On 1 March an important convoy left Rabaul, carrying 7,000 troops in eight transports. Major General George C. Kenney, MacArthur's air commander, had 336 American and Australian planes in Papua. On 3 March they set about the convoy, sinking seven of the transports and two of the escorting destroyers. Next day they sank two more destroyers while torpedo boats accounted for the remaining transport. At least 3,500 Japanese soldiers were killed. The Allies lost five planes. Never again did the Japanese expose such a target within the range of land-based aircraft.

On 16 April Yamamoto met his end. He was flying from Rabaul to the Solomon Islands on a tour of inspection. Decoded Japanese messages had given away his complete timetable. Sixteen Lightnings from Henderson Field were sent to intercept the Admiral and his escort of Zekes. Yamamoto, a martinet and a stickler for punctuality, turned up exactly on time. The Japanese considered his loss as a major defeat, but it may be questioned whether he was really the great strategist they thought him.

On 30 June MacArthur was at last ready. His objective was the airfield of Munda in New Georgia. His 34,000 raw troops, unaccustomed to jungle conditions, took six weeks to get the better of 8,000 Japanese. Munda fell on 5 August. (It was on the night of 1/2 August that the Japanese destroyer *Amagiri* ran down the PT-109 commanded by Lieutenant John F. Kennedy.)

On 15 August the Americans landed on Vella Lavella which was required as a fighter base. The final Japanese evacuation on the night 6/7 October led to the sea battle of Vella Lavella. This brisk engagement marks the end of the Central Solomons campaign in which the Americans had lost six warships and the Japanese 17.

The last three months had brought the Allies within 300 miles of Rabaul – albeit somewhat slowly. The Americans now had the initiative. Their next objective was Bougainville. On 1 November 14,000 Marines landed in Empress Augusta Bay, half way along the SW coast, opposed only by 270 Japanese infantry.

In the early hours of 2 November Rear Admiral Omori came on the scene, hoping to get in among the transports as the Japanese had done in the Battle of Savo Island (9 August 1942). Rear Admiral Merrill handled his force notably well, and sank a cruiser and a destroyer. Omori departed well contented with the thought that he had sunk two cruisers – which was not the case. The transports were unscathed.

Halsey now retaliated with carrier strikes at Rabaul, intended to destroy aircraft and attack seven heavy cruisers which were coming down from Truk to give Merrill the *coup de grâce* for which Omori imagined he had prepared him. The Japanese cruisers were all badly damaged (5 November). On 11 November a new task group, including the *Essex, Bunker Hill* and *Independence*, enjoyed a highly satisfactory baptism of fire when they destroyed a large number of planes from Rabaul. Admiral Koga, discomfited, withdrew his remaining warships and planes from Rabaul to Truk.

By 14 November the build-up on Bougainville had reached 33,861 men and 23,137 tons of stores.

Off New Ireland on 25 November Captain Arleigh A. ('31-knot') Burke's flotilla sank three new destroyers which were trying to run reinforcements into Buka. The Japanese did not score a single hit.

There were still some 60,000 Japanese on Bougainville. It took General Hyakutake a long time to concentrate them for an attack on the American perimeter, but during January and February he moved them up along the jungle tracks. By the time the attack began (9 March) General Griswold had about 27,000 fighting troops ashore. Japanese artillery destroyed or damaged over 20 planes, and their infantry made some impression on the American perimeter, but they sustained heavy losses, and by 17 March the battle had died down. Another

Above right: **The first step across the Central Pacific took the US Navy to the Gilbert Islands. The US suffered heavy casualties on Tarawa.**

Right: **The Australian 7th Division penetrated the jungle to attack Lae, which fell on 16 September 1943.**

Far right: **Australian troops in the New Guinea jungle pick off Japanese soldiers fleeing from a tank-blasted pillbox.**

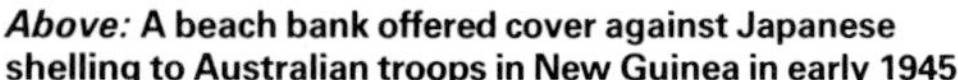

Above: **A beach bank offered cover against Japanese shelling to Australian troops in New Guinea in early 1945.**

general assault began on 23 March, but largely due to artillery counter-preparation made little progress. On the 27th the Japanese began to withdraw from the Empress Augusta Bay area.

Meanwhile MacArthur was mounting another offensive in New Guinea. His aim was to take Salamaua, Lae and Finschhafen. He prepared the way establishing local air superiority. On 17–18 August a raid on the Japanese base at Wewak destroyed over 100 planes. General Kenney followed this up by taking the airstrip at Nadzab with 1,700 paratroops.

The Australians seized Lae (6 September) and Finschhafen (2 October) by seaborne landings. The Japanese fell back from Salamaua towards Lae on 8 September.

On 26 December MacArthur landed the 1st Marine Division on Cape Gloucester, New Britain, so as to secure control of the Dampier Strait. It was, however, no longer intended to attack Rabaul and its garrison of 100,000 men. It had been decided at Quebec in August to bypass the place by occupying Manus in the Admiralties and Kavieng in New Ireland. On 29 February the 1,000 troopers of 1st Cavalry Division landed unopposed on Los Negros Island, which an airman had reported to be unoccupied. The garrison of 4,000 failed to eject these amphibious cavaliers.

The capture of Manus Island (15 March–25 March) was effected with remarkably little difficulty. The Seventh Fleet now controlled 'the magnificent, deep, landlocked Seeadler Harbour, fifteen miles long and four wide. Far better as a base than Rabaul, and nearer Japan'.

The last of the three offensives to get under way was that against the Gilberts and Marshalls.

The first objectives were Tarawa and Makin, both of which were heavily bombed between 12–20 November, while from New Zealand, Hawaii, San Diego and even Alaska the Fifth Fleet (Vice-Admiral Raymond A. Spruance) closed in upon them. The combat troops were under the command of Major-General Holland M. ('Howling Mad') Smith, USMC, while V Amphibious Force was under Rear-Admiral R. Kelly Turner, who had already won much experience in Guadalcanal.

Tarawa, resolutely defended by Rear Admiral Shibasaki and 4,500 men, of whom only 17 were made prisoners, cost the Marines about 3,000 casualties (19–23 November). The techniques of amphibious warfare were being learned the hard way, but they *were* learned, for the Americans, with customary thoroughness, made the operation the object of intensive study, and reaped the benefit during the rest of the war. It was sheer bad luck that the leading waves had had to wade 500 yards under fire because their landing craft could not get over the coral reef offshore. But the amount of preliminary bombardment needed to soften-up the garrison was seriously underestimated by the Navy. In the event the Marines won the battle in old-fashioned style at squad level, officers in front. When the chips are down the primitive virtues still count – and they always will.

Makin was taken between 20 and 24 November. The 27th Infantry Division, stale from over-training, took their time crushing a garrison of 800 Japanese. Their losses were slight but while they were making heavy weather of their task a Japanese submarine sank the escort carrier *Liscome Bay* (24 November). Kwajalein Atoll was a different story.

Nimitz now had at his disposal the powerful Fast Carrier Force Pacific Fleet, which included the *Enterprise*, the *Saratoga*, the *Essex* and three more of her class, and six light carriers. To some strategists it seemed that this force should be employed to help General MacArthur in his thrust along the New Guinea-Netherlands East Indies-Philippines axis. This would be in keeping with the principle of concentration of force. Nevertheless the Americans needed bases in the Marianas (Guam, Tinian and Saipan) in order to bomb Japan with Superfortresses (B-29s). At the Cairo Conference (3 December 1943) Admiral King won approval for the dual approach.

This strategy threw the Japanese off balance. They already had plenty on their hands trying to cope with MacArthur in the Bismarck Archipelago. They decided to sacrifice their garrisons in the Marshalls and to concentrate on holding their next line of defence: the Marianas-Truk-New Guinea-Timor.

Between 29 January and 6 February four carrier task groups softened up the Marshalls, practically wiping out the Japanese air and sea forces in the process. Simultaneously Kwajalein was heavily bombarded and then taken by a series of well-co-ordinated amphibious assaults. The atoll, consisting of 100 coral islands grouped round a great lagoon, is the largest in the world. At least ten of the islands were defended, and Kwajalein itself, where Rear-Admiral Akiyama was well dug in with 5,000 men, had to be taken yard by yard. Only 35 prisoners were captured. The attackers, who by this time had mastered the techniques of the amphibious assault, had only 372 soldiers and Marines killed out of the 41,000 who landed.

The Americans now proceeded to knock out the bases at Ponape and Truk. Liberators from Tarawa dealt with Ponape (15–26 February) and the fast carrier forces with Truk, sinking 200,000 tons of merchant shipping and two destroyers besides destroying about 275 planes (17–18 February).

Truk has been called the 'Gibraltar of the Pacific'. It was now so vulnerable as to be practically useless, and the Americans were able to bypass it with impunity. For the first time a major base had been neutralized by carriers without the aid of a single land-based bomber. With Ponape and Truk out of action the capture of Eniwetok Atoll, some 330 miles WNW of the Marshalls, was effected without the interference of a single Japanese plane. The fighting followed the Kwajalein pattern. A novel feature

Below: **Four riflemen creep forward carefully. They had volunteered to go on an advance patrol and later received DSCs for their bravery. By December 1944 the Americans had neutralized the Japanese force on Bougainville.**

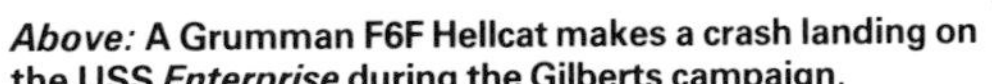

Above: **A Grumman F6F Hellcat makes a crash landing on the USS *Enterprise* during the Gilberts campaign.**

Above right: **Admiral William Halsey (centre with glasses) goes over the details of a future operation with Major General Turnage (on his right) and Major General Geiger.**

Right: **Marines prepare to land at Cape Gloucester, New Britain.**

was that the 2,000 Japanese on Parry and Eniwetok Island itself had hidden with such skill that the islands appeared to be unoccupied. Fortunately papers found elsewhere gave the game away. Once more Japanese casualties, 2,677, were far heavier than American, 339 killed and missing. But the winkling-out of a tough and fanatical enemy from bunker to bunker, with grenades and flame-throwers, was a desperate business calling for courage and training of the highest order. Robert Sherrod, a war correspondent, writing of Tarawa, gives a glimpse of one such fight.

'A Marine jumped over the seawall and began throwing blocks of fused TNT into a coconut-log pillbox about fifteen feet back of the seawall against which we sat. Two more Marines scaled the seawall, one of them carrying a twin-cylindered tank strapped to his shoulders, the other holding the nozzle of the flamethrower. As another charge of TNT boomed inside the pillbox, causing smoke and dust to billow out, a khaki-clad figure ran out the side entrance. The flamethrower, waiting for him caught him in its withering stream of fire. . . .'

The capture of the Marshall Islands meant that the Americans had broken through the outer crust of the Japanese defences. The strategy of the dual thrust had proved its worth.

25 THE WAR AT SEA, 1942-45

'The decisive point in warfare against England lies in attacking her merchant shipping in the Atlantic.'

Admiral Dönitz. September 1939

'The defeat of the U-Boat . . . is the prelude to all effective aggressive operations.'

Winston S. Churchill. 11 February 1943

Above: **Tankers were a prime target for U-Boats in the Battle of the Atlantic. One torpedo was enough to set the whole tanker ablaze and few of the crew survived.**

By the end of 1942 the Allies were slowly beginning to win back their mastery at sea, for the U-Boat 'wolf-packs', in their hunt for unescorted merchantmen, had been driven from the east coast of America to the Caribbean and the Gulf of Mexico. By October the American 'Interlocking Convoy System' extended as far south as Trinidad and Pernambuco. In the North Atlantic severe battles still continued. For example in August 18 U-Boats sank 11 ships (53,000 tons) of convoy SC. 94 in a five-day struggle. Two submarines were sunk and four severely damaged, so this battle could perhaps be called a draw. But in September the attack on convoy ON. 127, which claimed seven victims, cost the enemy not a single U-Boat. It was at this juncture, however, that Admiral Noble, Commander-in-Chief, Western Approaches, at last found that he had sufficient escorts to be able to form specially trained 'Support Groups'. New escort carriers; a short-wave (10 centimetre) radar which could detect a surfaced U-Boat several miles away; and heavier depth charges, all came into service. British aircraft could now patrol 800 miles out to sea, and the area which could not be covered from Iceland, Newfoundland, North Ireland or Gibraltar was diminishing.

On 12 September *U.156* sank the troopship *Laconia* with 1,800 Italian prisoners aboard. The German captain, Hartenstein, sent out messages promising not to torpedo rescue ships so long as he himself was not attacked. Several French and British ships, including the cruiser *Gloire* from Dakar, went to pick up survivors. On the afternoon of the 13th an American Army plane from Ascension Island, after flying around for about an hour, bombed the submarine. It is not known who ordered this attack, though 'the balance of probabilities suggests that it was an American authority'. The upshot was that Dönitz gave an order that 'all attempts to rescue the crews of sunken ships will cease forthwith', an order for which he would have to answer to the Nuremberg Tribunal.

Between July and October 1942 the Allies lost 396 ships (over 2,000,000 tons), though many of the sinkings were far from the main Atlantic routes.

Disguised raiders were still a menace. The *Stephen Hopkins*, an American 'Liberty ship', sank the *Stier* in the South Atlantic on 27 September, a fine achievement. Two others, *Komet* and *Thor*, were accounted for soon after. The Japanese sent two 10,400 ton ships, the *Hokoku Maru* and *Aikoku Maru*, each armed with six 6-inch guns, into the Indian Ocean, where, on 17 November, an incredible fight took place. The Royal Indian Navy's minesweeper *Bengal* (733 tons), armed with a 12-pounder, and the Dutch tanker *Ondina*, with one 4-inch gun, met these formidable opponents 1,300 miles NW of Perth. They sank the *Hokoku Maru* and drove off the *Aikoku Maru*, without themselves suffering serious damage.

Dönitz continued to probe deep. In October he had five U-Boats off Capetown, and in December nine off the coast of Brazil. Both groups scored heavily for a time.

Those who served in the Royal Navy in the War usually look upon the Russian convoys as the most exacting of the many duties that fell to their lot. The chances of survival if torpedoed in the Arctic were practically non-existent. Two convoys (PQ. 18 and QP. 14) fought their way through in the autumn of 1942. PQ. 18 lost 13 out of 43 ships, but shot down 41 German aircraft based on Norway, the escort carrier *Avenger* playing a decisive part. This was the turning point in the Arctic war.

Operation *Torch* made very heavy claims on the Royal Navy, and for a time the number of ships arriving at Archangel and Murmansk was much diminished. *En passant* it may be remarked that the Russians were not the easiest of Allies, even refusing the British permission to land medical staff to look after sick and wounded seamen. Yet whenever a convoy was postponed for any reason Stalin protested loudly.

Malta convoys were still demanding a tremendous effort on the part of the Royal Navy. Of 82 merchantmen that attempted to reach the island between January 1941 and August 1942 only 49 had arrived safely.

There is no evidence that at this period Hitler himself was taking much interest in the war at sea. It is true that Directive No. 23 was 'Directions for operations against the English war economy', but that was dated 6th February 1941. The *Führer* was preoccupied with the land fighting in Russia and in Africa. Even so the U-Boat fleet had continued to expand and now numbered nearly 400 boats, of which about half were fully operational. Admiral Raeder's requests that U-Boat construction be given the highest priority had – belatedly – been granted.

There were now some 450 British and Canadian escort vessels in the Atlantic, a very inadequate number if the crews were not to become utterly exhausted; 1942 had been a black year, even if prospects were beginning to look a little brighter. The Allies had lost 1,664 merchantmen (nearly 8,000,000 tons), and only a small proportion of these had been replaced. Britain's imports had dropped to one-third less than the 1939 figure. Stocks of commercial oil fuel in Britain had fallen very low, and only about two months' supply remained.

Hitler, obsessed with the notion that the Allies might invade Norway, had concentrated the *Tirpitz, Lützow, Hipper, Nürnberg, Köln* and some 12 big destroyers in Norwegian waters. When on 30 December a U-Boat from the strong flotilla based on Narvik reported the whereabouts of a Russian convoy, JW.51.B, Vice Admiral Kummetz came out of Altenfiord with the *Hipper, Lützow* and six destroyers.

Captain R. St. V. Sherbrooke, the commander of the escorts, had briefed his subordinates and the Convoy Commodore with great care and foresight. The cruisers *Sheffield* and *Jamaica* (Rear-Admiral R. L. Burnett) were coming from Murmansk to meet the convoy.

Contact was made at 8.30 and for three hours Sherbrooke with five destroyers and five smaller escorts had to fight off a converging attack. The two British cruisers made a belated appearance at 11.30 – they had been pursuing a radar contact to the east instead of steering for the gun flashes – and soon made themselves felt. By 2 p.m. the battle was over and the enemy were withdrawing. The British lost the destroyer *Achates* and the little minesweeper *Bramble*. The Germans lost the large destroyer *Friedrich Eckholdt*, while the *Hipper* herself was damaged and her speed reduced. None of the convoy was sunk, largely because in the Arctic twilight the *Lützow* had behaved with undue prudence.

Thus, thanks to the skill of Sherbrooke, who was badly wounded, and the devotion of his men, five British destroyers supported by two 6-inch cruisers foiled a pocket-battleship, an 8-inch cruiser and six large destroyers. The German Naval Staff described the battle as 'obviously unsatisfactory', while Hitler had one of his rages and was so rude about the German Navy that Grand Admiral Raeder resigned. Dönitz became Commander-in-Chief.

Above: **Admiral Karl Dönitz was an experienced submariner and he believed that the U-Boat could win the war for the Germans.**

Below: **The *U-132*.**

Above: **The destroyers *Saumarez* and *Mahratta* on duty in the Arctic. The *Saumarez* was the leader of the group of destroyers which torpedoed the *Scharnhorst* in the Battle of the North Cape.**

The Casablanca conference rightly decided that the defeat of the U-Boats was a necessary preliminary to the invasion of Europe. For this reason the USAAF and Bomber Command, much to the disgust of the latter's Commander-in-Chief, Harris, were ordered to divert a large part of their effort to the U-Boat bases. Between January and May 1943, 11,000 tons of high explosive and 8,000 tons of incendiaries were dropped on bases and building yards, but in vain: owing to the skilful construction of their pens not a single U-Boat was put out of action. This fruitless offensive was one of the most serious miscalculations made by the Allied planners during the whole war.

By the beginning of February Dönitz had 100 U-Boats on patrol, 37 of which were in the 'air gap' south of Greenland. Losses for February were heavy, a total of 63 ships (360,000 tons). March was even worse. Dönitz concentrated 40 U-Boats against convoys SC. 121, SC. 122 and HX. 229 from New York, and 21 merchantmen were lost. 'Our escorts are everywhere too thin,' Mr Churchill told President Roosevelt, 'and the strain upon the British Navy is becoming intolerable.' Altogether in March, in all theatres, 108 ships (627,000 tons) were lost. But the worst was over. By the end of the month the support groups were operating and the pendulum began to swing the other way.

In May, thanks to Admiral Horton's skilful handling of his support groups, losses dropped still further. The SC. 130 from Halifax, escorted by B.7 Group (Commander P. W. Gretton) and supported by No. 120 Squadron's Liberators from Iceland, got through unscathed in a battle which cost the enemy five U-Boats, and Dönitz one of his sons.

The month of May marks the climax of the Battle of the Atlantic. The number of merchantmen lost fell to 50 (265,000 tons), while the enemy, in all theatres, lost 41 U-Boats. On 22 May Dönitz, unable to accept such losses, withdrew his submarines from the North Atlantic. Although it was some time before the Admiralty realized it, a decisive victory had been won and the Germans' grip on our lifeline had at last been loosened – and not a day too soon.

A lull followed, but Dönitz was far from abandoning the struggle. U-Boats were to be produced at the rate of 40 per month. The construction of new types with a higher underwater speed was to receive the highest priority. The older boats were to be fitted with the 'schnorkel', a breathing-tube which enabled them to recharge their batteries while submerged, making them much more difficult to locate by radar. A new acoustic torpedo was to be used against escorts, and the U-Boats, which had suffered much during the summer from the attentions of Coastal Command, were to be given a more powerful anti-aircraft armament.

The month of June passed without a single convoy on the North Atlantic route being attacked, though the Germans lost 17 U-Boats that month.

Dönitz's strategy was always to thrust deep in search of soft spots, and his submarines scored heavily in the Indian Ocean (June) and in the West Indies and off the coasts of Brazil and West Africa. These far-flung forays depended very much on U-tankers or 'milch-cows', of which only 10 were ever completed. Four of them were sunk during the summer.

At the same period American escort carrier groups had a number of successes in the Germans' refuelling area about 400 miles NW of the Azores. Between June and August the Germans sank 58 merchantmen, but at a cost of 74 U-Boats, the majority being destroyed by aircraft.

By this time only the Indian Ocean was a really profitable hunting ground for the enemy. Between June and December 1943 seven German and eight Japanese submarines succeeded in sinking 57 merchantmen (337,000 tons) in those waters. The demands of the amphibious operations against Sicily and Italy had deprived the Eastern Fleet of escorts, and demonstrated once more how difficult it is for the Royal Navy – or any other – to be strong everywhere.

In mid-September Dönitz sent 28 U-Boats into the North Atlantic in an effort to reassert his grip on the British lifeline. The Submarine Tracking Room in the Admiralty was alert to this development, and escort groups which had been co-operating with Coastal Command in the Bay of Biscay were re-deployed between Iceland and Northern Ireland. In a fierce battle in mid-September the enemy sank three escorts and six merchantmen at a cost of three U-Boats, one of which (*U.229*) was rammed by the destroyer *Keppel*.

In October two escort groups fought a double convoy through, losing only one merchantman and accounting for six U-Boats.

The tactics developed by the renowned Captain F. J. Walker (2nd Escort Group) against U-Boats which sought safety by diving deep are of interest.

'His method was to station a "directing ship" astern of the enemy to hold asdic contact, while two others, not using their asdics crept up on either side, to release a barrage of depth charges by signal from the directing ship at the critical moment. The U-Boat thus never knew when the depth charges were released, and could not take avoiding action while they were descending.'

The escorts supported by long-range aircraft were proving more than a match for the submarine, despite its new torpedoes and other devices. Of 2,468 merchantmen which crossed the Atlantic in September and October only nine were sunk.

In October an agreement was made with Portugal by which Allied air and naval bases were established in the Azores. By the end of 1943 the Allies had definitely gained the upper hand in the Atlantic.

In mid-1943 the Home Fleet had been much reduced by the need to send ships to take part in the invasion of Sicily, though the Americans generously lent Admiral Fraser a battleship squadron and the carrier *Ranger*. The Fleet was able to reinforce Spitzbergen in June and to carry out a deception plan designed to make the Germans think that the British meant to invade southern Norway – an idea to which, as we know, Hitler was always receptive.

On 15 October Sir Andrew Cunningham became First Sea Lord in place of Sir Dudley Pound, who had become ill and who died on 21 October 1943 – Trafalgar Day.

In the summer of 1943 President Roosevelt was pressing for the renewal of the convoys to Russia. The Admiralty and Admiral Fraser were agreed as to the need to immobilize the *Tirpitz*, and, if possible, the *Scharnhorst* beforehand. On 22 September two midget submarines, *X.6* and *X.7*, commanded by Lieutenant D. Cameron, RNR and Lieutenant B. G. C. Place, RN, got into Altenfiord, despite mines and defensive nets. Two-ton charges, skilfully positioned, made the giant *Tirpitz* leap out of the water and put all three of her main turbines out of action.

Russian convoys began again in November, and the first two got through unscathed. In December Rear-Admiral Bey came out of Altenfiord with the *Scharnhorst* and five destroyers to attack Convoy JW. 55.B. Admiral Fraser had foreseen this move and had taken the *Duke of York* all the way to Kola Inlet to cover the previous convoy (JW. 55.A).

In the first phase of the Battle of the North Cape Vice-Admiral Burnett handled his cruisers most intelligently and, although *Norfolk* was badly hit gave the *Duke of York* time to join in. At 4.50 *Scharnhorst*, her guns trained fore and aft, was taken by surprise when *Belfast* illuminated her with star shell. Battered by the *Duke of York* and *Jamaica* from one side and Burnett's cruisers (*Belfast, Norfolk* and *Sheffield*) from the other, she fought bravely for an hour. Then, with her main armament silenced and her speed reduced, she was torpedoed by destroyers. At 7.45 she sank into the icy waters of the Barents Sea, taking with her all but 36 of her crew of 2,000.

The U-Boats had a bad time in the early days of 1944. Escorts were numerous, well-trained and alert. Sloops like *Wild Goose* and *Woodpecker,* to name but two, had brought submarine hunting to a fine art. It was a relentless struggle. Take the case of *U.358* sunk in February; 'four frigates of the 1st Escort Group held contact for 38 hours before success came to them, and when their victim was *in extremis* she managed to sink the frigate *Gould* with an acoustic torpedo.' It is hardly strange that Dönitz now gave up the unequal struggle. Between January and March 105 convoys (3,360 ships) crossed the Atlantic with a loss of only three merchantmen. Their escorts sank 29 U-Boats.

With the increase in the number of escorts and escort carriers the Russian convoys were now getting through, despite every effort on the part of the enemy.

On 3 April *Tirpitz* was the victim of a surprise attack by Barracudas from carriers of the Home Fleet. She was put out of action for another three months, and her crew suffered 400 casualties. The Royal Navy lost three aircraft.

In June the German Navy and *Luftwaffe* were hard-pressed to oppose the invasion of Normandy. A number of U-Boats, E-Boats and destroyers lay in French ports, but the destroyers were routed by the 10th Destroyer Flotilla west of Cherbourg on 9 June and the U-Boats, except for *U.984* which sank four ships in a Channel convoy on 29 June, did little to impede the Allied build-up. The elusive E-Boats, for all their dash, had little more than nuisance value. In fact the enemy's most dangerous weapon proved to be the pressure-operated mine.

In August the new Commander-in-Chief Home Fleet, Sir Henry Moore, began a new series of Russian convoys. As a preliminary, several abortive attempts on the *Tirpitz* were made by carrier-borne aircraft. Then on 15 September 28 RAF Lancasters operating from a primitive Russian airfield near Archangel scored a hit and two near misses with 12,000 pound bombs.

Finding it impossible to repair *Tirpitz* in Norway the Germans moved her to Tromsö, to be used as a floating battery, when – as they never ceased to expect – the Allies should invade Norway. This success meant that the Home Fleet could spare the carriers *Formidable* and *Indefatigable*, which left for the Far East. *Tirpitz* met her end on 12 November, when 32 Lancasters scored three hits and several near misses with 'block-busters' – 'and the battleship turned turtle with nearly 1,000 of her crew trapped

Above: **Dawn breaks over an Atlantic convoy in February 1944. Once the Allies decided to convoy their merchant shipping, losses were greatly reduced.**

Below: **Hitler visits his Grand Admiral Raeder (left). Hitler was disappointed with Raeder's results and after the Battle of Barents Sea Raeder was dismissed.**

Above: Admiral Sir Bruce Fraser.

Left: The *Tripitz* in its base at Narvik-Bagen Fjord, July 1942.

Right: A captured U-Boat is towed to Bermuda.

Far right: The captain of the gun relays a message aboard the *Duke of York* on 26 December 1944.

Below: The *U-236* surrenders at Loch Eriboll.

inside her'. *Tirpitz* had fired her big guns once – at Spitzbergen; but if her tactical career had been undistinguished, her strategic influence, while she was intact in Altenfjord, had been of great importance.

The well-escorted Russian convoys in the second half of 1944 were extremely successful. Every one of 159 ships sent to Russia got through, and only two out of 100 merchantmen in homeward convoys were sunk. In their unavailing attacks nine U-Boats were lost.

From first to last, in 40 outward convoys, 811 ships were sent to Russia of which 720 arrived. They delivered 4,000,000 tons of cargo, 5,000 tanks and 7,000 planes. This was a great achievement on the part of the Royal Navy, and the Merchant Navies of Britain and the USA.

Only in the Indian Ocean were the Germans still scoring fairly heavily, due to the lack of escorts in the Eastern Fleet, but by the autumn this campaign too was on the wane, largely due to heavy casualties among the boats sent out from Germany to reinforce the enemy.

A form of stalemate had developed by the end of 1944, for although the schnorkelling U-Boats were not sinking many ships, the escorts were not finding as many of them as in the days when they had ventured to operate on the surface in 'wolf-packs'. The number of German U-Boats was still increasing and reached its peak of 463 boats as late as March 1945. The war was nearing its close, but still these were anxious days for the Admiralty, because, in addition, mines laid by E-Boats and aircraft were taking a steady toll in coastal waters. Raids also caused some trouble. The German garrison in the Channel Islands reminded the Allies of its presence when on the night 8/9 March it surprised the little port of Granville on the neighbouring coast of the Cherbourg Peninsula, a place which had recently been the Headquarters of General Eisenhower, and Admiral Ramsay. On the night 11/12 a foray by the German naval forces in West Holland into the Scheldt was sharply repulsed.

On the credit side long-range aircraft of Bomber Command had sown so many mines in the Western Baltic that the Germans had to carry out their U-Boat training in Oslo Fjord, and by March their minesweeping service was beginning to break down. Beaufighters were ranging as far as the Kattegat to prey on coastal shipping.

The U-Boat struggle continued bitter to the end. In April 44 boats sailed out from Norway and, using their 'schnorkels', got busy off the north-east coast of Britain. One, *U.1199,* actually remained submerged for 50 days! During the last five weeks of the war they sank 10 merchantmen (52,000 tons) and two small warships, though the Germans lost 23 submarines. These last did not, however, include any of the new Type XXIII which, fortunately for the Allies, came on the scene too late to be decisive. As the Russians drew near to the Baltic coast in April the Germans moved their remaining U-Boats to Norway. When the surrender came 156 obeyed Dönitz's orders to surrender; 221 scuttled themselves.

Altogether the Germans had 1,162 U-Boats at one time or another, of which 785 were destroyed. British ships or planes sank 500. Enemy submarines sank 2,828 Allied or neutral ships, an astronomical total of 14,687,231 tons, of which the British Merchant Navy lost nearly 11,500,000 tons. Moreover, most of the 175 warships sunk by German submarines were British. During the war the Merchant Navy lost 30,248 men, and the Royal Navy, 51,578 killed and missing: of these a very large number fell victim to the U-Boats.

The Germans too suffered severely. By the end of the war their mercantile traffic had ceased. Mines laid by ships and planes had sunk 604 ships (660,000 tons); and air attacks had accounted for 289 (574,000 tons). Surface ships of the Royal Navy dealt with 86 more (303,000 tons). From 1940 onwards British submarines had sunk 104 ships (318,000 tons). The Royal Navy and the RAF between them had destroyed the German Merchant Navy.

When the surrender came the Germans still had the cruisers *Prinz Eugen* and *Nürnberg* fit for sea. The *Scheer, Lützow, Köln* and *Emden* had been destroyed by bombing. The *Seydlitz* and *Hipper* were scuttled by their own crews. The British took possession of the damaged *Leipzig,* while the wrecked *Gneisenau* and the uncompleted *Graf Zeppelin* fell into the hands of the Russians, the one at Stettin, the other at Gdynia.

These bare statistics of the war at sea give some idea of the awful struggle for sea-power, especially in the Atlantic and the Arctic; of the deadly menace of the U-Boat, and the sacrifices made in the long and doubtful campaign which was only brought to its conclusion by the collapse of the German power on land.

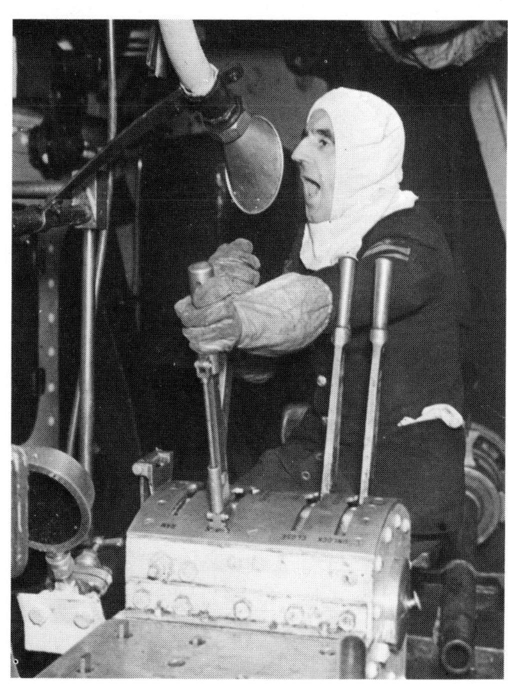

26 OPERATION OVERLORD

'He either fears his fate too much,
Or his deserts are small,
Who dare not put it to the touch,
To win or lose it all.'

Lines by James Graham, Marquis of Montrose, as quoted by Montgomery in his Personal Message to 21st Army Group before D-Day

The ten weeks' campaign of Normandy was one of the decisive struggles of modern times. The destruction of the German Seventh Army, half a million strong, and the liberation of France after four years of humiliating occupation, were results of the first importance, and placed the eventual outcome of the German War beyond all doubt.

The Germans, with 60 divisions, failed to repel the Allies, who could muster only 37. But the Anglo-American forces had complete command on the sea and in the air, and so it was once again a case of the victory of the better balanced force.

At the end of 1943 the Allied commanders for the invasion of Europe were appointed. General Eisenhower was to be in supreme command, with Air Chief Marshal Sir Arthur Tedder as his Deputy Commander and Lieutenant-General Bedell Smith as his Chief of Staff. For *Neptune*, the cross-channel phase of the operation, all three Commanders-in-Chief were British: Admiral Sir Bertram Ramsay, General Sir Bernard Montgomery (21st Army Group), and Air Chief Marshal Sir Trafford Leigh-Mallory. For the actual invasion there were to be two armies – the American 1st Army under Lieutenant-General Omar Bradley and the British 2nd Army under General Miles Dempsey.

Planning had been going on in London since 1943. During the Casablanca Conference Lieutenant-General F. E. Morgan had been appointed 'Chief of Staff to the Supreme Allied Commander (Designate)', better known as COSSAC. The number of divisions which could be landed on D-Day was limited by the availability of landing craft, but Montgomery, supported by Eisenhower and Mr Churchill, succeeded in getting the force increased to five seaborne divisions and three airborne. It seemed little enough. Indeed the success of the whole operation depended upon the speed of the German concentration to meet the landings, and the success of the measures devised to distract and delay them.

Eight divisions may not sound very much, but in fact the Allies were putting forth a stupendous effort in Operation *Overlord*. The force included:

5,300 ships and craft,
150,000 men,
1,500 tanks,
12,000 planes.

The German Commander-in-Chief, West, was Field-Marshal von Rundstedt, who had 60 divisions, 11 of them armoured, with which to hold France, Belgium and Holland. He considered that the German armies were over-extended, especially in face of Allied air superiority, and suggested a withdrawal to the German frontier. This was not well-received by Hitler, who in February appointed Rommel to command the troops in France, while retaining Rundstedt in overall command. Since the two field marshals differed as to the way in which their task was to be carried out, the arrangement was not a happy one. Von Rundstedt and Rommel were agreed that the French ports should be held to the last man, but whereas the latter wanted to fight the invaders on the beaches the former thought in terms of counter-attacking before their beach-head could be consolidated. Eventually they decided upon an unsatisfactory compromise, with most of the infantry well forward and most of the armour kept back. After the arrival of Rommel a great deal of work was done on the defences.

The German layout revealed von Rundstedt's preoccupation with the Pas de Calais. The enemy were convinced, and Eisenhower's deception plan encouraged them in their conviction, that the Allies would strike there. Here they constructed their strongest defences, and deployed their most powerful formations. Here, at least, the defence had some depth. But for the most part the famous Atlantic Wall had no more depth than the Maginot Line, which these same Germans had bypassed so readily in 1940.

In 1944 the Germans had very much more and better armour than the French had had in 1940, but in many ways their situation bore an ironic similarity to that of Gamelin's army. Deprived of air support the Germans now sat in a long thin crust of defences and awaited their fate, unaware of the strength of their enemy, or where to expect him.

In fact, as we have seen, there were only 37 divisions under SHAEF, and it was calculated that it would take seven weeks to get this force to France. Allied superiority at sea and in the air more than redressed the balance, for they enabled Eisenhower to keep the Germans dispersed before D-Day and to delay their concentration in the days that followed.

The pre-D-Day bombing of the French railway system did a great deal to hinder rapid troop movement. The French Resistance also played its part, by ambush and sabotage.

Still more important was the Allied Deception Plan. The 'First Army Group', a phantom formation, was concentrated in South-East England. Its wireless traffic did much to prevent the Germans drawing troops from the coast between Antwerp and Le Havre. Security leaks were prevented by the prohibition of travel

Below: **Landing craft head for the Normandy shore.**

between England and Ireland, and by the sealing off at the end of May of a stretch of the south coast, 10 miles deep. The pre-D-Day bombing, though it isolated the Normandy battlefield by destroying the bridges of the Seine and the Loire, was so intense in the Pas de Calais and elsewhere that it did not betray the area selected for the invasion.

In outline, Montgomery's plan, after establishing a beach-head, was to draw the German armour into battle with the British round Caen, while the Americans, after overrunning the Cotentin Peninsula and taking Cherbourg, were to break out and then, wheeling left, drive the Germans up against the River Seine. It was a masterly concept, based not only on Montgomery's knowledge of his immediate opponent, Rommel, but on the characteristics of the two great Allied armies committed to his charge – the stubbornness of the British, the dash of the Americans. As things turned out the campaign followed with fair accuracy the course Montgomery had predicted.

The chosen lodgement area was the Bay of the Seine between Cabourg and Valognes. It was selected as being the nearest stretch of beaches where the defenders were not altogether too thick on the ground. It was within range of Allied air support, and the Cotentin Peninsula gave some protection to the anchorage.

The Pas de Calais, though much nearer, was much more strongly defended; the straits were commanded by a great number of coast defence guns; and high chalk cliffs made it difficult to get away from many of the beaches.

The landings began in the early hours of 6 June when three airborne divisions were dropped to secure the flanks of the lodgement area.

On the American flank no less than 12,000 parachute troops were dropped. The US 82nd Division was to prevent a quick counter-attack from the West against the beaches, and ensure that the American seaborne divisions could break out of their beach-head so as to cut off the Cotentin Peninsula and Cherbourg. This was an essential part of Montgomery's plan.

Above left: **General Dwight D Eisenhower seen at his first press conference as Supreme Commander of the Allied Expeditionary Force, January 1944.**

Above: **General Eisenhower talks to paratroopers who are about to take part in the D-Day invasion.**

A good deal of cloud over the coast that night hampered the navigation of pilots, many of whom were on their first operation. The anti-aircraft fire, though not very destructive, induced many of them to take evasive action, and in so doing to lose their bearings. Men of the two American airborne divisions were landed all over a twenty-mile stretch of country, but many of their objectives were taken, including Ste. Mère Eglise and Pouppeville. A party from 82nd Division ambushed Major-General Falley, commander of the German 91st Division, while another paralyzed his Battle Headquarters. 91st Division had nobody to spare to counter-attack Utah beach.

The very chaos of the American airborne landings added to the bewilderment of their enemies. What tidy-minded German intelligence

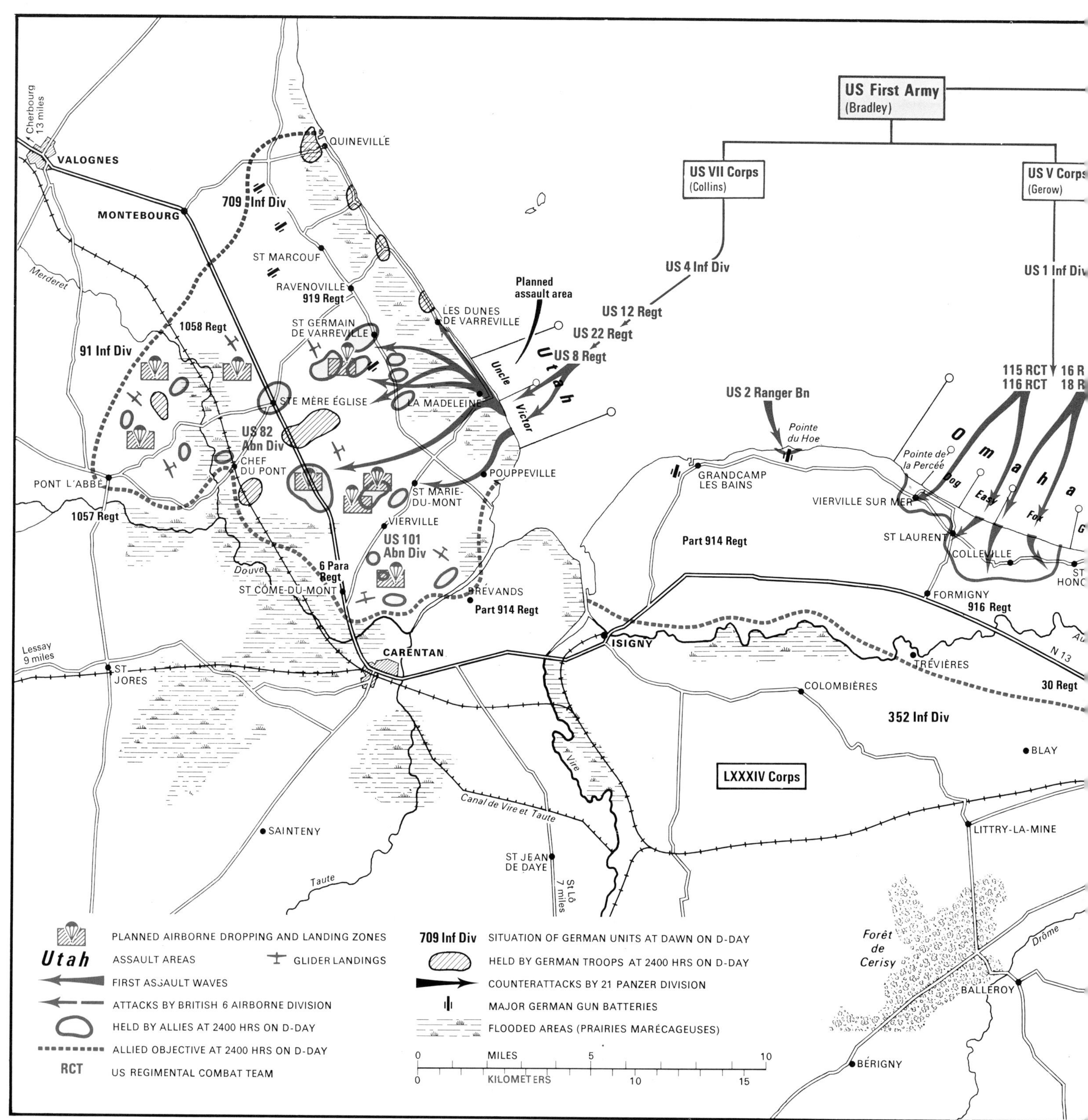

officer could be expected to sort out a pattern from the far-flung reports of parachute landings that came flooding in to their headquarters?

The task of 6th Airborne Division was to seize and hold the left flank of the beach-head, so as to give the seaborne divisions time to get set. Here the full force of the counter-attacking Panzer divisions was to be expected. Disaster here could mean that the British would be outflanked and rolled up from east to west. Were the Le Plein ridge, east of the Orne, to remain in enemy hands, the British beach-head would be displayed like a map to the German observation posts.

The bridges over the Orne and the canal at Benouville were captured by a glider-borne *coup-de-main* soon after midnight, and, although 6th Airborne's drop, like those of the American divisions, was scattered, the parachutists mustered in sufficient force to secure the bridges and most of the landing-zone, where at 3.30 a.m. gliders brought in the anti-tank guns designed to receive the expected onslaught of 21st Panzer Division. At the same time five bridges over the Dives had been blown up, and Lieutenant-Colonel Otway's 9th Parachute Battalion, which could muster only 150 men, had stormed the Merville Battery. Reinforced early in the afternoon by the 1st Commando Brigade, and at about 9 p.m. by the 6th Air-Landing Brigade, the 6th Airborne Division had that evening a firm grip on the eastern flank of the bridgehead.

The assault on Utah Beach went pretty well according to plan; battleships, aircraft, rocket ships and destroyers neutralized the defences and cut their telephone wires. They may not have caused many casualties, but they made the Germans unhappy, confused them and kept their heads down. At 0630 the ramps went down and the leading infantry got ashore without many casualties.

Only one thing had gone wrong. The whole of the first flight had landed in the wrong place. This was partly due to the strong tide and partly to accidents to the craft responsible for navigation. The Americans proceeded to turn this accident to their advantage. Appropriately enough it fell to a Roosevelt to make one of the big decisions of D-Day. Brigadier-General Theodore Roosevelt, a somewhat rheumatic veteran of 57, had persuaded his divisional commander to let him go in with the first wave

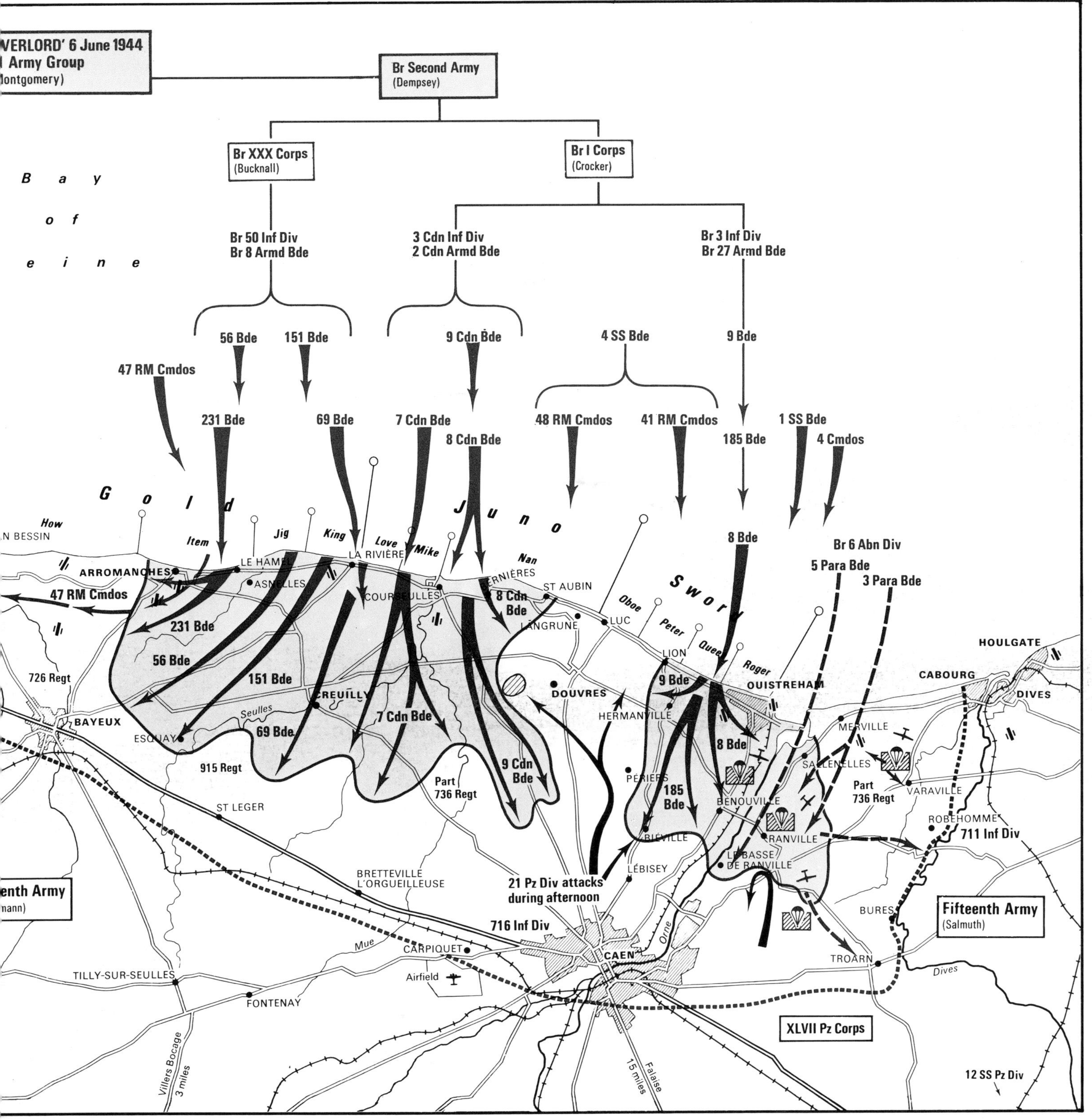

'to steady the boys'. Finding that the two leading battalions were more or less opposite the Pouppeville causeway he decided to make do with the beach he had got rather than try to fight his way along the beach to secure the correct beach-head. It was a brave decision, for should his men fail to capture the single causeway ahead of them by nightfall there was going to be the world's biggest traffic jam on Utah beach – some 36,250 men and 3,500 vehicles. But an outlet from Utah was secured. It was now only a matter of time before the seaborne troops could relieve their airborne comrades beyond Ste. Mère Eglise.

At no point were the D-Day landings nearer to failure than on Omaha beach. For this reason the landing is worth describing in some detail.

The German defensive position was naturally strong, and had been elaborately fortified. The Germans had big guns in eight concrete bunkers, 35 anti-tank guns in pill-boxes and 85 machine-guns. These were sited to cover three rows of obstacles planted below high-water mark. Inshore of these was a shingle belt, too steep for tanks and garnished with mines and barbed wire. The four beach exits were mined.

The fortified villages of Vierville, St. Laurent, and Colleville gave depth to the position, which was backed by the flooded valley of the River Aure. In sum it was a strong position, though, given reasonably expert planning, not an impregnable one. The American planning for this particular landing was not, however, of a high order.

Unduly impressed by the possibility that German shellfire would interfere with the lowering of the landing craft, the American admirals decided to perform this operation 12 miles offshore! The sea was so rough that a number of the craft were actually swamped, many were swept far to the east of their objectives, and landed their sea-sick soldiers not only in the wrong place, but late.

The frail canvas sides of the amphibious tanks were not designed for a heavy sea. One battalion was expected to swim about four miles. Of the 29 tanks launched, 27 either sank at once or were gradually swamped. The other battalion was sent in later, dryshod. Thus the first wave of infantry was left to storm the Atlantic Wall without the close support of armour.

The American planners had been offered large numbers of the 'Funnies' which their British allies had developed to deal with pillboxes, barbed wire and mines. These were Shermans converted for specialized purposes. Some were equipped to flail a way through minefields, others to lay tracks or to bridge anti-tank ditches. Some had flame-throwers or huge charges for destroying pillboxes. Such devices might be all right for the cautious and war-weary British: the Americans preferred to see what could be done by straightforward frontal assault. Dieppe might never have been fought!

Bad luck played at least as malignant a part as bad planning. Ten landing craft of the first wave sank during the run in. Wind and tide conspired to land most of the survivors in the wrong place. Most of the supporting fire, whether from the sea or the air, came down too far inland, missing the actual beach defences. The shells of the battleship *Nevada* had made such a screen of dust that observers could no longer make out their targets or perceive where the leading American troops had got to.

At close range the Germans opened a heavy fire from machine-guns, artillery, and mortars, which reached a crescendo as the leading landing craft touched down on the sandbanks, and the soldiers scrambled out to make their way across the last 600 yards of flat sand, shingle, wire, and mines. Many, burdened down by their heavy equipment, fell into pools or runnels and were drowned. Some sought cover behind the beach obstacles, others could only conceal themselves by lying where the sea lapped the shore, with only their heads exposed to the merciless fire of weapons so cunningly defiladed as to be practically invulnerable.

Here an LCA suffered four direct hits from mortar bombs and disintegrated; there a craft foundered 1,000 yards off-shore, and men were seen jumping overboard and being dragged down by their heavy loads.

Twenty-five minutes passed and the second wave touched down to find the first pinned at the water's edge. Already many of the leaders had fallen. No group had suffered more severely than the Army-Navy Special Engineer Task Force, who, burdened with their equipment, were invited to perform on foot the tasks carried out on the British beaches by 'the Funnies'. Only six out of sixteen bulldozers got ashore and of these three were knocked out almost at once by artillery fire. Casualties among these unfortunate engineers amounted to 41 per cent of their strength, the majority being mown down in the first half hour. As often as not when they managed to prepare an obstacle for demolition they could not blow it up because their comrades were taking cover behind it.

Here and there an officer or a sergeant got his men going. One was Colonel Canham, who remarked: 'They're murdering us here. Let's move inland and get murdered.'

Waves of men and vehicles continued to pile up along the foreshore, only to add to the confusion. At 1.30 p.m. the German commandant told 352nd Division's Headquarters that the invasion had been stopped on the beaches. Five minutes later the Chief of Staff passed the news to von Rundstedt that they had 'thrown the invaders back into the sea'. He spoke too soon.

About 10 a.m. General Huebner, the assault commander, had already taken a firm grip on the proceedings. Realizing the position on the beaches he stopped the waves of vehicles going in, and threw in more fighting troops. He called for naval gunfire support, and in response destroyers ran in to within a thousand yards of the shore.

On the American left the 1st Division, veterans of Sicily and Salerno, though hard-hit, rallied and began to fight their way inland. One battalion made its way through a minefield to attack the village of Colleville.

On the right 29th Division, in action for the first time, was badly shaken. But small groups pushed on from the sea wall, and infiltrated as far as Vierville and St. Laurent. By midday the German artillery was beginning to run short of ammunition and in face of Allied air superiority it was impossible for columns to get through.

Nightfall found the 1st Division fairly well established round Colleville, with a bridgehead two miles deep on a front of four miles; 29th Division had a precarious hold on a strip of France two miles long and three-quarters of a mile deep. During the night the Americans were

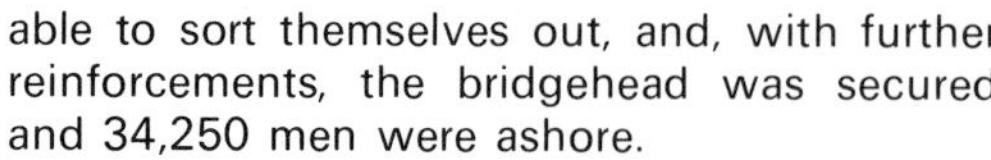

able to sort themselves out, and, with further reinforcements, the bridgehead was secured and 34,250 men were ashore.

The day's fighting had cost the Americans 3,000 casualties – about 1,000 from each of the two leading regimental combat teams. Material losses included more than 50 tanks, 26 guns and some 50 landing craft, besides 10 larger vessels. But their task had not been an easy one, and nobody could reasonably hope that a beach-head could be won without an ugly butcher's bill.

The Germans had been within an ace of repulsing the Omaha assault. But a purely static defence was not enough. A strong counter-attack was needed and this, thanks to 352nd Division's misleading optimistic reports, was never laid on. General Marcks, the corps commander, launched his reserves elsewhere.

The British landings were extremely well supported by the Royal Navy. The bombardment was long and accurate, the run-in comparatively short, and the navigation accurate. There were the usual accidents inevitable in a combined operation, but most of the troops landed in the right place and at the right time. The sea was very rough, and the swimming tanks in some cases had to be landed dryshod after the infantry were already ashore. The tide was racing in and most of the under-water obstacles were already submerged when the first troops landed. This made demolition by the Sappers unexpectedly difficult, and many of the landing craft were seriously damaged.

Many of 'the Funnies' were already on the

Below: Hundreds of troops surge onto a beach-head on the Normandy coast on 7 June 1944. Four of the landings were accomplished quite easily but on the fifth on Omaha the US 1st Division suffered heavy casualties. Once the bridgehead was established the Americans were able to get 34,250 men ashore.

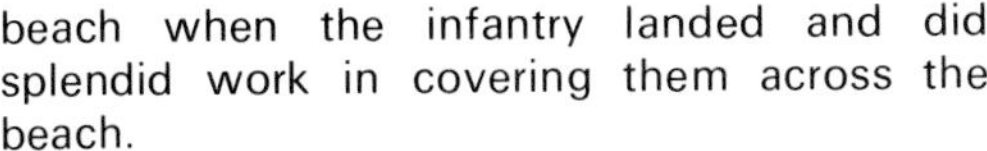

beach when the infantry landed and did splendid work in covering them across the beach.

On their right, by nightfall, the British were six miles inland, with their patrols already in the outskirts of Bayeux. The veterans of 50th Division and 7th Armoured had done their work well. They had secured a beach-head big enough to allow XXX Corps to deploy properly. They had secured Arromanches so that the Mulberry harbour could be built without delay. They had attracted a substantial portion of the German reserves, which spent an uncomfortable afternoon bicycling towards the coast under continuous attack from the RAF. Already that evening Major-General Richter with tears in his eyes was bewailing the fate of 716th Division: 'My troops are lost, my whole division is finished'. It was little more than the truth.

In the centre and on the left there had been

Above: **Troops land from *LCI-412* during the assault on Omaha beach.**

Above left: **After their landing craft was sunk, survivors struggle to the shore at Utah beach.**

Below: **Once the US 1st Division had established themselves on Omaha, there was an immense logistics problem to cope with. The American Mulberry (artificial harbour) near St Laurent-sur-Mer was never used. In a terrible gale from 19–22 June it was destroyed. The Mulberry at Arromanches worked extremely well.**

Above: **Landing ships unload cargo onto one of the invasion beaches during the first few days of the Normandy invasion. In the foreground there is a convoy of trucks forming up.**

substantial gains, with the 3rd Canadian and 3rd British Divisions thrusting towards Caen.

Fortunately for the Allies D-Day found the Germans still at loggerheads over the employment of their armour. Certain divisions were not to be committed without Hitler's orders. Major-General Feuchtinger's 21st Panzer – the nearest to Caen – was not to move without orders from Army Group B. The strange German chain of command was greatly to Montgomery's advantage. Better still, certain of the links were actually missing – Rommel was near Ulm; Dollmann (Seventh Army) was at Rennes, running an exercise to study the defence of Brittany; Sepp Dietrich (1st SS Panzer Corps) was in Brussels. Even so it was as early as 6.45 a.m. that Speidel (Rommel's Chief of Staff) authorized the employment of 21st Panzer in the Caen area. Feuchtinger sent a battle-group against 6th Airborne, but this was later called off because of the deteriorating situation on the Caen-Bayeux front. During the evening some of his tanks actually reached the sea at Luc-sur-Mer (8 p.m.), but their real achievement was to hold up the British thrust at Caen from the north.

As Colonel von Oppeln-Bronowski took his battle group into action, General Marcks said to him: 'Oppeln, the future of Germany may very well rest on your shoulders. If you don't push the British back, we've lost the war.' This was exactly the situation. Everything depended on hurling the Allies back into the Channel on D-Day itself, without giving them time to get dug-in. And this is precisely what the Germans failed to do.

And so in a single day the Allies had broken the Atlantic Wall – an obstacle at least as formidable as anything seen in the 1914–18 War. And yet the casualties – 9,000 out of 156,000 – did not compare with those suffered on the first day of the battle of the Somme. This is the measure of the technical and tactical advantages made in the intervening generation.

Counter-attack followed counter-attack during the first week, but all the time the Allies were building up more quickly than the Germans. The latter hoped to split the Allied front in two by a great armoured counter-offensive. This they entrusted to General Freiherr Geyr von Schweppenberg, who had been a successful corps commander in Russia. Geyr was not accustomed to operating against an enemy who had complete air superiority. He set up the Battle HQ of Panzer Group West in an orchard 12 miles South of Caen, with four large wireless trucks and a conspicuous group of office caravans clearly arrayed in the open. On the evening

of 10 June the RAF bombed the HQ, killed or wounded all the staff officers, knocked out the wireless trucks and most of the transport. Geyr, who was wounded, was one of the few survivors. The command now passed to Sepp Dietrich, who had no intention of carrying out the offensive Geyr had planned. Thus Rommel's hopes of putting in a counter-attack before it was too late were rudely dispelled.

By 11 June the beach-heads had been linked, as gradually the invaders won more elbow-room. By the 12th 326,547 men were ashore with 54,186 vehicles and 104,428 tons of stores. But the great gale of 19–22 June was a fearful setback, for it completely destroyed the American 'Mulberry', besides wrecking or damaging 415 vessels.

The early capture of Cherbourg was now more vital than ever. Operations on this flank were in the capable hands of Lieutenant-General J. Lawton Collins, who had commanded an infantry division in the jungles of Guadalcanal. Wilmot describes his tactics:

'In the Cotentin Collins' answer to the bocage was to attack on very narrow fronts and to deliver a series of short, sharp thrusts astride two main roads. He had four regiments advancing in column of battalions, each regiment on a frontage of a thousand yards. He could afford to ignore his flanks, for the enemy had poor communications, small reserves and no tanks except obsolete French models manned by a training battalion. He drove his men hard in brief spells, relieving his leading battalions two or three times a day. In 48 hours the Americans advanced five miles and fought the enemy to a standstill.'

Hitler allowed his local commanders very little tactical discretion. Wilmot relates a typical instance of the kind of remote-control generalship of which the Dictator was so fond.

'When it was pointed out that there was no possibility of the existing positions being held, he shouted, "Very well then, if they won't hold there (meaning Montebourg), they must hold here", and, taking a red pencil, he slashed a line straight across the map from one side of the peninsula to the other just south of Cherbourg.'

Neither von Rundstedt nor Rommel felt strong enough to stand up to Hitler on this occasion.

Thanks to the *Führer* the Americans had already broken the four divisions that ought to have defended Cherbourg, before they actually reached that formidable fortress. Major-General von Schlieben's garrison, some 21,000 strong, included many low-category troops, and Todt workers as well as Russians and Poles. But the very nature of the defences made the task a most difficult one and the American technique of attack is worth study.

'Dive-bombers and artillery drove the defenders in the outer entrenchments to seek the shelter of the concrete. Then the infantry, covered by a light bombardment, advanced rapidly until they were 300 to 400 yards from their objective. From there, machine-guns and anti-tank guns directed intense fire into the embrasures while demolition squads worked round to the rear of the pillbox. Then they dashed in and blew down the steel door with "beehives" or "bazookas", thrust in pole-charges and phosphorus grenades and left the explosives and the choking smoke to do the rest. It was a slow process, but it was sure and comparatively inexpensive.'

Von Schlieben surrendered on 26 June and the naval forts and arsenal capitulated next day.

The early fall of Cherbourg was a great prize for the Allies, who now possessed a first-class port even though its harbour could not be used straight away. The confidence of the German commanders in their coastal fortresses was much shaken. Hitler's inept generalship had certainly speeded up the proceedings, but the skill and certainty of General Collins's operations were most remarkable.

On the British flank no comparable progress was being made simply because the Germans had concentrated the bulk of their armour against that sector. By mid-July Dempsey's 14 divisions were pinning down 14 German divisions, including seven out of nine armoured divisions (600 tanks). Bradley's 15 divisions, with four of Patton's in reserve, were opposed by the equivalent of nine divisions with 110 tanks. It was the long slogging match round Caen which paved the way, as Montgomery had always intended, for the breakout on the American sector.

Bradley's plan for the breakout, *Cobra*, could well have foundered in the *bocage*. As he tells us:

'Previous attempts to force the Normandy hedgerows had failed when our Shermans bellied up over the tops of those mounds instead of crashing through them. There they exposed their soft undersides to the enemy while their own guns pointed helplessly toward the sky.'

At this juncture Sergeant Curtis G. Culin, Jr., devised a solution. He fitted four tusks to a light tank.

'The tank backed off and ran head-on toward a hedgerow at ten miles an hour. Its tusks bored into the wall, pinned down the belly, and the tank broke through under a canopy of dirt.'

Using Rommel's underwater obstacles for tusks every ordnance unit in Bradley's command set to and within a week three/fifths of the tanks taking part in *Cobra* had tusks – an organizational feat only possible to a nation as technically-minded as the Americans. (Sergeant Culin was awarded the Legion of Merit.)

Within the German High Command all was not well. On 17 June Hitler himself had put in a brief appearance and had held a conference at Margival near Soissons. He had demanded explanations from von Rundstedt and Rommel, and had received from the latter a forthright assessment of Allied strength which provoked an outburst from the *Führer*: 'Don't you worry about the future course of the war. Stick to your own invasion front!'

Left: **American paratroopers carefully edge forward in a field outside Carentan, at the foot of the Cotentin peninsula. They pass by the bodies of members of their unit, who fell to sniper fire on 14 June 1944.**

By this time Hitler was depending to some extent on his secret weapons, including the V-1 with which he had begun to bombard London on 12 June. One of these 'buzz bombs' developed a mechanical fault, changed direction and burst near the *Führer's* command post during the Margival Conference. Hitler, who had talked of visiting Cherbourg next day, promptly flew back to Berchtesgaden. From this time forward he preferred to run the Western Front entirely by remote control.

Von Rundstedt continued in command until 1 July, when he had a telephone conversation with Keitel and warned him that a counter-attack on the Odon by four SS Panzer divisions was being held by the British.

Keitel: 'What shall we do? What shall we do?'

Von Rundstedt: 'Make peace you fools. What else can you do?'

Von Kluge, in whose loyalty Hitler had a somewhat misplaced confidence, was sent to replace von Rundstedt. On the afternoon of the 15 July Rommel was attacked by fighters, his driver was hit, and the car crashed into a tree. Seriously injured, the Field Marshal was carried to the nearby village of Ste Foy de Montgommery. His fighting days were done.

Five days later came the famous *Attentat* of 20 July. Hitler was holding a conference in a wooden *Gästebaracke* at the Wolf's Lair in East Prussia. Colonel Count Claus Schenck von Stauffenberg, an officer who had been terribly wounded in Tunisia and was now Chief of Staff of the Replacement Army, smuggled in a bomb in his briefcase. At 12.42 the bomb went off. Stauffenberg returned to Berlin convinced that Hitler was dead, but in fact only four out of more than 20 people present were killed outright. Hitler's right ear was deafened, his legs were burned and his right arm was temporarily paralyzed, but that was all.

Hitler had the presence of mind to forbid the release of any information about the *Attentat*. This completely cut the ground from under the feet of the conspirators for generals who were in sympathy with them were not prepared to act unless they were absolutely certain that the tyrant was dead.

For a time the conspirators held the War Office in Berlin and their supporters in Vienna and Paris came out into the open. But that evening it was announced that the *Führer* was still alive.

Hitler's vengeance was swift and medieval. He denounced the conspirators as 'a small clique of criminally stupid, ambitious officers, devoid of conscience'. He saw them as blue-blooded Prussian swinehounds who could not comprehend the beauties of Nazism. In his mood of self-pity he mourned: 'The German people are unworthy of my greatness. No one appreciates what I have done for them.'

As for the plotters it was his wish that 'they be hanged like cattle.' Eight of them were, with the Reich Film Corporation's cameramen in attendance to film the scene as they hung naked and strangling. Each man took about five minutes to die. That evening in the *Reichskanzlerei* Hitler enjoyed the film not once but several times, and had it put into the syllabus of the Cadet Schools in Berlin.

The leaders of the plot had included Colonel-General Ludwig Beck, a former chief of the General Staff, and serving officers like General von Stülpnagel the governor of Paris. Von Kluge and Rommel were both to some extent implicated.

In Normandy the Allies had by this time practically fought their way out of the *bocage*. Caen fell on 9 July and St Lô on the 18th. On 26 July General Patton's fresh US Third Army broke out from the beach-head and began to overrun Brittany. The Battle of Normandy had become the Battle of France. It was high time for the Germans to withdraw if they were to save anything from the wreck. But Hitler had not finished. On 7 August a desperate German counter-thrust was launched in the direction of Avranches. Bradley's US First Army held the Mortain offensive, while Patton, swinging north, drove in towards Argentan, the British Second Army held firm and the Canadian First Army thrust south-east from Caen towards Falaise. For five awful days the German Fifth Panzer and the Seventh Armies struggled desperately to get out of the sack so formed. They left behind them 50,000 prisoners and 10,000 dead.

On 15 August the Allies landed 10 divisions near Cannes (Operation *Anvil* or *Dragoon*). The Germans now evacuated the South of France and departed up the Rhône valley with all speed.

By this time Hitler had produced yet another C.-in-C. West. This was Field Marshal Walther Model, an energetic and resourceful officer, who had the great virtue in Hitler's eyes that he did not belong to the old Prussian military families.

Von Kluge committed suicide on 19 August, after sending Hitler a final letter urging him to make up his mind to end the war. But Hitler still strove to convince his followers that the Allies would fall out among themselves, 'Whatever happens we shall carry on this struggle, until, as Frederick the Great said, "one of our damned enemies gives up in despair!"'

There was little enough that Model could do to save the situation in France. All he could hope to do was to rally the remnants of his armies along the Siegfried Line.

By this time Paris itself had risen in revolt (19 August), with the gendarmerie seizing the Ile de la Cité, and the FFI, 20,000 strong, fighting a pitched battle with General Choltitz's garrison, which surrendered, to the number of 10,000 on 25 August. On the 26th the great day came when at last General de Gaulle walked down the Champs Elysées in the midst of a delirious population.

The battles of Normandy and of France had cost the Germans dearly. Half a million casualties, including 210,000 prisoners, and more than 2,000 tanks and assault guns had been left behind. Everywhere the Allies were surging forward. Patton was in Lorraine. Montgomery, confounding the critics who thought him slow, had sped forward to Brussels and Antwerp. And far away in Belorussia the Red Army had destroyed Army Group Centre.

When on 1 September Eisenhower himself took over control of the campaign the question was where to strike next. Montgomery felt that the Allies had not the administrative backing for two simultaneous thrusts, one at Strasbourg, another to the Ruhr. Yet Eisenhower, whose tactical ideas were often illustrated in terms of the American football field, was unwilling to hold up Patton, 'the man with the ball'.

Montgomery still hoped to bring the European war to a swift conclusion. It was to this end that Operation *Market Garden* was planned. The three airborne divisions of the First Allied Airborne Army (Lieutenant-General Lewis H. Brereton) were to capture the key bridges of Holland and thus open the way for the British Second Army to outflank the Siegfried Line.

The American landings at Eindhoven and Nijmegen secured the passage of the Maas and the Waal (17 September). Only at Arnhem on the Lower Rhine did this ambitious plan go awry. The 1st Airborne Division was landed too far from the bridge and this was the fundamental cause of the troubles that followed. The flak was not so heavy as it had been when Gale seized the Orne crossings on D-Day. As ill luck would have it Model himself and 9th SS Panzer were in the Arnhem area when the drop took place and German reaction was swift. Bad weather and inefficient signals communications contributed to the disaster that followed. The Guards Armoured Division fought with great determination to break through to the relief of the Airborne Division.

On the night 25/26 September 2,162 survivors broke out. Of 10,000 who had landed 1,130 had been killed and 6,450 captured. The Germans estimated their losses at 3,300 killed and wounded.

It is wrong to look upon Operation *Market Garden* as a complete failure, for it had secured the passages of the Maas and the Waal. But it fell far short of the decisive results that had been hoped for, and with its end the great

Allied impetus, which had carried them triumphantly forward from the Normandy beaches, seemed – almost literally – to have 'run out of petrol'.

With the Russians still held up east of Warsaw, the capture of the approaches to Antwerp and its establishment as a forward base would probably have been a sounder operation of war than *Market Garden*. The fall of Walcheren on 8 November ended this phase of the campaign in north-west Europe. The Germans had been granted a breathing-space. They made full use of it.

Left: **Following the Anvil landings in the south of France, units of the US Seventh Army, which included the French 1st Division, rolled up the Rhône Valley. A tank advances through the rubble of a village, north of Montelimar. Note the bodies of the horses on the side of the road. They were used by the Germans to drag guns.**

Right: **German snipers surrender in a small town east of Toulon, end of August 1944.**

Below: **American soldiers march down the Champs Elysées in Paris on their way to the front. Some 10,000 German soldiers surrendered on the 25 August. Hitler's orders to destroy the French capital were ignored.**

27 THE EASTERN FRONT, 1944

'The Year of the Ten Victories.'

The spring of 1944 found the Germans everywhere on the defensive. In Italy the Allies were held at Anzio and Cassino; in the West Hitler conceived that a landing might take place as early as mid-February, so the withdrawal of troops or material from France, Belgium, Holland and Denmark had been forbidden (29 December 1943). In the East the *Führer* hoped to be able to hold the line of the old (1938) Russian frontier, and on 8 March, in *Führer* Order No. 11, he listed a chain of 'fortified areas' from Reval to Nikolayev, among them Vinnitsa, which had once been not one of his outposts but his Headquarters. Hitler remained surprisingly optimistic. On 2 April he outlined his current thinking in Operation Order No. 7.

'The Russian offensive in the south of the Eastern front has passed its climax. The Russians have exhausted and divided their forces.

The time has now come to bring the Russian advance to a final standstill . . .

It is now imperative, while holding firm to the Crimea, to hold or win back the following line:

Dniestr to north-east of Kishinev-Jassy-Targul Neamt – the Eastern exit from the Carpathians between Targul Neamt and Kolomyya-Ternopol-Brody-Kovel.'

One wonders whether Hitler expected his followers to believe that the Russians had exhausted their forces. It is impossible to be certain of the strength of the Russian services, but at the beginning of 1944 there were probably not less than 7,000,000 men in the Red Army alone. In addition the Soviet Air Force was now vastly superior to the enemy's. Werth records a revealing conversation with an air force colonel at Uman in March 1944.

'The German air force is much weaker now than it used to be. Very occasionally they send fifty bombers over, but usually they don't use more than twenty. There's no doubt that all this bombing of Germany has made a lot of difference to the German equipment, both in the air and on land. Our soldiers realize the importance of the Allied bombings; the British and Americans, they call them "*nashi*" – that is "*our*" people. . . . A lot of Germany fighters now have to operate in the west and we can do a lot of strafing of German troops, sometimes without much air opposition.'

And he added:

'Those Kittyhawks and Airacobras are damned good – not like last year's Tomahawks and Hurricanes – which were pretty useless. But here we mostly use Soviet planes, especially low-flying *sturmoviks* which scare the pants off the Germans . . .'

To the Russians 1944 is the year of the Ten Victories. Of these the first two have already received some mention in Chapter 22. The third victory came when in April the Fourth Ukrainian Front attacked Seventeenth Army in the Crimea and drove it back to Sevastopol. The Germans evacuated some 30,000 men by sea to Constanza in Rumania, but as many were left in Sevastopol, and much shipping was lost in this 'Dunkirk'. Sevastopol fell on 9 May, and Odessa had already fallen to Tolbukhin's army in April.

The fourth Russian triumph came in June when Marshal Govorov knocked Finland out of the war by breaking through the Mannerheim Line and taking Viborg (Viipuri). The Russians, with noteworthy restraint, halted at the 1940 Finnish frontier and did not push on to Helsinki.

Victory Number Five, the greatest of them all, was the liberation of Belorussia which began on 22 June. The Germans expected an offensive in the south designed to drive Army Group North Ukraine back against the Carpathians and Army Group South Ukraine into the Balkans. Hoping for a quiet summer on the central front they transferred a Panzer corps to the south, depriving Army Group Centre (Field-Marshal Busch) of about 80 per cent of its tanks. On 23 June the third anniversary of the German invasion of Russia, four Soviet armies began a double offensive on a 450-mile front. Zhukov, with the First and Second Belorussian Fronts, attacked towards Mogilev and Bobruisk; Vasilievski, with the First Baltic and Third Belorussian Fronts, advanced on Vitebsk and Orsha.

The Russians had made their preparations with all the thoroughness they had shown before Kursk. They had, including reserves, 166 divisions in Belorussia, with 31,000 guns and mortars, 5,200 tanks and self-propelled guns, and some 6,000 planes. A fleet of 12,000 lorries, mostly American, assured their administrative backing. For the wounded 294,000 hospital beds were in readiness.

Behind the German lines 143,000 partisans were operating, and between 20 and 23 June they put practically all the Belorussian railways out of action, paralyzing the German supply system.

In the first five days the Russians drove deep into the enemy lines, breaking them in six places, but Hitler, determined not to give up any more of the ground he had conquered in 1941, refused to allow his troops to fall back from parts of the front which had been by-passed. In consequence – as might have been foreseen – large numbers were cut off. The Third Panzer Army lost touch with Army Group North, the flanks of the Fourth and Ninth Armies were broken, and by the end of June the last-named had been trapped and destroyed round Bobruisk, only its Headquarters and one corps escaping. Another large body of German troops was cut off at Vitebsk and these two encirclements cost the Germans 20,000 prisoners.

Hitler now gave orders that the line of the Beresina must be held, but the Russians moved too fast and on 3 July they closed the pincers behind Minsk.

'In view of these shattering events,' writes Guderian,

'Hitler moved his headquarters in mid-July from the Obersalzberg to East Prussia. All units that could be scraped together were rushed to the disintegrating front. In place of Field-Marshal Busch, Field-Marshal Model, who already commanded Army Group A, was also given command of Army Group Centre – or to be more precise of the gap where that army had been . . . I knew Model well from the days when he commanded the 3rd Panzer Division in 1941 . . . ; he was a bold, inexhaustible soldier, who knew the front well and who won the confidence of his men by his habitual disregard for his personal safety. He had no time for lazy or incompetent subordinates. He carried out his intentions in a most determined fashion. He was the best possible man to perform the fantastically difficult task of reconstructing a line in the centre of the Eastern Front.'

The difficulty of his task will be readily appreciated from the fact that German casualties at Minsk numbered 100,000. On 17 July Werth saw 57,000 prisoners, including several generals, paraded through Moscow.

'Particularly striking was the attitude of the Russian crowds lining the streets. Youngsters booed and whistled, and even threw things at the Germans, only to be immediately restrained by the adults; men looked on grimly and in silence; but many women, especially elderly women, were full of commiseration (some even had tears in their eyes) as they looked at these bedraggled "Fritzes". I remember one old woman murmuring, "Just like our poor boys . . . also driven into the war." '

Through the 250 mile gap in the German front the Russians advanced at a rate of 10 or 15 miles a day. Vilna fell into their hands on 13 July, while on the 18th Rokossovsky crossed into Poland, taking Lublin (23 July) and Brest-Litovsk (28 July). Belorussia was free and the German army had suffered a worse defeat than Stalingrad, for 25 divisions had been destroyed with casualties amounting to 350,000 men. The Russians felt that this rout avenged the terrible defeats that they had suffered in the same area in 1941. Their morale and their attitude to the Communist régime is well-illustrated by a letter which Werth received during this Battle of Belorussia. It was from Mitya Khludov, aged 19, who came from a well-known Moscow family of merchants.

'I am proud,' he wrote, 'to tell you that my battery has done wonders in knocking the hell out of the Fritzes. Also, for our last engagement, I have been proposed for the Patriotic War Order, and, better still, I have been accepted into the Party. Yes, I know, my father and my mother were bourgeois, but what the hell! I am a Russian, a hundred per cent Russian, and I am proud of it, and our people have made this victory possible, after all the terror and humiliation of 1941; and I am ready to give my life for my country and for Stalin; I am proud to be in the Party, to be one of Stalin's victorious soldiers. If I'm lucky enough I'll be in Berlin yet. We'll get there – and we deserve to get there – before our Western Allies do. If you see Ehrenburg, give him my regards. Tell him we all have been reading his stuff. . . . Tell him we really hate the Germans after seeing so many horrors they have committed here in Belorussia. Not to mention all the destruction they've caused. They've pretty well turned this country into a desert.'

When Hitler moved to Rastenburg in July, the invasion of the Reich seemed imminent; indeed as early as 31 May Martin Bormann, the Nazy Party Chancellor, had sent a circular letter to all Gauleiters explaining the task of the Party in such an eventuality. It was at Rastenburg, while the Battle of Belorussia was drawing to its bloody close, that the *Führer* so narrowly escaped Colonel von Stauffenberg's time-bomb. His survival clinched the struggle for power between the Party and the Army, 'at once the most suspect and the most dangerous body in the State'. The plot has already been discussed in this work, but certain appointments that followed may be mentioned here. One was that of Colonel General Schörner, an officer whose loyalty to the Nazi party was only equalled by his self-esteem, to command Army Group North. Hitler empowered him to employ

'all available forces and materials of the Armed Forces and the Waffen SS, of non-military organizations and formations, of Party and civilian authorities in order to repel enemy attacks and preserve our Baltic territories (Ostland).'

Another was the selection of the Reichsführer S.S. Herr Himmler to replace General Fromm, the commander of the Replacement Army, who had been hanged for his part in the plot.

A third was the appointment of Guderian, who had played no part in the attempt on Hitler's life, as Chief of Staff of the OKH in place of Zeitzler, who had been sick for some time, and whose relations with his master had not been improved by the series of disasters on the front for which OKH had to answer.

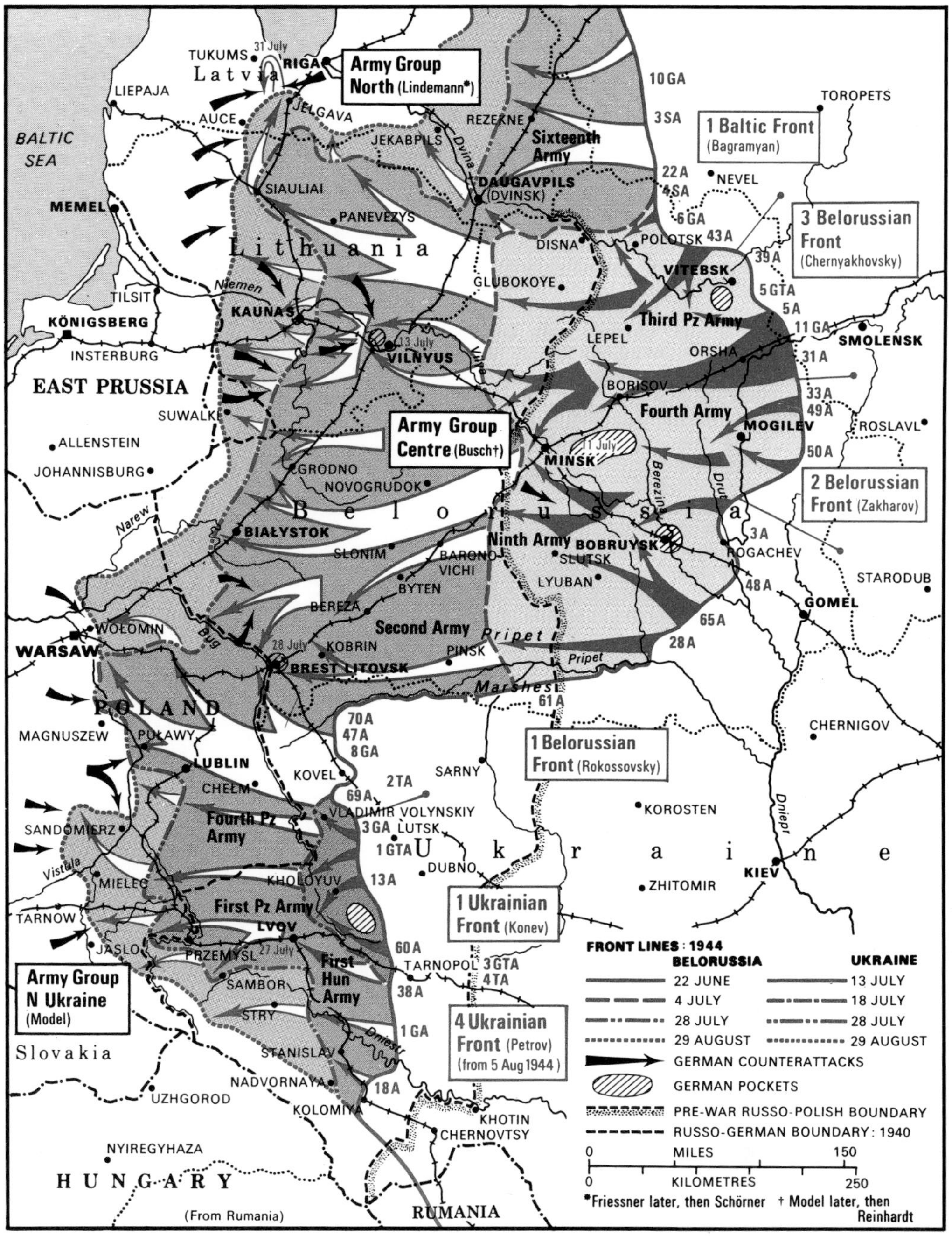

Left: **In June 1944 the Soviet Army launched a massive offensive to reach Poland. Men of the 1st Baltic Front liberate the town of Vitebsk, near the Lithuanian border.**

Right: **Hitler and his generals, August 1944. At this point Hitler's relationship with his generals was deteriorating badly after the July Bomb Plot.**

Guderian reached the *Wolfsschanze* on 21 July and reported to Hitler, who

'seemed to be in rather poor shape; one ear was bleeding; his right arm, which had been badly bruised and was almost unusuable, hung in a sling. But his manner was one of astonishing calm as he received me.'

According to Guderian the *Führer* soon got over the physical effects of the bomb.

'His already existing malady, plain for all to see in the trembling of his left hand and left leg, had no connection with the attempt on his life. But more important than the physical were the moral effects. In accordance with his character, the deep distrust he already felt for mankind in general, and for General Staff Corps officers and generals in particular, now became profound hatred. A by-product of the sickness from which he suffered is that it imperceptibly destroys the powers of moral judgment; in his case what had been hardness became cruelty, while a tendency to bluff became plain dishonesty. He often lied without hesitation, and assumed that others lied to him. He believed no one any more. It had already been difficult enough to deal with him; it now became a torture that grew steadily worse from month to month. He frequently lost all self-control and his language grew increasingly violent. In his intimate circle he now found no restraining influence, since the polite and gentlemanly Schmundt had been replaced by the oafish Burgdorf.'

The failure of the attempt to assassinate Hitler (20 July) was hardly less of a relief to Stalin than to the intended victim. The last thing the former wanted was to see the Nazi regime replaced by a pro-Western Government, now that the Anglo-American armies were established on the Continent. Having battered the Germans unmercifully, he meant to give them the *coup de grâce* in their home country.

With the Germans in flagrant disarray the Russians scored Victory Number Six. In July they overran the Western Ukraine, including Lvov, and won a bridgehead beyond the Vistula at Sandomierz, south of Warsaw. The victory was marred in Western eyes by the failure to take that city, or to relieve its heroic inhabitants who rose on 1 August, under the leadership of General Bór-Komorowski, in a desperate endeavour to throw off the German yoke.

There has been no lack of Polish, British and American writers to put a sinister interpretation upon this episode. Captain Cyril Falls, whose work is distinguished by his balanced judgment, concludes that it is 'most improbable' that the Red Army 'stood by and watched with satisfaction the slaughter and capture of elements which might have proved troublesome to it when it set about organizing as Soviet territory the belt of Poland which it had recovered'. Werth, who goes into the whole question most thoroughly, comes to much the same conclusion, while admitting that the Russians would have eliminated Bór-Komorowski himself one way or another. Werth had the advantage of discussing the whole question with General Rokossovsky, the commander responsible, at Lublin on 26 August, 1944, while the struggle was still in progress. Rokossovsky, who was himself of Polish blood, told Werth that on about 1 August a German counter-attack by three or four armoured divisions had driven his troops back about 65 miles. The insurgents, he said, had started their uprising on their own without co-ordinating it with the Russians. Even in the best circumstances the Red Army could not have got to Warsaw before mid-August. At the time of the interview the Germans were doing their damnedest to reduce the Russian bridgeheads across the Vistula. 'Mind you,' Rokossovsky continued, not without reason, 'we have fought non-stop for over two months now. We've liberated the whole of Belorussia and nearly one fourth of Poland; but, even the Red Army gets tired after a while. Our casualties have been very heavy.'

The Russians were bitterly criticized at the time for not allowing British and American planes to land behind their lines, after dropping supplies to the insurgents. Rokossovsky explained that the military situation east of the Vistula was very complicated – presumably due to his recent reverse. 'And we just don't want any British and American planes mucking around here at the moment.' He was of the opinion that, since General Bór's men were only holding out in isolated spots, most of the supplies would fall into German hands anyway. Allied experience at Arnhem and elsewhere seems rather to support this view.

Guderian's comments are also of interest:

'It may be assumed that the Soviet Union had no interest in seeing these (pro-London) elements strengthened by a successful uprising and by the capture of their capital. . . . But be that as it may, an attempt by the Russians . . . to cross the Vistula at Deblin on July 25 failed, with the loss of thirty tanks. . . . We Germans had the impression that it was our defence which halted the enemy rather than a Russian desire to sabotage the Warsaw uprising.'

It is hardly surprising that the Germans should have massed strong forces around Warsaw, since they blocked the direct Russian route to the Fatherland.

Ill-armed though they were, the Poles were remarkably successful at first. By 6 August much of the city was in their hands. On the 8th the sadistic *Gruppenführer* S.S. von dem Bach-Zelewski, an expert in anti-partisan warfare, came on the scene. He had at his command the Kaminski Brigade, composed largely of Russian turncoats and the Dirlewanger S.S. Brigade, recruited from paroled German convicts. These formations were not squeamish. According to Clark 'Prisoners were burned alive with petrol; babies were impaled on bayonets . . .; women were hung upside down from balconies in rows.' Still the Poles held out with the utmost tenacity. Rumours of the atrocities reached Guderian, who taxed von dem Bach with them, and was told that because of the desperate nature of the street-fighting his men had abandoned all moral standards. He had lost control of them. This was too much for Guderian, who complained to Hitler. The latter had been privy to Himmler's plan to extinguish the revolt by sheer violence and terror, but even so Guderian had his way. Von dem Bach, finding the wind had changed, sent the Kaminski Brigade to the rear and had its commander shot! In another age the Borgias might have found employment for such an officer.

The Poles held out with desperate courage, prolonging the unequal struggle in the sewers of their city. But at length they were compelled to surrender (2 October); 300,000 had lost their lives. The Ghetto had been destroyed in 1943. Now Hitler ordered that the whole city be razed to the ground (9 October). When the Russians entered in January 1945 they found that about nine-tenths of it had been demolished.

While the struggle for Warsaw was in progress, the Red Army was winning Victory Number Seven. On 20 August the Russians thrust southwards into Moldavia and Rumania with an army consisting of about 90 infantry divisions besides 41 tank and three cavalry formations. Army Group South Ukraine (General Friessner) was partly German and partly Rumanian. The Russian onslaught was deliberately directed against the latter, with the aim of knocking Rumania out of the war. They offered little resistance and some even turned against their allies. The Germans, though they resisted fiercely, were cut off by 23 August and 16 divisions were destroyed. Losses were estimated at 60,000 killed and 106,000 prisoners. The bag is said to have included 338 planes, 830 tanks and self-propelled guns, 5,500 pieces of artillery and 33,000 trucks. On 30 August Malinovsky entered Bucharest and Ploesti, while Tolbukhin pushed on into Bulgaria.

The Rumanian troops had shown themselves rather less than enthusiastic for Hitler's cause and on 23 August King Michael showed him-

Below right: A *Volkssturm* or People's Guard poster.

Below: The poster asks people to donate clothes to the war effort.

self to be of their mind when he had Marshal Antonescu imprisoned in the Palace. General Hansen and his German Military Mission were interned and an armistice with Russia was signed on 12 September.

Victory Number Eight was the freeing of Estonia and most of Latvia. This had the effect of alarming the Finns, who now sued for peace. The armistice was signed on 19 September. The Russians refrained from occupying Finland, a gesture calculated to reassure the Scandinavian peoples.

In October the Russians invaded Hungary and Czechoslovakia, and joined hands with the Yugoslavs in liberating Belgrade: Victory Number Nine. In Hungary fierce fighting continued well into 1945.

The last Russian success of this their year of victories took place in the far north when the Germans were expelled from Petsamo and driven back into northern Norway.

No objective account of the war on the Eastern Front can avoid the question of German war crimes and atrocities. It is thought that the Germans took well over 3,000,000 prisoners in 1941 alone, and in all perhaps 5,000,000. Of these, it seems that only about 1,000,000 survived. It is, of course, impossible to produce accurate statistics, but it is certain that very many died while prisoners. Nor did they succumb to starvation alone. There is ample evidence that great numbers were shot, gassed, or tortured to death. It is easy to say that these crimes were committed by the S.D. or the S.S., but the German Army cannot escape a share of the responsibility. General Reinecke, Chief of the General Army Office of the OKW, known as *'der kleine Keitel'*, excused the killing of Commissars and Bolsheviks on the grounds 'that the war between Germany and Russia was unlike any other war. The Red Army soldier . . . was not a soldier in the ordinary sense, but an ideological enemy. An enemy to the death of National-Socialism, and he had to be treated accordingly.' The Russians were *Untermensch* – sub-human – that was the underlying concept of the arrogant conquerors.

Nearly 3,000,000 Russians were deported to Germany for slave labour. They were not well treated. Early in 1942 Rosenberg complained to Keitel that only a few hundred thousands were still fit for work, and Göring told Ciano that some of the prisoners of war had resorted to cannibalism. Wittily he added that some had gone rather too far and had eaten a German sentry. The *Reichsmarschall* had a sense of humour all his own.

The extermination of the Jewish population was systematic. Alexander Werth cites the example of Klooga in Estonia where he 'saw the charred remains of some 2,000 Jews, brought from Vilno and other places, who had been shot and then burned on great bonfires they themselves had been ordered to build and light.' A few had escaped. One told Werth of a kindly

Left: T-34 tanks of the 3rd Belorussian Front advance through Poland.

Above: After the failure of the Warsaw Uprising, General Bór-Komorowski surrenders to General Bach-Zelewski on 3 October 1944.

Right: A wrecked Finnish floatplane with Nazi markings was smashed during the Soviet advance.

Far right: In the wake of the Red Army, Germans living in Eastern European countries fled.

Below: In March 1945 Soviet troops advance through the streets of Köslin, Pomerania.

S.D. man who comforted a weeping child with the words 'My little one, don't cry like this, death will soon come.'

The Germans have only themselves to thank if their critics see among their less lovable characteristics a pleasure in inflicting pain, which accords oddly with their well-known vein of self-pity. Forgetfulness one would not expect in people so efficient. Yet such an ornament of the German Army as Field Marshal von Manstein could allege at Nuremberg that an order he had signed had 'escaped his memory entirely'. It stated that:

'The Jewish-Bolshevist system must be exterminated. . . . The German soldier comes as the bearer of a racial concept. (He) must appreciate the necessity for the harsh punishment of Jewry. . . . The food situation at home makes it essential that the troops should be fed off the land, and the largest possible stocks should be placed at the disposal of the homeland. In enemy cities, a large part of the population will have to go hungry. Nothing, out of a misguided sense of humanity, may be given to prisoners-of-war or to the population, unless they are in the service of the German Wehrmacht.'

Himmler put things rather more bluntly when, speaking at Poznan in 1941, he said:

'I am not interested in the slightest if 10,000 Russian females die of exhaustion digging an anti-tank ditch for us, provided the ditch is dug.'

Even so Manstein's order was in the best Nazi manner, and he belonged neither to the S.S. nor the S.D. but to the German Army which, we are invited to believe, knew nothing of the barbarities committed by their fellow-countrymen – nothing of Belsen, nothing of Auschwitz, nothing of the systematic devastation as they fell back from Belorussia.

By comparison the atrocities committed at random by the Russians were child's play. Arson, murder, robbery and rape marked their conquering progress, but at least these crimes were not organized or even condoned by higher authority. A Russian major told Werth that 'many German women somehow assumed that "it was now the Russians' turn", and that it was no good resisting.' The most ignorant Kazakh knew enough German to say *'Frau, komm'*. It was sufficient. The wheel had come full circle.

SAROTTI
Danzig 191 Km
Neustettin 68 Km
Bublitz 38 Km
2
160
XII

28 FROM THE MARIANAS TO THE PHILIPPINES

'Dawn came none too soon for the Marines – but it found them still there.'
Samuel Eliot Morison

In the Pacific the two-pronged thrust drove deeper. In the south-west General MacArthur's operations were designed to pave the way for a landing on Mindanao in the Philippines on 15 November. In the Central Pacific the objective was the Marianas – a thousand-mile leap on the way to Japan.

With Manus in his hands and Rabaul sealed off, MacArthur lost no time in completing the conquest of New Guinea. Early in April General Kenney knocked out the Japanese air base at Hollandia with massive bombing attacks. MacArthur followed up with a well-planned combined operation (22 April) and by 3 May the place was in his hands. During the next three months he pushed westwards and in a series of four seaborne landings secured the rest of New Guinea as well as the island of Biak, which was needed for its airfields. The garrison, 10,000 men under Colonel Kuzume, was almost as numerous as the American landing force, and it was well dug-in.

The aggressive Admiral Toyoda was planning a big naval battle and realized that American heavy bombers from Biak might intervene. He decided to reinforce the island from Mindanao but was foiled twice. He then concentrated a really strong force, including the big battleships *Yamato* and *Musashi*, which might well have done the trick. But before he could strike he became aware of the threat to the Marianas from Spruance's Fifth Fleet and felt compelled to concentrate in the Philippine Sea. Colonel Kuzume was left to his fate, though he contrived to hold out until 22 June, and exacted a toll of 6,238 casualties.

With Hollandia, Wakde and Biak in his hands, MacArthur could prepare to fulfil the vow he had made when he left Corregidor.

In the Central Pacific the Americans now faced the vast leap from the Marshalls to the Marianas. Vice-Admiral Kelly Turner, who with Guadalcanal, Tarawa and the Marshalls behind him, qualified as *the* expert on amphibious warfare, had 535 ships and 127,571 troops at his disposal.

In Saipan, which the Japanese regarded as part of the homeland, General Saito had 22,700 men, while the unfortunate Admiral Nagumo – the man who had lost the carriers, and indeed the Pacific War, at Midway – had a flotilla of small craft and 6,700 sailors. After April, thanks to the successes of American submarines, the garrison received no reinforcements.

On 11 June Admiral Mitscher's four fast carrier groups began bombing the Japanese airfields. On 13 and 14 June the battleships carried on the softening-up process. D-Day was the 15th. By nightfall 20,000 troops were ashore, though 2,000 of them were casualties. The Japanese fought skilfully, making excellent use of artillery and mortars to compel the American amphtracs to disgorge their troops at the water's edge instead of carrying them well inland.

The Marines spent a bad night.

'The Japanese saw to it that nobody slept for more than a few minutes. After a series of probes, their big effort was announced at 0300 June 16 by a bugler; and with much screaming, brandishing of swords and flapping of flags the enemy launched an attack that was supposed to drive the Marines into the sea. As the Japanese fell others replaced them, and the fighting on this flank did not reach its climax until sunrise, at 0545. Five Marine Corps tanks then stopped the last attack, and the Japanese withdrew under a blanket of gunfire from the cruiser *Louisville* and destroyers *Phelps* and *Monssen*, leaving about 700 dead on the battlefield. Dawn came none too soon for the Marines – but it found them still there.'

The Japanese had no intention of leaving the Marianas to their fate as they had the Marshalls. Already a powerful fleet was on its way. The American commanders, Spruance, Turner and Holland Smith, knew this as well as Saito. Cancelling the landing on Guam due to take place on 18 June, they put their reserve infantry division ashore and sent the transports off to the eastward until such time as the crisis should blow over.

Admiral Toyoda, with new air groups at his command, was determined to try the old Yamamoto strategy of annihilating the US Pacific Fleet at one fell swoop. First Mobile Fleet (Vice-Admiral Ozawa) had concentrated at Tawi Tawi, west of Mindanao, on 16 May. The Japanese had hoped to lure the Americans south, but the news from Saipan told Toyoda that he must seek his decisive battle in the Marianas.

The Japanese fleet was thoroughly outclassed by the Americans:

	United States	*Japanese*
Fleet carriers	7	5
Light carriers	8	4
Battleships	7	5
Heavy cruisers	8	11
Light cruisers	13	2
Destroyers	69	28
Aircraft		
Fighters	475	222
Dive-bombers	232	113
Torpedo-bombers	184	95
Float planes	65	43

Spruance's main handicap was that he was more or less anchored to Saipan, since he had to cover the troops ashore.

June 19 was fair and cloudless. Still unaware of Ozawa's position the Americans began operations by attacking Guam, and a series of dogfights ensued, in which the Hellcats shot down more than their own number of Japanese aircraft.

Meanwhile the first wave was coming over from Ozawa's carriers and 'The Great Marianas Turkey Shoot' was on. The Japanese got one hit on *South Dakota* in Admiral Lee's battle line, but not one reached the carriers. The Hellcats got 45 out of 69 enemy planes.

During this phase American submarines had sunk two Japanese carriers, first the *Shokaku*, a veteran of Pearl Harbor; then the big new flagship *Taiho*, which, struck by a single torpedo, plunged swiftly to the cold depths of the Pacific, taking three-quarters of the crew with her.

Six of Ozawa's second raid got through to the carriers, only to be shot down by combat air patrols or anti-aircraft fire. About 20 attacked the battle line, and there were near-misses on several battleships. This time the Japanese lost 98 out of 130 planes. Most of the third wave of 47 aircraft got safely back to the *Junyo* and the *Ryuho* for the simple reason that they failed to find their target. Of about a dozen which did get through seven were shot down. The fourth raid, 82 planes, was launched at 1100. Nine survived.

While this was going on, Mitscher's bombers had been making heavy attacks on Guam.

The Philippine Sea was by far the biggest carrier battle of the war. In the unequal struggle the Japanese lost two carriers and 346 planes. The United States lost 30 planes, besides taking

Above: Marines dug in once they had established themselves on the Saipan beach.

Above left: Units of the Japanese fleet manoeuvre to avoid damaging hits from American aircraft. In the centre the burning *Zuikaku* has already suffered severe damage.

Left: A *New Mexico* class battleship bombards the Saipan coast as part of the build up to the landings. Note the middle gun in recoil position.

one single hit on a battleship. The Japanese pilots, outnumbered and seriously short of training, were simply shot out of the skies by vastly more experienced aviators.

On the 20th three American carrier groups pursued Ozawa eastwards. They did not find him until 1540. Then Mitscher launched 216 planes in an all-out strike, which sank the carrier *Hiyo* besides damaging the *Zuikaku* and other vessels. The Americans shot down 65 of Ozawa's 100 surviving carrier planes, for a loss of 20. It was pitch dark by the time they got back to their carriers, and, although in defiance of Japanese submarines Mitscher ordered his ships to light up, 80 planes crashed or were ditched, having run out of fuel. Even so the Americans lost no more than 130 aircraft and 76 airmen in the two days of battle. The Japanese got back to Okinawa (22 June) with 35 out of 430 planes. Once more their carrier air groups had been practically wiped out, and Spruance had hit the Japanese Navy in the way that hurt most.

It was now only a matter of time before the Marianas must fall. Resistance on Saipan ended on 9 July. The Americans had 14,000 casualties, the Japanese at least 24,000 killed. Although 1,780 prisoners were taken, half of them Koreans, hundreds of Japanese civilians committed suicide by jumping off the cliffs. Saito and Nagumo themselves committed *hara-kiri*.

On Guam, the most important of the Marianas, resistance was less determined than on Saipan. Even so its capture cost 7,081 casualties. By mid-August the Americans were in effective control of the Marianas. And on 18 July the cabinet of General Tojo had resigned.

The Americans were now thinking ahead to the final assault on Japan. One school of thought, which included Admirals King and Nimitz, wished to take Formosa and either make their base there or on the China coast. MacArthur headed the other school which wished to retake Luzon and make that the jumping-off place. He felt that not to liberate the Filipinos at the earliest possible moment would be a betrayal, and that thereafter no Asiatic would ever trust an American again. But it was not only for political reasons that the General had his way. Formosa was very strongly defended and, since most of the coast of China was in Japanese hands, there was little real prospect of establishing a base in the area.

In September Admiral Halsey with his *Essex* class carriers boldly sailed up within sight of land and bombarded the Japanese air bases in the Philippines. The few enemy planes that appeared were shot down. So much for the theory that carriers could never operate within range of shore-based planes. Meanwhile the Quebec Conference was thrashing out the course of future operations. The news of Halsey's success came in time for President Roosevelt and Winston Churchill to agree to the invasion of Leyte on 20 October. The projected operation to take Mindanao was cancelled, and the whole programme was speeded up by two months. This was a remarkable demonstration

Below: The first wave of landing craft approaches the Saipan beach in June 1944. The Marianas were heavily bombarded prior to the invasion.

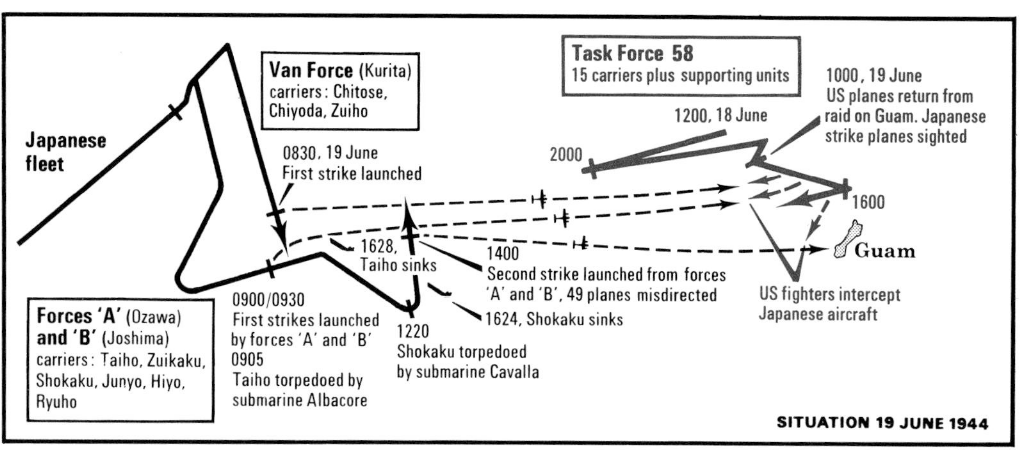

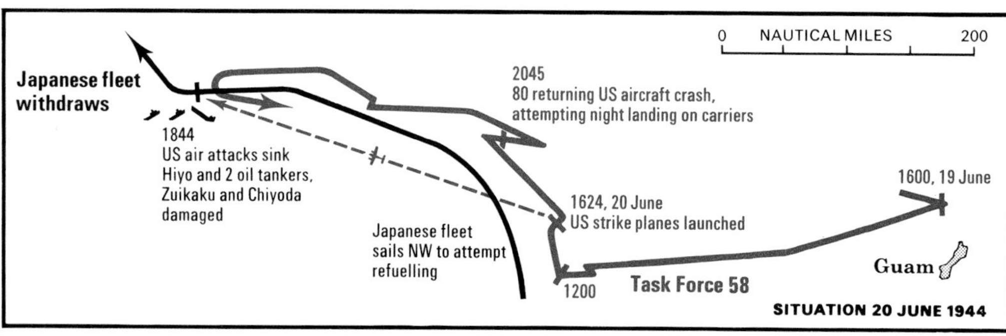

of strategic flexibility, but the administrative backing was there, and the amphibious assault that followed was a model.

Peleliu in the Palau Group was one of those islands which Nimitz might well have by-passed. But he felt that the Palaus would be needed as staging points and, as the veteran 1st Marine Division was already at sea, he ordered that the operation go forward, despite the recent change of plan.

By this time the Japanese were trying new tactics. Instead of meeting the Americans on the beach, as they had done in the past with such notable lack of success, their idea now was to site their main position well in rear, and to keep a strong reserve for counter-attack.

On Peleliu Colonel Nakagawa adopted a cross between the old and the new tactics, for his men fought hard for the beaches and inflicted 1,110 casualties on D-Day. By the 18th the Marines had fought their way to the airfields, but north of it they were faced by Umurbrogal Ridge, which was honey-combed with strong-points hewn out of the soft coral rock and immune from bombardment from ship or plane. The Americans

'. . . would reach a cave mouth after a bloody battle, only to find that it was deserted, or capture a peak and smell cooking being done by cave-dwelling Japanese resting comfortably beneath. The biggest cave, encountered on 17 September, contained more than a thousand Japanese. The only weapon to cope with them was a new long-range flame-thrower, first mounted on LVTs and later on Sherman tanks, which threw a wicked tongue of fire that could penetrate 40 or 50 feet and even lick around a corner.'

Nakagawa held out until the night of 24/25 November, when he committed suicide. His 5,300 men were no more. They had taken 1,950 Americans with them.

As a preliminary to the invasion of Leyte four carrier groups attacked Formosa and neighbouring airfields in China (12/14 October). The Americans destroyed over 500 planes for the loss of 76, besides inflicting immense bomb damage on military installations. Three American ships were damaged, but none of them fatally.

For the assault on Leyte the Americans assembled 738 ships, including 17 carriers. The landings went with great precision, and were comparatively uneventful (20 October). By midnight on the 21st the Americans had landed 132,000 men and 200,000 tons of stores, besides taking the harbour of Tacloban and the airfields there and at Dulag.

The Japanese Navy was too scattered to concentrate in time to interfere with the vulnerable ship-to-shore movement phase of the Leyte landings. But, undeterred by the debacle in the Marianas, Admiral Toyoda was still seeking the opportunity for a knock-out blow. Japanese strategists believed quite rightly in keeping the enemy guessing. They liked to achieve this not only by deception, which was very reasonable, but by dividing their forces in the hope of putting in an appearance suddenly where they were least expected. This called for good timing, which in turn demanded a higher standard of communications than the Japanese had achieved.

One would think that by October 1944 the

Above left: **A 37 mm artillery gun fires at enemy positions on Saipan.**

Left: **Some Japanese were trapped in a pocket north of Garapan. A few managed to escape on ships leaving Tanapag Harbour; on the beach one of the ones who did not make it.**

most obtuse and reactionary admiral would have noticed the value of air power. In this respect the Combined Fleet, though it still had four carriers, was completely outclassed. Ozawa came out of the Inland Sea with no more than 116 planes. There simply had not been time to train new pilots since their air groups had had the stuffing knocked out of them over the Philippine Sea. The wonder is that the Japanese gave their opponents such a run for their money in the battle of Leyte Gulf, one of the most intricate of the whole war.

The Japanese approached from two directions: the main force under Vice-Admiral Kurita coming from North Borneo and Ozawa from Japan. Kurita was to destroy the fleet under Kinkaid which was supporting the landing. Ozawa was to lure Halsey away to the north.

Kurita had five battleships, including the giants *Yamato* and *Musashi*, 12 heavy cruisers and 19 destroyers. A smaller force under Vice-Admiral Nishimura and including two battleships was to co-operate with Kurita. Since all four carriers were with Ozawa, the striking force depended for its air support on such land-based planes as were in range.

Ozawa was an officer of great ability, second only to Yamamoto, and he played his part with skill. As in the Philippine Sea battle American submarines scored heavily. They shadowed Kurita and sank his flagship, the heavy cruiser *Atago*, in the early stages of the operation (23 October). Then a carrier-borne attack smote the *Musashi* which turned turtle and plunged to the depths with most of the crew.

Convinced that Kurita had been hard hit and was probably retiring, Halsey turned north to oppose Ozawa and his carriers. Kinkaid was left to his own devices. But Kurita, so far from withdrawing, pushed on at 20 knots, making for the San Bernardino Straits. Nishimura was also bearing down on Kinkaid who, to meet this two-pronged thrust, had battleships, intended for ship-to-shore bombardment (and already seriously short of ammunition), and small escort carriers, devoid of armour and intended only for troop and convoy support. Halsey spent the night 24/25 October speeding away from Leyte in search of Ozawa. Kurita spent that same night dashing in towards the invasion fleet. Kinkaid was ready to repel an attack from the southward, where Rear-Admiral Oldendorf lay in wait for Nishimura in the Surigao Straits with six battleships and eight cruisers arrayed to cross the T as the Japanese approached. It was the school-solution to a sort of naval problem which hardly ever actually occurs. Nishimura, who forged ahead with determined gallantry, was practically blasted out of the water. This Battle of Surigao Straits was Tsushima over again. Admiral Shima, who was supporting Nishimura, withdrew with a discretion unusual in a Japanese commander. The cruiser *Mogami*, a survivor of Midway, was sunk, as well as the battleship *Yamashiro*. The dawn of 25 October found Halsey 300 miles north of Leyte, still looking for Ozawa; Kinkaid's covering force preening itself on one of the most satisfactory night actions ever fought; and the main Japanese striking force, all unsuspected, steaming down the east side of Samar towards Leyte, having traversed the San Bernardino Strait during the night without the least opposition.

The Battle of Samar began when at 6.45 a.m. Kurita sighted the northern group of Kinkaid's escort carriers under Rear-Admiral C. A. F. Sprague. They were operating about 40 miles offshore, providing support for the troops already ashore.

Both sides were equally surprised. In theory Sprague's force had no chance. With his speed and firepower Kurita should have been able to make short work of these carriers. But Sprague kept his head, and he and his command improvised tactics suitable to an occasion for which no manual caters. Airmen and light surface craft alike attacked with reckless courage, as the carriers made off eastwards at 17½ knots. The Americans lost three escort vessels but they managed to hit two cruisers and to check Kurita's onslaught.

Even before Sprague ordered the three destroyers *Hoel, Heermann* and *Johnston* to counter-attack, the commander of the last-named, Commander Ernest E. Evans, a Cherokee, 'called all hands to General Quarters, and passed the word "Prepare to attack major portion of Japanese Fleet".' *Johnston* went down fighting, but not before she had torpedoed *Kumano* and engaged the battleship *Kongo* with 5-inch gunfire.

While the fumbling Japanese admiral paused to ascertain damage, Avengers and Hellcats from all three American carrier groups set about him with sufficient fury to cripple two cruisers and to convince Kurita that he had the main American carrier force on his back. He sank the carrier *Gambier Bay*, but at 0911 he decided to withdraw. His staff had mistaken destroyers for cruisers and escort for fleet carriers. When he should have formed battle line he was worrying about cruising in anti-aircraft formation. He estimated that Sprague's force, whose maximum speed was 17½ knots, was making 30.

As if the escort carriers had not had enough to put up with for one day, the 25 October saw the first of the celebrated *Kamikaze* raids. They hit two carriers among other vessels and sank the carrier *St. Lo*.

Above: **An aerial view of the Leyte landings taken by an SOC Seagull from the USS *Portland* (CA-33) on 20 October 1944**

Below: **Captain Settle, on board the USS *Portland*, observes the shore-bombardment operations.**

Above: **Vice-Admiral Takeo Kurita was commander of the First Striking Force at the Battle of Leyte Gulf. He still believed battleships could win naval battles.**

On 25 October Halsey's aircraft discovered Ozawa and sank all four of his aircraft carriers and a destroyer in the Battle of Cape Engano.

Brooding over a supposed affront the American admiral then wasted a vital hour and failed to block Kurita's escape route through the San Bernardino Strait, thus robbing Admiral Lee of his chance of a good old-fashioned battle-wagon shooting match.

The complicated Japanese plan had failed; Ozawa, playing the part of the tethered goat, had sacrificed his carriers in vain. Kurita, cast in the role of the hunter, had missed a sitting target.

Halsey made two grave errors in the battle of Leyte Gulf, but by sinking all four carriers he more than compensated for these lapses. Oldendorf showed how to carry out one of the classic manoeuvres of naval warfare. Sprague showed how to play a completely unpredictable battle 'off the cuff'. But no amount of cleverness will win a battle. Without the cool courage of men like his Cherokee captain, Sprague's battle would have been lost.

The fighting for Leyte soon began to resemble the struggle for Guadalcanal two years earlier.

The Japanese had 365,000 troops in the Philippines and by 'Tokyo Express' tactics built up their forces on Leyte to about 45,000. But by 1 November 101,635 Americans were ashore under General Krueger (Sixth Army).

The *Kamikaze* campaign got into its stride and the carriers *Belleau Wood, Intrepid* and *Franklin* were badly damaged, and at least 45 planes destroyed. *Lexington* was hit a little later.

Severe American air strikes against Japanese reinforcement shipping (13/14 and 25 November) provoked a fierce reaction. The *Kamikazes* hit *Intrepid, Cabot* and *Essex* (25 November).

General Yamashita, the conqueror of Singapore, was sent to take command of the defence. As General Eichelberger (Eighth US Army) put it . . . 'Yamashita, the rainy season, and evil terrain made Leyte hard going for the military calendar-keepers.' By the end of November most of the island was in American hands and 35,000 Japanese who could no longer look for any reinforcement faced 183,242 Americans. Already 24,000 Japanese had died. American casualties included 2,260 killed, and considerable numbers died of dysentery and tropical diseases.

Their desperate resort to *Kamikaze* tactics brought the Japanese a real revival of air power. The *Kamikaze* Corps had been organized in 1944 by Rear-Admiral Arima. What with the American introduction of proximity fuses for anti-aircraft shells, and the ever-growing skill of their fighter pilots, it had become virtually impossible for a conventional bomber to hit an American ship.

The Japanese tactics were now to crash onto an enemy ship and obsolescent aircraft could be used – at twice the normal range. The spread of petrol and the explosion of the bombs were bound to inflict heavy casualties and damage for the loss of one semi-trained pilot. Nor did the Japanese temperament reject such desperate measures.

The *Kamikazes* had considerable successes against convoys between Leyte Gulf and Mindoro, where the Americans had landed on 15 December. But this was nothing to the attack on the Luzon Attack Force. During the three days bombardment (6/9 January) which preceded the landing in Lingayen Gulf, the *Kamikazes* struck time and again. The vessels hit during this nightmare period included the battleship *New Mexico*, the light cruiser *California*, HMAS *Australia* – four times – and several destroyers. But by 12 January the Japanese had practically used up every plane they had in the Philippines.

The US Sixth Army's fight for Manila itself was bitter, for, although Yamashita had ordered the evacuation of the capital, Rear-Admiral Iwabachi held out with the 20,000 men of his naval base. In his fanatical defence, the beautiful city with the ancient Spanish walled town of Intramuros was razed to the ground – the price of liberation. The Sixth Army's campaign for Luzon lasted 173 days and cost it 37,854 casualties.

On 30 June Eighth Army, which had finished off the Japanese on Leyte, took over on Luzon. Its commander, Lieutenant-General Eichelberger, claims that his Army 'set up an all-time record for swift amphibious movements' and had fifty-two D-Days between Christmas 1944 and the Japanese surrender.

'In one forty-four day period alone these troops conducted fourteen major landings and twenty-four minor ones. . . . 8 Army fought on Leyte, on Luzon, on Palwan and the Zamboanga Peninsula, on Panay and Bohol and Negros, on Mindanao, Mindoro, and Marinduque, on Cebu and Capul and Samar. And on a score of smaller islands which . . .are remembered by most G.Is only as "faraway places with strange-sounding names".'

The Philippines were recovered island by

Below: **The USS *White Plains* comes under attack from *kamikaze* aircraft during the Philippine operations.**

Above: The 5-inch guns of the *New Mexico* in action off Guam in July 1944.

Above right: Vice-Admiral Marc Mitscher.

island, and it was not until after the end of the war that Yamashita surrendered with the 50,000 men that remained to him. When soldiers of 11 Airborne Division fighting their way to Manila found the Japanese position protected by salvaged 5-inch naval guns, they sent word to their HQ saying; 'Tell Bill Halsey to stop looking for the Jap fleet. It's dug in on Nichols Field.' By the time the Americans had successfully challenged it in the Marianas and at Leyte Gulf, it might just as well have been.

Right: Vice-Admiral William Halsey and Rear Admiral John McCain aboard Halsey's flagship.

Below right: Marines use a boat hook mast to display the Stars and Stripes as they claw their way on a Guam beach.

29 BURMA VICTORY

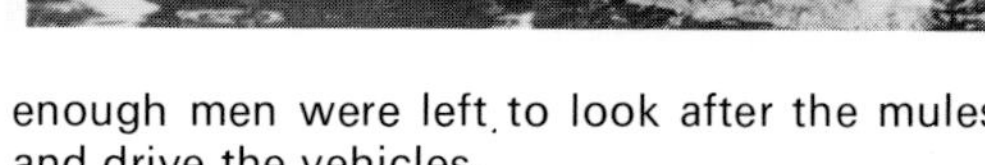

'On the other side of the room, seated by the situation map, lit by a shaded light, were the officer on duty and a younger colleague who had recently joined the Headquarters. The older officer was speaking in the voice of assured authority. He placed his finger firmly on the map. "Uncle Bill", he announced, "will fight a battle here", "Why?" not unreasonably asked the youngster. "Because", came the answer, "he always fights a battle going in where he took a licking coming out!" '

Field Marshal Slim

The British reconquered Burma, only to give the country its independence almost immediately afterwards. In consequence there are those among the veterans of the Fourteenth Army who wonder what they were fighting for in that far-away corner of an Empire which was on the eve of voluntary dissolution. But their contribution to the strategy of the Far East War was very real. The 'Forgotten Army' did not fight in vain. Its efforts not only saved India from invasion, but, still more important, helped to keep China in the fight, and thereby enabled the Chinese to tie down at least one-third of the Japanese army throughout the war. Although the Burma Road had been cut, the Allies still managed to supply the Chinese by the air-ferry service over the 'Hump Route' which cleared the Himalayas at an altitude of 23,000 feet.

General Marshall had no illusions as to the importance of keeping Chiang Kai-shek in the war.

'If the armies and government of Generalissimo Chiang Kai-shek had been fully defeated, Japan would have been left free to exploit the tremendous resources of China without harassment. It might have made it possible when the United States and Britain had finished the job in Europe, and assaulted the Japanese home islands, for the government to flee to China, and continue the war on a great and rich land mass.'

The Americans put enormous resources into the campaign in Burma. By the end of 1942 the British were beginning to think once more in terms of the offensive.

A new and strange British commander had appeared on the scene. This was Brigadier Ordê Wingate an officer who had already acquired something of a reputation in Abyssinia. He had managed to 'sell' to Churchill the idea of long-range penetration and between February and May 1943 waged a private war beyond the Chindwin, where his men cut the railway from Mandalay to Myitkyina in 75 places (March). The survivors of the Chindits returned after suffering immense hardships, and abandoning considerable numbers of sick and wounded to the Japanese, who, for their part, reacted very little to these pinpricks. The press made much of the exploits of these men, which was justifiable at a time when morale in Burma was still being built-up after the retreat of 1942. Wingate himself became a sort of reincarnation of 'Lawrence of Arabia'. It must, however, be conceded that the first Wingate expedition showed that in the jungle the Japanese were not invincible. More important it demonstrated the value of the new technique of air supply. It also offset the grim failure of attempts, early in 1943, to recapture Akyab and its important airfield, by means of an advance down the Arakan coast.

In August 1943 South-East-Asia Command (SEAC) came into being. The Supreme Commander was Lord Louis Mountbatten, who as Chief of Combined Operations had already gained an intimate knowledge of inter-service co-operation, besides being an inspiring leader, at a time when leadership and training were the key to the situation. The men of the Fourteenth Army – British, Indian, Gurkha, Africa – had to be made to believe that they were as good as the Japanese 'supermen'. They had to learn to live and move in the jungle, to patrol with boldness and cunning, to get used to having Japanese parties behind them trying to draw their fire and make them give their positions away.

In a war where no man was a non-combatant, and a country of rivers and jungle-clad mountains, physical fitness was of paramount importance. It was a tremendous problem in an army where in 1942 120 men were evacuated sick for every one wounded. Malaria, dysentery, mite typhus and skin troubles were the chief diseases. At the end of 1942 one division of 17,000 had 5,000 sick. In some units hardly enough men were left to look after the mules and drive the vehicles.

It was partly a question of discipline. The strictest health precautions were imposed, especially against malaria. Research into tropical diseases; the introduction of mepacrine and other drugs and the treatment of the sick in forward areas instead of evacuating them to India meant an absence from duty of weeks instead of months. The arrival forward of surgical teams; evacuation by light aircraft from airstrips cut out of jungle or ricefield, the innovation of jeep ambulances; and the gallant, devoted work of doctors, nurses, the American Field Service volunteers and others – all served to diminish the ravages of disease and to increase the chances of recovery for the wounded.

The immediate aim of Mountbatten's command was straightforward. It was to re-establish land communications with China. The methods of achieving this aim were necessarily complex. There was to be an offensive in northern Burma in the winter of 1943–4; the Ledo Road from Assam, which was then being built, was to be extended so as to join the old Burma Road at Mongyu near Lashio. A pipeline was to be built from Calcutta to Assam, and another parallel to the Ledo Road. Supplies flown over 'the Hump' were to be doubled – 20,000 tons a month was the new target. Advanced bases were to be set

Above: **An armed detachment of Burmese guerrilla fighters accompanied by American soldiers wades through a jungle stream in Northern Burma.**

up in China, from which Allied aircraft could bomb Japan and Manchukuo.

The main objective was Myitkyina with its three airfields. Once they were in Allied hands it would be possible to shorten the journey to China and cut out the climb over 'the Hump'.

Three Allied offensives were to take place simultaneously. Stilwell's Chinese-American Army (two Chinese divisions trained in India and 'Merrill's Marauders') was to thrust down the Chindwin to Myitkyina. The Chindits were to be flown into Burma to cut the communications of the Japanese facing Stilwell and to disrupt an expected offensive into Manipur. In the Arakan XV Corps (Lieutenant-General A. P. F. Christison) was to retake Akyab.

The British offensive in the Arakan was violently counter-attacked. The Japanese in their usual fashion went round the flanks and got behind their opponents. There was no lack of confusion and affright, hospitals and head-

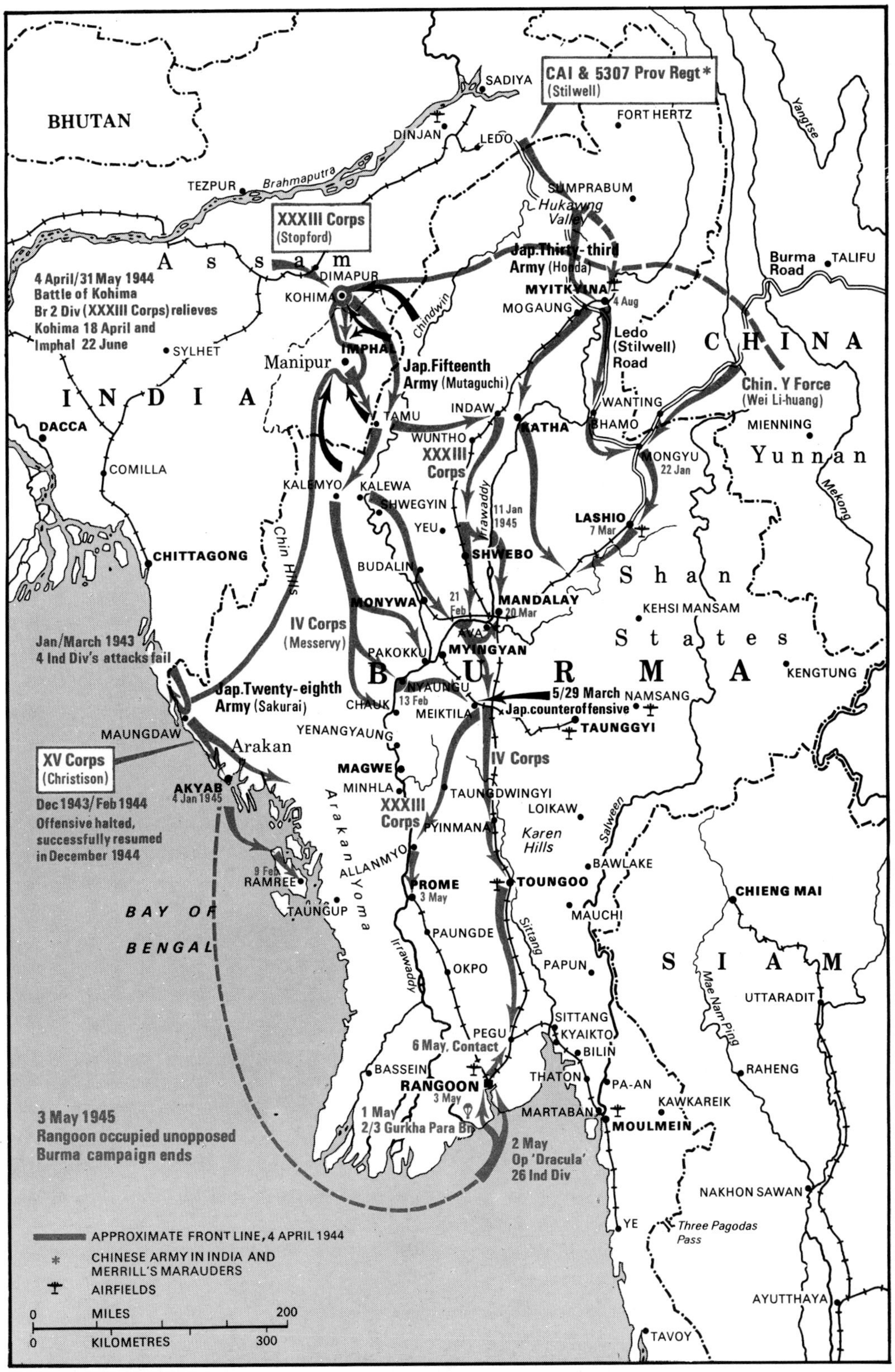

Below right: **Allied troops are ferried up the Chindwin River.**

Below: **British troops poised for action cross the Irawaddy River.**

quarters were overrun, general officers vanished into the jungle in their pyjamas, but instead of pulling out as they had so often been compelled to do in the past, the British stuck tight, formed brigade and divisional boxes and hung on. That this was possible was due entirely to command of the air. At last the British had a secure line of communications. The boxes were able to hold out simply because they were supplied from the air. This was to be the great feature of the war in Burma. The Chindits were supplied from the air, and so, when the Japanese invaded Assam, were Imphal and Kohima. Reinforcements – a complete division – were flown in from the Arakan.

Admiral Mountbatten has emphasized the extent to which the reconquest of Burma depended upon air supply:

'It was not just a question of auxiliary air supply, because 96 per cent of our supplies to the Fourteenth Army went by air. In the course of this campaign we lifted 615,000 tons of supplies to the armies, three quarters of it by the US Air Force and one quarter by the Royal Air Force; 315,000 reinforcements were flown in, . . . ; 110,000 casualties were flown out, . . . In our best month – March, 1945 – we actually lifted 94,300 tons. During that time the American Air Transport Command were building up their 'Hump' traffic, so that by July they had reached their peak of 77,500 tons per month.'

And this in spite of the fact that they had only about half the aircraft they needed for their exacting task. The American pilots aimed to get the war over as quickly as possible. If that meant flying all day, seven days a week, for 18 months on end, they were prepared to give it a try.

On 15 March 1944 the Japanese took the offensive. They meant to get into the Brahmaputra valley and overrun the airfields which were supplying China. Had they been successful they might well have pushed on to invade eastern India.

Slim, with singular foresight, had flown out many administrative troops – *bouches inutiles* – before the storm came. The battle lasted three months. By the beginning of June the two armies were strangely interlocked: in the north two British divisions round Kohima; between them and Imphal two Japanese divisions; around Imphal and Palel four more British divisions; and south of them a Japanese division and a brigade. Outnumbered by two to one, the Japanese eventually cracked and recrossed the Chindwin in disorder. They had lost most of their tanks and lorries, and at a conservative estimate 250 guns and 53,000 men. Five divisions could no longer be called fighting formations, and most of the survivors were exhausted. Well might Field Marshal Slim comment that 'the Japanese Army had suffered the greatest defeat in its history'. It was the decisive battle of the whole campaign.

This great victory was not lightly won. Fourteenth Army alone had suffered some 16,700 casualties, but had not lost a single gun. The desperate nature of the fighting is illustrated by the defence of Kohima.

The 13-day siege (5–18 April) was an epic to rival Lucknow or Hazebrouck. Colonel H. U. Richards who, fortunately, had been considered too old to command a brigade in Wingate's 'Special Force', held out with a scratch garrison, some 2,500 strong, whose main units were the 4th Queen's Own Royal West Kent Regiment and the 1st Assam Regiment. A series of determined attacks gradually reduced the perimeter. The main water supply was lost and by the end men were crawling out to get water from a spring only 30 yards from a Japanese position. No-man's-land was the width of the District Commissioner's tennis court. At night jitter raids deprived the defenders of sleep, by day the Japanese infantry hurled themselves in waves at the perimeter. The wounded were often compelled to lie out in the open, and many were hit a second time. Their stout resistance gave time for the 5th Division to be flown in from the Arakan, but before relief came Richards' men had been squeezed into a narrow perimeter on the single feature known as Garrison Hill. Here they had determined to make their last stand.

Meanwhile the Chindits, whose leader had been killed in an air crash on 24 March, were waging their second campaign. Tribute must be paid to their valour and endurance. At the same time it must be admitted that although they cut the railway and road from Mandalay to Myitkyina and the road from Bhamo to Myitkyina, the Japanese fighting Stilwell did not detach any troops to clear their lines of communications. Instead Take Force, about 6,000 strong, was formed from 53 Japanese Division, which was then arriving in Burma. This improvised formation attempted to capture 'White City' and destroy 77 Brigade, but was bloodily repulsed after heavy fighting. The chief effect of the second Chindit expedition 'was to delay for a couple of months two infantry and one artillery battalions of the Japanese 15 Division on their way to take part in the offensive against Imphal'. All in all it seems that these excellent troops would have been far better employed in the vital battle for Imphal.

Stilwell himself advanced but slowly and it was not until 4 August that he took Myitkyina. In October Chiang Kai-shek, who disliked his rugged mentor, contrived to get him recalled to America.

In December the British crossed the Chindwin and the Japanese retired to the Irrawaddy. Slim now confused them by bringing his left-hand corps across to his right flank and effecting a crossing of the Irrawaddy south of Mandalay.

The motto of the Fourteenth Army was 'God helps those who help themselves' and not the least remarkable feature of this campaign was the way in which a flotilla was improvised to cross the river.

By the end of February 1945 the Fourteenth Army had reached the vital communications centre of Meiktila. Bitter fighting followed. The Army Commander himself witnessed the last stage of a minor attack typical of thousands made in the three long years of the Burma campaign.

'The fire of Brens and rifles swelled in volume; the tank's gun thudded away. Suddenly three Gurkhas sprang up simultaneously and dashed forward. One fell, but the other two covered the few yards to the bunkers and thrust tommy-guns through the loopholes. Behind them surged an uneven line of their comrades; another broke from the spinney, bayonets glinting. They swarmed around the bunkers and for a moment all firing ceased. Then from behind one of the hummocks appeared a ragged group of half a dozen khaki-clad figures, running for safety. They were led . . . by a man exceptionally tall for a Japanese. . . . Twenty Gurkha rifles came up and crashed a volley. Alas for Gurkha marksmanship! Not a Japanese fell; zigzagging

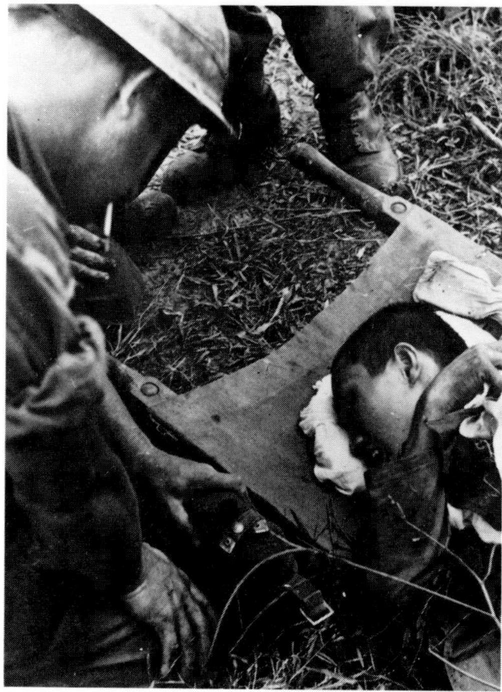

Above: **A wounded Japanese prisoner is given drink during the advance to Mawlu.**

Above right: **Japanese troops mend a puncture.**

Below: **Six mortars fire in salvo on Japanese positions near Pinwe station. Pinwe and Mawlu were the scenes of the 2nd Chindits operation.**

Right: The crew of a US 81mm mortar of the Mars Task Force pound Japanese supply and communications line during the Battle to take Lashio.

Below: British and Indian troops wait to be flown into Burma.

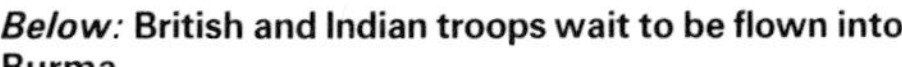

they ran on. But in a few seconds, as the Gurkhas fired again, they were all down, the last to fall being the tall man. The tank lumbered up, dipped its gun and, with perhaps unnecessary emphasis, finished him off. Within ten minutes, having made sure no Japanese remained alive in the bunkers, the two platoons of Gurkhas and their Indian-manned tank moved on to their next assignment. . . . A rear party appeared, attended to their own casualties, and dragged out the enemy bodies to search them for papers and identifications. It was all very business-like.'

Meanwhile in the Arakan XV Corps suddenly came to life again and in a fast moving amphibious campaign retook Akyab (3 January 1945), and inflicted a sharp reverse on the Japanese at Myebon (12–13 January). This was followed up by further amphibious landings on Ramree Island which proved the decisive battle of that campaign.

The fighting for Meiktila and Mandalay, the great battle for Central Burma, had exhausted General Kimura's reserves. Too late he decided to withdraw, and Fourteenth Army beat him in the race for Toungoo, largely because a secret force of Karen Guerrillas, organized well in advance, delayed the retreating Japanese with ambush after ambush.

It was now a question whether the British could reach Rangoon before the monsoon should break. On 3 May that race too was won.

Below: **Tanks and soldiers advance on Santhama.**

By that time the survivors of Kimura's broken army were scattered all over the country, and, although there was still a great deal of mopping-up to be done before the final Japanese surrender, the campaign in Burma was won.

The Fourteenth Army had the defeats of 1942 behind it; the jungle, malaria, and the monsoon to contend with; it was always low in priority for equipment of every kind, from landing-craft and parachutes to more mundane comforts such as a bottle of beer or a loaf of bread instead of the eternal 'compo' rations. Its triumph against every adversity has a dramatic quality all its own. Many contributed nobly to the good work, but one will be remembered when all the rest are forgotten – Field Marshal Slim.

Left: The amphibious landings at Akyab.

Right: **Chinese troops advance on the Burma Road.**

Far right: **Units of the 17th Division overrun the beautiful city of Meiktila.**

30 THE ARDENNES

'Soldiers of the West Front, your great hour has struck. Everything is at stake!'

Gerd von Rundstedt, 15 December 1944

Above: **US artillerymen knock out German positions in southern Belgium.**

Below: **A US Army tank destroyer takes cover behind a knocked-out pillbox on the Maginot Line at the French frontier.**

Far right: **After the Stauffenberg assassination attempt Mussolini visited Hitler. Also in attendance are Bormann and Dönitz (between Hitler and Mussolini) and Göring.**

Not since Pearl Harbor had the Americans received so rude a shock as when the dawn of 16 December 1944 was broken by the thunder of a thousand guns: German guns, heralding a most determined onslaught.

Ever since July, Hitler, with a strategic sense which one is compelled to admire, had been building up a reserve, a *masse de manoeuvre*, of 250,000 men. It was little enough for a two-front war, nor were they the soldiers of 1940, but it was still a force capable of delivering a heavy blow. And it was commanded by von Rundstedt, a man of whom miracles could still be expected. He had already performed one when he stabilized the German line on the Western Front after the débâcle in Normandy. Now he performed another by concentrating Hitler's last army (Model's Army Group B) in the Eifel area without attracting the attention of the American High Command. How did the Allied intelligence fail to see a quarter of a million men, their vehicles and 1,100 tanks? They saw what they wanted to see. The Germans, they thought, were licked – and anyway who would think of mounting an offensive in the Ardennes in the middle of winter? A certain number of suspicious troop movements were reported by prisoners, civilians and by airmen, but their significance was discounted. As the Germans hoped, these were thought to be reinforcements for the fighting round Aachen.

Although von Rundstedt was to command the offensive, he did not favour it. It was Hitler's own brain-child. Physically the *Führer* was not the man he had been before the bomb attempt of 20 July. Lieutenant-General Hasso von Manteuffel saw him as 'a stooped figure with a pale and puffy face, hunched in his chair, his hands trembling, his left arm subject to a violent twitching which he did his best to conceal, a sick man apparently borne down by the burden of his responsibility. When he walked he dragged one leg behind him.' But this miserable, shambling creature could still make himself obeyed. Whatever his physical condition his will-power was unimpaired. Temperamentally unstable, he was incapable of playing a waiting game. He deliberately sought a decision. Moreover that acute if unbalanced mind could detect certain factors in favour of his plan.

In 1940 the Ardennes had been the weak link in the French chain. Now the Monschau-Echternach sector was the weakest part of Eisenhower's front. Lieutenant-General Courtney H. Hodges (First Army) was holding 85 miles with only five divisions and three of them (2, 4 and 28) had suffered heavily in the recent fighting round Aachen. Only about 100 miles to the NW was Antwerp, the great Allied supply base, which had recently been opened to seaborne traffic. The German commanders knew the narrow roads of the Ardennes with their hairpin bends and steep hillsides very well. They had come that way in 1940. Bad weather could be expected to nullify the Allied air superiority. Otto Skorzeny's Panzer Brigade 150, disguised in American uniforms, would cause confusion behind the lines.

Von Manteuffel had a conversation with Hitler on 2 December, when the latter admitted that there was

'a certain disparity between the distant objective of Antwerp and the forces which were to capture it. However, he said, this was the time to put everything on one throw of the dice, "for Germany needs a pause to draw breath". Even a partial success, he believed, would retard the plans of the Allies by eight to ten weeks. . . . Temporary stabilization on the Western Front would enable the Supreme Command to move forces from there to the threatened central sector of the Eastern Front.'

The German generals were not unnaturally concerned about the question of air cover. After the Berlin Conference Manteuffel told Hitler that 'in our sector of the front we never saw or heard a German aeroplane these days'. He received this curious reply:

'The *Luftwaffe* is being deliberately held back. Göring has reported that he has three thousand fighters available for the operation. You know Göring's reports. Discount one thousand, and that still leaves a thousand to work with you and a thousand for Sepp Dietrich.'

Above: General 'Nuts' McAuliffe had a reputation for plain-speaking.

When the attack came the S.S. General Sepp Dietrich with the Sixth S.S. Panzer Army fell upon the US V Corps (Major-General Leonard T. Gerow) and thrust towards Liège. The Americans were driven back to the Eisenborn Ridge, but in three days desperate fighting they denied the enemy the direct road to Liège, the main communications centre of Bradley's 12th Army Group. A German armoured column did succeed in thrusting forward through Malmédy, Stavelot, and Stoumont, but as luck would have it narrowly missed not only the Allies' main fuel dump but Hodges' H.Q. at Spa. By 19 December it had been brought to a halt.

Fifth Panzer Army, though weaker than Sixth made much more progress. Von Manteuffel achieved tactical surprise by attacking without a preliminary bombardment, relying on close co-operation between his armour and his infantry. His onslaught shattered the US VIII Corps (Major-General Troy H. Middleton), which was strung out upon a long front. On Manteuffel's right a corps cut off two regiments of the inexperienced US 106th Division in the Schnee Eifel. On his left two Panzer corps broke through the US 28th Division, and reached the outskirts of Houffalize and Bastogne.

Seventh Army (General Erich Brandenberger) was supposed to cover Manteuffel's left flank by thrusting forward towards the Meuse. It made some progress at first especially on the right, but after a few days was held up by the US 4th Infantry Division and elements of the 9th Armoured Division.

Dietrich's failure meant that the Germans were not going to retake Antwerp. Hitler determined nonetheless to exploit Manteuffel's narrow breakthrough.

In 1940 Gamelin had had no theatre reserve, no *masse de manoeuvre.* Eisenhower had the XVIII Airborne Corps; this he now sent to General Hodges.

Eisenhower ordered General Omar N. Bradley (12th Army Group) to attack each flank of the German breakthrough with an armoured division. But he saw that if Model succeeded in widening the shoulders of the breakthrough Bradley's army group might be split right down the middle. Practical as ever, he placed all the US forces north of the breakthrough (First and Ninth Armies) under Montgomery (21st Army Group), leaving Bradley in command of the forces to the south.

Like Joffre in 1914 Eisenhower was willing to give up ground rather than let his line break. Patton (Third Army) was to disengage, make a tremendous left wheel, and drive northwards. The 6th Army Group in Alsace would have to take over Patton's sector in the Saar even if this meant giving ground in Alsace and perhaps abandoning Strasbourg. General de Gaulle was *not* pleased. But in fact the Germans were in no position to mount another offensive, and although the northern corner of Alsace was evacuated, Strasbourg itself was saved.

While Eisenhower was taking a grip on the situation, his front line troops, though hard-pressed, were putting up a fight which compared more than favourably with the resistance of the French IXth Army in 1940. The unfortunate Corap had had few if any tanks. It was the American armour that won time for Eisenhower's measures to take effect. The 7th Armoured Division denied St Vith to the enemy until 21 December. Part of the 10th Armoured Division delayed von Manteuffel just long enough to allow 101st Airborne Division to establish itself in Bastogne.

Bastogne stood like a rock. Fifth Panzer Army unable to drive through had to go round, shedding considerable forces to contain the improvised fortress. Summoned to surrender (22 December) Brigadier-General Anthony McAuliffe, a modern Cambronne, curtly answered 'Nuts'.

The Germans had not quite shot their bolt. Sixth Panzer Army got going again and Manteuffel's two Panzer corps drove on westward and on Christmas Eve his 2nd Panzer Division was in sight of the Meuse, near Celles, three miles east of Dinant. But the attack had lost its momentum.

Meanwhile the Allied counter-attack was getting under way. The weather had cleared and 5,000 Allied planes were strafing the transport strung out nose to tail all the way to the German frontier. In the words of General Arnold 'We prepared to isolate the battlefield.' Moreover it was air supply that saved Bastogne, while Patton pushed up from the south to its relief.

In the line north of the gap Montgomery had three American corps under Hodges (V, XVIII Airborne and VII) with the British XXX Corps in reserve on the Meuse. Hodges' centre was still vulnerable and to shorten it Montgomery evacuated a salient round Vielsalm – *reculer pour mieux sauter* is no bad tactical axiom.

The US 2nd Armoured Division (VII Corps) cut off and destroyed Manteuffel's spearhead at Celles on Christmas Day. Next day the US 4th Armoured Division broke through to Bastogne. Thus ended the first phase of the battle.

Below: British soldiers move down to the beach at Breskens, Netherlands to board landing craft for the attack on Flushing, November 1944.

Below right: From left to right: General Hodges, Field Marshal Montgomery, Generals Bradley and Dempsey.

Below: American airborne troops examine the wreckage of one of their gliders used in the Nijmegen operation. This operation to secure bridgeheads over the Rhine in September failed and the Allied advance was held up.

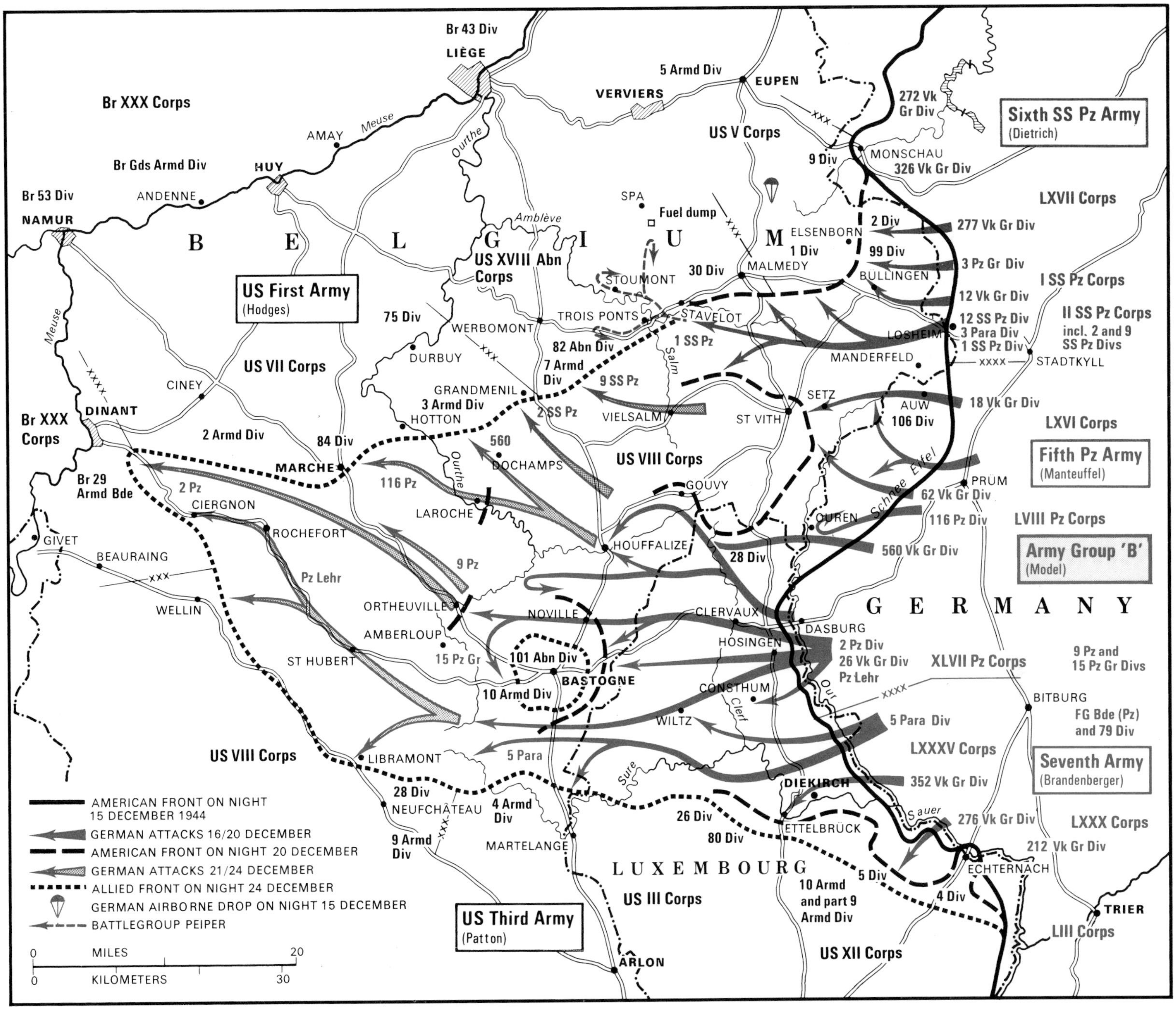

Br 43 Div
LIÈGE
5 Armd Div
EUPEN
VERVIERS
Br XXX Corps
AMAY
Meuse
Ourthe
US V Corps
272 Vk Gr Div
Sixth SS Pz Army
(Dietrich)
Br Gds Armd Div
HUY
9 Div
MONSCHAU
326 Vk Gr Div
Br 53 Div
ANDENNE
SPA
Fuel dump
LXVII Corps
NAMUR
Amblève
2 Div
ELSENBORN
277 Vk Gr Div
B E L G I U M
US XVIII Abn Corps
1 Div
99 Div
3 Pz Gr Div
STOUMONT
30 Div
MALMEDY
BULLINGEN
I SS Pz Corps
US First Army
(Hodges)
12 Vk Gr Div
75 Div
TROIS PONTS
STAVELOT
12 SS Pz Div
3 Para Div
1 SS Pz Div
II SS Pz Corps
incl. 2 and 9 SS Pz Divs
WERBOMONT
LOSHEIM
1 SS Pz
82 Abn Div
DURBUY
US VII Corps
7 Armd Div
MANDERFELD
STADTKYLL
Salm
9 SS Pz
CINEY
GRANDMENIL
3 Armd Div
SETZ
AUW
18 Vk Gr Div
Br XXX Corps
DINANT
HOTTON
2 SS Pz
VIELSALM
ST VITH
106 Div
LXVI Corps
2 Armd Div
84 Div
560
DOCHAMPS
US VIII Corps
Fifth Pz Army
(Manteuffel)
MARCHE
Schnee Eifel
Br 29 Armd Bde
116 Pz
PRUM
2 Pz
GOUVY
62 Vk Gr Div
CIERGNON
LAROCHE
OUREN
116 Pz Div
LVIII Pz Corps
GIVET
ROCHEFORT
HOUFFALIZE
28 Div
560 Vk Gr Div
Army Group 'B'
(Model)
BEAURAING
9 Pz
Pz Lehr
WELLIN
ORTHEUVILLE
NOVILLE
CLERVAUX
G E R M A N Y
AMBERLOUP
DASBURG
HOSINGEN
2 Pz Div
26 Vk Gr Div
Pz Lehr
XLVII Pz Corps
9 Pz and 15 Pz Gr Divs
ST HUBERT
15 Pz Gr
101 Abn Div
BASTOGNE
10 Armd Div
CONSTHUM
Our
BITBURG
Clerf
WILTZ
5 Para Div
FG Bde (Pz) and 79 Div
US VIII Corps
LIBRAMONT
5 Para
LXXXV Corps
Seventh Army
(Brandenberger)
Sure
DIEKIRCH
352 Vk Gr Div
28 Div
NEUFCHÂTEAU
4 Armd Div
26 Div
Sauer
276 Vk Gr Div
LXXX Corps
80 Div
ETTELBRÜCK
9 Armd Div
MARTELANGE
212 Vk Gr Div
L U X E M B O U R G
5 Div
ECHTERNACH
10 Armd and part 9 Armd Div
US III Corps
4 Div
TRIER
US Third Army
(Patton)
LIII Corps
US XII Corps
ARLON
AMERICAN FRONT ON NIGHT 15 DECEMBER 1944
GERMAN ATTACKS 16/20 DECEMBER
AMERICAN FRONT ON NIGHT 20 DECEMBER
GERMAN ATTACKS 21/24 DECEMBER
ALLIED FRONT ON NIGHT 24 DECEMBER
GERMAN AIRBORNE DROP ON NIGHT 15 DECEMBER
BATTLEGROUP PEIPER
0 MILES 20
0 KILOMETERS 30

By Christmas Day von Rundstedt realized that the battle had been lost, but Hitler was not the man to admit defeat or to cut his losses. Instead he thought up a new double offensive. He would begin by taking Bastogne and then, wheeling north, would take the First Army in flank while a secondary attack engaged it from the direction of Roermond. In the New Year he would mount yet another offensive in Alsace.

At the same time Eisenhower was planning a counter-offensive which had rather more substance. Bradley and Montgomery were to strike simultaneously.

Bastogne was still the storm centre. The corridor to the town was only a mile wide in places. Patton was determined to drive off the two German corps that were squeezing its lifeline. At the same time Manteuffel was concentrating for the attack which would rid him once and for all of this thorn in his flesh. On 30 December they met head on, and locked in a deadly winter battle which ranged blindly and fiercely through the snow-clad woods and ravines of the Ardennes.

By the time the battle died down the Germans were spent. On 8 January 1945 Hitler reluctantly agreed to limited withdrawals, and next day Patton broke out of Bastogne. Model, helped by a break in the weather, began to disengage his forces. On the 13th, owing to the Russian winter offensive, the German Supreme Command withdrew Sixth S.S. Panzer Army from the Ardennes battle, and permitted a general retreat. Patton and Hodges joined hands at Houffalize on the 16th and Bradley was able to resume command of his army and restore his original line. By 28 January it was all over.

The battle cost the Allies 76,980 casualties, but it ruined Hitler's last reserve army both morally and physically. The Germans lost 70,000 casualties and 50,000 prisoners, besides 5–600 tanks and 1,600 planes. The Russians had launched their great winter offensive on 12 January, and Hitler no longer had his *masse de manoeuvre* to meet it: a terrible price to pay for the six weeks delay it imposed on the Western Allies.

It was a great victory. Even so the Germans, though less well trained than three years earlier, had hacked a wound 50 miles deep in the American line. They had fought with all their old devotion. The more credit to the Americans who beat such men.

The part of the air forces must not be underrated. The *Luftwaffe* was still able to send over 700 aircraft on New Year's Day, 1945 to attack Allied airfields and to destroy nearly 200 planes on the ground. On 22 January the Anglo-American air forces claimed to have destroyed 4,200 pieces of heavy equipment; railway engines and trucks, tanks, motor and horse-drawn vehicles.

There are those who regard General Eisenhower as a very indifferent general, little more than a sort of Grand Liaison Officer. It is true that in the battle of the Ardennes his original lay-out was faulty. Major-General Fuller even goes so far as to say:

'The enormity of Eisenhower's distribution can be measured by supposing that it had been made in May, 1940. Had it been, then there can be little doubt that his armies would have suffered a similar fate to Gamelin's.'

But this is going altogether too far, and ignores the fact that up to mid-December 1944 Eisenhower had had the initiative on the Western front, and was not simply sitting waiting to be attacked. Once the battle began he made the right decisions and he made them in time. In the event his 33 divisions mauled 26 German divisions. One can only judge a general by his works, good or ill, and it seems to the present writer that Eisenhower's stature is greatly enhanced by this macabre winter battle.

'Few, few shall part where many meet
The snow shall be their winding sheet
And every turf beneath their feet
Shall be a soldier's sepulchre.' (Thomas Campbell.)

Above left: **Casualties on both sides were heavy in the Battle of the Bulge.**

Above far left: **Bastogne, Belgium was the scene of some of the bitterest fighting during the Battle of the Bulge.**

Below: **A German tank on its way to the front passes columns of American prisoners.**

31 ITALY, 1944-45

'The Italian campaign – more, probably than any other – abounds with drama and romance. The background as it unfolded evoked continual memories of Italy's great past; in the foreground in sharp strident contrast there was the momentous advance of modern armies. . . . The scene called to mind Italian masters of every age and school: if the ruins of Cassino resembled the cold desolation of Dante's Nine Circles of Hell, the countryside very often recalled the canvases of Bellini.'

Field Marshal Alexander

Above: A dead German lies in the ruins of a town outside Rome.

Right: The Fifth Army enters the Santa Maria area, east of Pisa.

With the invasion of Normandy, Italy took second priority among the campaigns of the Anglo-American Allies in Europe. Even so their presence in the peninsula was a standing threat not only to Germany's southern frontier, but also to her position in the Balkans – a third front.

The Allies were to milk their Italian armies to find divisions for *Dragoon* – the invasion of the South of France – and other fronts. The Germans did not venture to thin out the troops opposing them, continuing to maintain 25 divisions in Italy. The value of the great Allied victory in the Battle for Rome may be measured by the number of divisions which the Germans were compelled to subtract from their armies elsewhere to reinforce Italy. The Hermann Göring Division from France, the 20th *Luftwaffe* Field Division from Denmark, the 42nd Jäger and the 162nd Turkoman Divisions from the Balkans, and the 19th *Luftwaffe* Field Division from Belgium.

His defeat compelled Kesselring to fall back 150 miles to the Gothic Line, a strong defensive position running from Pisa to Rimini. General Alexander, for his part, saw his opportunity of breaching the northern Apennines before the Germans could get set there. On 7 June he ordered Eighth Army to advance 'with all possible speed direct on the general area Florence-Bibbiena-Arezzo and Fifth Army direct on the general area Pisa-Lucca-Pistoia'. The two Army Commanders were authorized to take extreme risks in order to secure these vital strategic areas. They were not to concern themselves unduly with the security of their flanks. The aim was to get into the valley of the Arno and break the Apennine line from Florence to Bologna. In order to save transport and bridging material for this dual offensive, the advance on the Adriatic flank was temporarily halted.

The Allies crossed the Tiber without delay and thrust forward in pursuit of the defeated enemy, advancing 75 miles in 12 days. The arrival of XIV Panzer Corps slowed down the American advance up the coast of the Tyrrhenian Sea, but they had advanced another 35 miles by 23 June.

In the centre the British Eighth Army fought its way forward against resolute opposition, taking Perugia on 20 June. There followed the fierce eight day battle for the Lake Trasimene line, which was broken by the 28th.

Meanwhile on the Adriatic coast, after a lull, with both sides thin on the ground, the Polish Corps, rested after Cassino, had come into the line. Pressing forward with characteristic impetuosity it took Ancona on 18 July.

Next day the US Fifth Army reached Leghorn. Working with their usual skill and efficiency the American engineers soon had the port in working order. By 23 July Fifth Army had occupied Pisa. There followed a lull, with the Americans still south of the River Arno.

The Eighth Army entered Florence, wounded but still beautiful, on 4 August.

As early as the autumn of 1943 the Todt Organization, with plenty of forced Italian labour at its command, had been constructing the Gothic Line. This position in the Etruscan Apennines was designed to deny the Po Valley to the Allies, and so protect 'the under-belly of Europe'. The fall of Cassino and Rome had galvanized the German engineers who, while their compatriots were winning them time by their dogged rearguard actions at Lake Trasimene and elsewhere, were working hard to complete their defences. But, formidable though these were, they were never completely finished.

The departure of the French Expeditionary Corps to take part in the landing in the south of France had deprived General Alexander of his best mountain-troops. Beyond question they would have been invaluable, and as Linklater has pointed out, might have found and exploited the weak point in the German position at Firenzuola.

General Leese now put forward a plan to surprise the Germans by an attack on the Adriatic flank, and roll up their line from the east, instead of continuing to thrust northwards from Florence. General Truscott's successes in the south of France, where he had rapidly taken Marseilles and Toulon, seemed to augur well for the prospects of the assault on the Gothic Line. And indeed at first all went well, for it was breached at the first assault. But unfortunately, the Line backed by range after range of forbidding mountains and the excellent road system in the Po Valley permitted Kesselring to make the best possible use of his mobile reserves. The breaching of the Gothic Line was not followed by any rapid progress. Although 3,000 prisoners were taken in the first fortnight's fighting, British casualties numbered 8,000. About 100 tanks had been lost and the Germans' Panzer, which outgunned any Allied tank except the Churchill, besides being very well-armoured, was causing a good deal of concern.

Meanwhile the Fifth Army, gravely weakened by the demands of *Dragoon*, had regrouped with the British XIII Corps under its command, and was also pushing forward towards the Gothic Line. The Germans, who had had to send troops to face the British on the Adriatic Coast, now fell back to the main defences of the Line.

The Germans laboured under the disadvantage that they could not tell where General Clark would strike. When it did come, his blow fell on Il Giogo Pass. Tremendous artillery fire demoralized the defenders: one corps' artillery fired nearly 13,000 rounds on 17 September, which 'was quite a normal day'. After a fortnight's fighting the Fifth Army also had broken the Gothic Line in several places.

The Eighth Army was now at the southern edge of the Po delta, a complex of canalized rivers and streams, where the Germans had systematically demolished bridges and culverts. The area was thickly populated, and the strongly-built farms and villages lent themselves to defence. The weather, too, favoured the defenders. It was a terrible autumn. Rain and floods turned streams to torrents and brought mud to rival the Flanders variety of the First World War. Not only was the tactical situation affected: the administrative machinery of the army became seriously clogged. To the tired troops the lack of warm clothing, and of reasonable accommodation, were very real hardships.

At this juncture General Leese was appointed Commander-in-Chief of the Allied Land Forces in South-East Asia, and was succeeded in command of the Eighth Army by General McCreery (8 August).

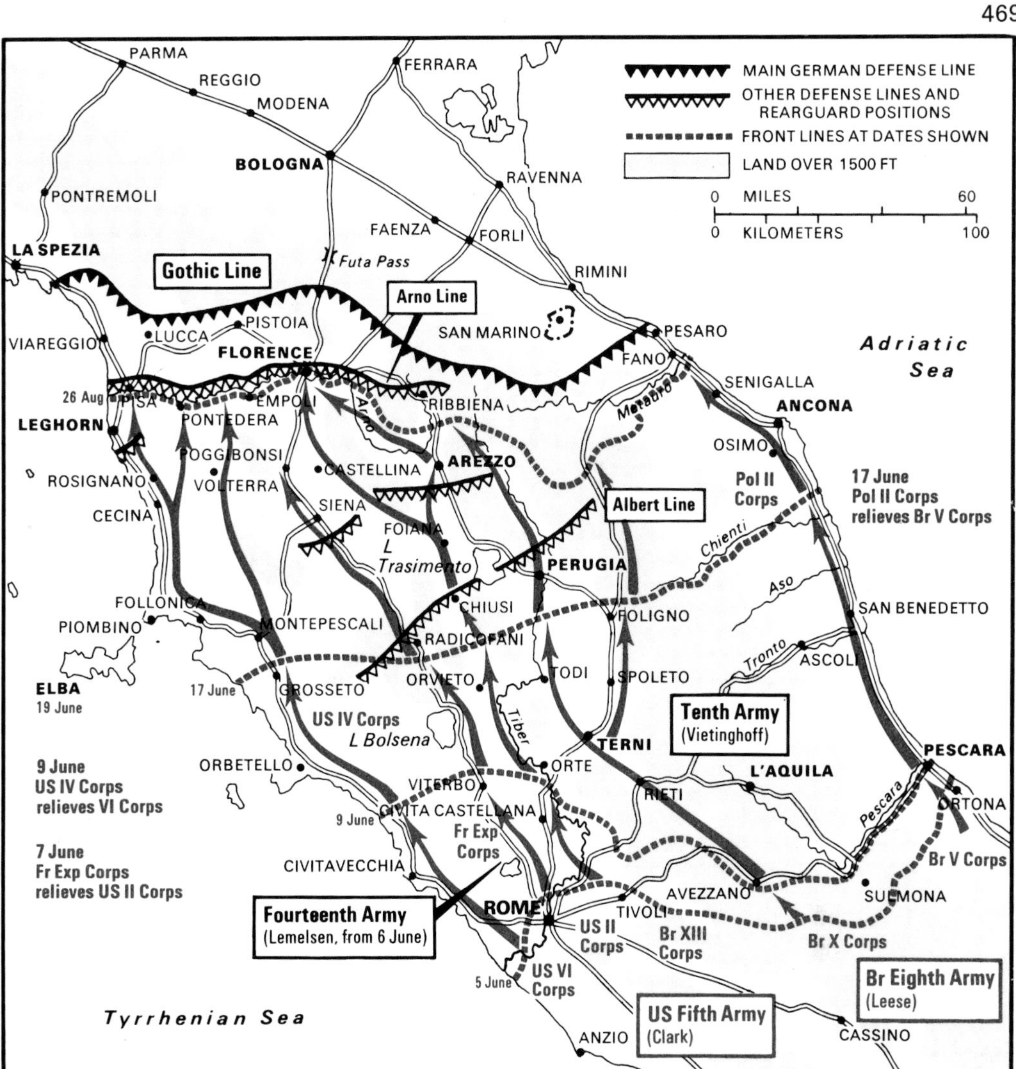

MAIN GERMAN DEFENSE LINE
OTHER DEFENSE LINES AND REARGUARD POSITIONS
FRONT LINES AT DATES SHOWN
LAND OVER 1500 FT
0 MILES 60
0 KILOMETERS 100
PARMA
REGGIO
MODENA
FERRARA
BOLOGNA
RAVENNA
PONTREMOLI
FAENZA
FORLI
LA SPEZIA
Futa Pass
RIMINI
Gothic Line
Arno Line
SAN MARINO
PESARO
Adriatic Sea
VIAREGGIO
LUCCA
PISTOIA
FLORENCE
FANO
SENIGALLA
26 Aug
PISA
EMPOLI
RIBBIENA
Metauro
ANCONA
LEGHORN
PONTEDERA
POGGIBONSI
AREZZO
OSIMO
ROSIGNANO
VOLTERRA
CASTELLINA
Pol II Corps
17 June
Pol II Corps relieves Br V Corps
CECINA
SIENA
Albert Line
FOIANA
L Trasimento
PERUGIA
Chienti
Aso
FOLLONICA
CHIUSI
FOLIGNO
SAN BENEDETTO
PIOMBINO
MONTEPESCALI
RADICOFANI
Tronto
ASCOLI
ELBA
19 June
17 June
GROSSETO
ORVIETO
TODI
SPOLETO
Tenth Army
(Vietinghoff)
US IV Corps
L Bolsena
Tiber
TERNI
PESCARA
9 June
US IV Corps relieves VI Corps
ORBETELLO
ORTE
L'AQUILA
VITERBO
RIETI
Pescara
ORTONA
9 June
CIVITA CASTELLANA
Fr Exp Corps
7 June
Fr Exp Corps relieves US II Corps
CIVITAVECCHIA
Br V Corps
AVEZZANO
SULMONA
Fourteenth Army
(Lemelsen, from 6 June)
ROME
TIVOLI
US II Corps
Br XIII Corps
Br X Corps
5 June
US VI Corps
Br Eighth Army
(Leese)
Tyrrhenian Sea
US Fifth Army
(Clark)
ANZIO
CASSINO

Above: **A shell explodes near a British jeep in Northern Italy.**

Despite the weather and the flooding the Eighth Army made considerable progress in mid-October by a series of attacks astride Highway 9. As each river obstacle was reached the British crossed the upper waters and turned it by moving through the foothills. This offensive had, however, the effect of shortening the German line in the hills south of Bologna, which city was now seriously threatened by the US Fifth Army.

It had become evident to the Allied Commanders that it was not going to be possible to give the Germans in Italy the *coup de grâce* until the spring of 1945. The aim of the Allied operations was now to keep the Germans fully occupied so as to prevent them withdrawing troops to their Eastern or Western Fronts. Starved of replacements the Allies did not find this easy, particularly as they had at the same time to find a garrison for Greece. The more tired the troops became the more they needed gunfire support, and by October the shortage of ammunition had become a serious problem, and the allotment of shells was down to 25 rounds per gun per day for field guns, and 15 for medium and heavy.

At the same time General von Vietinghoff's Tenth Army, though it had been able to meet the first phase of the Eighth Army's winter offensive without drawing on his general reserve, had also been severely mauled. The Allies kept up the pressure as best they could and by Christmas were established on their winter line, the River Senio. The Canadians had taken Ravenna on 5 December, but the Fifth Army's offensive had still not captured Bologna.

There was some local fighting during the winter, as when at Christmas the Germans launched a sudden counter-attack, routed the US 92nd Negro Division and threatened the Fifth Army's communications with Leghorn. This particular situation was restored by 8th Indian Division, borrowed from Eighth Army. But on the whole the winter was quiet and the Allies rested and built-up their armies for the final onset. Replacements of men and materials were now plentiful. By the time the spring weather came morale was high.

Both sides now withdrew troops from Italy. The Combined Chiefs of Staff moved the 1st Canadian Corps to North-Western Europe, while the Germans' 16th S.S. and 356 Divisions were taken from von Vietinghoff, who had succeeded Kesselring in command of Army Group C. The Germans still had rather more than 23 divisions besides six of Italian Fascists. The US Fifth Army (now under General Truscott) was faced by the Fourteenth Army; the Eighth by the German Tenth. And behind the lines some 50,000 Italian Partisans were amusing themselves with sabotage and guerrilla warfare.

By this time the Allied air offensive had wrecked the German lines of communications. All the Po bridges had been destroyed in the autumn of 1944. Fine weather in February and March left railway-yards, roads, bridges, and supply-dumps at the mercy of the XXIInd Tactical Air Command and the Desert Air Force. The railway through the Brenner Pass was almost continuously interrupted. According to von Senger the Allied 'air superiority had become so preponderant that nobody dared show himself on the roads in daylight'.

On 24 March General Mark Clark, the commander of the Fifteenth Army Group, issued orders for the final offensive. His aim was to destroy the German armies south of the Po, to force the passage of that river, and to take Verona.

The Eighth Army attacked on 9 April after a tremendous artillery bombardment, and with strong support from fighter-bombers. The Germans were holding the banks of the Senio in force, and five of their forward battalions were practically obliterated by the preliminary bombardment. The flame-throwing Crocodile tanks played a decisive part, and everywhere good progress was made.

Above: **A Bren gunner watches from his hideout in Tavoleto in September 1944.**

On the 14th the US Fifth Army began its attack, and achieved a considerable degree of surprise. At first the Germans regarded it as a diversionary operation. A breakthrough was made between LI Mountain Corps and XIV Panzer Corps. This the Germans had insufficient reserves to meet. Since all his communications with Germany ran through Verona, von Vietinghoff was particularly sensitive to the pressure from Eighth Army near Comacchio. For this reason he had concentrated two of his three reserve divisions there. Thus the American attack, the second phase of the Allied offensive against the so-called Genghiz Khan Line, was very successful and on 21 April Bologna was at last occupied by Polish and American troops.

The German army was beginning to disintegrate. General von Senger describes the hazards of re-crossing the Po.

'My H.Q. staff was dissolved into separate groups. At dawn on the 23rd we found a ferry at Bergantino. Of the thirty-six Po ferries in the zone of 14th Army, four only were still serviceable. Because of the incessant fighter-bomber attacks it was useless to cross in daylight. As the level of water in the Po was low, many officers and men were able to swim across. The access road at Revere was blocked by many columns of burning vehicles. I had to leave my cars behind. In the twilight we crossed the river, and together with my operations staff I marched the twenty-five kilometres to Legnano. We were unable to establish any communications. Major-General von Schellwitz, who after General Pfeiffer's death had assumed command of the remnants of 65 and 305 Inf. Divs., was captured south of the river.'

Later he was able to organize some sort of front between Lake Garda and the Pasubio Pass, with a few fresh troops – including a Parachute officers' School and an S.S. Mountain School – but there were no guns, and the roads to the North were 'filled with an unending stream of stragglers'.

With the fall of Verona on the 26th the German forces in Italy had been cut in two. The same day Genoa surrendered to the Partisans.

On the Eighth Army front only the German Parachute Divisions were still in good order. All the rest had been well battered. On 19 April General Keightley sent his Vth Corps through

Above right: **Piedimonte, a village beyond Cassino, fell to Polish troops on 26 May 1944.**

Right: **Mussolini boards a plane shortly after he had been rescued from captivity by Skorzeny.**

Left: **French troops take Siena, the last German strongpoint before Florence.**

the Argenta Gap, making for Ferrara and Bondeno to cut off the Germans retreating from Bologna. There were a few formations, notably the 29th Panzer Grenadier Division, still prepared to put up a desperate resistance in the face of grievous losses. But by the 25th April it was all over. On that day

'Lieutenant-General Graf von Schwerin, commanding the LXXVIth Corps, surrendered with some formality – and the remnants of his champagne – to the 27th Lancers, and declared his inability to continue fighting with a few Divisional Headquarters which had no troops under command. His opinion was substantiated by the wreckage on the river bank, where among hundreds of loose horses and draught oxen a thousand pieces of artillery and eighty tanks lay in the discard, and a vast concourse of carts and wagons – pressed into service and crowded with the accoutrements of flight – stood smouldering or lamed on broken wheels. Fourteen thousand prisoners were in the Vth Corps's cages to increase the evidence of an Army's mortality.'

The end came when on 2 May General von Vietinghoff's plenipotentiaries presented themselves at the palace of Caserta to surrender.

Benito Mussolini had not survived the collapse of his Allies. Rescued by the daring of Otto Skorzeny, the German partisan leader, from his inaccessible prison in the Gran Sasso, he had become once more the figurehead of Fascism – or what remained of it – in Northern Italy. As the Allies closed in on Milan, Mussolini, his mistress, Clara Petacci, and a few diehard adherents, taking with them a fortune in gold, made for Switzerland. On the night of 28 April, by the merest chance, a Communist, Lieutenant-Colonel Valerio, discovered them in a farmhouse near Lake Como. Soon afterwards he shot them. When Clara Petacci pleaded for their lives he said: 'I execute the will of the Italian people.' It is charitable to doubt whether his countrymen would have wished her death as well as that of the fallen dictator, but in the

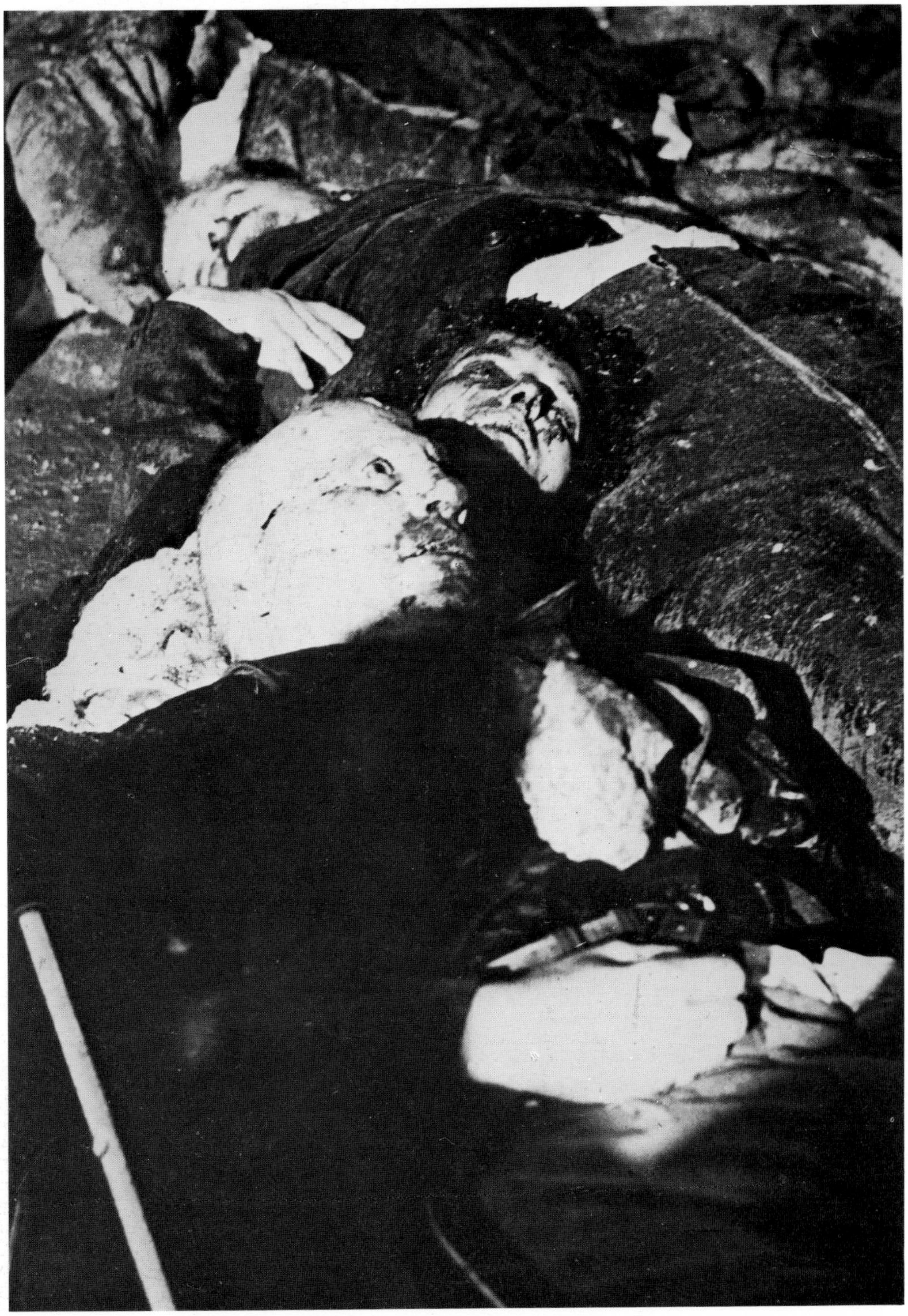

Above: **Mussolini, in capitivity, in the Abruzzi mountains.**

Above left: **German officers and men captured in the area around Lake Trasimeno, July 1944.**

Left: **Colonel Otto Skorzeny effected the brilliant operation to release Mussolini from captivity.**

Above right: **A machine gun post of the 143rd Infantry Division outside Giugliano on the Gothic Line.**

Right: **The bodies of Mussolini and his mistress, Clara Petacci.**

temper of the hour she may have been spared worse things. In Milan an hysterical mob subjected the lifeless corpses and those of a dozen other dead Fascists to revolting indignities.

The long campaign, which had lasted 600 days, was over. Even before the final surrender the defence of Italy had cost the Germans 556,000 casualties. The Allies had lost 312,000 killed and wounded, of which 59,000 was the 8th Army's share.

Once the concentration for Normandy had got under way the Allied commanders had been handicapped because they never received strategic priority. Indeed, at one time or another 21 divisions were withdrawn to fight in other theatres. Even so, in 1944 the presence of the Allied armies in Italy had contained no less than 55 enemy divisions in the Mediterranean area.

General Fuller is pleased to describe the Italian campaign as one 'which for lack of strategic sense and tactical imagination is unique in military history.' No doubt the tactics of the campaign could have been more enterprising had it been possible to have provided more landing craft, or more formations specially trained in mountain warfare.

Perhaps, at times, the campaign lacked subtlety both in its strategy and its tactics. Nevertheless by the crude yet warlike standards of divisions employed and casualties inflicted, the Allies had very much the better of the bargain in Italy.

32 THE END IN GERMANY

'Even if we could not conquer, we should drag half the world into destruction with us, and leave no one to triumph over Germany . . . We shall never capitulate, no never! We may be destroyed, but if we are we shall drag a world with us – a world in flames.' *Hitler, 1934*

His morale bolstered by the flattery of such courtiers as Göring and Ribbentrop, Hitler remained singularly unmoved by the disasters of 1944. When on 24 December Guderian outlined the Russian dispositions, the Dictator ridiculed his forecasts. Himmler echoed his leader.

'You know, my dear Colonel-General, I don't really believe the Russians will attack at all. It's all an enormous bluff. The figures given by your department "Foreign Armies East" are grossly exaggerated. They're far too worried, I'm convinced there's nothing going on in the East.'

The demands of the Ardennes offensive and the refusal to withdraw the 30 divisions from the Courland peninsula left the Eastern front of 750 miles relatively thinly held. Guderian worked hard to build up a reserve but was far from satisfied with the result. When Hitler, in one of his more gracious moments, thanked him for his efforts, Guderian gloomily replied:

'The Eastern Front is like a house of cards. If the front is broken through at one point all the rest will collapse, for twelve and a half divisions are far too small a reserve for so extended a front.'

It was fair comment.

When the Ardennes offensive was still raging, Churchill sent a message to Stalin (6 January) in which he described the battle as 'very heavy' and asked whether the Western Allies could 'count on a major Russian offensive on the Vistula front, or elsewhere, during January. . . .'

It was with profound relief that Churchill received Stalin's reply which said that:

'in view of the position of our allies on the Western Front, Headquarters of the Supreme Command has decided to complete the preparations at a forced pace and, disregarding the weather, to launch wide-scale offensive operations against the Germans all along the Central Front not later than the second half of January.'

He was better than his word. The Red Army began its offensive on 12 January and was rewarded with a swift breakthrough. By the 17th they were in Warsaw. Koniev overran southern Poland, making for Silesia. Zhukov pushed on through central Poland, thrusting for the very heart of Germany; Rokossovsky advanced northwards on Danzig. In the north Cherniakhovsky was overrunning East Prussia and in the south Petrov was crossing the Carpathians.

By the end of the month the Red Army was on the Oder, and had penetrated the provinces of Silesia and Brandenberg. In Berlin there was panic, and thousands of Germans, slave labourers, and prisoners of war, trekked westwards through the freezing winter.

On 30 January the doomed Dictator broadcast to his followers for the last time, assuring them that by sparing his life on 20 July the Almighty had shown that he wished him to continue as their *Führer*, a conclusion which the events of his career scarcely seem to have warranted. He adjured the people to fight on and defeat 'the hordes that England had called up from the steppes of central Asia'.

On 3 February the Russian advance reached the Oder, only 36 miles east of Berlin, and by early March had cleared Silesia. Hitler used up most of his remaining reserves in a vain attempt to relieve Budapest, which fell on 13 February.

The conclusion of the Ardennes battle (28 January) left the Germans facing seven great armies west of the Rhine. Despite unfavourable weather in February the Allies fought their way forward, and by 13 March the whole of the west bank of the river was in their hands. It was bitter fighting all the way, for now the Germans were fighting for the Fatherland. If there was despair in their hearts, there was fanaticism as well. The British and Canadian soldiers who battled their way through the forests of the Reichswald and the Hochwald have grim memories of those days. But it was fighting that cost the enemy dear. The Germans lost 60,000 casualties and 293,000 prisoners between the start of the Reichswald offensive and the day (23 March) when the Allies stood poised and ready to cross the Rhine.

Meanwhile an all-out air offensive struck at German communications. Sometimes as many as 16,000 sorties were made in a day. On both 22 and 23 February 20,000 tons of bombs were dropped. The *Luftwaffe* could do nothing to protect the Reich from this devastating onslaught.

At one vital point the watch on the Rhine proved less than vigilant. On 7 March Sergeant Alexander A. Drabik of Holland, Ohio, led a platoon of the US 9th Armoured Division across the Ludendorff bridge at Remagen between Bonn and Cologne.

'We ran down the middle of the bridge, shouting as we went. I didn't stop because I knew that if we kept moving they couldn't hit me. My men were in squad column and not one of them was hit. We took cover in some bomb craters. Then we just sat and waited for the others to come. That's the way it was.'

This was a windfall indeed – well might Eisenhower call it 'One of my happy moments of the war.'

Hitler reacted in his usual heavy-handed way. Four officers whom he considered to blame were court-martialled and shot. Von Rundstedt was dismissed for the last time, and to take his place Field Marshal Kesselring was summoned from Italy. He introduced himself to his new staff with the words 'Well, gentlemen, I am the new V-3'.

The Germans fought hard to seal off the Remagen bridge-head. Jet dive bombers, V-2 rockets and long-range artillery shells were hurled at the bridge, but when on 17 March it eventually collapsed the Americans had already pushed several divisions across.

Still Germany struggled on, and despite the decision to give Herr Himmler command of Army Group Vistula – a truly astonishing appointment – even managed to stage a brief counter-offensive in mid-February.

Every day now brought Hitler some evil tidings, but with the portrait of Frederick the Great hanging over his desk he could still take heart: 'When bad news threatens to crush my

Right: **Soviet tanks pound into Berlin.**

Below left: **The first Soviet tanks to enter Berlin.**

Bottom left: **Citizens of Kronach leave their burning homes after the US 11th Armoured Division had entered the town.**

Below: **The supposedly impassable Siegfried Line or West Wall is breached by the 33rd Infantry, 3rd Armoured Division in September 1944.**

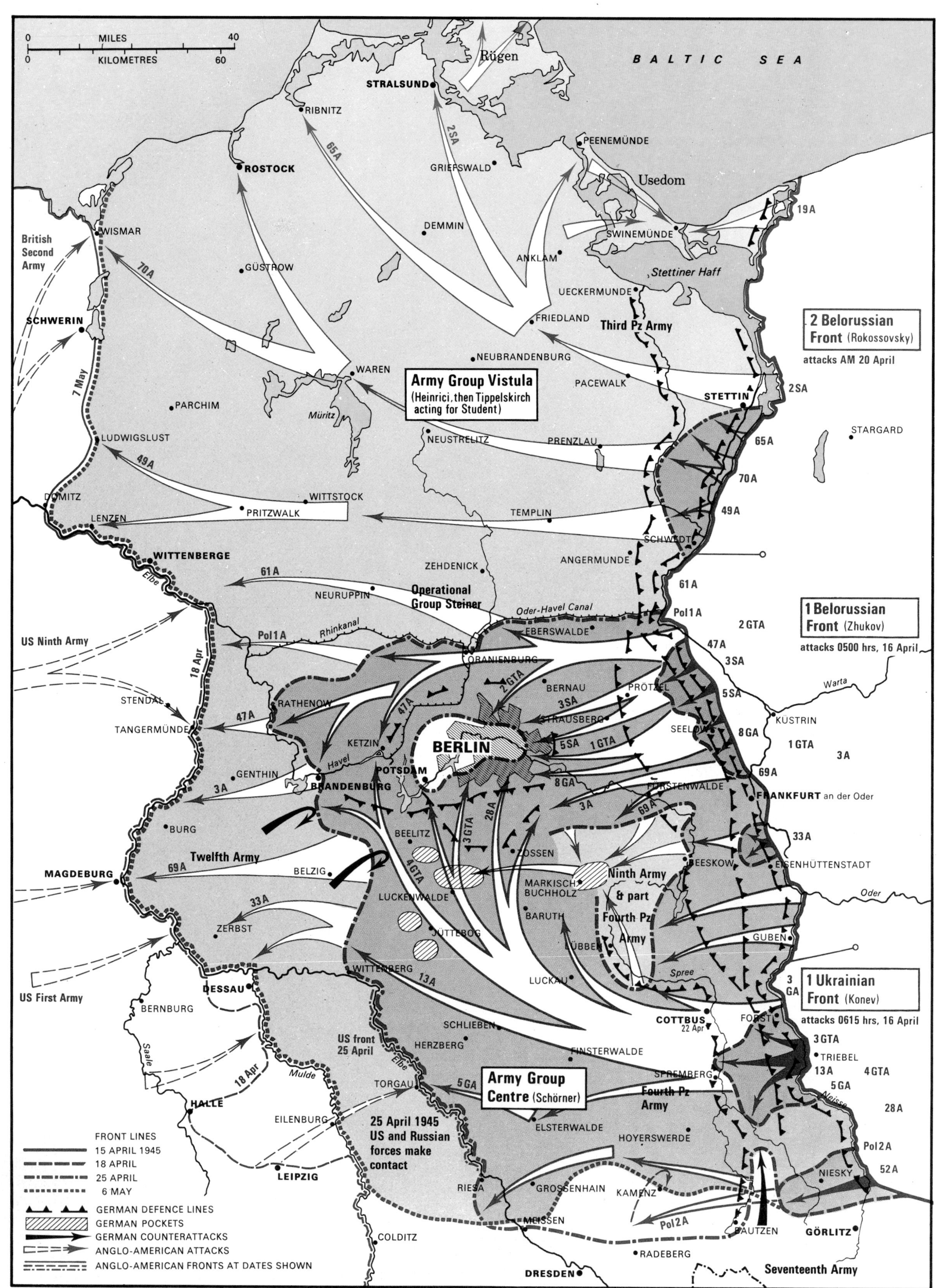

MILES 0 40
KILOMETRES 0 60
BALTIC SEA
Rügen
STRALSUND
RIBNITZ
ROSTOCK
GRIEFSWALD
PEENEMÜNDE
Usedom
SWINEMÜNDE
Stettiner Haff
DEMMIN
ANKLAM
UECKERMUNDE
FRIEDLAND
Third Pz Army
2 Belorussian Front (Rokossovsky)
attacks AM 20 April
WISMAR
British Second Army
GÜSTROW
SCHWERIN
NEUBRANDENBURG
WAREN
Army Group Vistula
(Heinrici, then Tippelskirch acting for Student)
PACEWALK
STETTIN
PARCHIM
Müritz
7 May
LUDWIGSLUST
NEUSTRELITZ
PRENZLAU
STARGARD
DÖMITZ
WITTSTOCK
PRITZWALK
LENZEN
TEMPLIN
SCHWEDT
ANGERMUNDE
WITTENBERGE
Elbe
ZEHDENICK
NEURUPPIN
Operational Group Steiner
Oder-Havel Canal
EBERSWALDE
1 Belorussian Front (Zhukov)
attacks 0500 hrs, 16 April
US Ninth Army
Rhinkanal
ORANIENBURG
18 Apr
STENDAL
RATHENOW
BERNAU
PRÖTZEL
Warta
STRAUSBERG
KÜSTRIN
TANGERMÜNDE
SEELOW
KETZIN
BERLIN
Havel
GENTHIN
POTSDAM
BRANDENBURG
FÜRSTENWALDE
FRANKFURT an der Oder
BURG
BEELITZ
ZOSSEN
Twelfth Army
BEESKOW
EISENHÜTTENSTADT
MAGDEBURG
BELZIG
MARKISCH BUCHHOLZ
Ninth Army & part Fourth Pz Army
Oder
LUCKENWALDE
BARUTH
ZERBST
JÜTTEBOG
LÜBBEN
GUBEN
WITTENBERG
Spree
LUCKAU
1 Ukrainian Front (Konev)
attacks 0615 hrs, 16 April
DESSAU
US First Army
BERNBURG
COTTBUS 22 Apr
FORST
SCHLIEBEN
US front 25 April
HERZBERG
Saale
FINSTERWALDE
TRIEBEL
18 Apr
Mulde
Elbe
TORGAU
Army Group Centre (Schörner)
SPREMBERG
Fourth Pz Army
Neisse
HALLE
EILENBURG
25 April 1945 US and Russian forces make contact
ELSTERWALDE
HOYERSWERDE
LEIPZIG
RIESA
GROSSENHAIN
KAMENZ
NIESKY
MEISSEN
BAUTZEN
GÖRLITZ
COLDITZ
RADEBERG
DRESDEN
Seventeenth Army
65A 2SA 70A 49A 61A Pol1A 47A 3SA 2GTA 5SA 1GTA 8GA 3A 69A 33A 3GTA 28A 4GTA 13A 5GA 19A 1GTA 3 GA 4GTA Pol2A 52A
FRONT LINES
15 APRIL 1945
18 APRIL
25 APRIL
6 MAY
GERMAN DEFENCE LINES
GERMAN POCKETS
GERMAN COUNTERATTACKS
ANGLO-AMERICAN ATTACKS
ANGLO-AMERICAN FRONTS AT DATES SHOWN

spirit I derive fresh courage from the contemplation of this picture. Look at those strong blue eyes, that wide brow. What a head!' Certainly the *Führer* did not lack tenacity – and like his hero he couldn't be sacked!

Meanwhile in the south Patton's US Third Army had been reducing the Saar-Moselle area, a task he had completed by 23 February, and clearing the west bank of the Rhine. On the night of 22 March he suddenly crossed south of Mainz, losing only 28 casualties in the process. Far away in Berlin Hitler and his staff discussed this disaster on a sector that they knew only too well was practically unguarded – 'Is there no Panzer brigade or something like that which could be sent there?' the *Führer* demanded, to be told that except for five tank-destroyers (*Jagdtiger*) in a repair shop at Sennelager everything had been committed.

With his world collapsing about him, Hitler, showing a determination worthy of a better cause, maintained the unequal struggle. He now decided to proclaim a 'Scorched Earth' policy, telling Speer, when he protested:

'If the war is lost, the German nation will also perish. This fate is inevitable. There is no need to take into consideration the basic requirements of the people for continuing even a most primitive existence . . . Those who will remain after the battle are those who are inferior; for the good will have fallen.'

Such was the man in whom the Germans had, with so few exceptions, put their trust.

North of the Ruhr the crossing of the Rhine was effected in more formal style than on Patton's front. The nature of the obstacle, which is lucidly described by Fuller, made this imperative:

'The width of the Rhine on Montgomery's front was between four hundred and five hundred yards, liable to increase from seven hundred to one thousand two hundred yards at high water, and the mean velocity of the current was about three and a half knots. With this breadth of water to cross, the whole operation was organized on amphibious lines – it was an inland waterborne invasion.'

Montgomery, in his precise, calculating way, laid on a set-piece attack. A shattering bombardment, of an hour's duration, opened the proceedings, then the 1st Commando Brigade crossed and seized Wesel. Meanwhile the 2nd British Army and the US Ninth Army were crossing north and south of that town respectively.

These strokes were followed up next day by a massive demonstration of airborne power. The British 6th Airborne from East Anglia and the US 17th Airborne from near Paris, escorted by 2,153 planes of the Tactical Air Forces, and carried in 1,572 planes and 1,326 gliders, landed beyond the Rhine. They were within range of artillery support from the west bank, and happily their casualties were not heavy.

Once across the Rhine the Allies could at last strike into the Ruhr, the industrial heart of Germany, the home of Krupp of Essen, Thyssen of Mülheim and a hundred lesser firms sprawled from Dortmund and Duisburg to Solingen and Hamm. In vain the *Führer* declared that the Ruhr was a fortress. There was no longer any magic in that formula. As March drew to its close the US First and Ninth Armies swung round the Ruhr in a double envelopment; the classic pincers movement in which the Nazis had so often crushed their foes. The two armies met near Paderborn on 1 April, trapping Model in a vast net 80 miles in diameter. By 18 April 400,000 Germans had been taken, and on the 21st Model, who had been declared a war criminal by the Russians, shot himself in a wood near Duisberg.

While Army Group B was being crushed in the vice, the German front was everywhere disintegrating. To the southward the American and French armies drove forward with unrelenting vigour. Patton reached Frankfurt on 29 March. Mannheim, Magdeburg, Leipzig, Bayreuth, all fell with bewildering speed. On 12 April the US Ninth Army reached the Elbe near Magdeburg. They were now only 60 miles from Berlin.

By the end of March the Red Army had

Above: **One of the last photographs taken of Hitler in his headquarters in Prenzlau, East Germany. He is surrounded by lesser known generals.**

entered Austria and on 13 April Vienna itself was taken. In the north Danzig had fallen on 30 March.

By this time the German soldiers scarcely knew what was going on. The support of tanks or planes was a thing of the past. Supply was uncertain, communications broke down. Units and formations, left for days on end without orders, had to sort things out for themselves as best they could. The number of 'missing' began to increase, as at long last defeatism began to spread through the *Wehrmacht.* The long-deferred Allied victory was in sight.

President Roosevelt did not live to see it. On 12 April he died suddenly of a cerebral haemorrhage, and was succeeded by the Vice-President, a former county judge from Missouri, Harry S. Truman. Hitler had long hoped for an event such as 'the miracle of the House of Brandenburg', which had saved Frederick the Great in the Seven Years War. This miracle he saw in the

Below: **Soviet tanks in Berlin. The final battle for Berlin lasted from 19 April to 2 May when General Weidling officially surrendered.**

Instrument of Surrender

of

All German armed forces in HOLLAND, in

northwest Germany including all islands,

and in DENMARK.

1. The German Command agrees to the surrender of all German armed forces in HOLLAND, in northwest GERMANY including the FRISIAN ISLANDS and HELIGOLAND and all other islands, in SCHLESWIG-HOLSTEIN, and in DENMARK, to the C.-in-C. 21 Army Group. This to include all naval ships in these areas. These forces to lay down their arms and to surrender unconditionally.

2. All hostilities on land, on sea, or in the air by German forces in the above areas to cease at 0800 hrs. British Double Summer Time on Saturday 5 May 1945.

3. The German command to carry out at once, and without argument or comment, all further orders that will be issued by the Allied Powers on any subject.

4. Disobedience of orders, or failure to comply with them, will be regarded as a breach of these surrender terms and will be dealt with by the Allied Powers in accordance with the accepted laws and usages of war.

5. This instrument of surrender is independent of, without prejudice to, and will be superseded by any general instrument of surrender imposed by or on behalf of the Allied Powers and applicable to Germany and the German armed forces as a whole.

6. This instrument of surrender is written in English and in German.

The English version is the authentic text.

7. The decision of the Allied Powers will be final if any doubt or dispute arises as to the meaning or interpretation of the surrender terms.

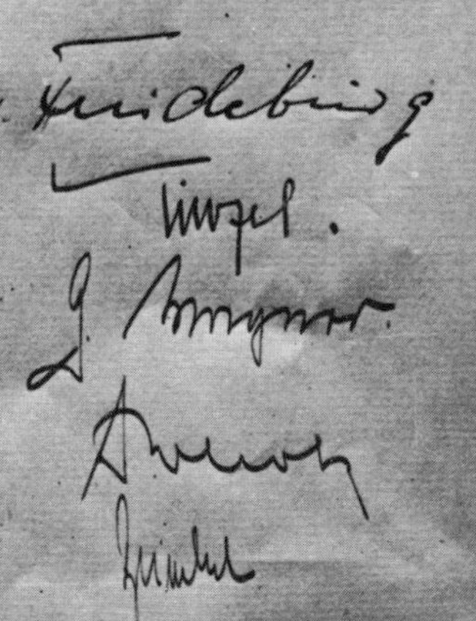

B. L. Montgomery
Field-Marshal

4 May 1945
1830 hrs

death of the great American who had dealt him so many mortal blows. Yet, though Hitler himself did not live long enough to discover it, he had as relentless an enemy in Truman as in Roosevelt.

It was not until 16 April that Zhukov and Koniev launched their final offensive. Within two days the T-34s were racing through Saxony. In Berlin Hitler prepared to make his last stand. On the 16th April the *Führer*, living to the last in his fantasy world, issued an Order of the Day to his soldiers on the Eastern Front.

> 'The hordes of our Judeo-Bolshevist foe have rallied for the last assault. They want to destroy Germany and to extinguish our people . . . Colossal artillery forces are welcoming the enemy. Countless new units are replacing our losses . . .
>
> This moment, which has removed from the face of the earth the greatest war criminal of all ages, will decide the turn in the fortunes of war.'

But his course was run. This was to be his last Order of the Day; he had little more than a week to live. His last days were bitter. On 23 April a telegram came from Göring, suggesting that as Hitler had decided to remain at his post in the fortress of Berlin, he, Göring, should 'take over, immediately, the total leadership of the Reich'. This provoked an explosion! Göring was a *Schweinhund*, and a drug addict! It was a stab-in-the-back! Göring, guilty of high treason, would be spared the death penalty, but must resign his high offices forthwith.

Next came the news that Himmler, his *treuer Heinrich*, through the mediation of the Swedish Count Folke Bernadotte, had endeavoured to open surrender negotiations. When the news filtered through to his Berlin bunker, Hitler went into another paroxysm of frustrated fury. 'Nothing is spared me! No loyalty is kept, no honour observed! There is no bitterness, no betrayal that has not been heaped upon me!'

On the night of 28/29 April, with the Russians only a few hundred yards away in the Potsdamer Platz, he married the faithful Eva Braun in the bunker in the garden of the Chancellery. Next day, after naming Admiral Dönitz as his successor, and poisoning his dog, he shot himself and went to join the 30 million who had fallen victim to his ambitions. His body was burnt. On 2 May the survivors of the Berlin garrison surrendered.

The British had crossed the Elbe on 29 April and on 2 May British, American and Russian troops met on the shores of the Baltic. On 4 May Field Marshal Montgomery accepted the unconditional surrender of Dönitz's plenipotentiaries, Admiral von Friedeburg and General Kinzel, on Lüneberg Heath. Hostilities were over, but the document which formally concluded the Second German War was that signed at Rheims on 7 May, by Air Chief Marshal Tedder, representing Eisenhower, and by Marshal Zhukov and Field Marshal Keitel. The document signed, a telegram was sent to the Combined Chiefs of Staff. It read:

'The mission of this Allied Force was fulfilled at 3 a.m., local time, 7 May 1945. Eisenhower.'

Above left: **Victorious Soviet soldiers.**

Left: **The document of surrender of German troops in Holland, Belgium and Northern Germany, signed by Field Marshal Montgomery.**

Above right: **The Red Flag is raised on the Reichstag on 2 May 1945.**

Far right: Marshal Zhukov signs the act of German Capitulation on 8 May 1945.

Right: **The centre of Berlin was flattened by the intensive bombardment prior to and during the 18-day battle.**

33 IWO JIMA AND OKINAWA

O Lord! Thou knowest how busy I must be this day:
If I forget Thee, do not Thou forget me.

Sir Jacob Astley at Edgehill, 23 October 1642

At last the time for the assault on Japan itself drew near.

Iwo Jima, $4\frac{1}{2}$ miles by $2\frac{1}{2}$, is the central island of the Volcano group and lies half way between Saipan in the Marianas and Tokyo. It was uninhabited except for its garrison. The Americans wanted it as an emergency landing place for their B-29s from the Marianas, which had begun bombing Japan on 24 November 1944. The Americans had given the Japanese plenty of time to make a fortress of an island which, had the Joint Chiefs of Staff decided to capture it immediately after the Marianas, could have been taken practically unopposed. Iwo Jima took 6,800 tons of bombs and 22,000 shells, from 5-inch to 16-inch in calibre, before the invasion began. But the defences, skilfully tunnelled into the sides of the extinct volcano, Mount Suribachi, were immune to this.

D-Day was 19 February 1945. The run-in went like clockwork, but once ashore things were different. The amphtracs found volcanic ash and cinders poor going and the terraces of Mount Suribachi practically insurmountable. The Japanese brought down a tremendous volume of mortar fire from the mouths of cleverly constructed tunnels. Of the 30,000 Marines landed that day 2,400 were hit. The beach-head was far short of that planned, but there was no counter-attack. General Kuribayashi was conserving his strength.

Iwo Jima was one more island which the US Marines had to take yard by yard, fighting up bare slopes against a strongly entrenched enemy. The Japanese fought to the last and of a garrison of over 20,000 only 216 were taken prisoner. Thirty per cent of the American landing force became casualties.

The *Kamikazes* could play little part, for their bases were too far away. 21 February was a bad day, however, for one crashed the *Saratoga* and destroyed 42 planes. Another wrecked the *Bismarck Sea*.

Okinawa, 67 miles long by from three to 20 miles wide, was defended by Lieutenant-General Mitsuru Ushijima and some 90,000 men. Tenth Army (Lieutenant-General Simon Bolivar Buckner), not far short of 300,000 strong, was given the task of taking it.

By this time very heavy raids by B-29s were going in against Japanese cities. These 'rocked the nation to its very foundations'. Fast carrier raids (18–21 March) were not so successful, *Wasp, Yorktown* and *Franklin* all suffering serious damage from *Kamikazes.* Even so 161 Japanese aircraft were shot down.

The landings on Okinawa began on 1 April 1945 after five days of preliminary bombardment. All went well that Easter Sunday and by the evening Yontan and Kadena airfields were in American hands. The Japanese had retired from the beach area and 50,000 troops were ashore. General Ushijima did not intend to try conclusions with the invaders until they were beyond the effective range of naval gunfire support. Thus a week elapsed before the real fighting began.

Before that time a serious attempt was made to relieve the garrison. A sortie by the beautiful giant *Yamato* (72,908 tons), the light cruiser *Yahagi* and eight destroyers was to follow up a mass attack by *Kamikazes.*

On 7 April Mitscher's task groups found the 'Special Surface Attack Force' (Vice-Admiral Ito) as it passed through Van Diemen Strait. From 1232–1417 plane after plane bombed and torpedoed the force, reducing the decks of the *Yamato* to a shambles. At 1423 she went down with 2,488 men. *Yahagi* and four destroyers were sunk. The Americans lost 15 planes. Japan now had only one battleship left, *Haruna.*

Her fleet crippled, Japan now depended on the *Kamikazes,* although conventional bombing continued. The period 6 April to 22 June was made hideous by the massed attacks bearing the charming title of *Kikusui,* which, being translated, means 'floating chrysanthemum'. It has been estimated that more than 3,000 *Kamikazes* were flown in these weeks. They sank 21 ships, and damaged 66. When one adds to this hundreds of attacks by conventional aircraft one begins to comprehend the ordeal of the fleet supporting the Okinawa invasion. It was the most costly naval campaign of the war. But statistics do not really tell us what it was like. One example must suffice.

There were 355 *Kamikazes* in the first *Kikusui* attack which concentrated against the destroyers *Leutze* and *Newcomb.* The latter was attacked five times in swift succession. The first *Kamikaze* hit her after-stack, the second was splashed, and the third crashed right down through the ship and blew up, destroying the engine rooms.

'"With intentions of polishing us off," wrote her skipper, Commander I. E. McMillan, "a fourth plane raced toward *Newcomb* from the port beam and although under fire by her forward batteries came through to crash into the forward stack, spraying the entire amidships section of *Newcomb,* which was a raging conflagration, with a fresh supply of gasoline." Flames shot up hundreds of feet, followed by a thick pall of smoke and spray which so completely covered the destroyer that sailors in nearby battleships thought that she had gone down.'

The British carriers of the Pacific Fleet (Vice-Admiral Sir Bernard Rawlings), which had been operating with the Americans since 26 March, though their fuel capacity did not compare with that of the American carriers, were better able to cope with the *Kamikazes,* which did only local damage to their steel decks.

As early as 8 April 82 Marine Corsairs were operating from the captured airfields of Yontan and Kadena, though both were still under shell-fire. Land-based planes were soon able to thicken up the carrier-based Combat Air Patrols and bring some relief to the destroyers on radar picket duty.

Above right: **The Japanese airstrips on Iwo Jima were clearly visible to American bombers.**

Right: **The 4th Marine Division moves up the beach on Iwo Jima, 19 February 1945. This was the fourth amphibious assault in eighteen months that the division took part in.**

Below: **On the second day of the invasion of Iwo Jima two men from the 5th Marines Division walk past the dead bodies of Japanese soldiers.**

Below: **Left to right, Vice-Admiral Kelly Turner, Major General Harry Schmidt and Lieutenant General Holland Smith who directed the landing operations on Iwo Jima.**

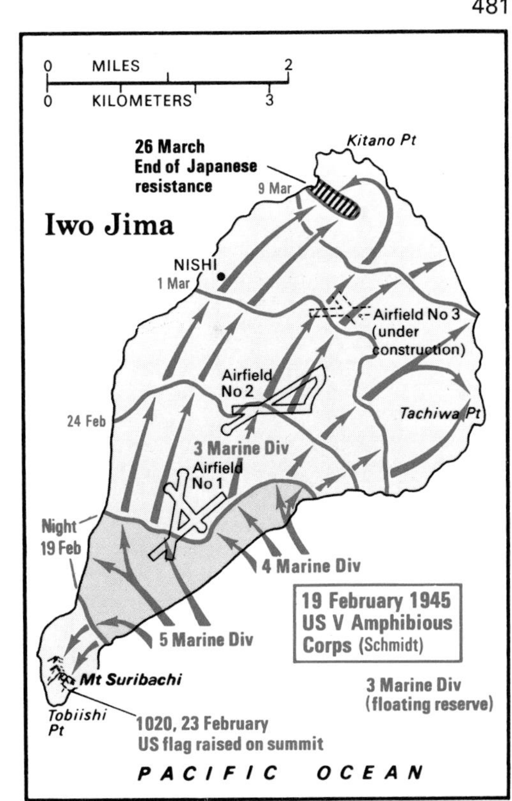
0 MILES 2
0 KILOMETERS 3
Kitano Pt
26 March
End of Japanese
resistance
9 Mar
Iwo Jima
NISHI
1 Mar
Airfield No 3
(under
construction)
Airfield
No 2
Tachiwa Pt
24 Feb
3 Marine Div
Airfield
No 1
Night
19 Feb
4 Marine Div
19 February 1945
US V Amphibious
Corps (Schmidt)
5 Marine Div
Mt Suribachi
3 Marine Div
(floating reserve)
Tobiishi
Pt
1020, 23 February
US flag raised on summit
PACIFIC OCEAN

By 19 April the Americans, with four-fifths of the island in their hands, had 160,000 men ashore. They were up against the fortified Japanese position across the three-mile waist of the island. The defences were as tough as anything the Americans had met on the long road from Guadalcanal. But by mid-June the Japanese were almost worn down. When on 18 June Lieutenant-General Buckner was killed by shellfire, while observing one of the last attacks of the campaign, his work was nearly complete.

On 20 June civilians were surrendering *en masse* and next day Major-General Geiger was able to report that organized resistance was at an end. At dawn on 22 June, when American grenades were already exploding nearby, Lieutenant-General Ushijima, in full uniform, accompanied by his Chief of Staff, Lieutenant-General Cho, in a white *kimono*, emerged from their Headquarters cave, seated themselves on a quilt covered by a white cloth, bowed to the eastern sky, and, with the assistance of an Adjutant, committed *hari-kiri*. In the words of a Japanese eye-witness 'both generals had nobly accomplished their last duty to the Emperor'

They had certainly exacted a heavy toll of American life. The war might be long lost but there was no falling-off in the resolute resistance of the obedient, fanatical, fatalistic Japanese soldier. In taking Okinawa, Tenth Army lost 7,613 killed and 31,800 wounded. The United States Navy had 4,900 sailors killed and 4,800 wounded; 34 ships and craft sunk, 368 damaged.

As it turned out, General Carl Spaatz's US Army Strategic Air Force was to strike the mortal blow against Japan. He had the Eighth Air Force (Lieutenant-General J. H. Doolittle) in Okinawa and the Twentieth (Lieutenant-General N. F. Twining) in the Marianas. With amazing speed the Americans constructed 23 airstrips on Okinawa, and by the end of the war 18 groups of heavy and medium bombers and fighters were operating from that hard-won base.

Okinawa was, however, much more than an air base. Admiral Nimitz summarized its strategic value thus:

'Establishment of our forces on Okinawa has practically cut off all Japanese positions to the southward as far as sea communications are concerned. It has made the Japanese situation in China, Burma, and the Dutch East Indies untenable and has forced withdrawals which are now being exploited by our forces in China.'

That Japan was beaten was clear enough. But would she surrender without an invasion that could cost another 50,000 American lives? President Roosevelt had not lived to see victory. While the fight for Okinawa was at its height he had died suddenly. His successor, the unknown Harry S. Truman, was to have an early opportunity to show the world the calibre of his decisions.

Above: **The Japanese surrendered in large numbers on Okinawa.**

Right: **An M-18 of the 306th Anti-tank Company, 77th Division fires onto the enemy lines at Shuri, Okinawa.**

Below right: **Units of the 15th Regiment, 6th Marines Division roll on to the outskirts of Naha, the capital of Okinawa.**

Below: **Captured Japanese battle flags.**

34 THE BOMB

'A fission bomb of superlatively destructive power will result from bringing quickly together a sufficient mass of element U-235. This seems as sure as any untried prediction based upon theory and experiment can be.'
Report of the secret committee of the National Academy of Science. Washington, 6 November 1941

By May 1945 the Japanese knew they were beaten, but President Truman did not know they knew. The Japanese wanted to find a way out of their predicament, but always in the background was the stumbling block of Unconditional Surrender. After the loss of Manila in February the Emperor consulted certain elder statesmen including Prince Konoye. All were agreed that peace was desirable, but they did not know how to bring it about.

When in April the *Yamato*, newest and biggest of Japanese battleships, was sunk, all hope of victory at sea vanished. Nothing could be done to help the armies in Burma and Yunan. The Emperor resolved to seek peace. On 22 June he summoned the Imperial Presence Conference, and gave orders that the question of ending the war as quickly as possible should be considered. This, commented a Court official, 'in those days of frenzied chauvinism was an act which required an extraordinary resolution, involving a grave risk even to the august person of an emperor'.

Hiroshima ('the broad island'), the seventh largest town in Japan, stood where the seven arms of the river Ota pour into the inland sea. Arsenal, harbour, factories, oil refineries and warehouses formed a triangle, inhabited by 343,000 civilians and a garrison of perhaps 150,000 soldiers. For all the horror of its fate it was certainly 'a military target' by the standards already established in World War II. Estimates vary as to how much it had already suffered from bombing during raids in March and April.

At nine minutes past seven on the morning of 6 August four B-29s appeared in the cloudless sky and the sirens sounded. By 7.31 they had disappeared and the all-clear went.

Meanwhile a single Superfortress, named the *Enola Gay*, and piloted by Colonel Paul W. Tibbetts, had released one bomb, which had descended five miles by parachute and burst over the target. It left no crater.

The casualties were approximately 78,000 killed, 10,000 missing, and 37,000 injured, not counting those who were to suffer later from exposure to gamma rays.

So bald a statement hardly conveys the horror of what happened. A Japanese journalist describes the scene:

'Suddenly a glaring whitish pinkish light appeared in the sky accompanied by an unnatural tremor which was followed almost immediately by a wave of suffocating heat and a wind which swept away everything in its path.

Within a few seconds the thousands of people in the streets and the gardens in the centre of the town were scorched by a wave of searing heat.

Many were killed instantly, others lay writhing on the ground screaming in agony from the intolerable pain of their burns. Everything standing upright in the way of the blast – walls, houses, factories, and other buildings – was annihilated and the debris spun round in a whirlwind and was carried up into the air. Trams were picked up and tossed aside as though they had neither weight nor solidity. Trains were flung off the rails as though they were toys. Horses, dogs and cattle suffered the same fate as human beings. Every living thing was petrified in an attitude of indescribable suffering. Even the vegetation did not escape. Trees went up in flames, the rice plants lost their greenness, the grass burned on the ground like dry straw.

Above: Colonel Paul Tibbetts, pilot of the B-29 *Enola Gay*, stands by the plane which dropped the atomic bomb of Hiroshima.

Beyond the zone of utter death in which nothing remained alive houses collapsed in a whirl of beams, bricks and girders. Up to about three miles from the centre of the explosion lightly-built houses were flattened as though they had been built of cardboard. Those who were inside were either killed or wounded. Those who managed to extricate themselves by some miracle found themselves surrounded by a ring of fire. And the few who succeeded in making their way to safety generally died twenty or thirty days later from the delayed effects of the deadly gamma-rays. Some of the reinforced concrete or stone buildings remained standing, but their interiors were completely gutted by the blast.

About half an hour after the explosion, whilst the sky all around Hiroshima was still cloudless, a fine rain began to fall on the town and went on for about five minutes. It was caused by the sudden rise of overheated air to a great height, where it condensed and fell back as rain. Then a violent wind rose and the fires extended with terrible rapidity, because most Japanese houses are built only of timber and straw.

By the evening the fire began to die down and then it went out. There was nothing left to burn. Hiroshima had ceased to exist.'

Stunned by the blast, the Jesuit priest Father Wilhelm Kleinsorge found himself wandering round the garden of his mission, dressed only in his underclothes. Nearby he could hear his housekeeper crying in Japanese: 'Our Lord Jesus Christ, have pity on us!' And on the other side of the world Winston Churchill attributed to 'God's mercy' the fact that American and British, not German, scientists had discovered the secret of atomic power.

On 25 August Minoru Suzuki dictated a

Left: Victims of the bomb that hit Hiroshima.

Right: The now-familiar mushroom cloud which formed over Nagasaki on 9 August 1945. It is estimated that 35,000 were killed outright, 5,000 went missing and 6,000 were seriously injured.

The ruins of Tokyo, which bore the brunt of the Allied bombing offensive against Japan.

letter to his parents thanking them because despite their meagre resources they had allowed him to study first at college, then at Tokyo University. He was going to die. 'Autumn will come, the chirping of the crickets, the forest despoiled of its foliage will remind you of my death, but do not weep.' It was in exquisite taste. His hands had been burnt away.

The dropping of the Hiroshima bomb was followed by an ultimatum, which was ignored.

On 9 August a second bomb was dropped on the port of Nagasaki, a city of 250,000 inhabitants. Unconditional surrender followed on 14 August.

The Imperial Rescript

We, the Emperor, have ordered the Imperial Government to notify the four countries, the United States, Great Britain, China and the Soviet Union, that We accept their Joint Declaration. To ensure the tranquillity of the subjects of the Empire and share with all the countries of the world the joys of co-prosperity, such is the rule that was left to Us by the Founder of the Empire of Our Illustrious Imperial Ancestors, which We have endeavoured to follow. Today, however, the military situation can no longer take a favourable turn, and the general tendencies of the world are not to our advantage either.

What is worse, the enemy, who has recently made use of an inhuman bomb, is incessantly subjecting innocent people to grievous wounds and massacre. The devastation is taking on incalculable proportions. To continue the war under these conditions would not only lead to the annihilation of Our Nation, but the destruction of human civilization as well. How could We then protect Our innumerable subjects, who are like new-borne babes for Us? How could We ask the forgiveness of the divine spirits of Our Imperial Ancestors? When Our thoughts dwell on those of Our subjects who died in battle, those who fell as victims of their duty, those who perished by a premature death, and on the families they have left behind them, We feel profoundly upset.

. . . It is Our desire to initiate an era of peace for future generations by tolerating the intolerable and enduring the unendurable. Capable of maintaining the national policy and placing Our trust in the perfect sincerity of Our good and faithful subjects, We will always be with you. Let all the countries, like one single family where tradition is handed down from son to grandson, have firm faith in the indestructible character of the Land of the Gods. Remembering Our heavy responsibilities and the length of road yet to be covered, concentrating all Our strength on the construction of the future, animated by deep morality and firm honesty, We swear to hold the flower of Our National policy very high, resolved not to remain backward in the general progress of the world. We ask you, Our subjects, to be the incarnation of Our will.

Hirohito.

All over Japan his people listened to the Emperor addressing them for the first time. When it was over many wept, then, bowing to each other politely, they went their way. 'The Emperor knows better than we do what should be done.'

A few, like Vice-Admiral Onishi, the commander of the *Kamikaze*, and General Sugiyama, the Chief of Staff, committed *hara-kiri*, but there was no wave of suicides.

The surrender was signed aboard the US battleship *Missouri* anchored in Tokyo Bay on Sunday 2 September 1945. For the Americans the war had lasted three years, eight months, and 25 days. At the ceremony the Americans flew not only the flag that had been flying over the Capitol in Washington on the day of Pearl Harbor, but oddly enough, the historic flag – with only 31 stars – which Commodore Perry had flown when he first landed on Japanese soil in 1853. Perhaps some who were present reflected that it might have been better had he never set foot there!

General MacArthur made a short speech and announced that he meant to discharge his

Above: The HMS *Duke of York* proudly flies the Allies' flags for the Japanese surrender ceremony in Tokyo Bay.

Top left: 62,000 of Hiroshima's 90,000 houses were destroyed by the atomic bomb.

Left: General MacArthur and Emperor Hirohito.

Right: Sugiyama killed himself on 12 September 1945.

responsibilities with justice and tolerance. Next the instrument was signed by two delegations. General MacArthur then led a short prayer for peace – which was followed closely by the flight of 436 Superfortresses over Tokyo.

Japan too saw its version of the Nuremberg tribunal. On 19 November MacArthur ordered the arrest of 11 Japanese war leaders. With an accurate historical sense he sought to punish war crimes that had taken place as long ago as the 'thirties when the Japanese had seized Nanking. Prince Konoye, who had thrice been premier of Japan, and who, had justice been done, would probably have been acquitted, committed suicide before he could be taken. Tojo, the brains of the war party and virtual

Above: **Lieutenant General Roy Geiger at the Japanese surrender ceremony.**

Left: **The Japanese delegation about to sign the official surrender on board the USS *Missouri* in Tokyo Bay on 2 September 1945.**

dictator, had not been so lucky. He wished to commit *hara-kiri*, but had nobody to assist by decapitating him after the ceremonial disembowelment. When he was about to be arrested on 11 September he shot himself in the chest. The Americans found him wearing full uniform and six rows of medal ribbons. He was not mortally wounded – his pistol was only a .32.

While a prisoner he said to a Japanese reporter: 'I am sorry for the peoples of Greater East Asia. I will shoulder the whole responsibility. I hope they will not go amiss in dealing with the situation. The war of Greater East Asia was a just war. With all our strength gone we finally fell. I do not wish to stand before the victor and be tried as the vanquished. . . .' To some Americans he said: 'You are the victors and you are now able to name who was responsible for the war. But historians 500 or 1,000 years from now may judge differently.' It is a thought that no victor can afford to ignore.

He went to the gallows on 22 December leaving this valedictory verse:

It is good-bye,
Over the mountains I go today
To the bosom of Buddha
So, happy am I.

Who are we to condemn those who play the game by an altogether different set of rules?

The case of General Yamashita, the Tiger of the Philippines, excites less pity. The sadism of his troops was well attested. There were those who alleged that, among other atrocities, his soldiers had poured petrol on women's heads and then set fire to them. Yamashita's denial that he had any knowledge of such doings was unconvincing. He was executed on 7 December 1945, the fourth anniversary of Pearl Harbor.

Wisely the Americans kept Emperor Hirohito on the throne of his ancestors, and refrained from trying him as a war criminal. He had, of course, attended meetings of those who planned the war, but his spiritual control over his subjects was such that it was clearly simpler for the occupation forces to support him. At a time when the Japanese nation had been shaken to its very soul by an unbelievable and unparalleled defeat at the hands of a despised enemy, they needed something to cling to. Loyalty to their Emperor must at least be left them. Doubtless this decision prevented terrible disorders and accelerated the process of rebuilding the democratic and industrious Japan we know today.

35 PARTING SHOTS

'We are now about to enter upon a new chapter in the history of mankind. We should thank God for Hitler. He has done a great service to the world. He has brought us back to a realization of brute facts. He has got us away from ideals and rhetoric. Facts are the only things that matter. Hitler has shown that Hell is still here on Earth. He has, in fact, taken the lid off Hell, and we have all looked into it. That is his service to the human race.'

Field Marshal Smuts, 1944

An international tribunal sat at Nuremberg from 20 November 1945 to 1 October 1946 and tried 24 of Hitler's chief associates, some of whom have figured in these pages. Göring, von Ribbentrop, Keitel, Jodl and Bormann were among those condemned to hang. Admiral Raeder was sent to prison for life; Dönitz and Speer for 20 years. In 1965 the time limit for Nazi trials was extended until 31 December 1969.

A generation that has only seen him ranting on some ancient newsreel might be inclined to underrate Hitler, but though unbalanced he was a formidable opponent. General von Mellenthin, a keen observer and no friendly critic, gives an interesting thumbnail sketch:

'. . . Hitler was an incredibly clever man, with a memory far beyond the average. He had terrific will-power and was utterly ruthless; he was an orator of outstanding quality, able to exercise an hypnotic influence on those in his immediate surroundings. In politics and diplomacy he had an extraordinary flair for sensing the weakness of his adversaries, and for exploiting their failings to the full. He used to be a healthy man, a vegetarian who neither smoked nor drank, but he undermined his constitution by taking sleeping powders and pep pills, chiefly during the later years of the war. Although his health deteriorated, his mind remained amazingly alert and active until the very end.'

Why, despite these powers and his undoubted tenacity, did he lose?

It may be that he underrated his opponents. Despising democracy and the quest for peace, he evidently came to regard Great Britain and the United States as utterly effete. In this he fell victim to his own rhetoric and the wishful thinking of the incompetent von Ribbentrop. His own service as a front-line soldier in the First World War should have warned him against this line of thought.

It is easy to criticize the Allies for going into the war ill-prepared. But while Hitler's preparations for a land campaign were excellent it is usually forgotten that the *Wehrmacht* was only ready for campaigns on the continent. When in 1940 Great Britain failed to surrender after the fall of France the *Luftwaffe*, largely for lack of long-range bombers, was not quite up to the task of subduing the RAF. The German navy was inadequate to clear the Channel, and the U-Boat fleet, which at the outbreak of war was rather weaker than the British submarine force, was not able to cut Britain's Atlantic life-line, though later it came near to doing so.

Hitler certainly had a high opinion of himself as a soldier. He had been decorated twice in the First World War and his experiences then had probably given him confidence. He had a certain tactical flair, demonstrated by his supporting Manstein's plans for the 1940 campaign. He alleged that he had studied Clausewitz and Schlieffen. The German victories in Poland and France appeared to him in the light of personal triumphs. Then when his will-power enabled his army to ride the storm, when his generals wanted to retreat in that awful Russian winter, he became convinced that he was another Frederick.

But in fact his personal command on the Eastern Front was disastrous for Germany. His habit of playing off OKW and OKH against each other – divide and rule – made for inefficiency and confusion. His continual interference in detail – so contrary to Roosevelt's methods – was the root of countless calamities. His main fault was his inability to concentrate on one aim at a time.

After the Axis defeats of November 1942, when Faith took the place of Reason in German planning, his already unscrupulous character rapidly deteriorated. It says much for the tactical power of the defensive and the tenacity of the German soldier that the Reich kept going for another three years after such blows as Stalingrad and Tunis. Thanks to the *Schnorkel* and the V.2 Hitler remained dangerous to the last – particularly to Britain.

The inordinate length of the war is easily explained by Allied unpreparedness and the devastating series of early defeats.

The war had certain general features which are worthy of comment, and some may be the pattern of things still to come. Most of the campaigns began without the formality of a declaration of war. The use of the 'fifth column', of guerrillas and partisans was widespread, and though often effective frequently led to brutal atrocities by either side.

The value of a balanced force was forcibly demonstrated by the early German campaigns, when aircraft and tanks were such successful ingredients of the *Blitzkrieg*.

The interrelation of land, sea and air was well-illustrated. It was, for example, the capture of their bases by land forces that put an end to the V.2 and U-Boat campaigns. The bomber offensive, by drawing the *Luftwaffe* home to defend the Fatherland, paved the way for the amphibious operations against Sicily, Italy and Normandy. A fresh idea, still of great military use, was air-supply.

The verdict of history will probably be that the admirals, generals and air-marshals of the Second World War, Allied and Axis alike, were a far more competent lot than their predecessors of the First. Even so, one detects at times a certain conservatism – reluctance to admit that the carrier is mightier than the battleship; a tendency to combat the *Blitzkrieg* with methods already inappropriate in 1918. But this criticism could be taken too far.

The power of broadcasting to enable the war leaders to indoctrinate their followers was amply demonstrated by such masters as Churchill, Roosevelt, and, it must be said, Goebbels.

It may be that minor tactics have changed very little in the last twenty years. One captures a pillbox or destroys a tank much as one did in those distant days. But the grand tactics of war were changed at a blow when the bomb fell on Hiroshima.

It is easy to condemn President Truman for ordering that the bombs be dropped, and indeed, Mr Churchill for his concurrence. Living as we do in an age when not one but several nations have far more destructive weapons, we may well regret the opening of the nuclear period of Military History. But to be fair we must look at the situation as President Truman saw it in August 1945. He did not know that the Emperor had already (8 June) ordered his ministers to seek to end the war as quickly as possible. He *did* know the desperate devotion of the Japanese forces, the *Kamikaze* spirit, their 'no surrender' attitude. However much he may have exaggerated probable Allied losses in the invasion of Japan, his statement that he saved every one of them cannot be parried. Few modern generals would hesitate to slay the enemy, military and civilian, guilty or innocent, if by so doing they could save their own men. How long would they enjoy their confidence if they did?

From a moral point of view the bombing of cities from the air, a form of war in which the Axis rather than the Allies led the way, is hard to justify. At the same time one can make a case for saying that the bombing of Hamburg (July 1943) was just as atrocious as that of Hiroshima. A bomb is still a bomb, however big its destructive potential. If the equivalent of 20,000 tons of TNT is coming does it matter whether it comes from one or 1,000?

From the strictly military point of view it is worth pointing out that one atomic bomb was a more effective weapon than a number of bombs dropped in a conventional raid by Superfortresses, even supposing that the capacity of the latter exactly equalled one atomic bomb. The principles of war, which guide commanders in their conduct of operations, call attention to the need to plan for Surprise and Concentration of Force. Nor is this view entirely cynical. The Germans had stood up to terrible bombing. Let none think that the Japanese did not equal, or indeed excel, in courage their allies: chauvinistic, patriotic, fatalistic, obedient, they were ready to go on as long as the Emperor required them to. Only the grim reaping scythe of Hiroshima and Nagasaki could prepare them for his change of mind.

But if, reluctantly, one must conclude that Mr Truman's decision was justified, this is not to say that the whole sorry tale of bombing from Warsaw and Rotterdam to Dresden and Nagasaki does anything but dishonour to the human

Above right: **Vidkun Quisling, Norway's dictator under the Nazis, on trial for high treason after the war. He was found guilty and executed on 24 November 1945.**

Right: **Pierre Laval was Marshal Pétain's Foreign Minister during the Vichy regime. When France was liberated by the Allies Laval withdrew to Germany but at the end of the war he was found in Spain and deported to France. He was found guilty of treason and shot in Fresnes prison.**

The bomb-damaged drydock at Kure in Japan. The drydock contained some sixty two-man submarines and was flooded by American soldiers shortly after the occupation of Japan, August 1945.

race. World War II was total, military and economic. Almost everywhere military targets were surrounded by the dwellings of ordinary people. Seldom did the attacker, like the British at Dieppe (19 August 1942), spare the civilians at the risk of adding to their own military casualties. The history of war is a tale of violence in which civilian and soldier suffer.

Even the limited wars of the eighteenth century show this. Frederick the Great was not notably squeamish, to take only one example. Faced with a life and death struggle, there are no holds barred and atrocities find justification whenever their perpetrators 'get away' with them. Any weapon is permissible so long as it is effective. If poison gas was not employed in World War II it was not because it had been found too horrible in World War I but because it had proved insufficiently destructive. Such is the morality of war.

If there is any hope for the future it is that the powers will dread the use of weapons so world-ravaging as those they now possess. But history does not support the view that people are either so prudent or so benevolent. Who can tell whether we may not see the day when the United States will use the bomb against China, rather than see her equally well armed?

Military History is about people, about how they react to the stresses and strains of war. If the techniques of war change, the human spirit remains immutable. In war primitive virtues still count. It follows that, however much weapons development may alter tactics, the study of past wars is still worth while, and especially so if one is capable of recognizing one's own bias, and setting aside such things as inter-service rivalry and jealousy of one's allies.

It is as yet too early to expect the final verdict of History on the rights and wrongs of World War II, and the way it was conducted. The full story has not yet been told. We are too near the events which this book attempts to outline.

But it is not too early to say something of the nature of war itself, its strange fascination. It is easy to denounce it for its horrors and its hardships; to condemn it for its cruelty and the suffering it brings. Dr. Johnson once said: 'Every man thinks meanly of himself for not having been a soldier, or not having been at

sea.' To which Boswell replied: 'Lord Mansfield does not.' Johnson: 'Sir if Lord Mansfield were in a company of admirals and generals who'd seen service he'd wish to creep under the table!'

The veteran has compassion for the civilians hurt, the soldiers slain – even the enemy soldiers – but, having survived a hundred perils, he would not have things other than they were, for he thinks the better of himself for his campaigning days. He remembers the good times, the careless – almost carefree – life of disinterested comradeship amidst brave and generous friends. His senses reject the memory of the butcher's shop that was an observation post until the Japanese scored a direct hit, and the sickly sweet smell of corpses rotting in a Sicilian farmyard. He is glad that when the challenge came he achieved rather more than he thought he would. However regrettable it may be, there are still a great many men in this world who feel quite different from the common run of mortals because they have been under fire. It is as though it were some sort of hallmark. And, though they may not admit it, there are thousands who would like to have proved themselves in the ancient ordeal of combat. The marvels of the Industrial Revolution and of modern science must not conceal from us the primitive being that lurks within us all. The peaceful British, driven into a corner in 1940, fought back with a determination that almost amounted to savagery. In some this atavistic reaction may have left a sense of guilt. The majority, though they had not previously regarded themselves as warriors, look back on the part they played in overthrowing the Axis, with nothing but satisfaction.

We live in a technological age. But it is an age in which people whose interests are opposed still strive to solve their problems by force, though their methods may be those of the economist, the politician and the diplomat. Perhaps two World Wars have bred a brand of statesman capable of keeping the lid on Hell. It does not seem likely, for we are not specially skilful in selecting our masters. Let us therefore remember the words of Santayana: 'He who forgets his History is condemned to relive it.'

Damaged Japanese AF aircraft in Atsugi Airport in September 1945.

THE MODERN WORLD

THE KOREAN WAR

The postwar Western world soon found that it could not subside into complacency even after years of harrowing conflict. The agreements reached with the Soviet Union at Yalta and Potsdam were leavened with the potential for renewed hostilities from Eastern Europe to Eastern Asia. Far-sighted observers who warned against giving the Soviets too strong a hand – Churchill, Harriman, Eisenhower and Patton among them – were largely ignored. US President Harry S Truman chose to honor the commitments made by a mortally stricken Roosevelt at Yalta and by himself at Potsdam. Josef Stalin was not the man to throw away an opportunity of this kind. He capitalized on Allied wishful thinking by tightening his hold on Eastern Europe as quickly as possible. Not until Stalin refused to allow free elections in occupied Poland did Truman become more realistic.

The Iron Curtain Closes

Before the 1940s were out, Russia had attempted to extend its hegemony to Greece and Turkey by taking advantage of the dismal postwar condition of these troubled lands. Greek Communist insurgents received major Soviet assistance, which was countered first by Britain, then by the United States through the newly announced Truman Doctrine. Initially, this appropriated $400 million to assist the embattled Greek and Turkish Governments, in a departure from the norm of US foreign policy, which was historically isolationist in peacetime. Concurrently, the Western European powers sought unity through alliances concluded in 1947-8. They received liberal assistance from the United States through the Marshall Plan, which was originally conceived as a means of strengthening all the European economies that had been devastated by World War II. As it turned out, only Western Europe accepted American financial and technological help; the Soviet Union and its satellites in Eastern Europe held aloof.

The burgeoning 'cold war' was intensified by the presence of strong, well-organized Communist Parties in such former Allied states as France and Italy. Their influence was often disproportionate to their numbers, as the Communists had been in the vanguard of resistance to Nazi Germany in Western Europe after 1941. They commanded a sizable minority of the vote in France and Italy, and there was widespread – and well-founded – apprehension that they might achieve power democratically, even without overt aid from Soviet Russia. If so, their orientation would be toward Moscow rather than Washington. This fear was addressed in the containment policy formulated by George Kennan, which gave birth to the Marshall Plan. Between the dictatorships of Hitler and Stalin, there was little to choose, and few could face the possibility that the continent which had been so dearly bought from Nazi Germany should pass entirely under the Hammer and Sickle.

A Test of Western Will

As Western Europe's war wounds began to heal, Russia achieved a nearly bloodless coup in Czechoslovakia – the last democratic government in Eastern Europe until Jan Masaryk's mysterious death and the ousting of the broken Eduard Benes in 1948. Klement Gottwald enthroned Stalinism in Prague, while the West did nothing – just as a decade before when Hitler's army strode through the Sudetenland. However, when the Soviet blockade of Berlin went into effect later that same year, the former Allies were galvanized into activity. America joined the airlift of food and other necessities into the Western sectors of a city deep within Soviet territory. It took over a year to convince the Soviets that the West would defend its interests in Europe: daily airlifts finally broke the blockade in 1949. Not coincidentally, this was the year that the North Atlantic Treaty Organization (NATO) was formed. It pledged the United States to defend Western Europe by force of arms in case of an attack – a promise that stands to this day, with all its implications in a nuclear age. However, since the United States alone possessed atomic weapons in 1949, the Soviets backed down on Berlin and focused their attention on rebuilding their own nation, which had suffered and lost more than any other during World War II. Berlin had proved that the newly forged NATO alliance would defend Western interests in Europe, but the question of US interests in Asia remained untested until the following year.

Previous page: Israeli Centurion tank unit parades in 1967.

Below: US representatives meet with Mao in 1946 to mediate between the Communists and Nationalists.

Communist Inroads in the East

The Chinese Civil War had resumed and escalated in 1947, but President Truman was unwilling to risk American lives in Chiang Kai-shek's Nationalist struggle against the Communist armies of Mao Tse-tung. Some three billion dollars' worth of US aid had shored up Chiang's dubious government since the mid-1940s, but in 1949 this succumbed to Mao's forces and fled to the island of Formosa (Taiwan). American critics charged Truman with being 'soft on Communism,' and alleged that he and Secretary of State Dean Acheson had 'lost' Czechoslovakia and China (which were scarcely theirs to lose) to atheistic warmongers whose aim was world conquest. Such influential right-wing Republicans as Senators William Jenner, Joseph McCarthy and William Knowland spearheaded this attack, which damaged the administration's credibility with the American people. The political stage was set for the decisions that followed upon Acheson's call to Truman at his home in Independence, Missouri, on 24 June 1950: 'Mr President, I have some very serious news. The North Koreans have invaded South Korea.'

Violation of the 38th Parallel

Acheson recommended to Truman that the Security Council of the United Nations meet immediately to declare that an act of aggression had been committed. Events soon proved that this was the case; the North Korean incursion was no mere border skirmish. Some 150 Russian-built T-34 tanks and seven infantry divisions had crossed the dividing line between North and

Above: Dr Syngman Rhee, President of South Korea, and General MacArthur take the salute during the former's visit to Japan in early 1950.

Above left: General MacArthur visiting the fighting front in February 1951.

Right: The Korean War, Sept-Oct 1950.

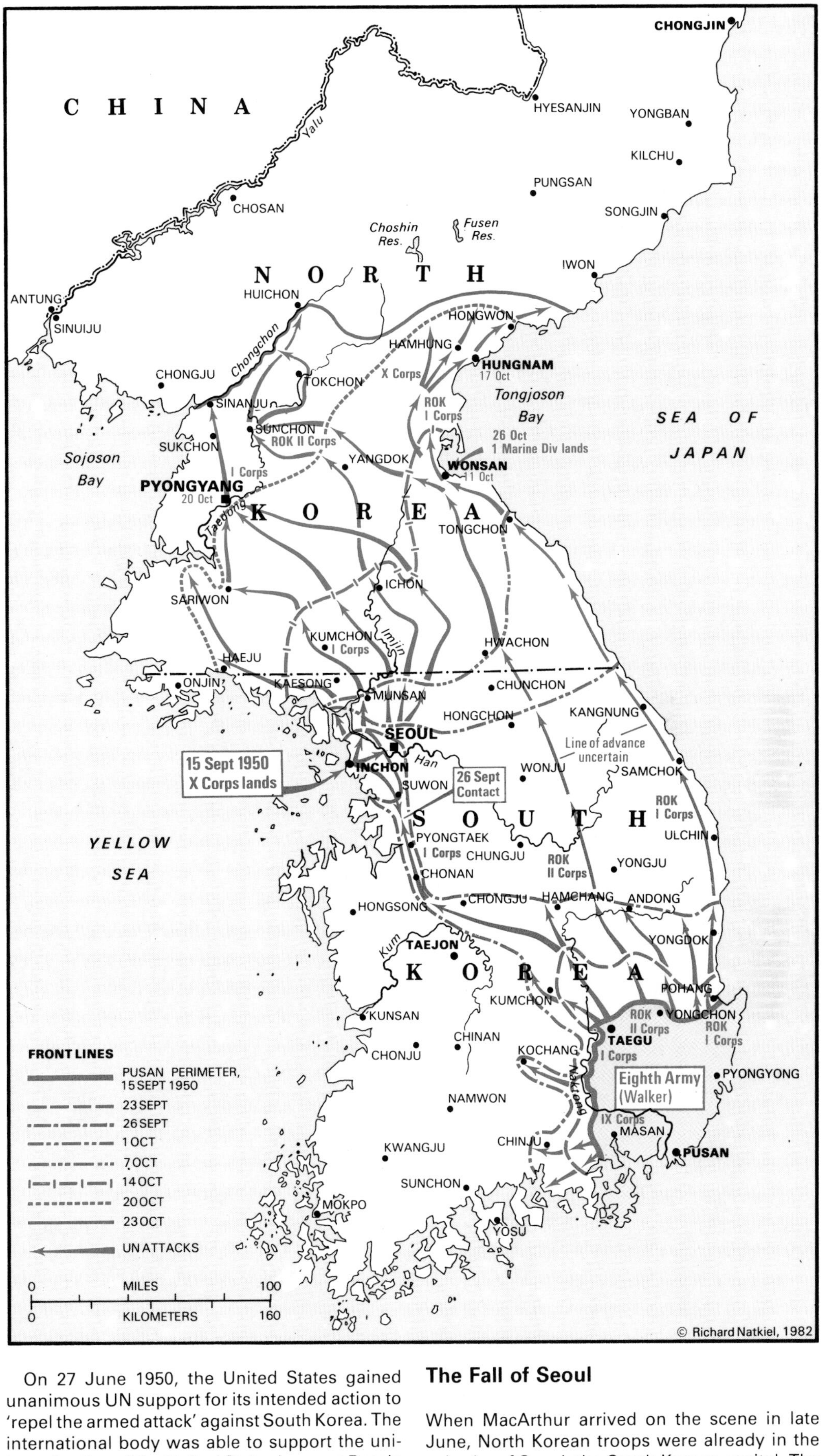

South Korea, the 38th Parallel, along a 150-mile front. During the night of 24 June 1950, it became clear that a full-scale invasion was underway. Trygve Lie, Secretary General of the UN, was asked to convene the special Security Council session that would deal with the emergency.

As anticipated, the UN resolution of 25 June 1950 did nothing to stop the North Korean advance. A hastily called meeting of the Joint Chiefs of Staff with Truman and Acheson that same day resulted in a unanimous decision to act forcefully against the aggressors. General Douglas MacArthur, Supreme Commander of Allied Powers in Japan, was ordered to evacuate all Americans from Korea but to keep the airports open, if possible. He was to send ammunition and other supplies from American-occupied Japan to South Korea. The US Seventh Fleet was ordered to the Formosa Strait, both to protect the Nationalist Chinese and to prevent their attempting to reoccupy parts of mainland China. In a word, MacArthur was to contain the war – to prevent its spread to other parts of East Asia. This meant an extended regional defense perimeter, which had formerly excluded both Formosa and the Republic of Korea. American troops had withdrawn from the Korean peninsula, leaving the South Koreans with an army of only 100,000, plus some 48,000 local militia – no tanks, no warplanes, no heavy artillery. The North Korean Army, by contrast, had some 135,000 well-trained and experienced troops plus Russian arms and advisers, 120 tanks and an armored brigade of about 6000. They also had fighters and bombers – some 180 planes.

MacArthur's intelligence team in Korea had discerned the buildup north of the 38th Parallel well before the attack, and the veteran commander was eager to resume a real military career (with all its headline potential) after years of occupation duty. His long-range goal was the US Presidency, for which he was prepared to take on either Truman or Dwight D Eisenhower, his second-in-command in the Philippines before World War II. (MacArthur and Truman had never met, but the President and the general were mutually disposed to dislike one another.)

On 27 June 1950, the United States gained unanimous UN support for its intended action to 'repel the armed attack' against South Korea. The international body was able to support the unilateral action of the United States because Russia had boycotted the UN since early in the year, when it took Nationalist China's part against the Chinese Communists. However, UN sanction would hamper US actions in many ways, since the UN mandate was to restore the *status quo ante bellum*. America, in fact, wanted first to repel the North Koreans (Truman's major purpose) and then to unite Korea under its client Syngman Rhee, President of South Korea (an objective dear to MacArthur, his Republican supporters and Rhee himself).

The Fall of Seoul

When MacArthur arrived on the scene in late June, North Korean troops were already in the suburbs of Seoul, the South Korean capital. The city fell on 28 June, with Republic of Korea (ROK) casualties of almost 50 percent. It was clear to MacArthur that only US ground troops could prevent the takeover of South Korea, and he so advised both Truman and the Pentagon. He wanted to bring in two of his four Eighth Army divisions from Japan, but Truman balked at first. He did not want a wider war, but US air and naval forces were not containing the North Koreans (MacArthur had ordered bombing north of the 38th Parallel even before he landed in South

Below: A British unit arrives to take over a position from American troops on the Naktong River sector of the Pusan perimeter.

Korea). US forces worldwide had been depleted from some 15 million in 1945 to about a million in 1950. There was fear of European repercussions. However, when these did not materialize, Truman ordered a naval blockade of all Korean coasts (30 June), as the first two companies of the 24th Infantry Division arrived in Pusan by air. This began the first US experiment in limited war after World War II.

Truman made a point of calling the Korean conflict a police action, and stressed the idea that 'we are not at war.' For this reason, he rejected Chiang Kai-shek's less-than-altruistic offer to send Chinese troops to Korea, which would have provoked Communist China into entering the conflict – if not into attacking Formosa itself. This meant that all four Eighth Army divisions in Japan had to be committed to Korea, under command of General Walton H Walker. Australian troops joined MacArthur's command on 8 July 1950, and he was then designated Commander-in-Chief United Nations Command. This title was distinct from MacArthur's original American appointment as Commander-in-Chief Far East, which MacArthur saw as his primary role. Thus he considered himself responsible only to the President, to whom he left the fine points of UN involvement. This fact would become crucial during the following year.

Above: **American artillerymen try to make the most of a few minutes rest.**

Far right: **MacArthur meets with Marguerite Higgins, correspondent of the New York *Herald Tribune*, during the first weeks of the fighting.**

Below: **Landing craft approach the sea wall at Inchon complete with scaling ladders to help the Marines get ashore.**

A Wider 'Non-War'

MacArthur made immediate plans for an invasion of Inchon, for which he requested five more divisions and three tank battalions. The Joint Chiefs of Staff turned him down initially, on the ground that European military installations could not be depleted for the sake of South Korea (echoes of the 'Europe-First' policy of World War II, which made MacArthur furious all over again). He improvised by adding ROK forces to American units, but the military picture was bleak. Half the ROK Army had been destroyed in some 10 days of hostilities. Other Korean troops were streaming south in a headlong retreat. Walker's understrength army, with its outmoded equipment, arrived only to be driven back with the indigenous forces. In B-29 Superfortress raids between 2 and 4 July, however, many North Korean aircraft were destroyed on the ground, and the enemy air force was effectively neutralized by the end of the month.

On the ground, North Korean T-34 tanks and accompanying infantry made steady gains all the way down the peninsula. Walker sought to block their path near Taejon with the 25th Infantry Division under Major-General William B Kean, and the 1st Cavalry Division led by Major-General Hobart R Gay. Taejon commanded the road south to Pusan, the only possible evacuation point for UN forces if they should be overwhelmed. The area could well have become another Dunkirk, with its roads radiating south and west behind the Kum River. The Americans dug in for the city's defense, but 4000 men were not enough for the job. T-34s rolled into Taejon on 19 July, driving all before them. The city was evacuated and Kean escaped with many of his men only to be captured in the nearby hills. He spent the rest of the war in a People's Republic of Korea prison camp.

Superior tactics and experience had much to do with the early North Korean success. Surprise was another factor, enhanced by South Korean unpreparedness. The North Koreans developed frontal pressure through infantry assault teams, often supported by tanks. Once their opponents were pinned down, flanking forces proceeded to the rear to complete the envelopment.

The Race to Pusan

By the end of July 1950, Walker was concentrating on holding the Pusan Perimeter – a semicircular enclave in the peninsula's southeast corner. Reinforcements continued to arrive through Pusan, which was the country's only deep-water port. Intelligence reports showed that the North Koreans were advancing on Pusan at a steady rate of two miles an hour, night and day. On the plus side, reinforcements were being mobilized in the States to be funneled through Hawaii, Tacoma, San Diego and Okinawa. By the end of August, many of these units had arrived, along with some 2000 men from the British 27th Infantry Brigade based in Hong Kong. Additionally, five new armored battalions brought tank strength in the Pusan Perimeter to some 500 – a superiority of roughly five to one. Air superiority

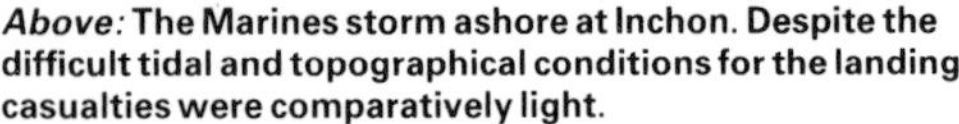

Above: **The Marines storm ashore at Inchon. Despite the difficult tidal and topographical conditions for the landing casualties were comparatively light.**

had been established at the outset, so American forces were now in a good position to hold their lines and, eventually, to counterattack.

On the night of 31 August-1 September, the North Koreans launched a new offensive that came within 10 miles of Taegu. The British 27th Brigade held the line as the Americans retreated. Marine units came in at General Walker's orders and threw back the enemy between 3 – 5 September, in what Walker would later describe as the war's most critical phase. Had the front been breached at Taegu, the Communists would almost certainly have taken Pusan, effectively ending UN participation in the war. Walker was everywhere on the front in an armored jeep, or overflying it to observe the progress of battle. He communicated directly via teleprinter with MacArthur, who had returned to his Tokyo headquarters. When morale began to flag, Walker braced up his men with the promise of a major amphibious assault that was preparing to land at Inchon, near Seoul. MacArthur won Joint-Chief approval of this plan for an invasion behind enemy lines on 29 August. Despite UN naval and air superiority, the project was fraught with risk.

Below: **A weary member of the 5th Regimental Combat Team takes a well-earned rest.**

Tides at Inchon were enormous for the Far East: high tide reached a coastal depth of around 30 feet, while low tide turned the harbor into a huge mudflat reaching three miles out to sea. Landing-craft drafts of 23 to 29 feet dictated a rapid in-and-out operation to avoid being stranded by low tide. Three hours was the maximum allowable time for landing and departure. The tides would be high enough for the projected assault only around mid-September or mid-October, and the Inchon area presented additional hazards in the form of numerous rocks, reefs and shoals. The final obstacle was a 12-foot-high seawall that would have to be scaled by the first US Marines ashore with the help of ladders. Upon this dangerous mission rested the success or failure of the entire Korean war effort.

The Inchon Landing

Under threat of an impending typhoon, the Inchon invasion force (code-named Operation Chromite) set out from Japan on 5 September 1950. It consisted of some 260 ships and 70,000 men, with vessels from many nations: Britain, France, Canada, New Zealand, Australia, the Netherlands, the United States and others. A record-breaking storm broke over the area the following day, but the typhoon itself passed out to sea. MacArthur boarded the *Mount McKinley* at Sasebo on 12 September, even as naval bombardment began near Inchon, against the island of Wolmi-do. This objective was connected to the mainland by a causeway, and fell to US Marine amphibious assault on 15 September. Wolmi-do was taken without a single fatality, and two mainland landings were effected with the next high tide. Serious fighting raged in Inchon, but by the next morning the North Koreans had been driven from the city, and UN nations received their first good news from the Korean front.

MacArthur's bold gamble had paid off, but heavily fortified Seoul remained to be taken. A swift UN advance to the capital was followed by a stubborn two-week struggle that ended only on 28 September, when 130,000 North Koreans had been captured. MacArthur presided over a dramatic public ceremony in the South Korean National Assembly Hall, in which he formally restored Seoul to President Rhee as the seat of government. Rhee wept with gratitude and hailed MacArthur as 'the savior of our race.' The

triumphant general then returned to Tokyo in full possession of the most remarkable victory of his illustrious career.

Conflict on Strategy

The United Nations now had to decide whether to pursue the North Koreans across the 38th Parallel, or to allow them privileged sanctuary there. Truman concluded that the war must be carried into North Korea, thus departing from the original UN aim of defending South Korea against aggression. The new objective was nothing less than the unification of Korea under the

Left: **A Marine armed with a Browning Automatic Rifle moves to a new position as his buddy waits to give covering fire.**

Right: **A bazooka team knocks out an isolated communist position left behind during the communist retreat in September 1950.**

Below: **South Korean troops escort Communist prisoners into captivity as Marine tanks pass by.**

government of Syngman Rhee. On 27 September 1950, the Pentagon authorized MacArthur to cross the 38th Parallel, but specified that no UN troops could be used on the borders of Communist China or the Soviet Union; nor could the air space of these nations be violated.

MacArthur then requested and obtained approval to send the Eighth Army north to seize Pyongyang, the North Korean capital, while the 10th Corps effected a landing at Wonsan to join the Eighth Army. On 1 October, the day he received approval, MacArthur asked the North Korean commander-in-chief to surrender. He refused, despite the fact that his forces were surrounded and hampered from regrouping north of the 38th Parallel by the Eighth Army breakout from the Pusan Perimeter. Then Chou En-lai warned that Communist China would not countenance an 'imperialist' invasion of North Korea. MacArthur suspected that Chinese 'volunteers' were already bolstering defenses around Pyongyang, but Truman, the Pentagon and many European allies were reluctant to give the general his head in the drive across the 38th Parallel.

Truman made a very large concession when he invited MacArthur to meet with him on strategy at Wake Island – geographically, at least, the president was going more than halfway. But the 15 October Wake Island conference between

Above: **Bridges at Sinuiju, North Korea, under attack by aircraft from the carrier USS *Leyte* in November 1950. Naval forces played an important supporting role throughout the war for the UN forces.**

Below: **Landing craft are loaded at Inchon, ready for the move of the 1st Marine Division to Wonsan in October 1950.**

Above: A somewhat makeshift Thanksgiving Dinner on the banks of the Yalu for men of the 8th Division, 23 November 1950.

Above left: Chinese communist leader Mao Tse-tung.

Above: **Marines of the 5th and 7th Regiments during the epic retreat from the Choshin Reservoir.**

Truman and MacArthur – their first and last meeting – was a failure. Neither man budged from his original point of view: MacArthur's aggressiveness versus Truman's anxiety to prevent Chinese intervention at all cost. The general minimized the danger of the massive Chinese forces then assembling north of the Yalu River, the Sino-Korean border. Even if they were used, he asserted, and even if Russian forces came into play, the two Communist nations would not cooperate with one another, and UN air superiority would nullify either threat. Truman insisted that the war must be contained, that neither Russia nor China could be involved. On the surface, the two men parted amicably, but the gulf between them became apparent after the Eighth Army entered Pyongyang five days later. MacArthur had anticipated the victorious UN drive across the 38th Parallel by authorizing his forces to advance within 30–40 miles of the Yalu (well above the line fixed by his original plan). On 24 October he lifted all restrictions on the movement of UN troops in Korea, in flat contradiction of orders. The Pentagon did nothing.

Successful amphibious operations at Wonsan and a second objective farther north were unopposed, as the North Koreans were in chaotic retreat. After airborne troops landed well behind enemy lines, MacArthur landed in Pyongyang and declared that the war was all but over. However, he and General Walker kept a wary eye on the massive Chinese buildup across the Yalu, in Manchuria. On 5 November, the Joint Chiefs received word that MacArthur had ordered the bombing of bridges across the Yalu. He was directed not to bomb within five miles of the frontier, and his request for permission to pursue North Korean planes into Chinese air space was denied. Then the Pentagon caved in again to MacArthur's *fait accompli* and asked only that he refrain from bombing power plants that supplied electricity to Manchuria or Siberia.

The War Goes Wrong

This time MacArthur had overreached himself. The war was escalating by the day, and it was clear by early November that two full Communist Chinese divisions were in Korea. American forward units had advanced on the Yalu far too rapidly, imperiling their supply lines, and Chinese formations began to encircle them. Most US units were able to fight their way out, but it was obvious that MacArthur had underestimated the Chinese threat. Communist commanders were battle-hardened veterans leading equally seasoned fighting men. The overconfident American general now had to ask for additional arms, as he made a worried aerial survey of the border region. He was concerned that a mid-winter freeze of the Yalu would expedite Chinese infiltration; as a result, he ordered new advances, rather than a retreat to a viable defense line. General Walker's objections were overridden, and the Eighth Army pushed forward on 25 November. Next day the Chinese commander, Lin Piao, threw 200,000 men into a new offensive. The Eighth Army and US Marines around the Choshin Reservoir had to fight their way back to the coast, and by the month's end UN forces were in full retreat. Pyongyang was evacuated on 5 December.

Truman wanted MacArthur to hold the line at the 38th Parallel, but he refused to send massive reinforcements lest the general launch another offensive. MacArthur argued hotly that the UN would lose the war without reinforcements, but the Pentagon sided with Truman on this and other points. No blockade could be instated along the Chinese coast; no Nationalist Chinese troops could be brought in; no air raids could be carried out against Chinese installations, including military and industrial facilities in Manchuria. To MacArthur, this policy spelled acceptance of total defeat. Additional bad news arrived when General Walker died in the crash of his jeep on an icy road (23 December) and Matthew B Ridgway was named as his successor. Ridgway's loyalty to the Pentagon would curb MacArthur's penchant for independent action, although the new field commander's abilities inspired real confidence in his leadership. MacArthur gave Ridgway *carte blanche* to re-evacuate Seoul and establish a defense line at the Han River, whence UN forces fought their way back to within 30 miles of the 38th Parallel. Seoul was retaken on 14 March 1951, and a cease-fire was seen as the optimum alternative to continued hostilities that risked all-out war with China.

Below: **Trucks are hurried aboard landing craft during the evacuation of Hungnam in December 1950.**

MacArthur's Dismissal

MacArthur's public criticism of what he called Truman's 'no-win policy' in Korea, plus his disobedience of orders on several occasions, finally angered the president to the point where he obtained Pentagon approval for a change of command in Korea. The breaking point came on 24 March 1951, when MacArthur publicly denigrated China's strength and advocated bombardment of the China coast and interior bases. High-level meetings in Washington in early April resulted in the 11 April announcement that MacArthur was relieved of his command. Matthew Ridgway was named as his replacement. It was the end of a distinguished military career of 52 years' duration.

Public reaction to MacArthur's dismissal in the United States was one of shock and outrage. Criticism of Truman was rampant, and an outpouring of popular enthusiasm and support greeted MacArthur upon his arrival in San Fran-

Right: **Men of the 25th Infantry Division move warily down a village street during fighting near Seoul in February 1951.**

Below: **Men of the 1st Marine Division watch the effects of an air strike by Corsair fighter-bombers in December 1950.**

FINAL DAILY NEWS 3¢

NEW YORK'S PICTURE NEWSPAPER

Vol. 32. No. 249 New York 17, Wednesday, April 11, 1951 28 Main+12 Brooklyn+8 Queens Pages

EXTRA

TRUMAN FIRES M'ARTHUR

Gives Ridgway Command Of U.S. Forces in Far East

Special to The News.

Washington, D. C., Wednesday, April 11.—President Truman early today relieved Gen. MacArthur of his command in the Far East and appointed Gen. Matthew B. Ridgway as his successor.

Truman said at 1 A. M. in a news conference unprecedented since World War II:

"With deep regret I have concluded that General of the Army Douglas MacArthur is unable to give his wholehearted support to the policies of the United States Government and the United Nations in matters pertaining to his official duties.

"In view of these specific responsibilities imposed upon me by the Constitution of the United States and the United Nations, I have decided that I must make a change in the command of the Far East.

"Full and vigorous debate on matters of national policy is a vital element in the Constitutional system of our democracy.

"It is fundamental, however, that military commanders must be governed by the public directives issued to them in the matter provided by our laws and Constitution.

"In time of crisis, this consideration is particularly compelling."

For the days' events leading up to the ouster of Gen. MacArthur, turn to page 2.

Above: MacArthur gives his famous address to Congress on 19 April 1951. Behind him are Vice President Alben Barkley (left) and Speaker Sam Rayburn.

Above left: Banner headlines announce MacArthur's dismissal.

Left: US Navy Skyraiders attack the Hwachon Dam.

cisco. A 'MacArthur for President' drive gathered national momentum. On 19 April America's favorite hero addressed Congress in a televised broadcast that provided a forum for his views on winning the war in Korea – and for justifying his actions there. It was his *ave atque vale,* a famous address in which MacArthur reiterated his argument that 'In war . . . there can be no substitute for victory.' He advocated economic sanctions against China, a naval blockade on her coasts, freedom from restrictions on aerial reconnaissance and involvement of the Nationalist Chinese in the Korean conflict. In closing, he described himself as an 'old soldier' who would now 'fade away,' in the words of the time-honored barracks ballad, having done his duty as he saw it. Congress and the nation wept. The 'old soldier' then embarked on a national tour which drew enthusiastic crowds but failed to support his hopes for

Right: Paratroops of the 187th Regiment make a training drop from C-119 transport planes in Korea in April 1951.

Below: General of the Army Dwight D. Eisenhower meets with President Truman in November 1951. Eisenhower was then Supreme Commander in Europe but was soon to announce his presidential hopes.

a presidential candidacy. During the course of his triumphal progress across the country, it gradually dawned on the American people that MacArthur had, in fact, defied his commander-in-chief and disobeyed written orders from his superiors, leaving Truman no choice except to replace him.

Meanwhile, the fortunes of war in Korea swung back and forth between UN and Communist forces during the spring of 1951. By July, UN troops were across the 38th Parallel everywhere except Kaesong, in the extreme northwest corner of South Korea. Peace talks were first held in that city, then moved to Panmunjon, where they went on for another two years. North Korean, Chinese and UN representatives took part.

A New Kind of Peace

The American public was increasingly frustrated and disaffected by the long-drawn-out war of attrition that ensued after MacArthur's dismissal. The final armistice, signed on 27 July 1953, came as an anti-climax, since it embodied roughly the same provisions agreed upon two years before. South Korea's independence was secured, but the MacArthur-Truman controversy would have repercussions on US national life for years to come.

Russia and China had learned that the United States would defend what it saw as its interests in Asia, and America had made its first essay of limited war. The frustrations experienced in this new kind of conflict – which could be summed up as fighting a war with one hand tied behind one's back – would be repeated on a much greater scale in the following decade, as the United States sank deeply into the quagmire that was Vietnam.

Above left: A mortar team with the British forces in Korea looks out for targets, c 1952.

Left: A Marine patrol returns to the front lines in typically bitter Korean winter weather, December 1951.

Right: The British light carrier HMS _Ocean_ en route to join the supporting naval forces off Korea in July 1952.

Below: President-elect Eisenhower during his famous fact-finding visit to Korea in late 1952.

THE VIETNAM WAR

The conflict that has gone on in Vietnam and Indochina since World War II, with no end in sight at this writing, is a tragic mask with two faces – those of civil and guerrilla warfare. It has pitted hill tribesmen against lowland farmers, country against city, Christian against animist and Buddhist, Communist against bourgeois, and a seemingly vain hope of freedom against a series of despotic rulers. Vietnam labored for centuries to throw off the yoke of Chinese oppression, only to become a French conquest under Napoleon III. The Indo-Chinese masses pursued their traditional ways of life while French settlers and planters holidayed in Saigon, where they tried to replicate Paris among the rice paddies. The French presence remained even after Paris fell before Nazi Germany and Japan conquered Indo-China. Then the power vacuum created by the Japanese defeat of 1945 brought indigenous leaders to the fore, most prominently the dedicated Communist Ho Chi Minh (Nguyen Ai Quoc). Ho had become a Marxist-Leninist in his early youth, and had spent almost a decade studying and working for the Comintern at Moscow's 'Stalin School for the Toilers of the East,' which trained third-world revolutionary leaders. During World War II, he had patiently built a guerrilla organization whose eventual goal was a unified, independent Indo-China under Vietnamese Communist control. Ho saw America as a possible source of support in achieving this goal, but this hope failed to materialize when the French chose to prop up his rival, Bao Dai, the former Emperor of Annam and self-appointed heir apparent to the government of Vietnam. Thus Vietnam had two rival governments when the Japanese surrendered, and the French were ready to reclaim their former colony while paying lip service to Vietnamese nationalism. Ho Chi Minh's Communist army, popularly known as the Viet Minh, was grandiosely named 'League for the Independence of Vietnam' - a name considerably longer than the organization's list of resources when it was formed in 1941. But it was gifted with a brilliant leader and strategist: Vo Nguyen Giap. He astutely predicted 'a war of long duration' against the French, which the Europeans would lose because they lacked the will and support to sustain such a protracted conflict. The French failed to reckon with the obdurate resolve of the Communists to fight for Vietnamese independence (later, the Americans would make the same fatal error). They also chose a poor focal point for Vietnamese nationalist sentiment: their client, Bao Dai, was an accommodating Gallicized aristocrat, who stood little chance of matching the charisma of the driven ascetic and visionary Ho Chi Minh. By 1946, when the French reasserted their authority over Indo-China, the Communist army under Giap numbered some 50,000. It was equipped with a heterogeneous collection of arms and other matériel begged, borrowed or stolen from Chinese, French, American and other forces over the years. The French looked down their noses at this motley crew, whom they saw as no match for the experienced and well-equipped legions of the French Empire. The Haiphong Incident of 20 November 1946 provided the only missing element.

Above: **Vietnamese communist leader Ho Chi Minh.**

Right: **An American tank knocked-out by a land mine, 1966.**

Below right: **Newly-arrived American troops are instructed in Viet Cong booby trap techniques.**

Below: **French soldiers dash for cover as Viet Minh artillery continues the bombardment of Dien Bien Phu.**

The Viet Minh Declares Itself

It began as a seemingly innocuous incident, when a French naval boat stopped a Chinese junk loaded with contraband and brought it into the port of Haiphong, where local Vietnamese forces opened fire on both vessels as they anchored. The sound of gunfire brought nearby Viet Minh soldiers across French barricades, and some 23 French soldiers were killed in the ensuing fight. Two days later, a French burial detail was ambushed by the Viet Minh, and six more French soldiers died. This elicited an ultimatum that the Viet Minh evacuate the Chinese quarter of Haiphong, which they had occupied. The French moved in in force, and fierce fighting broke out, joined by salvoes from the French cruiser *Suffren,* fired directly into the city. In a pattern that would become only too familiar, over 6000 Vietnamese civilians were killed by gunfire, street fighting and the panicked rush from the city. Then a rumor spread among French circles (19 December) that an uprising in Hanoi was imminent. That night, the northern capital's power plant was blown up, and within hours, every French garrison in the country was under attack.

The Viet Minh had planned and executed their coup in the hope of a blitzkrieg-style victory. The French clung to their determination to regain hegemony, and turned to Bao Dai, who had his own agenda for an independent Vietnam. The Americans wanted to support their French ally, but drew back from the imperialism inherent in the French position. The resulting ambivalence and confusion played into the hands of Ho Chi Minh and his irregulars, who held on to the cities they had seized as long as they could before melting back into the countryside. In the process, they elicited popular admiration and support for their nationalist initiative, which was untainted by the involvement of any outside power. The creation of a quasi-independent Vietnam under Bao Dai in 1948 came too late to salvage the French investment – political, economic and military – in Indo-China.

The French Field a Leader

Guerrilla warfare intensified for several years, as the French maintained control over cities, railways and ports, while the Viet Minh made gains in the northern countryside: this pattern, too, would repeat itself for years with a changing cast of characters. Then flagging French morale was

U.S. ARMY 9A 6326

Above: **Napalm bombs explode into flame during an attack by B-57 bombers on suspected Viet Cong positions.**

bolstered by the appointment of a new High Commissioner and Commander-in-Chief of Indo-China, who combined a heroic military record with the qualities of a true statesman. General Jean de Lattre de Tassigny personified the best of the French aristocracy, and he addressed the problem of guerrilla warfare with characteristic resolve. He introduced the use of napalm, a shock/surprise tactic that pushed the Viet Minh back throughout the north. Most importantly, he drove the overconfident Giap from the Red River Delta in northern Tonkin early in 1951 – a lesson the Communist general would never forget in subsequent operations. The French people were tiring of the war in Vietnam, and de Lattre took it upon himself to provide the victories that were needed to maintain the French presence and hold the line against Communism. He achieved wonders in a short twelve months, but in December 1951, mortally ill, he returned to France, where he died the following month.

In 1952 the Viet Minh were on the offensive again, having consolidated their hold on the northwest, especially around the Laotian border. US aid began pouring in to support the French, and a native Vietnamese force was created to take its part in the fight. Henri Navarre replaced de Lattre as Commander-in-Chief in Indo-China, and sent bad news on the French situation back to his government. The United States pressured Paris to take action or make a truce, as US aid since 1950 had amounted to some $500 million per year (with the proviso that Laos, Cambodia and Vietnam would become independent in time). Meanwhile, the Viet Minh were infiltrating Laos, and Navarre made the worst possible decision under the multiple pressures that were coming to bear upon him. He elected to seize and hold a forward base near the Laotian border, in the Communists' strongest area. This was to be a show of French strength that would restore confidence in Paris, in Washington and among his own troops. The objective selected was Dien Bien Phu.

End of a century's occupation

In itself, the village of Dien Bien Phu had little strategic significance, but it commanded routes into China and Laos and had an airstrip that could be used to airlift supplies into the fortress, which lay on a plateau surrounded by hills. The French controlled these hills from three defensive positions. Giap saw the potential for breaking the French will to stay in Indo-China, and he put everything he could muster into the assault on Dien Bien Phu, which began on 13 March 1954. He overran the outlying French posts at a heavy cost in Communist lives and pressed toward the

Below: **The burned-out remains of an F-4 Phantom fighter-bomber following a Viet Cong rocket attack on Da Nang.**

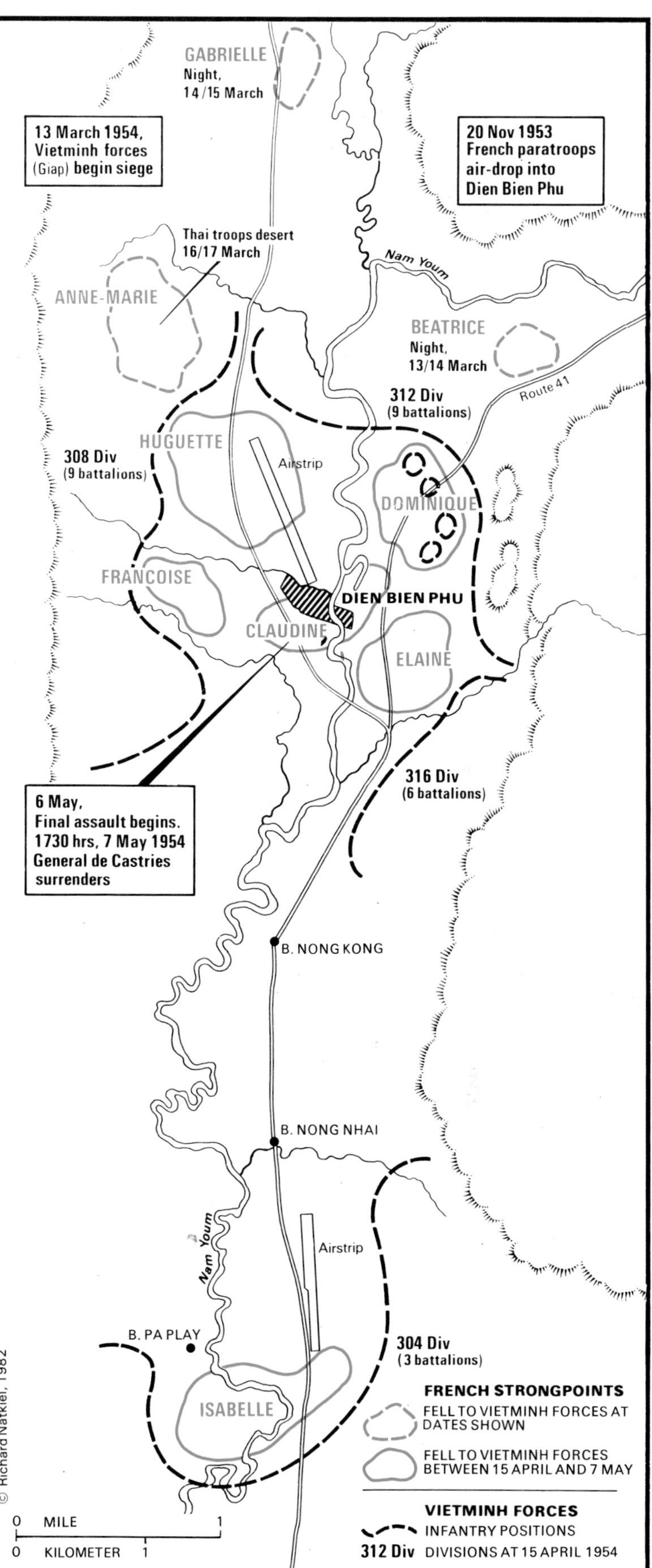

Top: **Marines during a patrol operation in 1967.**

Above: **American troops try to befriend villagers in Qui Nhon province in 1967.**

Above right: **The battle for Dien Bien Phu.**

perimeter of the fortress. The French had discounted Viet Minh ability to bring in heavy artillery and anti-aircraft guns through the mountainous terrain of northern Tonkin, but the Communists achieved this feat – largely by bicycle - and used their guns to good effect. Many French supply planes were shot down, as the garrison waited eagerly for food and ammunition that never reached it. Wounded French soldiers could not be evacuated. On 30 March, the massive Communist assault began; many Viet Minh soldiers were sacrificed in human-wave attacks that broke against the French perimeter until 7 May, when the defenses were finally breached. The French surrendered that afternoon, and the news sped to Geneva, where the international conference on the future of Indo-China and Korea had just begun. The Army of the Republic of Vietnam (ARVN) was going to pieces, and with it the last French hope of maintaining a hold on Indo-China. Would the Americans take up the struggle against Communism there, or would they yield up the whole area? The answer was yet another partition like that of Korea, with the same potential for ongoing conflict: territory north of the 17th Parallel would go to the government of Ho Chi Minh, while South Vietnam, Laos and Cambodia would be independent states protected by the newly formed SEATO (South-East Asia Treaty Organization) Pact. Bao Dai was out, and Ngo

Dinh Diem, an aristocratic Catholic with American backing, was in, as President of South Vietnam. Elections were promised to unite Vietnam under one government by 1956. These elections would never take place, since Ho Chi Minh was certain to win them. Instead, the Americans built up, re-trained and re-equipped the South Vietnamese Army, while Giap began infiltrating the south via the Ho Chi Minh Trail through Laos.

The Communists Move South

Over a five-year period, the Communists built up their strength in the South to a level that threatened even major cities. The Viet Cong, made up mainly of Southern forces, became the equivalent of the Viet Minh, assisted and advised by North Vietnamese Army (NVA) regulars. In late 1960 a major but unsuccessful effort to unseat Diem was launched by South Vietnamese forces, and his tenuous grasp on power became apparent even to his American backers, including newly elected President John F Kennedy. But if America was to maintain its anti-Communist stance in Indo-China, it would have to keep South Vietnam going. The best to be hoped for in Laos was a neutralist government, as the Communist Pathet Lao were growing in strength from day to day. Thus US efforts concentrated on shoring up Diem and his unpopular government, which included his widely hated brother, Ngo Dinh Nhu. America extorted half-hearted promises of land reform as the price of continued aid, but guerrilla strength continued to grow; US military advisers had increased to 16,000 by 1963. Buddhist and other opposition to Diem surfaced and the 'strategic hamlet' program imposed by the South Vietnamese Government forced many peasants to relocate into defensible fortified villages. This policy did violence to the national ethos, which was characterized by deep ties to family and land. Only middle-class elements supported the strategic-hamlet approach to South Vietnamese defense.

Above: **A team leader gives instructions to his squad in the typically unpleasant conditions of a fire-fight in a rice paddy.**

Left: **A Marine marksman tries to pick off a Viet Cong observer during the famous siege of Khe Sanh in 1968.**

Below: **A Phantom strike takes effect just outside the Khe Sanh defensive perimeter. American air power was vital in sustaining the defending forces.**

Diem's Overthrow and US Escalation

On 1 November 1963, both Diem and his brother Nhu were overthrown by a military coup that had tacit American approval (the fact that both were killed in the takeover was seen by some as an unfortunate byproduct of the unhealthy political climate of Saigon). However, the media in Washington displayed much hand-wringing over the deaths and gave considerable play to the histrionics of Madame Nhu, who survived the coup. In fact, her excesses had helped to bring it about. President Kennedy himself was assassinated three weeks later, leaving Lyndon Johnson to preside over the next stage of the war in Vietnam. Johnson declared privately that he would never be the first US President to lose a war, but he concealed his bellicose views from the American public until after the 1964 elections. Meanwhile, he took immediate steps to escalate the war against the Communists. Johnson had amassed great personal power during his years as a notoriously ruthless politician; now he used that power – reinforced by his new office – to influence his Cabinet and advisers in favor of full US involvement in Vietnam. His inner circle consisted mainly of holdovers from the Kennedy regime – a group that had been widely known as 'the best and the brightest' – and his opportunity came with the Tonkin Gulf incident of 2 August 1964. The USS *Maddox* was attacked in the Gulf of Tonkin by North Vietnamese PT boats, one of which it hit in returning fire. Johnson claimed that the *Maddox* and its companion ship, the USS *C Turner Joy,* were 30 miles offshore (where they had a right to be) and not 13 miles from a North Vietnamese island. The whole issue was deliberately confused to win approval for what amounted to a blank check for executive war: Johnson's request to Congress for presidential power to wage aerial war against North Vietnam and build up US troops in Indo-China. When it passed the Tonkin Gulf Resolution, Congress

abdicated its power to restrain Johnson's hawkish approach to North Vietnam (which he referred to among intimates in his down-home way as 'that sorry little raggedy-ass country').

Saturation bombing that would culminate in Operation Rolling Thunder began during Johnson's first year in office. (By the end of hostilities, over six million tons of bombs had been dropped over North and South Vietnam.) All this destructive power had little strategic effect upon a country that was non-urban and non-industrialized, consisting mainly of jungles, plains and scattered populations. Hanoi and Haiphong – the important targets – remained off-limits to US Air Force bombers. This failure of the air-war approach necessitated a major buildup of ground troops, which were commanded in 1965 by General Maxwell Taylor. Early that year, Taylor asked for 75,000 men. In July, this figure jumped to 125,000. It was only the beginning.

By 1968 General William Westmoreland was in charge in Vietnam, and the US presence there approached half a million troops. The American public grew increasingly restive and critical of this war that seemed to have no clear-cut objective – and in which many American lives were now being lost. The Domino Theory had worn thin since the days of Eisenhower and John Foster Dulles: some Americans doubted that all of South-east Asia would inevitably fall to Communism if Vietnam succumbed. Others felt that American interests would not be affected either way. The majority simply grew sick of the bloodshed on both sides and the waste of lives and money that reached them graphically on the nightly news broadcasts. Meanwhile, American prestige abroad was sinking along with domestic self-esteem and solidarity. It was a repeat of what had happened in France during the early 1950s: escalation of an unpopular – and unsuccessful – war effort in an obscure part of the world (most Americans had never even heard of Vietnam before 1960) that received ever-diminishing support on the home front.

Bogged Down

As the Communist insurgents gained ground in South Vietnam, the North sent additional regular troops in to support them. Russia and China supplied arms to North Vietnam, and it was not un-

Above: American self-propelled guns bombard suspected Viet Cong concentrations from a fire base. Accurate detection of Viet Cong and NVA positions was a continual problem.

Right: Vietnamese farmers are interrogated concerning suspected contacts with the communists.

Below right: A fuel store burns following a Viet Cong rocket attack on Da Nang.

Below, far right: A GI carefully fords a river, keeping watch for booby traps.

known for South Vietnamese soldiers to sell their US-made weapons on the black market. These, too, found their way into enemy hands.

By this time, the protracted war effort was undermining the very fabric of Vietnamese society. The presence of numerous affluent foreigners in an underdeveloped country long ravaged by war contributed to black marketing, drug traffic, prostitution, broken families and a flight from the land. Inflation in Vietnam had its mirror image in the United States, where the balance-of-payments deficit soared. Public unrest and war-weariness in Vietnam were echoed in America, where anti-war demonstrations and civil-rights riots spilled from the campuses into the streets. It needed only another Dien Bien Phu to break the Americans' will to stay in the fight.

The Tet Offensive

On the morning of 31 January 1968, the Vietnamese New Year, the American Embassy in Saigon and almost every important US base in South Vietnam came under attack by Communist forces. Surprise was total, and allied forces were stunned into massive retaliation. Whole cities like Kontum, My Tho, Ben Tre and the historic Annamese capital of Hué were destroyed by bombing and fighting between US and Viet Cong forces. The US Marines acquitted themselves courageously at Khe Sanh, Hué and Saigon, where the National Liberation Front sought to seize control. Not until early March was the offensive contained, at a cost of 165,000 civilian lives. It was carnage on a scale never seen before in the war, and it turned a resounding Communist defeat into a political victory. Lyndon Johnson's credibility was destroyed by it; he had to bow out of the 1968 Presidential elections.

Above: **Oil storage tanks burn furiously following an American air attack on the North Vietnamese port of Haiphong in April 1972.**

Opposite: **Men of the 12th Infantry return to their base after a search mission in September 1970. Note how each hut is protected by numerous sandbags.**

Left: **A Marine base comes under mortar attack.**

General Westmoreland was requesting an additional 200,000 men, the dollar faced devaluation and the American public was through with the war at the very moment the Communists had shot their bolt and were on the defensive for the first time in years. The traumatic 1968 assassinations of the popular Robert F Kennedy, Democratic candidate for the presidency, and civil-rights leader Martin Luther King Jr, completed the case against continued involvement in Vietnam. The nation turned to a familiar if uninspiring candidate, and elected Richard M Nixon President.

Propping up a Reluctant Client

Nixon's policy was essentially one of a slow American withdrawal from Indo-China, as the ARVN was trained and equipped to hold South Vietnam against the Communists alone. 'Vietnamization' was the new magic word, as 'counter-insurgency' had been during the Kennedy era. General Creighton Abrams replaced Westmoreland, and President Thieu was pressured into ordering full mobilization of South Vietnamese youth (for the first time in the war). By 1970 the ARVN had over a million men – perhaps half the eligible males in the country. Indigenous troops were equipped with the new M-16 rifles, rocket launchers, helicopters, tanks and F-5 bombers – in short, with everything they needed except unanimity.

April 1970 brought a short US offensive into Cambodia to strike North Vietnamese bases there, but public reaction at home was so hostile to this apparent re-escalation of the war that Nixon had to step up the US withdrawal. A similar operation against Viet Cong bases in Laos the following year saw ARVN casualties so high that the offensive had to be abandoned. Thus Communist strength built up in these nations adjacent to South Vietnam, while US troop strength dwindled to 20 percent of what it had once been. In 1972 (another election year), Nixon had to promise to get the United States out of the war or face defeat. Presidential adviser Henry Kissinger gained Chinese and Russian agreement not to support North Vietnam, and the administration announced that the end of the war was imminent. Nixon's electoral majority was overwhelming, and the last American troops left Indo-China in 1973. Many prisoners of war had been returned in the interim, but the fate of others is unknown to this day.

America continued to send military equipment to the precarious South Vietnamese and Cambodian Governments, but Laos-based attacks on South Vietnamese cities increased in 1974. By that time, Cambodia, too, had come increasingly under Communist control, which became complete the following year when the Khmer Rouge captured Phnom Penh in mid-April. Meanwhile, Nixon's presidency had been wrecked by the Watergate scandal, and he had resigned on 9 August 1974. Congress was increasingly reluctant to commit funds to Indo-China, and it was now only a question of when the Communists

Right: **South Vietnamese troops with an M113 armored personnel carrier during operations near the Ho Chi Minh trail in Laos in 1971.**

Below: **The Ninh Binh rail and road bridge destroyed by 'smart' bombs from American aircraft in 1972.**

Above: **An air strike goes in on North Vietnamese positions. The close-quarter style of fighting favored by the communists made the direction of air strikes very difficult.**

Right: **An exhausted American soldier waits to be evacuated from Con Thieu.**

would launch their decisive blow against South Vietnam.

When the Viet Cong seized Phuoc Benh, northwest of Saigon, in January 1975, the anticipated US reaction did not materialize. No new supplies were sent to the hopeful South; no bombers overflew the North. Both sides realized that this time, America had meant what it said. On 4 March, the NVA 968th Division attacked the fortress at Pleiku, in the Central Highlands. President Thieu responded by dispatching the 23rd ARVN Division, which was unable to hold either the Central Highlands or the coastal plain. An evacuation of Kontum and Pleiku was ordered, after which panic-stricken refugees streamed south alongside the demoralized South Vietnamese Army. Desertion was epidemic, as conscripts and even officers jettisoned their commitment to the military for the more urgent and compelling ties of family loyalty. They simply went home to salvage what they could. Longtime strongholds fell without a fight: Quang Tri, Hué, Da Nang. Those government troops that were still prepared to fight (and many South Vietnamese soldiers fought with exemplary courage) were impeded from moving up to the front by the flight of the refugees, during which many thousands simply vanished out of human knowledge.

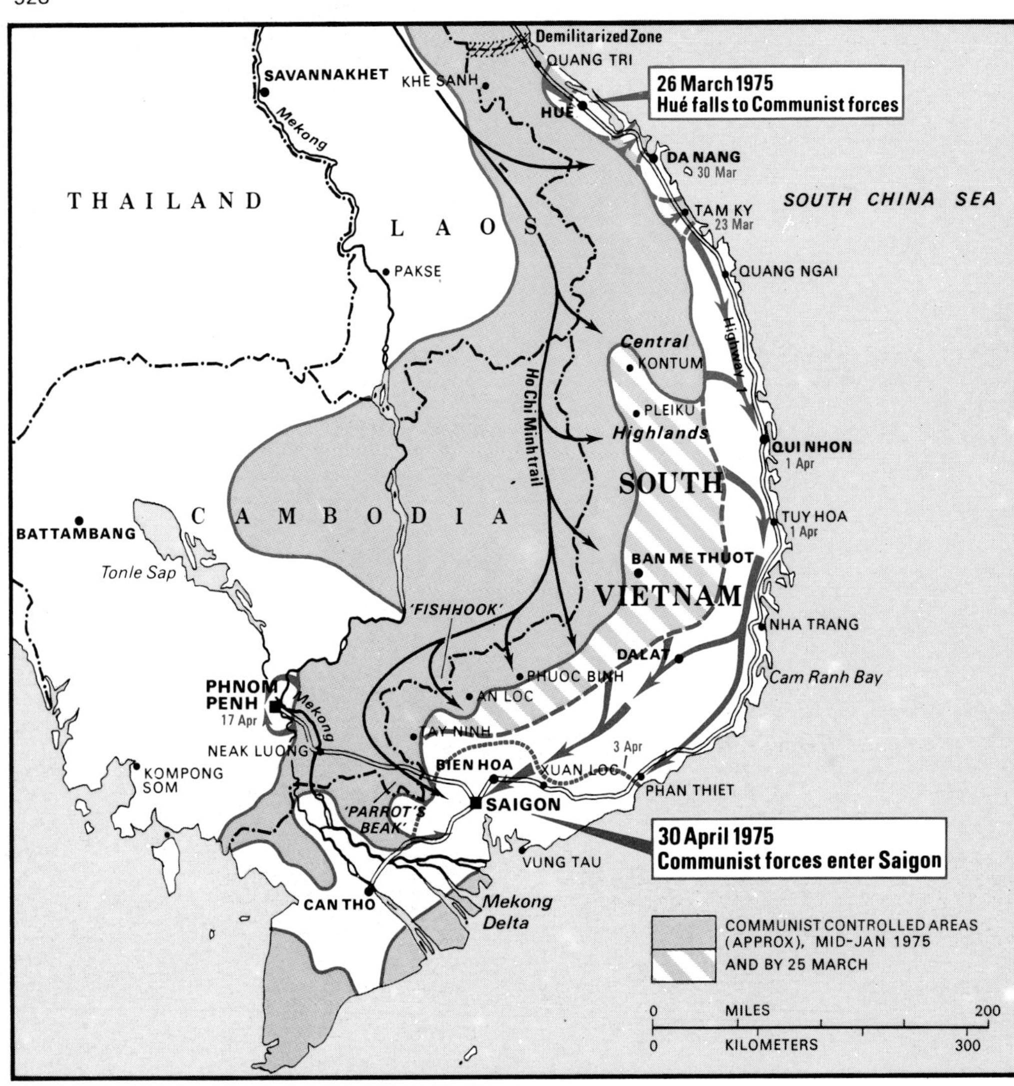

Above: **American troops in Saigon during the Tet Offensive.**

Left: **The fall of South Vietnam.**

By mid-April Saigon and its environs were almost the only South Vietnamese territory still under government control. President Thieu was pressured into resigning after the fall of Xuan Loc put the Bien Hoa airfield into enemy hands. His successor lasted only two days, before Duong Van Minh (called Big Minh) took power – it was he who had succeeded Diem in 1963. Minh had always favored a negotiated end to the war, but the Communists gave him no chance to negotiate. US and ARVN helicopters flew thousands of Americans, journalists and children out of imperiled Saigon, and every kind of vessel was commandeered at Vung Tau to bring additional refugees to the US Fleet offshore. Residents of Saigon were frantic to get out, as many remembered the horrific reprisals carried out in the past by victorious Communist forces. However, there was no way to evacuate everyone who wanted to leave the city. Saigon fell on 30 April 1975, after 30 years of war. It was immediately renamed Ho Chi Minh City – fittingly enough, on 1 May, the major Communist holiday. Some South Vietnamese greeted the Communists as liberators. Even former ARVN soldiers threw away their uniforms and joined the mass looting and destruction that followed upon South Vietnam's unconditional surrender. The tragedy of South Vietnam was far from over, but US involvement was at an end. The war had cost the United States thousands of lives, billions of dollars, international prestige and basic trust between its people and their government. Vietnam veterans (except for prisoners of war) did not find the heroes' welcome that had greeted the combatants in previous wars. It would be years before the Vietnam War dead were memorialized in their nation's capital. Only recently has the nation been able to look at the war again, to study and re-evaluate its implications for American and for the world. Tragically, in Cambodia, Laos and Thailand, the fighting continues to this day.

Left: **Marines, laden with machine gun ammunition, move in on Viet Cong positions.**

Above right: **Cambodian government troops with a dead comrade during fighting against the Khmer Rouge in 1974.**

Right: **A South Vietnamese river patrol boat at work near Saigon in 1972.**

THE MIDDLE EAST WARS

Hitler's genocidal attack on European minorities during World War II slaughtered millions of Jews, Slavs, gypsies and other targets of systematic extermination in Nazi death camps. The world averted its face from the horrifying scenes that came to light as the Allies liberated the skeletal survivors of Dachau, Auschwitz and other charnel houses in Germany and Eastern Europe. History could offer no parallel to the mindless ferocity of this assault on human life, which devoured men, women and children indiscriminately, like the Phoenician Baal. The collective tragedy known as the Holocaust was imprinted indelibly on the Western mind. It affected the international quest for a new home for Jewish survivors who could not, or would not, return to their places of origin, primarily in Eastern Europe and Germany.

The British had held Palestine under a UN mandate since 1919, after it was taken from the decrepit Ottoman Empire during World War I. Since 1917, when the Balfour Declaration promised a 'national homeland' in Palestine for Jews of the Diaspora, the Zionist movement had gathered momentum. As more Jews entered Palestine after World War I, the Arab majority there protested, and the British were forced to limit Jewish immigration. They could not afford to jeopardize relations with the Arabs, who helped to maintain Anglo-French hegemony in the Middle East, especially in the vital Suez Canal Zone.

A New Israel

After World War II, international pressure mounted to open Palestine to multitudes of Jewish refugees. Britain's Labour Government tried to balance its sympathy for the refugees with its interest in Arab support, which became more compelling when the Indian Empire was relinquished in 1947. Suez and oil tipped the balance toward limiting Jewish immigration to Palestine, as the British prepared to abandon their mandate. The United Nations sought to prevent the inevitable clash between Arabs and Jews by partitioning Palestine: the Jews were to inhabit a large area in the Negev Desert, and a series of ephemeral borderlines were established with the Arab part of the country, based on heavy Jewish concentrations in various areas. A state of Israel was declared under Chaim Weizmann, and it received substantial US aid from the outset in the form of money, goods and military equipment. When the British mandate ended on the night of 14-15 May 1948, the first Arab-Israeli War followed immediately.

Egypt, Syria and Jordan made a concerted attack on the Israelis from three sides, but the embattled Jewish state astonished the world with the intensity and skill of its defense. By the year's end, the Israelis had extended their borders up to Jerusalem and occupied half the city – historically a source of conflict among Moslems, Christians and Jews because of its sacred implications for all three faiths. Truce lines established in 1949 confirmed that well over half of Palestine was now under Jewish control.

Those Arabs who remained in the new state of Israel were hounded into the nearby Gaza Strip – Egyptian territory – and across the Jordan River, whose west bank belonged to the Hashemite Kingdom of Jordan. Arab families who had lived in Palestine for centuries were killed or driven out by the Israelis, who felt that their claim to the land had the sanction of millennia. Ancient animosities among these Semitic inhabitants of the Middle East flared into open hatred. Western Europe and the United States sided with Israel, partly out of guilt at their own refusal to accept large numbers of Jewish refugees after World War II. On a deeper level, they blamed themselves for the covert anti-Semitism that pointed the finger at Nazi Germany but shared in the general culpability for the persecution of the Jews through recorded history. Zionism would never have become an issue were it not for widespread animosity toward the Jewish minority. In addition, the United States had a relatively large and influential Jewish population that worked tirelessly on behalf of Israel, which became a focal point of Jewish identity everywhere.

Above: **Israeli Minister of Defense in 1956, Pinchas Lavan.**

Right: **Divers at work to clear blockships from the Suez canal after the 1956 war.**

Egypt Ascendant

The 1952 revolution that ousted the corrupt regime of Egypt's King Farouk culminated in the accession to power of Gamal Abdel Nasser, who aspired to Pan-Arab leadership. His simultaneous goal was to break the British grip on

Right: **A member of the Israeli Irgun organization in action in March 1948.**

Below: **Lt Col Izaat Bey Dessonky, Egyptian commander in Gaza in 1948.**

Below: **Arab fighters move away after just having ambushed an Israeli truck in Jerusalem in 1948.**

Above: Former Israeli Prime Minister Golda Meir.

Below: The Israeli and Anglo-French attacks in 1956.

Right: Cheerful Israeli troops advance against the Egyptians in 1967.

Far right: Algerian rebel troops training for the independence struggle against the French in 1959.

Below right: Israeli troops stand guard over prisoners.

Egyptian affairs that had lasted for 70 years, even after Egypt gained its independence. The corridors of power in Cairo and Alexandria had never ceased to resound to British footsteps. Nasser brought formidable abilities to his position, and used them to woo the Soviet Union, which agreed readily to finance a great dam at Aswan (the United States had turned it down). When British forces finally left the Suez in 1954, they maintained a base at Ismailia with an eye to returning if necessary. Continued US refusal to supply unrestricted military aid to Egypt enhanced the romance between Nasser and the Soviets, and encouraged the Egyptian leader to essay guerrilla activity inside Israel. His credibility as a champion of Arab interests required that he challenge the Jewish state, but Britain was outraged and collaborated with both France and Israel to invade Egypt in 1956. The Americans were kept in the dark about this plan, which they would certainly see as a neo-colonial enterprise that could redound unfavorably on US interests in the region's oil-producing states. The Anglo-French Israeli plot against Egypt was implemented in October 1956. By this time, Nasser had nationalized the Suez Canal, and Anglo-French power in the Middle East was already becoming a memory.

The Suez War

Israel opened hostilities against Egypt on 29 October, and Britain and France justified their intervention on the basis of preserving the Suez Canal from possible damage in the course of hostilities. British bombers joined Israeli planes in the skies over Sinai; French ships stood by to

Above: A Palestinian refugee camp in Jordan in 1969. The Palestinian question remains a most intractable problem in the Middle East.

cover Israeli paratroop landings at the strategic Mitla Pass to the canal. Egypt began sinking ships in the canal by way of reprisal, as Israeli soldiers entered the Gaza Strip. America was increasingly affronted by the Anglo-French involvement. By 5 November, Gaza had fallen to the Israelis, and Anglo-French paratroops were descending on Port Said. President Eisenhower put pressure on French and British leaders to desist, and Russia joined the chorus of protest, in a rare show of US-Soviet concurrence. The demand was backed by withdrawal of US support for the British pound, which had plummeted with record sales of sterling on world money markets. As Anglo-French forces advanced down the canal, the United Nations called for a cease-fire, and the European powers had to give way. In December 1956, Britain and France withdrew from Egypt with their international prestige in tatters.

Meanwhile, the Israelis had taken possession of Sharm-el-Sheikh, on the Gulf of Aqaba, and of the whole Sinai Peninsula. When their European allies withdrew, they had to pull back. UN troops entered the Gaza Strip and positioned themselves at strategic points on the Israeli-Egyptian frontier in 1957. The Suez Canal was blocked by sunken ships for almost a year, and oil shortages were widely felt. Both Britain and France experienced changes of government as a result of the ill-advised Suez adventure, and it took over a year to normalize Anglo-French and US relations.

Above right: **Prisoners take their exercise in an Israeli jail, a picture released by the Israeli authorities in 1970 following allegations of torture of Arab detainees.**

Below: **An Israeli M48 tank unit advances in the Sinai during the 1973 war.**

Israel had now emerged as the strongest military power in the Middle East, and an uneasy pseudo-peace descended upon the region for the next decade, as Arab nations jostled one another for pre-eminence and Russia supplied the more militant among them - notably Egypt and Syria – with weapons and money. Israel was plentifully supplied by the United States, and experienced phenomenal economic growth during the 1960s. An influx of emigrants from the Afro-Asian world more than doubled the Israeli population, which had formerly comprised mainly Jews of European origin. Then skirmishes along the borders of Syria and Egypt became more numerous, and Nasser sent UN forces out of Egypt, threatening the use of the Soviet armor and aircraft he had amassed. The Israelis prepared for a second pre-emptive strike against their Arab enemies – the phalanx of Egypt, Jordan and Syria.

The Six-Day War

In May 1967 Egypt deployed its army on the border with Israel and at Sharm-el-Sheikh. The excuse for this was imminent Israeli reprisals against Syria, which had launched numerous bombardments on Israeli settlements from the Golan Heights, along the Syrian border. Israel appealed to the United Nations, but received no reassurances. It appeared that she was about to be attacked from three sides, outnumbered in men, planes and armor. General Moshe Dayan and the Israeli General Staff decided to strike Egypt first – from the west, where it was least expected – and destroy the Egyptian Air Force on the ground. Just after dawn on 5 June 1967,

Israeli Mystères, covered by 40 Mirages, struck nine Egyptian airfields, avoiding the radar screen until the last moment. Then they climbed to visibility so as to catch enemy pilots along with their planes, as the Egyptians tried to man their aircraft against the attack. Successive waves of Israeli planes faced increasing anti-aircraft fire, but only two Mirages were shot down: the Egyptians lost all but eight of their MiG-21s before they could reach the skies. The attack kept up for over an hour, hitting eight more Egyptian airfields in the process. By mid-morning, the Egyptian Air Force was destroyed, and Israel turned her planes against Syria and Jordan, whose airfields were similarly wiped out. In fact, Israel won the Six-Day War in something like four hours by seizing the initiative in the air. Three days later, the Egyptian Army was driven from Sinai, despite its massive numerical superiority.

Jerusalem and the Golan Heights

The main confrontation with Jordan took place in Jerusalem, half of which was under Jordanian control at the outset. House-to-house fighting raged for three days, but ended in Israeli conquest not only of Jerusalem, but of the whole West Bank of the Jordan. King Hussein had lost the richest part of his domain, and was only thankful that the Israelis did not follow up their success by crossing the river.

The Golan Heights cost Israel more lives than the other two fronts combined, but this position was vital to Israeli security. It commanded the approach to Damascus, capital of Syria, and had served the Syrians as a launching pad for bombardments against Israel since 1948. Brigadier Elazar led the Israeli advance against the Golan Heights on Day Four of the war, and gained air-force cover the following day, when the Syrian front became the focus of all-out effort. Two days of heavy fighting secured the Golan Heights to Israel.

In a six-day offensive, Israel had more than doubled its territory and lost only 778 soldiers and 26 civilians. Some 150,000 Palestinian Arabs had fled into Jordan, but well over a million more were now in Israeli territory. The magnitude of this victory would create serious problems for the Jewish state in years to come, both internally and with surrounding Arab nations. Egypt and Syria increased their ties to the Soviet Union after the Six-Day War, receiving new matériel that included missiles. These were installed near the Suez Canal – the new Israeli-Egyptian border. Nasser's offer to resign after Egypt's humiliation was refused by his people, and he remained to preside over an increasingly serious war of attrition along the new frontier until his death in 1970. His successor, President Anwar Sadat, demanded an Israeli withdrawal from former Egyptian territory, but without success. Syria, too, was involved in border hostilities and by 1972 tensions had reached the boiling point again.

The Arab Buildup

The Middle East was increasingly polarized by Soviet support of the Arab bloc *vis-à-vis* US support of Israel after the Six-Day War. The United States was ambivalent about arming Israel, since

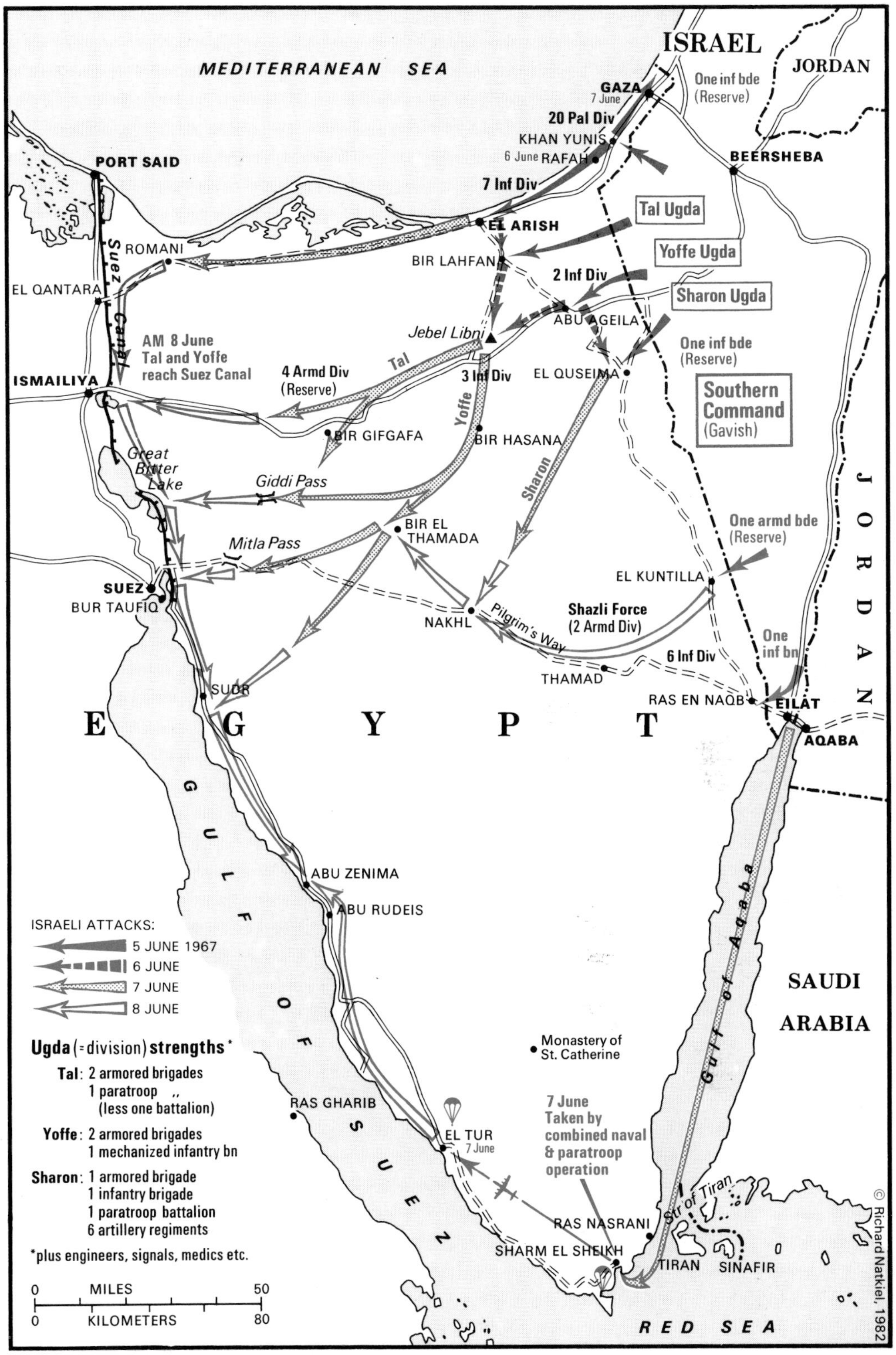

ISRAELI ATTACKS:
5 JUNE 1967
6 JUNE
7 JUNE
8 JUNE

Ugda (= division) **strengths***
Tal: 2 armored brigades
1 paratroop „ (less one battalion)
Yoffe: 2 armored brigades
1 mechanized infantry bn
Sharon: 1 armored brigade
1 infantry brigade
1 paratroop battalion
6 artillery regiments
*plus engineers, signals, medics etc.

© Richard Natkiel, 1982

Above left: **Russian made tanks of the Syrian Army captured by the Israelis in 1973.**

Left: **Egyptian troops cross the Suez canal at the start of the Yom Kippur War.**

Above right: **The Israel–Egypt battles in 1967.**

Right: **Moshe Dayan (with eyepatch) visits the Golan in 1973.**

Above: Scenes in the Sabra refugee camp in Beirut following the widely-condemned massacre in September 1982.

Left: An Israeli M48 tank moves up to the front.

Right: Israeli shells explode along the waterfront of Beirut in 1982.

she knew that a lasting peace in the Middle East could not be achieved unless Israel made some concession of territory. On the contrary, the Jewish state continued to appropriate parts of formerly Arab Palestine, where some 600,000 Arabs were now in refugee camps. The annexation of Jerusalem's Old City was a particular affront to the Moslem nations, as that quarter housed the Dome of the Rock, from which tradition held that Mohammed had ascended into heaven. After Mecca and Medina, it was Islam's holiest shrine. It occupied the same 35-acre site as the Wailing Wall – all that remained of Herod's Temple, and the paramount holy place of Judaism. Christians, too, venerated the Temple area as one of the scenes of Christ's ministry. As so often in history, religious differences generated the most virulent kind of conflict.

In 1972 Palestinian guerrillas attacked Israeli athletes at the Munich Olympics, in a display of terrorism that extended to threats against Israeli businesses and institutions worldwide. Prominent Jews were killed or kidnapped. It was clear that the Palestinian situation had to be resolved before another full-scale war broke out in the Middle East. Sadat encouraged the Soviet presence in Egypt until 17 July 1972, when he unexpectedly expelled some 40,000 Russian advisers and their families and took over the missile sites and airfields they had installed. This raised his stock among disaffected Egyptian military and student elements, and was followed by diplomatic initiatives that resulted in a united Arab front: Egypt, Jordan, Syria, Saudi Arabia and the Gulf States. Egyptian armor began massing near the Suez Canal in September, but the overconfident Israelis regarded this as a regular fall exercise. Dayan warned of a similar buildup near the Golan Heights, but he went unheeded on the eve of the Jewish High Holy Day, Yom Kippur.

Left: Soldiers of the US and Egyptian armies discuss the workings of a Soviet-made heavy machine gun during joint exercises in 1980. The opportunity to examine the equipment of former Soviet friends was one bonus for the United States of the changed political patterns in the Middle East following the Camp David agreement.

The Yom Kippur War

Most Israeli soldiers were off duty when Egypt and Syria launched their surprise attack on Israel on the Day of Atonement, 6 October 1973. Some 700 Syrian tanks converged on the Golan Heights, as Egyptian units crossed the Suez Canal into Sinai. The Bar-Lev Line of Israeli defense crumpled, and air-raid warnings shocked the people of Jerusalem from their devotions. Soldiers on leave were pulled from their synagogues and rushed to the front, as the Syrians captured Mount Hermon and ranged their artillery against Israeli positions. Egyptian forces poured into Sinai for six days, achieving a broad front that controlled the entire west bank of the Suez Canal. Meanwhile, Syrian troops had gone on the defensive, and were now driven back to Sassa, where they held a second line of defense for Damascus.

On 14 October an epic tank battle took place in the Sinai Desert: Israeli Super-Shermans, Centurions and Pattons fought Egyptian T-34s, -55s and -62s to a standstill near the Gidi and Mitla Passes. Some 2000 tanks were involved, and the British and American armor fielded by Israel proved superior under torrid desert conditions. The Egyptian thrust was blunted, and the Israelis prepared to counterattack.

Next day, 15 October, General Ariel Sharon discovered a gap in Egyptian lines west of the canal and exploited it to establish a bridgehead. The Egyptians failed to repel this incursion in the Battle of Chinese Farm (16 October), and the fortunes of war shifted toward Israel's side. Meanwhile, the oil-producing nations had raised their prices by 70 percent to pressure the United States and Western Europe into subduing the Israelis. President Richard Nixon declined to be coerced, and put US troops in Europe on full alert. Massive American aid continued to flow into Israel, and Russia reacted to this threat to her recent détente with the West by urging Egypt to pull out of the war before it was too late.

On 24 October 1973, a cease-fire was effected. Israeli forces were then deep in Egyptian territory – some 60 miles from Cairo – but Egypt clung to some holdings east of the canal. The truce patched up by Nixon's Secretary of State, Henry Kissinger, was no ideal solution to the Middle Eastern problem. However, several factors did become clear: the Arab states had finally achieved both unity and strength; Israel could not simultaneously expand and secure her frontiers indefinitely; and the Western world was dangerously dependent upon Middle Eastern oil.

In the months after the war, the balance of power in the region shifted from Russia to the United States. Even Syria, perhaps the most militantly anti-Israeli Arab nation, was wooed by Kissinger toward the US camp. Sadat and his supporters along the Persian Gulf finally realized that the Soviet Union would never sanction the total destruction of Israel if it meant a nuclear confrontation with the United States. Thus another uneasy peace settled over the ancient crossroads of two continents.

Left: **Israeli troops in southern Lebanon in 1982 with the Lebanese Christian militia leader Major Haddad.**

Below: **The aftermath of the Sabra refugee camp massacre; victims of the Christian militia await burial.**

Above: **Israeli troops during street fighting in Beirut in August 1982. Note the Palestinian poster on the wall.**

EPILOGUE

The Middle Eastern conflict did not end with the 1973 war. The Palestine Liberation Organization, under the episodic leadership of Yasser Arafat, continued to harass the Israelis from positions in Jordan and, later, the Lebanon, from which it launched sporadic raids. Although Egypt's Sadat reached a *modus vivendi* with Israel in the late 1970s, an act for which he subsequently was assassinated, the PLO continued to operate from its sanctuary in the Lebanon. Eventually the Israelis invaded the south of that country, supported by many Christian groups who were being besieged in their enclaves by Islamic forces supported by Iraq and more notably, Syria. Despite UN efforts to end the conflict, a full-scale attack to take over the whole of southern Lebanon was launched by Israel in the summer of 1982. By the end of August, Israeli forces had reached the capital, Beirut, and PLO and Syrian forces were obliged to withdraw. The Israeli withdrawal to the Awali River was accompanied by the movement of a protective force into the Beirut area, principally American, but also British, Italian and French troops. Under heavy Syrian/Islamic Lebanese bombardment in Beirut, and equally heavy political pressure in their home countries to withdraw, they did so throughout 1983. With Syrians and Israelis occupying large parts of Lebanon in 1985, the Middle East crisis – a war which had continued for almost 40 years with hardly a respite – seemed no nearer to resolution. Until the problem of the Palestinian Arabs was solved definitively, and the Israelis had retreated to more realistic frontiers, no permanent peace in the Middle East could be envisaged. But the likelihood of a Middle East flare-up mushrooming into a general world war had greatly receded.

By the 1980s, the United States was rearming during a period of prosperity, low inflation and a strong dollar. This was in contrast to the previous decade – a period of US political retreat after Vietnam and Watergate, when Jimmy Carter's Presidency was marked by high inflation, high unemployment and a weak dollar. With this recovery, the prospects for world war diminished. The Soviet Union, in the early 1980s, was undergoing a series of crises. The first was a crisis of leadership, as three of its central figures died within a year or two of each other. Brezhnev's long reign was followed by Andropov's and Chernenko's equally short ones. Struggles for succession in the Kremlin made it difficult for the Soviet Union to make dramatic power plays after its invasion of Afghanistan in 1979, which initiated a guerrilla struggle that continues at the time of writing. There was also a twofold crisis in the Soviet economy: grain had to be imported from the West in annually increasing quantities, while the Soviet people demanded a greater share of the national wealth in the form of consumer goods, which were often unavailable and almost invariably of poor quality. At the same time, the share of the GNP taken by the Soviet armed forces grew dramatically to meet the demand of the arms race. Soviet leadership, di-

Above: **A young Palestinian waves farewell to his father, one of the PLO fighters evacuated from Beirut in 1982.**

Right: **Part of the small British component of the multinational peacekeeping force patrols a Beirut street.**

Below: **The ruins of the US Marine compound destroyed by a suicide bomber in October 1983.**

ARA
VANLIAN
02 DA 26

vided against itself, could not choose between consumer demands and military exigencies, and therefore satisfied neither. The third crisis, and perhaps most important in the longer term, was the crisis of confidence. Few Soviet leaders of the 1980s still believed, apart from official statements, in the inevitability of Communism's triumph. It can only be imagined what the Soviet people believed. Even more significant is the obvious doubt the Soviets felt in the efficacy of the Communist system for themselves. A system which cannot feed itself, or even adequately arm itself for global conflict on all fronts, in the end performs no function. In this context of political turmoil, economic crisis and the deeper crisis of confidence, the possibility of nuclear war, which everyone in the world fears, seemed further away than ever. Emboldened by the unaccustomed lack of thrust of Soviet political and military power, the Western Allies, Britain and the United States, embarked upon two quite independent military adventures which, in the 1970s, would have seemed unthinkable.

When Argentina invaded the Falkland Islands, a residual British colony in the South Atlantic, in April 1982, the British struck back quickly. A task force was mounted in the British Isles and steamed some 8000 miles to retake the rocky and sparsely inhabited archipelago. The task force arrived in mid-May and within a few weeks wiped out all Argentine resistance in the Falklands, re-establishing the British colony. The Soviets said and did little to thwart the invasion, and Prime Minister Margaret Thatcher was subsequently re-elected by a greatly increased majority thanks to this bold enterprise, which, in retrospect, showed courage but to no particular point – discussions continue on the eventual turnover of the islands to the Argentinians.

The Americans, emboldened by the ease with which the British had gotten away with their military adventure, decided to invade the island of Grenada in the Caribbean in 1983. Grenada had recently fallen under the leadership of left-wing groups that were far from hostile to the Soviet Union. The Soviets were building a large air base which, if completed, would have been used as a launching pad to assist their client states in the region, notably Nicaragua. President Ronald Reagan used establishment of the air base and the unrest within the island community to justify an attack led by the 82nd Airborne, which had achieved fame in D-Day and Market-Garden operations during World War II. The few Cuban and Grenadan troops defending the island were quickly overrun. Within a few months, a new government friendly to American interests was established, and almost all American troops were withdrawn. Again, the Soviets said little and did nothing. It was clear that a counteroffensive in the Third World by the United States and its allies in NATO was at hand. France subsequently sent paratroops into Chad, and anti-Communist forces throughout the world were heartened. Cuba began negotiations for a détente with the United States, and Libya and Iran lost much of their economic power when the price of oil dropped precipitously in the mid-1980s.

Above: **Israeli Minister of Defense Moshe Arens meets US diplomat Jeanne Kirkpatrick in March 1983.**

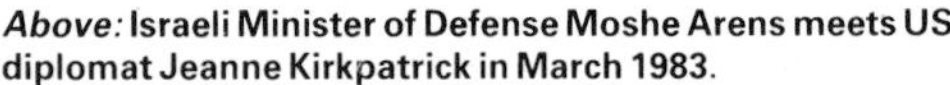

Right: **A patrol from the US peacekeeping unit moves through downtown Beirut in September 1983. The soldiers are from the 24th Marine Amphibious Unit.**

By mid-decade, it had become clear that nuclear war was unlikely, but that localized wars, like those seen in Korea, Vietnam and the Middle East, would continue, however unlikely the prospect that they might lead to a wider conflict. The two World Wars of the 20th century had proved that such bloodlettings were senseless in their own time and fatally futile in the nuclear age. The modern superpowers will never go to war with one another as long as credible defenses still exist on both sides of the Iron Curtain. Wars will continue as long as human pride and folly endure, but they need not necessarily result in human annihilation. If the wars of the 20th century teach us anything, it is this: wars, like life, never turn out the way one thinks they will at the outset. As long as this is remembered, it is safe to say, with a fair degree of certainty, that the lessons of recent history will have been learned, and that no wide-scale conflict can possibly bring success to the victors. It is equally safe to say that in a large-scale nuclear conflict, there can be no victors – only the vanquished, heaped upon the ruins of dead civilizations. Wars bring rapid and violent change. No sane person seeks such change, in an age when change itself has accelerated beyond our ability to assimilate it. If the tragic conflicts of the 20th century have brought us to an age in which wars have been limited, if not abolished, the dreams of Woodrow Wilson and other idealists of the early part of this century will have been, at least in part, fulfilled.

Left: **US Secretary of State Alexander Haig and Israeli Foreign Minister Yitzhak Shamir meet in January 1982 during Haig's visit to Israel.**

Right: **Fresh US Marine units arrive for a tour of duty with the Beirut peacekeeping force in late 1982.**

INDEX

Page numbers in *italics* refer to illustrations.

ACKNOWLEDGMENTS

The Publishers would like to thank the Robert Hunt Library for supplying most of the pictures used in this book. They would also like to thank the agencies listed below for allowing the reproduction of the following pictures.

AP/Wide World Photos: pp 513, 516 (bottom), 530 (bottom right) 531 (both), 533 (top right), 534 (top), 538 (right), 541 (bottom), 542 (both).
BBC Hulton Picture Library: pp 16 (bottom, left and right), 100 (center), 142 (top right), 145 (top), 157 (top), 165 (bottom right), 243 (bottom right).
Bison Picture Library: pp 260, 263 (top), 264, 265, 276, 280, 283, 284-5, 291, 292 (top), 292-3, 295 (top), 297 (top), 298 (top), 299, 303 (top left), 307 (top right), 309 (top and bottom right), 312 (top), 312 (bottom), 313, 314 (bottom), 319, 322 (bottom), 323 (bottom left), 323 (bottom right), 325 (top left), 326 (top), 327 (top right), 330 (top), 334-5, 338, 339 (bottom left and right), 339-40, 340 (bottom), 347 (top), 350 (top), 351 (top both), 352 (top right), 354, 360 (bottom), 367 (top and bottom), 370 (top), 376 (bottom left), 377 (bottom), 378 (top), 379 (top), 387 (top), 388 (top), 390 (top), 392 (bottom), 391 (top), 394, 395 (top left and bottom left), 406, 408, 411 (center), 412 (top right), 414, 415 (top right and center), 416 (top), 429 (top right), 431, 432 (bottom), 433 (top), 464 (top), 471 (bottom), 484 (bottom), 486-7, 488 (bottom), 493 (top), 498-9, 500 (both), 508-8 (below), 509 (top left), 530 (top & bottom left), 532 (top left), 532-3 (top center & bottom), 535 (top), 536 (bottom), 537, 539, 540, 541 (top), 544 (both).
Mr Bredewold: p 294 (top right).
Bundesarchiv: pp 21 (bottom right), 22 (top left), 23 (top right), 64-5, 64 (bottom left), 88 (top), 98 (bottom), 100 (top left), 138-9, 146 (top), 148-9 (top), 160-61, 162-3, 180-81 (top), 182 (bottom), 188-9, 189 (top right), 199 (center right), 203 (top left), 206-7, 221 (bottom), 258-9, 266-7, 268-9 (top), 271, 280-81 (top), 282, 286-7, 287 (top), 289, 290 (bottom), 292 (bottom), 294 (top left), 294-5, 296, 297 (top), 298 (bottom), 300, 301 (top), 301 (bottom right), 302 (top), 303 (top right), 324-5, 325 (top right), 326 (center), 327 (top left), 328-9, 330-31, 331 (top right), 332, 333, 340 (top), 343 (top), 346, 347 (center and bottom), 363 (top right), 364-5, 366 (top), 366-7, 368-9, 376 (bottom right), 381 (left), 384 (center), 407 (top right), 410-11, 421 (bottom left), 428-9 (top and bottom), 433 (top left), 445, 446, 463 (center), 477 (top).
Dwight D. Eisenhower Library: 514 (right).
Imperial War Museum: pp 8-9, 14, (top), 15 (main picture), 20 (top right), 27 (bottom), 34, 38 (top right), 38 (center), 40 (top left), 40-41, 41 (bottom right), 43 (both), 46-7, 46 (top both), 48 (top right), 49 (top left, bottom left and center right), 54 (center), 55 (center), 56 (top), 57 (top), 58-9, 59 (center), 60 (center), 61 (center), 62-3, 63 (top), 65 (top left), 66 (top), 67 (top right), 69 (top both), 70 (center), 71 (top right and center), 72-3, 88 (bottom), 89 (all three), 90-91 (all five), 92-3, 92 (top), 94-5 (all four), 99 (bottom), 100-101, 101 (top three), 102-3, 102 (center), 103 (top left), 104 (bottom right), 105 (top left and bottom right), 106-7, 107 (center), 108-9, 110-11, 111 (center), 112-13, 113 (top), 114-15, 121 (top both), 123 (center and bottom right), 124, 125 (bottom both), 126-7, 128 (bottom right), 129 (top left and bottom both), 130 (top), 133 (center), 136, 149 (top), 150-51, 156 (top right), 158-9 (top), 163 (top), 164 (bottom left), 168 (top and center left), 170-71, 172 (top), 172-3, 174-5, 176-7, 178-9 (all five), 180 (top), 181, 182-3 (top), 196-7, 198-9 (top and bottom), 202 (top), 203 (top right and center left), 212-13, 214-15 (bottom), 215 (bottom), 218 (both), 219 (bottom), 221 (top), 222-3, 222 (top), 224-5, 226-7, 228 (bottom), 233 (bottom), 234 (top), 242-3 (bottom), 244 (center0, 246-7, 252-3, 270, 277, 278-9, 286 (top), 288, 290 (inset), 295 (center), 301 (bottom left), 301 (center), 304 (top both), 304 (bottom right), 307 (top left), 306-7, 307 (top left), 308 (bottom), 309 (bottom left), 310-11, 318, 320-21, 321 (top right), 322 (top), 323 (top), 326-7, 331 (top left), 342-3, 355 (bottom right), 362-3, 363 (center), 376 (center), 378-9, 380, 381 (right), 385 (top), 386 (bottom), 387 (bottom center), 395 (bottom right), 397 (center), 405 (top), 415 (top left), 418-19, 420 (top), 421 (bottom right), 422 (top), 424-5 (bottom), 433 (top right), 435 (top left), 442, 448 (top right), 456-7 (top), 457 (bottom), 458, 459, 460 (top), 461 (top right), 462-3 (bottom), 465 (bottom right), 470 (top), 471 (top left), 473 (top), 514 (top), 515.
Israeli Government Press Office: 534-5 (below).
National Archives (US): pp 194 (top), 195 (top left), 198 (top), 200 (top), 206 (top), 213 (top), 215 (top), 230-31, 235 (bottom), 236-7, 238-9, 240 (bottom), 315 (top), 316 (top), 350 (center and bottom), 371 (top), 371 (center left), 372-3, 374-5, 383 (top right), 399 (top left and bottom), 400 (top), 401 (bottom), 413, 422-3, 425 (top), 427 (top left, top right and bottom), 435 (top right), 439 (top right), 440, 451 (top left), 453 (top), 454 (bottom), 455 (center), 508 (top), 510 (bottom), 512 (bottom left).
National Maritime Museum (UK): pp 98 (top), 99 (top), 106 (top both), 107 (top), 344-5, 348-9 (top), 395 (top right), 396-7, 396 (top), 397 (top left and right), 411 (top), 415 (bottom), 416 (bottom and center), 417, 430, 432 (top right), 489 (top).
New York Daily News: 512 (top left).
Novosti: pp 18 (bottom), 21 (bottom left), 140 (bottom), 154-5, 336-7, 339 (top), 388-9, 390 (top right), 393, 395 (top right), 396-7, 444, 448 (top left), 449, 474 (center), 475 (top), 477 (bottom), 478 (top), 479.
Rijksinstitut: p 293 (both).
Ullstein: pp 74-5, 75 (top left), 77 (bottom), 78-9, 79 (center), 80 (top right), 81 (top both), 96-7, 100 (top right).
USAF: pp 119 (top both), 120 (bottom), 133 (top right), 134 (bottom), 383 (top left), 386 (top), 402 (center), 403 (top), 404-5 (bottom three), 407 (top left and bottom), 481 (top), 484 (top), 485, 494-5, 496-7, 525 (bottom).
US Army: pp 235 (top left), 382-3, 382 (top), 384 (bottom), 385 (bottom), 420 (bottom), 426-7 (bottom), 438, 439 (top left and bottom), 441, 443 (bottom), 466 (top), 466-7 (bottom), 468, 469, 475 (bottom), 488 (top), 517 (both), 529 (bottom).
US Department of Defense: 501 (left), 504-5 (all), 506-7 (all), 509 (top right), 510 (top), 511 (both), 512 (top & bottom right), 514 (bottom left), 518 (both), 519 (both), 620-1 (all), 522-3 (all), 525 (top), 526 (top), 527 (both), 528 (both), 538 (left), 543, 545 (both).
USIS: pp 190-91, 216-17.
US Marine Corps: pp 250-51, 262-3, 450-51, 451 (top right), 452, 455 (bottom), 480, 482-3, 490-91.
US Navy: pp 196-7, 351 (bottom), 352 (top left), 352 (bottom), 370-71, 371 (center), 399 (top right), 400 (bottom), 434-5, 451 (center), 453 (bottom), 454 (top), 455 (top), 481 (bottom), 489 (bottom), 493 (bottom), 526 (bottom).